GO!

Learn | Practice | Succeed

Microsoft®
Office 365®

Word™ 2019

Shelley Gaskin | Alicia Vargas

Series Editor: Shelley Gaskin

Pearson

VP Courseware Portfolio Management: Andrew Gilfillan
Executive Portfolio Manager: Jenifer Niles
Team Lead, Content Production: Laura Burgess
Content Producer: Shannon LeMay-Finn
Development Editor: Ginny Munroe
Portfolio Management Assistant: Bridget Daly
Director of Product Marketing: Brad Parkins
Director of Field Marketing: Jonathan Cottrell
Product Marketing Manager: Heather Taylor
Field Marketing Manager: Bob Nisbet
Product Marketing Assistant: Liz Bennett
Field Marketing Assistant: Derrica Moser
Senior Operations Specialist: Diane Peirano

Senior Art Director: Mary Seiner
Interior and Cover Design: Pearson CSC
Cover Photo: Jag_cz/Shutterstock, everything possible/Shutterstock
Senior Product Model Manager: Eric Hakanson
Manager, Digital Studio: Heather Darby
Digital Content Producer, MyLab IT: Becca Golden
Course Producer, MyLab IT: Amanda Losonsky
Digital Studio Producer: Tanika Henderson
Full-Service Project Management: Pearson CSC, Katie Ostler
Composition: Pearson CSC
Printer/Binder: LSC Communications, Inc.
Cover Printer: Phoenix Color/Hagerstown

Credits and acknowledgments borrowed from other sources and reproduced, with permission, in this textbook appear on appropriate page within text.

Many of the designations by manufacturers and seller to distinguish their products are claimed as trademarks. Where those designations appear in this book, and the publisher was aware of a trademark claim, the designations have been printed in initial caps or all caps.

Library of Congress Cataloging-in-Publication Data

On file with the Library of Congress.

ISBN-10: 0-13-544284-2
ISBN-13: 978-0-13-544284-5

Brief Contents

Table of Contents

Microsoft Word 2019   101

Chapter 1 Creating Documents with Microsoft Word   103

Chapter 2 Creating Cover Letters and Using Tables to Create Resumes   169

About the Authors

Shelley Gaskin, Series Editor, is a professor in the Business and Computer Technology Division at Pasadena City College in Pasadena, California. She holds a bachelor's degree in Business Administration from Robert Morris College (Pennsylvania), a master's degree in Business from Northern Illinois University, and a doctorate in Adult and Community Education from Ball State University (Indiana). Before joining Pasadena City College, she spent 12 years in the computer industry, where she was a systems analyst, sales representative, and director of Customer Education with Unisys Corporation. She also worked for Ernst & Young on the development of large systems applications for their clients. She has written and developed training materials for custom systems applications in both the public and private sector, and has also written and edited numerous computer application textbooks.

This book is dedicated to my husband Fred, and to my students, who inspire me every day.

Alicia Vargas is a faculty member in Business Information Technology at Pasadena City College. She holds a master's and a bachelor's degree in business education from California State University, Los Angeles, and has authored several textbooks and training manuals on Microsoft Word, Microsoft Excel, and Microsoft PowerPoint.

This book is dedicated with all my love to my husband Vic, who makes everything possible; and to my children Victor, Phil, and Emmy, who are an unending source of inspiration and who make everything worthwhile.

GO! with Microsoft Word 2019 Comprehensive

Introducing seamless digital instruction, practice, and assessment

Using GO! with MyLab IT has never been better! With the integrated etext and pre-built learning modules, instructors can assign learning easily and students can get started quickly.

▶ **Proven content and pedagogical approach of *guided instruction, guided practice,* and *mastery*** is effective for all types of learners and all types of course delivery—face-to-face in the classroom, online, and hybrid.

▶ **Students learn Microsoft Office skills by creating practical projects** they will see in their academic and professional lives.

▶ **With GO! MyLab IT students can learn, practice, and assess live or in authentic simulations of Microsoft Office.**

- **Microsoft Office autograded Grader** projects for the instructional, mastery, and assessment projects allow students to work live in Excel, Word, Access, or PPT so that during each step of the learning process, they can receive immediate, autograded feedback!

- **Microsoft Office authentic simulations** allow students to practice what they are learning in a safe environment with learning aids for instant help—*Read*, *Watch*, or *Practice*. Authentic simulations can also be used for assessment without learning aids.

What's New?

- The **book (print or etext) is the student's guide** to completing all autograded Grader projects for instruction, practice, and assessment.
- The **GO!** *Learn How* **videos**, integrated in the etext, give students an instructor-led, step-by-step guide through the A & B projects.
- **Improved business case connection** throughout the instruction so students always understand the *what* and *why*.
- **Mac tips** ⬜ are woven into the instruction for each project so Mac students can proceed successfully.
    - All text and Grader projects created and tested by the authors on both a Mac and a PC.
    - Content not limited by Mac compatibility! Everything students need to know for MOS exams, Excel, and Access that are not possible on the Mac are still covered!
- **MyLab IT Prebuilt Learning modules** make course setup a snap. The modules are based on research and customer use, and can be easily customized to meet your course requirements.
- **Critical Thinking assessments and badges** expand coverage of Employability Skills.
- **New combined Office Features and Windows chapter** with Grader projects and auto-graded Windows projects for a fast and concise overview of these important features. Shorter and easier to assign.

- **Regular content updates to stay current with Office 365** updates and new features:
  - New *Semester Updates* for the etext and Grader projects through MyLab IT
  - New *Lessons on the GO!* to help you teach new features

What's New for Grader Projects

- **Autograded *Integrated Projects*** covering Word, Excel, Access, and PPT.
- Projects **A & B Grader reports now include *Learning Aids*** for immediate remediation.
- Autograded Critical Thinking Quizzes and Badges
  - Critical Thinking Modules include a Capstone and Quiz that enable students to earn a Critical Thinking Badge
  - Critical Thinking quizzes for the A & B instructional projects
- A **final output image** is provided so students can visualize what their solution should look like.
- **Mac Compatibility:** All Grader projects are built for PC and Mac users, excluding Access. Only projects that have features not supported on the Mac are not 100% compatible.

What's New for Simulations

- Simulations are updated by the authors for improved reinforcement of the software navigation in each instructional project—as always, they are matched one-to-one with the text Activities.
- *Student Action Visualization* provides an immediate playback for review by students and instructors when there's a question about why an action is marked as incorrect.

The Program

The GO! series has been used for over 17 years to teach students Microsoft Office successfully because of the *Quality of Instruction*, *Ease of Implementation*, and *Excellence in Assessment*. Using the hallmark Microsoft Procedural Syntax and Teachable Moment approach, students understand how to navigate the Microsoft Office ribbon so they don't get lost, and they get additional instruction and tips *when* they need them. Learning by doing is a great approach for skill-based learning, and creating a real-world document, spreadsheet, presentation, or database puts the skills in context for effective learning!

To improve student results, we recommend pairing the text content with **MyLab IT,** which is the teaching and learning platform that empowers you to reach every student. By combining trusted author content with digital tools and a flexible platform, MyLab personalizes the learning experience and will help your students learn and retain key course concepts while developing skills that future employers are seeking in their candidates.

Solving Teaching and Learning Challenges

The GO! series continues to evolve based on author interaction and experience with real students. GO! is written to ensure students know where they are going, how to get there, and why. Today's software is cloud based and changes frequently, so students need to know how the software functions so they can adapt quickly.

Each chapter is written with two instructional projects organized around **student learning outcomes** and **numbered objectives,** so that students understand what they will learn and be able to do when they finish the chapter. The **project approach** clusters the learning objectives around the projects rather than around the software features. This tested pedagogical approach teaches students to solve real problems as they practice and learn the software features. By using the textbook (print or digital), students can complete the A & B instructional projects as autograded Grader projects in MyLab IT. The *Learn How* videos, integrated in the etext or learning modules, give students an instructor-led, step-by-step guide through the project. This unique approach enhances learning and engages students because they receive immediate feedback. Additionally, students can practice the skills they are learning in the MyLab IT simulations, where they also get immediate feedback and help when needed! Both *Graders* and *Simulations* are available in assessment form so that students can demonstrate mastery.

The **Clear Instruction** in the project steps is written following *Microsoft Procedural Syntax* to guide students where to go and *then* what to do, so they never get lost! With the **Teachable Moment** approach, students learn important concepts when they need to as they work through the instructional projects. No long paragraphs of text. And with the integrated etext in MyLab IT, students can access their book anywhere, anytime.

The page design drives effective learning; textbook pages are clean and uncluttered, with screenshots that validate the student's actions and engage visual learners. Important information is boxed within the text so that students won't miss or skip the *Mac Tips*, *Another Way*, *By Touch*, *Note*, *Alert*, or *More Knowledge* details. **Color-Coded Steps** guide students through the projects with colors coded by project and the **End-of-Project Icon** helps students know when they have completed the project, which is especially useful in self-paced or online environments.

Students can engage in a wide variety of end-of-chapter projects where they apply what they learned in outcomes-based, problem-solving, and critical thinking projects—many of which require students to create a complete project from scratch.

Within the GO! etext and MyLab IT, students also have access to the *GO! Learn How* training videos, the *GO! to Work* videos (which demonstrate how Microsoft Office is used in a variety of jobs), the GO! for Job Success videos (which teach essential employability skills), and the *Where We're Going* videos, which provide a clear and concise overview of the instructional projects to ensure student success!

This complete, highly effective offering ensures students can learn the skills they need to succeed!

Developing Employability Skills

For students to succeed in a rapidly changing job market, they should be aware of their career options and how to go about developing a variety of skills. With MyLab IT and GO! we focus on developing these skills in the following ways:

High-Demand Office Skills are taught to help students gain these skills and prepare for the Microsoft Office Specialist (MOS) certification exams. The MOS objectives are covered throughout the content and highlighted with the MOS icons.

Essential Employability Skills are taught throughout the chapters using GO! for Job Success Videos and discussions, along with the new Critical Thinking badge students can earn by successfully completing the Critical Thinking Modules.

Employability Skills Matrix (ESM)								
	Grader Projects	Project K	Project M	Project O Group Project	Critical Thinking Projects and Badge	GO! To Work and Job Success Videos	MOS Practice Exams	MOS Badges
Critical Thinking	X	X	X		X		X	X
Communication	X			X		X		
Collaboration				X		X		
Knowledge Application and Analysis	X	X	X		X		X	X
Social Responsibility						X		

Real-World Projects and GO! To Work Videos

The projects in GO! help you learn skills you'll need in the workforce and everyday life. And the GO! to Work videos give you insight into how people in a variety of jobs put Microsoft Office into action every day.

Projects in GO! are real-world projects you create from start to finish, so that you are using the software features and skills as you will on the job and in everyday life.

GO! to Work videos feature people from a variety of real jobs explaining how they use Microsoft Office every day to help you see the relevance of learning these programs.

GO! for Job Success Videos and Discussions

Important professional skills you need to succeed in a work environment, such as Accepting Criticism, Customer Service, and Interview Skills, are covered in a video with discussion questions or an overall discussion topic. These are must-have skills.

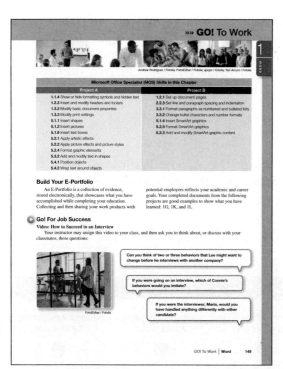

Skills Badging

Within MyLab IT 2019, you can earn digital badges that demonstrate mastery of specific skills related to Office 2019 or Critical Thinking. These badges can be easily shared across social networks, such as LinkedIn, leading to real opportunities to connect with potential employers.

Applied Learning Opportunities

Throughout the chapters there are two projects for instruction, two for review, and a variety of outcomes-based projects to demonstrate mastery, critical thinking, and problem solving. In addition, within MyLab IT, GO! Learn How videos walk students through the A & B instructional project objectives. Grader projects and simulations provide hands-on instruction, training, and assessment.

▼ Live-in-the-Application Grader Projects

The MyLab IT Grader projects are autograded so students receive immediate feedback on their work. By completing these projects, students gain real-world context as they work live in the application, to learn and demonstrate an understanding of how to perform specific skills to complete a project.

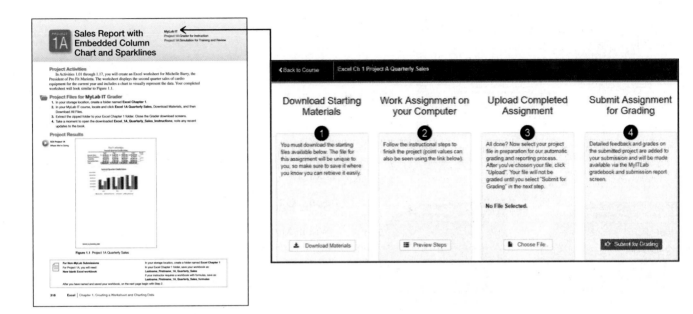

▼ Microsoft Office Simulations

The realistic and hi-fidelity simulations help students feel like they are working in the real Microsoft applications and enable them to explore, use 96% of Microsoft methods, and do so without penalty.

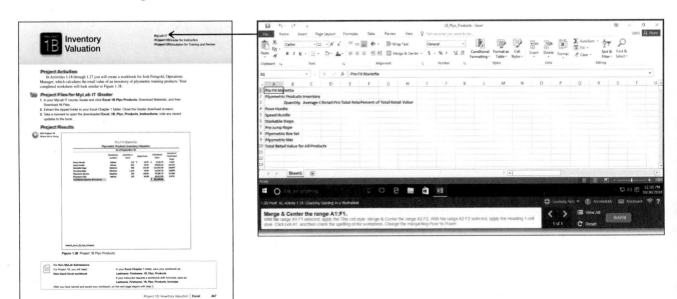

Instructor Teaching Resources

This program comes with the following teaching resources.

Resources available to instructors at www.pearsonhighered.com/go	Features of the Resources
Annotated Instructor Edition Tabs	Available for each chapter and include: • Suggested course implementation strategies and resources for the instructional portion of the chapter • Suggested strategies and resources for the Review, Practice, and Assessment portion of the chapter • Teaching tips
Annotated Solution Files	Annotated solution files in PDF feature callouts to enable easy grading.
Answer Keys for Chapter, MOS, and Critical Thinking Quizzes	Answer keys for each matching and multiple choice question in the chapter.
Application Capstones	Capstone projects for Word, Excel, Access, and PowerPoint that cover the objectives from all three chapters of each application. These are available as autograded Grader projects in MyLab IT, where students can also earn a proficiency badge if they score 90% or higher.
Collaborative Team Project	An optional exercise to assign to students to learn to work in groups.
Content Updates	A living document that features any changes in content based on Microsoft Office 365 changes as well as any errata.
Critical Thinking Quiz and Answers	Additional quiz and answers.
End-of-Chapter Online Projects H-J and M-O	Additional projects that can be assigned at instructor discretion.
Image Library	Every image in the book.
Instructor Manual	Available for each chapter and includes: • Suggested course implementation strategies and resources for the instructional portion of the chapter • Suggested strategies and resources for the Review, Practice, and Assessment portion of the chapter • Objectives • Teaching notes • Discussion questions
List of Objectives and Outcomes	Available for each chapter to help you determine what to assign • Includes every project and identifies which outcomes, objectives, and skills are included from the chapter
Lessons on the GO!	Projects created to teach new features added to Office 365. Available online only.
MOS Mapping and Additional Content	Based on the Office 2019 MOS Objectives • Includes a full guide of where each objective is covered in the textbook. • For any content not covered in the textbook, additional material is available in the Online Appendix document.
PowerPoint Presentations	PowerPoints for each chapter cover key topics, feature key images from the text, and include detailed speaker notes in addition to the slide content. PowerPoints meet accessibility standards for students with disabilities. Features include, but are not limited to: • Keyboard and screen reader access • Alternative text for images • High color contrast between background and foreground colors Audio PPTs contain spoken audio within traditional PowerPoint presentations.
Prepared Exams by Project, Chapter, and Application	An optional exercise that can be used to assess students' ability to perform the skills from each project, chapter, or across all chapters in an application • Each Prepared Exam folder includes the needed data files, instruction file, solution, annotated solution, and scorecard.

Resources available to instructors at www.pearsonhighered.com/go	Features of the Resources
Scorecards and Rubrics	Scorecards allow for easy scoring when hand-grading projects with definitive solutions.
	Rubrics are for projects without a definitive solution. These are available in Microsoft Word format, enabling instructors to customize the assignments for their classes.
Scripted Lectures	A lecture guide that provides the actions and language to help instructors demonstrate skills from the chapter.
Skills and Procedures Summary Charts	Concise list of key skills, including software icon and keyboard shortcut.
Solution Files, Solution File PDFs, and Solution Files with Formulas (Excel only)	Available for all exercises with definitive solutions.
Student Assignment Trackers	Document with a grid of suggested student deliverables per chapter that can be provided to students with columns for Due Date, Possible Points, and Actual Points.
Student Data Files	Files that students need to complete projects that are not delivered as Grader projects in MyLab IT.
Syllabus Template	Syllabus templates set up for 8-week, 12-week, and 16-week courses.
TestGen and Test Bank	TestGen enables instructors to: • Customize, save, and generate classroom tests • Edit, add, or delete questions from the Test Item Files • Analyze test results • Organize a database of tests and student results. The Test Gen contains approximately 75–100 total questions per chapter, made up of multiple-choice, fill-in-the blank, true/false, and matching. Questions include these annotations: • Correct answer • Difficulty level • Learning objective Alternative versions of the Test Bank are available for the following LMS: Blackboard CE/Vista, Blackboard, Desire2Learn, Moodle, Sakai, and Canvas.
Transition Guide	A detailed spreadsheet that provides a clear mapping of content from GO! Microsoft Office 2016 to GO! Microsoft Office 365, 2019 Edition.

Reviewers of the GO! Series

Carmen Montanez	Allan Hancock College	Therese ONeil	Indiana University of Pennsylvania
Jody Derry	Allan Hancock College	Bradley Howard	Itawamba Community College
Roberta McDonald	Anoka-Ramsey Community College	Edna Tull	Itawamba Community College
Paula Ruby	Arkansas State University	Pamela Larkin	Jefferson Community and Technical College
Buffie Schmidt	Augusta University	Sonya Shockley	Madisonville Community College
Julie Lewis	Baker College	Jeanne Canale	Middlesex Community College
Melanie Israel	Beal College	John Meir	Midlands Technical College
Suzanne Marks	Bellevue College	Robert Huyck	Mohawk Valley Community College
Ellen Glazer	Broward College	Mike Maesar	Montana Tech
Charline Nixon	Calhoun Community College	Julio Cuz	Moreno Valley College
Joseph Cash	California State University, Stanislaus	Lynn Wermers	North Shore Community College
Shaun Sides	Catawba Valley Community College	Angela Mott	Northeast Mississippi Community College
Linda Friedel	Central Arizona College	Connie Johnson	Owensboro Community & Technical College
Vicky Semple	Central Piedmont Community College	Kungwen Chu	Purdue University Northwest
Amanda Davis	Chattanooga State Community College	Kuan Chen	Purdue University Northwest
Randall George	Clarion University of Pennsylvania	Janette Nichols	Randolph Community College
Beth Zboran	Clarion University of Pennsylvania	Steven Zhang	Roane State Community College
Lee Southard	College of Coastal Georgia	Elizabeth Drake	Santa Fe College
Susan Mazzola	College of the Sequoias	Sandy Keeter	Seminole State
Vicki Brooks	Columbia College	Pat Dennis	South Plains College
Leasa Richards-Mealy	Columbia College	Tamara Dawson	Southern Nazarene University
Heidi Eaton	Elgin Community College	Richard Celli	SUNY Delhi
Ed Pearson	Friends University	Lois Blais	Walters State Community College
Nancy Woolridge	Fullerton College	Frederick MacCormack	Wilmington University
Wayne Way	Galveston College	Jessica Brown	Wilmington University
Leslie Martin	Gaston College	Doreen Palucci	Wilmington University
Don VanOeveren	Grand Rapids Community College	Rebecca Anderson	Zane State College

Microsoft Office Features and Windows 10 File Management

1

OFFICE AND
WINDOWS

Petar Djordjevic/Shutterstock

In This Chapter

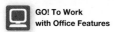

GO! To Work
with Office Features

In this chapter, you will practice using the features of Microsoft Office that work similarly across Word, Excel, Access, and PowerPoint. These features include performing commands, adding document properties, applying formatting to text, and searching for Office commands quickly. You will also practice using the file management features of Windows 10 so that you can create folders, save files, and find your documents easily.

The projects in this chapter relate to the **Bell Orchid Hotels**, headquartered in Boston, and which own and

operate restaurants, resorts, and business-oriented hotels. Resort property locations are in popular destinations, including Honolulu, Orlando, San Diego, and Santa Barbara. The resorts offer deluxe accommodations and a wide array of dining options. Other Bell Orchid hotels are located in major business centers and offer the latest technology in their meeting facilities. Bell Orchid offers extensive educational opportunities for employees. The company plans to open new properties and update existing properties over the next decade.

Chef Notes

Project Activities

In Activities 1.01 through 1.19, you will create a handout for the Executive Chef at Skyline Metro Grill to give to her staff at a meeting where they will develop new menu ideas for wedding rehearsal dinners. The restaurant is located within Bell Orchid's San Diego resort hotel. Your completed notes will look similar to Figure 1.1.

Project Files for MyLab IT Grader

1. For Project 1A, you will start with a blank Word document, and then you will learn how to create a folder for your **MyLab IT** files as you work through the Project instruction. At the appropriate point in the Project, you will be instructed to download your files from your **MyLab IT** course.

Project Results

GO! Project 1A

Where We're Going

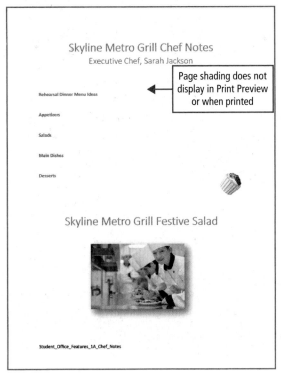

Figure 1.1 (Wavebreakmedia/Shutterstock)

For Non-MyLab Submissions   **Start with a blank Word document**

For Project 1A, you will begin with a blank Word document and then learn how to create a folder and save a Word document as you work through the Project instruction.

NOTE   If You Are Using a Touch Screen

Tap an item to click it.

Press and hold for a few seconds to right-click; release when the information or commands display.

Touch the screen with two or more fingers and then pinch together to zoom out or stretch your fingers apart to zoom in.

Slide your finger on the screen to scroll—slide left to scroll right and slide right to scroll left.

Slide to rearrange—similar to dragging with a mouse.

Swipe to select—slide an item a short distance with a quick movement—to select an item and bring up commands, if any.

Objective 1 | Explore Microsoft Office

ALERT   Because Office 365 is a cloud-based subscription service that receives continuous updates, you may encounter some variations in what appears on your screen and what is shown in this instruction. Microsoft Office 365 is fully installed on your PC or Mac; no internet access is necessary to create or edit documents. When you *are* connected to the internet, you will receive monthly upgrades and new features, so you always have the latest versions of Office apps as soon as they are available. Your subscription gives you continuous free access to the latest innovations and refinements.

ALERT   Is Your Screen More Colorful and a Different Size Than the Figures in This Textbook?

Your installation of Microsoft Office may use the default Colorful theme, where the ribbon in each application is a vibrant color and the title bar displays with white text. In this textbook, figures shown use the White theme, but you can be assured that all the commands are the same. You can keep your Colorful theme, or if you prefer, you can change your theme to White to match the figures here. To do so, open any application and display a new document. On the ribbon, click the File tab, and then on the left, click Options. With General selected on the left, under Personalize your copy of Microsoft Office, click the Office Theme arrow, and then click White. Change the Office Background to No Background. (In macOS, display the menu bar, click the application name—Word, Excel, and so on—click Preferences, and then click General. Under Personalize, click the Office Theme arrow to select either Colorful or Classic.)

Additionally, the figures in this book were captured using a screen resolution of 1280 x 768. If that is not your screen resolution, your screen will closely resemble, but not match, the figures shown. To view or change your screen's resolution, on the desktop, right-click in a blank area, click Display settings, click the Resolution arrow, and then select the resolution you want.

GO! Learn How
Video OF1-1

The term *desktop application* or *desktop app* refers to a computer program that is installed on your PC and that requires a computer operating system such as Microsoft Windows to run. The programs in Office 365 and in Microsoft Office 2019 are considered to be desktop apps. A desktop app typically has hundreds of features and takes time to learn.

Activity 1.01 | Exploring Microsoft Office

1 On the computer you are using, start Microsoft Word, and then compare your screen with Figure 1.2.

Depending on which operating system you are using and how your computer is set up, you might start Word from the taskbar or from the Start menu. On an Apple Mac computer, you might start the program from the Dock.

On the left, the Home tab is active in this view, referred to as *Backstage view*, which is a centralized space for all your file management tasks such as opening, saving, printing, publishing, or sharing a file—all the things you can do *with* a file. In macOS the File tab is on the menu bar.

Documents that you have recently opened, if any, display under the Recent tab. You can also click the Pinned tab to see documents you have pinned there, or you can click the Shared with Me tab to see documents that have been shared with you by others.

On the left, you can click New to find a *template*—a preformatted document that you can use as a starting point and then change to suit your needs. Or you can click Open to navigate to your files and folders. You can also look at Account information, give feedback to Microsoft, or look at the Word Options dialog box.

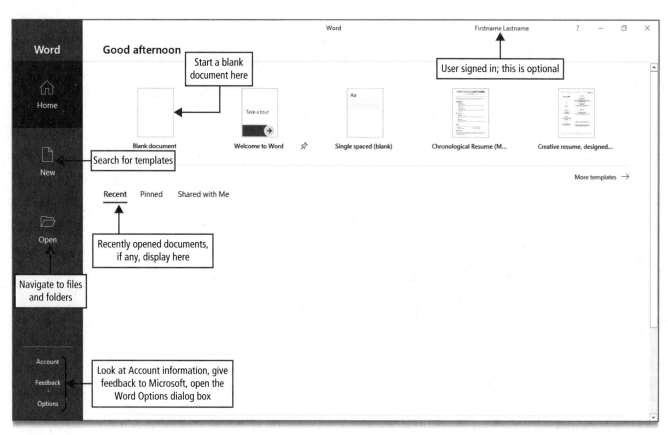

Figure 1.2

2 ▶ Click **Blank document**. Compare your screen with Figure 1.3, and then take a moment to study the description of the screen elements in the table in Figure 1.4.

> **NOTE** **Displaying the Full Ribbon**
>
> If your full ribbon does not display, click any tab, and then at the right end of the ribbon, click [📌] to pin the ribbon to keep it open while you work.

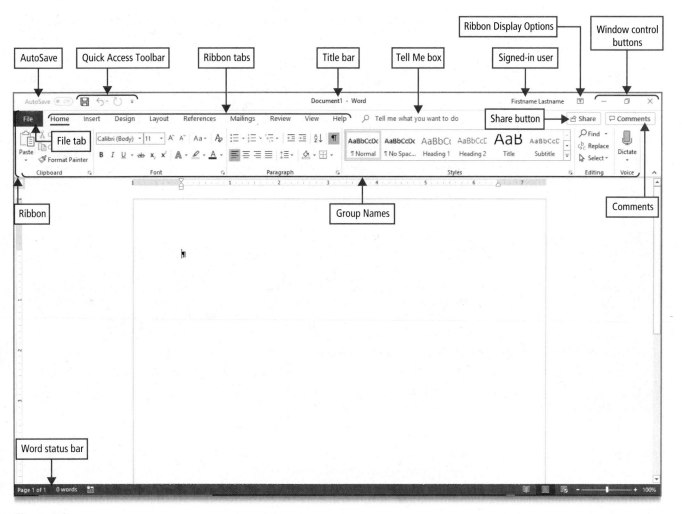

Figure 1.3

Screen Element	Description
AutoSave (off unless your document is saved to OneDrive using an Office 365 subscription)	Saves your document every few seconds so you don't have to. On a Windows system, AutoSave is available in Word, Excel, and PowerPoint for Office 365 subscribers. AutoSave is enabled only when a file is stored on OneDrive, OneDrive for Business, or SharePoint Online. Changes to your document are saved to the cloud as you are working, and if other people are working on the same file, AutoSave lets them see your changes in a matter of seconds.
Comments	Displays a short menu from which you can add a comment to your document or view other comments already in the document.
File tab	Displays Microsoft Office Backstage view, which is a centralized space for all your file management tasks such as opening, saving, printing, publishing, or sharing a file—all the things you can do *with* a file. (In macOS the File tab is on the menu bar.)
Group names	Indicate the name of the groups of related commands on the displayed ribbon tab.
Quick Access Toolbar	Displays buttons to perform frequently used commands and resources with a single click. The default commands include Save, Undo, and Redo. You can add and delete buttons to customize the Quick Access Toolbar for your convenience.
Ribbon	Displays a group of task-oriented tabs that contain the commands, styles, and resources you need to work in Microsoft Office desktop apps. The look of your ribbon depends on your screen resolution. A high resolution will display more individual items and button names on the ribbon.
Ribbon Display Options	Displays three ways you can display the ribbon: Auto-hide Ribbon, Show Tabs, or Show Tabs and Commands; typically, you will want to use Show Tabs and Commands, especially while you are learning Office.
Ribbon tabs	Display the names of the task-oriented tabs relevant to the open document.
Share	Opens the Share dialog box from which you can save your file to the cloud—your OneDrive—and then share it with others so you can collaborate. Here you can also email the Office file or a PDF of the file directly from Outlook if you are using Outlook to view and send email. A *dialog box* enables you to make decisions about an individual object or topic.
Signed-in user	Identifies the user who is signed in to Office.
Status bar	Displays file information on the left; on the right displays buttons for Read Mode, Print Layout, and Web Layout views; on the far right edge, displays Zoom controls.
Tell me what you want to do	Provides a search feature for Microsoft Office commands that you activate by typing what you are looking for in the *Tell me what you want to do* area. As you type, every keystroke refines the results so that you can click the command as soon as it displays.
Title bar	Displays the name of the file and the name of the program; the window control buttons are grouped on the right side of the title bar.
Window control buttons	Displays buttons for commands to Minimize, Restore Down, or Close the window.

Figure 1.4

Objective 2 Create a Folder for File Storage

GO! Learn How
Video OF1-2

A *location* is any disk drive, folder, or other place in which you can store files and folders. A *file* is information stored on a computer under a single name. A *folder* is a container in which you store files. Where you store your files depends on how and where you use your data. For example, for your college classes, you might decide to store your work on a removable USB flash drive so that you can carry your files to different locations and access your files on different computers.

If you do most of your work on a single computer, for example your home desktop system or your laptop computer that you take with you to school or work, then you can store your files in one of the folders on your hard drive provided by your Windows operating system—Documents, Music, Pictures, or Videos.

The best place to store files if you want them to be available anytime, anywhere, from almost any device is on your *OneDrive*, which is Microsoft's free *cloud storage* for anyone with a free Microsoft account. Cloud storage refers to online storage of data so that you can access your data from different places and devices. *Cloud computing* refers to applications and services that are accessed over the internet, rather than to applications that are installed on your local computer.

Besides being able to access your documents from any device or location, OneDrive also offers *AutoSave*, which saves your document every few seconds, so you don't have to. On a Windows system, AutoSave is available in Word, Excel, and PowerPoint for Office 365 subscribers. Changes to your document are saved to the cloud as you are working, and if other people are working on the same file—referred to as *real-time co-authoring*—AutoSave lets them see your changes in a matter of seconds.

If you have an *Office 365* subscription—one of the versions of Microsoft Office to which you subscribe for an annual fee or download for free with your college *.edu* address—your storage capacity on OneDrive is a terabyte or more, which is more than most individuals would ever require. Many colleges provide students with free Office 365 subscriptions. The advantage of subscribing to Office 365 is that you receive monthly updates with new features.

Because many people now have multiple computing devices—desktop, laptop, tablet, smartphone—it is common to store data *in the cloud* so that it is always available. *Synchronization*, also called *syncing*—pronounced SINK-ing—is the process of updating computer files that are in two or more locations according to specific rules. So, if you create and save a Word document on your OneDrive using your laptop, you can open and edit that document on your tablet in OneDrive. When you close the document again, the file is properly updated to reflect your changes. Your OneDrive account will guide you in setting options for syncing files to your specifications. You can open and edit Office files by using Office apps available on a variety of device platforms, including iOS, Android, in a web browser, and in Windows.

MORE KNOWLEDGE | **Creating a Microsoft Account**

Use a free Microsoft account to sign in to Microsoft Office so that you can work on different PCs and use your free OneDrive cloud storage. If you already sign in to a Windows PC or tablet, or you sign in to Xbox Live, Outlook.com, or OneDrive, use that account to sign in to Office. To create a new Microsoft account, in your browser, search for *sign up for a Microsoft account*. You can use any email address as the user name for your new Microsoft account—including addresses from Outlook.com or Gmail.

Activity 1.02 | Creating a Folder for File Storage

Your computer's operating system, either Windows or macOS, helps you to create and maintain a logical folder structure, so always take the time to name your files and folders consistently.

NOTE This Activity is for Windows PC users. Mac users refer to the document *Creating a Folder for File Storage on a Mac*.

Mac users can refer to the document Creating a Folder for File Storage on a Mac available within **MyLab IT** or, for non-MyLab users, your instructor can provide this document to you from the Instructor Resource Center.

In this Activity, you will create a folder in the storage location you have chosen to use for your files, and then you will save your file. This example will use the Documents folder on the PC at which you are working. If you prefer to store on your OneDrive or on a USB flash drive, you can use similar steps.

1 Decide where you are going to store your files for this Project.

As the first step in saving a file, determine where you want to save the file, and if necessary, insert a storage device.

2 At the top of your screen, in the title bar, notice that *Document1 – Word* displays.

The Blank option on the opening screen of an Office program displays a new unsaved file with a default name—*Document1, Presentation1*, and so on. As you create your file, your work is temporarily stored in the computer's memory until you initiate a Save command, at which time you must choose a file name and a location in which to save your file.

3 In the upper left corner of your screen, click the **File tab** to display **Backstage** view, and then on the left, if necessary, click **Info**. Compare your screen with Figure 1.5.

Recall that Backstage view is a centralized space that groups commands related to *file* management; that is why the tab is labeled *File*. File management commands include opening, saving, printing, or sharing a file. The **Backstage tabs**—*Info, New, Open, Save, Save As, Print, Share, Export*, and *Close*—display along the left side. The tabs group file-related tasks together.

Here, the **Info tab** displays information—*info*—about the current file, and file management commands display under Info. For example, if you click the Protect Document button, a list of options that you can set for this file that relate to who can open or edit the document displays.

On the right, you can also examine the **document properties**. Document properties, also known as **metadata**, are details about a file that describe or identify it, such as the title, author name, subject, and keywords that identify the document's topic or contents.

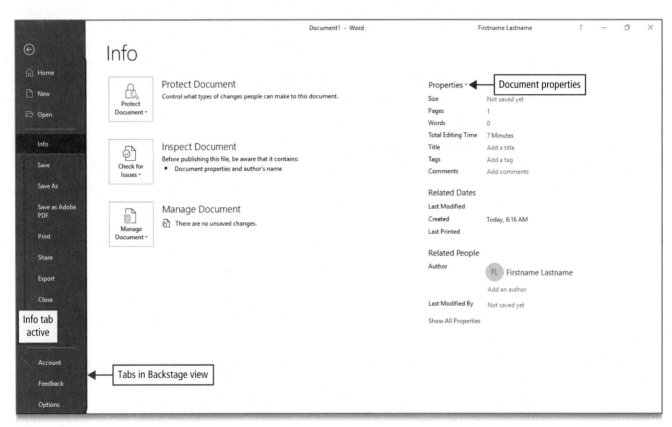

Figure 1.5

4 On the left, click **Save As**, and notice that, if you are signed into Office with a Microsoft account, one option for storing your files is your **OneDrive**. Compare your screen with Figure 1.6.

When you are saving something for the first time, for example a new Word document, the Save and Save As commands are identical. That is, the Save As commands will display if you click Save or if you click Save As.

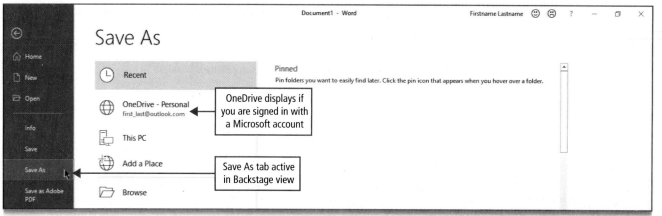

Figure 1.6

NOTE   Saving After Your File Is Named

After you name and save a file, the Save command on the Quick Access Toolbar saves any changes you make to the file without displaying Backstage view. The Save As command enables you to name and save a *new* file based on the current one—in a location that you choose. After you name and save the new document, the original document closes, and the new document—based on the original one—displays.

5 To store your Word file in the **Documents** folder on your PC, click **Browse** to display the **Save As** dialog box. On the left, in the **navigation pane**, scroll down; if necessary click **>** to expand This PC, and then click **Documents**. Compare your screen with Figure 1.7.

In the Save As dialog box, you must indicate the name you want for the file and the location where you want to save the file. When working with your own data, it is good practice to pause at this point and determine the logical name and location for your file.

In the Save As dialog box, a *toolbar* displays, which is a row, column, or block of buttons or icons, that displays across the top of a window and that contains commands for tasks you perform with a single click.

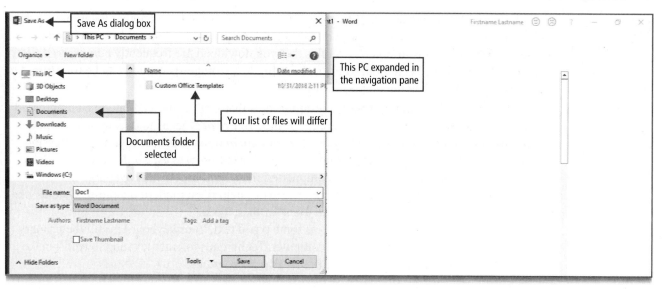

Figure 1.7

6 On the toolbar, click **New folder**.

In the file list, Windows creates a new folder, and the text *New folder* is selected.

7 Type **Office Features Chapter 1** and press Enter. In the **file list**, double-click the name of your new folder to open it and display its name in the **address bar**. Compare your screen with Figure 1.8.

In Windows-based programs, the Enter key confirms an action.

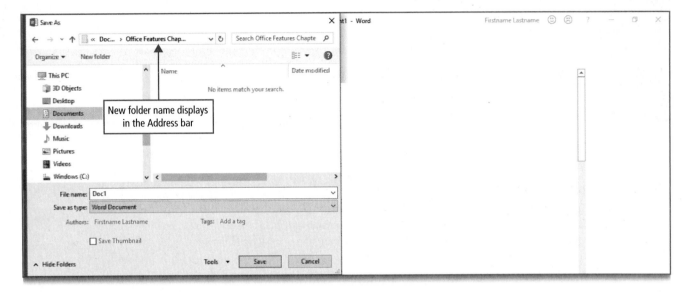

New folder name displays in the Address bar

Figure 1.8

8 In the lower right corner of the **Save As** dialog box, click **Cancel**. In the upper left corner of Backstage view, click the **Back** arrow.

9 In the upper right corner of the Word window, click **Close** ⌧. If prompted to save your changes, click Don't Save. Close any other open windows or programs.

Objective 3	**Download and Extract Zipped Files, Enter and Edit Text in an Office Application, and Use Editor to Check Documents**

GO! Learn How
Video OF1-3

Download refers to the action of transferring or copying a file from another location—such as a cloud storage location, your college's Learning Management System, or from an internet site like **MyLab IT**—to your computer. Files that you download are frequently *compressed files*, which are files that have been reduced in size, take up less storage space, and can be transferred to other computers faster than uncompressed files.

A compressed folder might contain a group of files that were combined into one compressed folder, which makes it easier to share a group of files. To *extract* means to decompress, or pull out, files from a compressed form. The terms *zip* and *unzip* refer to the process of compressing (zipping) and extracting (unzipping). Windows 10 includes *Compressed Folder Tools*, available on the ribbon, to assist you in extracting compressed files. Similar tools are available in macOS. You do not need to install a separate program to zip or unzip files; modern operating systems like Windows and macOS provide sophisticated tools for these tasks.

All programs in Microsoft Office require some typed text. Your keyboard is still the primary method of entering information into your computer. Techniques to enter text and to *edit*—make changes to—text are similar across all Microsoft Office programs.

For Non-MyLab Submissions

Start Word and click Blank document. Click the File tab, on the left click Save As, click Browse, and then navigate to your **Office Features Chapter 1 folder.** At the bottom of the **Save As** dialog box, in the **File name** box, using your own name, name the file **Lastname_Firstname_Office_Features_1A_Chef_Notes** and then click Save. Then, move to Step 3 in Activity 1.03.

Activity 1.03 | **Downloading and Extracting Zipped Files from MyLab IT and Entering and Editing Text in an Office Program**

1 ▶ Sign in to your **MyLab IT** course. Locate and click the Grader project **Office Features 1A Chef Notes**, click **Download Materials**, and then click **Download All Files**. Using the Chrome browser (if you are using a different browser see notes below), extract the zipped folder to your **Office Features Chapter 1 folder** as follows (or use your favorite method to download and extract files):

- In the lower left, next to the downloaded zipped folder, click the small **arrow**, and then click **Show in folder**. The zipped folder displays in *File Explorer*—the Windows program that displays the contents of locations, folders, and files on your computer—in the Downloads folder. (Unless you have changed default settings, downloaded files go to the Downloads folder on your computer.)
- With the zipped folder selected, on the ribbon, under **Compressed Folder Tools**, click the **Extract tab**, and then at the right end of the ribbon, click **Extract all** (you may have to wait a few seconds for the command to become active).
- In the displayed **Extract Compressed (Zipped) Folders** dialog box, click **Browse**. In the **Select a destination** dialog box, use the navigation pane on the left to navigate to your **Office Features Chapter 1 folder**, and double-click its name to open the folder and display its name in the **Address bar**.
- In the lower right, click **Select Folder**, and then in the lower right, click **Extract**; when complete, a new File Explorer window displays showing the extracted files in your chapter folder. Take a moment to open **Office_Features_1A_Chef_Notes_Instructions**; note any recent updates to the book.
- **Close** ⊠ both File Explorer windows, close any open documents, and then close the Grader download screens. You can also close **MyLab IT** and, if open, your Learning Management system.

> **NOTE**   **Using the Edge Browser or Firefox Browser to Extract Files**
>
> Microsoft Edge: At the bottom, click Open, click Extract all, click Browse, navigate to and open your Chapter folder, click Select Folder, click Extract.
> Firefox: In the displayed dialog box, click OK, click Extract all, click Browse, navigate to and open your Chapter folder, click Select Folder, and then click Extract.

> 🖥 **MAC TIP**   Using the Chrome browser, in **MyLab IT**, after you click Download Materials, in the lower left, to the right of the zipped folder, click the arrow. Click Open. Click the blue folder containing the unzipped files. Use Finder commands to move or copy the files to your Office Features Chapter 1 folder.

2 ▶ On the Windows taskbar, click **File Explorer** ▣. Navigate to your **Office Features Chapter 1 folder**, and then double-click the Word file you downloaded from **MyLab IT** that displays your name—**Student_Office_Features_1A_Chef_Notes**. In this empty Word document, if necessary, at the top, click **Enable Editing**.

> 🖥 **MAC TIP**   When the Word application is not open, on the Dock, use the macOS Finder commands to locate your Word document. When the Word application is open, use the File tab on the menu bar.

3 ▶ On the ribbon, on the **Home tab**, in the **Paragraph group**, if necessary, click **Show/Hide** ¶ so that it is active—shaded. On the **View tab**, if necessary, in the **Show group**, select the **Ruler** check box so that rulers display below the ribbon and on the left side of your window, and then redisplay the **Home tab**.

The *insertion point*—a blinking vertical line that indicates where text or graphics will be inserted—displays. In Office programs, the mouse *pointer*—any symbol that displays on your screen in response to moving your mouse device—displays in different shapes depending on the task you are performing and the area of the screen to which you are pointing.

When you press Enter, Spacebar, or Tab on your keyboard, characters display to represent these keystrokes. These screen characters do not print and are referred to as **formatting marks** or **nonprinting characters**.

When working in Word, display the rulers so that you can see how margin settings affect your document and how text and objects align. Additionally, if you set a tab stop or an indent, its location is visible on the ruler.

NOTE   Activating Show/Hide in Word Documents

When Show/Hide is active—the button is shaded—formatting marks display. Because formatting marks guide your eye in a document—like a map and road signs guide you along a highway—these marks will display throughout this instruction. Expert Word users keep these marks displayed while creating documents.

4 ▶ Type **Skyline Grille Info** and notice how the insertion point moves to the right as you type. Point slightly to the right of the letter *e* in *Grille* and click to place the insertion point there. Compare your screen with Figure 1.9.

A **paragraph symbol** (¶) indicates the end of a paragraph and displays each time you press Enter. This is a type of formatting mark and does not print.

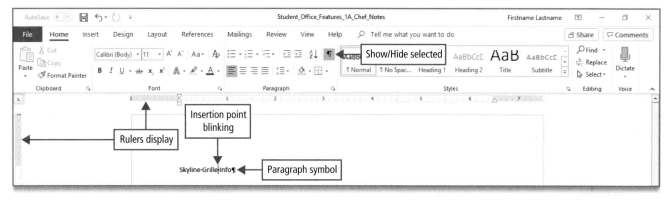

Figure 1.9

5 ▶ On your keyboard, locate and then press the Backspace key one time to delete the letter *e*.

Pressing Backspace removes a character to the left of the insertion point.

6 ▶ Press → one time to place the insertion point to the left of the *I* in *Info*. Type **Chef** and then press Spacebar one time.

By **default**, when you type text in an Office program, existing text moves to the right to make space for new typing. Default refers to the current selection or setting that is automatically used by a program unless you specify otherwise.

7 ▶ Press Del four times to delete *Info* and then type **Notes**

Pressing Del removes a character to the right of the insertion point.

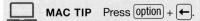

8 With your insertion point blinking after the word *Notes*, on your keyboard, hold down the Ctrl key. While holding down Ctrl, press ← three times to move the insertion point to the beginning of the word *Grill*.

> This is a ***keyboard shortcut***—a key or combination of keys that performs a task that would otherwise require a mouse. This keyboard shortcut moves the insertion point to the beginning of the previous word.

> A keyboard shortcut is indicated as Ctrl + ← (or some other combination of keys) to indicate that you hold down the first key while pressing the second key. A keyboard shortcut can also include three keys, in which case you hold down the first two and then press the third. For example, Ctrl + Shift + ← selects one word to the left.

MAC TIP Press option + ←.

9 With the insertion point blinking at the beginning of the word *Grill*, type **Metro** and press Spacebar one time.

10 Click to place the insertion point after the letter *s* in *Notes* and then press Enter one time. With the insertion point blinking, type the following and include the spelling error: **Exective Chef, Madison Dunham** (If Word autocorrects *Exective* to *Executive*, delete *u* in the word.)

11 With your mouse, point slightly to the left of the *M* in *Madison*, hold down the left mouse button, and then ***drag***—hold down the left mouse button while moving your mouse—to the right to select the text *Madison Dunham* but not the paragraph mark following it, and then release the mouse button. Compare your screen with Figure 1.10.

> The ***mini toolbar*** displays commands that are commonly used with the selected object, which places common commands close to your pointer. When you move the pointer away from the mini toolbar, it fades from view.

> ***Selecting*** refers to highlighting—by dragging or clicking with your mouse—areas of text or data or graphics so that the selection can be edited, formatted, copied, or moved. The action of dragging includes releasing the left mouse button at the end of the area you want to select.

> The Office programs recognize a selected area as one unit to which you can make changes. Selecting text may require some practice. If you are not satisfied with your result, click anywhere outside of the selection, and then begin again.

MAC TIP The mini toolbar may not display; use ribbon commands.

BY TOUCH Tap once on *Madison* to display the gripper—a small circle that acts as a handle—directly below the word. This establishes the start gripper. If necessary, with your finger, drag the gripper to the beginning of the word. Then drag the gripper to the end of *Dunham* to select the text and display the end gripper.

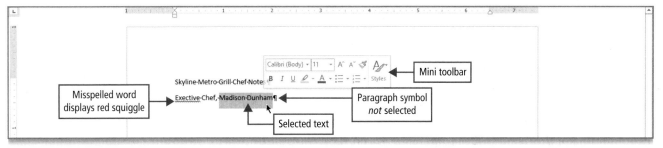

Figure 1.10

12 With the text *Madison Dunham* selected, type **Sarah Jackson**

In any Windows-based program, such as the Microsoft Office programs, selected text is deleted and then replaced when you begin to type new text. You will save time by developing good techniques for selecting and then editing or replacing selected text, which is easier than pressing [Backspace] or [Del] numerous times to delete text.

Activity 1.04 | Checking Spelling

ALERT   The Display of Spelling Suggestions Varies Among Office Versions

Depending on your version of Office (Office 365 or Office 2019), you may see variations in how the spelling checking displays suggestions for corrections. You will still be able to follow the screen prompts to select the correct spelling.

Microsoft Office has a dictionary of words against which all entered text is checked. In Word and PowerPoint, words that are not in the dictionary display a red squiggle, indicating a possible misspelled word, a proper name, or an unusual word—none of which are in the Office dictionary. In Excel and Access, you can initiate a check of the spelling, but red squiggles do not display.

1 Notice that the misspelled word *Exective* displays with a red squiggle.

2 Point to *Exective* and then **right-click**—click your right mouse button one time.

A **shortcut menu** displays, which displays commands and options relevant to the selected text or object. These are **context-sensitive commands** because they relate to the item you right-clicked. These are also referred to as **context menus**. Here, the shortcut menu displays commands related to the misspelled word.

BY TOUCH   Tap and hold a moment—when a square displays around the misspelled word, release your finger to display the shortcut menu.

3 Press [Esc] two times to cancel the shortcut menus, and then in the lower left corner of your screen, on the status bar, click the **Proofing** icon ▣, which displays an *X* because some errors are detected. In the **Editor** pane that displays on the right, if necessary, click the Results button, and then under **Suggestions**, to the right of *Exective*, click ▾, and then compare your screen with Figure 1.11.

The Editor pane displays on the right. **Editor**, according to Microsoft, is your digital writing assistant in Word and also in Outlook. Editor displays misspellings, grammatical mistakes, and writing style issues as you type by marking red squiggles for spelling, blue double underlines for grammar, and dotted underlines for writing style issues.

Here you have many more options for checking spelling than you have on the shortcut menu. The suggested correct word, *Executive*, displays under Suggestions. The displayed menu provides additional options for the suggestion. For example, you can have the word read aloud, hear it spelled out, change all occurrences in the document, or add to AutoCorrect options.

In the Editor pane, you can ignore the word one time or in all occurrences, change the word to the suggested word, select a different suggestion, or add a word to the dictionary against which Word checks.

MAC TIP   In the Spelling and Grammar dialog box, click Executive, and then click Change. The Editor pane is not available on a Mac.

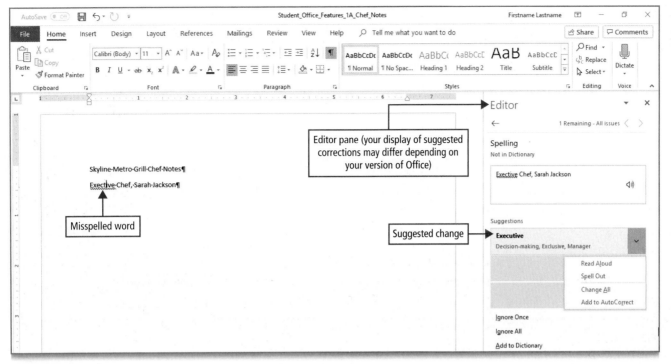

Figure 1.11

 ANOTHER WAY Press [F7] to display the Editor pane; or, on the Review tab, in the Proofing group, you can check your document for Spelling.

4 In the **Editor** pane, under **Suggestions**, click *Executive* to correct the spelling. In the message box that displays, click **OK**.

5 If necessary **Close** the **Editor** pane by clicking ⊠ in the upper right corner.

Objective 4 Perform Office Commands and Apply Office Formatting

GO! Learn How
Video OF1-4

Formatting refers to applying Office commands to make your document easy to read and to add visual touches and design elements to make your document inviting to the reader. This process establishes the overall appearance of text, graphics, and pages in your document.

Activity 1.05 Performing Commands from a Dialog Box

MOS
1.2.4

In a dialog box, you make decisions about an individual object or topic. In some dialog boxes, you can make multiple decisions in one place.

1 On the ribbon, click the **Design tab**, and then in the **Page Background group**, click **Page Color**.

2 At the bottom of the menu, notice the command **Fill Effects** followed by an **ellipsis** (. . .). Compare your screen with Figure 1.12.

An *ellipsis* is a set of three dots indicating incompleteness. An ellipsis following a command name indicates that a dialog box will display when you click the command.

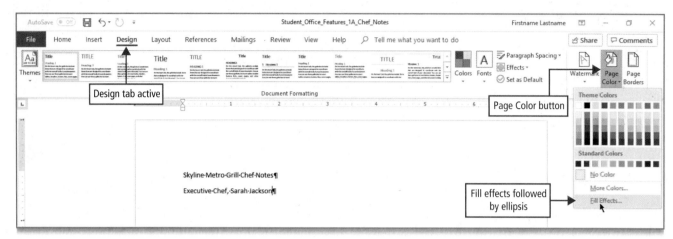

Figure 1.12

3 Click **Fill Effects** to display the **Fill Effects** dialog box. Compare your screen with Figure 1.13.

Fill is the inside color of a page or object. Here, the dialog box displays a set of tabs across the top from which you can display different sets of options. Some dialog boxes display the option group names on the left. The Gradient tab is active. In a *gradient fill*, one color fades into another.

MAC TIP Click More Colors to display the Colors dialog box.

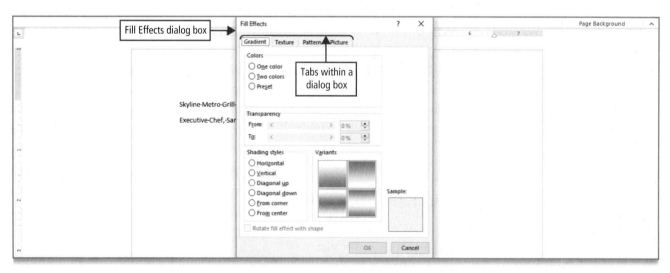

Figure 1.13

4 ▶ Under **Colors**, click the **One color** option button.

The dialog box displays settings related to the *One color* option. An ***option button*** is a round button that enables you to make one choice among two or more options.

MAC TIP On the first tab, drag your cursor on the color wheel until you see a color in the small box similar to the background color shown in Figure 1.1.

5 ▶ Click the **Color 1 arrow**—the arrow under the text *Color 1*—and then in the eighth column, point to the second color to display a ScreenTip with the name of the color.

When you click an arrow in a dialog box, additional options display. A ***ScreenTip*** displays useful information about mouse actions, such as pointing to screen elements or dragging.

6 ▶ Click the color, and then notice that the fill color displays in the **Color 1** box. In the **Dark Light** bar, click the **Light arrow** as many times as necessary until the scroll box is all the way to the right—or drag the scroll box all the way to the right. Under **Shading styles**, click the **From corner** option button. Under **Variants**, click the **upper right variant**. Compare your screen with Figure 1.14.

This dialog box is a good example of the many different elements you may encounter in a dialog box. Here you have option buttons, an arrow that displays a menu, a slider bar, and graphic options that you can select.

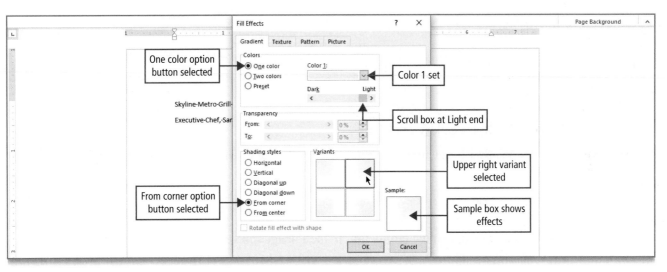

Figure 1.14

BY TOUCH In a dialog box, you can tap option buttons and other commands just as you would click them with a mouse. When you tap an arrow to display a color palette, a larger palette displays than if you used your mouse. This makes it easier to select colors with your finger in a dialog box.

7 ▶ At the bottom of the dialog box, click **OK**, and notice the subtle page color.

In Word, the gold shading page color will not print—even on a color printer—unless you set specific options to do so. However, a subtle background page color is effective if people will be reading the document on a screen. Microsoft's research indicates that two-thirds of people who open Word documents on a screen never print or edit them; they only read them.

Activity 1.06 | Using Undo and Applying Text Effects

1 Point to the *S* in *Skyline*, and then drag down and to the right to select both paragraphs of text and include the paragraph marks. On the mini toolbar, click **Styles**, and then *point to* but do not click **Title**. Compare your screen with Figure 1.15.

A *style* is a group of formatting commands, such as font, font size, font color, paragraph alignment, and line spacing that can be applied to a paragraph with one command.

Live Preview is a technology that shows the result of applying an editing or formatting change as you point to possible results—before you actually apply it.

MAC TIP The mini toolbar and Live Preview are not available; use ribbon commands.

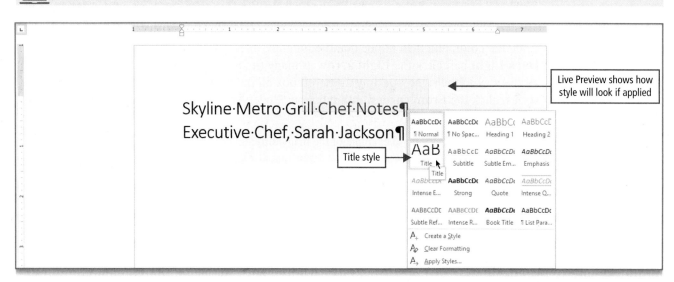

Figure 1.15

2 In the **Styles** gallery, click **Title**.

A *gallery* is an Office feature that displays a list of potential results.

MAC TIP On the Home tab, in the Styles gallery, click Title.

3 On the ribbon, on the **Home tab**, in the **Paragraph group**, click **Center** ≡ to center the two paragraphs.

Alignment refers to the placement of paragraph text relative to the left and right margins. *Center alignment* refers to text that is centered horizontally between the left and right margins. You can also align text at the left margin, which is the default alignment for text in Word, or at the right.

ANOTHER WAY Press Ctrl + E to use the Center command.

MAC TIP Press command ⌘ + E to use the Center command.

4 With the two paragraphs still selected, on the **Home tab**, in the **Font Group**, click **Text Effects and Typography** Ⓐ ▾ to display a gallery.

5 In the second row, click the first effect. Click anywhere to *deselect*—cancel the selection—the text and notice the text effect.

6 Because this effect might be difficult to read, in the upper left corner of your screen, on the **Quick Access Toolbar**, click **Undo** ↺.

The *Undo* command reverses your last action.

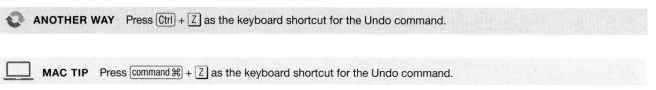

ANOTHER WAY   Press `Ctrl` + `Z` as the keyboard shortcut for the Undo command.

MAC TIP   Press `command ⌘` + `Z` as the keyboard shortcut for the Undo command.

7 Select the two paragraphs of text again, display the **Text Effects and Typography** gallery again, and then in the first row, click the fifth effect. Click anywhere to deselect the text and notice the text effect. Compare your screen with Figure 1.16.

As you progress in your study of Microsoft Office, you will practice using many dialog boxes and commands to apply interesting effects such as this to your Word documents, Excel worksheets, Access database objects, and PowerPoint slides.

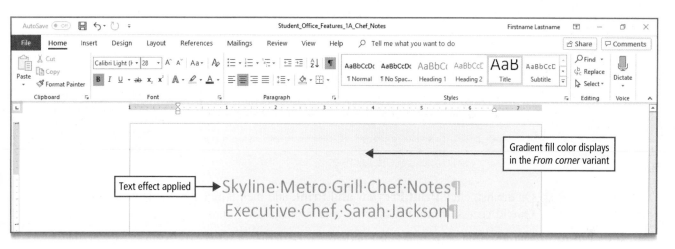

Figure 1.16

Activity 1.07 | Performing Commands from and Customizing the Quick Access Toolbar

The ribbon that displays across the top of the program window groups commands in the way that you would most logically use them. The ribbon in each Office program is slightly different, but all contain the same three elements: *tabs*, *groups*, and *commands*.

Tabs display across the top of the ribbon, and each tab relates to a type of activity; for example, laying out a page. Groups are sets of related commands for specific tasks. Commands—instructions to computer programs—are arranged in groups and might display as a button, a menu, or a box in which you type information.

You can also minimize the ribbon so only the tab names display, which is useful when working on a smaller screen such as a tablet computer where you want to maximize your screen viewing area.

1 In the upper left corner of your screen, above the ribbon, locate the **Quick Access Toolbar**.

Recall that the Quick Access Toolbar contains commands that you use frequently. By default, only the commands Save, Undo, and Redo display, but you can add and delete commands to suit your needs. Possibly the computer at which you are working already has additional commands added to the Quick Access Toolbar.

2 At the end of the **Quick Access Toolbar**, click the **Customize Quick Access Toolbar** button ⏷, and then compare your screen with Figure 1.17.

A list of commands that Office users commonly add to their Quick Access Toolbar displays, including New, Open, Email, Quick Print, and Print Preview and Print. Commands already on the Quick Access Toolbar display a check mark. Commands that you add to the Quick Access Toolbar are always just one click away.

Here you can also display the More Commands dialog box, from which you can select any command from any tab to add to the Quick Access Toolbar.

BY TOUCH Tap once on Quick Access Toolbar commands.

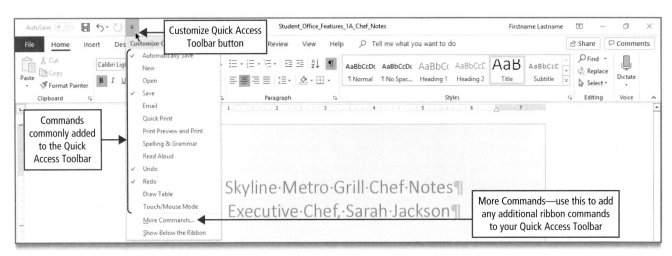

Figure 1.17

3 On the list, click **Print Preview and Print**, and then notice that the icon is added to the **Quick Access Toolbar**. Compare your screen with Figure 1.18.

The icon that represents the Print Preview command displays on the Quick Access Toolbar. Because this is a command that you will use frequently while building Office documents, you might decide to have this command remain on your Quick Access Toolbar.

ANOTHER WAY Right-click any command on the ribbon, and then on the shortcut menu, click Add to Quick Access Toolbar.

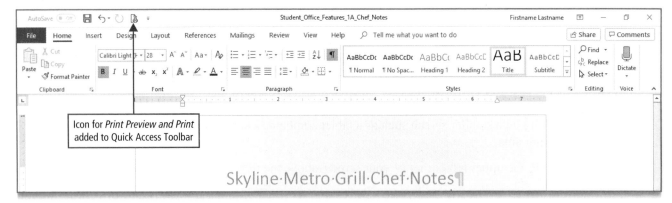

Figure 1.18

Activity 1.08 | Performing Commands from the Ribbon

> **1** ▶ In the second line of text, click to place the insertion point to the right of the letter *n* in *Jackson*. Press ⸨Enter⸩ three times. Compare your screen with Figure 1.19.

Word creates three new blank paragraphs, and no Text Effect is applied.

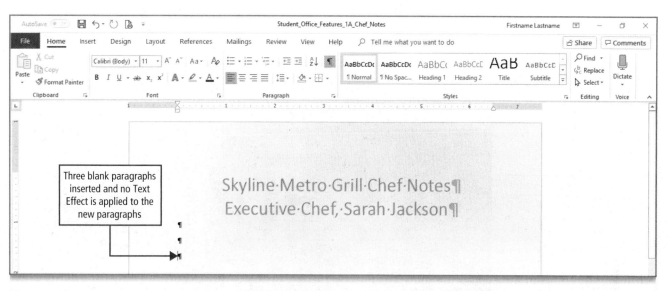

Figure 1.19

> **2** ▶ Click to position the insertion point to the left of the **second blank paragraph** that you just inserted. On the ribbon, click the **Insert tab**. In the **Illustrations group**, *point* to **Pictures** to display its ScreenTip.

Many buttons on the ribbon have this type of *enhanced ScreenTip*, which displays useful descriptive information about the command.

> **3** ▶ Click **Pictures**. In the **Insert Picture** dialog box, navigate to your **Office Features Chapter 1 folder**, double-click the **of01A_Chefs** picture, and then compare your screen with Figure 1.20.

The picture displays in your Word document.

 MAC TIP Click Picture from File, then navigate to your Office Features Chapter 1 folder.

For Non-MyLab Submissions
The of01A_Chefs picture is included with this chapter's Student Data Files, which you can obtain from your instructor or by downloading the files from www.pearsonhighered.com/go

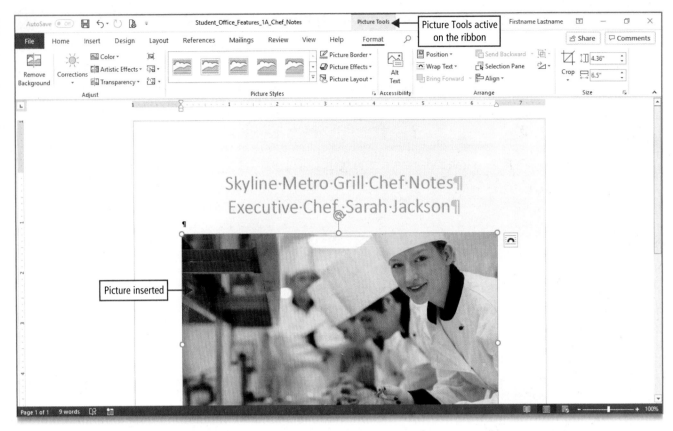

Figure 1.20

4 In the upper right corner of the picture, point to the **Layout Options** button ![icon] to display its ScreenTip, and then compare your screen with Figure 1.21.

> *Layout Options* enable you to choose how the *object*—in this instance an inserted picture— interacts with the surrounding text. An object is a picture or other graphic such as a chart or table that you can select and then move and resize.
>
> When a picture is selected, the Picture Tools become available on the ribbon. Additionally, *sizing handles*—small circles or squares that indicate an object is selected—surround the selected picture.

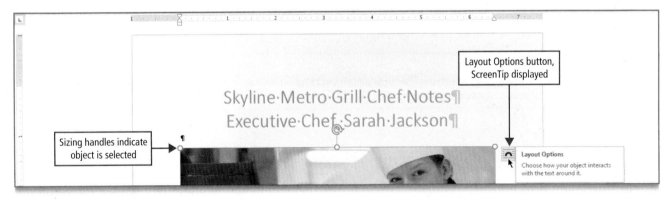

Figure 1.21

5 With the image selected, click **Layout Options** ![icon], and then under **With Text Wrapping**, in the second row, click the first layout—**Top and Bottom**. In the upper right corner of the Layout Options dialog box, click **Close** ![icon].

6 On the ribbon, with the **Picture Tools Format tab** active, at the right, in the **Size group**, click in the **Shape Height** box ⬚ 0.29" ⬚ to select the existing text. Type **2** and press Enter.

7 On the **Picture Tools Format tab**, in the **Arrange group**, click **Align**, and then at the bottom of the list, locate **Use Alignment Guides**. If you do not see a checkmark to the left of **Use Alignment Guides**, click the command to enable the guides.

8 If necessary, click the image again to select it. Point to the image to display the 🔅 pointer, hold down the left mouse button and move your mouse slightly to display a green line at the left margin, and then drag the image to the right and down slightly until a green line displays in the center of the image as shown in Figure 1.22, and then release the left mouse button.

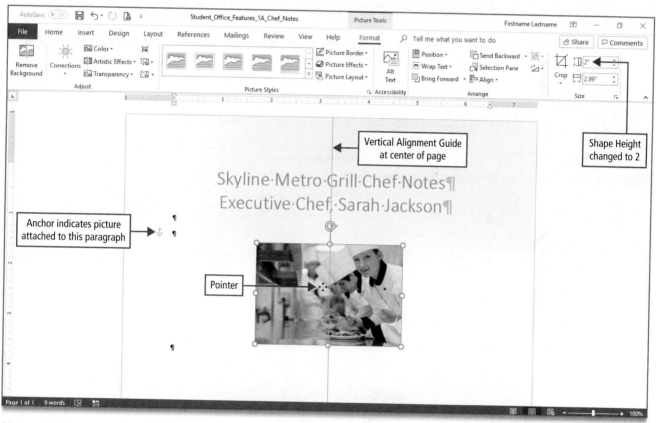

Figure 1.22

9 Be sure that there are two blank paragraphs above the image and that the anchor symbol is attached to the second blank paragraph mark—if necessary, drag the picture up slightly or down slightly. If you are not satisfied with your result, on the Quick Access Toolbar, click Undo ↺ and begin again.

> *Alignment guides* are green lines that display to help you align objects with margins or at the center of a page.

> Inserted pictures anchor—attach to—the paragraph at the insertion point location—as indicated by an anchor symbol.

10 On the ribbon, on the **Picture Tools Format tab**, in the **Picture Styles group**, point to the first style to display the ScreenTip *Simple Frame, White*, and notice that the image displays with a white frame.

MAC TIP Preview may not be available.

NOTE   The Size of Groups on the Ribbon Varies with Screen Resolution

Your monitor's screen resolution might be set higher than the resolution used to capture the figures in this book. At a higher resolution, the ribbon expands some groups to show more commands that are available with a single click, such as those in the Picture Styles group. Or, the group expands to add descriptive text to some buttons, such as those in the Arrange group. Regardless of your screen resolution, all Office commands are available to you. In higher resolutions, you will have a more robust view of the ribbon commands.

11 Watch the image as you point to the second picture style, and then to the third, and then to the fourth.

Recall that Live Preview shows the result of applying an editing or formatting change as you point to possible results—*before* you actually apply it.

12 In the **Picture Styles group**, click the fourth style—**Drop Shadow Rectangle**. Reposition the picture up or down so that it is anchored to the second blank paragraph above the image, and then click anywhere outside of the image to deselect it. Notice that the Picture Tools no longer display on the ribbon. Compare your screen with Figure 1.23.

Contextual tabs on the ribbon display only when you need them.

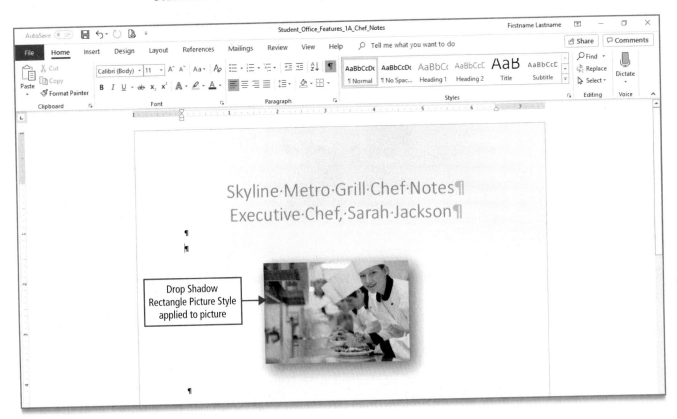

Figure 1.23

13 On the **Quick Access Toolbar**, click **Save** 🖫 to save the changes you have made.

2.2.5

1 If necessary, on the right edge of your screen, drag the vertical scroll box to the top of the scroll bar. To the left of *Executive Chef, Sarah Jackson*, point in the margin area to display the pointer and click one time to select the entire paragraph. Compare your screen with Figure 1.25.

Use this technique to select complete paragraphs from the margin area—drag downward to select multiple-line paragraphs—which is faster and more efficient than dragging through text.

Figure 1.25

2 On the **Home tab**, in the **Font Group**, click **Clear All Formatting** . Compare your screen with Figure 1.26.

This command removes all formatting from the selection, leaving only the normal, unformatted text.

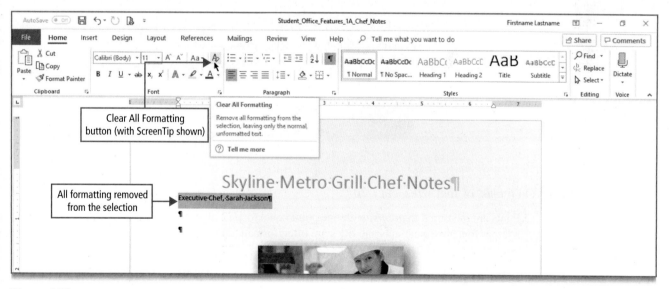

Figure 1.26

3 With the text still selected, on the **Home tab**, in the **Paragraph group**, click **Center** .

4 With the text still selected, on the **Home tab**, in the **Font group**, click the **Font button arrow** . On the alphabetical list of font names, scroll down and then locate and *point to* **Cambria**.

A *font* is a set of characters with the same design and shape. The default font in a Word document is Calibri, which is a *sans serif font*—a font design with no lines or extensions on the ends of characters.

The Cambria font is a *serif font*—a font design that includes small line extensions on the ends of the letters to guide the eye in reading from left to right.

The list of fonts displays as a gallery showing potential results. For example, in the Font gallery, you can point to see the actual design and format of each font as it would look if applied to text.

5 ▶ Point to several other fonts and observe the effect on the selected text. Then, scroll back to the top of the **Font** gallery. Under **Theme Fonts**, click **Calibri Light**.

A *theme* is a predesigned combination of colors, fonts, line, and fill effects that look good together and is applied to an entire document by a single selection. A theme combines two sets of fonts—one for text and one for headings. In the default Office theme, Calibri Light is the suggested font for headings.

6 ▶ With the paragraph *Executive Chef, Sarah Jackson* still selected, on the **Home tab**, in the **Font group**, click the **Font Size button arrow** 11 ▾, point to **20**, and then notice how Live Preview displays the text in the font size to which you are pointing. Compare your screen with Figure 1.27.

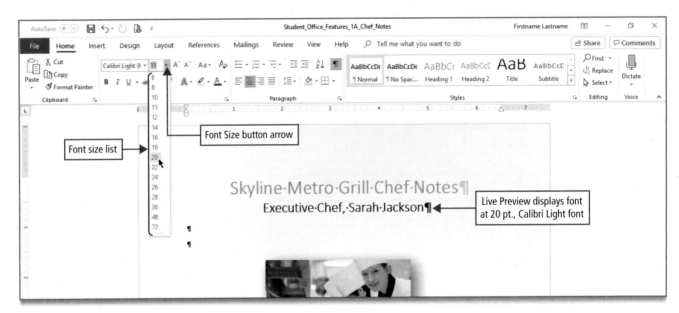

Figure 1.27

7 ▶ On the list of font sizes, click **20**.

Fonts are measured in *points*, with one point equal to 1/72 of an inch. A higher point size indicates a larger font size. Headings and titles are often formatted by using a larger font size. The word *point* is abbreviated as *pt*.

8 ▶ With *Executive Chef, Sarah Jackson* still selected, on the **Home tab**, in the **Font group**, click the **Font Color button arrow** A ▾. Under **Theme Colors**, in the sixth column, click the fifth (next to last) color, and then click in the last blank paragraph to deselect the text.

9 ▶ With your insertion point in the blank paragraph below the picture, type **Rehearsal Dinner Menu Ideas** and then press Enter two times.

10 Type **Appetizers** and press `Enter` two times. Type **Salads** and press `Enter` two times. Type **Main Dishes** and press `Enter` two times.

11 Type **Desserts** and press `Enter` four times. Compare your screen with Figure 1.28.

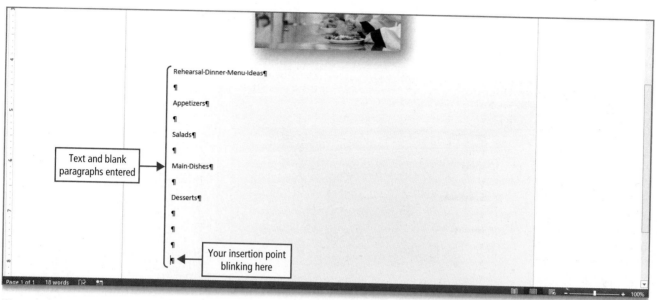

Figure 1.28

12 Click anywhere in the word *Dinner* and then ***triple-click***—click the left mouse button three times—to select the entire paragraph. If the entire paragraph is not selected, click in the paragraph and begin again.

13 With the paragraph selected, on the mini toolbar, click the **Font Color** button [A ▾], and notice that the text color of the selected paragraph changes.

The font color button retains its most recently used color—the color you used to format *Executive Chef, Sarah Jackson* above. As you progress in your study of Microsoft Office, you will use other commands that behave in this manner; that is, they retain their most recently used format. This is commonly referred to as ***MRU***—most recently used.

Recall that the mini toolbar places commands that are commonly used for the selected text or object close by so that you reduce the distance you must move your mouse to access a command. If you are using a touch screen device, most commands that you need are close and easy to touch.

MAC TIP   Use commands on the ribbon, on the Home tab.

14 With the paragraph *Rehearsal Dinner Menu Ideas* still selected and the mini toolbar displayed, on the mini toolbar, click **Bold** [B] and **Italic** [I].

Font styles include bold, italic, and underline. Font styles emphasize text and are a visual cue to draw the reader's eye to important text.

15 On the mini toolbar, click **Italic** $\boxed{I}$ again to turn off the Italic formatting. Click anywhere to deselect, and then compare your screen with Figure 1.29.

> A *toggle button* is a button that can be turned on by clicking it once, and then turned off by clicking it again.

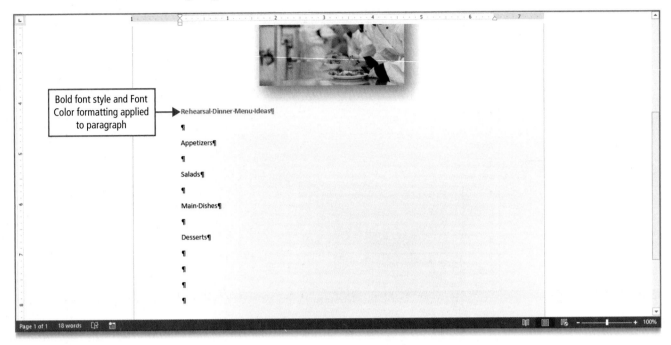

Figure 1.29

Activity 1.12 | Using Format Painter

Use the *Format Painter* to copy the formatting of specific text or copy the formatting of a paragraph and then apply it in other locations in your document.

1 To the left of *Rehearsal Dinner Menu Ideas*, point in the left margin to display the $\boxed{\text{\LARGE\textit{A}}}$ pointer, and then click one time to select the entire paragraph. Compare your screen with Figure 1.30.

> Use this technique to select complete paragraphs from the margin area. This is particularly useful if there are many lines of text in the paragraph. You can hold down the left mouse button and drag downward instead of trying to drag through the text.

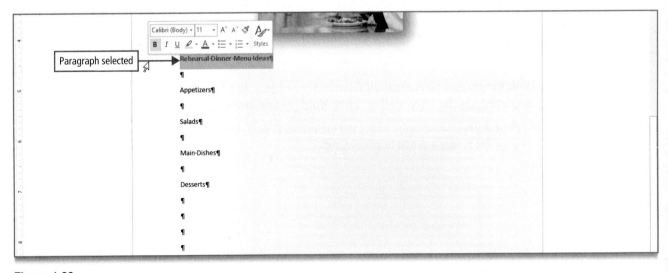

Figure 1.30

2 With *Rehearsal Dinner Menu Ideas* still selected, on the mini toolbar, click **Format Painter** . Then, move your mouse to the right of the word *Appetizers*, and notice the mouse pointer. Compare your screen with Figure 1.31.

> The pointer takes the shape of a paintbrush and contains the formatting information from the paragraph where the insertion point is positioned or from what is selected. Information about the Format Painter and how to turn it off displays in the status bar.

MAC TIP On the Home tab, in the Clipboard group, click Format Painter.

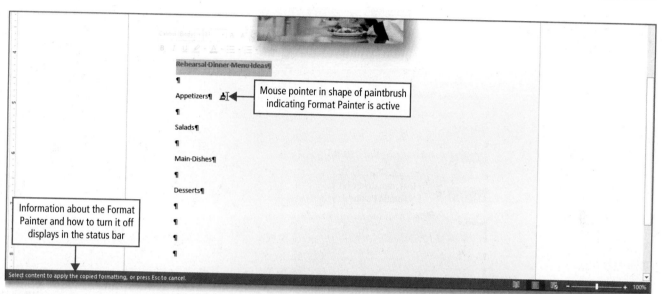

Mouse pointer in shape of paintbrush indicating Format Painter is active

Information about the Format Painter and how to turn it off displays in the status bar

Figure 1.31

3 With the pointer, drag to select the paragraph *Appetizers* and notice that the font color and Bold formatting is applied. Then, click anywhere in the word *Appetizers*, right-click to display the mini toolbar, and on the mini toolbar, *double-click* **Format Painter** .

4 Select the paragraph *Salads* to copy the font color and Bold formatting, and notice that the pointer retains the shape. You might have to move the mouse slightly to see the paintbrush shape.

> When you *double-click* the Format Painter button, the Format Painter feature remains active until you either click the Format Painter button again, or press [Esc] to cancel it—as indicated on the status bar.

5 With Format Painter still active, drag to select the paragraph *Main Dishes*, and then on the ribbon, on the **Home tab**, in the **Clipboard group**, notice that **Format Painter** ⊲ is selected, indicating that it is active. Compare your screen with Figure 1.32.

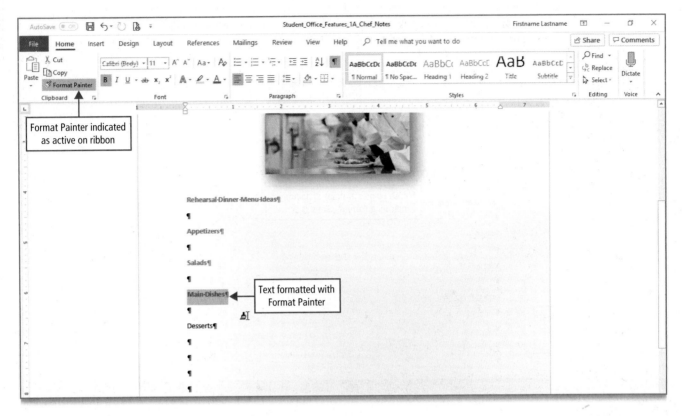

Figure 1.32

6 Select the paragraph *Desserts* to copy the format, and then on the ribbon, click **Format Painter** ⊲ to turn the command off.

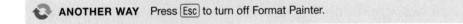

ANOTHER WAY Press (Esc) to turn off Format Painter.

7 On the **Quick Access Toolbar**, click **Save** 🖫 to save the changes you have made to your document.

Activity 1.13 | **Using Keyboard Shortcuts and Using the Clipboard to Copy, Cut, and Paste**

The ***Clipboard*** is a temporary storage area that holds text or graphics that you select and then cut or copy. When you ***copy*** text or graphics, a copy is placed on the Clipboard and the original text or graphic remains in place. When you ***cut*** text or graphics, a copy is placed on the Clipboard, and the original text or graphic is removed—cut—from the document.

After copying or cutting, the contents of the Clipboard are available for you to ***paste***—insert—in a new location in the current document, or into another Office file.

1 On your keyboard, hold down Ctrl and press Home to move to the beginning of your document, and then take a moment to study the table in Figure 1.33, which describes similar keyboard shortcuts with which you can navigate quickly in a document.

MAC TIP Press command ⌘ + fn + to move to the top of a document.

To Move	On a Windows PC press:	On a Mac press:
To the beginning of a document	Ctrl + Home	command ⌘ + fn + ←
To the end of a document	Ctrl + End	command ⌘ + fn + →
To the beginning of a line	Home	command ⌘ + ←
To the end of a line	End	command ⌘ + →
To the beginning of the previous word	Ctrl + ←	option + ←
To the beginning of the next word	Ctrl + →	option + →
To the beginning of the current word (if insertion point is in the middle of a word)	Ctrl + ←	option + ←
To the beginning of the previous paragraph	Ctrl + ↑	command ⌘ + ↑
To the beginning of the next paragraph	Ctrl + ↓	command ⌘ + ↓
To the beginning of the current paragraph (if insertion point is in the middle of a paragraph)	Ctrl + ↑	command ⌘ + ↑
Up one screen	PgUp	fn + ↑
Down one screen	PgDn	fn + ↓

Figure 1.33

2 To the left of *Skyline Metro Grill Chef Notes*, point in the left margin area to display the ⇗ pointer, and then click one time to select the entire paragraph. On the **Home tab**, in the **Clipboard group**, click **Copy** 🗎.

Because anything that you select and then copy—or cut—is placed on the Clipboard, the Copy command and the Cut command display in the Clipboard group of commands on the ribbon. There is no visible indication that your copied selection has been placed on the Clipboard.

ANOTHER WAY Right-click the selection, and then click Copy on the shortcut menu; or, use the keyboard shortcut Ctrl + C.

MAC TIP Press command ⌘ + C as a keyboard shortcut for the Copy command.

3 On the **Home tab**, in the **Clipboard group**, to the right of the group name *Clipboard*, click the **Dialog Box Launcher** button ⬚, and then compare your screen with Figure 1.34.

The Clipboard pane displays with your copied text. In any ribbon group, the ***Dialog Box Launcher*** displays either a dialog box or a pane related to the group of commands. It is not necessary to display the Clipboard in this manner, although sometimes it is useful to do so.

> 🖳 **MAC TIP** On a Mac, you cannot view or clear the Clipboard. Use the ribbon commands.

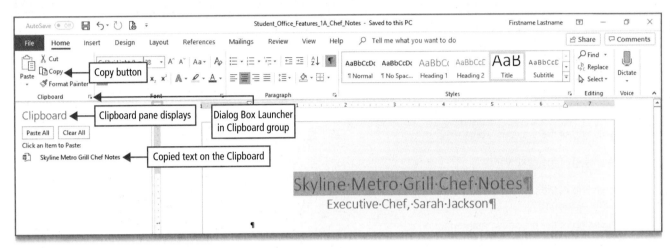

Figure 1.34

4 In the upper right corner of the **Clipboard** pane, click **Close** ☒.

5 Press ⌃Ctrl + End to move to the end of your document. On the **Home tab**, in the **Clipboard group**, point to **Paste**, and then click the *upper* portion of this split button.

The Paste command pastes the most recently copied item on the Clipboard at the insertion point location. If you click the lower portion of the Paste button, a gallery of Paste Options displays. A ***split button*** is divided into two parts; clicking the main part of the button performs a command, and clicking the arrow displays a list or gallery with choices.

> 🖳 **MAC TIP** Press ⌘ command + fn + → to move to the end of a document. The Paste button is not split; instead, display the dropdown menu; or use ⌘ command + V to paste.

> 🔄 **ANOTHER WAY** Right-click, on the shortcut menu under Paste Options, click the desired option button; or, press ⌃Control + V.

6 Below the pasted text, click **Paste Options** 📋 as shown in Figure 1.35.

Here you can view and apply various formatting options for pasting your copied or cut text. Typically, you will click Paste on the ribbon and paste the item in its original format. If you want some other format for the pasted item, you can choose another format from the ***Paste Options gallery***, which provides a Live Preview of the various options for changing the format of the pasted item with a single click. The Paste Options gallery is available in three places: on the ribbon by clicking the lower portion of the Paste button—the Paste button arrow; from the Paste Options button that displays below the pasted item following the paste operation; or on the shortcut menu if you right-click the pasted item.

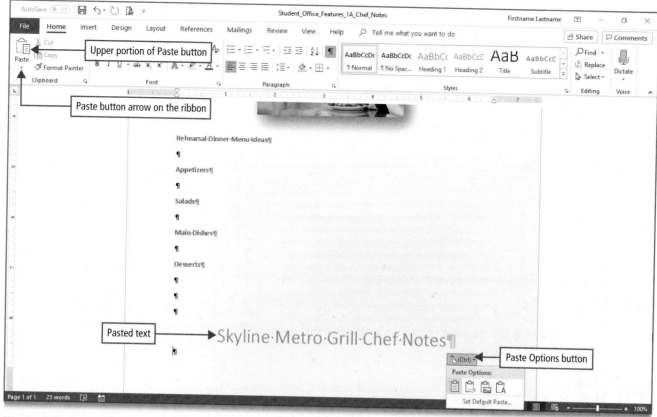

Figure 1.35

> **7** In the **Paste Options** gallery, *point* to each option to see the Live Preview of the format that would be applied if you clicked the button.

> The contents of the Paste Options gallery are contextual; that is, they change based on what you copied and where you are pasting.

> **8** Press Esc to close the gallery; the button will remain displayed until you take some other screen action.

> **9** On your keyboard, press Ctrl + Home to move to the top of the document, and then click the **chefs image** one time to select it. While pointing to the selected image, right-click, and then on the shortcut menu, click **Cut**.

> Recall that the Cut command cuts—removes—the selection from the document and places it on the Clipboard.

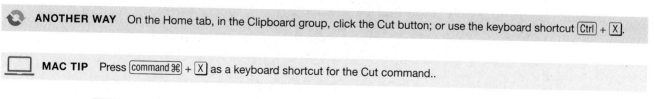

ANOTHER WAY On the Home tab, in the Clipboard group, click the Cut button; or use the keyboard shortcut Ctrl + X.

MAC TIP Press command ⌘ + X as a keyboard shortcut for the Cut command..

> **10** Press Ctrl + End to move to the end of the document.

11 With the insertion point blinking in the blank paragraph at the end of the document, right-click, and notice that the **Paste Options** gallery displays on the shortcut menu. Compare your screen with Figure 1.36.

Figure 1.36

12 On the shortcut menu, under **Paste Options**, click the first button—**Keep Source Formatting**.

MAC TIP On the shortcut menu, click Paste, click the Paste Options button, and then click Keep Source Formatting.

13 Point to the picture to display the ⚞ pointer, and then drag to the right until the center green **Alignment Guide** displays and the blank paragraph is above the picture. Release the left mouse button.

MAC TIP In the Arrange group, on the Picture Format tab, click Align, click Align Center.

14 Above the picture, select the text *Chef Notes*, type **Festive Salad** and then compare your screen with Figure 1.37.

Figure 1.37

15 Click **Save** 🖫.

Activity 1.14 | Adding Alternative Text for Accessibility

1 Point to the **chefs picture** and right-click. On the shortcut menu, click **Edit Alt Text** to display the **Alt Text** pane.

Alternative text helps people using a *screen reader*, which is software that enables visually impaired users to read text on a computer screen to understand the content of pictures. *Alt text* is the term commonly used for this feature.

2 In the **Alt Text** pane, notice that Word generates a suggested description of the picture. Click in the box, select the existing text, and then type **Young chefs making salads in a restaurant kitchen** and then compare your screen with Figure 1.38.

Anyone viewing the document with a screen reader will see the alternative text displayed instead of the picture.

Figure 1.38

3 **Close** ☒ the **Alt Text** pane. Press [Ctrl] + [Home] to move to the top of your document. On the Quick Access Toolbar, click **Save** 🖫 to the changes you have made to your document.

Objective 5 | Finalize an Office Document

GO! Learn How
Video OF1-5

There are steps you will want to take to finalize your documents. This typically includes inserting a footer for identifying information and adding Document Properties to facilitate searching. Recall that Document Properties—also known as metadata—are details about a file that describe or identify it, such as the title, author name, subject, and keywords that identify the document's topic or contents. You might also want to take some security measures or mark information to find later.

Activity 1.15 | Inserting a Footer, Inserting Document Info, and Adding Document Properties

MOS
1.3.2

1 On the **Insert tab**, in the **Header & Footer group**, click **Footer**. At the bottom of the list, click **Edit Footer**, and then with the **Header & Footer Tools Design tab** active, in the **Insert group**, click **Document Info**. Click **File Name** to add the file name to the footer.

A *footer* is a reserved area for text and graphics that displays at the bottom of each page in a document. It is common in organizations to add the file name to the footer of documents so that documents are easily identified.

 MAC TIP In the Insert group, click Field. In the dialog box, under Categories, click Document Information. Then under Field names, click FileName. Click OK.

2 On the right end of the ribbon, click **Close Header and Footer**.

3 On the **Quick Access Toolbar**, point to the **Print Preview and Print** button 🖺 you placed there, right-click, and then click **Remove from Quick Access Toolbar**.

> If you are working on your own computer and you want to do so, you can leave the icon on the toolbar; in a college lab, you should return the software to its original settings.

4 Click the **File tab** to display **Backstage** view. With the **Info tab** active, in the lower right corner, click **Show All Properties**. Click in the **Tags** box, and then type **rehearsal dinners, menus**

> *Tags*—also referred to as *keywords*—are custom file properties in the form of words that you associate with a document to give an indication of the document's content. Use tags to assist in searching for and organizing files.

🖥 **MAC TIP** On the menu bar, click File, click Properties, click the Summary tab, and then type the tags in the Keywords box. Click OK.

---

5 Click in the **Subject** box, and then type your course name and number—for example, *CIS 10, #5543*. Under **Related People**, be sure your name displays as the author. (To edit the Author, right-click the name, click Edit Property, type the new name, click in a white area to close the list, and then click OK.)

6 On the left, click **Save** to save your document and return to the Word window.

Activity 1.16 | Inspecting a Document

Word, Excel, and PowerPoint all have the same commands to inspect a file before sharing it.

🖥 **MAC TIP** On the menu bar, click Tools. Here you can click Protect Document and Check Accessibility.

MOS
1.4.1, 1.4.2, 1.4.3

1 With your document displayed, click the **File tab**, on the left, if necessary, click **Info**, and then on the right, click **Check for Issues**.

2 On the list, click **Inspect Document**.

> The *Inspect Document* command searches your document for hidden data or personal information that you might not want to share publicly. This information could reveal company details that should not be shared.

3 In the lower right corner of the **Document Inspector** dialog box, click **Inspect**.

> The Document Inspector runs and lists information that was found and that you could choose to remove.

4 In the lower right corner of the dialog box, click **Close**, and then click **Check for Issues** again. On the list, click **Check Accessibility**.

> The *Check Accessibility* command checks the document for content that people with disabilities might find difficult to read. The Accessibility Checker pane displays on the right and lists objects that might require attention.

5 Close ☒ the **Accessibility Checker** pane, and then click the **File tab**.

6 Click **Check for Issues**, and then click **Check Compatibility**.

> The *Check Compatibility* command checks for features in your document that may not be supported by earlier versions of the Office program. This is only a concern if you are sharing documents with individuals with older software.

7 Click **OK**. Leave your Word document displayed for the next Activity.

Activity 1.17 | Inserting a Bookmark and a 3D Model

1.1.2, 5.2.6

A *bookmark* identifies a word, section, or place in your document so that you can find it quickly without scrolling. This is especially useful in a long document.

3D models are a new kind of shape that you can insert from an online library of ready-to-use three-dimensional graphics. A 3D model is most powerful in a PowerPoint presentation where you can add transitions and animations during your presentation, but you can also insert a 3D model into a Word document for an impactful image that you can position in various ways.

1 In the paragraph *Rehearsal Dinner Menu Items*, select the word *Menu*.

2 On the **Insert tab**, in the **Links group**, click **Bookmark**.

3 In the **Bookmark** name box, type **menu** and then click **Add**.

4 Press Ctrl + Home to move to the top of your document.

5 On the **Home tab**, at the right end of the ribbon, in the **Editing group**, click the **Find button arrow**, and then click **Go To**.

> **ANOTHER WAY** Press Ctrl + G, which is the keyboard shortcut for the Go To command.

> **MAC TIP** On the menu bar, click Edit, point to Find, click Go To. In the dialog box, click Bookmark.

6 Under **Go to what**, click **Bookmark**, and then with *menu* indicated as the bookmark name, click **Go To**. **Close** the **Find and Replace** dialog box, and notice that your bookmarked text is selected for you.

7 Click to position your insertion point at the end of the word *Desserts*. On the **Insert tab**, in the **Illustrations group**, click the upper portion of the **3D Models button** to open the **Online 3D Models** dialog box.

> **NOTE   3D Models Not Available?**
>
> If the 3D Models command is not available on your system, in the **Illustrations group**, click **Pictures**, and then from the files downloaded with this project, click of01A_Cupcake. Change the Height to .75" and then move to Step 12.

8 In the search box, type **cupcake** and then press Enter.

9 Click the image of the **cupcake in a pink and white striped wrapper**—or select any other cupcake image. At the bottom, click **Insert**.

10 Point to the **3D control** in the center of the image, hold down the left mouse button, and then rotate the image so the top of the cupcake is pointing toward the upper right corner of the page—your rotation need not be exact. Alternatively, in the 3D Model Views group, click the More button ⮟, and then locate and click Above Front Left.

11 With the cupcake image selected, on the **3D Model Tools Format tab**, in the **Size group**, click in the **Height** box, type **.75"** and press Enter.

12 In the **Arrange group**, click **Wrap Text**, and then click **In Front of Text**. Then, in the **Arrange group**, click **Align**, and click **Align Right** to position the cupcake at the right margin.

13 Press Ctrl + Home to move to the top of your document. On the **Quick Access Toolbar**, click **Save** 🖫.

Activity 1.18 | Printing a File and Closing a Desktop App

1 Click the **File tab** to return to **Backstage** view, on the left click **Print**, and then compare your screen with Figure 1.39.

Here you can select any printer connected to your system and adjust the settings related to how you want to print. On the right, the ***Print Preview*** displays, which is a view of a document as it will appear on paper when you print it. Your page color effect will not display in Print Preview nor will the shading print. This effect appears only to anyone viewing the document on a screen.

At the bottom of the Print Preview area, in the center, the number of pages and page navigation arrows with which you can move among the pages in Print Preview display. On the right, the Zoom slider enables you to shrink or enlarge the Print Preview. ***Zoom*** is the action of increasing or decreasing the viewing area of the screen.

🔄 **ANOTHER WAY** From the document screen, press Ctrl + P or Ctrl + F2 to display Print in Backstage view.

💻 **MAC TIP** Press command ⌘ + P.

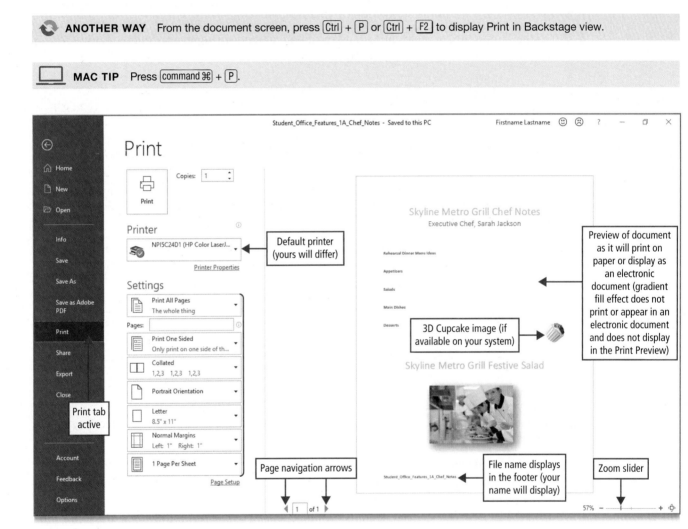

Figure 1.39

2 On the left, click **Save**. In the upper right corner of your screen, click **Close** ☒ to close Word. If a message displays regarding copied items, click No.

💻 **MAC TIP** On the menu bar, click File, click Close.

---

3 In **MyLab IT**, locate and click the Grader Project **Office Features 1A Chef Notes**. In **step 3**, under **Upload Completed Assignment**, click **Choose File**. In the **Open** dialog box, navigate to your **Office Features Chapter 1 folder**, and then click your **Student_Office_Features_1A_ Chef_Notes** file one time to select it. In the lower right corner of the **Open** dialog box, click **Open**.

> The name of your selected file displays above the Upload button.

4 To submit your file to **MyLab IT** for grading, click **Upload**, wait a moment for a green **Success!** message, and then in **step 4**, click the blue **Submit for Grading** button. Click **Close Assignment** to return to your list of **Course Materials**.

MORE KNOWLEDGE **Creating an Electronic Image of Your Document**

You can create an electronic image of your document that looks like a printed document. To do so, in Backstage view, on the left click Export. On the right, click Create PDF/XPS, and then click the Create PDF/XPS button to display the Publish as PDF or XPS dialog box.

PDF stands for **Portable Document Format**, which is a technology that creates an image that preserves the look of your file. This is a popular format for sending documents electronically, because the document will display on most computers. **XPS** stands for **XML Paper Specification**—a Microsoft file format that also creates an image of your document and that opens in the XPS viewer.

ALERT **The Remaining Activities in This Chapter Are Optional**

The following Activities describing the Office Help features are recommend but are optional to complete.

Objective 6 | Use the Office Help Features

GO! Learn How
Video OF1-6

Within each Office program, you will see the **Tell Me** feature at the right end of the ribbon—to the right of the Help tab. This is a search feature for Microsoft Office commands that you activate by typing in the *Tell me what you want to do* box. Another way to use this feature is to point to a command on the ribbon, and then at the bottom of the displayed ScreenTip, click *Tell me more*.

Activity 1.19 | Using Microsoft Office Tell Me, Tell Me More, the Help Tab, and Adding Alt Text to an Excel Chart

MOS
5.3.3

1 Start Excel and open a **Blank workbook**. With cell **A1** active, type **456789** and press Enter. Click cell **A1** again to make it the active cell.

2 At the top of the screen, click in the *Tell me what you want to do* box, and then type **format as currency** In the displayed list, to the right of **Accounting Number Format**, click the ▶ arrow. Compare your screen with Figure 1.40.

As you type, every keystroke refines the results so that you can click the command as soon as it displays. This feature helps you apply the command immediately; it does not explain how to locate the command.

MAC TIP Click the Help tab on the menu bar.

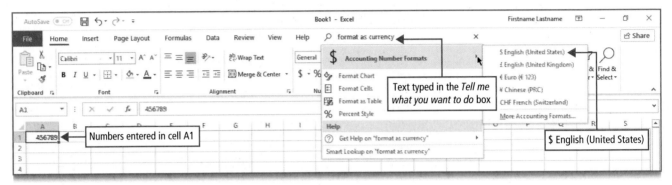

Figure 1.40

3 Click **$ English (United States)**.

4 On the **Home tab**, in the **Font group**, *point* to the **Font Color** button 🅰▾ to display its ScreenTip, and then click **Tell me more**.

Tell me more is a prompt within a ScreenTip that opens the Office online Help system with explanations about how to perform the command referenced in the ScreenTip.

5 In the **Help** pane that displays on the right, if necessary, click **Change the color of text**. Compare your screen with Figure 1.41.

As you scroll down, you will notice that the Help pane displays extensive information about the topic of changing the color of text, including how to apply a custom color.

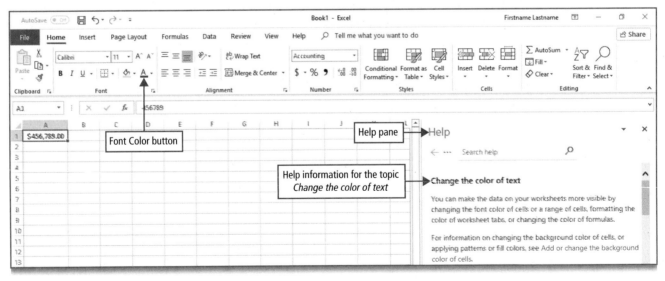

Figure 1.41

6 **Close** ✕ the **Help** pane.

7 On the ribbon, click the **Help tab**. In the **Help** group, click **Help**. In the **Help** pane, type **3D models** and then click the **Search** button. Click **Get creative with 3D models**, and then compare your screen with Figure 1.42.

Some Help topics include videos like this one to demonstrate and explain the topic.

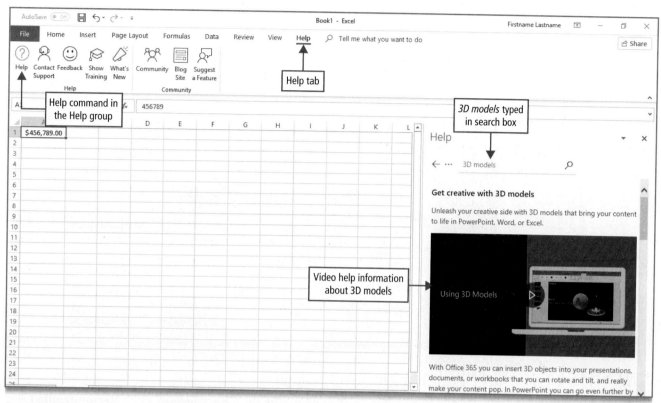

Figure 1.42

8 In the **Help** group and the **Community** group, look at the buttons.

Here you can Contact Support, send Feedback, Show Training developed by Microsoft, and see new features. In the Community group, you can visit the Excel Community, read the Excel Blog, and suggest new features.

9 ▷ Click **Show Training**, and then compare your screen with Figure 1.43.

Here you can view training videos developed by Microsoft.

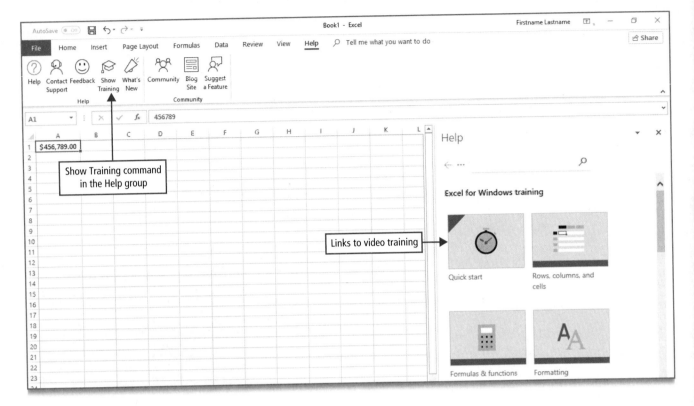

Figure 1.43

10 ▷ Click cell **A1**, and then click the **Insert tab**. In the **Charts group**, click **Recommended Charts**, and then in the **Insert Chart** dialog box, with the first chart selected, click **OK**.

11 ▷ Click the **Chart Tools Format tab**, and then in the **Accessibility group**, click **Alt Text**.

Here you can add text to describe the chart, similar to the Alt Text you added for the chef's image.

12 ▷ **Close** ☒ the **Help** pane, **Close** ☒ the **Alt Text** pane, and then in the upper right corner of the Excel window, click **Close** ☒. Click **Don't Save**.

MORE KNOWLEDGE **Don't Type, Talk! With the New Dictate Feature**

Office 365 subscribers will see the *Dictate* feature in Word, PowerPoint, Outlook, and OneNote for Windows 10. When you enable Dictate, you start talking and as you talk, text appears in your document or slide. Dictate is one of Microsoft's Office Intelligent Services, which adds new cloud-enhanced features to Office. Dictate is especially useful in Outlook when you must write lengthy emails. The Dictate command is on the Home tab in Word and PowerPoint and on the Message tab in Outlook.

You have completed Project 1A **END**

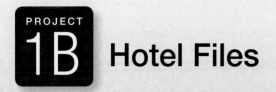

PROJECT 1B

Hotel Files

Project Activities

In Activities 1.20 through 1.38, you will assist Barbara Hewitt and Steven Ramos, who work for the Information Technology Department at the Boston headquarters office of the Bell Orchid Hotels. Barbara and Steven must organize some of the files and folders that comprise the corporation's computer data. As you progress through the project, you will insert screenshots of windows that you create into a PowerPoint presentation with five slides that will look similar to Figure 1.44.

Project Files for MyLab IT Grader

For Project 1B, you will start with the Windows 10 desktop displayed, and then learn how to create a folder for your **MyLab IT** files as you work through the project instruction. At the appropriate point in the project, you will be instructed to download your files from your **MyLab IT** course.

Project Results

GO! Project 1B
Where We're Going

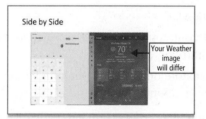

Figure 1.44

For Non-MyLab Submissions Start with the Windows 10 Desktop Displayed

For Project 1B, you will start with the Windows 10 desktop displayed and learn how to create a folder and save a new PowerPoint presentation as you work through the project instruction. Additionally, you will need the Student Data Files **win01_1B_Bell_Orchid** from your instructor or from www.pearsonhighered.com/go.

Objective 7 | Explore Windows 10

A *program* is a set of instructions that a computer uses to accomplish a task. A computer program that helps you perform a task for a specific purpose is referred to as an *application*. As an example, there are applications to create a document using word processing software, to play a game, to view the latest weather report, to edit photos or videos, or to manage financial information.

An *operating system* is a specific type of computer program that manages the other programs on a computing device such as a desktop computer, a laptop computer, a smartphone, a tablet computer, or a game console. You need an operating system to:

- Use application programs.
- Coordinate the use of your computer hardware such as a keyboard, mouse, touchpad, touchscreen, game controller, or printer.
- Organize data that you store on your computer and access data that you store on your own computer and in other locations.

Windows 10 is an operating system developed by Microsoft Corporation that works with mobile computing devices and also with traditional desktop and laptop PCs.

The three major tasks of an operating system are to:

- Manage your computer's hardware—the printers, scanners, disk drives, monitors, and other hardware attached to it.
- Manage the application software installed on your computer—programs like those in Microsoft Office and other programs you might install to edit photos and videos, play games, and so on.
- Manage the *data* generated from your application software. Data refers to the documents, worksheets, pictures, songs, and so on that you create and store during the day-to-day use of your computer.

The Windows 10 operating system continues to perform these three tasks, and additionally is optimized for touchscreens; for example, tablets of all sizes and convertible laptop computers. Windows 10 works equally well with any input device, including a mouse, keyboard, touchscreen, and *pen*—a pen-shaped stylus that you tap on a computer screen.

In most instances, when you purchase a computer, the operating system software is already installed. The operating system consists of many smaller programs, stored as system files, which transfer data to and from the disk and transfer data in and out of your computer's memory. Other functions performed by the operating system include hardware-specific tasks such as checking to see if a key has been pressed on the keyboard and, if it has, displaying the appropriate letter or character on the screen.

Windows 10, in the same manner as other operating systems and earlier versions of the Windows operating system, uses a ***graphical user interface***—abbreviated as ***GUI*** and pronounced *GOO-ee*. A graphical user interface uses graphics such as an image of a file folder or wastebasket that you click to activate the item represented. A GUI commonly incorporates the following:

- A ***pointer***—any symbol that displays on your screen in response to moving your mouse and with which you can select objects and commands.
- An ***insertion point***—a blinking vertical line that indicates where text will be inserted when you type or where an action will take place.
- A ***pointing device***, such as a mouse or touchpad, to control the pointer.
- ***Icons***—small images that represent commands, files, applications, or other windows.
- A ***desktop***—a simulation of a real desk that represents your work area; here you can arrange icons such as shortcuts to programs, files, folders, and various types of documents in the same manner you would arrange physical objects on top of a desk.

In Windows 10, you also have a Start menu with tiles that display when you click the Start button in the lower left corner of your screen. The array of tiles serves as a connected dashboard to all of your important programs, sites, and services. On the Start menu, your view is tailored to your information and activities.

The physical parts of your computer such as the central processing unit (CPU), memory, and any attached devices such as a printer, are collectively known as ***resources***. The operating system keeps track of the status of each resource and decides when a resource needs attention and for how long.

Application programs enable you to do work on, and be entertained by, your computer—programs such as Word and Excel found in the Microsoft Office suite of products, Adobe Photoshop, and computer games. No application program, whether a larger desktop app or smaller ***Microsoft Store app***—a smaller app that you download from the Store—can run on its own; it must run under the direction of an operating system.

For the everyday use of your computer, the most important and most often used function of the operating system is managing your files and folders—referred to as ***data management***. In the same manner that you strive to keep your paper documents and file folders organized so that you can find information when you need it, your goal when organizing your computer files and folders is to group your files so that you can find information easily. Managing your data files so that you can find your information when you need it is one of the most important computing skills you can learn.

Activity 1.20 | Recognizing User Accounts in Windows 10

On a single computer, Windows 10 can have multiple user accounts. This is useful because you can share a computer with other people in your family or organization and each person can have his or her own information and settings—none of which others can see. Each user on a single computer is referred to as a ***user account***. Figure 1.45 shows the Settings screen where you can add additional users to your computer.

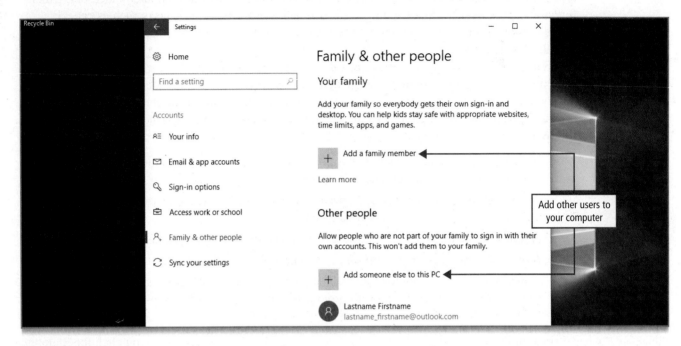

Figure 1.45

ALERT   Variations in Screen Organization, Colors, and Functionality Are Common in Windows 10

Individuals and organizations can determine how Windows 10 displays; therefore, the colors and the organization of various elements on the screen can vary. Your college or organization may customize Windows 10 to display a college picture or company logo or restrict access to certain features. The basic functions and structure of Windows 10 are not changed by such variations. You can be confident that the skills you will practice in this instruction apply to Windows 10 regardless of available functionality or differences between the figures shown and your screen.

NOTE   Comparing Your Screen with the Figures in This Textbook

Your screen will more closely match the figures shown in this textbook if you set your screen resolution to 1280 x 768. At other resolutions, your screen will closely resemble, but not match, the figures shown. To view your screen's resolution, on the desktop, right-click in a blank area, click *Display settings*, and then click the Resolution arrow. To adjust the resolution, select the desired setting, and then click OK.

With Windows 10, you can create a ***Microsoft account***, and then use that account to sign in to *any* Windows 10 computer on which you have, or create, a user account. By signing in with a Microsoft account you can:

- Download apps from the Microsoft Store
- Get your online content—email, social network updates, updated news—automatically displayed in an app when you sign in

Optionally, you can create a local account for use only on a specific PC. On your own Windows 10 computer, you must establish and then sign in with either a local account or a Microsoft account. Regardless of which one you select, you must provide an email address to associate with the user account name. If you create and then sign in with a local account, you can still connect to the internet, but you will not have the advantage of having your personal arrangement of apps displayed on your Start menu every time you sign in to that PC. You can use any email address to create a local account—similar to other online services where an email address is your user ID. You can also use any email address to create a Microsoft account.

To enjoy and get the full benefit of Windows 10, Microsoft Office, Skype, and free OneDrive cloud storage, if you have not already done so, create a Microsoft account. To do so, in your preferred web search engine, search for *create a Microsoft account*.

You can create an account using any email address. By signing in with a Microsoft account, your computer becomes your connected device where *you*—not your files—are the center of activity. At your college or place of employment, sign-in requirements will vary, because those computers are controlled by the organization's IT (Information Technology) professionals who are responsible for maintaining a secure computing environment for the entire organization.

Activity 1.21 | Turning On Your Computer, Signing In, and Exploring the Windows 10 Environment

Before you begin any computer activity, you must, if necessary, turn on your computer. This process is commonly referred to as *booting the computer*. Because Windows 10 does not require you to completely shut down your computer except to install or repair a hardware device, in most instances moving the mouse or pressing a key will wake your computer in a few seconds. So, most of the time you will skip the lengthier boot process.

In this Activity, you will turn on your computer and sign in to Windows 10. Within an organization, the sign-in process may differ from that of your own computer.

ALERT   The look and features of Windows 10 will differ between your own PC and a PC you might use at your college or workplace.

The Activities in this project assume that you are working on your own PC and signed in with a Microsoft account, or that you are working on a PC at your college or workplace where you are permitted to sign into Windows 10 with your own Microsoft account.

If you do not have a Microsoft account, or are working at a computer where you are unable to sign in with your Microsoft account, you can still complete the Activities, but some steps will differ.

On your own computer, you created your user account when you installed Windows 10 or when you set up your new computer that came with Windows 10. In a classroom or lab, check with your instructor to see how you will sign in to Windows 10.

NOTE   Create your Microsoft account if you have not already done so.

To benefit from this instruction and understand your own computer, be sure that you know your Microsoft account login and password and use that to set up your user account. If you need to create a Microsoft account, in your preferred web search engine, search for *create a Microsoft account* and click the appropriate link.

1 If necessary, turn on your computer, and then examine Figure 1.46.

The Windows 10 *lock screen* fills your computer screen with a background—this might be a default picture from Microsoft such as one of the ones shown in the Lock screen settings in Figure 1.46 or a picture that you selected if you have personalized your system already. You can also choose to have a slide show of your own photos display on the lock screen.

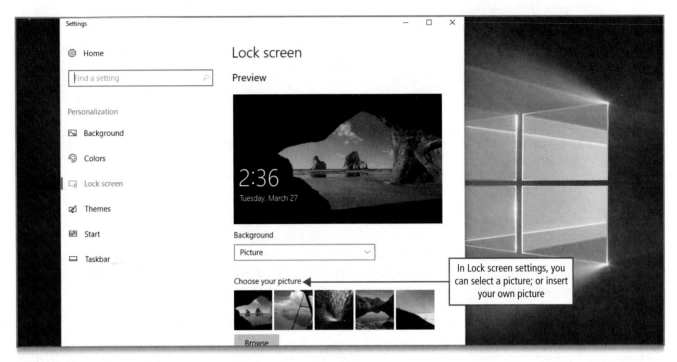

In Lock screen settings, you can select a picture; or insert your own picture

Figure 1.46

2 Determine whether you are working with a mouse and keyboard system or with a touchscreen system. If you are working with a touchscreen, determine whether you will use a stylus pen or the touch of your fingers.

NOTE **This Book Assumes You Are Using a Mouse and Keyboard, but You Can Also Use Touch**

This instruction uses terminology that assumes you are using a mouse and keyboard, but you need only touch gestures (described at the beginning of Project 1A in this chapter) to move through the instruction easily using touch. If a touch gesture needs more clarification, a *By Touch* box will assist you in using the correct gesture. Because more precision is needed for desktop operations, touching with a stylus pen may be preferable to touch using your fingers. When working with Microsoft Store apps, finger gestures are usually precise enough.

3 Press Enter to display the Windows 10 sign-in screen. If you are already signed in, go to Step 5.

BY TOUCH On the lock screen, swipe upward to display the sign-in screen. Tap your user image if necessary to display the Password box.

4 If you are the displayed user, type your password (if you have established one) and press Enter. If you are not the displayed user, click your user image if it displays or click the Switch user arrow → and then click your user image. Type your password.

The Windows 10 desktop displays with a default desktop background, a background you have selected, or perhaps a background set by your college or workplace.

5 In the lower left corner of your screen, move the mouse pointer over—*point to*—**Start** ■ and then *click*—press the left button on your mouse pointing device—to display the **Start menu**. Compare your screen with Figure 1.47, and then take a moment to study the table in Figure 1.48. If your list of programs does not display, in the upper left, click the ≡.

The *mouse pointer* is any symbol that displays on your screen in response to moving your mouse.

The Windows 10 *Start menu* displays a list of installed programs on the left and a customizable group of square and rectangular boxes—referred to as *tiles*—on the right. You can customize the arrangement of tiles from which you can access apps, websites, programs, folders, and tools for using your computer by simply clicking or tapping them.

Think of the right side of the Start menu as your connected *dashboard*—a one-screen view of links to information and programs that matter to *you*—through which you can connect with the people, activities, places, and apps that you care about.

Some tiles are referred to as *live tiles*, because they are constantly updated with fresh information relevant to you—the number of new email messages you have or new sports scores that you are interested in. Live tiles are at the center of your Windows 10 experience.

Figure 1.47

Parts of the Windows 10 Start Menu	
Create	Apps pinned to the Start menu that relate to your own information; for example, your Mail, your Calendar, and apps with which you create things; for example, your Office apps.
Apps list	Displays a list of the apps available on your system (yours will differ).
Play and Explore	Apps pinned to the Start menu that relate to games or news apps that you have installed; you can change this heading or delete it.
Power button	Enables you to set your computer to Sleep, Shut down, or Restart.
Settings	Displays the Settings menu to change any Windows 10 setting.
Signed-in User	Displays the icon for the signed-in user.

Figure 1.48

6 Click **Start** ⊞ again to close the Start menu. Compare your screen with Figure 1.49, and then take a moment to study the parts of the Windows desktop as shown in the table in Figure 1.50.

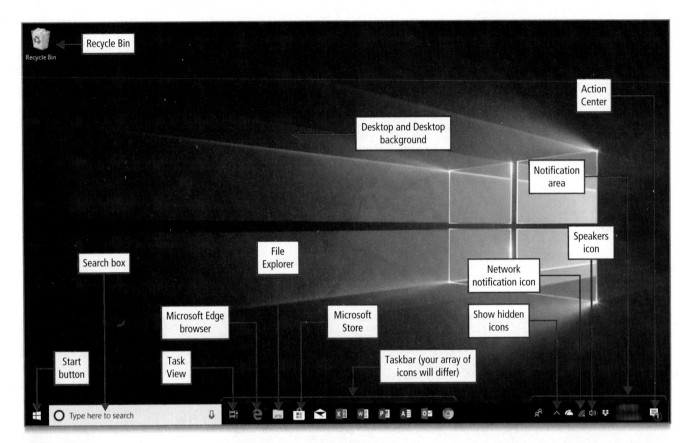

Figure 1.49

Parts of the Windows 10 Desktop	
Action Center	Displays the Action Center in a vertical pane on the right of your screen where you can see notifications—such as new mail or new alerts from social networks—at the top and access commonly used settings at the bottom.
Desktop	Serves as a surface for your work, like the top of an actual desk. Here you can arrange icons—small pictures that represent a file, folder, program, or other object.
Desktop background	Displays the colors and graphics of your desktop; you can change the desktop background to look the way you want it, such as using a picture or a solid color. Also referred to as *wallpaper*.
File Explorer	Launches the File Explorer program, which displays the contents of folders and files on your computer and on connected locations and also enables you to perform tasks related to your files and folders such as copying, moving, and renaming. If your File Explorer icon does not display, search for it, right-click its name in the search results, and then click Pin to taskbar.
Microsoft Edge browser	Launches Microsoft Edge, the web browser program developed by Microsoft that is included with Windows 10.
Microsoft Store	Opens the Microsoft Store where you can select and download Microsoft Store apps.
Network notification icon	Displays the status of your network.
Notification area	Displays notification icons and the system clock and calendar; sometimes referred to as the *system tray*.
Recycle Bin	Contains files and folders that you delete. When you delete a file or folder, it is not actually deleted; it stays in the Recycle Bin if you want it back, until you take an action to empty the Recycle Bin.
Search box	If *Cortana*—Microsoft's intelligent personal assistant—is enabled, a small circle will display on the left edge of the Search box. If Cortana is not enabled, a search icon displays at the left edge.

Parts of the Windows 10 Desktop

Show hidden icons	Displays additional icons related to your notifications.
Speakers icon	Displays the status of your computer's speakers (if any).
Start button	Displays the Start menu.
Task View	Displays your desktop background with a small image of all open programs and apps. Click once to open, click again to close. May also display the Timeline.
Taskbar	Contains buttons to launch programs and buttons for all open programs; by default, it is located at the bottom of the desktop, but you can move it. You can customize the number and arrangement of buttons.

Figure 1.50

Activity 1.22 | Pinning a Program to the Taskbar

Snipping Tool is a program within Windows 10 that captures an image of all or part of your computer's screen. A *snip*, as the captured image is called, can be annotated, saved, copied, or shared via email. Any capture of your screen is referred to as a *screenshot*, and there are many other ways to capture your screen in addition to the Snipping Tool.

> **NOTE** **Snip & Sketch Offers Improved Snipping Capabilities**
>
> Although Snipping Tool will be available for several more years, a newer tool for snipping, called Snip & Sketch, will roll out to Windows 10 users. Find it by typing Snip & Sketch in the search box.

1 In the lower left corner of your screen, click in the **Search box**.

Search relies on *Bing*, Microsoft's search engine, which enables you to conduct a search on your PC, your apps, and the web.

2 With your insertion point in the search box, type **snipping** Compare your screen with Figure 1.51.

BY TOUCH On a touchscreen, tap in the Search box to display the onscreen keyboard, and then begin to type *snipping*.

Figure 1.51

3 With the **Snipping Tool Desktop app** shaded and displayed at the top of the search results, press Enter one time.

> The Snipping Tool program's ***dialog box***—a small window that displays options for completing a task—displays on the desktop, and on the taskbar, the Snipping Tool program button displays underlined and framed in a lighter shade to indicate that the program is open.

BY TOUCH In the search results, tap the Snipping Tool app.

4 On the taskbar, point to the **Snipping Tool** button ![icon] and then ***right-click***—click the right mouse button one time. On the displayed **Jump List**, click **Pin to taskbar**.

> A ***Jump List*** displays destinations and tasks from a program's taskbar icon when you right-click the icon.

BY TOUCH On the taskbar, use the *Swipe to select* technique—swipe upward with a short quick movement—to display the Jump List. On the list, tap *Pin to taskbar*.

5 Point to the upper right corner of the **Snipping Tool** dialog box, and then click **Close** ☒.

> Because Snipping Tool is a useful tool, while completing the Projects in this textbook, it is recommended that you leave Snipping Tool pinned to your taskbar.

Objective 8 | Prepare to Work with Folders and Files

A ***file*** is a collection of information stored on a computer under a single name. Examples of a file include a Word document, an Excel workbook, a picture, a song, or a program. A ***folder*** is a container in which you store files. Windows 10 organizes and keeps track of your electronic files by letting you create and label electronic folders into which you can place your files.

Activity 1.23 | Creating a New Folder to Store a File

In this Activity, you will create a new folder and save it in a location of your choice. You might decide to use a ***removable storage device***, such as a USB flash drive, which is commonly used to transfer information from one computer to another. Such devices are also useful when you want to work with your files on different computers. For example, you probably have files that you work with at your college, at home, and possibly at your workplace.

A ***drive*** is an area of storage that is formatted with a file system compatible with your operating system and is identified by a drive letter. For example, your computer's ***hard disk drive***—the primary storage device located inside your computer where some of your files and programs are typically stored—is usually designated as drive *C*. Removable storage devices that you insert into your computer will be designated with a drive letter—the letter designation varies depending on how many input ports you have on your computer.

You can also use ***cloud storage***—storage space on an internet service that can also display as a drive on your computer. When you create a Microsoft account, free cloud storage called ***OneDrive*** is provided to you. If you are signed in with your Microsoft account, you can access OneDrive from File Explorer.

Increasingly, the use of removable storage devices for file storage is becoming less common, because having your files stored in the cloud where you can retrieve them from any device is more convenient and efficient.

1 Be sure your Windows desktop is still displayed. If you want to do so, insert your USB flash drive. If necessary, close any messages.

Plugging in a device results in a chime sound—if sound is enabled. You might see a message in the taskbar or on the screen that the device software is being installed.

2 On your taskbar, check to see if the **File Explorer** icon displays. If it does, move to Step 3. If not, in the search box, type **file explorer** under **Best match**, point to **File Explorer Desktop app**, right-click, and then click **Pin to taskbar**.

In an enterprise environment such as a college or business, File Explorer may not be pinned to the taskbar by default, so you might have to pin it there each time you use the computer. Windows 10 Home, the version of Windows that comes on most consumer PCs, typically has File Explorer pinned to the taskbar by default.

3 On the taskbar, click **File Explorer**. If necessary, in the upper right corner of the **File Explorer** window, click Expand the Ribbon.

File Explorer is the program that displays the contents of locations, folders, and files on your computer and also in your OneDrive and other cloud storage locations.

The *ribbon* is a user interface in Windows 10 that groups commands for performing related tasks on tabs across the upper portion of a window. Commands for common tasks include copying and moving, creating new folders, emailing and zipping items, and changing the view.

Use the *navigation pane*—the area on the left side of File Explorer window—to get to locations— your OneDrive, folders on your PC, devices and drives connected to your PC, and other PCs on your network.

4 ▶ On the ribbon at the top of the window, click the **View tab**, and then in the **Layout group**, click **Tiles**. Compare your screen with Figure 1.52, and then take a moment to study the parts of the File Explorer window as shown in the table in Figure 1.53.

NOTE   Does your ribbon show only the tab names? Does your Quick Access toolbar display below the ribbon?

By default, the ribbon is minimized and appears as a menu bar, displaying only the ribbon tabs. If your ribbon displays only tabs, click the Expand the Ribbon arrow ⌄ on the right side to display the full ribbon. If your Quick Access toolbar displays below the ribbon, point to it, right-click, and then click Show Quick Access Toolbar above the Ribbon.

The *File Explorer window* displays with the Quick access area selected by default. A File Explorer window displays the contents of the current location and contains helpful parts so you can *navigate*—explore within the file organizing structure of Windows. A *location* is any disk drive, folder, network, or cloud storage area in which you can store files and folders.

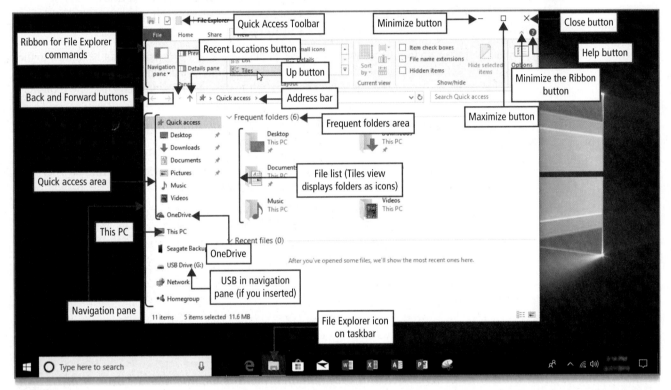

Figure 1.52

Parts of the File Explorer Window	
Address bar	Displays your current location in the folder structure as a series of links separated by arrows.
Back and Forward buttons	Provides the ability to navigate to other folders you have already opened without closing the current folder window. These buttons work with the address bar; that is, after you use the address bar to change folders, you can use the Back button to return to the previous folder.
Close button	Closes the window.
File list	Displays the contents of the current folder or location; if you type text into the Search box, only the folders and files that match your search will display here—including files in subfolders.
Frequent folders area	When Quick access is selected in the navigation pane, displays the folders you use frequently.
Help button	Opens a Bing search for Windows 10 help.
Maximize button	Increases the size of a window to fill the entire screen.
Minimize button	Removes the window from the screen without closing it; minimized windows can be reopened by clicking the associated button in the taskbar.

Parts of the File Explorer Window

Minimize the Ribbon button	Collapses the ribbon so that only the tab names display.
Navigation pane	Displays—for the purpose of navigating to locations—the Quick access area, your OneDrive if you have one and are signed in, locations on the PC at which you are working, any connected storage devices, and network locations to which you might be connected.
OneDrive	Provides navigation to your free file storage and file sharing service provided by Microsoft that you get when you sign up for a Microsoft account; this is your personal cloud storage for files.
Quick access area	Displays commonly accessed locations—such as Documents and Desktop—that you want to access quickly.
Quick Access Toolbar	Displays commonly used commands; you can customize this toolbar by adding and deleting commands and by showing it below the ribbon instead of above the ribbon.
Recent Locations button	Displays the path to locations you have visited recently so that you can go back to a previously working directory quickly.
Ribbon for File Explorer commands	Groups common tasks such as copying and moving, creating new folders, emailing and zipping items, and changing views.
Search box	Locates files stored within the current folder when you type a search term.
This PC	Provides navigation to your internal storage and attached storage devices including optical media such as a DVD drive.
Up button	Opens the location where the folder you are viewing is saved—also referred to as the *parent folder*.

Figure 1.53

> **5** In the **navigation pane**, click **This PC**. On the right, under **Devices and drives**, locate **Windows (C:)**—or **OS (C:)**—point to the device name to display the ▢ pointer, and then right-click to display a shortcut menu. Compare your screen with Figure 1.54.
>
> A *shortcut menu* is a context-sensitive menu that displays commands and options relevant to the active object. The Windows logo on the C: drive indicates this is where the Windows 10 operating system is stored.

BY TOUCH Press and hold briefly to display a shaded square and then release.

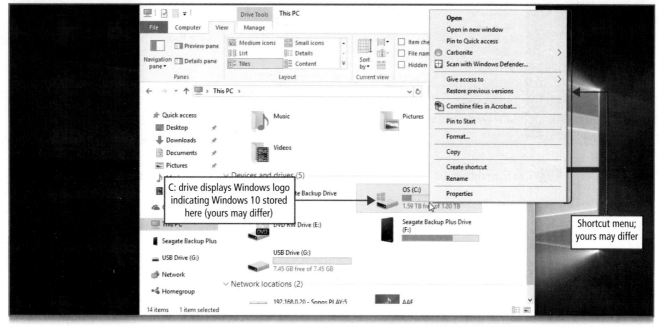

Figure 1.54

6 On the shortcut menu, click **Open** to display the *file list* for this drive.

A file list displays the contents of the current location. This area is also referred to as the *content pane*. If you enter a search term in the search box, your results will also display here. Here, in the C: drive, Windows 10 stores various files related to your operating system.

ANOTHER WAY   Point to the device name and double-click to display the file list for the device.

7 On the ribbon, notice that the **Drive Tools** tab displays above the **Manage tab**.

This is a *contextual tab*, which is a tab added to the ribbon automatically when a specific object is selected and that contains commands relevant to the selected object.

8 To the left of the **address bar**, click **Up** ⬆ to move up one level in the drive hierarchy and close the file list.

The *address bar* displays your current location in the folder structure as a series of links separated by arrows. Use the address bar to enter or select a location. You can click a part of the path to go to that level. Or, click at the end of the path to select the path for copying.

9 Under **Devices and drives**, click your **USB flash drive** to select it—or click the folder or location where you want to store your file for this project—and notice that the drive or folder is highlighted in blue, indicating it is selected. At the top of the window, on the ribbon, click the **Computer tab**, and then in the **Location group**, click **Open**. Compare your screen with Figure 1.55.

The file list for the selected location displays. There may be no files or only a few files in the location you have selected. You can open a location by double-clicking its name, using the shortcut menu, or by using this ribbon command.

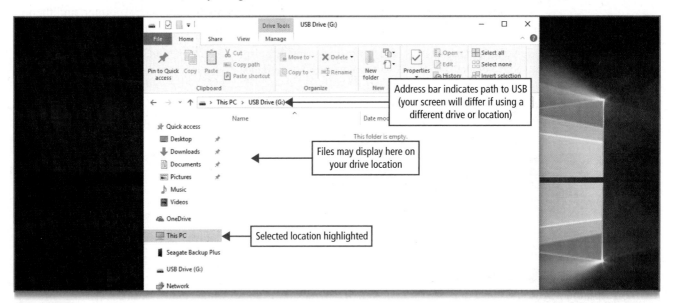

Figure 1.55

10 On the ribbon, on the **Home tab**, in the **New group**, click **New folder**.

11 With the text *New folder* highlighted, type **Windows 10 Chapter 1** and then press Enter to confirm the folder name and select—highlight—the new folder. With the folder selected, press Enter again to open the File Explorer window for your **Windows 10 Chapter 1** folder. Compare your screen with Figure 1.56.

Windows creates a new folder in the location you selected. The address bar indicates the *path* from This PC to your folder. A path is a sequence of folders that leads to a specific file or folder.

To *select* means to specify, by highlighting, a block of data or text on the screen with the intent of performing some action on the selection.

BY TOUCH You may have to tap the keyboard icon in the lower right corner of the taskbar to display the onscreen keyboard.

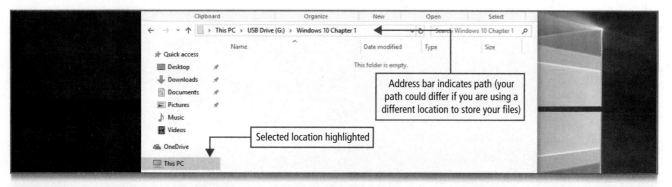

Figure 1.56

MORE KNOWLEDGE **Use OneDrive as Cloud Storage**

OneDrive is Microsoft's **cloud storage** product. Cloud storage means that your data is stored on a remote server that is maintained by a company so that you can access your files from anywhere and from any device. The idea of having all your data on a single device—your desktop or laptop PC—has become old fashioned. Because cloud storage from large companies like Microsoft are secure, many computer users now store their information on cloud services like OneDrive. Anyone with a Microsoft account has a large amount of free storage on OneDrive, and if you have an Office 365 account—free to most college students—you have 1 terabyte or more of OneDrive storage that you can use across all Microsoft products. That amount of storage is probably all you will ever need—even if you store lots of photos on your OneDrive. OneDrive is integrated into the Windows 10 operating system.

Activity 1.24 | **Creating and Saving a File**

1 In the upper right corner of your **Windows 10 Chapter 1** folder window, click **Close** ⊠.

2 In the lower left corner, click **Start** ▦.

3 Point to the right side of the **apps list** to display a **scroll bar**, and then drag the **scroll box** down to view apps listed under **T**. Compare your screen with Figure 1.57.

To *drag* is to move something from one location on the screen to another while holding down the left mouse button; the action of dragging includes releasing the mouse button at the desired time or location.

A vertical *scroll bar* displays on the right side of the menu area. A scroll bar displays when the contents of a window or pane are not completely visible. A scroll bar can be vertical as shown or horizontal and displayed at the bottom of a window.

Within the scroll bar, you can move the *scroll box* to bring the contents of the window into view. The position of the scroll box within the scroll bar indicates your relative position within the window's contents. You can click the *scroll arrow* at either end of the scroll bar to move within the window in small increments.

Figure 1.57

MORE KNOWLEDGE **Jump to a Lettered Section of the Apps List Quickly**

To move quickly to an alphabetic section of the apps list, click an alphabetic letter on the list to display an onscreen alphabet, and then click the letter of the alphabet to which you want to jump.

---

4 Click **Tips**. If necessary, in the upper right, click **Maximize** ⬜ so that the **Tips** window fills your entire screen. Then, move your mouse pointer to the right edge of the screen to display the **scroll bar**. Compare your screen with Figure 1.58.

In any window, the *Maximize* button will maximize the size of the window to fill the entire screen.

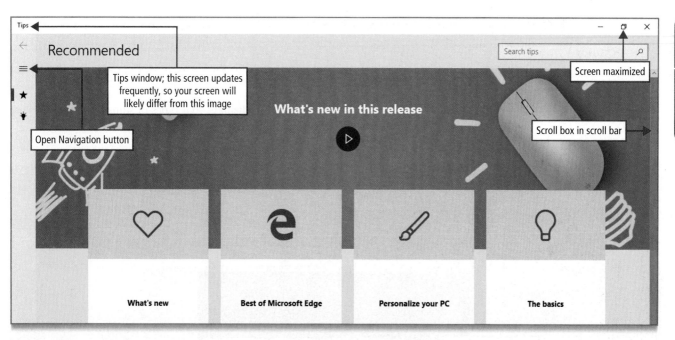

Figure 1.58

5 In the upper left corner, click **Open Navigation** ≡.

This icon is commonly referred to as a *menu icon* or a *hamburger menu* or simply a *hamburger*. The name derives from the three lines that bring to mind a hamburger on a bun. This type of button is commonly used in mobile applications because it is compact to use on smaller screens.

When you click the hamburger icon, a menu expands to identify the icons on the left—Recommended and Collections.

6 Click **Collections**, and then click **Windows**. Click **Get organized**. Move your mouse within the center right side of the screen to display a slideshow arrow ⟩, and then click the arrow until you get to the tip **Snap apps side by side**; if this tip is not available, pause at another interesting tip. Compare your screen with Figure 1.59.

To find interesting new things about Windows, Office, Microsoft Mixed Reality, and other topics, take time to explore the Tips app.

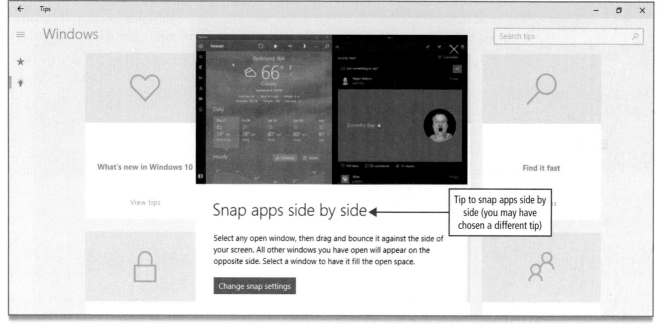

Figure 1.59

7 On the taskbar, click **Snipping Tool** 📷 to display the small **Snipping Tool** dialog box over the screen.

8 On the **menu bar** of the **Snipping Tool** dialog box, to the right of *Mode*, click the **arrow**. Compare your screen with Figure 1.60.

This *menu*—a list of commands within a category—displays four types of snips. A group of menus at the top of a program window is referred to as the *menu bar*.

Use a *free-form snip* to draw an irregular line such as a circle around an area of the screen. Use a *rectangular snip* to draw a precise box by dragging the mouse pointer around an area of the screen to form a rectangle. Use a *window snip* to capture the entire displayed window. Use a *full-screen snip* to capture the entire screen.

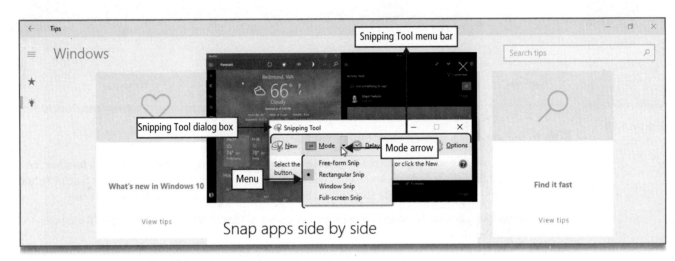

Figure 1.60

9 On the menu, click **Rectangular Snip**, and move your mouse slightly. Notice that the screen dims and your pointer takes the shape of a plus sign ⊞.

10 Move the ⊞ pointer to the upper left corner of the slide portion of the screen, hold down the left mouse button, and then drag down and to the right until you have captured the slide portion of the screen, as shown in Figure 1.61 and then release the mouse button. If you are not satisfied with your result, close the Snipping Tool window and begin again.

The Snipping Tool mark-up window displays the portion of the screen that you snipped. Here you can annotate—mark or make notes on—save, copy, or share the snip.

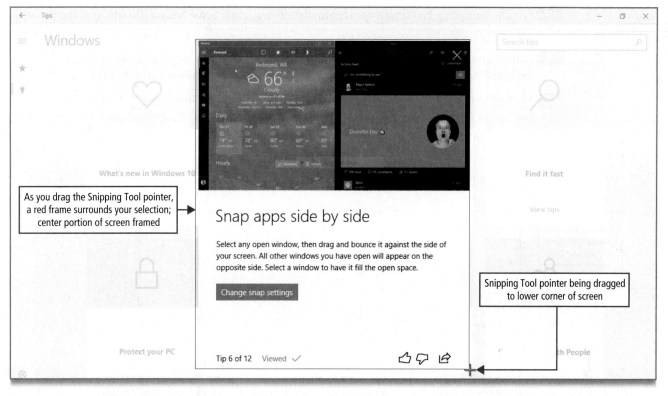

As you drag the Snipping Tool pointer, a red frame surrounds your selection; center portion of screen framed

Snipping Tool pointer being dragged to lower corner of screen

Figure 1.61

11 On the toolbar of the displayed **Snipping Tool** mark-up window, click the **Pen button arrow** ▋, and then click **Red Pen**. Notice that your mouse pointer displays as a red dot.

12 On the snip—remember that you are now looking at a picture of the portion of the screen you captured—use the red mouse pointer to draw a circle around the text *Snap apps side by side*—or whatever the name of the tip you selected is. The circle need not be precise. If you are not satisfied with your circle, on the toolbar, click the Eraser button ▋, point anywhere on the red circle, click to erase, and then begin again. Compare your screen with Figure 1.62.

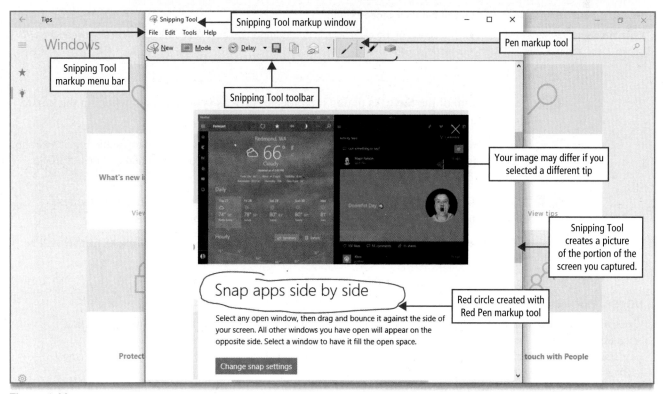

Snipping Tool markup window

Pen markup tool

Snipping Tool markup menu bar

Snipping Tool toolbar

Your image may differ if you selected a different tip

Snipping Tool creates a picture of the portion of the screen you captured.

Red circle created with Red Pen markup tool

Figure 1.62

On the **Snipping Tool** mark-up window's toolbar, click **Save Snip** 🖫 to display the **Save As** dialog box.

14 In the **Save As** dialog box, in the **navigation pane**, drag the scroll box down as necessary to find and then click the location where you created your **Windows 10 Chapter 1** folder.

15 In the **file list**, scroll as necessary, locate and *double-click*—press the left mouse button two times in rapid succession while holding the mouse still—your **Windows 10 Chapter 1** folder. Compare your screen with Figure 1.63.

🔄 **ANOTHER WAY**   Right-click the folder name and click Open.

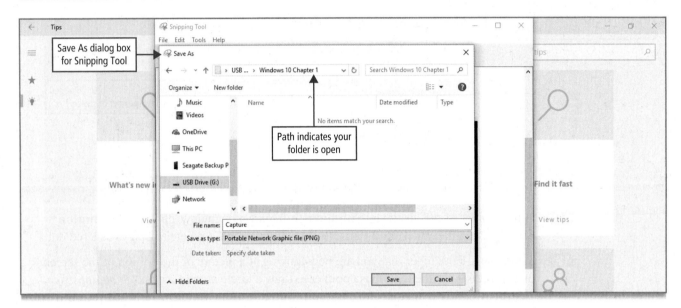

Figure 1.63

NOTE   Successful Double-Clicking Requires a Steady Hand

Double-clicking needs a steady hand. The speed of the two clicks is not as important as holding the mouse still between the two clicks. If you are not satisfied with your result, try again.

---

16 At the bottom of the **Save As** dialog box, locate **Save as type**, click anywhere in the box to display a list, and then on the displayed list click **JPEG file**.

JPEG, which is commonly pronounced *JAY-peg* and stands for Joint Photographic Experts Group, is a common file type used by digital cameras and computers to store digital pictures. JPEG is popular because it can store a high-quality picture in a relatively small file.

17 At the bottom of the **Save As** dialog box, click in the **File name** box to select the text *Capture*, and then using your own name, type **Lastname_Firstname_1B_Tip_Snip**

Within any Windows-based program, text highlighted in blue—selected—in this manner will be replaced by your typing.

NOTE   File Naming in This Textbook

Windows 10 recognizes file names with spaces. You can use spaces in file names, however, some programs, especially when transferring files over the internet, may insert the extra characters %20 in place of a space. In this instruction you will be instructed to save files using an underscore instead of a space. The underscore key is the shift of the ⎯ key—on most keyboards located two or three keys to the left of ⎆Backspace.

---

18 In the lower right corner of the window, click **Save**.

19 **Close** ☒ the **Snipping Tool** mark-up window, and then **Close** ☒ the **Tips** window.

20 Close any open windows and display your Windows desktop.

You have successfully created a folder and saved a file within that folder.

MORE KNOWLEDGE **The Hamburger**

For a brief history of the hamburger icon, visit http://blog.placeit.net/history-of-the-hamburger-icon

---

For Non-MyLab Submissions

Start PowerPoint and click Blank Presentation. Click the File tab, on the left click Save As, click Browse, and then navigate to your Windows 10 Chapter 1 folder. At the bottom of the Save As dialog box, in the File name box, using your own name, name the file **Lastname_Firstname_Windows_10_1B_Hotel_Files** and then click Save. Move to Activity 1.26.

Activity 1.25 | Downloading and Extracting Zipped Files

1 If the Microsoft PowerPoint application is not pinned to your taskbar, use the same technique you used to search for and pin the Snipping Tool application to search for and pin the PowerPoint application to your taskbar.

2 Sign in to your **MyLab IT** course. In your course, locate and click **Windows 10 1B Hotel Files**, click Download Materials, and then click Download All Files. Using the Chrome browser (if you are using a different browser see notes below), use the steps below to extract the zipped folder to your **Windows 10 Chapter 1** (or use your favorite method to download and extract files):

- In the lower left, next to the downloaded zipped folder, click the small **arrow**, and then click **Show in folder**. The zipped folder displays in *File Explorer*—the Windows program that displays the contents of locations, folders, and files on your computer—in the Downloads folder. (Unless you have changed default settings, downloaded files go to the Downloads folder on your computer.)
- With the zipped folder selected, on the ribbon, under **Compressed Folder Tools**, click the **Extract tab**, and then at the right end of the ribbon, click **Extract all**.
- In the displayed **Extract Compressed (Zipped) Folders** dialog box, click **Browse**. In the **Select a destination** dialog box, use the navigation pane on the left to navigate to your **Windows 10 Chapter 1 folder**, and double-click its name to open the folder and display its name in the **Address bar**.
- In the lower right, click **Select Folder**, and then in the lower right, click **Extract**; when complete, a new File Explorer window displays showing the extracted files in your chapter folder. For this Project, you will see a PowerPoint file with your name and another zipped folder named **win01_1B_Bell_Orchid**, which you will extract later, a result file to check against, and an Instruction file. Take a moment to open **Windows_10_1B_Hotel_Files_Instructions**; note any recent updates to the book.
- **Close** ☒ both File Explorer windows, close the Grader download screens, and close any open documents For this Project, you should close MyLab and any other open windows in your browser.

NOTE **Using the Edge Browser or Firefox Browser to Extract Files**

Microsoft Edge: At the bottom click Open, click Extract all, click Browse, navigate to and open your Chapter folder, click Select Folder, click Extract.

Firefox: In the displayed dialog box, click OK, click Extract all, click Browse, navigate to and open your Chapter folder, click Select Folder, click Extract.

3 From the taskbar, click **File Explorer**, navigate to and reopen your **Windows 10 Chapter 1 folder**, and then double-click the PowerPoint file you downloaded from **MyLab IT** that displays your name—**Student_Windows_10_1B_Hotel_Files**. In your blank PowerPoint presentation, if necessary, at the top click **Enable Editing**.

Activity 1.26 | Locating and Inserting a Saved File Into a PowerPoint Presentation

1 Be sure your PowerPoint presentation with your name is displayed. Then, on the **Home tab,** in the **Slides group**, click **Layout**. In the displayed gallery, click **Title Only**. If necessary, on the right, close the Design Ideas pane. Click anywhere in the text *Click to add title*, and then type **Tip Snip**

2 Click anywhere in the empty space below the title you just typed. Click the **Insert tab**, and then in the **Images group**, click **Pictures**. In the **navigation pane**, click the location of your **Windows 10 Chapter 1** folder, open the folder, and then in the **Insert Picture** dialog box, click one time to select your **Lastname_Firstname_1B_Tip_Snip** file. In the lower right corner of the dialog box, click **Insert**. If necessary, close the Design Ideas pane on the right. If necessary, drag the image to the right so that your slide title *Tip Snip* displays.

3 On the Quick Access Toolbar, click **Save** 🖫, and then in the upper right corner of the PowerPoint window, click **Minimize** ⊟ so that PowerPoint remains open but not displayed on your screen; you will need your PowerPoint presentation as you progress through this project.

4 **Close** ☒ the File Explorer window and close any other open windows.

Activity 1.27 | Using Snap and Task View

Use *Snap* to arrange two or more open windows on your screen so that you can work with multiple screens at the same time.

Snap with the mouse by dragging the *title bar*—the bar across the top of the window that displays the program, file, or app name—of one app to the left until it snaps into place, and then dragging the title bar of another app to the right until it snaps into place.

Snap with the keyboard by selecting the window you want to snap, and then pressing ⊞ + ←. Then select another window and press ⊞ + →. This is an example of a *keyboard shortcut*—a combination of two or more keyboard keys used to perform a task that would otherwise require a mouse.

1 From your desktop, click **Start** ⊞. In the list of apps, click the letter **A** to display the alphabet, and then click **W**. Under **W**, click **Weather**. If necessary, personalize your weather content by typing your zip code into the Search box, selecting your location, and clicking Start.

2 By using the same technique to display the alphabet, click **C**, and then click **Calculator**. On the taskbar, notice that icons display to show that the Weather app and the Calculator app are open. Notice also that on the desktop, the most recently opened app displays on top and is also framed on the taskbar. Compare your screen with Figure 1.64.

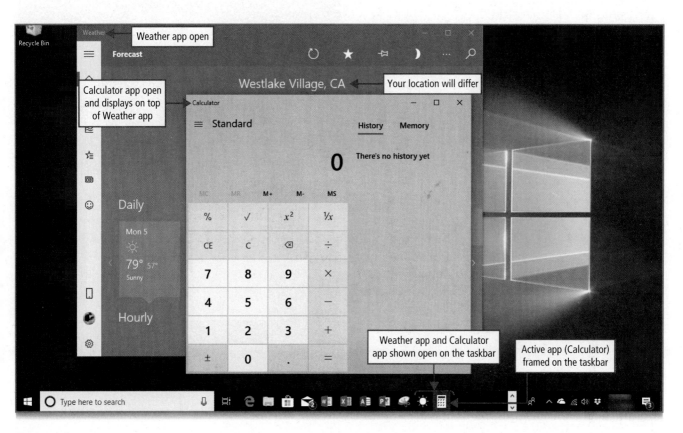

Figure 1.64

3 Point to the word *Calculator* at the top of this open app, hold down your left mouse button, drag your mouse pointer to the left edge of your screen until an outline displays to show where the window will snap, and then release the mouse button. Compare your screen with Figure 1.65.

On the right, all open windows display—your PowerPoint presentation and the Weather app. This feature is **Snap Assist**—after you have snapped a window, all other open windows display as *thumbnails* in the remaining space. A thumbnail is a reduced image of a graphic.

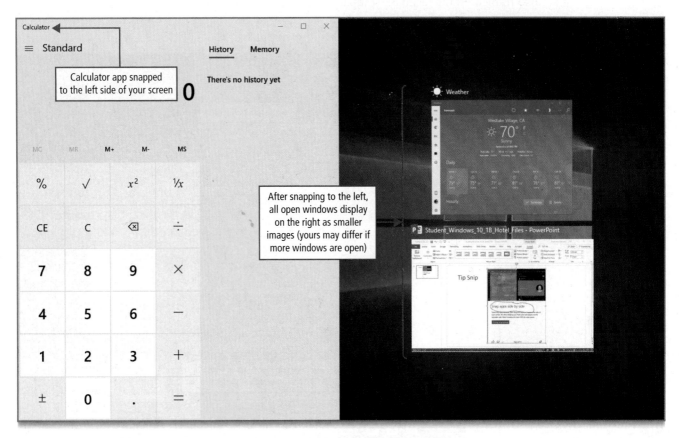

Figure 1.65

4 Click the **Weather** app to have it fill the right half of your screen.

5 In the lower left of your keyboard, press and hold down ⊞ and then in upper right of your keyboard, locate and press and release (PrintScrn). Notice that your screen dims momentarily.

This is another method to create a screenshot. This screenshot file is automatically stored in the Screenshots folder in the Pictures folder of your hard drive; it is also stored on the Clipboard if you want to copy it immediately.

A screenshot captured in this manner is saved as a *.png* file, which is commonly pronounced PING, and stands for Portable Network Graphic. This is an image file type that can be transferred over the internet.

6 On the taskbar, click **Task View** 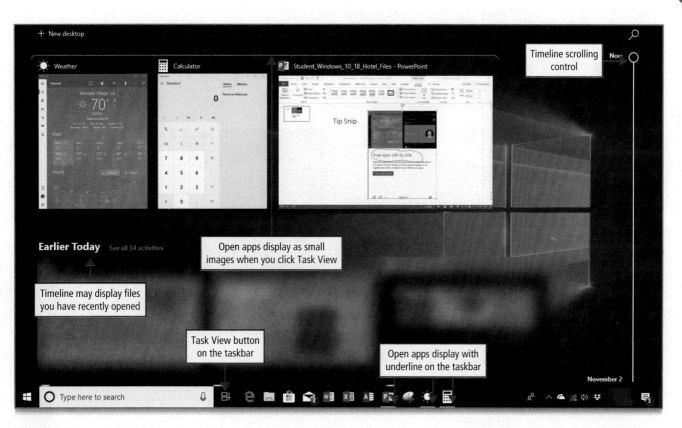, point to one of the open apps, and then compare your screen with Figure 1.66.

Use the *Task View* button on the taskbar to see and switch between open apps—including desktop apps. You may see the Windows 10 feature *Timeline*, with which, when you click the Task View button, you can see your activities and files you have recently worked on across your devices. For example, you can find a document, image, or video you worked on yesterday or a week ago.

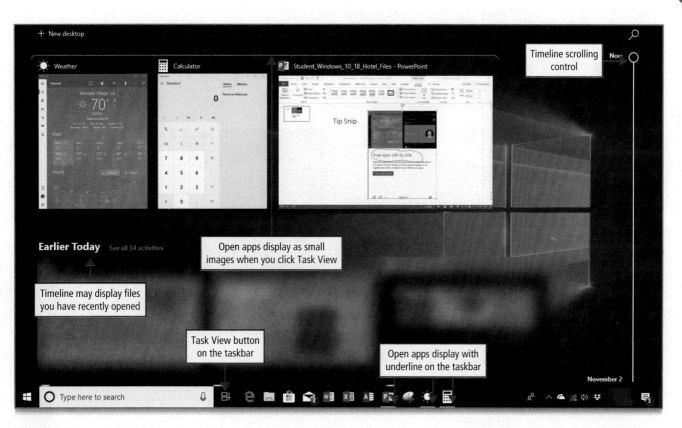

Figure 1.66

7 From **Task View**, click your **PowerPoint** window. On the **Home tab**, in the **Slides group**, click the upper portion of the **New Slide** button to insert a new slide in the same layout as your previous slide.

An arrow attached to a button will display a menu when clicked. Such a button is referred to as a *split button*—clicking the main part of the button performs a command and clicking the arrow opens a menu with choices.

8 As the title type **Side by Side** and then click in the blank space below the title. On the ribbon, on the **Home tab**, in the **Clipboard group**, click the upper portion of the **Paste** button to paste your screenshot into the slide.

Recall that by creating a screenshot using the 🖼 + PrintScrn command, a copy was placed on the Clipboard. A permanent copy is also stored in the Screenshots folder of your Pictures folder. This is a convenient way to create a quick screenshot.

9 With the image selected, on the ribbon, under **Picture Tools**, click **Format**. In the **Size group**, click in the **Shape Height** box, type 5 and press Enter. Drag the image down and into the center of the space so that your slide title is visible. Compare your screen with Figure 1.67.

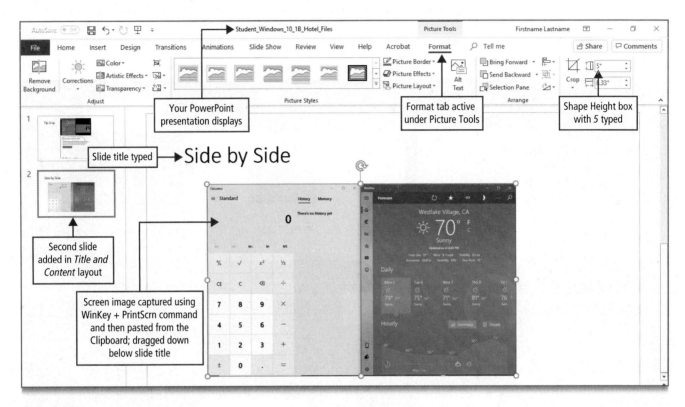

Figure 1.67

10 On the Quick Access Toolbar, click **Save**, and then in the upper right corner of the PowerPoint window, click **Minimize** so that PowerPoint remains open but not displayed on your screen.

11 Close the **Calculator** app and the **Weather** app to display your desktop.

Objective 9   **Use File Explorer to Extract Zipped Files and to Display Locations, Folders, and Files**

A file is the fundamental unit of storage that enables Windows 10 to distinguish one set of information from another. A folder is the basic organizing tool for files. In a folder, you can store files that are related to one another. You can also place a folder inside of another folder, which is then referred to as a *subfolder*.

Windows 10 arranges folders in a structure that resembles a *hierarchy*—an arrangement where items are ranked and where each level is lower in rank than the item above it. The hierarchy of folders is referred to as the *folder structure*. A sequence of folders in the folder structure that leads to a specific file or folder is a *path*.

Activity 1.28 | Navigating with File Explorer

Recall that File Explorer is the program that displays the contents of locations, folders, and files on your computer and also in your OneDrive and other cloud storage locations. File Explorer also enables you to perform tasks related to your files and folders such as copying, moving, and renaming. When you open a folder or location, a window displays to show its contents. The design of the window helps you navigate—explore within the file structure so you can find your files and folders—and so that you can save and find your files and folders efficiently.

In this Activity, you will open a folder and examine the parts of its window.

1 With your desktop displayed, on the taskbar, *point to* but do not click **File Explorer** , and notice the ScreenTip *File Explorer*.

> A *ScreenTip* displays useful information when you perform various mouse actions, such as pointing to screen elements.

2 Click **File Explorer** to display the **File Explorer** window.

> File Explorer is at work anytime you are viewing the contents of a location or the contents of a folder stored in a specific location. By default, the File Explorer button on the taskbar opens with the *Quick access* location—a list of files you have been working on and folders you use often—selected in the navigation pane and in the address bar.

> The default list will likely display the Desktop, Downloads, Documents, and Pictures folders, and then folders you worked on recently or work on frequently will be added automatically, although you can change this behavior.

> The benefit of the Quick access list is that you can customize a list of folders that you go to often. To add a folder to the list quickly, you can right-click a folder in the file list and click Pin to Quick Access.

> For example, if you are working on a project, you can pin it—or simply drag it—to the Quick access list. When you are done with the project and not using the folder so often, you can remove it from the list. Removing it from the list does not delete the folder, it simply removes it from the Quick access list.

3 On the left, in the **navigation pane**, scroll down if necessary, and then click **This PC** to display folders, devices, and drives in the **file list** on the right. Compare your screen with Figure 1.68.

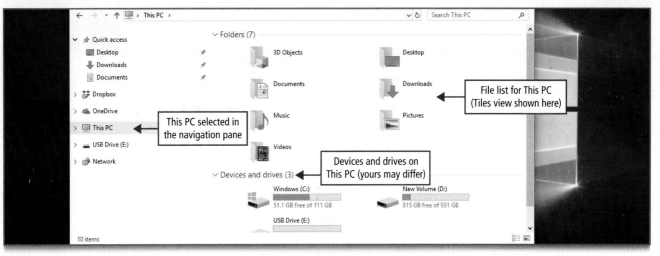

Figure 1.68

4 If necessary, in the upper right corner, click Expand the Ribbon ⌄. In the **file list**, under **Folders**—click **Documents** one time to select it, and then on the ribbon, on the **Computer tab**, in the **Location group**, click **Open**.

5 On the ribbon, click the **View tab**. In the **Show/Hide group**, be sure that **Item check boxes** is selected—select it if necessary, and then in the **Layout group**, if necessary, click **Details**.

The window for the Documents folder displays. You may or may not have files and folders already stored here. Because this window typically displays the file list for a folder, it is also referred to as the *folder window*. Item check boxes make it easier to select items in a file list and also to see which items are selected in a file list.

ANOTHER WAY   Point to Documents, right-click to display a shortcut menu, and then click Open; or, point to Documents and double-click.

6 Compare your screen with Figure 1.69, and then take a moment to study the parts of the window as described in the table in Figure 1.70.

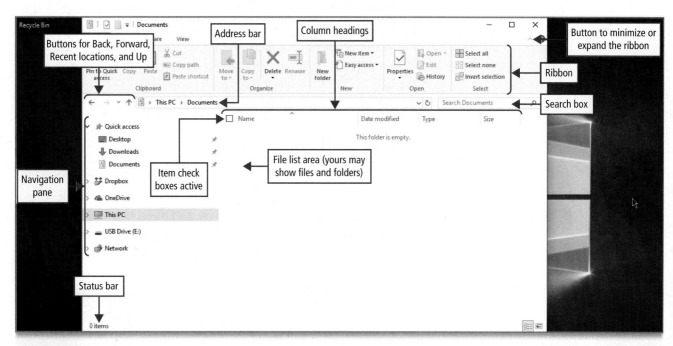

Figure 1.69

Parts of the File Explorer Window	
Window Part	**Function**
Address bar	Displays your current location in the file structure as a series of links separated by arrows. Tap or click a part of the path to go to that level or tap or click at the end to select the path for copying.
Back, Forward, Recent locations, and Up buttons	Enable you to navigate to other folders you have already opened without closing the current window. These buttons work with the address bar; that is, after you use the address bar to change folders, you can use the Back button to return to the previous folder. Use the Up button to open the location where the folder you are viewing is saved—also referred to as the *parent folder*.
Column headings	Identify the columns in Details view. By clicking the column heading name, you can change how the files in the file list are organized; by clicking the arrow on the right, you can select various sort arrangements in the file list. By right-clicking a column heading, you can select other columns to add to the file list.
File list	Displays the contents of the current folder or location. If you type text into the Search box, a search is conducted on the folder or location only, and only the folders and files that match your search will display here—including files in subfolders.
Minimize the Ribbon or Expand the Ribbon button	Changes the display of the ribbon. When minimized, the ribbon shows only the tab names and not the full ribbon.
Navigation pane	Displays locations to which you can navigate; for example, your OneDrive, folders on This PC, devices and drives connected to your PC, folders listed under Quick access, and possibly other PCs on your network. Use Quick access to open your most commonly used folders and searches. If you have a folder that you use frequently, you can drag it to the Quick access area so that it is always available.
Ribbon	Groups common tasks such as copying and moving, creating new folders, emailing and zipping items, and changing views of the items in the file list.
Search box	Enables you to type a word or phrase and then searches for a file or subfolder stored in the current folder that contains matching text. The search begins as soon as you begin typing; for example, if you type *G*, all the file and folder names that start with the letter *G* display in the file list.
Status bar	Displays the total number of items in a location, or the number of selected items and their total size.

Figure 1.70

7 Move your ◦ pointer anywhere into the **navigation pane**, and notice that a downward pointing arrow ˅ displays to the left of *Quick access* to indicate that this item is expanded, and a right-pointing arrow > displays to the left of items that are collapsed.

You can click these arrows to collapse and expand areas in the navigation pane.

Activity 1.29 | Using File Explorer to Extract Zipped Files

 For Non-MyLab Users
From your instructor or from www.pearsonhighered.com/go download the zipped folder **win01_1B_Bell_Orchid** to your **Windows 10 Chapter 1** folder.

1 In the **navigation pane**, if necessary expand **This PC**, scroll down if necessary, and then click your **USB flash drive** (or the location where you have stored your chapter folder) one time to display its contents in the **file list**. Double-click to open your **Windows 10 Chapter 1 folder** and locate the zipped folder **win01_1B_Bell_Orchid**.

2 Use the steps below to extract this zipped folder to your **Windows 10 Chapter 1 folder** as follows (or use your favorite method to unzip):

- On the **Home tab**, click **New folder**, and then name the folder **win01_1B_Bell_Orchid**
- Click the zipped folder **win01_1B_Bell_Orchid** one time to select it.

- With the zipped folder selected, on the ribbon, under **Compressed Folder Tools**, click the **Extract tab**, and then at the right end of the ribbon, click **Extract all**.
- In the displayed **Extract Compressed (Zipped) Folders** dialog box, click **Browse**. In the **Select a destination** dialog box, use the navigation pane on the left to navigate to your **Windows 10 Chapter 1 folder**, and then double-click the name of the new folder you just created to open the folder and display its name in the **Address bar**.
- In the lower right, click **Select Folder**, and then in the lower right, click **Extract**. When complete, click the Up button ↑ one time. You will see the extracted folder and the zipped folder.
- To delete the unneeded zipped version, click it one time to select it, and then on the **Home tab**, in the **Organize group**, click **Delete**. If necessary, click Yes. Now that the files are extracted, you do not need the zipped copy.

3 ▶ **Close** ☒ all File Explorer windows to display your desktop.

Activity 1.30 | Using File Explorer to Display Locations, Folders, and Files

1 ▶ From the taskbar, open **File Explorer** 📁. In the **navigation pane**, if necessary expand **This PC**, scroll down if necessary, and then click your **USB flash drive** (or the location where you have stored your chapter folder) one time to display its contents in the **file list**. In the **file list**, double-click your **Windows 10 Chapter 1 folder** to display its contents. Compare your screen with Figure 1.71.

In the navigation pane, *This PC* displays all of the drive letter locations attached to your computer, including the internal hard drives, CD or DVD drives, and any connected devices such as a USB flash drive.

Your PowerPoint file, your *Tip_Snip* file, and your extracted folder *win01_1B_Bell_Orchid* folder display if this is your storage location.

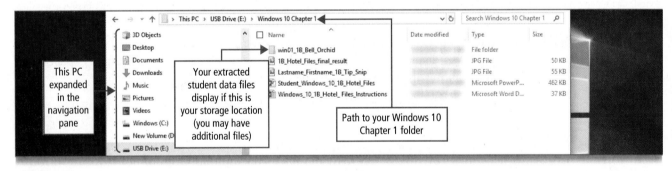

Figure 1.71

2 In the **file list**, double-click the **win01_1B_Bell_Orchid** folder to display the subfolders and files.

Recall that the corporate office of the Bell Orchid Hotels is in Boston. The corporate office maintains subfolders labeled for each of its large hotels in Honolulu, Orlando, San Diego, and Santa Barbara.

ANOTHER WAY   Right-click the folder, and then click Open; or, select the folder and then on the ribbon, on the Home tab, in the Open group, click Open.

3 In the **file list**, double-click **Orlando** to display the subfolders, and then look at the **address bar** to view the path. Compare your screen with Figure 1.72.

Within each city's subfolder, there is a structure of subfolders for the Accounting, Engineering, Food and Beverage, Human Resources, Operations, and Sales and Marketing departments.

Because folders can be placed inside of other folders, such an arrangement is common when organizing files on a computer.

In the address bar, the path from the flash drive to the win01_1B_Bell_Orchid folder to the Orlando folder displays as a series of links.

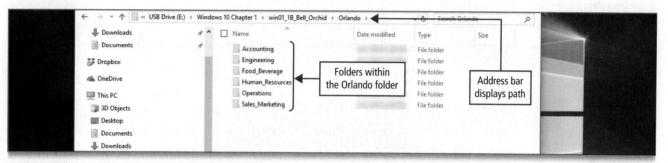

Figure 1.72

4 In the **address bar**, to the right of **win01_1B_Bell_Orchid**, click the ▸ arrow to display a list of the subfolders in the **win01_1B_Bell_Orchid** folder. On the list that displays, notice that **Orlando** displays in bold, indicating it is open in the file list. Then, on the list, click **Honolulu**.

The subfolders within the Honolulu folder display.

5 In the **address bar**, to the right of **win01_1B_Bell_Orchid**, click the ▸ arrow again to display the subfolders in that folder. Then, on the **address bar**—not on the list—point to **Honolulu** and notice that the list of subfolders in the **Honolulu** folder displays.

After you display one set of subfolders in the address bar, all of the links are active and you need only point to them to display the list of subfolders.

Clicking an arrow to the right of a folder name in the address bar displays a list of the subfolders in that folder. You can click a subfolder name to display its contents. In this manner, the address bar is not only a path, but it is also an active control with which you can step from the current folder directly to any other folder above it in the folder structure just by clicking a folder name.

6 On the list of subfolders for **Honolulu**, click **Sales_Marketing** to display its contents in the **file list**. On the **View tab**, in the **Layout group**, if necessary, click **Details**. Compare your screen with Figure 1.73.

 ANOTHER WAY   In the file list, double-click the Sales_Marketing folder.

The files in the Sales_Marketing folder for Honolulu display in the Details layout. To the left of each file name, an icon indicates the program that created each file. Here, there is one PowerPoint file, one Excel file, one Word file, and four JPEG images.

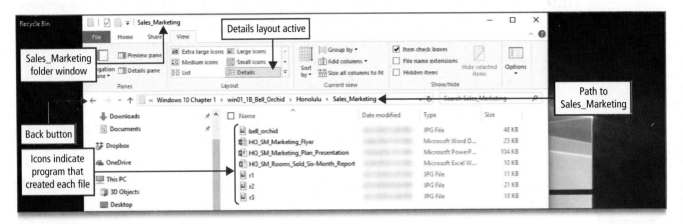

Figure 1.73

7 In the upper left portion of the window, click **Back** ← one time.

The Back button retraces each of your clicks in the same manner as clicking the Back button when you are browsing the internet.

8 In the **file list**, point to the **Human_Resources** folder, and then double-click to open the folder.

9 In the **file list**, click one time to select the PowerPoint file **HO_HR_New_Employee_ Presentation**, and then on the ribbon, click the **View tab**. In the **Panes group**, click **Details pane**, and then compare your screen with Figure 1.74.

The **Details pane** displays the most common *file properties* associated with the selected file. File properties refer to information about a file, such as the author, the date the file was last changed, and any descriptive *tags*—properties that you create to help you find and organize your files.

Additionally, a thumbnail image of the first slide in the presentation displays, and the status bar displays the number of items in the folder.

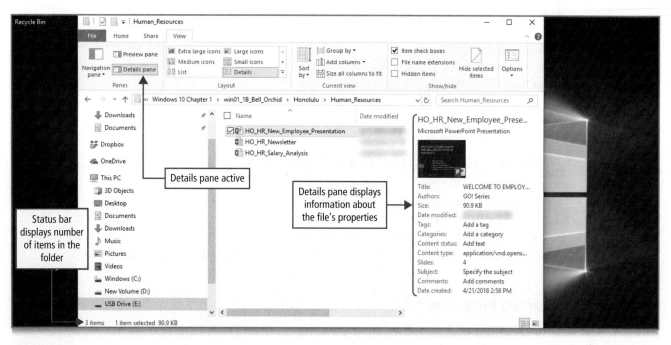

Figure 1.74

> **10** On the right, in the **Details pane**, click **Add a tag**, type **New Employee meeting** and then at the bottom of the pane click **Save**.
>
> Because you can search for tags, adding tags to files makes them easier to find.

🔄 **ANOTHER WAY** With the file selected, on the Home tab, in the Open group, click Properties to display the Properties dialog box for the file, and then click the Details tab.

> **11** On the ribbon, on the **View tab**, in the **Panes group**, click **Preview pane** to replace the **Details pane** with the **Preview pane**. Compare your screen with Figure 1.75.
>
> In the Preview pane that displays on the right, you can use the scroll bar to scroll through the slides in the presentation; or, you can click the up or down scroll arrow to view the slides as a miniature presentation.

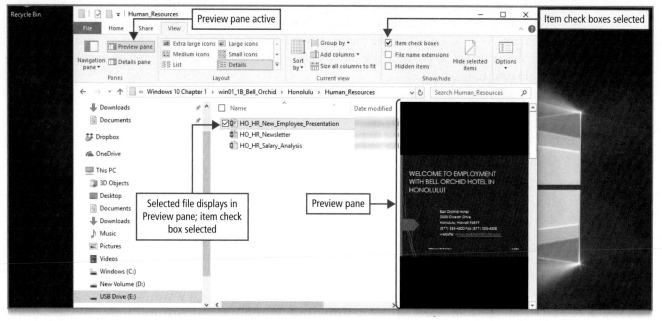

Figure 1.75

12 On the ribbon, click **Preview pane** to close the right pane.

Use the Details pane to see a file's properties and the Preview pane when you want to look at a file quickly without actually opening it.

13 Close ☒ the **Human_Resources** window.

When you are using the software programs installed on your computer, you create and save data files—the documents, workbooks, databases, songs, pictures, and so on that you need for your job or personal use. Therefore, most of your work with Windows 10 desktop applications is concerned with locating and starting your programs and locating and opening your files.

Activity 1.31 | Starting Programs

You can start programs from the Start menu or from the taskbar by pinning a program to the taskbar. You can open your data files from within the program in which they were created, or you can open a data file from a window in File Explorer, which will simultaneously start the program and open your file.

1 Be sure your desktop displays and that your PowerPoint presentation is still open but minimized on the taskbar. You can point to the PowerPoint icon to have a small image of the active slide display. Click **Start** ⊞ to place the insertion point in the search box, type **wordpad** and then click the **WordPad Desktop app**.

2 With the insertion point blinking in the document window, type your first and last name.

3 From the taskbar, open your PowerPoint presentation. On the **Home tab**, click the upper portion of the **New Slide** button to insert a blank slide in the Title Only layout. Click anywhere in the text *Click to add title*, and then type **Wordpad**

4 Click anywhere in the lower portion of the slide. On the **Insert tab**, in the **Images group**, click **Screenshot**, and then under **Available Windows**, click the image of the WordPad program with your name typed to insert the image in the PowerPoint slide. Click in a blank area of the slide to deselect the image; if necessary, close the Design Ideas pane on the right. As necessary, drag the image down so that the title displays, and if necessary, use the Shape Height box to decrease the size of the screenshot slightly. Compare your screen with Figure 1.76.

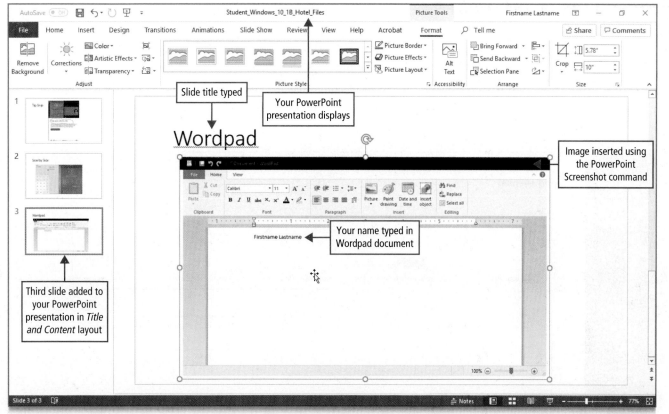

Figure 1.76

5 On the Quick Access toolbar, click **Save** 🔲 and then in the upper right corner of the PowerPoint window, click **Minimize** ⊟ so that PowerPoint remains open but not displayed on your screen.

6 Close ✕ **WordPad**, and then click **Don't Save**.

Activity 1.32 | Opening Data Files

1 Open **Microsoft Word** from your taskbar, or click **Start** ▦, type **Microsoft word** and then open the **Word** desktop app. Compare your screen with Figure 1.77.

The Word program window has features that are common to other programs you have opened; for example, commands are arranged on tabs. When you create and save data in Word, you create a Word document file.

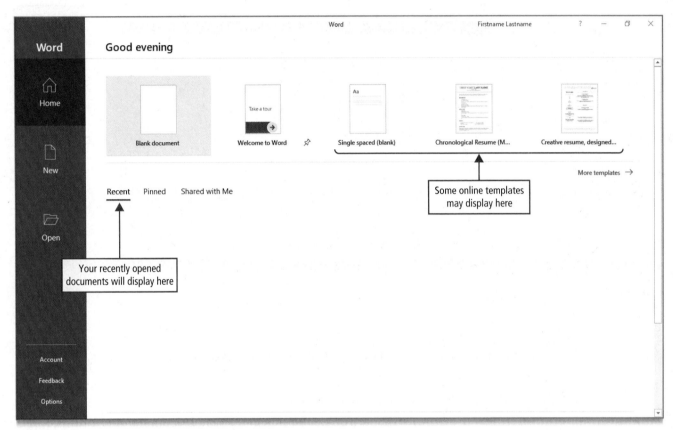

Figure 1.77

2 On the left, click **Open**. Notice the list of places from which you can open a document, including your OneDrive if you are logged in. Click **Browse** to display the **Open** dialog box. Compare your screen with Figure 1.78, and then take a moment to study the table in Figure 1.79.

Recall that a dialog box is a window containing options for completing a task; the layout of the Open dialog box is similar to that of a File Explorer window. When you are working in a desktop application, use the Open dialog box to locate and open existing files that were created in the desktop application.

When you click Browse, typically the Documents folder on This PC displays. You can use the skills you have practiced to navigate to other locations on your computer, such as your removable USB flash drive.

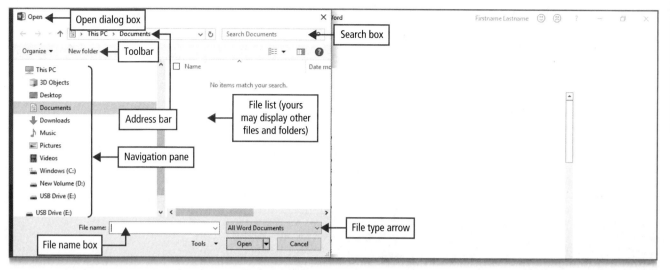

Figure 1.78

Dialog Box Element	Function
Address bar	Displays the path in the folder structure.
File list	Displays the list of files and folders that are available in the folder indicated in the address bar.
File name box	Enables you to type the name of a specific file to locate it—if you know it.
File type arrow	Enables you to restrict the type of files displayed in the file list; for example, the default *All Word Documents* restricts (filters) the type of files displayed to only Word documents. You can click the arrow and adjust the restrictions (filters) to a narrower or wider group of files.
Navigation pane	Navigate to files and folders and get access to Quick access, OneDrive, and This PC.
Search box	Search for files in the current folder. Filters the file list based on text that you type; the search is based on text in the file name (and for files on the hard drive or OneDrive, in the file itself), and on other properties that you can specify. The search takes place in the current folder, as displayed in the address bar, and in any subfolders within that folder.
Toolbar	Displays relevant tasks; for example, creating a new folder.

Figure 1.79

3 In the **navigation pane**, scroll down as necessary, and then under **This PC**, click your **USB flash drive** or whatever location where you have stored your files for this project. In the **file list**, double-click your **win01_1B_Bell_Orchid** folder to open it and display its contents.

4 In the upper right portion of the **Open** dialog box, click the **More options arrow** ▾, and then set the view to **Large icons**. Compare your screen with Figure 1.80.

The Live Preview feature indicates that each folder contains additional subfolders.

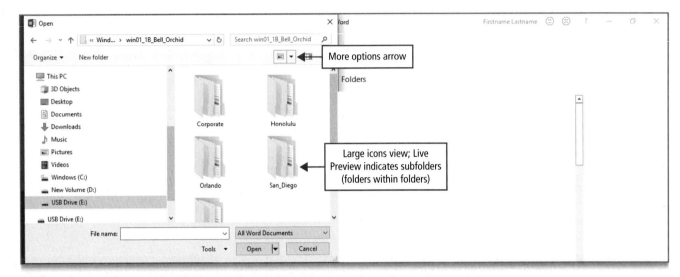

Figure 1.80

5 In the **file list**, double-click the **Corporate** folder, and then double-click the **Accounting** folder.

The view returns to the Details view.

6 In the **file list**, notice that only one document—a Word document—displays. In the lower right corner, locate the **File type** button, and notice that *All Word Documents* displays as the file type. Click the **File type arrow**, and then on the displayed list, click **All Files**. Compare your screen with Figure 1.81.

When you change the file type to *All Files*, you can see that the Word file is not the only file in this folder. By default, the Open dialog box displays only the files created in the active program; however, you can display variations of file types in this manner.

Microsoft Office file types are identified by small icons, which is a convenient way to differentiate one type of file from another. Although you can view all the files in the folder, you can open only the files that were created in the active program, which in this instance is Microsoft Word.

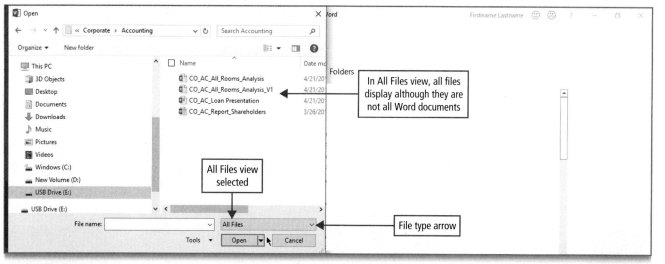

Figure 1.81

7 Change the file type back to **All Word Documents**. Then, in the **file list**, double-click the **CO_AC_Report_Shareholders** Word file to open the document. Take a moment to scroll through the document. If necessary, Maximize ⬜ the window.

8 **Close** ☒ the Word window.

9 Click **Start** ⊞, and then search for **.txt** At the top, click **Filters**, click **Documents**, and then on the list, click **Structure.txt in Future_Hotels**.

The file opens using the Windows 10 *Notepad* desktop app—a basic text-editing program included with Windows 10 that you can use to create simple documents.

In the search box, you can search for files on your computer, and you can search for a file by its *file name extension*—a set of characters at the end of a file name that helps Windows understand what kind of information is in a file and what program should open it. A *.txt file* is a simple file consisting of lines of text with no formatting that almost any computer can open and display.

10 **Close** ☒ the Notepad program.

MORE KNOWLEDGE **Do Not Clutter Your Desktop by Creating Desktop Shortcuts or Storing Files**

On your desktop, you can add or remove *desktop shortcuts*, which are desktop icons that can link to items accessible on your computer such as a program, file, folder, disk drive, printer, or another computer. In previous versions of Windows, many computer users commonly did this.

Now the Start menu is your personal dashboard for all your programs and online activities, and increasingly you will access programs and your own files in the cloud. So do not clutter your desktop with shortcuts—doing so is more confusing than useful. Placing desktop shortcuts for frequently used programs or folders directly on your desktop may seem convenient, but as you add more icons, your desktop becomes cluttered and the shortcuts are not easy to find. A better organizing method is to use the taskbar for shortcuts to programs. For folders and files, the best organizing structure is to create a logical structure of folders within your Documents folder or your cloud-based OneDrive.

You can also drag frequently-used folders to the Quick access area in the navigation pane so that they are available any time you open File Explorer. As you progress in your use of Windows 10, you will discover techniques for using the taskbar and the Quick access area of the navigation pane to streamline your work instead of cluttering your desktop.

Activity 1.33 | Searching, Pinning, Sorting, and Filtering in File Explorer

1 From the taskbar, open **File Explorer** 📁. On the right, at the bottom, you may notice that under **Recent files**, you can see files that you have recently opened.

2 In the **navigation pane**, click your **USB flash drive**—or click the location where you have stored your files for this project. Double-click your **Windows 10 Chapter 1 folder** to open it. In the upper right, click in the **Search** box, and then type **pool** Compare your screen with Figure 1.82.

> Files that contain the word *pool* in the title display. If you are searching a folder on your hard drive or OneDrive, files that contain the word *pool* within the document will also display. Additionally, Search Tools display on the ribbon.

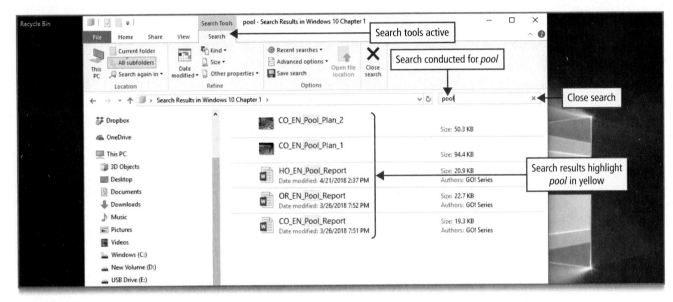

Figure 1.82

3 In the search box, clear the search by clicking ✕, and then in the search box type **Paris.jpg** Notice that you can also search by using a file extension as part of the search term.

4 **Clear** ✕ the search. Double-click your **win01_1B_Bell_Orchid** folder to open it.

5 On the **Home tab**, in the **Clipboard group**, click **Pin to Quick access**. If necessary, scroll up in the navigation pane. Compare your screen with Figure 1.83.

> You can pin frequently used folders to the Quick access area, and then unpin them when you no longer need frequent access. Folders that you access frequently will also display in the Quick access area without the pin image. Delete them by right-clicking the name and clicking Unpin from Quick access.

Figure 1.83

🔄 **ANOTHER WAY** In the file list, right-click a folder name, and then click Pin to Quick access; or, drag the folder to the Quick access area in the navigation pain and release the mouse button when the ScreenTip displays Pin to Quick access.

6 In the **file list**—double-click the **Corporate** folder and then double-click the **Engineering** folder.

7 On the **View tab**, in the **Current view group**, click **Sort by**, and then click **Type**. Compare your screen with Figure 1.84.

Use this technique to sort files in the file list by type. Here, the JPG files display first, and then the Microsoft Excel files, and so on—in alphabetic order by file type.

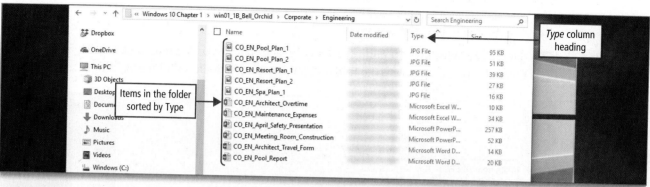

Figure 1.84

8 Point to the column heading **Type**, and then click **^**.

9 Point to the column heading **Type** again, and on the right, click ☑. On the displayed list, click **Microsoft PowerPoint Presentation**, and notice that the file list is filtered to show only PowerPoint files.

A *filtered list* is a display of files that is limited based on specified criteria.

10 To the right of the **Type** column heading, click the check mark and then click **Microsoft PowerPoint Presentation** again to clear the Microsoft PowerPoint filter and redisplay all of the files.

11 **Close** ☒ the File Explorer window.

ALERT **Allow Time to Complete the Remainder of This Project in One Session**

If you are working on a computer that is not your own, for example in a college lab, plan your time to complete the remainder of this project in one working session. Allow 45 to 60 minutes.

Because you will need to store and then delete files on the hard disk drive of the computer at which you are working, it is recommended that you complete this project in one working session—*unless you are working on your own computer or you know that the files will be retained*. In your college lab, files you store on the computer's hard drive will not be retained after you sign off.

Objective 11 | Create, Rename, and Copy Files and Folders

File management includes organizing, copying, renaming, moving, and deleting the files and folders you have stored in various locations—both locally and in the cloud.

Activity 1.34 | Copying Files from a Removable Storage Device to the Documents Folder on the Hard Disk Drive

Barbara and Steven have the assignment to transfer and then organize some of the corporation's files to a computer that will be connected to the corporate network. Data on such a computer can be accessed by employees at any of the hotel locations through the use of sharing technologies. For example, *SharePoint* is a Microsoft technology that enables employees in an organization to access information across organizational and geographic boundaries.

1 Close any open windows, but leave your open PowerPoint presentation minimized on the taskbar.

2 From the taskbar, open **File Explorer** 📁. In the **navigation pane**, if necessary expand **This PC**, and then click your USB flash drive or the location where you have stored your chapter folder to display its contents in the file list.

> Recall that in the navigation pane, under This PC, you have access to all the storage areas inside your computer, such as your hard disk drives, and to any devices with removable storage, such as CDs, DVDs, or USB flash drives.

3 Open your **Windows 10 Chapter 1** folder, and then in the **file list**, click **win01_1B_Bell_Orchid** one time to select the folder. Compare your screen with Figure 1.85.

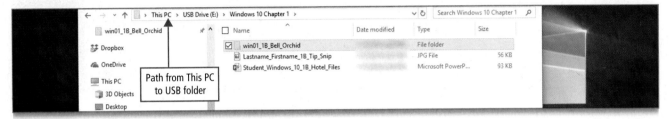

Figure 1.85

4 With the **win01_1B_Bell_Orchid** folder selected, on the ribbon, on the **Home tab**, in the **Clipboard group**, click **Copy**.

> The Copy command places a copy of your selected file or folder on the *Clipboard* where it will be stored until you use the Paste command to place the copy somewhere else. The Clipboard is a temporary storage area for information that you have copied or moved from one place and plan to use somewhere else.

> In Windows 10, the Clipboard can hold only one piece of information at a time. Whenever something is copied to the Clipboard, it replaces whatever was there before. In Windows 10, you cannot view the contents of the Clipboard nor place multiple items there in the manner that you can in Microsoft Word.

🔄 **ANOTHER WAY**   With the item selected in the file list, press ⌃ Ctrl + C to copy the item to the clipboard.

5 To the left of the address bar, click **Up** ↑ two times. In the **file list**, double-click your **Documents** folder to open it, and then on the **Home tab**, in the **Clipboard group**, click **Paste**.

> A *progress bar* displays in a dialog box and also displays on the taskbar button with green shading. A progress bar indicates visually the progress of a task such as a copy process, a download, or a file transfer.

> The Documents folder is one of several folders within your *personal folder* stored on the hard disk drive. For each user account—even if there is only one user on the computer—Windows 10 creates a personal folder labeled with the account holder's name.

🔄 **ANOTHER WAY**   With the destination location selected, press ⌃ Ctrl + V to paste the item from the clipboard to the selected location. Or, on the Home tab, in the Organize group, click Copy to, find and then click the location to which you want to copy. If the desired location is not on the list, use the Choose location command at the bottom.

6 Close ✕ the **Documents** window.

Activity 1.35 | Creating Folders, Renaming Folders, and Renaming Files

Barbara and Steven can see that various managers have been placing files related to new European hotels in the *Future_Hotels* folder. They can also see that the files have not been organized into a logical structure. For example, files that are related to each other are not in separate folders; instead they are mixed in with other files that are not related to the topic.

In this Activity, you will create, name, and rename folders to begin a logical structure of folders in which to organize the files related to the European hotels project.

1 From the taskbar, open **File Explorer** 🗔, and then use any of the techniques you have practiced to display the contents of the **Documents** folder in the **file list**.

NOTE   Using the Documents Folder and OneDrive Instead of Your USB Drive

In this modern computing era, you should limit your use of USB drives to those times when you want to quickly take some files to another computer without going online. Instead of using a USB drive, use your computer's hard drive, or better yet, your free OneDrive cloud storage that comes with your Microsoft account.

There are two good reasons to stop using USB flash drives. First, searching is limited on a USB drive—search does not look at the content inside a file. When you search files on your hard drive or OneDrive, the search extends to words and phrases actually *inside* the files. Second, if you delete a file or folder from a USB drive, it is gone and cannot be retrieved. Files you delete from your hard drive or OneDrive go to the Recycle Bin where you can retrieve them later.

---

2 In the **file list**, double-click the **win01_1B_Bell_Orchid** folder, double-click the **Corporate** folder, double-click the **Information_Technology** folder, and then double-click the **Future_Hotels** folder to display its contents in the file list; sometimes this navigation is written as *Documents > win01_1B_Bell_Orchid > Corporate > Information_Technology > Future_Hotels*.

Some computer users prefer to navigate a folder structure by double-clicking in this manner. Others prefer using the address bar as described in the following Another Way box. Use whatever method you prefer—double-clicking in the file list, clicking in the address bar, or expanding files in the Navigation pane.

ANOTHER WAY   In the navigation pane, click Documents, and expand each folder in the navigation pane. Or, In the address bar, to the right of Documents, click >, and then on the list, click win01_1B_Bell_Orchid. To the right of win01_1B_Bell_Orchid, click the > and then click Corporate. To the right of Corporate, click > and then click Information_Technology. To the right of Information_Technology, click >, and then click Future_Hotels.

---

3 In the **file list**, be sure the items are in alphabetical order by **Name**. If the items are not in alphabetical order, recall that by clicking the small arrow in the column heading name, you can change how the files in the file list are ordered.

4 On the ribbon, click the **View tab**, and then in the **Layout group**, be sure **Details** is selected.

The *Details view* displays a list of files or folders and their most common properties.

ANOTHER WAY   Right-click in a blank area of the file list, point to View, and then click Details.

---

5 On the ribbon, click the **Home tab**, and then in the **New group**, click **New folder**. With the text *New folder* selected, type **Paris** and press Enter. Click **New folder** again, type **Venice** and then press Enter. Create a third **New folder** named **London**

In a Windows 10 file list, folders are listed first, in alphabetic order, followed by individual files in alphabetic order.

6 Click the **Venice** folder one time to select it, and then on the ribbon, on the **Home tab**, in the **Organize group**, click **Rename**. Notice that the text *Venice* is selected. Type **Rome** and press Enter.

⟳ **ANOTHER WAY**   Point to a folder or file name, right-click, and then on the shortcut menu, click Rename.

---

7 In the **file list**, click one time to select the Word file **Architects**. With the file name selected, click the file name again to select all the text. Click the file name again to place the insertion point within the file name, edit the file name to **Architects_Local** and press Enter. Compare your screen with Figure 1.86.

You can use any of the techniques you just practiced to change the name of a file or folder.

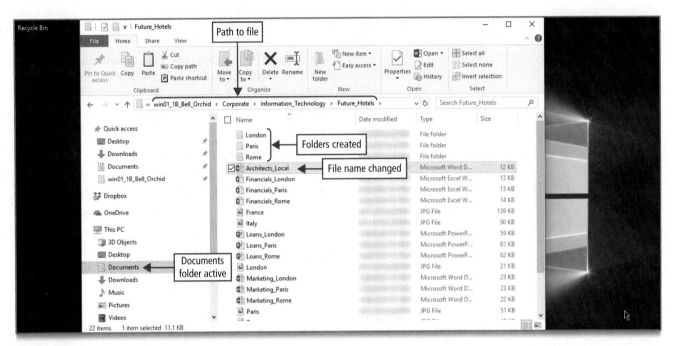

Figure 1.86

8 On the taskbar, click the **PowerPoint** icon to redisplay your **Windows_10_1B_Hotel_Files** presentation, and then on the **Home tab**, click the upper portion of the **New Slide** button to insert a new slide with the Title Only layout.

9 Click anywhere in the text *Click to add title*, type **Europe Folders** and then click anywhere in the empty space below the title.

10 On the **Insert tab**, in the **Images group**, click **Screenshot**, and then under **Available Windows**, click the image of your file list. On the **Picture Tools Format tab**, in the **Size group**, click in the **Shape Height** box, [⬆ 0.05"], type **5** and then press Enter. As necessary, drag the image down so that the title you typed is visible; your presentation contains four slides.

11 Above the **File tab**, on the Quick Access toolbar, click **Save** 🖫, and then in the upper right corner, click **Minimize** [–] so that PowerPoint remains open but not displayed on your screen.

12 Close ☒ the **Future_Hotels** window.

Activity 1.36 | Copying Files

Copying, moving, renaming, and deleting files and folders comprise the most heavily used features within File Explorer. Probably half or more of the steps you complete in File Explorer relate to these tasks, so mastering these techniques will increase your efficiency.

When you *copy* a file or a folder, you make a duplicate of the original item and then store the duplicate in another location. In this Activity, you will assist Barbara and Steven in making copies of the Staffing_Plan file, and then placing the copies in each of the three folders you created—London, Paris, and Rome.

1 From the taskbar, open **File Explorer** 🔲, and then by double-clicking in the file list or following the links in the address bar, navigate to **This PC > Documents > win01_1B_Bell_Orchid > Corporate > Information_Technology > Future_Hotels**.

2 In the upper right corner, **Maximize** 🔲 the window. On the **View tab**, if necessary set the **Layout** to **Details**, and then in the **Current view group**, click **Size all columns to fit** 🔳.

3 In the **file list**, click the file **Staffing_Plan** one time to select it, and then on the **Home tab**, in the **Clipboard group**, click **Copy**.

4 At the top of the **file list**, double-click the **London folder** to open it, and then in the **Clipboard group**, click **Paste**. Notice that the copy of the **Staffing_Plan** file displays. Compare your screen with Figure 1.87.

Figure 1.87

> **ANOTHER WAY** Right-click the file you want to copy, and on the menu click Copy. Then right-click the folder into which you want to place the copy, and on the menu click Paste. Or, select the file you want to copy, press [Ctrl] + [C] to activate the Copy command, open the folder into which you want to paste the file, and then press [Ctrl] + [V] to activate the Paste command.

5 With the **London** window open, by using any of the techniques you have practiced, rename this copy of the **Staffing_Plan** file to **London_Staffing_Plan**

6 To the left of the **address bar**, click **Up** ↑ to move up one level in the folder structure and to redisplay the **file list** for the **Future_Hotels** folder.

> **ANOTHER WAY** In the address bar, click Future_Hotels to redisplay this window and move up one level in the folder structure.

7 Click the **Staffing_Plan** file one time to select it, hold down Ctrl, and then drag the file upward over the **Paris** folder until the ScreenTip + *Copy to Paris* displays, and then release the mouse button and release Ctrl.

> When dragging a file into a folder, holding down Ctrl engages the Copy command and places a *copy* of the file at the location where you release the mouse button. This is another way to copy a file or copy a folder.

8 Open the **Paris** folder, and then rename the **Staffing_Plan** file **Paris_Staffing_Plan** Then, move up one level in the folder structure to redisplay the **Future_Hotels** window.

9 Double-click the **Rome** folder to open it. With your mouse pointer anywhere in the **file list**, right-click, and then from the shortcut menu click **Paste**.

> A copy of the Staffing_Plan file is copied to the folder. Because a copy of the Staffing_Plan file is still on the Clipboard, you can continue to paste the item until you copy another item on the Clipboard to replace it.

10 Rename the file **Rome_Staffing_Plan**

11 On the **address bar**, click **Future_Hotels** to move up one level and open the **Future_Hotels** window—or click Up ↑ to move up one level. Leave this folder open for the next Activity.

Activity 1.37 | Moving Files

When you *move* a file or folder, you remove it from the original location and store it in a new location. In this Activity, you will move items from the Future_Hotels folder into their appropriate folders.

1 With the **Future_Hotels** folder open, in the **file list**, click the Excel file **Financials_London** one time to select it. On the **Home tab**, in the **Clipboard group**, click **Cut**.

> The file's Excel icon dims. This action places the item on the Clipboard.

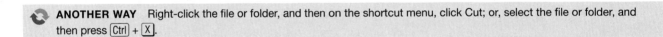

ANOTHER WAY   Right-click the file or folder, and then on the shortcut menu, click Cut; or, select the file or folder, and then press Ctrl + X.

2 Double-click the **London** folder to open it, and then on the **Home tab**, in the **Clipboard group**, click **Paste**.

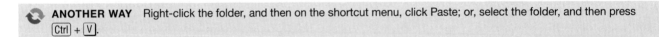

ANOTHER WAY   Right-click the folder, and then on the shortcut menu, click Paste; or, select the folder, and then press Ctrl + V.

3 Click **Up** ↑ to move up one level and redisplay the **Future_Hotels** folder window. In the **file list**, point to **Financials_Paris**, hold down the left mouse button, and then drag the file upward over the **Paris** folder until the ScreenTip *Move to Paris* displays, and then release the mouse button.

4 Open the **Paris** folder, and notice that the file was moved to this folder. Click **Up** ↑—or on the address bar, click Future_Hotels to return to that folder.

5 In the **file list**, click **Loans_London** one time to select it. hold down Ctrl, and then click the photo image **London** and the Word document **Marketing_London** to select the three files. Release the Ctrl key. Compare your screen with Figure 1.88.

Use this technique to select a group of noncontiguous items in a list.

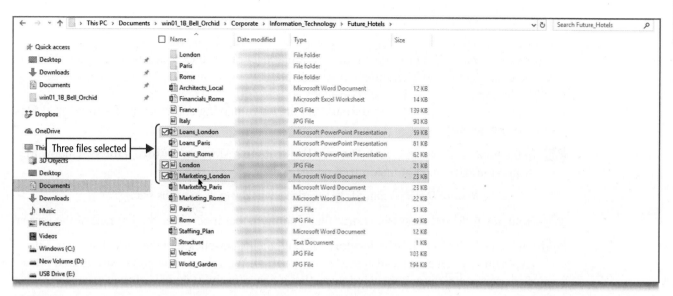

Figure 1.88

6 Point to any of the selected files, hold down the left mouse button, and then drag upward over the **London** folder until the ScreenTip →*Move to London* displays and *3* displays over the files being moved, and then release the mouse button.

You can see that by keeping related files together—for example, all the files that relate to the London hotel—in folders that have an appropriately descriptive name, it will be easier to locate information later.

7 By dragging, move the **Architects_Local** file into the **London** folder.

8 In an empty area of the file list, right-click, and then click **Undo Move**. Leave the **Future_Hotels** window open for the next Activity.

Any action that you make in a file list can be undone in this manner.

ANOTHER WAY Press Ctrl + Z to undo an action in the file list.

MORE KNOWLEDGE **Using Shift + Click to Select Files**

If a group of files to be selected are contiguous (next to each other in the file list), click the first file to be selected, hold down Shift and then click the left mouse button on the last file to select all of the files between the top and bottom file selections.

Activity 1.38 | Copying and Moving Files by Snapping Two Windows

Sometimes you will want to open, in a second window, another instance of a program that you are using; that is, two copies of the program will be running simultaneously. This capability is especially useful in the File Explorer program, because you are frequently moving or copying files from one location to another.

In this Activity, you will open two instances of File Explorer, and then use snap, which you have already practiced in this chapter, to display both instances on your screen.

To copy or move files or folders into a different level of a folder structure, or to a different drive location, the most efficient method is to display two windows side by side and then use drag and drop or copy (or cut) and paste commands.

In this Activity, you will assist Barbara and Steven in making copies of the Staffing_Plan files for the corporate office.

1 In the upper right corner, click **Restore Down** ⬓ to restore the **Future_Hotels** window to its previous size and not maximized on the screen.

> Use the *Restore Down* command ⬓ to resize a window to its previous size.

2 Hold down ⊞ and press ← to snap the window so that it occupies the left half of the screen.

3 On the taskbar, *point* to **File Explorer** 🗂 and then right-click. On the jump list, click **File Explorer** to open another instance of the program. With the new window active, hold down ⊞ and press → to snap the window so that it occupies the right half of the screen.

4 In the window on the right, click in a blank area to make the window active. Then navigate to **Documents > win01_1B_Bell_Orchid > Corporate > Human_Resources**. Compare your screen with Figure 1.89.

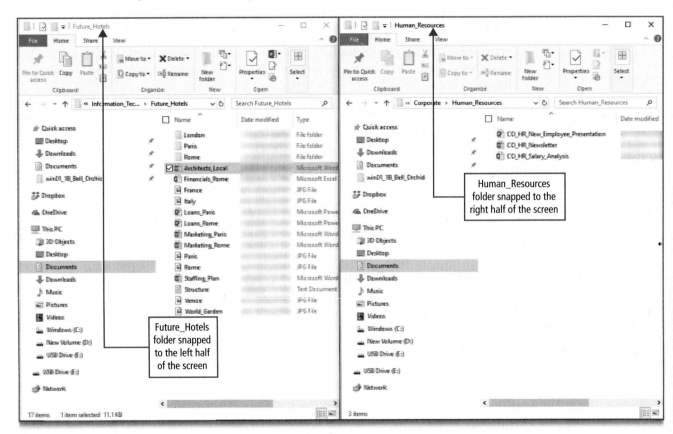

Figure 1.89

5 In the left window, double-click to open the **Rome** folder, and then click one time to select the file **Rome_Staffing_Plan**.

6 Hold down Ctrl, and then drag the file into the right window, into an empty area of the **Human_Resources file list**, until the ScreenTip + *Copy to Human_Resources* displays and then release the mouse button and Ctrl.

7 In the left window, on the **address bar**, click **Future_Hotels** to redisplay that folder. Open the **Paris** folder, point to **Paris_Staffing_Plan** and right-click, and then click **Copy**.

> You can access the Copy command in various ways; for example, from the shortcut menu, on the ribbon, or by using the keyboard shortcut Ctrl + C.

8 In the right window, point anywhere in the **file list**, right-click, and then click **Paste**.

9 On the taskbar, click the PowerPoint icon to redisplay your **Windows_10_1B_Hotel_Files** presentation, and then on the **Home tab**, click the upper portion of the **New Slide** button to insert a new slide with the **Title Only** layout; this will be your fifth slide.

10 Click anywhere in the text *Click to add title*, type **Staffing Plan Files** and then click anywhere in the empty space below the title.

11 On the **Insert tab**, in the **Images group**, click **Screenshot**, and then click **Screen Clipping**. When the dimmed screen displays, move the ⊞ pointer to the upper left corner of the screen, hold down the left mouse button, and drag to the lower right corner but do not include the taskbar. Then release the mouse button.

> Because you have two windows displayed side by side, each window displays under Available Windows. Recall that to capture an entire screen that contains more than one window, use the Screen Clipping tool with which you can capture a snapshot of your screen.

12 If necessary, close the Design Ideas pane on the right. On the **Picture Tools Format tab**, in the **Size group**, click in the **Shape Height** box, type **5** and press Enter. As necessary, drag the image down so that the title you typed is visible.

13 Click outside of the image to deselect it, and then press Ctrl + Home to display the first slide in your presentation; your presentation contains five slides.

14 In the upper right, **Close** ✕ the **PowerPoint** window, and when prompted, click **Save**.

15 **Close** ✕ all open windows.

For Non-MyLab Submissions Determine What Your Instructor Requires for Submission
As directed by your instructor, submit your completed PowerPoint file.

---

16 In **MyLab IT**, locate and click the Grader Project **Windows 10 1B Hotel Files**. In **step 3**, under **Upload Completed Assignment**, click **Choose File**. In the **Open** dialog box, navigate to your **Windows 10 Chapter 1 folder**, and then click your **Student_Windows_10_1B_ Hotel_Files** file one time to select it. In the lower right corner of the **Open** dialog box, click **Open**.

> The name of your selected file displays above the Upload button.

17 To submit your file to **MyLab IT** for grading, click **Upload**, wait a moment for a green **Success!** message, and then in **step 4**, click the blue **Submit for Grading** button. Click **Close Assignment** to return to your list of **Course Materials**.

Deleting Files and Using the Recycle Bin

It is good practice to delete files and folders that you no longer need from your hard disk drive and removable storage devices. Doing so makes it easier to keep your data organized and also frees up storage space.

When you delete a file or folder from any area of your computer's hard disk drive or from OneDrive, the file or folder is not immediately deleted. Instead, the deleted item is stored in the **Recycle Bin** and remains there until the Recycle Bin is emptied. Thus, you can recover an item deleted from your computer's hard disk drive or OneDrive so long as the Recycle Bin has not been emptied. Items deleted from removable storage devices like a USB flash drive and from some network drives are immediately deleted and cannot be recovered from the Recycle Bin.

To permanently delete a file without first moving it to the Recycle Bin, click the item, hold down Shift, and then press Delete. A message will display indicating *Are you sure you want to permanently delete this file?* Use caution when using Shift + Delete to permanently delete a file because this action is not reversible.

You can restore items by dragging them from the file list of the Recycle Bin window to the file list of the folder window in which you want to restore. Or, you can restore them to the location they were deleted from by right-clicking the items in the file list of the Recycle Bin window and selecting Restore.

You have completed Project 1B **END**

wavebreakmedia/Shutterstock, Monkey Business Images/Fotolia, Ivanko80/Shutterstock, Monkey Business Images/Shutterstock

Microsoft Office Specialist (MOS) Skills in This Chapter
Project 1A
Microsoft Word
1.1.1 Search for text
1.2.1 Set up document pages
1.2.4 Configure page background elements
1.2.4 Modify basic document properties
1.3.1 Modify basic document properties
1.4.1 Locate and remove hidden properties and personal information
1.4.2 Locate and correct accessibility issues
1.4.3 Locate and correct compatibility issues
2.2.5 Clear formatting
5.2.6 Format 3D models
5.4.3 Add alternative text to objects for accessibility
Microsoft Excel
5.3.3 Add alternative text to charts for accessibility

Build Your E-Portfolio

An E-Portfolio is a collection of evidence, stored electronically, that showcases what you have accomplished while completing your education. Collecting and then sharing your work products with potential employers reflects your academic and career goals. Your completed documents from the following projects are good examples to show what you have learned: 1A and 1B.

GO! For Job Success

Discussion: Managing Your Computer Files

Your instructor may assign this discussion to your class, and then ask you to think about, or discuss with your classmates, these questions:

g-stockstudio/Shutterstock

> **Why do you think it is important to follow specific guidelines when naming and organizing your files?**

> **Why is it impractical to store files and shortcuts to programs on your desktop?**

> **How are you making the transition from storing all your files on physical media, such as flash drives or the hard drive of your computer, to storing your files in the cloud where you can access them from any computer with an internet connection?**

End of Chapter

Summary

Many Office features and commands, such as accessing the Open and Save As dialog boxes, performing commands from the ribbon and from dialog boxes, and using the Clipboard are the same in all Office desktop apps.

A desktop app is installed on your computer and requires a computer operating system such as Microsoft Windows or Apple's macOS to run. The programs in Microsoft Office 365 and Office 2019 are considered to be desktop apps.

The Windows 10 Start menu is your connected dashboard—this is your one-screen view of information that updates continuously with new information and personal communications that are important to you.

File Explorer is at work anytime you are viewing the contents of a location, a folder, or a file. Use File Explorer to navigate your Windows 10 folder structure that stores and organizes the files you create.

GO! Learn It Online

Review the concepts, key terms, and MOS skills in this chapter by completing these online challenges, which you can find at **MyLab IT**.

Chapter Quiz: Answer matching and multiple-choice questions to test what you have learned in this chapter.

Lessons on the GO!: Learn how to use all the new apps and features as they are introduced by Microsoft.

Quiz: Answer questions to review the MOS skills that you practiced in this chapter.

Monkey Business Images/Fotolia

Glossary

Glossary of Chapter Key Terms

.png file An image file type that can be transferred over the internet, an acronym for Portable Network Graphic.

.txt file A simple file consisting of lines of text with no formatting that almost any computer can open and display.

3D models A new kind of shape that you can insert from an online library of ready-to-use three-dimensional graphics.

Address bar In a File Explorer window, the area that displays your current location in the folder structure as a series of links separated by arrows.

Alignment The placement of text or objects relative to the margins.

Alignment guides Green lines that display when you move an object to assist in alignment.

Alt text Text added to a picture or object that helps people using a screen reader understand what the object is; also called *alternative text*.

Alternative text Text added to a picture or object that helps people using a screen reader understand what the object is; also called *alt text*.

Application A computer program that helps you perform a task for a specific purpose.

AutoSave An Office 365 feature that saves your document every few seconds—if saved on OneDrive, OneDrive for Business, or SharePoint Online—and enables you to share the document with others for real-time co-authoring.

Backstage tabs The area along the left side of Backstage view with tabs to display screens with related groups of commands.

Backstage view A centralized space for file management tasks; for example, opening, saving, printing, publishing, or sharing a file.

Bing Microsoft's search engine.

Bookmark A command that marks a word, section, or place in a document so that you can jump to it quickly without scrolling.

Booting the computer The process of turning on the computer.

Center alignment The alignment of text or objects centered horizontally between the left and right margin.

Check Accessibility A command that checks a document for content that people with disabilities might find difficult to read.

Check Compatibility A command that searches your document for features that may not be supported by older versions of Office.

Click The action of pressing the left button of the mouse pointing device.

Clipboard A temporary storage area that holds text or graphics that you select and then cut or copy.

Cloud computing Applications and services that are accessed over the internet.

Cloud storage Online storage of data so that you can access your data from different places and devices.

Commands An instruction to a computer program that causes an action to be carried out.

Compressed Folder Tools A command available in File Explorer with which you can extract compressed files.

Compressed files Files that have been reduced in size, take up less storage space, and can be transferred to other computers faster than uncompressed files.

Content pane In a File Explorer window, another name for the file list.

Context menus Menus that display commands and options relevant to the selected text or object; also called *shortcut menus*.

Context-sensitive commands Commands that display on a shortcut menu that relate to the object or text that is selected.

Contextual tab A tab added to the ribbon automatically when a specific object is selected and that contains commands relevant to the selected object.

Copy A command that duplicates a selection and places it on the Clipboard.

Cortana Microsoft's intelligent personal assistant in Windows 10 and also available on other devices; named for the intelligent female character in the video game Halo.

Cut A command that removes a selection and places it on the Clipboard.

Dashboard The right side of the Start menu that is a one-screen view of links to information and programs that matter to you.

Data The documents, worksheets, pictures, songs, and so on that you create and store during the day-to-day use of your computer.

Data management The process of managing files and folders.

Default The term that refers to the current selection or setting that is automatically used by a computer program unless you specify otherwise.

Deselect The action of canceling the selection of an object or block of text by clicking outside of the selection.

Desktop A simulation of a real desk that represents your work area; here you can arrange icons such as shortcuts to files, folders, and various types of documents in the same manner you would arrange physical objects on top of a desk.

Desktop app A computer program that is installed on your PC and requires a computer operating system such as Microsoft Windows to run; also known as a *desktop application*.

Desktop application A computer program that is installed on your PC and requires a computer operating system such as Microsoft Windows to run; also known as a *desktop app*.

Desktop shortcuts Desktop icons that can link to items accessible on your computer such as a program, file, folder, disk drive, printer, or another computer.

Details pane When activated in a folder window, displays—on the right—the most common file properties associated with the selected file.

Details view A command that displays a list of files or folders and their most common properties.

Dialog box A small window that displays options for completing a task.

Dictate A feature in Word, PowerPoint, Outlook, and OneNote for Windows 10; when you enable Dictate, you start talking and as you talk, text appears in your document or slide.

Dialog Box Launcher A small icon that displays to the right of some group names on the ribbon and that opens a related dialog box or pane providing additional options and commands related to that group.

Document properties Details about a file that describe or identify it, including the title, author name, subject, and keywords that identify the document's topic or contents; also known as *metadata*.

Double-click The action of pressing the left mouse button two times in rapid succession while holding the mouse still.

Glossary

Download The action of transferring or copying a file from another location—such as a cloud storage location, your college's Learning Management System, or from an internet site—to your computer.

Drag The action of holding down the left mouse button while moving your mouse.

Drive An area of storage that is formatted with a file system compatible with your operating system and is identified by a drive letter.

Edit The process of making changes to text or graphics in an Office file.

Editor A digital writing assistant in Word and Outlook that displays misspellings, grammatical mistakes, and writing style issues.

Ellipsis A set of three dots indicating incompleteness; an ellipsis following a command name indicates that a dialog box will display if you click the command.

Enhanced ScreenTip A ScreenTip that displays useful descriptive information about the command.

Extract To decompress, or pull out, files from a compressed form.

File Information stored on a computer under a single name.

File Explorer The Windows program that displays the contents of locations, folders, and files on your computer.

File Explorer window A window that displays the contents of the current location and contains helpful parts so that you can navigate—explore within the file organizing structure of Windows.

File list In a File Explorer window, the area that displays the contents of the current location.

File name extension A set of characters at the end of a file name that helps Windows understand what kind of information is in a file and what program should open it.

File properties Information about a file, such as the author, the date the file was last changed, and any descriptive tags.

Fill The inside color of an object.

Filtered list A display of files that is limited based on specified criteria.

Folder A container in which you can store files.

Folder structure The hierarchy of folders.

Folder window A window that typically displays the File List for a folder.

Font A set of characters with the same design and shape.

Font styles Formatting emphasis such as bold, italic, and underline.

Footer A reserved area for text or graphics that displays at the bottom of each page in a document.

Format Painter The command to copy the formatting of specific text or to copy the formatting of a paragraph and then apply it in other locations in your document; when active, the pointer takes the shape of a paintbrush.

Formatting The process of applying Office commands to make your documents easy to read and to add visual touches and design elements to make your document inviting to the reader; establishes the overall appearance of text, graphics, and pages in an Office file—for example, in a Word document.

Formatting marks Characters that display on the screen, but do not print, indicating where the Enter key, the Spacebar, and the Tab key were pressed; also called *nonprinting characters*.

Free-form snip From the Snipping Tool, a command that draws an irregular line such as a circle around an area of the screen.

Full-screen snip From the Snipping Tool, a command that captures the entire screen.

Gallery An Office feature that displays a list of potential results.

Gradient fill A fill effect in which one color fades into another.

Graphical user interface Graphics such as an image of a file folder or wastebasket that you click to activate the item represented.

Groups On the Office ribbon, the sets of related commands that you might need for a specific type of task.

GUI An abbreviation of the term graphical user interface.

Hamburger Another name for a hamburger menu.

Hamburger menu Another name for a menu icon, deriving from the three lines that bring to mind a hamburger on a bun.

Hard disk drive The primary storage device located inside your computer where some of your files and programs are typically stored, usually designated as drive C.

Hierarchy An arrangement where items are ranked and where each level is lower in rank than the item above it

Icons Small images that represent commands, files, applications, or other windows.

Info tab The tab in Backstage view that displays information about the current file.

Insertion point A blinking vertical line that indicates where text or graphics will be inserted.

Inspect Document A command that searches your document for hidden data of personal information that you might not want to share publicly.

JPEG An acronym that stands for *Joint Photographic Experts Group* and that is a common file type used by digital cameras and computers to store digital pictures.

Jump List A display of destinations and tasks from a program's taskbar icon when you right-click the icon.

Keyboard shortcut A combination of two or more keyboard keys, used to perform a task that would otherwise require a mouse.

KeyTip The letter that displays on a command in the ribbon and that indicates the key you can press to activate the command when keyboard control of the ribbon is activated.

Keywords Custom file properties in the form of words that you associate with a document to give an indication of the document's content.

Landscape orientation A page orientation in which the paper is wider than it is tall.

Layout Options A button that displays when an object is selected and that has commands to choose how the object interacts with surrounding text.

Live Preview A technology that shows the result of applying an editing or formatting change as you point to possible results—*before* you actually apply it.

Live tiles Tiles that are constantly updated with fresh information.

Location Any disk drive, folder, or other place in which you can store files and folders.

Lock screen A background that fills the computer screen when the computer boots up or wakes up from sleep mode.

Maximize A window control button that will enlarge the size of the window to fill the entire screen.

Menu A list of commands within a category.

Menu bar A group of menus at the top of a program window.

Menu icon A button consisting of three lines that, when clicked, expands a menu; often used in mobile applications because it is compact to use on smaller screens—also referred to a *hamburger menu*.

Glossary

Metadata Details about a file that describe or identify it, including the title, author name, subject, and keywords that identify the document's topic or contents; also known as *document properties*.

Microsoft account A user account with which you can sign in to any Windows 10 computer on which you have, or create, an account.

Microsoft Store app A smaller app that you download from the Microsoft Store.

Mini toolbar A small toolbar containing frequently used formatting commands that displays as a result of selecting text or objects.

Minimize A window control button that will keep a program open but will remove it from screen view.

Move In File Explorer, the action of removing a file or folder from its original location and storing it in a new location.

Mouse pointer Any symbol that displays on the screen in response to moving the mouse.

MRU Acronym for *most recently used*, which refers to the state of some commands that retain the characteristic most recently applied; for example, the Font Color button retains the most recently used color until a new color is chosen.

Navigate A process for exploring within the file organizing structure of Windows.

Navigation pane The area on the left side of the File Explorer window to access your OneDrive, folders on your PC, devices and drives connected to your PC, and other PCs on your network.

Nonprinting characters Characters that display on the screen, but do not print, indicating where the Enter key, the Spacebar, and the Tab key were pressed; also called *formatting marks*.

Notepad A basic text-editing program included with Windows 10 that you can use to create simple documents.

Object A text box, picture, table, or shape that you can select and then move and resize.

Office 365 A version of Microsoft Office to which you subscribe for an annual fee.

OneDrive Microsoft's free cloud storage for anyone with a free Microsoft account.

Operating system A specific type of computer program that manages the other programs on a computing device such as a desktop computer, a laptop computer, a smartphone, a tablet computer, or a game console.

Option button In a dialog box, a round button that enables you to make one choice among two or more options.

Page Width A command that zooms the document so that the width of the page matches the width of the window.

Paragraph symbol The symbol ¶ that represents the end of a paragraph.

Parent folder The location in which the folder you are viewing is saved.

Paste The action of placing text or objects that have been copied or cut from one location to another location.

Paste Options gallery A gallery of buttons that provides a Live Preview of all the Paste options available in the current context.

Path A sequence of folders that leads to a specific file or folder.

PDF The acronym for Portable Document Format, which is a file format that creates an image that preserves the look of your file, but that cannot be easily changed; a popular format for sending documents electronically, because the document will display on most computers.

Pen A pen-shaped stylus that you tap on a computer screen.

Personal folder The folder created on the hard drive for each Windows 10 user account on a computer; for each user account—even if there is only one user on the computer—Windows 10 creates a personal folder labeled with the account holder's name.

Point to The action of moving the mouse pointer over a specific area.

Pointer Any symbol that displays on your screen in response to moving your mouse.

Pointing device A mouse or touchpad used to control the pointer.

Points A measurement of the size of a font; there are 72 points in an inch.

Portable Document Format A file format that creates an image that preserves the look of your file, but that cannot be easily changed; a popular format for sending documents electronically, because the document will display on most computers.

Portrait orientation A page orientation in which the paper is taller than it is wide.

Print Preview A view of a document as it will appear when you print it.

Program A set of instructions that a computer uses to accomplish a task.

Progress bar A bar that displays in a dialog box—and also on the taskbar button—that indicates visually the progress of a task such as a copy process, a download, or a file transfer.

pt The abbreviation for *point* when referring to a font size.

Quick access In the navigation pane in a File Explorer window, a list of files you have been working on and folders you use often.

Real-time co-authoring A process where two or more people work on the same file at the same time and see changes made by others in seconds.

Rectangular snip From the Snipping Tool, a command that draws a precise box by dragging the mouse pointer around an area of the screen to form a rectangle.

Recycle Bin The area where deleted items are stored until you empty the bin; enables you to recover deleted items until the bin is emptied.

Removable storage device A device such as a USB flash drive used to transfer information from one computer to another.

Resources The collection of the physical parts of your computer such as the central processing unit (CPU), memory, and any attached devices such as a printer.

Restore Down A command that resizes a window to its previous size.

Ribbon In Office applications, displays a group of task-oriented tabs that contain the commands, styles, and resources you need to work in an Office desktop app. In a File Explorer window, the area at the top that groups common tasks on tabs. such as copying and moving, creating new folders, emailing and zipping items, and changing the view on related tabs.

Right-click The action of clicking the right mouse button one time.

Sans serif font A font design with no lines or extensions on the ends of characters.

Screen reader Software that enables visually impaired users to read text on a computer screen to understand the content of pictures.

Screenshot Any captured image of your screen.

ScreenTip A small box that displays useful information when you perform various mouse actions such as pointing to screen elements or dragging.

Glossary

Scroll arrow An arrow found at either end of a scroll bar that can be clicked to move within the window in small increments.

Scroll bar A vertical bar that displays when the contents of a window or pane are not completely visible; a scroll bar can be vertical, displayed at the side of the window, or horizontal, displayed at the bottom of a window.

Scroll box Within a scroll bar, a box that you can move to bring the contents of the window into view.

Select To specify, by highlighting, a block of data or text on the screen with the intent of performing some action on the selection.

Selecting Highlighting, by dragging with your mouse, areas of text or data or graphics, so that the selection can be edited, formatted, copied, or moved.

Serif font A font design that includes small line extensions on the ends of the letters to guide the eye in reading from left to right.

SharePoint A Microsoft technology that enables employees in an organization to access information across organizational and geographic boundaries.

Shortcut menu A menu that displays commands and options relevant to the selected text or object; also called a *context menu*.

Sizing handles Small circles or squares that indicate a picture or object is selected.

Snap An action to arrange two or more open windows on your screen so that you can work with multiple screens at the same time.

Snap Assist A feature that displays all other open windows after one window is snapped.

Snip An image captured by the Snipping tool that can be annotated, saved, copied, or shared via email.

Snipping tool A Windows 10 program that captures an image of all or part of your computer's screen.

Split button A button divided into two parts and in which clicking the main part of the button performs a command and clicking the arrow opens a menu with choices.

Start menu A Windows 10 menu that displays as a result of clicking the Start button and that displays a list of installed programs on the left and a customizable group of tiles on the right that can act as a user dashboard.

Style A group of formatting commands, such as font, font size, font color, paragraph alignment, and line spacing that can be applied to a paragraph with one command.

Subfolder The term for a folder placed within another folder.

Synchronization The process of updating computer files that are in two or more locations according to specific rules—also called *syncing*.

Syncing The process of updating computer files that are in two or more locations according to specific rules—also called *synchronization*.

System tray Another term for the notification area on the taskbar that displays notification icons and the system clock and calendar.

Tabs (ribbon) On the Office ribbon, the name of each activity area.

Tags Custom file properties in the form of words that you associate with a document to give an indication of the document's content; used to help find and organize files. Also called keywords.

Task View A taskbar button that displays your desktop background with small images of all open programs and apps and from which you can see and switch between open apps, including desktop apps.

Taskbar The bar at the bottom of your Windows screen that contains buttons to launch programs and buttons for all open apps.

Tell Me A search feature for Microsoft Office commands that you activate by typing what you are looking for in the Tell Me box.

Tell me more A prompt within a ScreenTip that opens the Office online Help system with explanations about how to perform the command referenced in the ScreenTip.

Template A preformatted document that you can use as a starting point and then change to suit your needs.

Theme A predesigned combination of colors, fonts, and effects that look good together and that is applied to an entire document by a single selection.

Timeline A Windows 10 feature that when you click the Task view button, you can see activities you have worked on across your devices; for example, you can find a document, image, or video you worked on yesterday or a week ago.

Thumbnail A reduced image of a graphic.

Tiles A group of square and rectangular boxes that display on the start menu.

Title bar The bar across the top of the window that displays the program, file, or app name.

Toggle button A button that can be turned on by clicking it once and then turned off by clicking it again.

Toolbar A row, column, or block of buttons or icons that displays across the top of a window and that contains commands for tasks you perform with a single click.

Triple-click The action of clicking the left mouse button three times in rapid succession.

Undo On the Quick Access Toolbar, the command that reverses your last action.

Unzip The process of extracting files that have been compressed.

User account A user on a single computer.

Wallpaper Another term for the Desktop background.

Window snip From the Snipping Tool, a command that captures the entire displayed window.

Windows 10 An operating system developed by Microsoft Corporation that works with mobile computing devices and also with traditional desktop and laptop PCs.

XML Paper Specification A Microsoft file format that creates an image of your document and that opens in the XPS viewer.

XPS The acronym for *XML Paper Specification*—a Microsoft file format that creates an image of your document and that opens in the XPS viewer.

Zip The process of compressing files.

Zoom The action of increasing or decreasing the size of the viewing area on the screen.

Introducing
Microsoft Word 2019

W

WORD 2019

TippaPatt/Shutterstock

Word 2019: Introduction   Introduction to Word

Content! Defined by Merriam-Webster's online dictionary as "the topic or matter treated in a written work" and also as "the principal substance (as written matter, illustrations, or music) offered by a World Wide Web site," content is what you consume when you read on paper or online, when you watch video, or when you listen to any kind of music—live or recorded.

Content is what you *create* when your own words or performances are recorded in some form. For creating content in the form of words, Microsoft Word is a great choice. Rather than just a tool for word processing, Word is now a tool for you to communicate and collaborate with others. When you want to communicate with pictures or images, Microsoft Word has many features to help you do so. You can use Word to complete complex tasks, such as creating sophisticated tables, embedding graphics, writing blogs, and creating publications. Word is a program that you can learn gradually, and then add more advanced skills one at a time.

Best of all, Microsoft Word is integrated into the cloud. If you save your documents to your cloud-based storage that comes with any free Microsoft account, you can retrieve them from any device and continue to work with and share your documents.

Creating Documents with Microsoft Word

1
WORD 2019

PROJECT 1A
Outcomes
Create a flyer with a picture.

Objectives
1. Create a New Document and Insert Text
2. Insert and Format Graphics
3. Insert and Modify Text Boxes and Shapes
4. Preview and Print a Document

PROJECT 1B
Outcomes
Format text, paragraphs, and documents.

Objectives
5. Change Document and Paragraph Layout
6. Create and Modify Lists
7. Set and Modify Tab Stops
8. Insert and Format a SmartArt Graphic and an Icon

Roman Belogorodov/Shutterstock

In This Chapter

GO! To Work with Word

In this chapter, you will begin your study of Microsoft Word, one of the most popular computer software applications and one that almost everyone has a reason to use. You can use Microsoft Word to perform basic word processing tasks, such as writing a memo, a report, or a letter. In this chapter, you will insert and format objects such as pictures, text boxes, SmartArt, and shapes, to improve the appearance of your documents and to better communicate your message. You will also practice formatting fonts, paragraphs, and the layout of your pages.

The projects in this chapter relate to **Sturgeon Point Productions**, an independent film company based in Miami with offices in Detroit and Milwaukee. The film professionals produce effective broadcast and branded content for many industries and provide a wide array of film and video production services. Sturgeon Point Productions has won awards for broadcast advertising, business media, music videos, and social media. The mission of the company is to help clients tell their stories—whether the story is about a social issue, a new product, a geographical location, a company, or a person.

PROJECT 1A Flyer

Project Activities

In Activities 1.01 through 1.16, you will create a flyer for Sharon Matsuo, Creative Director for Sturgeon Point Productions, announcing two internships for a short documentary. Your completed document will look similar to Figure 1.1.

Project Files for **MyLab IT** Grader

1. In your storage location, create a folder named **Word Chapter 1**.
2. In your **MyLab IT** course, locate and click **Word 1A Flyer**, Download Materials, and then Download All Files.
3. Extract the zipped folder to your Word Chapter 1 folder. Close the Grader download screens.
4. Take a moment to open the downloaded **Word_1A_Flyer_Instructions**; note any recent updates to the book.

Project Results

GO Project 1A
Where We're Going

Figure 1.1 Project 1A Internship Flyer

For Non-MyLab Submissions

For Project 1A, you will need:
New blank Word Document
w01A_Bird
w01A_Text

In your storage location, create a folder named **Word Chapter 1**
In your Word Chapter 1 folder, save your document as:
Lastname_Firstname_1A_Flyer

Start a new, blank Word document. After you have named and saved your document, on the next page begin with Step 2.

NOTE If You Are Using a Touch Screen

 Tap an item to click it.

 Press and hold for a few seconds to right-click; release when the information or commands display.

 Touch the screen with two or more fingers and then pinch together to zoom out or stretch your fingers apart to zoom in.

 Slide your finger on the screen to scroll—slide left to scroll right and slide right to scroll left.

 Slide to rearrange—similar to dragging with a mouse.

Swipe to select—slide an item a short distance with a quick movement—to select an item and bring up commands, if any.

Objective 1 | Create a New Document and Insert Text

ALERT Because Office 365 is a cloud-based subscription service that receives continuous updates, you may encounter some variations in what appears on your screen and what is shown in this instruction. Microsoft Office 365 is fully installed on your PC or Mac; no internet access is necessary to create or edit documents. When you *are* connected to the internet, you will receive monthly upgrades and new features, so you always have the latest versions of Office apps as soon as they are available. Your subscription gives you continuous free access to the latest innovations and refinements.

GO! Learn How
Video W1-1

When you create a new document, you can type all the document text, or you can type some of the text and then insert additional text from another source. Sharon Matsuo, Creative Director for Sturgeon Point Productions, created some of the document text in a Word document that you can insert in the flyer you are creating.

Activity 1.01 | Creating a New Word Document

MOS
1.1.4

1 Navigate to your **Word Chapter 1 folder**, and then double-click the Word file you downloaded from **MyLab IT** that displays your name—**Student_Word_1A_Flyer**. In your blank document, if necessary, at the top click **Enable Editing**.

MAC TIP If you are not submitting your file in **MyLab IT**, from the student data files that accompany this project, open the file Mac_w01A_Flyer. This is a blank document with default settings necessary to complete this project.

2 On the **Home tab**, in the **Paragraph group**, if necessary click Show/Hide ¶ so that it is active and the formatting marks display. If the rulers do not display, click the View tab, and then in the Show group, select the Ruler check box.

MAC TIP To display group names on the ribbon, display the menu, click Word, click Preferences, click View, select the Show group titles check box.

3 Type **Internships Available** and then press ⟨Enter⟩ two times. Then, type the following text: **This summer, Sturgeon Point Productions will be filming a short documentary in Costa Rica about its native birds and has positions available for two interns.**

As you type, the insertion point moves to the right, and when it approaches the right margin, Word determines whether the next word in the line will fit within the established right margin. If the word does not fit, Word moves the entire word down to the next line. This is *word wrap* and means that you press ⟨Enter⟩ *only* when you reach the end of a paragraph—it is not necessary to press ⟨Enter⟩ at the end of each line of text.

NOTE **Spacing Between Sentences**

Although you might have learned to add two spaces following end-of-sentence punctuation, the common practice now is to space only one time at the end of a sentence. Be sure to press ⟨Spacebar⟩ only one time following end-of-sentence punctuation.

---

4 Press ⟨Spacebar⟩ and then take a moment to study the table in Figure 1.2 to become familiar with the default document settings in Microsoft Word. Compare your screen with Figure 1.3.

When you press ⟨Enter⟩, ⟨Spacebar⟩, or ⟨Tab⟩ on your keyboard and Show/Hide is active, characters display in your document to represent these keystrokes. These characters do not print and are referred to as *formatting marks* or *nonprinting characters*. These marks will display throughout this instruction.

Default Document Settings in a New Word Document	
Setting	**Default format**
Font and font size	The default font is Calibri, and the default font size is 11 points.
Margins	The default left, right, top, and bottom page margins are 1 inch.
Line spacing	The default line spacing is 1.08, which provides slightly more space between lines than single spacing does.
Paragraph spacing	The default spacing after a paragraph is 8 points, which is slightly less than the height of one blank line of text.
View	The default view is Print Layout view, which displays the page borders and displays the document as it will appear when printed.

Figure 1.2

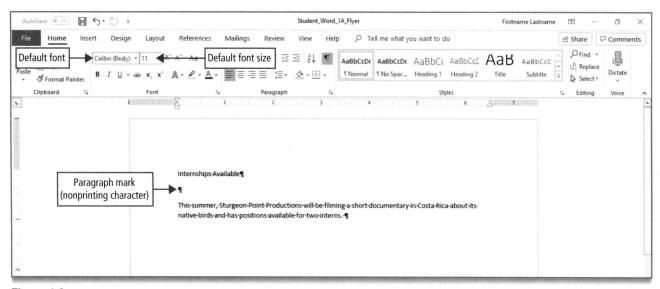

Figure 1.3

MORE KNOWLEDGE   **Word's Default Settings Are Easier to Read Online**

Until just a few years ago, word processing programs used single spacing, an extra blank paragraph to separate paragraphs, and 12 pt Times New Roman as the default formats. Now, studies show that individuals find the Word default formats described in Figure 1.2 to be easier to read online, where many documents are now viewed and read.

Activity 1.02 | Inserting Text from Another Document

You can create text in one Word document and insert it in another. Sharon Matsuo, Creative Director for Sturgeon Point Productions, created some of the document text for your flyer. You will insert the text from her document into the flyer you are creating.

1 ▶ On the ribbon, click the **Insert tab**. In the **Text group**, click the **Object button arrow**, and then click **Text from File**.

ALERT   **Does the Object dialog box display?**

If the Object dialog box displays, you probably clicked the Object *button* instead of the Object *button arrow*. Close the Object dialog box, and then in the Text group, click the Object button arrow, as shown in Figure 1.4. Click *Text from File*, and then continue with Step 2.

2 ▶ In the **Insert File** dialog box, navigate to the files you downloaded for this project, locate and select **w01A_Text**, and then click **Insert**. Compare your screen with Figure 1.4.

A *copy* of the text from the w01A_Text file displays at the insertion point location; the text is not removed from the original file.

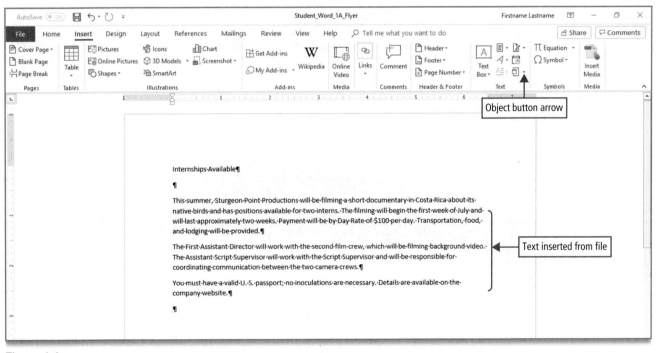

Figure 1.4

🔄 **ANOTHER WAY**   Open the file, copy the required text, close the file, and then paste the text into the current document.

3 ▶ On the **Quick Access Toolbar**, click **Save** 🖫 .

Objective 2 Insert and Format Graphics

GO! Learn How
Video W1-2

To add visual interest to a document, insert *graphics*. Graphics include pictures, online pictures, charts, and *drawing objects*—shapes, diagrams, lines, and so on. For additional visual interest, you can apply an attractive graphic format to text; add, resize, move, and format pictures; and add a page border.

Activity 1.03 | Formatting Text by Using Text Effects

Text effects are decorative formats, such as shadowed or mirrored text, text glow, 3-D effects, and colors that make text stand out. The flyer you are creating will be printed and posted online, and the use of text effects will draw attention to some of the important information.

1 Including the paragraph mark, select the first paragraph of text—*Internships Available*. On the **Home tab**, in the **Font group**, click **Text Effects and Typography** [A ▾].

2 In the **Text Effects and Typography** gallery, in the third row, click the first effect to apply it to the selection.

3 With the text still selected, in the **Font group**, click in the **Font Size** box [11 ▾] to select the existing font size. Type **52** and then press Enter.

When you want to change the font size of selected text to a size that does not display in the Font Size list, type the number in the Font Size box and press Enter to confirm the new font size.

4 With the text still selected, in the **Paragraph group**, click **Center** [≡] to center the text. Compare your screen with Figure 1.5.

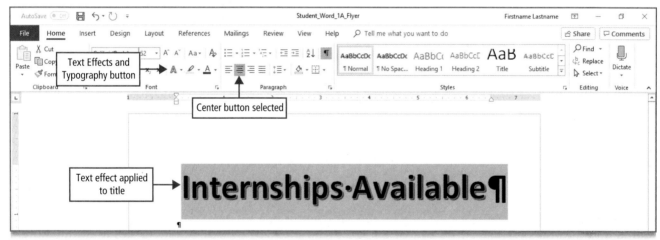

Figure 1.5

5 With the text still selected, in the **Font group**, click the **Font Color button arrow** [A ▾] to display the Font Color palette. Under **Theme Colors**, in the sixth column, click the first color.

6 With the text still selected, in the **Font group**, click **Text Effects and Typography** [A ▾]. Point to **Shadow**, and then under **Outer**, in the second row, click the third style.

7 Click anywhere in the document to deselect the text, click **Save** [🖫], and then compare your screen with Figure 1.6.

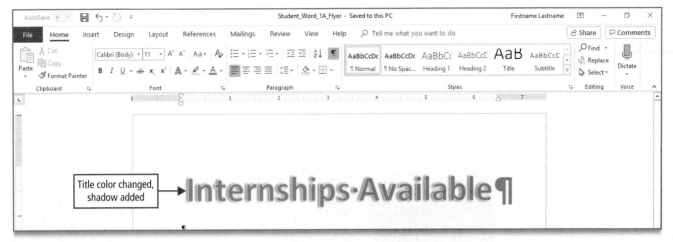

Figure 1.6

MORE KNOWLEDGE **Clear Existing Formatting**

If you do not like your text effect, you can remove all formatting from any selected text. To do so, on the Home tab, in the Font group, click Clear All Formatting [A₀].

Activity 1.04 | Inserting Pictures

5.1.2

Pictures that reflect document content can focus the reader's attention on the message. Sharon Matsuo asked that you insert a picture in the flyer that depicts the types of images that a photographer might capture during the internship.

1 In the paragraph that begins *This summer*, click to position the insertion point at the beginning of the paragraph.

2 On the **Insert tab**, in the **Illustrations group**, click **Pictures**. In the **Insert Picture** dialog box, navigate to the files you downloaded for this project, locate and click **w01A_Bird**, and then click **Insert**.

Word inserts the picture as an ***inline object***; that is, the picture is positioned directly in the text at the insertion point, just like a character in a sentence. The Layout Options button displays to the right of the picture. You can change the ***Layout Options*** to control the manner in which text wraps around a picture or other object. Sizing handles surround the picture indicating it is selected.

MAC TIP To insert the picture, on the Insert tab, click Pictures, and then click Picture from File.

3 Notice the sizing handles around the selected picture, as shown in Figure 1.7.

The corner sizing handles resize the graphic proportionally. The center sizing handles resize a graphic vertically or horizontally only; however, sizing with these will distort the graphic. A ***rotation handle***, with which you can rotate the graphic to any angle, displays above the top center sizing handle.

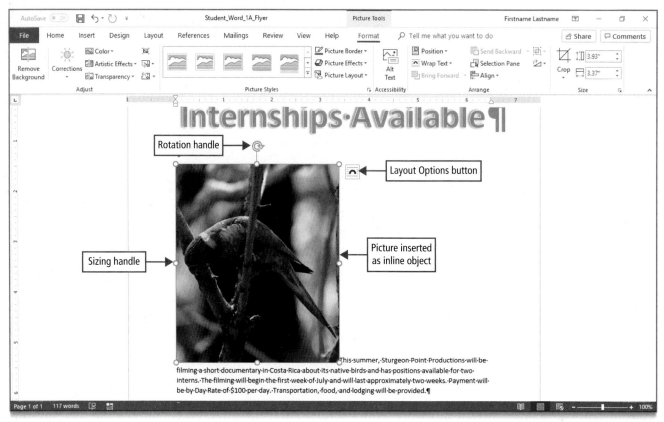

Figure 1.7

Activity 1.05 | Wrapping Text Around a Picture Using Layout Options

MOS
5.4.2

Recall that Layout Options enable you to control ***text wrapping***—the manner in which text displays around an object.

1 Be sure the picture is selected—you know it is selected if the sizing handles display.

2 To the right of the picture, click **Layout Options** 🖼 to display a gallery of text wrapping arrangements. Point to each icon layout option to view its ScreenTip.

Each icon visually depicts how text will wrap around an object.

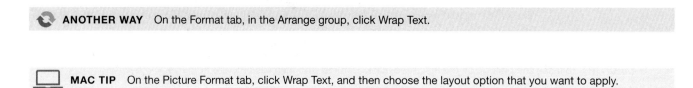

ANOTHER WAY On the Format tab, in the Arrange group, click Wrap Text.

MAC TIP On the Picture Format tab, click Wrap Text, and then choose the layout option that you want to apply.

3 From the gallery, under **With Text Wrapping**, click the first layout—**Square**. Compare your screen with Figure 1.8.

Select Square text wrapping when you want to wrap the text to the left or right of an image. To the left of the picture, an ***object anchor*** displays, indicating that the selected object is anchored to the text at this location in the document.

Figure 1.8

> **4** **Close** ⊠ the **Layout Options**, and then **Save** 🔲 your document.

Activity 1.06 | Resizing Pictures and Using Live Layout

When you move or size a picture, ***Live Layout*** reflows text as you move or size an object so that you can view the placement of surrounding text.

> **1** If necessary, scroll your document so the entire picture displays. At the lower right corner of the picture, point to the sizing handle until the 🔧 pointer displays. Drag slightly upward and to the left. As you drag, a green alignment guide may display. Compare your screen with Figure 1.9.

> ***Alignment guides*** may display when you are moving or sizing a picture to help you with object placement, and Live Layout shows you how the document text will flow and display on the page.

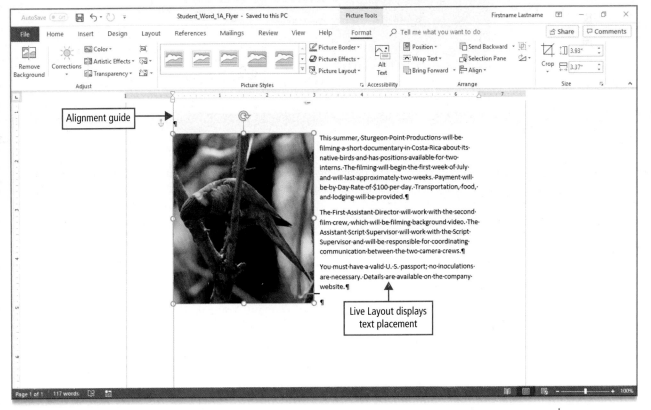

Figure 1.9

2 Continue to drag up and to the left until the bottom of the graphic is aligned at approximately **4 inches on the vertical ruler**. Notice that the graphic is proportionally resized.

3 On the **Quick Access Toolbar**, click **Undo** to restore the picture to its original size.

ANOTHER WAY On the Format tab, in the Adjust group, click Reset Picture.

---

4 On the ribbon, under **Picture Tools**, on the **Format tab**, in the **Size group**, click in the **Shape Height box** to select the number. Type **3.8** and then press [Enter]. If necessary, scroll down to view the entire picture on your screen, and then compare your screen with Figure 1.10.

When you use the Shape Height and Shape Width boxes to change the size of a graphic, the graphic will resize proportionally; that is, the width adjusts as you change the height and vice versa.

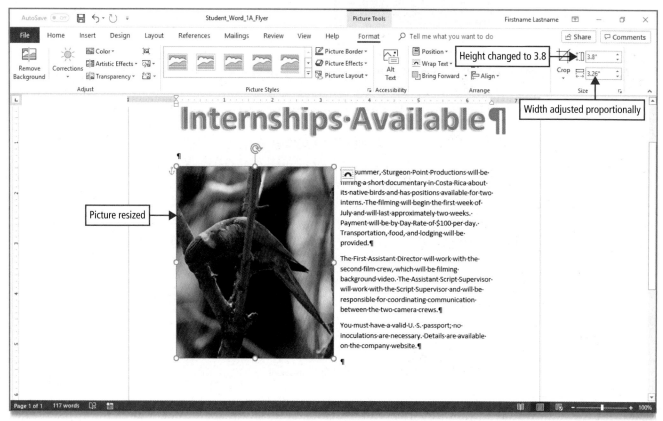

Figure 1.10

ANOTHER WAY A *spin box* is a small box with an upward- and downward-pointing arrow that lets you move rapidly through a set of values by clicking. You can change the height or width of a picture or object by clicking the Shape Height or Shape Width spin box arrows.

---

5 **Save** your document.

Activity 1.07 | Positioning a Picture

There are two ways to move a picture in a document. You can point to the picture and then drag it to a new position. You can also change the picture settings in a dialog box, which gives you more precise control over the picture location.

1 Be sure the picture is selected. On the ribbon, click the **Format tab**. In the **Arrange group**, click **Position**, and then click **More Layout Options**.

2 In the **Layout** dialog box, be sure the **Position tab** is selected. Under **Horizontal**, click the **Alignment** option button. To the right of **Alignment**, click the **arrow**, and then click **Right**. To the right of **relative to**, click the **arrow**, and then click **Margin**.

3 Under **Vertical**, click the **Alignment** option button. Change the **Alignment** options to **Top relative to Line**. Compare your screen with Figure 1.11.

With these alignment settings, the picture will move to the right margin of the page and the top edge will align with the top of the first line of the paragraph to which it is anchored.

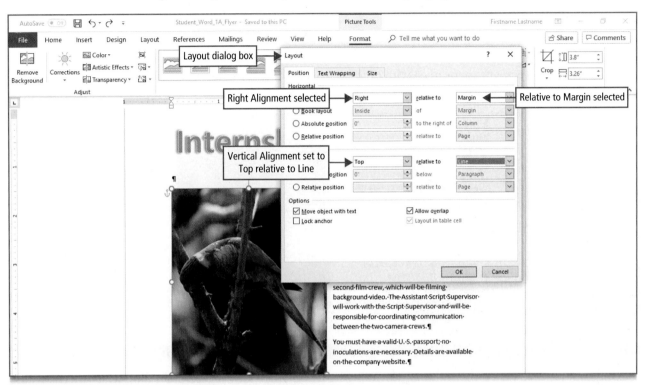

Figure 1.11

4 At the bottom of the **Layout** dialog box, click **OK**, and then on the **Quick Access Toolbar**, click **Save** 🖫. Notice that the picture moves to the right margin, and the text wraps on the left side of the picture. Compare your screen with Figure 1.12.

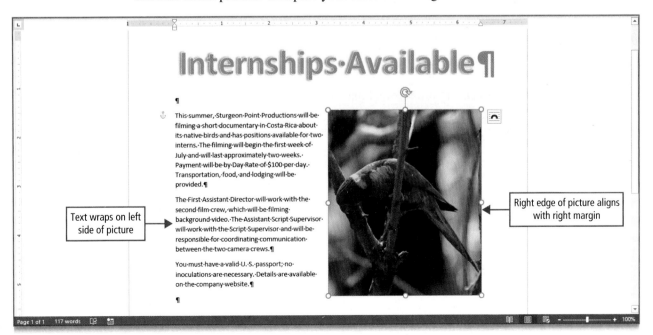

Figure 1.12

Activity 1.08 | Applying Picture Effects

Picture styles include shapes, shadows, frames, borders, and other special effects with which you can stylize an image. ***Picture Effects*** enhance a picture with effects such as a shadow, glow, reflection, or 3-D rotation.

1 Be sure the picture is selected. On the **Format tab**, in the **Picture Styles group**, click **Picture Effects**.

2 Point to **Soft Edges**. Use the ScreenTips to locate and then click **5 Point**.

The Soft Edges feature fades the edges of the picture. The number of points you choose determines how far the fade goes inward from the edges of the picture.

3 Compare your screen with Figure 1.13, and then **Save** your document.

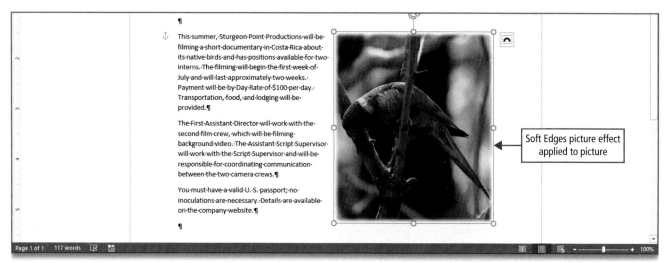

Figure 1.13

MORE KNOWLEDGE | **Applying Picture Styles**

To apply a picture style, select the picture. On the Format tab, in the Picture Styles group, click More, and then click the Picture Style that you want to apply.

Activity 1.09 | Applying Artistic Effects

Artistic effects are formats that make pictures look more like sketches or paintings.

1 Be sure the picture is selected. On the **Format tab**, in the **Adjust group**, click **Artistic Effects**.

2 In the first row of the gallery, point to, but do not click, the third effect.

Live Preview displays the picture with the third effect added.

3 In the second row of the gallery, click the third effect—**Paint Brush**. Paint Brush may be in another location in the gallery. If necessary, use the ScreenTips to locate the Paint Brush effect.

4 **Save** your document, and then notice that the picture looks more like a painting than a photograph. Compare your screen with Figure 1.14.

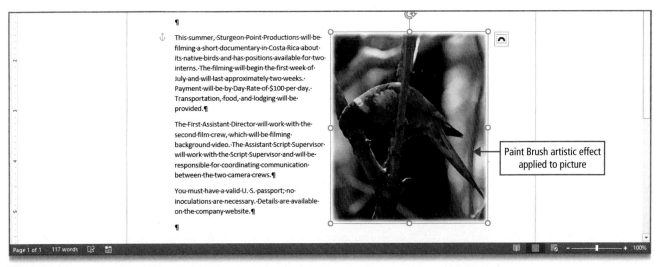

Figure 1.14

Activity 1.10 | Adding a Page Border

Page borders frame a page and help to focus the information on the page.

1 Click anywhere outside the picture to deselect it. On the **Design tab**, in the **Page Background group**, click **Page Borders**.

2 In the **Borders and Shading** dialog box, on the **Page Border tab**, under **Setting**, click **Box**. Under **Style**, scroll the list and click the seventh style—double lines.

3 Click the **Color arrow**, and then in the sixth column, click the first color.

4 Under **Apply to**, be sure *Whole document* is selected, and then compare your screen with Figure 1.15.

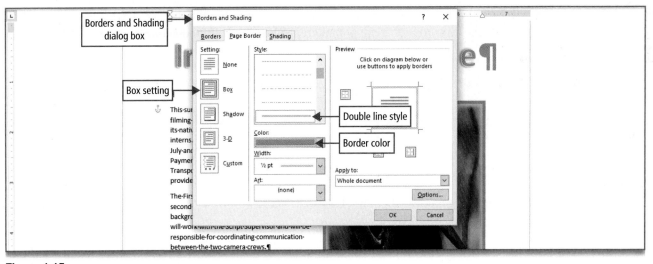

Figure 1.15

5 At the bottom of the **Borders and Shading** dialog box, click **OK**. Press Ctrl + Home to move to the top of the document.

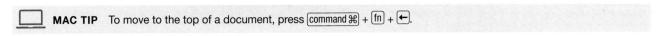

MAC TIP To move to the top of a document, press command ⌘ + fn + ←.

6 **Save** 🖫 your document, and then compare your screen with Figure 1.16.

Figure 1.16

🖥 **MAC TIP**   If your document page border does not display as shown in Figure 1.16, you may need to adjust the border margins. On the Design tab, click Page Borders. In the lower right corner of the Borders and Shading dialog box, click Options, and then change all the margins to 24 pt measured from Edge of page.

Objective 3   Insert and Modify Text Boxes and Shapes

▶
GO! Learn How
Video W1-3

Word has predefined *shapes* and *text boxes* that you can add to your documents. A shape is an object such as a line, arrow, box, callout, or banner. A text box is a movable, resizable container for text or graphics. Use these objects to add visual interest to your document.

Activity 1.11 │ Inserting, Sizing, and Positioning a Shape

MOS
5.1.1

Important information in a document needs to be easily recognized and noticed. Ms. Matsuo asked that you insert a shape with text in it to draw attention to the important information in the flyer.

1 ▶ Click in the blank paragraph below the title. Press Enter four times to create additional space for a text box, and then notice that the picture anchored to the paragraph moves with the text.

2 ▶ Press Ctrl + End to move to the bottom of the document, and then notice that your insertion point is positioned in the empty paragraph at the end of the document. Press Delete to remove the blank paragraph.

🖥 **MAC TIP**   To move to the bottom of a document, press command ⌘ + fn + →.

3 ▶ Click the **Insert tab**, and then in the **Illustrations group**, click **Shapes** to display the Shapes gallery. Compare your screen with Figure 1.17.

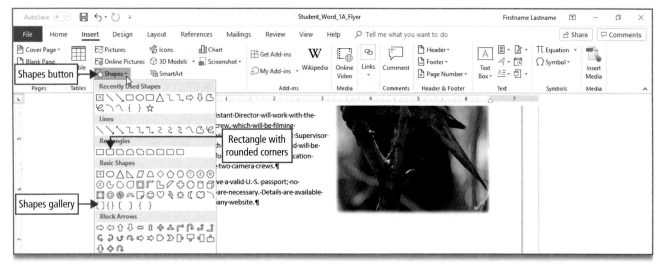

Figure 1.17

4 Under **Rectangles**, click the second shape—the rectangle that includes rounded corners, and then move your pointer. Notice that the ⊞ pointer displays.

5 Position the ⊞ pointer near the left margin at approximately **8 inches on the vertical** ruler. Click one time to insert a 1-inch by 1-inch rounded rectangle. The exact location is not important.

A blue rectangle with rounded edges displays.

MAC TIP You may need to drag your mouse to insert the rectangle. The exact size and location are not important as you will adjust both in a later step.

6 To the right of the rectangle object, click **Layout Options** ⊠, and then at the bottom of the gallery, click **See more** to display the Layout dialog box.

MAC TIP On the Shape Format tab, click Arrange, click Position, and then click More Layout Options.

7 In the **Layout** dialog box, under **Horizontal**, click **Alignment**. To the right of **Alignment**, click the **arrow**, and then click **Centered**. To the right of **relative to**, click the **arrow**, and then click **Page**. Under **Vertical**, select the existing number in the **Absolute position** box. Type **1** and then to the right of **below**, be sure that **Paragraph** displays. Click **OK**.

This action centers the rectangle on the page and positions the rectangle one inch below the last paragraph.

8 On the **Format tab**, in the **Shape Height box** ⬚ 0.29″ ⬚ select the existing number. Type **1.5** and then click in the **Shape Width box** ⬚ 1.07″ ⬚. Select the existing number, type **4.5** and then press Enter.

9 Compare your screen with Figure 1.18, and then **Save** 🖫 your document.

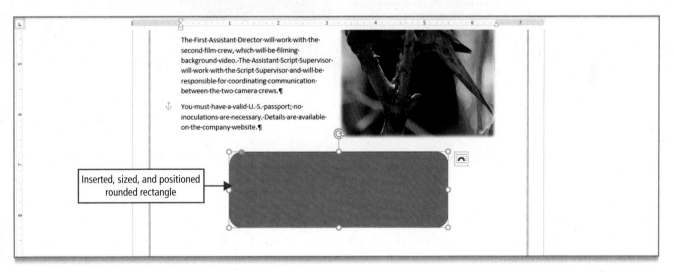

Figure 1.18

Activity 1.12 | Typing Text in a Shape and Formatting a Shape

MOS
5.2.4 and 5.3.2

1 If necessary, select the rectangle shape. Type **To set up an interview, apply online at:** and then press Enter. Type **www.SturgeonPointProductions.com**

2 Press Ctrl + A to select all of the text in the shape. Right-click over the selected text to display the mini toolbar, and then click **Bold** B. With the text still selected, click **Increase Font Size** A˄ three times to increase the font size to **16 pt**.

Use the keyboard shortcut Ctrl + A to select all of the text in a text box.

> **3** With the text still selected, on the **Home tab**, click the **Font Color button arrow**. Under **Theme Colors**, in the second column, click the first color.

> **4** Click outside the shape to deselect the text. Click the border of the shape to select the shape but not the text. On the **Format tab**, in the **Shape Styles group**, click **Shape Fill**. In the sixth column, click the fourth color.

> **5** With the shape still selected, in the **Shape Styles group**, click **Shape Outline**. In the sixth column, click the first color. Compare your screen with Figure 1.19, and then **Save** 🖫 your document.

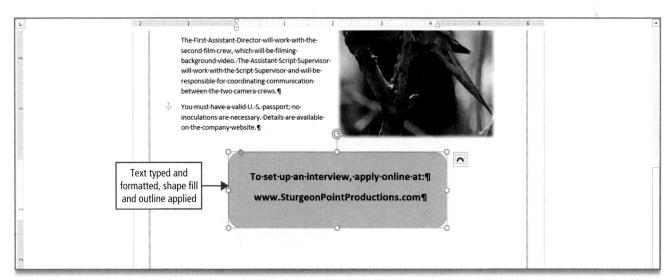

Figure 1.19

Activity 1.13 │ Inserting a Text Box

5.1.6

A text box is useful to differentiate portions of text from other text on the page. Because it is a *floating object*—a graphic that can be moved independently of the surrounding text characters— you can place a text box anywhere on the page.

> **1** Press ⌐Ctrl⌐ + ⌐Home⌐ to move to the top of the document.

> **2** On the **Insert tab**, in the **Text group**, click **Text Box**. At the bottom of the gallery, click **Draw Text Box**.

> **3** Position the ⊞ pointer over the first blank paragraph—aligned with the left margin and at approximately 1 inch on the vertical ruler. Drag down and to the right to create a text box approximately **1.5 inches** high and **4 inches** wide—the exact size and location need not be precise.

4 With the insertion point blinking in the text box, type the following, pressing Enter after each of the first *two* lines to create a new paragraph:

> **Interviews will be held:**
> **Friday and Saturday, January 14 and 15**
> **In the Career Services Conference Room**

5 Compare your screen with Figure 1.20, and then **Save** 💾 your document

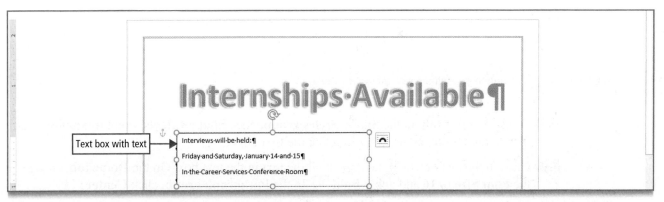

Figure 1.20

Activity 1.14 | Sizing and Positioning a Text Box and Formatting a Text Box Using Shape Styles

5.2.4

1 Point to the text box border to display the ⇱ pointer. In the space below the *Internships Available* title, by dragging, move the text box until a horizontal green alignment guide displays above the first blank paragraph mark and a vertical green alignment guide displays in the center of the page, as shown in Figure 1.21. If the alignment guides do not display, drag the text box to position it approximately as shown in the figure.

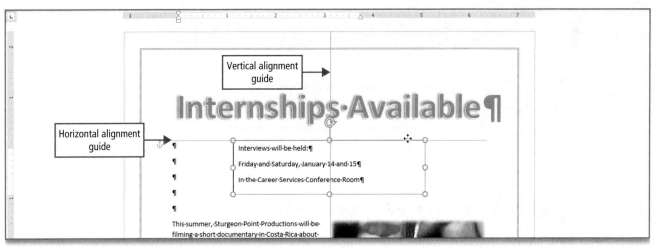

Figure 1.21

2 To place the text box precisely, on the **Format tab**, in the **Arrange group**, click **Position**, and then click **More Layout Options**.

3 In the **Layout** dialog box, under **Horizontal**, click **Alignment**. To the right of **Alignment**, click the **arrow**, and then click **Centered**. To the right of **relative to**, click the **arrow**, and then click **Page**.

4 Under **Vertical**, click in the **Absolute position** box, select the existing number, and then type **1.25** To the right of **below**, click the **arrow**, and then click **Margin**.

5 In the **Layout** dialog box, click the **Size tab**. Under **Height**, select the number in the **Absolute** box. Type **1.25** and then under **Width**, select the number in the **Absolute** box. Type **4** and then click **OK**.

> The text box is sized correctly, centered horizontally, and the top edge is positioned 1.25 inches below the top margin of the document.

6 On the **Format tab**, in the **Shape Styles group**, click **More**, and then in the first row, click the third style.

💻 **MAC TIP** The More button is located below the Shape Styles.

---

7 On the **Format tab**, in the **Shape Styles group**, click **Shape Effects**. Point to **Shadow**, and then under **Outer**, in the first row, click the first effect.

8 Click in the text box, and then select all the text in the text box. On the **Home tab**, change the **Font Size** to **16** and apply **Bold** B. In the **Paragraph group**, click **Center** ☰.

🔄 **ANOTHER WAY** The keyboard shortcut to center text in a document is Ctrl + E.

---

9 Click anywhere in the document to deselect the text box. Compare your screen with Figure 1.22, and then **Save** 🖫 your document.

Text formatted and centered, text box sized and positioned, shape style and Shadow effect applied

Internships·Available¶

Interviews·will·be·held:¶

Friday·and·Saturday,·January·14·and·15¶

In·the·Career·Services·Conference·Room¶

Figure 1.22

Objective 4 Preview and Print a Document

GO! Learn How
Video W1-4

While you are creating your document, it is useful to preview your document periodically to be sure that you are getting the result you want. Then, before printing or distributing electronically, make a final preview to be sure the document layout is what you intended.

Activity 1.15 | Adding a File Name to the Footer by Inserting a Field

1.3.4

Information in headers and footers helps to identify a document when it is printed or displayed electronically. Recall that a header is information that prints at the top of every page and a footer is information that prints at the bottom of every page. In this text book, you will insert the file name in the footer of every Word document.

1 Click the **Insert tab**, and then in the **Header & Footer group**, click **Footer**.

2 At the bottom of the gallery, click **Edit Footer**.

The footer area displays with the insertion point blinking at the left edge, and on the ribbon, the Header & Footer Tools display.

ANOTHER WAY At the bottom edge of the page, right-click; from the shortcut menu, click Edit Footer.

---

3 On the ribbon, under the **Header & Footer Tools**, on the **Design tab**, in the **Insert group**, click **Document Info**, and then click **File Name**. Compare your screen with Figure 1.23.

MAC TIP To insert the filename in the footer, on the Insert tab, click Footer, and then click Edit Footer. On the Header & Footer tab, click Field, and then under Categories, click Document Information. Under Field Names, click FileName, and then click OK.

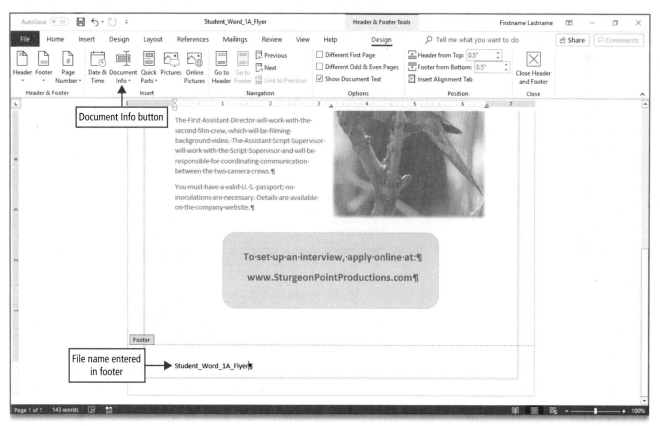

Figure 1.23

4 On the **Design tab**, click **Close Header and Footer**, and then **Save** 🖫 your document.

When the body of the document is active, the footer text is dimmed—it displays in gray. Conversely, when the footer area is active, the footer text is not dimmed; instead, the document text is dimmed.

ANOTHER WAY Double-click in the document outside of the footer area to close the footer and return to the document.

Activity 1.16 | Adding Document Properties and Previewing and Printing a Document

1.3.2 and 1.3.3

1 Press `Ctrl` + `Home` to move the insertion point to the top of the document. In the upper left corner of your screen, click the **File tab** to display **Backstage** view. Click **Info**, and then at the bottom of the **Properties** list, click **Show All Properties**.

2 As the **Tags** type **internship, documentary** In the **Subject** box, type your course name and section number. Be sure that your name displays in the **Author** box and edit if necessary.

MAC TIP To enter document properties, click File. At the bottom of the menu, click Properties, and then click the Summary tab. Click in the Keywords box to type the tags internship, documentary. Click in the Subject box, type your course name and section number, edit the Author if necessary, and then click OK. To print, click File, and then click Print.

---

3 On the left, click **Print** to display the **Print Preview**. Compare your screen with Figure 1.24.

Here you can select any printer connected to your system and adjust the settings related to how you want to print. On the right, Print Preview displays your document exactly as it will print; the formatting marks do not display. At the bottom of the Print Preview area, the number of pages and arrows with which you can move among the pages in Print Preview display. On the right, Zoom settings enable you to shrink or enlarge the Print Preview.

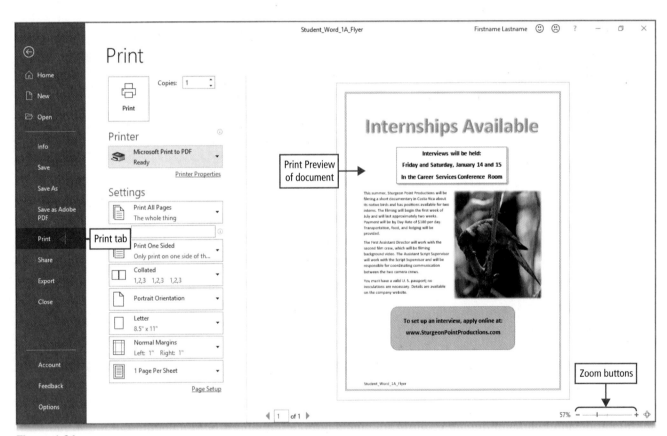

Figure 1.24

4 In the lower right corner of the window, click **Zoom In** ➕ several times to view the document at a larger size, and notice that a larger preview is easier to read. Click **Zoom to Page** 🔲 to view the entire page.

5 If you want to print your document on paper using the default printer on your system, in the upper left portion of the screen, click **Print**. If you do not print, click Save.

The document will print on your default printer; if you do not have a color printer, colors will print in shades of gray. Backstage view closes and your file redisplays in the Word window.

6 Save 🖫 your document. In the upper right corner of the Word window, click **Close** ☒.

For Non-MyLab Submissions Determine What Your Instructor Requires
As directed by your instructor, submit your completed Word file.

---

7 In **MyLab IT**, locate and click the Grader Project **Word 1A Flyer**. In **step 3**, under **Upload Completed Assignment**, click **Choose File**. In the **Open** dialog box, navigate to your **Word Chapter 1 folder**, and then click your **Student_Word_1A_Flyer** file one time to select it. In the lower right corner of the **Open** dialog box, click **Open**.

The name of your selected file displays above the Upload button.

8 To submit your file to **MyLab IT** for grading, click **Upload**, wait a moment for a green **Success!** message, and then in **step 4**, click the blue **Submit for Grading** button. Click **Close Assignment** to return to your list of **Course Materials**.

You have completed Project 1A   **END**

»»» GO! With Google Docs

ALERT **Working with Web-Based Applications and Services**

Computer programs and services on the web receive continuous updates and improvements, so the steps to complete this web-based Activity may differ from the ones shown. You can often look at the screens and the information presented to determine how to complete the Activity.

If you do not already have a Google account, you will need to create one before you begin this Activity. Go to **http://google.com** and in the upper right corner, click Sign In. On the Sign In screen, click Create Account. On the Create your Google Account page, complete the form, read and agree to the Terms of Service and Privacy Policy, and then click Next step. On the Welcome screen, click Get Started.

Activity | Creating a Flyer

In this Activity, you will use Google Docs to create a flyer.

1 From the desktop, open your browser, navigate to http://google.com, and then sign in to your Google account. In the upper right corner of your screen, click **Google apps** ⊞, and then click **Drive**.

2 To create a folder in which to store your web projects, click **New**, and then click **Folder**. In the **New folder** box, type **GO! Web Projects** and then click **Create** to create a folder on your Google drive. Double-click your **GO! Web Projects** folder to open it.

3 In the left pane, click **New**, and then click **Google Docs** to open a new tab in your browser and to start an Untitled document. At the top of the window, click **Untitled document** and then, using your own name as the file name, type **Lastname_Firstname WD_1A_Web** and then press Enter to change the file name.

4 To the right of the file name, point to the small file folder to display the ScreenTip **Move to**. Click the file folder and notice that your file is saved in the GO! Web Projects folder. Compare your screen with Figure A.

Figure A

5 Click in your document to close the Move to folder dialog box and to position the insertion point at the top of the document. Type **Internships Available** and then press Enter two times. Type **Interviews will be held Friday and Saturday, January 14 and 15 in the Career Services Conference Room.**

6 Press Ctrl + A to select all of the text. Click the **Font size arrow** 10 , and then click **24**. With the text still selected, click **Center** ≡.

7 Press Ctrl + End to move to the end of the document, and then press Enter. Click **Insert**, and then click **Image**. Click **Upload from computer**, and then navigate to your student data files. Click **w01A_Bird**, and then click **Open** to insert the picture.

8 Click the picture to select it, and then point to the square sizing handle at the upper left corner of the picture. Drag down and to the right until the sizing handle aligns with approximately **3 inches on the ruler**.

9 If necessary scroll up to view the image and the text above it. Click to the right of the picture and then press Enter twice. Type **Join our production crew in Costa Rica as we film a short documentary about its native birds. We are hiring two interns!**

10 Select the title *Internships Available* and then click **Text color** A . In the first column, click the last color, and then apply **Bold** B . Your document will look similar to Figure B.

11 Your document will be saved automatically. Sign out of your Google account. Submit as instructed by your instructor.

Internships Available

Interviews will be held Friday and Saturday, January 14 and 15 in the Career Services Conference Room.

Join our production crew in Costa Rica as we film a short documentary about its native birds. We are hiring two interns!

Figure B

Information Handout

Project Activities

In Activities 1.17 through 1.29, you will format an information handout from Sturgeon Point Productions that describes internships available to students. Your completed document will look similar to Figure 1.25.

Project Files for MyLab IT Grader

1. In your **MyLab IT** course, locate and click **Word 1B Programs**, Download Materials, and then Download All Files.
2. Extract the zipped folder to your Word Chapter 1 folder. Close the Grader download screens.
3. Take a moment to open the downloaded **Word_1B_Programs_Instructions**; note any recent updates to the book.

Project Results

GO! Project 1B
Where We're Going

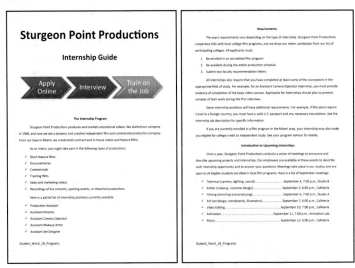

Figure 1.25 Project 1B Information Handout

For Non-MyLab Submissions

For Project 1B, you will need:
w01B_Programs

In your Word Chapter 1 folder, save your document as:
Lastname_Firstname_1B_Programs

After you have named and saved your document, on the next page continue with Step 2.

Objective 5 Change Document and Paragraph Layout

GO! Learn How
Video W1-5

Document layout includes *margins*—the space between the text and the top, bottom, left, and right edges of the paper. Paragraph layout includes line spacing, indents, and tabs. In Word, the information about paragraph formats is stored in the paragraph mark at the end of a paragraph. When you press Enter, the new paragraph mark contains the formatting of the previous paragraph, unless you take steps to change it.

Activity 1.17 │ Setting Margins

1.2.1

1 Navigate to your **Word Chapter 1 folder**, and then double-click the Word file you downloaded from **MyLab IT** that displays your name —**Student_Word_1B_Programs**. If necessary, at the top click **Enable Editing**. On the **Home tab**, in the **Paragraph group**, be sure **Show/Hide** ¶ is active so that you can view the formatting marks.

2 Click the **Layout tab**. In the **Page Setup group**, click **Margins**, and then take a moment to study the settings in the Margins gallery.

If you have recently used custom margins settings, they will display at the top of this gallery. Other commonly used settings also display.

3 At the bottom of the **Margins** gallery, click the command followed by an ellipsis—**Custom Margins . . .** —to display the **Page Setup** dialog box.

4 In the **Page Setup** dialog box, under **Margins**, press Tab as necessary to select the value in the **Left** box, and then, with *1.25″* selected, type **1**

This action will change the left margin to 1 inch on all pages of the document. You do not need to type the inch (″) mark.

5 Press Tab to select the margin in the **Right** box, and then type **1** At the bottom of the dialog box, notice that the new margins will apply to the **Whole document**. Compare your screen with Figure 1.26.

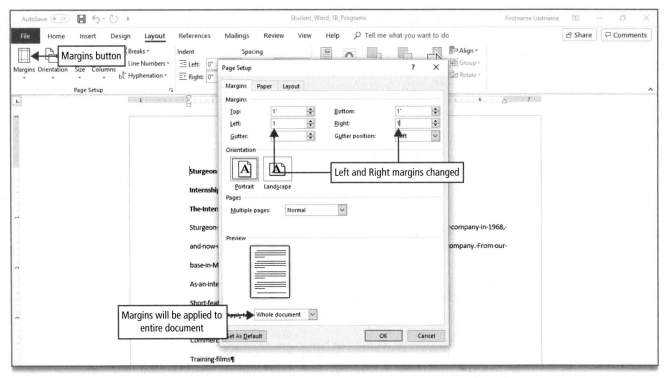

Figure 1.26

6 Click **OK** to apply the new margins and close the dialog box. If the ruler below the ribbon is not displayed, on the View tab, in the Show group, select the Ruler check box.

7 Scroll to position the bottom of **Page 1** and the top of **Page 2** on your screen. Notice that the page edges display, and the page number and total number of pages display on the left side of the status bar.

8 Near the bottom edge of **Page 1**, point anywhere in the bottom margin area, right-click, and then click **Edit Footer** to display the footer area. On the ribbon, under the **Header & Footer Tools**, on the **Design tab**, in the **Insert group**, click **Document Info**, and then click **File Name**.

MAC TIP In the bottom margin area, hold down [control] and then click to display the shortcut menu. Click Edit Footer. On the Header & Footer tab, click Field, and then under Categories, click Document Information. Under Field Names, click FileName, and then click OK.

---

9 Double-click anywhere in the document to close the footer area, and then **Save** 🖫 your document.

Activity 1.18 | Aligning Paragraphs

Alignment refers to the placement of paragraph text relative to the left and right margins. Most paragraph text uses *left alignment*—aligned at the left margin, leaving the right margin uneven. Three other types of paragraph alignment are: *center alignment*—centered between the left and right margins; *right alignment*—aligned at the right margin with an uneven left margin; and *justified alignment*—text aligned evenly at both the left and right margins. The table in Figure 1.27 shows examples of these alignment types.

Types of Paragraph Alignment		
Alignment	**Button**	**Description and Example**
Align Left	☰	Align Left is the default paragraph alignment in Word. Text in the paragraph aligns at the left margin, and the right margin is uneven.
Center	☰	Center alignment aligns text in the paragraph so that it is centered between the left and right margins.
Align Right	☰	Align Right aligns text at the right margin. Using Align Right, the left margin, which is normally even, is uneven.
Justify	☰	The Justify alignment option adds additional space between words so that both the left and right margins are even. Justify is often used when formatting newspaper-style columns.

Figure 1.27

1 Scroll to position the middle of **Page 2** on your screen, look at the left and right margins, and notice that the text is justified—both the right and left margins of multiple-line paragraphs are aligned evenly at the margins. On the **Home tab**, in the **Paragraph group**, notice that **Justify** ☰ is active.

> To achieve a justified right margin, Word adjusts the size of spaces between words, which can result in unattractive spacing in a document that spans the width of a page. Many individuals find such spacing difficult to read.

2 Press Ctrl + A to select all the text in the document, and then on the **Home tab**, in the **Paragraph group**, click **Align Left** ☰.

ANOTHER WAY   On the Home tab, in the Editing group, click Select, and then click Select All.

MAC TIP   Use command ⌘ + A to select all the text in a document.

---

3 Press Ctrl + Home to move to the beginning of the document. In the left margin area, point to the left of the first paragraph—*Sturgeon Point Productions*—until the ⟋ pointer displays, and then click one time to select the paragraph.

> Use this technique to select entire lines of text.

4 On the mini toolbar, in the **Font Size** box, select the existing number, type **40** and then press Enter.

> Use this technique to change the font size to a size that is not available on the Font Size list.

MAC TIP   On the Home tab, in the Font Size, select the existing number and type 40.

---

5 Select the second paragraph—*Internship Guide*—and then using the mini toolbar or the ribbon, change the **Font Size** to **26 pt**. Point to the left of the first paragraph—*Sturgeon Point Productions*—to display the ⟋ pointer again, and then drag down to select the first two paragraphs, which form the title and subtitle of the document.

6 On the **Home tab**, in the **Paragraph group**, click **Center** ☰ to center the title and subtitle between the left and right margins, and then compare your screen with Figure 1.28.

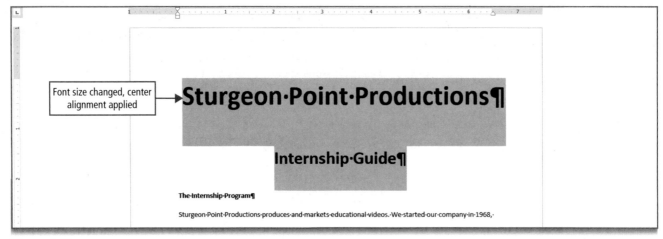

Figure 1.28

7 Near the top of **Page 1**, locate the first bold subheading—*The Internship Program*. Point to the left of the paragraph to display the 🔏 pointer, and then click one time to select the text.

8 With *The Internship Program* selected, use your mouse wheel or the vertical scroll bar to bring the bottom portion of **Page 1** into view. Locate the subheading *Requirements*. Move the pointer to the left of the paragraph to display the 🔏 pointer, hold down Ctrl, and then click one time. Release Ctrl, and then scroll to the middle of **Page 2**. Use the same technique to select the third subheading—*Introduction to Upcoming Internships*.

> Three subheadings are selected; in Windows-based programs, you can hold down Ctrl to select multiple items.

💻 **MAC TIP** Hold down command ⌘ when selecting multiple items.

9 Click **Center** ≡ to center all three subheadings, and then click **Save** 🖫.

Activity 1.19 | Setting Line Spacing

MOS
2.2.3

Line spacing is the distance between lines of text in a paragraph. Three of the most commonly used line spacing options are shown in the table in Figure 1.29.

Line Spacing Options	
Spacing	**Description, Example, and Information**
Single spacing	**This text in this example uses single spacing.** Single spacing was once the most commonly used spacing in business documents. Now, because so many documents are read on a computer screen rather than on paper, single spacing is becoming less popular.
Multiple 1.08 spacing	**This text in this example uses multiple 1.08 spacing.** The default line spacing in Microsoft Word is 1.08, which is slightly more than single spacing to make the text easier to read on a computer screen. Many individuals now prefer this spacing, even on paper, because the lines of text appear less crowded.
Double spacing	**This text in this example uses double spacing.** College research papers and draft documents that need space for notes are commonly double-spaced; there is space for a full line of text between each document line.

Figure 1.29

1 Move to the beginning of the document, and then press Ctrl + A to select all of the text in the document.

2 With all of the text in the document selected, on the **Home tab**, in the **Paragraph group**, click **Line and Paragraph Spacing**, and notice that the text in the document is double spaced—**2.0** is checked. Compare your screen with Figure 1.30.

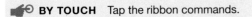

BY TOUCH Tap the ribbon commands.

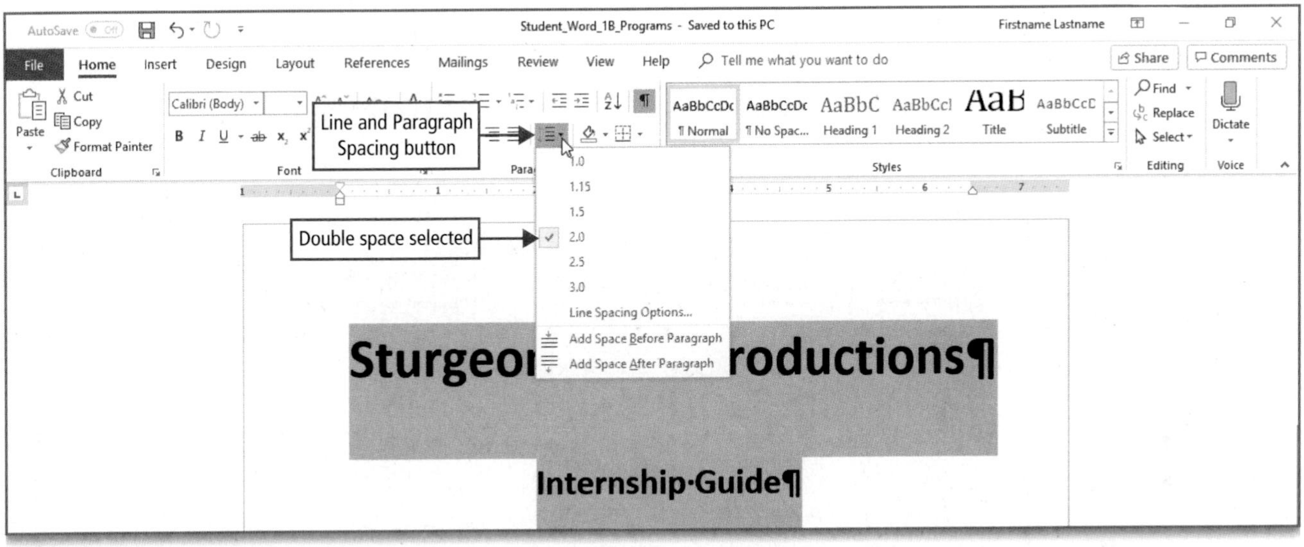

Figure 1.30

3 On the **Line Spacing** menu, click **1.5**, and then click anywhere in the document to deselect the text. Compare your screen with Figure 1.31, and then **Save** your document.

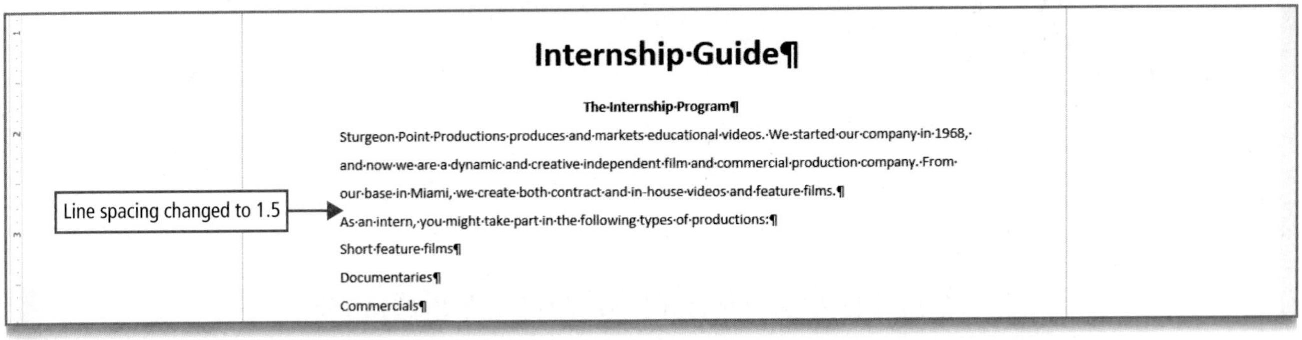

Figure 1.31

Activity 1.20 | Indenting Text

MOS 2.2.3

Indenting the first line of each paragraph is a common technique to distinguish paragraphs.

1 Below the title and subtitle of the document, click anywhere in the paragraph that begins *Sturgeon Point Productions produces*.

2 On the **Home tab**, in the **Paragraph group**, click the **Dialog Box Launcher**.

MAC TIP Click the Line and Paragraph Spacing button, and then click Line Spacing Options.

3 In the **Paragraph** dialog box, on the **Indents and Spacing tab**, under **Indentation**, click the **Special arrow**, and then click **First line** to indent the first line by 0.5", which is the default indent setting. Compare your screen with Figure 1.32.

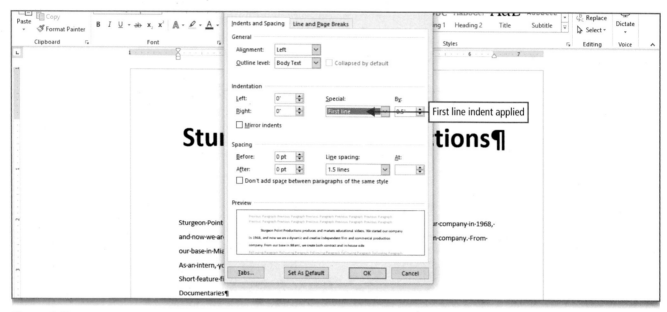

Figure 1.32

4 Click **OK**, and then click anywhere in the next paragraph, which begins *As an intern*. On the ruler under the ribbon, drag the **First Line Indent** marker ▽ to **0.5 inches on the horizontal ruler**, and then compare your screen with Figure 1.33.

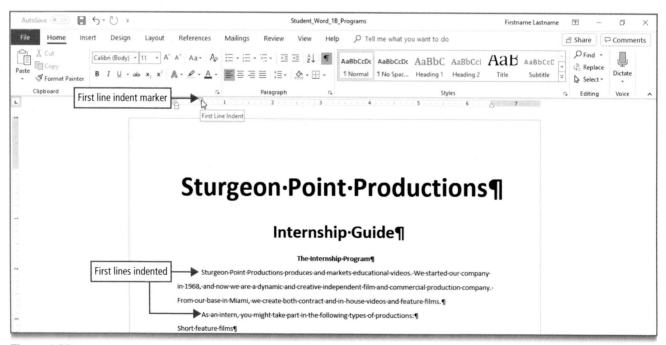

Figure 1.33

5 By using either of the techniques you just practiced, apply a first line indent of **0.5"** to the paragraph that begins *Here is a partial*.

6 **Save** 🖫 your document.

Activity 1.21 │ Setting Space Before and After Paragraphs

2.2.3

Adding space after each paragraph is another technique to differentiate paragraphs.

1 Press Ctrl + A to select all the text in the document. Click the **Layout tab**, and then in the **Paragraph group**, under **Spacing**, click the **After spin box up arrow** one time to change the value to **6 pt**.

To change the value in the box, you can also select the existing number, type a new number, and then press Enter. This document will use 6 pt spacing after paragraphs to add space.

ANOTHER WAY   On either the Home tab or the Layout tab, display the Paragraph dialog box from the Paragraph group, and then under Spacing, click the spin box arrows as necessary.

2 Press Ctrl + Home, and then compare your screen with Figure 1.34.

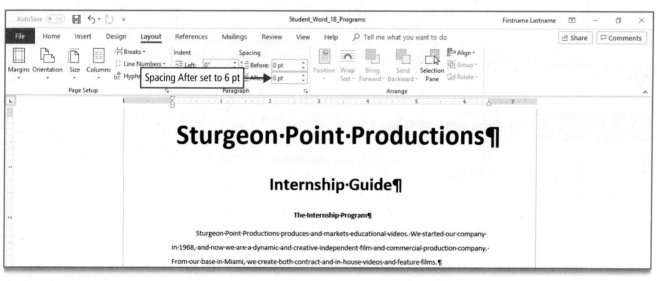

Figure 1.34

3 Near the top of **Page 1**, select the subheading *The Internship Program*, including the paragraph mark following it. Scroll down using the vertical scroll bar, hold down Ctrl, and then select the *Requirements* and *Introduction to Upcoming Internships* subheadings.

MAC TIP   Use command ⌘ to select multiple items.

ALERT   Did your screen zoom when you were selecting?

Holding down Ctrl and using the mouse wheel at the same time will zoom your screen.

4 With all three subheadings selected, in the **Paragraph group**, under **Spacing**, click the **Before up spin box arrow** two times to set the **Spacing Before** to **12 pt**. Compare your screen with Figure 1.35, and then **Save** 🖫 your document.

> This action increases the amount of space above each of the subheadings, which will make them easy to distinguish in the document. The formatting is applied only to the selected paragraphs.

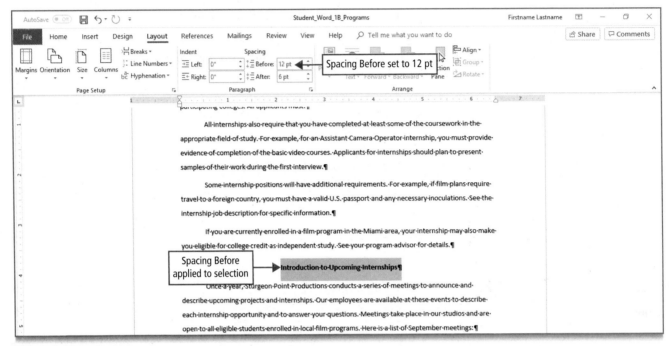

Figure 1.35

Objective 6 | Create and Modify Lists

GO! Learn How
Video W1-6

To display a list of information, you can choose a ***bulleted list***, which uses ***bullets***—text symbols such as small circles or check marks—to introduce each item in a list. You can also choose a ***numbered list***, which uses consecutive numbers or letters to introduce each item in a list.

Use a bulleted list if the items in the list can be introduced in any order; use a numbered list for items that have definite steps, a sequence of actions, or are in chronological order.

Activity 1.22 | Creating a Bulleted List

MOS
3.3.1

1 In the upper portion of **Page 1**, locate the paragraph *Short feature films*, and then point to this paragraph from the left margin area to display the ⌐𝒜⌐ pointer. Drag down to select this paragraph and the next five paragraphs—ending with the paragraph *Recordings of live concerts*.

2 On the **Home tab**, in the **Paragraph group**, click **Bullets** ⌐⌐ to change the selected text to a bulleted list.

> The spacing between each of the bulleted points is removed and each bulleted item is automatically indented.

3 On the ruler, point to **First Line Indent** ▽ and read the ScreenTip, and then point to **Hanging Indent** △. Compare your screen with Figure 1.36.

By default, Word formats bulleted items with a first line indent of 0.25" and adds a Hanging Indent at 0.5". The hanging indent maintains the alignment of text when a bulleted item is more than one line.

You can modify the list indentation by using Decrease Indent ⮜ or Increase Indent ⮞. Decrease Indent moves your paragraph closer to the margin. Increase Indent moves your paragraph farther away from the margin.

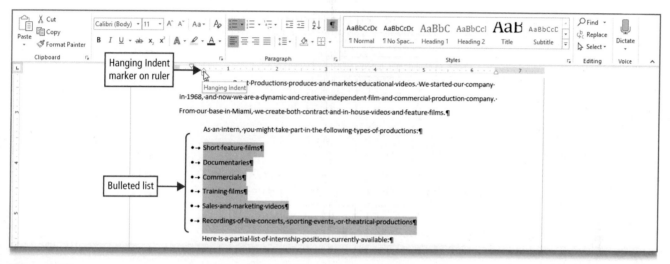

Figure 1.36

4 Scroll down slightly, and then by using the ⬀ pointer from the left margin area, select the five internship positions, beginning with *Production Assistant* and ending with *Assistant Set Designer*. In the **Paragraph group**, click **Bullets** ☷ ▾.

5 Scroll down to view **Page 2**. Apply bullets to all of the paragraphs that indicate the September meetings and meeting dates, beginning with *Technical* and ending with *Music*.

6 **Save** 🖫 your document.

Activity 1.23 | Creating a Numbered List

3.3.1

1 Under the subheading *Requirements*, in the paragraph that begins *The exact requirements*, click to position the insertion point at the *end* of the paragraph, following the colon. Press (Enter) to create a blank paragraph. Notice that the paragraph is indented because the First Line Indent from the previous paragraph carried over to the new paragraph.

2 To change the indent formatting for this paragraph, on the ruler, drag the **First Line Indent** marker ▽ to the left so that it is positioned directly above the lower button.

3 Being sure to include the period, type **1.** and press (Spacebar). Compare your screen with Figure 1.37.

Word determines that this paragraph is the first item in a numbered list and formats the new paragraph accordingly, indenting the list in the same manner as the bulleted list. The space after the number changes to a tab, and the AutoCorrect Options button displays to the left of the list item. The tab is indicated by a right arrow formatting mark.

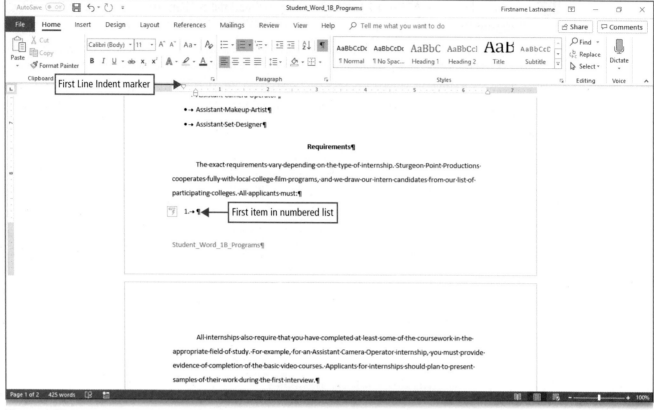

Figure 1.37

4 Click **AutoCorrect Options** 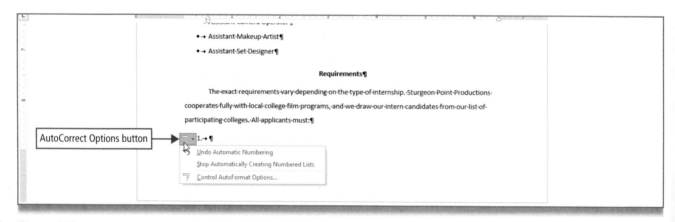, and then compare your screen with Figure 1.38.

From the displayed list, you can remove the automatic formatting here, or stop using the automatic numbered lists option in this document. You also have the option to open the AutoCorrect dialog box to *Control AutoFormat Options*.

Figure 1.38

5 Click **AutoCorrect Options** 🖅 again to close the menu without selecting any of the commands. Type **Be enrolled in an accredited film program** and press Enter. Notice that the second number and a tab are added to the next line.

6 Type **Be available during the entire production schedule** and press Enter. Type **Submit two faculty recommendation letters** and then compare your screen with Figure 1.39. **Save** 🖫 your document.

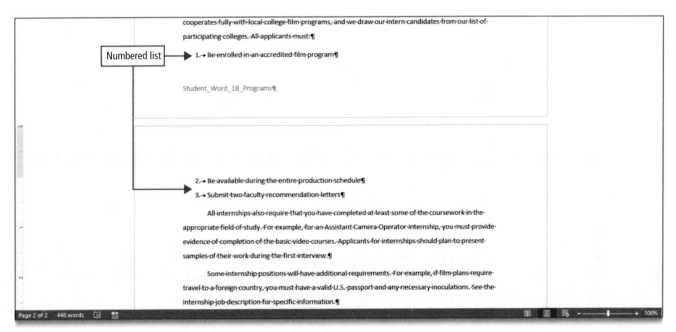

Figure 1.39

MORE KNOWLEDGE | **To End a List**

To turn a list off, you can press Backspace, click the Numbering or Bullets button, or press Enter two times. Both list buttons—Numbering and Bullets—act as *toggle buttons*; that is, clicking the button one time turns the feature on, and clicking the button again turns the feature off.

Activity 1.24 | Customizing Bullets

MOS
3.3.2

You can use any symbol from any font for your bullet characters.

1 Press Ctrl + End to move to the end of the document, and then scroll up as necessary to display the bulleted list containing the list of meetings.

2 Point to the left of the first list item to display the 🔊 pointer, and then drag down to select all six meetings in the list—the bullet symbols are not selected.

3 On the mini toolbar, click the **Bullets button arrow** ⋮≡⋅ to display the Bullet Library, and then compare your screen with Figure 1.40.

 MAC TIP On the Home tab, click the Bullets button arrow.

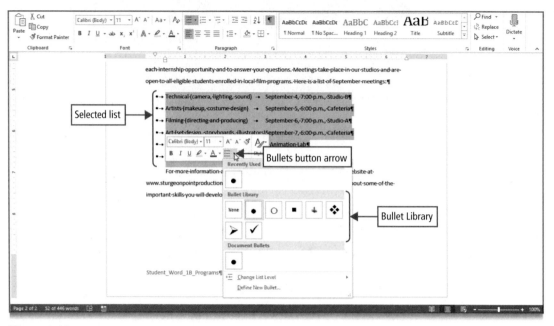

Figure 1.40

ALERT **Did your bullet symbols disappear?**

If the bullet symbols no longer display, then you clicked the Bullets button. The Bullets button is a toggle button that turns the bullet symbols on and off. Click Undo to reapply the bullets, and then repeat Step 3, making sure that you click the Bullets button arrow.

---

4 Under **Bullet Library**, click the **check mark** symbol.

MAC TIP If the check mark bullet is not available, click Define New Bullet. Click Bullet, click the Font arrow, click Wingdings, and then locate and click the check mark symbol. Click OK two times.

---

5 With the bulleted list still selected, on the **Home tab**, in the **Clipboard group**, double-click **Format Painter** to activate it for multiple use.

6 Use the vertical scroll bar or your mouse wheel to scroll to view **Page 1**. Move the pointer to the left of the first item in the first bulleted list to display the pointer, and then drag down to select all six items in the list and to apply the format of the third bulleted list—the check mark bullets—to this list. Repeat this procedure to change the bullets in the second list to check marks. Press Esc to turn off **Format Painter**, and then **Save** your document. Compare your screen with Figure 1.41.

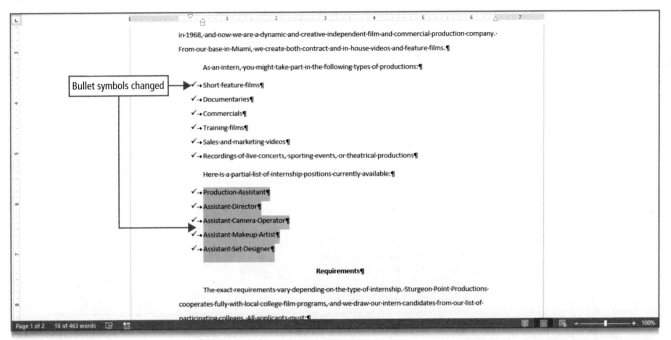

in·1968,·and·now·we·are·a·dynamic·and·creative·independent·film·and·commercial·production·company.·
From·our·base·in·Miami,·we·create·both·contract·and·in-house·videos·and·feature·films.¶

As·an·intern,·you·might·take·part·in·the·following·types·of·productions:¶

✓→Short·feature·films¶
✓→Documentaries¶
✓→Commercials¶
✓→Training·films¶
✓→Sales·and·marketing·videos¶
✓→Recordings·of·live·concerts,·sporting·events,·or·theatrical·productions¶

Here·is·a·partial·list·of·internship·positions·currently·available:¶

✓→Production·Assistant¶
✓→Assistant·Director¶
✓→Assistant·Camera·Operator¶
✓→Assistant·Makeup·Artist¶
✓→Assistant·Set·Designer¶

Requirements¶

The·exact·requirements·vary·depending·on·the·type·of·internship.·Sturgeon·Point·Productions·
cooperates·fully·with·local·college·film·programs,·and·we·draw·our·intern·candidates·from·our·list·of·
participating·colleges.·All·applicants·must·¶

Bullet symbols changed

Figure 1.41

Objective 7 | Set and Modify Tab Stops

GO! Learn How
Video W1-7

Tab stops mark specific locations on a line of text. Use tab stops to indent and align text and use the Tab key to move to tab stops.

Activity 1.25 | Setting Tab Stops

1 Scroll to view **Page 2**, and then by using the 🔊 pointer at the left of the first item, select all the items in the bulleted list. Notice that there is a tab mark between the name of the meeting and the date.

The arrow that indicates a tab is a nonprinting formatting mark.

2 To the left of the horizontal ruler, point to **Tab Alignment** ⌊ to display the *Left Tab* ScreenTip, and then compare your screen with Figure 1.42.

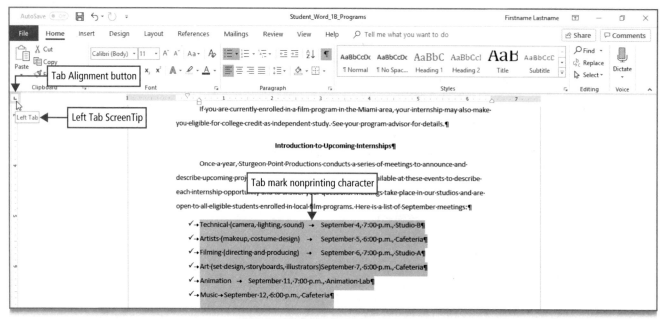

Figure 1.42

3 Click **Tab Alignment** ⌐ several times to view the tab alignment options shown in the table in Figure 1.43.

Tab Alignment Options		
Type	**Tab Alignment Button Displays This Marker**	**Description**
Left	⌐	Text is left aligned at the tab stop and extends to the right.
Center	⊥	Text is centered around the tab stop.
Right	⌐	Text is right aligned at the tab stop and extends to the left.
Decimal	⊥	The decimal point aligns at the tab stop.
Bar	I	A vertical bar displays at the tab stop.
First Line Indent	▽	Text in the first line of a paragraph indents.
Hanging Indent	△	Text in all lines indents except for the first line in the paragraph.

Figure 1.43

4 Display **Left Tab** ⌐. Along the lower edge of the horizontal ruler, point to and then click at **3.5 inches on the horizontal ruler**. Notice that all of the dates left align at the new tab stop location, and the right edge of the column is uneven.

5 Compare your screen with Figure 1.44, and then **Save** 🖫 your document.

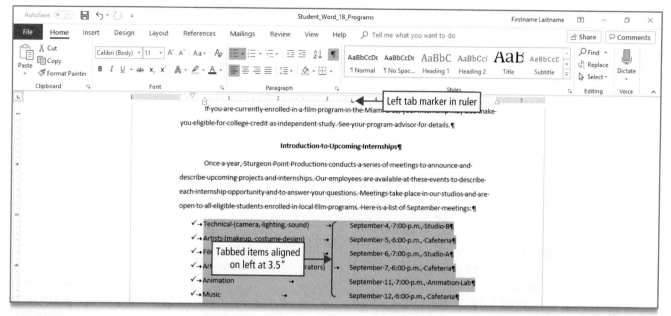

Figure 1.44

Activity 1.26 | Modifying Tab Stops

Tab stops are a form of paragraph formatting. Therefore, the information about tab stops is stored in the paragraph mark in the paragraphs to which they were applied.

1 With the bulleted list still selected, on the ruler, point to the new tab marker at *3.5 inches on the horizontal ruler*, and then when the *Left Tab* ScreenTip displays, drag the tab marker to **4 inches on the horizontal ruler**.

> In all of the selected lines, the text at the tab stop left aligns at 4 inches.

2 On the ruler, point to the tab marker that you moved to display the *Left Tab* ScreenTip, and then double-click to display the **Tabs** dialog box.

ANOTHER WAY On the Home tab, in the Paragraph group, click the Dialog Box Launcher. At the bottom of the Paragraph dialog box, click the Tabs button.

---

3 In the **Tabs** dialog box, under **Tab stop position**, if necessary select *4"*, and then type **6**

MAC TIP At the bottom of the Tabs dialog box, click Clear All. In the Tab stops box type 6. Under Alignment, click Right. Under Leader, click the option that is a series of dots, and then skip to step 6.

---

4 Under **Alignment**, click the **Right** option button. Under **Leader**, click the **2** option button. Near the bottom of the **Tabs** dialog box, click **Set**.

> Because the Right tab will be used to align the items in the list, the tab stop at 4" is no longer necessary.

5 In the **Tabs** dialog box, in the **Tab stop position** box, click **4"** to select this tab stop, and then in the lower portion of the **Tabs** dialog box, click the **Clear** button to delete this tab stop, which is no longer necessary. Compare your screen with Figure 1.45.

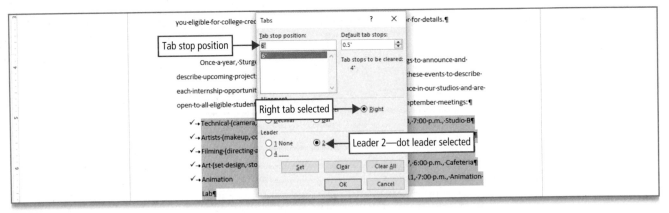

Figure 1.45

6 Click **OK**. On the ruler, notice that the left tab marker at *4″* no longer displays, a right tab marker displays at *6″*, and a series of dots—a *dot leader*—displays between the columns of the list. Notice also that the right edge of the column is even. Compare your screen with Figure 1.46.

> A *leader character* creates a solid, dotted, or dashed line that fills the space to the left of a tab character and draws the reader's eyes across the page from one item to the next. When the character used for the leader is a dot, it is commonly referred to as a dot leader.

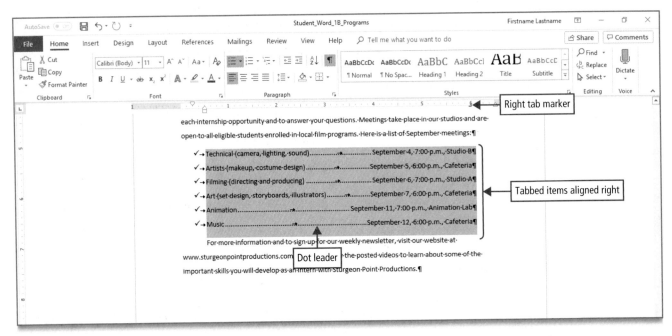

Figure 1.46

7 In the bulleted list that uses dot leaders, locate the *Art* meeting, and then click to position the insertion point at the end of that line, after the word *Cafeteria*. Press Enter to create a new blank bullet item.

8 Type **Video Editing** and press Tab. Notice that a dot leader fills the space to the tab marker location.

9 Type **September 10, 7:00 p.m., Cafeteria** and notice that the text moves to the left to maintain the right alignment of the tab stop.

10 **Save** 🖫 your document.

Objective 8 Insert and Format a SmartArt Graphic and an Icon

GO! Learn How
Video W1-8

SmartArt graphics are designer-quality visual representations of information, and Word provides many different layouts from which you can choose. *Icons* are pictures composed of straight and curved lines. SmartArt graphics and icons can communicate your messages or ideas more effectively than plain text, and these objects add visual interest to a document or web page.

Activity 1.27 │ Inserting a SmartArt Graphic

MOS
5.1.4 and 5.3.3

1 Press Ctrl + Home to move to the top of the document, and then click to the right of the subtitle *Internship Guide*.

2 Click the **Insert tab**, and then in the **Illustrations group**, point to **SmartArt** to display its ScreenTip. Read the ScreenTip, and then click **SmartArt**.

3 In the center portion of the **Choose a SmartArt Graphic** dialog box, examine the numerous types of SmartArt graphics available.

4 On the left, click **Process**, and then by using the ScreenTips, locate and click **Basic Chevron Process**. Compare your screen with Figure 1.47.

At the right of the dialog box, a preview and description of the SmartArt displays.

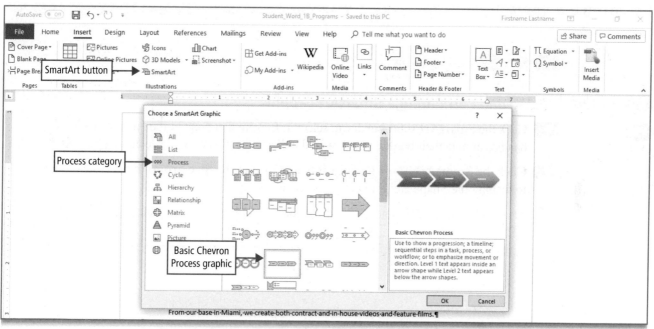

Figure 1.47

5 Click **OK** to insert the SmartArt graphic.

To the left of the inserted SmartArt graphic, the text pane may display. The *text pane* is used to type text and edit text in your SmartArt graphic. If you choose not to use the text pane to enter text, you can close it.

6 On the ribbon, under **SmartArt Tools**, on the **Design tab**, in the **Create Graphic group**, notice the Text Pane button. If the text pane button is selected, click **Text Pane** to close the pane.

7 In the SmartArt graphic, in the first blue arrow, click **[Text]**, and notice that *[Text]* is replaced by a blinking insertion point.

The word *[Text]* is called *placeholder text*, which is nonprinting text that indicates where you can type.

8 Type **Apply Online**

9 Click the placeholder text in the middle arrow. Type **Interview** and then click the placeholder text in the third arrow. Type **Train on the Job** and then compare your screen with Figure 1.48.

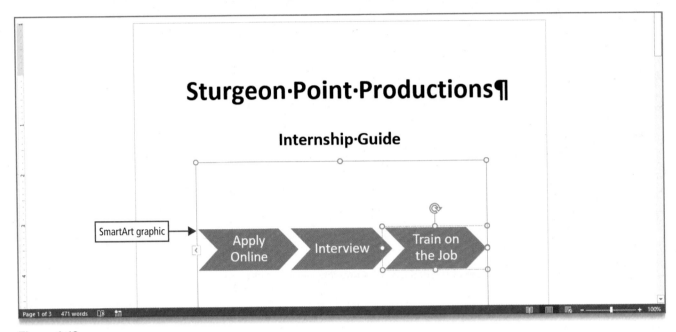

Figure 1.48

10 Save your document.

Activity 1.28 | **Sizing and Formatting a SmartArt Graphic**

1 Click the **SmartArt solid border** to select it. Be sure that none of the arrows have sizing handles around their border, which would indicate the arrow was selected, not the entire graphic.

2 Click the **SmartArt Tools Format tab**, and then in the **Size group**, if necessary, click Size to display the Shape Height and Shape Width boxes.

3 Set the **Height** to **1.75"** and the **Width** to **6.5"**, and then compare your screen with Figure 1.49.

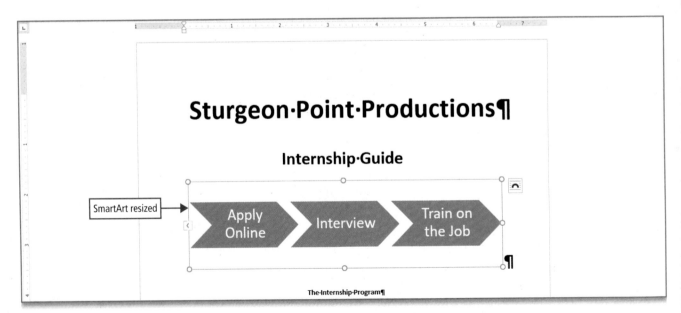

Figure 1.49

4 With the SmartArt graphic still selected, click the **SmartArt Tools Design tab**, and then in the **SmartArt Styles group**, click **Change Colors**. Under **Colorful**, click the fourth style—**Colorful Range - Accent Colors 4 to 5**.

5 On the **SmartArt Tools Design tab**, in the **SmartArt Styles group**, click **More** ⊡. Under **3-D**, click the second style—**Inset**. Compare your screen with Figure 1.50.

SmartArt color changed and SmartArt 3-D style applied

Sturgeon·Point·Productions¶

Internship·Guide

Apply Online   Interview   Train on the Job

Figure 1.50

6 Save 🖫 your document.

Activity 1.29 | Inserting an Icon

Many of the marketing materials at Sturgeon Point Productions use a clapperboard icon to represent the filmmaking and video production aspect of the business. In this Activity, you will insert a clapperboard icon at the end of the document.

1 Press [Ctrl] + [End] to move to the end of the document. Press [Enter] to insert a blank line and notice that a first line indent is applied. On the ruler, drag the **First Line Indent** marker back to the left margin.

2 On the **Insert tab**, in the **Illustrations group**, click **Icons**. On the left side of the **Insert Icons** dialog box, click **Arts**. Under **Arts**, click the **clapperboard icon** as shown in Figure 1.51 so that a check mark displays.

MAC TIP In the Icons pane, click the Jump to arrow, and then click Arts. Click the Clapperboard icon.

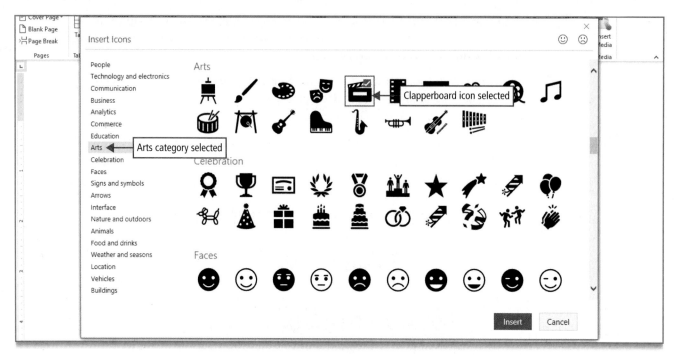

Figure 1.51

3 Click **Insert** to insert the icon. On the **Home tab**, in the **Paragraph group**, click **Center**.

4 **Save** 🖫 your document. In the upper right corner of the Word window, click **Close** ☒.

For Non-MyLab Submissions Determine What Your Instructor Requires
As directed by your instructor, submit your completed Word file.

---

5 In **MyLab IT**, locate and click the Grader Project **Word 1B Programs**. In step 3, under **Upload Completed Assignment**, click **Choose File**. In the **Open** dialog box, navigate to your **Word Chapter 1 folder**, and then click your **Student_Word_1B_Programs** file one time to select it. In the lower right corner of the **Open** dialog box, click **Open**.

The name of your selected file displays above the Upload button.

6 To submit your file to **MyLab IT** for grading, click **Upload**, wait a moment for a green **Success!** message, and then in **step 4**, click the blue **Submit for Grading** button. Click **Close Assignment** to return to your list of **Course Materials**.

You have completed Project 1B   **END**

Objective   Create an Information Handout

ALERT   Working with Web-Based Applications and Services

Computer programs and services on the web receive continuous updates and improvements, so the steps to complete this web-based Activity may differ from the ones shown. You can often look at the screens and the information presented to determine how to complete the Activity.

If you do not already have a Google account, you will need to create one before you begin this Activity. Go to http://google.com and in the upper right corner, click **Sign In**. On the Sign In screen, click **Create Account**. On the Create your Google Account page, complete the form, read and agree to the Terms of Service and Privacy Policy, and then click **Next step**. On the Welcome screen, click **Get Started**.

Activity │ Creating a Handout with Bulleted and Numbered Lists

In this Activity, you will use Google Docs to create an information handout.

1 From the desktop, open your browser, navigate to http://google.com. In the upper right corner of your screen, click **Google apps** ⊞, and then click **Drive** ☁. Sign in to your Google account, and then double-click your **GO! Web Projects** folder to open it. If you have not created this folder, refer to the instructions in the first Google Docs project in this chapter.

2 Click **New**, and then click **Google Docs**. Click **File**, and then click **Open**. Click **Upload**, and then click **Select a file from your computer**. From your student data files, click **w01_1B_Web** and then click **Open**.

3 In the upper left corner of the Google Docs window, select **w01_1B_Web**. Type **Lastname_Firstname_WD_1B_Web** and then press Enter to rename the file.

4 Press Ctrl + A to select all of the text. Click **Line spacing** ⌶, and then click **1.5**. Click **Left align** ≣.

5 Select the six lines of text beginning with *Short feature films* and ending with *Recording of live concerts*, and then click **Bulleted list** ≣ to apply bullets to the selected text. Select the list of internship positions beginning with *Production Assistant* and ending with *Assistant Set Designer*, and then click **Bulleted list**. Compare your screen with Figure A.

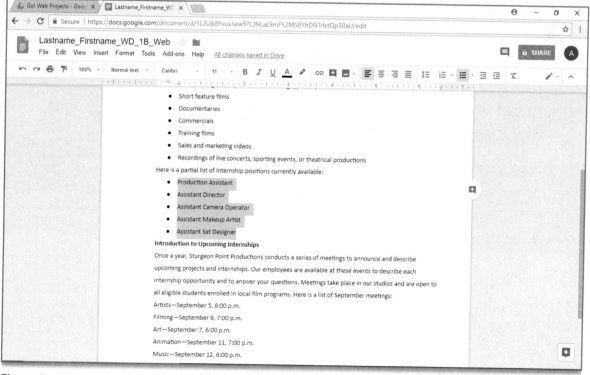

Figure A

»» **GO!** With Google continues on next page

6 Select the last five lines of the document beginning with *Artists* and ending with *Music*. To create a numbered list from the selection, click **Numbered list** ▤.

7 Select the first three lines of text in the document, and then click **Center** ▤. Click in the *Introduction to Upcoming Internships* heading, and then click **Center**.

8 Click at the beginning of the paragraph that begins *Sturgeon Point Production produces and markets*, and then press Tab. Look at the ruler and notice that the first line indent is applied.

9 With the insertion point in the same paragraph, double-click **Paint format** ▣. Then, click in the paragraphs that begin *As an intern*, *Here is a partial list*, and *Once a year* to apply the first line indent to each of the paragraphs. Click **Paint format** ▣ to turn it off. Compare your document with Figure B.

10 Your document will be saved automatically. Sign out of your Google account, and then submit as instructed by your instructor.

Sturgeon Point Productions

Internship Guide

The Internship Program

Sturgeon Point Productions produces and markets educational videos. We started our company in 1968, and now we are a dynamic and creative independent film and commercial production company. From our base in Miami, we create both contract and in-house videos and feature films.

As an intern, you might take part in the following types of productions:

- Short feature films
- Documentaries
- Commercials
- Training films
- Sales and marketing videos
- Recordings of live concerts, sporting events, or theatrical productions

Here is a partial list of internship positions currently available:

- Production Assistant
- Assistant Director
- Assistant Camera Operator
- Assistant Makeup Artist
- Assistant Set Designer

Introduction to Upcoming Internships

Once a year, Sturgeon Point Productions conducts a series of meetings to announce and describe upcoming projects and internships. Our employees are available at these events to describe each internship opportunity and to answer your questions. Meetings take place in our studios and are open to all eligible students enrolled in local film programs. Here is a list of September meetings:

1. Artists—September 5, 6:00 p.m.
2. Filming—September 6, 7:00 p.m.
3. Art—September 7, 6:00 p.m.
4. Animation—September 11, 7:00 p.m.
5. Music—September 12, 6:00 p.m.

Figure B

wavebreakmedia/Shutterstock, Monkey Business Images/Fotolia, Ivanko80/Shutterstock, Monkey Business Images/Shutterstock

Microsoft Office Specialist (MOS) Skills in This Chapter

Project A	Project B
1.1.4 Show or hide formatting symbols and hidden text	**1.2.1** Set up document pages
1.2.3 Insert and modify headers and footers	**2.2.3** Set line and paragraph spacing and indentation
1.3.2 Modify basic document properties	**3.3.1** Format paragraphs as numbered and bulleted lists
1.3.3 Modify print settings	**3.3.2** Change bullet characters and number formats
5.1.1 Insert shapes	**5.1.4** Insert SmartArt graphics
5.1.2 Insert pictures	**5.2.5** Format SmartArt graphics
5.1.6 Insert text boxes	**5.3.3** Add and modify SmartArt graphic content
5.2.1 Apply artistic effects	
5.2.2 Apply picture effects and picture styles	
5.2.4 Format graphic elements	
5.3.2 Add and modify text in shapes	
5.4.1 Position objects	
5.4.2 Wrap text around objects	

Build Your E-Portfolio

An E-Portfolio is a collection of evidence, stored electronically, that showcases what you have accomplished while completing your education. Collecting and then sharing your work products with potential employers reflects your academic and career goals. Your completed documents from the following projects are good examples to show what you have learned: 1G, 1K, and 1L

Go! For Job Success

Video: How to Succeed in an Interview

Your instructor may assign this video to your class, and then ask you to think about, or discuss with your classmates, these questions:

g-stockstudio/Shutterstock

> Can you think of two or three behaviors that Lee might want to change before he interviews with another company?

> If you were going on an interview, which of Connie's behaviors would you imitate?

> If you were the interviewer, Maria, would you have handled anything differently with either candidate?

End of Chapter

Summary

In this chapter, you started Word and practiced navigating the Word window, and you entered, edited, and formatted text. You also inserted text from another Word file.

Graphics include pictures, shapes, and text boxes. In this chapter, you formatted objects by applying styles, effects, and text-wrapping options, and you sized and positioned objects on the page.

SmartArt graphics visually represent your ideas, and there are many SmartArt graphics from which to choose. You added an icon to your document to provide visual interest.

Word documents can be formatted to display your information attractively. You can add a page border, add bulleted and numbered lists, change margins and tabs, and modify paragraph and line spacing.

GO! Learn It Online

Review the concepts, key terms, and MOS skills in this chapter by completing these online challenges, which you can find at **MyLab IT**.

Chapter Quiz: Answer matching and multiple-choice questions to test what you learned in this chapter.

Lessons on the GO!: Learn how to use all the new apps and features as they are introduced by Microsoft.

MOS Prep Quiz: Answer questions to review the MOS skills that you practiced in this chapter.

GO! Collaborative Team Project (Available in Instructor Resource Center)

If your instructor assigns this project to your class, you can expect to work with one or more of your classmates—either in person or by using Internet tools—to create work products similar to those that you created in this chapter. A *team* is a group of workers who work together to solve a problem, make a decision, or create a work product. *Collaboration* is when you work together with others as a team in an intellectual endeavor to complete a shared task or achieve a shared goal.

Monkey Business Images/Fotolia

Project Guide for Word Chapter 1

Your instructor will assign Projects from this list to ensure your learning and assess your knowledge.

	Project Guide for Word Chapter 1		
Project	**Apply Skills from These Chapter Objectives**	**Project Type**	**Project Location**
1A MyLab IT	Objectives 1–4 from Project 1A	**1A Instructional Project (Grader Project)** **Instruction** Guided instruction to learn the skills in Project A.	In **MyLab IT** and in text
1B MyLab IT	Objectives 5–8 from Project 1B	**1B Instructional Project (Grader Project)** **Instruction** Guided instruction to learn the skills in Project B.	In **MyLab IT** and in text
1C	Objectives 1–4 from Project 1A	**1C Skills Review (Scorecard Grading)** **Review** A guided review of the skills from Project 1A.	In text
1D	Objectives 5–8 from Project 1B	**1D Skills Review (Scorecard Grading)** **Review** A guided review of the skills from Project 1B.	In text
1E MyLab IT	Objectives 1–4 from Project 1A	**1E Mastery (Grader Project)** **Mastery and Transfer of Learning** A demonstration of your mastery of the skills in Project 2A with extensive decision-making.	In **MyLab IT** and in text
1F MyLab IT	Objectives 5–8 from Project 1B	**1F Mastery (Grader Project)** **Mastery and Transfer of Learning** A demonstration of your mastery of the skills in Project 1B with extensive decision-making.	In **MyLab IT** and in text
1G MyLab IT	Objectives 1–8 from Projects 1A and 1B	**1G Mastery (Grader Project)** **Mastery and Transfer of Learning** A demonstration of your mastery of the skills in Projects 1A and 1B with extensive decision-making.	In **MyLab IT** and in text
1H	Combination of Objectives from Projects 1A and 1B	**1H GO! Fix It (Scorecard Grading)** **Critical Thinking** A demonstration of your mastery of the skills in Projects 1A and 1B by creating a correct result from a document that contains errors you must find.	IRC
1I	Combination of Objectives from Projects 1A and 1B	**1I GO! Make It (Scorecard Grading)** **Critical Thinking** A demonstration of your mastery of the skills in Projects 1A and 1B by creating a result from a supplied picture.	IRC
1J	Combination of Objectives from Projects 1A and 1B	**1J GO! Solve It (Rubric Grading)** **Critical Thinking** A demonstration of your mastery of the skills in Projects 1A and 1B, your decision-making skills, and your critical thinking skills. A task-specific rubric helps you self-assess your result.	IRC
1K	Combination of Objectives from Projects 1A and 1B	**1K GO! Solve It (Rubric Grading)** **Critical Thinking** A demonstration of your mastery of the skills in Projects 1A and 1B, your decision-making skills, and your critical thinking skills. A task-specific rubric helps you self-assess your result.	In text
1L	Combination of Objectives from Projects 1A and 1B	**1L GO! Think (Rubric Grading)** **Critical Thinking** A demonstration of your understanding of the chapter concepts applied in a manner that you would outside of college. An analytic rubric helps you and your instructor grade the quality of your work by comparing it to the work an expert in the discipline would create.	In text
1M	Combination of Objectives from Projects 1A and 1B	**1M GO! Think (Rubric Grading)** **Critical Thinking** A demonstration of your understanding of the chapter concepts applied in a manner that you would outside of college. An analytic rubric helps you and your instructor grade the quality of your work by comparing it to the work an expert in the discipline would create.	IRC
1N	Combination of Objectives from Projects 1A and 1B	**1N You and GO! (Rubric Grading)** **Critical Thinking** A demonstration of your understanding of the chapter concepts applied in a manner that you would in a personal situation. An analytic rubric helps you and your instructor grade the quality of your work.	IRC
1O	Combination of Objectives from Projects 1A and 1B	**1O Cumulative Group Project for Word Chapter 1** A demonstration of your understanding of concepts and your ability to work collaboratively in a group role-playing assessment, requiring both collaboration and self-management.	IRC

Glossary

Glossary of Chapter Key Terms

Alignment The placement of paragraph text relative to the left and right margins.

Alignment guide A green vertical or horizontal line that displays when you are moving or sizing an object to assist you with object placement.

Artistic effects Formats applied to images that make pictures resemble sketches or paintings.

Bulleted list A list of items with each item introduced by a symbol such as a small circle or check mark, and which is useful when the items in the list can be displayed in any order.

Bullets Text symbols such as small circles or check marks that precede each item in a bulleted list.

Center alignment The alignment of text or objects that is centered horizontally between the left and right margin.

Collaboration The action of working together with others as a team in an intellectual endeavor to complete a shared task or achieve a shared goal.

Dot leader A series of dots preceding a tab that guides the eye across the line.

Drawing objects Graphic objects, such as shapes, diagrams, lines, or circles.

Floating object A graphic that can be moved independently of the surrounding text characters.

Formatting marks Characters that display on the screen, but do not print, indicating where the Enter key, the Spacebar, and the Tab key were pressed; also called nonprinting characters.

Graphics Pictures, charts, or drawing objects.

Icons Pictures composed of straight and curved lines.

Inline object An object or graphic inserted in a document that acts like a character in a sentence.

Justified alignment An arrangement of text in which the text aligns evenly on both the left and right margins.

Layout Options Picture formatting options that control the manner in which text wraps around a picture or other object.

Leader character Characters that form a solid, dotted, or dashed line that fills the space preceding a tab stop.

Left alignment An arrangement of text in which the text aligns at the left margin, leaving the right margin uneven.

Line spacing The distance between lines of text in a paragraph.

Live Layout A feature that reflows text as you move or size an object so that you can view the placement of surrounding text.

Margins The space between the text and the top, bottom, left, and right edges of the paper.

Nonprinting characters Characters that display on the screen, but do not print; also called formatting marks.

Numbered list A list that uses consecutive numbers or letters to introduce each item in a list.

Object anchor The symbol that indicates to which paragraph an object is attached.

Picture effects Effects that enhance a picture, such as a shadow, glow, reflection, or 3-D rotation.

Picture styles Frames, shapes, shadows, borders, and other special effects that can be added to an image to create an overall visual style for the image.

Placeholder text Nonprinting text that holds a place in a document where you can type.

Right alignment An arrangement of text in which the text aligns at the right margin, leaving the left margin uneven.

Rotation handle A symbol with which you can rotate a graphic to any angle; displays above the top center sizing handle.

Shapes Lines, arrows, stars, banners, ovals, rectangles, and other basic shapes with which you can illustrate an idea, a process, or a workflow.

SmartArt A designer-quality visual representation of your information that you can create by choosing from among many different layouts to effectively communicate your message or ideas.

Spin box A small box with an upward- and downward-pointing arrow that lets you move rapidly through a set of values by clicking.

Tab stop A specific location on a line of text, marked on the Word ruler, to which you can move the insertion point by pressing the Tab key, and which is used to align and indent text.

Team A group of workers tasked with working together to solve a problem, make a decision, or create a work product.

Text box A movable resizable container for text or graphics.

Text effects Decorative formats, such as shadowed or mirrored text, text glow, 3-D effects, and colors that make text stand out.

Text pane A pane that displays to the left of a SmartArt graphic and is used to type text and edit text in a SmartArt graphic.

Text wrapping The manner in which text displays around an object.

Toggle button A button that can be turned on by clicking it once, and then turned off by clicking it again.

Word wrap The feature that moves text from the right edge of a paragraph to the beginning of the next line as necessary to fit within the margins.

Chapter Review

In the following Skills Review, you will create a flyer advertising a photography internship with Sturgeon Point Productions. Your completed document will look similar to Figure 1.52.

Apply 1A skills from these Objectives:

1. Create a New Document and Insert Text
2. Insert and Format Graphics
3. Insert and Modify Text Boxes and Shapes
4. Preview and Print a Document

Project Files

For Project 1C, you will need the following files:

New blank Word document
w01C_Building
w01C_Job_Description

You will save your document as:

Lastname_Firstname_1C_Photography

Project Results

Internship Available for

Still Photographer

> This position requires skill in the use of:
>
> Professional full-frame DSLR cameras
>
> Tilt-shift lenses for tall buildings

This fall, Sturgeon Point Productions will film a documentary on the historic architecture in and around Milwaukee, Wisconsin.

The filming will take place during the last two weeks of September. If the weather is not conducive to outdoor shooting, it is possible that filming will continue into the first week of October.

The still photographer will accompany the director during the first two weeks of September to scout locations and take photographs for the purpose of planning the filming schedule. The photographer will also accompany the film crew throughout filming.

Photographs taken during pre-production and filming will be used for advertising and marketing and published in an upcoming book on the history of the city of Milwaukee.

Submit Your Application by June 30!

Student_Word_1C_Photography

Figure 1.52

Chapter Review

1 ▶ Start Word and then click **Blank document**. On the **Home tab**, in the **Paragraph group**, if necessary, click Show/Hide to display the formatting marks. If the rulers do not display, click the View tab, and then in the Show group, select the Ruler check box. (Mac users, from your student data files, open Mac_w01C_Photography and use this file instead of a new blank document.) **Save** the file in your **Word Chapter 1** folder as **Lastname_Firstname_1C_Photography**

a. Type **Internship Available for Still Photographer** and then press Enter two times. Type the following text: **This fall, Sturgeon Point Productions will film a documentary on the historic architecture in and around Milwaukee, Wisconsin.** Press Enter.

b. On the ribbon, click the **Insert tab**. In the **Text group**, click the **Object button arrow**, and then click **Text from File**. In the **Insert File** dialog box, from your student data files, locate and select **w01C_Job_Description**, and then click **Insert**. Delete the blank paragraph at the end of the document.

c. Including the paragraph mark, select the first paragraph of text—*Internship Available for Still Photographer*. On the **Home tab**, in the **Font group**, click **Text Effects and Typography**. In the **Text Effects and Typography** gallery, in the first row, click the fourth effect.

d. With the text still selected, in the **Font group**, click in the **Font Size** box to select the existing font size. Type **44** and then press Enter. In the **Font group**, click the **Font Color button arrow**. Under **Theme Colors**, in the fourth column, click the first color.

e. With the text still selected, in the **Font group**, click **Text Effects and Typography**. Point to **Shadow**, and then under **Outer**, in the second row, click the third style. In the **Paragraph group**, click **Center**.

2 ▶ In the paragraph that begins *The filming*, click to position the insertion point at the beginning of the paragraph. On the **Insert tab**, in the **Illustrations group**, click **Pictures**. (Mac users, after clicking Pictures, click Picture form File.) In the **Insert Picture** dialog box, navigate to your student data files, locate and click **w01C_Building**, and then click **Insert**.

a. To the right of the selected picture, click the **Layout Options** button, and then under **With Text Wrapping**, click the first option—**Square**. **Close** the Layout Options. (Mac users, on the Picture Format tab, click Wrap Text.)

b. On the **Format tab**, in the **Size group**, click in the **Shape Height** box to select the value, type **2.7** and then press Enter.

c. With the picture selected, on the **Format tab**, in the **Arrange group**, click **Position**, and then click **More Layout Options**. In the **Layout** dialog box, on the **Position tab**, in the middle of the dialog box under **Vertical**, click the **Alignment** option button. To the right of **Alignment**, click the arrow, and then click **Top**. To the right of **relative to**, click the arrow, and then click **Line**. Click **OK**.

d. On the **Format tab**, in the **Picture Styles group**, click **Picture Effects**. Point to **Soft Edges**, and then click **5 Point**. On the **Format tab**, in the **Adjust group**, click **Artistic Effects**. Use the ScreenTips to locate and click **Crisscross Etching**.

e. Click anywhere outside the picture to deselect it. On the **Design tab**, in the **Page Background group**, click **Page Borders**. In the **Borders and Shading** dialog box, on the **Page Border tab**, under **Setting**, click **Box**. Under **Style**, scroll the list and then click the third style from the bottom—a black line that fades to gray.

f. Click the **Color arrow**, and then in the next to last column, click the first color. Under **Apply to**, be sure **Whole document** is selected, and then click **OK**. Click **Save**.

3 ▶ Click the **Insert tab**, and then in the **Illustrations group**, click **Shapes** to display the gallery. Under **Basic Shapes**, use the ScreenTips to locate and then click **Frame**.

a. Position the ⊞ pointer anywhere in the blank area at the bottom of the document. Click one time to insert a 1" by 1" frame. The exact location need not be precise. To the right of the shape, click the **Layout Options** button, and at the bottom, click **See more**. (Mac users, drag a 1 × 1 shape, click to insert the shape. To display the Layout dialog box, on the Shape Format tab, click Arrange, click Position, click More Layout Options.)

b. In the **Layout** dialog box, under **Horizontal**, click the **Alignment** option button. To the right of **Alignment**, click the arrow, and then click **Centered**. To the right of **relative to**, click the arrow, and then click **Page**. Under **Vertical**, click the **Absolute position** option button. In the **Absolute position** box, select the existing number, and then type **1** To the right of **below**, click the arrow, and then click **Paragraph**. Click **OK**.

(continues on next page)

Chapter Review

c. On the **Format tab**, click in the **Shape Height** box. Type **1.5** and then select the number in the **Shape Width** box. Type **5.5** and then press Enter.

d. If necessary, select the frame shape. On the **Format tab**, in the **Shape Styles group**, click **More**. In the **Shape Styles** gallery, in the first row, click the sixth style. With the shape selected, type **Submit Your Application by June 30!** Select the text you just typed, and then change the **Font Size** to **22**.

4 Click outside of the frame to deselect it, and then to move to the top of the document. Click in the blank paragraph below the title. Press Enter four times to make space for a text box.

a. On the **Insert tab**, in the **Text group**, click **Text Box**. At the bottom of the gallery, click **Draw Text Box**. Position the ⊞ pointer over the first blank paragraph at the left margin. Drag down and to the right to create a text box approximately 1.5 inches high and 4 inches wide—the exact size and location need not be precise.

b. With the insertion point blinking in the text box, type the following, pressing Enter after the first two lines to create a new paragraph:

This position requires skill in the use of:
Professional full-frame DSLR cameras
Tilt-shift lenses for tall buildings

c. To precisely place the text box, on the **Format tab**, in the **Arrange group**, click **Position**, and then click **More Layout Options**. In the **Layout** dialog box, under **Horizontal**, click the **Alignment** button. To the right of **Alignment**, click the arrow, and then click **Centered**. To the right of **relative to**, click the arrow, and then click **Page**.

d. Under **Vertical**, click the **Absolute position** button. In the **Absolute position** box, select the existing number. Type **2** To the right of **below**, click the arrow, and then click **Margin**.

e. In the **Layout** dialog box, click the **Size tab**. Under **Height**, select the number in the **Absolute** box. Type **1** and then under **Width**, select the number in the **Absolute** box. Type **3.75** and then click **OK**.

f. In the text box, select all of the text. On the **Home tab**, change the **Font Size** to **12**, apply **Bold**, and then **Center** the text.

g. On the **Format tab**, in the **Shape Styles group**, click **Shape Effects**. Point to **Shadow**, and then under **Outer**, in the first row, click the first style.

h. In the **Shape Styles group**, click **Shape Outline**. In the fifth column, click the first color to change the color of the text box border. Click **Shape Fill**, and then in the fifth column, click the second color. Click **Save**.

5 Click the **Insert tab**, and then in the **Header & Footer group**, click **Footer**. At the bottom of the menu, click **Edit Footer**. On the **Header & Footer Tools Design tab**, in the **Insert group**, click **Document Info**, and then click **File Name**. Double-click in the document outside of the footer area to close the footer and return to the document. (Mac users, on the Header & Footer tab, click Field, click Document Information, click FileName.)

a. In the upper left corner of your screen, click the **File tab** to display **Backstage** view. Click **Info**, and then at the bottom of the **Properties list**, click **Show All Properties**. On the list of Properties, click to the right of **Tags**, and then type **internship, documentary** Click to the right of **Subject**, and then type your course name and section #. Under **Related People**, be sure that your name displays as the author. If necessary, right-click the author name, click Edit Property, type your name, and click OK. ((Mac users, click File, click Properties, click Summary. In the Keywords box type the tags. Type the Subject and Author. Click OK.)

b. **Save** and **Close** your document. Print or submit your workbook electronically as directed by your instructor.

You have completed Project 1C **END**

Chapter Review

Apply **1B** skills from these Objectives:

5. Change Document and Paragraph Layout
6. Create and Modify Lists
7. Set and Modify Tab Stops
8. Insert and Format a SmartArt Graphic and an Icon

Skills Review   Project 1D Internship

In the following Skills Review, you will edit an information handout regarding production and development internships with Sturgeon Point Productions. Your completed document will look similar to Figure 1.53.

Project Files

For Project 1D, you will need the following file:

w01D_Internship

You will save your document as:

Lastname_Firstname_1D_Internship

Project Results

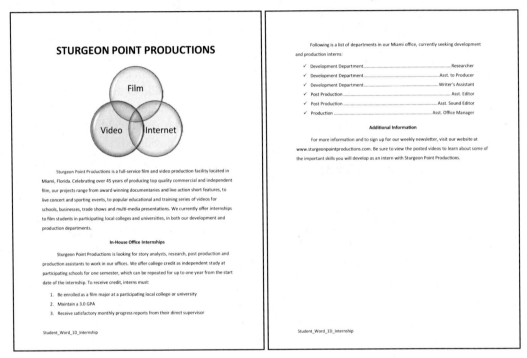

Figure 1.53

(continues on next page)

Chapter Review

Skills Review: Project 1D Internship (continued)

1 From your student data files, open **w01D_Internship**. On the **Home tab**, in the **Paragraph group**, be sure **Show/Hide** is active. **Save** the document to your **Word Chapter 1** folder, as **Lastname_Firstname_1D_Internship**

a. Click the **Layout tab**. In the **Page Setup group**, click **Margins**, and then click **Custom Margins**. In the **Page Setup** dialog box, press Tab as necessary to select the value in the **Left** box. Type **1** and then press Tab to select the value in the **Right** box. Type **1** and then click **OK**.

b. Scroll down to view the bottom of **Page 1**, point anywhere in the bottom margin area, right-click, and then click **Edit Footer** to display the footer area. On the **Header & Footer Tools Design tab**, in the **Insert group**, click **Document Info**, and then click **File Name**. Double-click anywhere in the document to close the footer area. (Mac users, double-click in the footer area. On the Header & Footer tab, click Field.)

c. Press Ctrl + A to select all the text in the document. (Mac users, press command ⌘ + A.) On the **Home tab**, in the **Paragraph group**, click **Align Left**.

d. Press Ctrl + Home. (Mac users, press command ⌘ + fn + ←.) Select the document title, and then on the **Home tab**, in the **Paragraph group**, click **Center**.

e. Locate the first bold subheading—*In-House Office Internships*. Point to the left of the paragraph to display the 📐 pointer, and then click one time to select the text. With *In-House Office Internships* selected, locate the subheading *Additional Information*. Move the pointer to the left of the paragraph to display the 📐 pointer, hold down Ctrl, and then click one time to select both paragraphs. (Mac users, press command ⌘.) In the **Paragraph group**, click **Center**.

f. Select all of the text in the document. On the **Home tab**, in the **Paragraph group**, click **Line and Paragraph Spacing**, and then click **1.5**.

2 Below the title of the document, click anywhere in the paragraph that begins *Sturgeon Point Productions is a full-service*. On the **Home tab**, in the **Paragraph group**, click the **Dialog Box Launcher**. (Mac users, on the Home tab, click Line and Paragraph Spacing, click Line Spacing Options.)

a. In the **Paragraph** dialog box, on the **Indents and Spacing tab**, under **Indentation**, click the **Special arrow**, and then click **First line** to indent the first line by 0.5". Click **OK**, and then click anywhere in the paragraph that begins *Sturgeon Point Productions is looking for*. On the ruler under the ribbon, drag the **First Line Indent** marker to **0.5 inches on the horizontal ruler**.

b. Select all the text in the document. Click the **Layout tab**, and then in the **Paragraph group**, under **Spacing**, click the **After spin box up arrow** one time to change the value to **6 pt**.

c. Select the subheading *In-House Office Internships*, including the paragraph mark following it. Scroll down, hold down Ctrl, and then select the subheading *Additional Information*. With both subheadings selected, in the **Paragraph group**, under **Spacing**, click the **Before up spin box arrow** two times to set the **Spacing Before** to **12 pt**. **Save** your document.

3 Locate the first paragraph that begins *Development Department*, and then point to this paragraph from the left margin area to display the 📐 pointer. Drag down to select this paragraph and the next five paragraphs so that six paragraphs are selected. On the **Home tab**, in the **Paragraph group**, click **Bullets** to change the selected text to a bulleted list.

a. Under the subheading *In-House Office Internships*, in the paragraph that begins *Sturgeon Point Productions is looking*, click to position the insertion point at the *end* of the paragraph, following the colon. Press Enter to create a blank paragraph. On the ruler, drag the **First Line Indent** marker to the left so that it is positioned directly above the lower button. Being sure to include the period, type **1.** and then press Spacebar to create the first item in a numbered list.

b. Type **Be enrolled as a film major at a participating local college or university** and then press Enter. Type **Maintain a 3.0 GPA** and then press Enter. Type **Receive satisfactory monthly progress reports from their direct supervisor**

c. Scroll down to view the bulleted list of departments, and then select all six bulleted items in the list. On the mini toolbar, click the **Bullets button arrow**, and then under **Bullet Library**, click the **check mark** symbol. If the check mark is not available, choose another bullet symbol.

4 With the list selected, move the pointer to the horizontal ruler, and then point to and click at **3.5 inches on the horizontal ruler** to align the job titles at the tab mark.

a. With the bulleted list still selected, on the ruler, point to the new tab marker at **3.5 inches on the horizontal ruler**, and then when the *Left Tab* ScreenTip displays, drag the tab marker to **4 inches on the horizontal ruler**.

(continues on next page)

Chapter Review

b. With the list still selected, on the ruler, point to the tab marker that you moved to display the *Left Tab* ScreenTip, and then double-click to display the **Tabs** dialog box.

c. In the **Tabs** dialog box, under **Tab stop position**, if necessary select *4"*, and then type **6** Under **Alignment**, click the **Right** option button. Under **Leader**, click the **2** option button. Near the bottom of the **Tabs** dialog box, click **Set**. Under **Tab stop position**, select **4"**, and then click **Clear** to delete the tab stop. (Mac users, click Clear All. In the Tab stops box, type 6, click Right, and then Under Leader, click the dot leader style.) Click **OK**. **Save** your document.

5 ▶ Press Ctrl + Home to move to the top of the document, and then in the title, click to the right of the *S* in *PRODUCTIONS*.

a. Click the **Insert tab**, and then in the **Illustrations group**, click **SmartArt**. On the left, click **Relationship**, and then scroll the list to the bottom. Locate and then click **Basic Venn**. Click **OK** to insert the SmartArt graphic. If necessary, close the Text Pane.

b. In the SmartArt graphic, click on *[Text]* in the top circle shape. Type **Film** and then in the lower left shape, click on the placeholder *[Text]*. Type **Video** and then in the third circle, type **Internet**

c. Click the SmartArt graphic border to select it. Click the **Format tab**, and then in the **Size group**, if necessary click **Size** to display the **Shape Height** and **Shape Width** boxes. Set the **Height** to **3"**.

d. With the SmartArt graphic still selected, on the ribbon, under **SmartArt Tools**, click the **Design tab**, and then in the **SmartArt Styles group**, click **Change Colors**. (Mac users, use the SmartArt Design tab.) Under **Colorful**, click the third style— **Colorful Range - Accent Colors 3 to 4**. On the **Design tab**, in the **SmartArt Styles group**, click **More**. Under **3-D**, click **Cartoon**.

e. Click the **File tab**, click **Info**, and then, click **Show All Properties**. In the **Tags** box, type **internship** and in the **Subject** box type your course name and section number. If necessary, in the **Author** box, replace the existing text with your first and last name. Click **Save**.

f. Click the **File tab** to display **Backstage** view, and then click **Print** to display **Print Preview**. At the bottom of the preview, click the **Next Page** and **Previous Page** buttons to move between pages. If necessary, return to the document and make any necessary changes.

g. **Save** and **Close** your document. Print or submit your workbook electronically as directed by your instructor.

You have completed Project 1D **END**

Content-Based Assessments (Mastery and Transfer of Learning)

Apply 1A skills from these Objectives:

1. Create a New Document and Insert Text
2. Insert and Format Graphics
3. Insert and Modify Text Boxes and Shapes
4. Preview and Print a Document

In the following Mastery project, you will create a flyer announcing a special event being hosted by Sturgeon Point Productions. Your printed results will look similar to those in Figure 1.54.

Project Files for **MyLab IT** Grader

1. In your **MyLab IT** course, locate and click **Word 1E Documentary**, Download Materials, and then Download All Files.
2. Extract the zipped folder to your Word Chapter 1 folder. Close the Grader download screens.
3. Take a moment to open the downloaded **Word_1E_Documentary_Instructions**; note any recent updates to the book.

Project Results

Sturgeon Point Productions
Presents Aria Pacheco

Sturgeon Point Productions will be hosting its **5th Annual Script to Screen** series, every Friday night this April in our Studio G screening room. All employees, interns, and film students with current school ID are welcome to share in this totally free, exciting evening, where our award-winning filmmakers from our Documentary and Short Feature Film Departments give a first-hand account of the filmmaking process and the challenges that went into their particular projects, from the script phase through production and finally, in distribution and marketing.

This year, we are proud to kick off the series with Aria Pacheco, who will discuss her multi-award winning documentary, **"Through the Cold."** This film documents the perils and triumphs of a team of scientists living in Antarctica. This compelling story, rich in visual complexity, follows the team as they prepare for the six months of darkness in the winter season. Celebrated film critic, Georges Harold, will be conducting an interview with Ms. Pacheco and select members of her crew following a screening of the film, which will take place on Friday, April 5th at 8 p.m. This event is guaranteed to fill up fast, so we suggest you get in line at least one hour prior to the screening.

"Through the Cold" has been heralded by critics across the country. Don't miss this chance to meet one of our greatest documentary filmmakers.

Date: April 5

Time 8 p.m.

Place: Studio G Screening Room

Student_Word_1E_Documentary

Figure 1.54 (Volodymyr Goinyk/Shutterstock)

For Non-MyLab Submissions

For Project 1E, you will need:

New blank Word Document
w01E_Antarctica
w01E_Filmmaker

In your Word Chapter 1 folder, save your document as:

Lastname_Firstname_1E_Documentary

Start with a new blank document. After you have named and saved your document, on the next page, begin with Step 2. After Step 16, save and submit your file as directed by your instructor.

1 Navigate to your **Word Chapter 1 folder**, and then double-click the Word file you downloaded from **MyLab IT** that displays your name— **Student_Word_1E_Documentary**. In your document, if necessary, at the top click **Enable Editing**. Display the rulers and verify that **Show/Hide** is active. (Mac users, If you are not submitting your file in **MyLab IT**, from the student data files that accompany this project, open the file **Mac_w01E_Documentary**.)

2 Type **Sturgeon Point Productions Presents Aria Pacheco** and then press Enter. From your downloaded files, insert the text file **w01E_Filmmaker**.

3 Select the title and then from the **Text Effects and Typography** gallery, in the first row apply the second effect. Change the **Font Size** to **36**.

4 With the title still selected, display the **Font Color** palette, and then in the fourth column apply the first color. Then, from the **Shadow** gallery, under **Outer**, apply the first **Shadow** style. **Center** the title.

5 Position the insertion point at the beginning of the paragraph that begins with *This year*, and then from your downloaded files, insert the picture **w01E_Antarctica**.

6 Change the **Layout Options** to **Square** and then change the **Height** of the picture to **2.25**.

7 Using the **Position** command, display the **Layout** dialog box, and then change the **Horizontal Alignment** to **Right relative to** the **Margin**.

8 Apply a **10 Point Soft Edges** picture effect to the image, and then display the **Artistic Effects** gallery. Apply the **Paint Brush** effect.

9 Deselect the picture. Apply a **Page Border** to the document using the **Shadow** setting, and then select the double lines style.

10 Below the last paragraph, draw a **Text Box** and then change the **Height** to **1.5** and the **Width** to **4.5**

11 To precisely place the text box, display the **Layout** dialog box. Change the **Horizontal Alignment** to **Centered, relative to** the **Page**, and then change the **Vertical Absolute position** to **0.5** below the **Paragraph**.

12 In the text box, type the following text:

> **Date: April 5**
> **Time: 8 p.m.**
> **Place: Studio G Screening Room**

13 In the text box, change the font size of all the text to **18**. Apply **Bold** and **Center**.

14 Apply a **Shape Style** to the text box—under **Theme Styles**, in the last row, select the second style.

15 Insert the **File Name** in the footer, and then display the document properties. As the **Tags**, type **documentary, interview** and as the **Subject**, type your course and section number. Be sure your name is indicated as the **Author**. **Save** your file.

16 Display the **Print Preview** and, if necessary, return to the document and make any necessary changes. **Save** your document and **Close** Word.

17 In **MyLab IT**, locate and click the Grader Project **Word 1E Documentary**. In **step 3**, under **Upload Completed Assignment**, click **Choose File**. In the **Open** dialog box, navigate to your **Word Chapter 1 folder**, and then click your **Student_Word_1E_Documentary** file one time to select it. In the lower right corner of the **Open** dialog box, click **Open**.

The name of your selected file displays above the Upload button.

18 To submit your file to **MyLab IT** for grading, click **Upload**, wait a moment for a green **Success!** message, and then in step 4, click the blue **Submit for Grading** button. Click **Close Assignment** to return to your list of **Course Materials**.

You have completed Project 1E **END**

Mastering Word | **Project 1F Pitch Festival**

In the following Mastery project, you will edit a document with information regarding an event that Sturgeon Point Productions is holding for college students. Your printed results will look similar to those in Figure 1.55.

Apply 1B skills from these Objectives:

5. Change Document and Paragraph Layout
6. Create and Modify Lists
7. Set and Modify Tab Stops
8. Insert and Format a SmartArt Graphic and an Icon

Project Files for MyLab IT Grader

1. In your **MyLab IT** course, locate and click **Word 1F Pitch Festival**, Download Materials, and then Download All Files. Close the Grader download screens.
2. Extract the zipped folder to your Word Chapter 1 folder. Close the Grader download screens.
3. Take a moment to open the downloaded **Word_1F_Pitch_Festival_Instructions**; note any recent updates to the book.

Project Results

Figure 1.55

For Non-MyLab Submissions

For Project 1F, you will need:
w01F_Pitch_Festival

In your Word Chapter 1 folder, save your document as:
Lastname_Firstname_1F_Pitch_Festival

After you have named and saved your document, on the next page, begin with Step 2.
After Step 13, save and submit your file as directed by your instructor.

1 Navigate to your **Word Chapter 1 folder**, and then double-click the Word file you downloaded from **MyLab IT** that displays your name—**Student_Word_1F_Pitch_Festival**. In your document, if necessary, at the top, click **Enable Editing**. Display the rulers and verify that **Show/Hide** is active.

2 Insert the **File Name** in the footer, and then change the **Line Spacing** for the entire document to **1.5. Center** the document title, and then change the title font size to **24**. Change the **Top** and **Bottom** margins to **0.5**

3 Select the paragraph below the title, and then apply a **First line** indent of **0.5"**. Then, apply the same indent to the paragraphs below the picture that begin *Sturgeon Point Productions* and *The Pitch Festival*.

4 Select the entire document, and then change the **Spacing Before** to **6 pt** and the **Spacing After** to **6 pt**.

5 Select the last three paragraphs containing the dates, and then apply the filled square bullets. With the bulleted list selected, set a **Right** tab with **dot leaders** at **6"**.

6 Locate the paragraph that begins *Sturgeon Point Productions*, and then click at the end of the paragraph, after the colon. Press [Enter] and remove the first line indent from the new paragraph.

7 In the blank line you inserted, create a numbered list with the following three numbered items:

Human interest or educational
Political or journalistic
Biographical or documentary

8 Position the insertion point at the end of the document after the word *Pitches*. Do *not* insert a blank line. Display the **SmartArt** gallery and the **Process** category. Select and insert the **Equation** SmartArt. Select the outside border of the SmartArt, and then change the **Height** of the SmartArt to **1** and the **Width** to **6.5**

9 With the SmartArt selected, change the layout to **Square**, and change the **Horizontal Alignment** to **Centered relative to** the **Page**. Change the **Vertical Alignment** to **Bottom relative to** the **Margin**.

10 In the first circle, type **Your Ideas** and in the second circle, type **Our Experts** In the third circle, type **Pitch Festival!**

11 Change the SmartArt color to **Colorful Range – Accent Colors 4 to 5**. Apply the **3-D Polished** style.

12 Display the document properties. As the **Tags**, type **pitch festival** and in the **Subject** box, type your course name and section number. In the **Author** box, replace the existing text with your first and last name. **Save** the file.

13 Display the **Print Preview** and if necessary, return to the document and make any necessary changes. **Save** your document and **Close** Word.

14 In **MyLab IT**, locate and click the Grader Project **Word 1F Pitch Festival**. In **step 3**, under **Upload Completed Assignment**, click **Choose File**. In the **Open** dialog box, navigate to your **Word Chapter 1 folder**, and then click your **Student_Word_1F_Pitch_Festival** file one time to select it. In the lower right corner of the **Open** dialog box, click **Open**.

The name of your selected file displays above the Upload button.

15 To submit your file to **MyLab IT** for grading, click **Upload**, wait a moment for a green **Success!** message, and then in step 4, click the blue **Submit for Grading** button. Click **Close Assignment** to return to your list of **Course Materials**.

You have completed Project 1F **END**

Content-Based Assessments (Mastery and Transfer of Learning)

Apply 1A and 1B skills from these Objectives:

1. Create a New Document and Insert Text
2. Insert and Format Graphics
3. Insert and Modify Text Boxes and Shapes
4. Preview and Print a Document
5. Change Document and Paragraph Layout
6. Create and Modify Lists
7. Set and Modify Tab Stops
8. Insert and Format a SmartArt Graphic and an Icon

In the following Mastery project, you will create a flyer that details a new educational website that Sturgeon Point Productions has developed for instructors. Your printed results will look similar to those in Figure 1.56.

Project Files for **MyLab IT** Grader

1. In your **MyLab IT** course, locate and click **Word 1G Educational Website**, Download Materials, and then Download All Files. Close the Grader download screens.
2. Extract the zipped folder to your Word Chapter 1 folder. Close the Grader download screens.
3. Take a moment to open the downloaded **Word_1G_Educational_Website_Instructions**; note any recent updates to the book.

Project Results

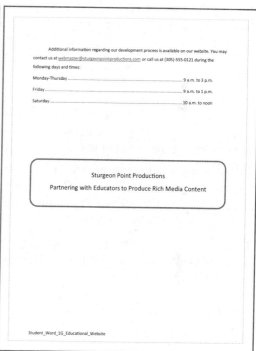

Figure 1.56

For Non-MyLab Submissions

For Project 1G, you will need:
New blank document
w01G_Education
w01G_Media

In your Word Chapter 1 folder, save your document as:
Lastname_Firstname_1G_Educational_Website

After you have named and saved your document, on the next page, begin with Step 2.
After Step 19, save and submit your file as directed by your instructor.

(continues on next page)

Content-Based Assessments (Mastery and Transfer of Learning)

1 Navigate to your **Word Chapter 1 folder**, and then double-click the Word file you downloaded from **MyLab IT** that displays your name—**Student_Word_1G_Educational_Website**. In your document, if necessary, at the top click **Enable Editing**. Display the rulers and verify that **Show/Hide** is active. (Mac users, If you are not submitting your file in **MyLab IT**, from the student data files that accompany this project, open the file **Mac_w01G_Educational_Website**.)

2 Type **Educational Websites** and then press Enter. Type **Sturgeon Point Productions is offering website tie-ins with every educational video in our catalog, at no additional cost.** Press Spacebar, and then with the insertion point positioned at the end of the sentence that you typed, insert the text from your downloaded file **w01G_Education**.

3 Change the **Line Spacing** for the entire document to **1.5** and the spacing **After** to **6 pt**. To each of the four paragraphs that begin *Sturgeon Point Productions*, *As educators*, *When submitting*, and *Additional information*, apply a **First Line** indent of **0.5"**.

4 Change the **font size** of the title to **50** and the **Line Spacing** to **1.0. Center** the title. With the title selected, display the **Text Effects and Typography** gallery. In the first row, apply the second effect.

5 Click at the beginning of the paragraph below the title, and then from your downloaded files, insert the picture **w01G_Media**. Change the picture **Height** to **2** and the **Layout Options** to **Square**. Format the picture with **Soft Edges** in **10 Point**.

6 Use the **Position** command to display the **Layout** dialog box. Change the picture position so that the **Horizontal Alignment** is **Right relative to** the **Margin**. Change the **Vertical Alignment** to **Top relative to** the **Line**.

7 Select the five paragraphs beginning with *Historic interactive timelines* and ending with *Quizzes and essay exams*, and then apply checkmark bullets. (Mac users, if the check mark bullet style does not display, click Define New Bullet, click Bullet, change the font to Wingdings, click the check mark symbol, and then click OK.)

8 In the paragraph below the bulleted list, click after the colon. Press Enter and remove the first line indent. Type a numbered list with the following three numbered items:

The title in which you are interested
The name of the class and subject
Online tools you would like to see created

9 With the insertion point located at the end of the numbered list, insert a **SmartArt** graphic. In the **Process** category, locate and select the **Basic Chevron Process**. In the first shape, type **View** In the second shape, type **Interact** and in the third shape, type **Assess**

10 Change the SmartArt color to **Colorful Range – Accent Colors 4 to 5**, and then apply the **3-D Flat Scene** style. Change the **Height** of the SmartArt to **1** and the **Width** to **6.5** Change the **Layout Options** to **Square**, the **Horizontal Alignment** to **Centered relative to** the **Page**, and the **Vertical Alignment** to **Bottom relative to** the **Margin**.

11 Select the days and times at the end of the document, and then set a **Right** tab with **dot leaders** at **6"**.

12 In the middle of **Page 2**, insert a **Shape**—the rectangle with rounded corners. The exact location need not be precise. Change the **Shape Height** to **1.5** and the **Shape Width** to **6.5** and then display the **Shape Styles** gallery. In the first row, apply the second style.

13 Use the **Position** command to display the **Layout** dialog box, and then change the position so that both the **Horizontal** and **Vertical Alignment** are **Centered relative to** the **Margin**. In the rectangle, type **Sturgeon Point Productions** and then press Enter. Type **Partnering with Educators to Produce Rich Media Content** and then change the font size to **16**.

14 Move to the top of the document and insert a **Text Box** above the title. The exact location need not be precise. Change the **Height** of the text box to the **0.5** and the **Width** to **3.7** Type **Sturgeon Point Productions** and then change the font size of all the text in the text box to **22. Center** the text.

15 Use the **Position** command to display the **Layout** dialog box, and then position the text box so that the **Horizontal Alignment** is **Centered relative to** the **Page** and the **Vertical Absolute position** is **0.5 below** the **Page**.

16 With the text box selected, display the **Shape Fill** gallery, and then in the next to last column, select the second color. Change the **Shape Outline** to the same color.

17 Deselect the text box. Apply a **Page Border** to the document. Use the **Box** setting, and then choose the first style. Display the **Color** palette, and then in the second to last column, apply the first color.

18 Change the **Top** margin to **1.25** and insert the **File Name** in the footer.

(continues on next page)

Content-Based Assessments (Mastery and Transfer of Learning)

19 Display the document properties. As the **Tags**, type **website** and as the **Subject**, type your course and section number. Be sure your name displays in the **Author** box. **Save** your document and **Close** Word.

20 In **MyLab IT**, locate and click the Grader Project **Word 1G Educational Website**. In **step 3**, under **Upload Completed Assignment**, click **Choose File**. In the **Open** dialog box, navigate to your **Word Chapter 1 folder**, and then click your **Student_Word_1G_Educational_ Website** file one time to select it. In the lower right corner of the **Open** dialog box, click **Open**.

The name of your selected file displays above the Upload button.

21 To submit your file to **MyLab IT** for grading, click **Upload**, wait a moment for a green **Success**! message, and then in step 4, click the blue **Submit for Grading** button. Click **Close Assignment** to return to your list of **Course Materials**.

You have completed Project 1G | **END**

GO! Fix It	**Project 1H Casting Call**	IRC
GO! Make It	**Project 1I Development Team**	IRC
GO! Solve It	**Project 1J Softball**	IRC
GO! Solve It	**Project 1K Production**	

Project Files

For Project 1K, you will need the following files:

w01K_Production

w01K_Studio

You will save your document as:

Lastname_Firstname_1K_Production

The Marketing Director for Sturgeon Point Productions is developing marketing materials aimed at filmmakers. From the student files that accompany this textbook, locate and open the file w01K_Production. Format the document using techniques you learned in this chapter to create an appropriate flyer aimed at filmmakers. From your student data files, insert the picture w01K_Studio, and then format the picture with an artistic effect. Insert a SmartArt graphic that illustrates two or three important points about the company. Use text effects so that the flyer is easy to read and understand and has an attractive design. Save the file in your Word Chapter 1 folder as **Lastname_Firstname_1K_Production** and submit it as directed.

		Performance Level		
		Exemplary: You consistently applied the relevant skills	**Proficient: You sometimes, but not always, applied the relevant skills.**	**Developing: You rarely or never applied the relevant skills.**
Performance Criteria	**Use text effects**	Text effects applied to text in an attractive and appropriate manner.	Text effects are applied but do not appropriately display text.	Text effects not used.
	Insert and format a picture	The picture is inserted; text wrapping and an artistic effect are applied.	The picture is inserted but not formatted properly.	No picture is inserted in the document.
	Insert and format SmartArt	The SmartArt is inserted and appropriately formatted.	The SmartArt is inserted but no formatting is applied.	A SmartArt is not inserted in the document.

You have completed Project 1K | **END**

Outcomes-Based Assessments (Critical Thinking)

Rubric

The following outcomes-based assessments are *open-ended assessments*. That is, there is no specific correct result; your result will depend on your approach to the information provided. Make *Professional Quality* your goal. Use the following scoring rubric to guide you in *how* to approach the problem and then to evaluate *how well* your approach solves the problem.

The *criteria*—Software Mastery, Content, Format and Layout, and Process—represent the knowledge and skills you have gained that you can apply to solving the problem. The *levels of performance*—Professional Quality, Approaching Professional Quality, or Needs Quality Improvements—help you and your instructor evaluate your result.

	Your completed project is of Professional Quality if you:	Your completed project is Approaching Professional Quality if you:	Your completed project Needs Quality Improvements if you:
1-Software Mastery	Choose and apply the most appropriate skills, tools, and features and identify efficient methods to solve the problem.	Choose and apply some appropriate skills, tools, and features, but not in the most efficient manner.	Choose inappropriate skills, tools, or features, or are inefficient in solving the problem.
2-Content	Construct a solution that is clear and well organized, contains content that is accurate, appropriate to the audience and purpose, and is complete. Provide a solution that contains no errors of spelling, grammar, or style.	Construct a solution in which some components are unclear, poorly organized, inconsistent, or incomplete. Misjudge the needs of the audience. Have some errors in spelling, grammar, or style, but the errors do not detract from comprehension.	Construct a solution that is unclear, incomplete, or poorly organized, contains some inaccurate or inappropriate content, and contains many errors of spelling, grammar, or style. Do not solve the problem.
3-Format and Layout	Format and arrange all elements to communicate information and ideas, clarify function, illustrate relationships, and indicate relative importance.	Apply appropriate format and layout features to some elements, but not others. Overuse features, causing minor distraction.	Apply format and layout that does not communicate information or ideas clearly. Do not use format and layout features to clarify function, illustrate relationships, or indicate relative importance. Use available features excessively, causing distraction.
4-Process	Use an organized approach that integrates planning, development, self-assessment, revision, and reflection.	Demonstrate an organized approach in some areas, but not others; or, use an insufficient process of organization throughout.	Do not use an organized approach to solve the problem.

Outcomes-Based Assessments (Critical Thinking)

Apply a combination of the 1A and 1B skills.

| GO! Think | Project 1L Classes |

Project Files

For Project 1L, you will need the following file:
New blank Word document
You will save your document as:
Lastname_Firstname_1L_Classes

The Human Resources director at Sturgeon Point Productions needs to create a flyer to inform full-time employees of educational opportunities beginning in September. The courses are taught each year by industry professionals and are designed to improve skills in motion picture and television development and production. Employees who have been with Sturgeon Point Productions for at least two years are eligible to take the courses free of cost. The classes provide employees with opportunities to advance their careers, gain valuable skills, and achieve technical certification. All courses take place in Studio G. Interested employees should contact Elana Springs in Human Resources to sign up. Information meetings are being held at 5:30 according to the following schedule: television development on June 15; motion picture production on June 17; and recording services on June 21.

Create a flyer with basic information about the courses and information meetings. Be sure the flyer is easy to read and understand and has an attractive design. Save the document as **Lastname_Firstname_1L_Classes** and submit it as directed.

You have completed Project 1L | END

| GO! Think | Project 1M Store | IRC |

| You and GO! | Project 1N Family Flyer | IRC |

| GO! Cumulative Team Project | Project 1O Bell Orchid Hotels | IRC |

Creating Cover Letters and Using Tables to Create Resumes

2

WORD 2019

PROJECT 2A

Outcomes
Create a resume by using a Word table.

Objectives
1. Create a Table for a Resume
2. Format a Table
3. Present a Word Document Online

PROJECT 2B

Outcomes
Write a cover letter, print an envelope, create a Word template, and use Learning Tools.

Objectives
4. Create a Letterhead for a Cover Letter
5. Create a Cover Letter and Correct and Reorganize Text
6. Use the Word Editor to Check Your Document
7. Print an Envelope, Change a Style Set, Create a Word Template, and Use Learning Tools

Dragan Grkic/Shutterstock

In This Chapter

 GO! To Work with Word

Tables are useful for organizing and presenting data. Because a table is so easy to use, many individuals prefer to arrange tabular information in a Word table rather than setting a series of tabs. For example, you can use a table when you want to present rows and columns of information or to create a format for a document such as a resume.

When using Word to write business or personal letters, use a commonly approved letter format, and always use a clear writing style. You will make a good impression with prospective employers if you use a standard business letter style when you are writing a cover letter for a resume.

The projects in this chapter relate to the **College Career Center at Florida Port Community College** in St. Petersburg, Florida, a coastal port city near the Florida High Tech Corridor. With 60 percent of Florida's high tech companies and a third of the state's manufacturing companies located in the St. Petersburg and Tampa Bay areas, the college partners with businesses to play a vital role in providing a skilled workforce. The College Career Center assists students in exploring careers, finding internships, and applying for jobs. The Center offers workshops for resume and cover letter writing and for practice interviews.

2A Resume

Project Activities

In Activities 2.01 through 2.11, you will create a table to use as the format for a resume. The director of the Career Center, Mary Walker-Huelsman, will use this model when assisting students with building their resumes. Your completed document will look similar to Figure 2.1.

Project Files for **MyLab IT Grader**

1. In your storage location, create a folder named **Word Chapter 2**.
2. In your **MyLab IT** course, locate and click **Word 2A Resume**, click Download Materials, and then click Download All Files.
3. Extract the zipped folder to your Word Chapter 2 folder. Close the Grader download screens.
4. Take a moment to open the downloaded **Word_2A_Resume_Instructions**; note any recent updates to the book.

Project Results

GO! Project 2A
Where We're Going

Figure 2.1 Project 2A Resume

For Non-MyLab Submissions

For Project 2A, you will need:

New blank Word document

w02A_Experience

In your storage location, create a folder named **Word Chapter 2**

In your Word Chapter 2 folder, save your document as:

Lastname_Firstname_2A_Resume

After you have named and saved your document, on the next page, begin with Step 2.

Objective 1 Create a Table for a Resume

ALERT Because Office 365 is a cloud-based subscription service that receives continuous updates, you may encounter some variations in what appears on your screen and what is shown in this instruction. Microsoft Office 365 is fully installed on your PC or Mac; no internet access is necessary to create or edit documents. When you are connected to the internet, you will receive monthly upgrades and new features, so you always have the latest versions of Office apps as soon as they are available. Your subscription gives you continuous free access to the latest innovations and refinements.

GO! Learn How
Video W2-1

A ***table*** is an arrangement of information organized into rows and columns. The intersection of a row and a column in a table creates a box called a ***cell*** into which you can type. Tables are useful to present information in a logical and orderly format. Using a Word table to create a resume will assure that your information is presented in an easy-to-read format.

Activity 2.01 | Inserting a Table by Defining Table Dimensions

MOS
1.1.4, 1.2.3, 3.1.3

1 Navigate to your **Word Chapter 2** folder, and then double-click the Word file you downloaded from **MyLab IT** that displays your name—**Student_Word_2A_Resume**. In your blank Word document, if necessary, at the top click **Enable Editing**.

MAC TIP If you are not submitting your file in **MyLab IT**, from the student data files that accompany this project, open the file Mac_w02A_Resume. This is a blank document with default settings necessary to complete this project.

To display group names, display the menu bar, click Word, click Preferences, click View, select Show group titles.

2 On the **Home tab**, in the **Paragraph group**, if necessary click **Show/Hide** ¶ to display the formatting marks. If the rulers do not display, click the View tab, and then in the Show group, select the Ruler check box.

3 On the **Insert tab**, in the **Header & Footer group**, click **Footer**, and then at the bottom of the list, click **Edit Footer**. On the ribbon, in the **Insert group**, click **Document Info**, click **File Name**, and then at the right end of the ribbon, click **Close Header and Footer**.

MAC TIP On the Header & Footer tab, in the Insert group, click Field. Under Categories, click Document Information. Under Field names, click FileName. Click OK.

4 On the **Insert tab**, in the **Tables group**, click **Table**. In the **Insert Table** grid, in the fourth row, point to the second square, and notice that the cells are bordered in orange and *2x4 Table* displays at the top of the grid. Compare your screen with Figure 2.2.

MAC TIP Cells are shaded in blue.

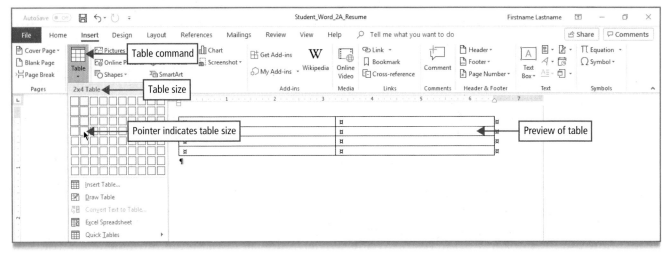

Figure 2.2

5 Click one time to create the table. Notice that formatting marks in each cell indicate the end of the contents of each cell; the mark to the right of each *row* indicates the row end. Compare your screen with Figure 2.3.

A table with four rows and two columns displays at the insertion point location, and the insertion point displays in the upper left cell. The table fills the width of the page from the left margin to the right margin. On the ribbon, Table Tools and two additional tabs—*Design* and *Layout*—display. Borders display around each cell in the table.

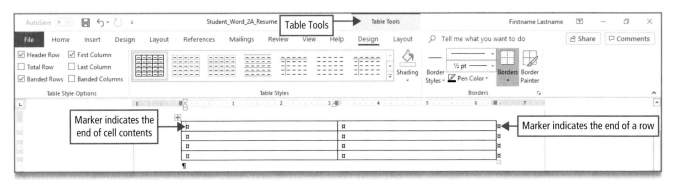

Figure 2.3

Activity 2.02 | Typing Text in a Table

In a Word table, each cell behaves similarly to a document. For example, as you type in a cell, when you reach the right border of the cell, wordwrap moves the text to the next line. When you press Enter, the insertion point moves down to a new paragraph in the same cell. You can also insert text from another document into a table cell.

There are numerous acceptable formats for resumes, many of which can be found in Business Communications textbooks. The layout in this project is suitable for a recent college graduate and places topics in the left column and details in the right column.

1 With the insertion point blinking in the first cell in the first row, type **OBJECTIVE** and then press Tab.

Pressing Tab moves the insertion point to the next cell in the row, or, if the insertion point is already in the last cell in the row, pressing Tab moves the insertion point to the first cell in the following row.

2 Type **Technology writing and editing position in the robotics industry, using research and advanced editing skills to communicate with customers.** Notice that the text wraps in the cell and the height of the row adjusts to fit the text.

3 Press Tab to move to the first cell in the second row. Type **SUMMARY OF QUALIFICATIONS** and then press Tab. Type the following, pressing Enter at the end of each line *except* the last line:

Two years' experience in robotics lab for Aerospace Instruction Team

Excellent interpersonal and communication skills

Proficiency using Microsoft Office and page layout and design software

Fluency in spoken and written Spanish

The default font and font size in a table are the same as for a document—Calibri 11 pt. The default line spacing in a table is single spacing with no space before or after paragraphs, which differs from the defaults for a document.

4 **Save** 🖫 your document, and then compare your screen with Figure 2.4.

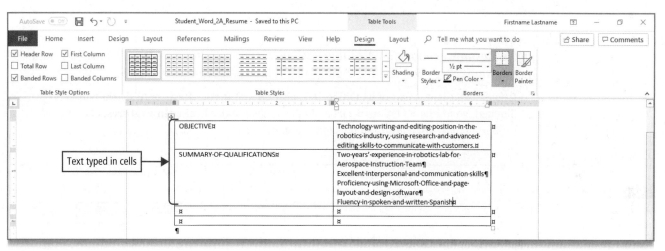

Figure 2.4

Activity 2.03 | Inserting Text From a File and Using Resume Assistant

Use the ***Text from File*** command to insert text from another file into your document. If you have text already created, this is much easier than retyping.

Resume Assistant enables you to view suggestions from ***LinkedIn*** to help you update your resume. LinkedIn is professional networking website that focuses on business and employment-oriented services and on which you can build and share your professional identity and connect with others in your field of interest. If you have not yet set up a LinkedIn profile, it's a good idea to do so to begin building your professional online presence. And it's a good place to find a new job!

1 Press Tab to move to the first cell in the third row. Type **EXPERIENCE** and then press Tab.

2 Be sure your insertion point is positioned in the second column to the left of the cell marker. Compare your screen with Figure 2.5.

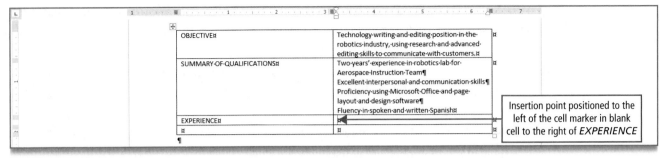

Figure 2.5

> **3** On the **Insert tab**, in the **Text group**, click the **Object button arrow**, and then click **Text from File**. Navigate to the downloaded files that accompany this project, select **w02A_Experience**, and then click **Insert**.

All of the text from the w02A_Experience document is added to the document at the insertion point.

ANOTHER WAY Open the second document and select the text you want. Copy the text, and then paste at the desired location.

> **4** At this point, you might see a message indicating *Working on a resume?* On the **Review tab**, in the **Resume group**, click **Resume Assistant**. If you do not have the Resume Assistant, just examine Steps 5–9 and the Figures that follow and begin with Step 9.

Resume Assistant is part of an Office 365 subscription. If your Resume Assistant button is dimmed, go to File > Options > General tab and then under **LinkedIn Features**, click *Enable (or Show) LinkedIn features in my Office applications*.

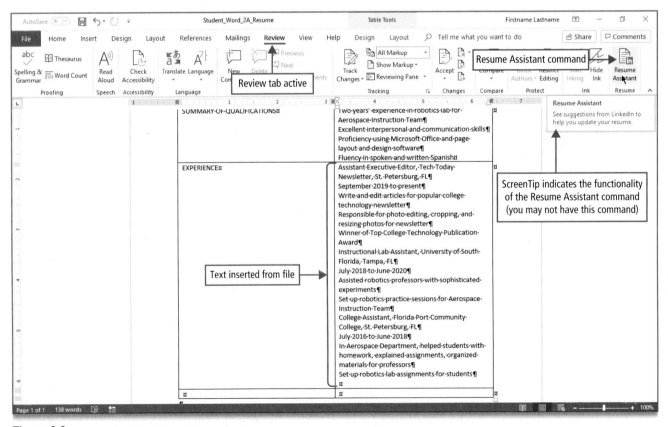

Figure 2.6

5 Click **Resume Assistant**. In the **Resume Assistant** pane on the right, if necessary, click **Get started**. Click **Add role**, and then type **Executive Editor** as shown in Figure 2.7.

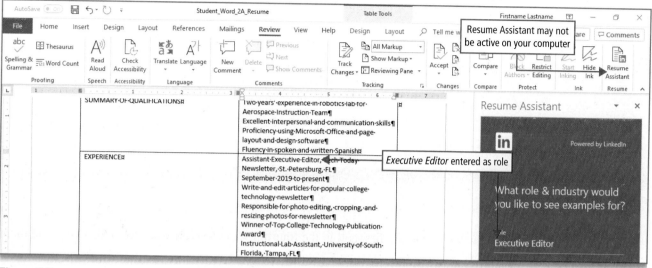

Figure 2.7

6 Click in **Add industry**, type **technology** and then click **Information Technology and Services**. Click **See examples**. Compare your screen with Figure 2.8.

Certainly you cannot copy someone else's resume. But you can see how people who are looking for the same type of job you are have talked about their experience. It can give you ideas about how you could word your own resume to make it more interesting and more descriptive of your experience.

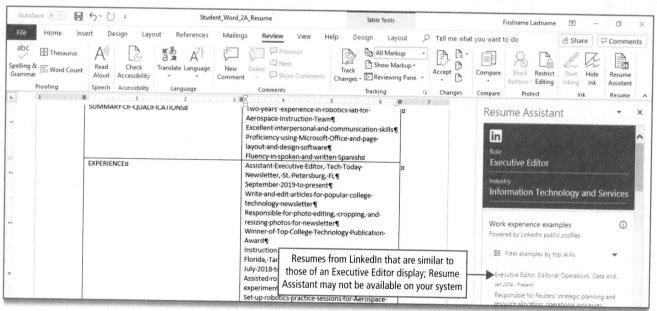

Figure 2.8

7 In the **Resume Assistant** pane, scroll down to view more resumes, interesting articles, and a link to get started on LinkedIn.

8 Close ☒ the **Resume Assistant** pane.

9 Locate, or click to position, the insertion point at the bottom of the text you just inserted, and then press ⌫Backspace one time to remove the blank line at the end of the inserted text. Compare your screen with Figure 2.9.

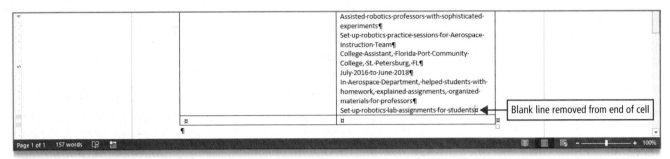

Figure 2.9

10 Press ⎋Tab to move to the first cell in the fourth row. Type **HONORS AND ACTIVITIES** and then press ⎋Tab.

11 Type the following, pressing ⏎Enter at the end of each item *except* the last one:

> **Elected to Pi Tau Sigma, honor society for mechanical engineers**
> **Qualified for Dean's List, six semesters**
> **Student Mentor, helped other students in engineering programs**

12 Save 🖫 your document, and then compare your screen with Figure 2.10.

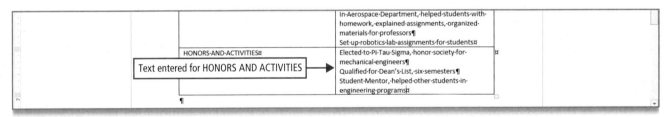

Figure 2.10

Activity 2.04 | Creating Bulleted Lists in a Table

1 Press ⌃Ctrl + ⌂Home to move to the top of your document, and then in the cell to the right of *SUMMARY OF QUALIFICATIONS*, select all of the text.

⌨ **MAC TIP** Press ⌘command ⌘ + fn + ←.

2 On the **Home tab**, in the **Paragraph group**, click **Bullets** ☰▾.

The selected text displays as a bulleted list to make each qualification more distinctive.

3 In the **Paragraph group**, click **Decrease Indent** ☷ one time to align the bullets at the left edge of the cell.

4 Scroll as necessary so that you can view the entire *EXPERIENCE* and *HONORS AND ACTIVITIES* sections on your screen. With the bulleted text still selected, in the **Clipboard group**, double-click **Format Painter**.

5 In the cell to the right of *EXPERIENCE*, select the third, fourth, and fifth paragraphs—beginning with *Write* and *Responsible* and *Winner*—to create the same style of bulleted list as you did in the previous step.

6 In the same cell, under *Instructional Lab Assistant*, select the two paragraphs that begin *Assisted* and *Set up* to create another bulleted list aligned at the left edge of the cell.

7 In the same cell, select the paragraphs that begin *In Aerospace* and *Set up robotics* to create the same type of bulleted list.

8 In the cell below, select the paragraphs that begin *Elected*, *Qualified*, and *Student* to create a bulleted list.

9 Press [Esc] to turn off the **Format Painter**. Click anywhere in the table to deselect the text; if blue lines display, right-click over them and click Ignore Once. **Save** 🖫 your document, and then compare your screen with Figure 2.11.

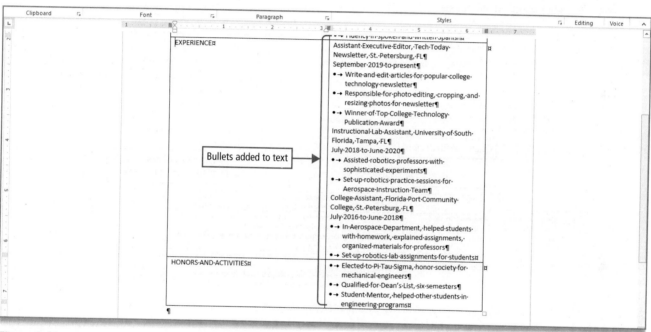

Figure 2.11

Objective 2 | Format a Table

GO! Learn How
Video W2-2

Use Word's formatting tools to make your tables attractive and easy to read. Types of formatting you can add to a table include changing the row height and the column width, removing or adding borders, increasing or decreasing the paragraph or line spacing, and enhancing the text.

Activity 2.05 | Changing the Width of Table Columns and Using AutoFit

3.2.4

When you create a table, all of the columns are of equal width. In this Activity, you will change the width of the columns.

1 Press [Ctrl] + [Home]. Click anywhere in the first column, and then on the ribbon, under **Table Tools**, click the **Layout tab**. In the **Cell Size group**, notice the **Width** box, which displays the width of the active column.

2 Look at the horizontal ruler and locate the **1.5-inch mark**. Then, in the table, in any row, point to the vertical border between the two columns to display the ⊞ pointer.

3 Hold down the left mouse button and drag the column border to the left until the white arrow on the ruler is at approximately **1.5 inches on the horizontal ruler** and then release the left mouse button.

4 In the **Cell Size group**, click the **Width box down spin arrow** as necessary to set the column width to **1.4"** and notice that the right border of the table moves to the left.

Adjusting column width by dragging a column border adjusts only the width of the column; adjusting column width with the Width box simultaneously adjusts the right border of the table.

5 In the **Cell Size group**, click **AutoFit**, and then click **AutoFit Window** to stretch the table across the page within the margins so that the right border of the table is at the right margin. **Save** and then compare your screen with Figure 2.12.

ANOTHER WAY You can adjust column widths by dragging the Move Table Column markers on the ruler. To maintain the right border of the table at the right margin, hold down [Shift] while dragging. To display measurements on the ruler, hold down [Alt] while dragging the marker.

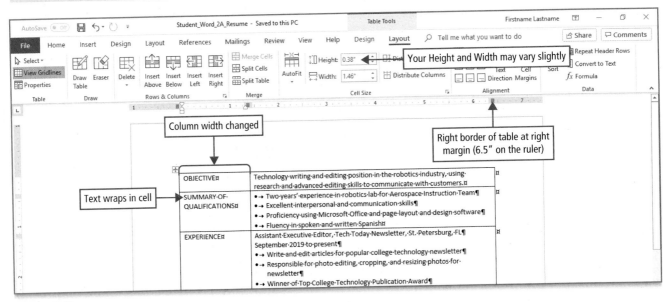

Figure 2.12

MORE KNOWLEDGE **Changing Column Widths**

You will typically get the best results if you change the column widths starting at the left side of the table, especially in tables with three or more columns. Word can also calculate the best column widths for you. To do this, select the table. Then, on the Layout tab, in the Cell Size group, click the AutoFit button and click AutoFit Contents.

Activity 2.06 | Using One-Click Row/Column Insertion to Modify Table Dimensions

One of the most common actions you will take in a table is adding another row or another column. By using *One-click Row/Column Insertion* you can do so in context by pointing to the left or top edge where you want the row or column to appear and then clicking the ⊕ button to add it.

1 Scroll to view the lower portion of the table. On the left border of the table, *point* to the upper left corner of the cell containing the text *HONORS AND ACTIVITIES* to display the **One-click Row/Column Insertion** button. Compare your screen with Figure 2.13.

MAC TIP In your table, click where you want to add a row or column. To the right of the Table Design tab, click the Layout tab, and then use the commands in the Rows & Columns group.

Figure 2.13

> **2** Click ⊕ one time to insert a new row above the *HONORS AND ACTIVITIES* row.

> **3** Click in the left cell of the new row, type **EDUCATION** and then press Tab.

> **4** Type the following, pressing Enter at the end of each item *except* the last one:

University of South Florida, Tampa, FL
Bachelor of Science, Mechanical Engineering, June 2020
Florida Port Community College, St. Petersburg, FL
Associate of Arts, Journalism, June 2018

> **5** **Save** 🖫 your document, and then compare your screen with Figure 2.14.

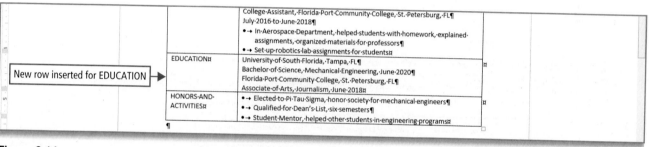

Figure 2.14

🔄 **ANOTHER WAY**   When the insertion point is in the last cell in the bottom row of a table, you can add a row by pressing the TAB key; the insertion point will display in the first cell of the new row.

Activity 2.07 | Adjusting Cell Margins and Merging Table Cells

MOS
3.2.3

Cell margins refer to the space inside a table cell between the text and the cell borders—top, bottom, left, and right. By increasing the cell margins, you can avoid having text so close to the cell borders that it is difficult to read.

The title of a table typically spans all of the columns. In this Activity, you will increase the cell margins and then merge cells so that you can position the personal information across both columns.

> **1** Click anywhere in the top row of the table, and then on the **Table Tools Layout tab**, in the **Alignment group**, click **Cell Margins**.

The Table Options dialog box displays showing the default cell margins.

> **2** In the **Table Options** dialog box, use the spin box arrows to change the **Top** cell margin to **0.04** and the **Bottom** cell margin to **0.04**. Compare your screen with Figure 2.15.

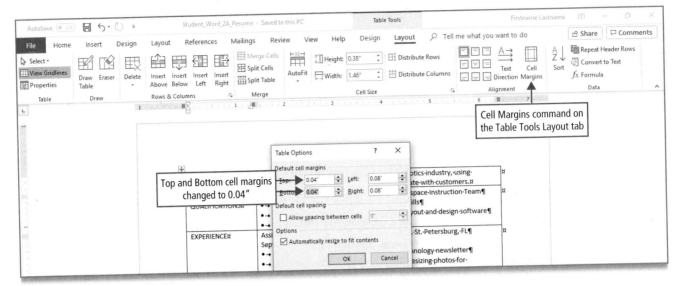

Figure 2.15

> 3 ▶ Click **OK**, and then compare your screen with Figure 2.16.

> The space between the text and the top and bottom of each cell increases, making it easier to read the text with in the table.

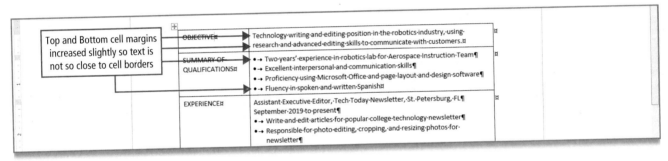

Figure 2.16

> 4 ▶ Click anywhere in the top row of the table, and then on the **Table Tools Layout tab**, in the **Rows & Columns group**, click **Insert Above**.

> A new row displays above the row that contained the insertion point, and the new row is selected. This is another method to insert rows and columns in a table; use this method to insert a new row at the top of a table.

🔄 **ANOTHER WAY**   Right-click in the top row, point to Insert, and then click Insert Rows Above.

> 5 ▶ Be sure the two cells in the top row are selected; if necessary, drag across both cells to select them.

> 6 ▶ On the **Table Tools Layout tab**, in the **Merge group**, click **Merge Cells**.

> The cell border between the two cells no longer displays.

🔄 **ANOTHER WAY**   Right-click the selected row and click Merge Cells on the shortcut menu.

Activity 2.08 | Setting Tabs in a Table

1 With the merged cell still selected, on the **Home tab**, in the **Paragraph group**, click the **Dialog Box Launcher** ⌐ to display the **Paragraph** dialog box.

MAC TIP To display the Paragraph dialog box, on the Home tab, in the Paragraph group, click Line and Paragraph Spacing. Click Line Spacing Options.

2 On the **Indents and Spacing tab**, in the lower left corner, click **Tabs** to display the **Tabs** dialog box.

3 Under **Tab stop position**, type **6.5** and then under **Alignment**, click the **Right** option button. Click **Set**, and then click **OK** to close the dialog box.

MAC TIP Instead of Set, click the add button (+).

4 Type **Josh Hayes** Hold down Ctrl and then press Tab. Notice that the insertion point moves to the right-aligned tab stop at 6.5".

In a Word table, you must use Ctrl + Tab to move to a tab stop, because pressing Tab is reserved for moving the insertion point from cell to cell.

5 Type **(727) 555-0313** and then press Enter.

6 Type **1541 Dearborn Lane, St. Petersburg, FL 33713** Hold down Ctrl and then press Tab.

7 Type **jhayes@alcona.net** Save 🖫 your document, and then compare your screen with Figure 2.17.

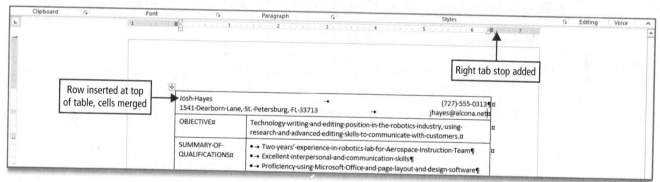

Figure 2.17

Activity 2.09 | Using Spacing After in a Table

1 In the first row of the table, select the name *Josh Hayes*, and then from the mini toolbar, apply **Bold** 🄱 and change the **Font Size** to **16**.

MAC TIP Use ribbon commands on the Home tab, in the Font group.

2 Under *Josh Hayes*, click anywhere in the second line of text, which contains the address and email address.

3 On the **Layout tab**, in the **Paragraph group**, click the **Spacing After up spin arrow** three times to add **18 pt** spacing between the first row of the table and the second row. Compare your screen with Figure 2.18.

This action separates the personal information from the body of the resume and adds focus to the name.

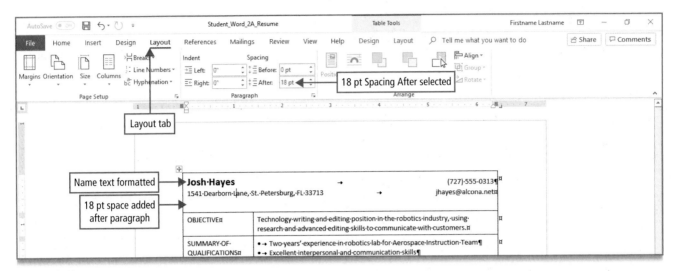

Figure 2.18

4 By using the technique you just practiced, in the second column, click in the last line of *every cell* and add **18 pt Spacing After** including the last row; later you will add a border to the bottom of the table, so spacing will be needed between the last row and the border.

5 In the second row, point to the word *OBJECTIVE*, hold down the left mouse button, and then drag downward in the first column only to select all the headings in uppercase letters. From the mini toolbar, click **Bold** [B].

NOTE **Selecting Only One Column**

When you drag downward to select the first column, a fast mouse might also begin to select the second column when you reach the bottom. If this happens, drag upward slightly to deselect the second column and select only the first column.

---

6 In the cell to the right of *EXPERIENCE*, without selecting the following comma, select *Assistant Executive Editor* and then on the mini toolbar, click **Bold** [B].

7 In the same cell, apply **Bold** [B] to the other job titles—*Instructional Lab Assistant* and *College Assistant*.

8 In the cell to the right of *EDUCATION*, apply **Bold** [B] to *University of South Florida, Tampa, FL* and *Florida Port Community College, St. Petersburg, FL*.

9 In the same cell, click anywhere in the line beginning *Bachelor*. On the **Layout tab**, in the **Paragraph group**, click the **Spacing After up spin arrow** two times to add **12 pt** spacing after the paragraph.

10 In the cell to the right of *EXPERIENCE*, under *Assistant Executive Editor*, click anywhere in the third bulleted item, and then add **12 pt Spacing After** the item.

11 In the same cell, repeat this process for the last bulleted item under *Instructional Lab Assistant*.

12 Scroll to view the top of your document, **Save** 🖫 your document, and then compare your screen with Figure 2.19.

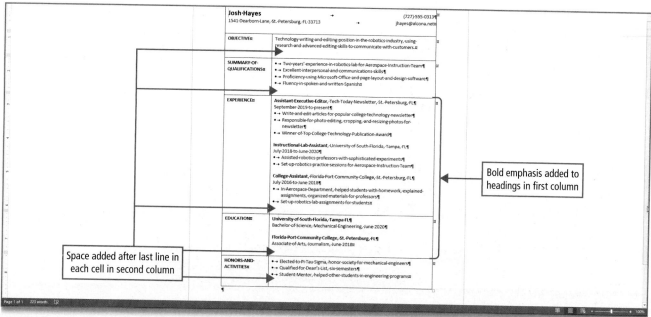

Bold emphasis added to headings in first column

Space added after last line in each cell in second column

Figure 2.19

Activity 2.10 | Modifying Table Borders, Using Spacing Before, and Viewing Gridlines in a Table

MOS
1.3.2

When you create a table, all of the cells have black 1/2-point, single-line, solid-line borders that print unless you remove them. Most resumes do not display any cell borders. A border at the top and bottom of the resume, however, is attractive and adds a professional look to the document.

1 Scroll as necessary to view the top margin area above the table, and then click anywhere in the top row of the table. In the upper left corner of the table, notice the **table move handle** ⊞, which indicates the table is active.

2 On the **Table Tools Layout tab**, in the **Table group**, click **Select**, and then click **Select Table**. Notice that the row markers at the end of each row are also selected.

Shaded row markers indicate that the entire row is selected.

ANOTHER WAY Click the table move handle ⊞ to select the table.

3 On the ribbon, click the **Table Tools Design tab**. In the **Borders group**, click the **Borders button arrow**, and then click **No Border**.

The black borders no longer display.

4 Click the **Borders button arrow** again, and then at the bottom of the menu, if necessary, click **View Gridlines** to view the gridlines in your table. Compare your screen with Figure 2.20.

When you turn off the display of borders, you can show table gridlines to help you see where each cell is located. Table gridlines do not print, but can be useful in visualizing a table in which borders do not display. This command is a toggle—clicking it once turns on the display of gridlines, clicking it again turns off the display of gridlines.

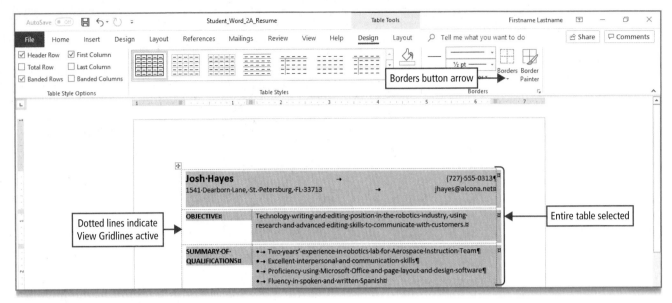

Figure 2.20

> **5** Click the **Borders button arrow** again, and then at the bottom of the menu, click **View Gridlines** to cancel the display of gridlines.

> **6** Press `Ctrl` + `P`, which is the keyboard shortcut to view the **Print Preview**, and notice that no borders display in the preview. Then, press **Back** ⊖ to return to your document.

🖥️ **MAC TIP** Press `command ⌘` + `P`; then click Cancel.

> **7** With the table still selected, on the **Table Tools Design tab**, in the **Borders group**, click the **Borders button arrow**, and then at the bottom of the **Borders** gallery, click **Borders and Shading**.

> **8** In the **Borders and Shading** dialog box, on the **Borders tab**, under **Setting**, click **Custom**. Under **Style**, scroll down about one-third of the way, and then click the style with a **thick upper line and a thin lower line**.

> **9** In the **Preview** box at the right, point to the *top* border of the small preview and click one time.

🔄 **ANOTHER WAY** Click the top border button, which is one of the buttons that surround the Preview.

> **10** Under **Style**, scroll down if necessary, click the opposite style—with the **thin upper line and the thick lower line**, and then in the **Preview** box, click the *bottom* border of the preview. Compare your screen with Figure 2.21.

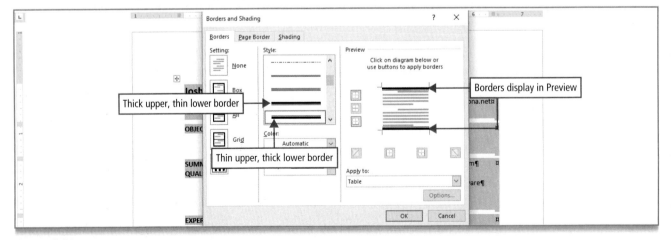

Figure 2.21

11 Click **OK**, click anywhere to cancel the selection, and then notice that there is only a small amount of space between the upper border and the first line of text.

12 Click anywhere in the text *Josh Hayes*, and then on the **Layout tab**, in the **Paragraph group**, click the **Spacing Before up spin arrow** as necessary to add **6 pt** spacing before the first paragraph.

13 Click the **File tab**, and then on the left click **Print** to display the Print Preview. Compare your screen with Figure 2.22.

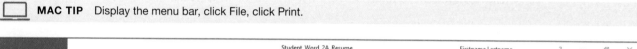

MAC TIP Display the menu bar, click File, click Print.

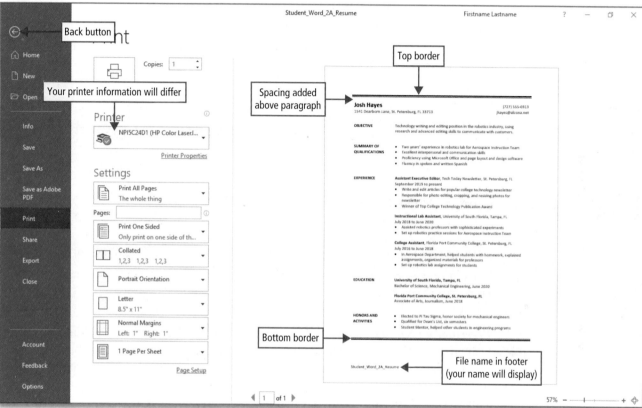

Figure 2.22

14 On the left, click **Info**, and then in the lower right corner, click **Show All Properties**. In the **Tags** box, type **resume, Word table** and in the **Subject** box, type your course name and section number. In the **Author** box, be sure your name is indicated and edit if necessary.

MAC TIP On the menu bar, click File, click Properties, click the Summary tab. For Tags, use Keywords.

15 Press **Back** to return to your document, and then on the Quick Access Toolbar, click **Save**.

MAC TIP Click OK to return to your document.

16 In the upper right corner of the Word window, click **Close** ✕.

For Non-MyLab Submissions Determine What Your Instructor Requires for Submission
As directed by your instructor, submit your completed Word file.

17 In **MyLab IT**, locate and click the Grader Project **Word 2A Resume**. In **step 3**, under **Upload Completed Assignment**, click **Choose File**. In the **Open** dialog box, navigate to your **Word Chapter 2 folder**, and then click your **Student_Word_2A_Resume** file one time to select it. In the lower right corner of the **Open** dialog box, click **Open**.

The name of your selected file displays above the Upload button.

18 To submit your file to **MyLab IT** for grading, click **Upload**, wait a moment for a green **Success!** message, and then in **step 4**, click the blue **Submit for Grading** button. Click **Close Assignment** to return to your list of **Course Materials**.

MORE KNOWLEDGE   **Converting a Table to Text**

You can convert a table to regular text and choose which text character to use to separate the columns. To do so, on the Table Tools Layout tab, in the Data group, click Convert to Text.

You have completed Project 2A   **END**

ALERT   **This Activity in Objective 3 is Optional**

This Activity is optional. Check with your instructor to see if you should complete this Activity. This Activity is not included in the **MyLab IT** Grader system for this project; however, you may want to practice this on your own.

GO! Learn How
Video W2-3

Office Presentation Service enables you to present your Word document to others who can watch in a web browser. No preliminary setup is necessary; Word creates a link to your document that you can share with others via email or instant message. Anyone to whom you send the link can see your document while you are presenting online.

Individuals watching your presentation can navigate within the document independently of you or others in the presentation, so they can use a mouse, keyboard, or touch input to move around in the document while you are presenting it. If an individual is viewing a different portion of the document than the presenter, an alert displays on his or her screen. To return to the portion of the document that the presenter is showing, a Follow Presenter button displays.

While you are presenting, you can make minor edits to the document. If you want to share a copy of the document to the presentation attendees, you can select *Enable remote viewers to download the document* when you start the presentation. You can also share any meeting notes that you or others created in OneNote.

Activity 2.11 | **Presenting a Word Document Online**

If you are creating your own resume, it will be valuable to get feedback from your friends, instructors, or Career Center advisors before you submit your resume for a job application. In this Activity, you will present the resume document online for others to look at.

NOTE   **You must sign in with your Microsoft account.**

You must sign in with your Microsoft account, even if you are already signed in, to present your document online.

1 With your resume document displayed, click **Save** 🗔.

2 Click the **File tab**, on the left click **Share**, and then under **Share**, click **Present Online**.

3 On the right, click **Present Online**. Wait a moment for the service to connect, and then compare your screen with Figure 2.23.

> There are several methods to send your meeting invitation to others. You can click Copy Link to copy and paste the hyperlink; for example, you could copy the link into a *Skype* window. Skype is a Microsoft product with which you can make voice calls, make video calls, transfer files, or send messages—including instant messages and text messages—over the internet.
> You can also select Send in Email, which will open your Outlook email window if you use Outlook as your mail client.

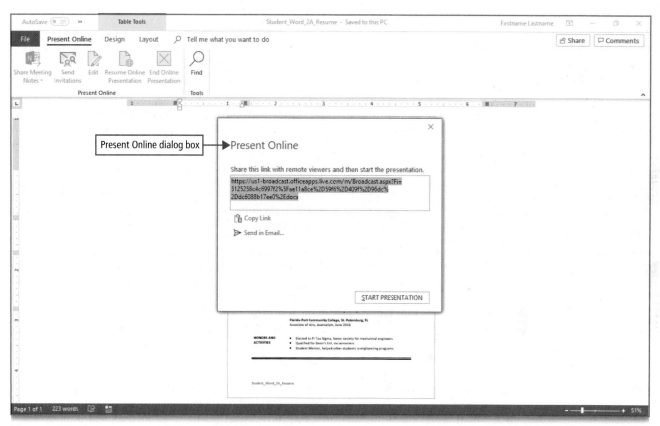

Figure 2.23

4 If you want to do so, identify a classmate or friend who is at a computer and available to view your presentation, select one of the methods to share, click **START PRESENTATION**, and when you are finished, on the ribbon, click **End Online Presentation**. Otherwise, **Close** ⊠ the **Present Online** dialog box.

> If you present online, you will need to initiate voice communication using Skype or by simply phoning the other person.

You have completed the optional portion of this project | END

»»» GO! With Google Docs

Objective	Edit a Resume in Google Docs

ALERT **Working with Web-Based Applications and Services**

Computer programs and services on the web receive continuous updates and improvements, so the steps to complete this web-based Activity may differ from the ones shown. You can often look at the screens and the information presented to determine how to complete the Activity.

If you do not already have a Google account, you will need to create one before you begin this Activity. Go to http://google.com and, in the upper right corner, click Sign In. On the Sign In screen, click Create Account. On the Create your Google Account page, complete the form, read and agree to the Terms of Service and Privacy Policy, and then click Next step. On the Welcome screen, click Get Started.

Activity | Editing a Resume in Google Docs

In this Activity, you will use Google Docs to open and edit a Word table containing a resume similar to the resume you created in Project 2A.

1 From the desktop, open your browser, navigate to **http://google.com**, and then click the **Google apps** menu ⚏. Click **Drive**, and then if necessary, sign in to your Google account.

2 Open your **GO! Web Projects** folder—or click New to create and then open this folder if necessary.

3 In the upper left corner, click **New**, and then click **File upload**. In the **Open** dialog box, navigate to the files you downloaded with this chapter, and then in the **File List**, double-click to open **w02_2A_Web**.

4 When the upload is complete, in the **Google Drive file list**, double-click the document to open it in Google Docs. If necessary, at the top of the screen, click Open with Google Docs.

5 Click anywhere in the word *OBJECTIVE*. On the menu bar, click **Format**, point to **Table**, and then click **Insert row above**. In the first cell of the new row, type **Daniela Frank** Select the text you just typed, and then on the toolbar, click the **Font size arrow**, and then click **18**.

6 Press Tab to move to the second cell of the new row, and then type **1343 Siena Lane, Deerfield, WI 53531** Hold down Shift and press Enter. Type **(608) 555-0588** Hold down Shift and press Enter. Type **dfrank@alcona.net** Select all the text in the second cell that you just typed, and then on toolbar, locate and click **Right align**.

7 Drag to select the two cells in the top row, right-click over the selection, and then click **Merge cells**. With the newly merged cell still selected, right-click over the selection again, and then click **Table properties**.

8 Under **Cell background color**, click the arrow, and then in the top row, click the seventh color—**light gray 1**. Click **OK**.

9 Scroll down and click anywhere in the *EXPERIENCE* cell. Right-click, and then click **Insert row below**. In the first cell of the new row, type **EDUCATION**

10 Press Tab to move to the second cell in the new row, and then type **Madison Area Technical College, Madison, WI** Hold down Shift and press Enter.

11 On the toolbar, click **Bold** B to turn off bold formatting, and then type **Associate of Arts in Information Systems, June 2020** and press Enter.

12 Press Ctrl + P to view the Print Preview, and then compare your screen with Figure A.

13 In the upper left corner, click **Cancel** to close the Print Preview. Submit the file as directed by your instructor. In the upper right, click your user name, and then click **Sign out**. **Close** your browser window. Your file is automatically saved in your Google Drive.

Figure A

Cover Letter and Envelope

Project Activities

In Activities 2.12 through 2.20, you will create a letterhead, and then use the letterhead to create a cover letter to accompany a resume. Optionally, in Activities 2.21 through 2.24 you will format and print an envelope, change a style set, create a Word template for a letterhead, and use Word's Learning Tools. Your completed cover letter will look similar to Figure 2.24.

Project Files for MyLab IT Grader

1. In your **MyLab IT** course, locate and click **Word 2B Cover Letter**, Download Materials, and then Download All Files.
2. Extract the zipped folder to your Word Chapter 2 folder. Close the Grader download screens.
3. Take a moment to open the downloaded **Word_2B_Cover_Letter_Instructions**; note any recent updates to the book.

Project Results

GO! Project 2B
Where We're Going

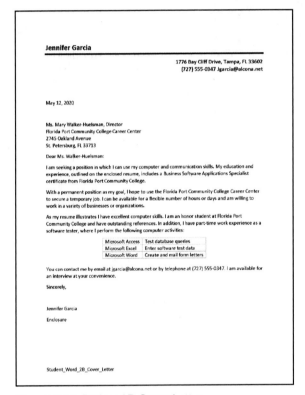

Figure 2.24 Project 2B Cover Letter

Objective 4　Create a Letterhead for a Cover Letter

GO! Learn How

Video W2-4

A *letterhead* is the personal or company information that displays at the top of a letter, and which commonly includes a name, address, and contact information. The term also refers to a piece of paper imprinted with such information at the top.

Activity 2.12　Inserting a Manual Line Break

In this Activity, you will create a personal letterhead for the top of your cover letter.

1 Navigate to your **Word Chapter 2 folder**, and then double-click the Word file you downloaded from **MyLab IT** that displays your name—**Student_Word_2B_Cover_Letter**. If necessary, at the top click **Enable Editing**.

2 On the **Design tab**, in the **Document Formatting group**, click **Paragraph Spacing**. Notice that **Default** is shaded in blue indicating this is the active Style Set for paragraphs in this document. (If this is not the active style set, click Default to make it active.)

A *style set* is a collection of character and paragraph formatting that is stored and named.

MAC TIP　If you are not submitting your file in **MyLab IT**, from the student data files that accompany this project, open the file Mac_w02B_Cover_Letter and begin with that file instead of a blank document. If group names do not display on your ribbon, display the menu bar, click Word, click Preferences, under Authoring and Proofing tools, click View, and then at the bottom of the View dialog box, select the Show group titles check box. Close the dialog box.

3 *Point* to **Default**, and then compare your screen with Figure 2.25.

MAC TIP　No ScreenTip displays.

This is the default paragraph spacing for a new Word document when you open Word and click Blank document, which is 0 points of blank space before a paragraph, 8 points of blank space following a paragraph, and line spacing of 1.08. This is also referred to as the Normal style. Microsoft's research shows that these settings make documents easier to read both on paper and on a screen.

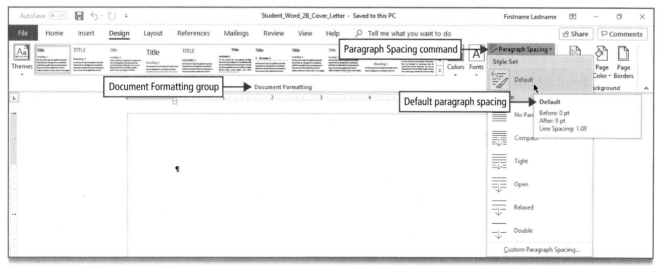

Figure 2.25

4 On the list, under **Built-In**, *point* to **No Paragraph Space**, and then examine the ScreenTip. Compare your screen with Figure 2.26.

The *No Paragraph Space* style inserts *no* extra space before or after a paragraph and uses line spacing of 1. This is the format commonly referred to as *single spacing*.

Some Business Communications texts describe business letters, for example a cover letter, in terms of single spacing. However, it is more modern, and will make your documents easier to read, if you use Word's default paragraph spacing for all of your documents.

Single spacing—where you must press Enter two times to create a new paragraph and where the lines of text within a paragraph are very close together—is an old-fashioned method designed for typewriters in the previous century!

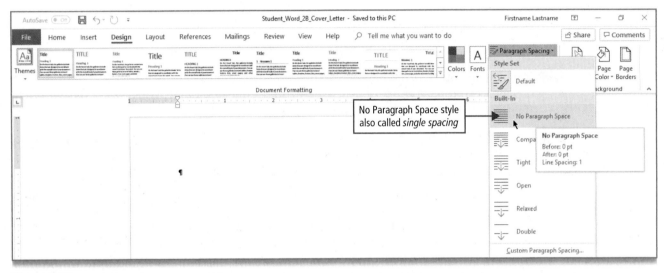

Figure 2.26

5 Be sure that **Default** is the active style set, and then click anywhere outside of the menu to close the menu without making any changes.

6 As the first paragraph, type **Jennifer Garcia** and then press Enter.

7 Type **1776 Bay Cliff Drive, Tampa, FL 33602** hold down Shift and then press Enter. Compare your screen with Figure 2.27.

Holding down Shift while pressing Enter inserts a *manual line break*, which moves the text to the right of the insertion point to a new line while keeping the text in the same paragraph. A *line break indicator*, in the shape of a bent arrow, indicates a manual line break.

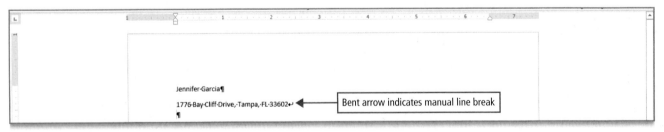

Figure 2.27

8 Type **(727) 555-0347 jgarcia@alcona.net** and then press Enter. If the email address changes to blue text, right-click the address, and then click **Remove Hyperlink**. (Mac users: Point to the beginning of the hyperlink, click AutoCorrect Options button, click Undo Hyperlink.)

9 Select the first paragraph—*Jennifer Garcia*—and then apply **Bold** B and change the **Font Size** to **16**.

10 Select the two address lines that form the second paragraph. Apply **Bold** B and change the Font Size to **12**.

11 With the two-line paragraph still selected, on the **Home tab**, in the **Paragraph group**, click **Align Right** ≡.

ANOTHER WAY   Press Ctrl + R to align text to the right.

Activity 2.13 | Applying a Bottom Border to a Paragraph

1 Click anywhere in the first paragraph—*Jennifer Garcia*. In the **Paragraph group**, click the **Borders button arrow** ⊞ ▾, and then at the bottom, click **Borders and Shading**.

2 In the **Borders and Shading** dialog box, on the **Borders tab**, under **Style**, be sure the first style—a single solid line—is selected.

3 Click the **Width arrow**, and then click **3 pt**. To the right, under **Preview**, click the bottom border of the diagram. Under **Apply to**, be sure *Paragraph* displays. Compare your screen with Figure 2.28.

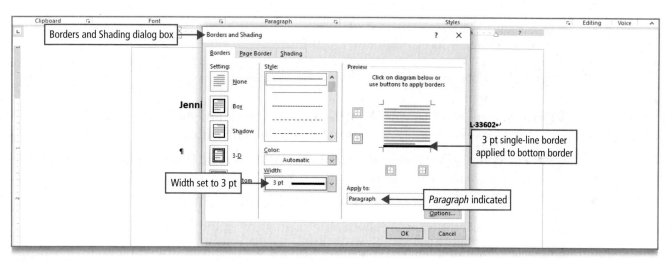

Figure 2.28

ANOTHER WAY   Under Preview, click the bottom border button ⊞ ▾. Mac users: press command ⌘ + R.

4 Click **OK** to display a 3 pt line below *Jennifer Garcia*, which extends from the left margin to the right margin.

The border is a paragraph command and uses the same margins as the paragraph to which it is applied.

5 On the **Insert tab**, in the **Header & Footer** group, click **Footer**, at the bottom click **Edit Footer**, and then in the **Insert group**, click **Document Info**. Click **File Name**, and then click **Close Header and Footer**.

MAC TIP   On the Header & Footer tab, in the Insert group, click Field, click Document Information, click FileName.

6 Save 🖫 your document.

GO! Learn How
Video W2-5

A *cover letter* is a document that you send with your resume to provide additional information about your skills and experience. An effective cover letter includes specific information about why you are qualified for the job for which you are applying. Use the cover letter to explain your interest in the position and the organization.

Business letters follow a standard format and contain the following parts: the current date, referred to as the *dateline*; the name and address of the person receiving the letter, referred to as the *inside address*; a greeting, referred to as the *salutation*; the text of the letter, usually referred to as the *body* of the letter; a closing line, referred to as the *complimentary closing*; and the *writer's identification*, which includes the name of the writer and sometimes the writer's job title and which is also referred to as the *writer's signature block*.

Some letters also include the initials of the person who prepared the letter, an optional *subject line* that describes the purpose of the letter, or a list of *enclosures*—documents included with the letter.

Activity 2.14 | Adding AutoCorrect Entries

Word's *AutoCorrect* feature corrects commonly misspelled words automatically; for example *teh* instead of *the*. If you have words that you frequently misspell, you can add them to the list for automatic correction.

1 Click the **File tab** to display **Backstage** view. On the left, click **Options** to display the **Word Options** dialog box.

MAC TIP Display the menu bar, click Tools, click AutoCorrect; move to Step 3.

2 On the left side of the **Word Options** dialog box, click **Proofing**, and then under **AutoCorrect options**, click the **AutoCorrect Options** button.

3 In the **AutoCorrect** dialog box, click the **AutoCorrect tab**. Under **Replace**, type **resumee** and under **With**, type **resume**

If another student has already added this AutoCorrect entry, a Replace button will display.

4 Click **Add**. If the entry already exists, click Replace instead, and then click Yes.

5 In the **AutoCorrect** dialog box, under **Replace**, with the existing text highlighted in blue, type **computr** and under **With**, type **computer** Compare your screen with Figure 2.29.

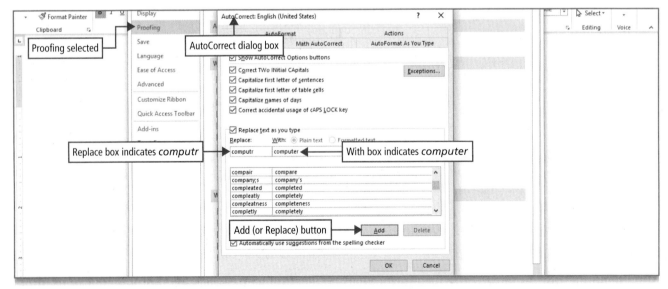

Figure 2.29

6 ▶ Click **Add** (or Replace) and then click **OK** two times to close the dialog boxes.

Activity 2.15 | Inserting the Current Date and Creating a Cover Letter

Typically you send a cover letter with your resume to provide additional information about your skills and experience. An effective cover letter includes specific information about why you are qualified for the job for which you are applying. Use the cover letter to explain your interest in the position and the organization.

By using the *Date & Time* command, you can select from a variety of formats to insert the current date and time in a document.

For cover letters, there are a variety of accepted letter formats that you will see in reference manuals and Business Communications texts. The one used in this chapter is a block format following the style in Courtland Bovee and John Thill, *Business Communication Today*, Fourteenth Edition, Pearson, 2018, p. 584.

1 ▶ Press Ctrl + End to move the insertion point to the blank line below the letterhead, and then press Enter two times.

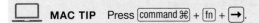

MAC TIP   Press command ⌘ + fn + →.

2 ▶ On the **Insert tab**, in the **Text group**, click **Insert Date & Time**, and then click the third date format. Click **OK** to create the dateline. Compare your screen with Figure 2.30

Most Business Communication texts recommend that the dateline be positioned at least 0.5 inch below the letterhead; or, position the dateline approximately 2 inches from the top edge of the paper.

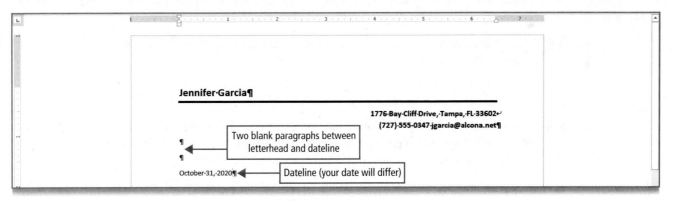

Figure 2.30

3 ▶ Press Enter two times. Type **Ms. Mary Walker-Huelsman, Director** and press Enter.

The recommended space between the dateline and inside address varies slightly among experts in Business Communication texts and office reference manuals. However, all indicate that the space can be from 2 to 10 blank paragraphs (sometimes referred to as blank *lines* in a single-spaced document) depending on the length of your letter. You can adjust the number of blank paragraphs to balance the layout of your letter.

4 ▶ Type **Florida Port Community College Career Center** and press Enter. Type **2745 Oakland Avenue** and press Enter.

5 ▶ Type **St. Petersburg, FL 33713** and press Enter.

6 Select the first three lines of the inside address, and then on the **Layout tab**, in the **Paragraph group**, change **Spacing After** to **0**. Compare you screen with Figure 2.31.

Two parts of a business letter—the inside address and the writer's signature block if it is more than one line—are commonly described in terms of single-spaced paragraphs where there is no blank space following a paragraph. By changing the spacing after paragraphs for all but the last line of the inside address, you will be following the prescribed format of a letter.

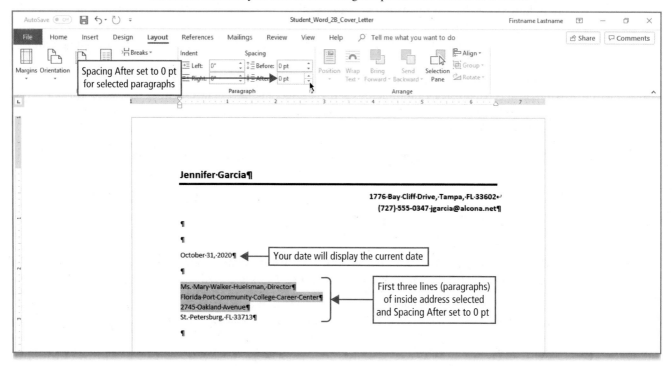

Figure 2.31

7 Click in the blank paragraph below the inside address. Type the salutation **Dear Ms. Walker-Huelsman:** and then press ⎆Enter.

Because the Word default settings automatically apply 8 pt spacing after a paragraph, pressing ⎆Enter one time to begin a new paragraph inserts appropriate space between the parts of the letter.

8 Type, exactly as shown, the following opening paragraph that includes an intentional word usage error: **I am seek a position in which I can use my** and press ⎵Spacebar. Type, exactly as shown, **computr** and then watch *computr* as you press ⎵Spacebar.

The AutoCorrect feature recognizes the misspelled word, and then changes *computr* to *computer* when you press ⎵Spacebar, ⎆Enter, or type a punctuation mark.

9 Type the following, including the misspelled last word: **and communication skills. My education and experience, outlined on the enclosed resumee** and then type **,** (a comma). Notice that when you type the comma, AutoCorrect replaces *resumee* with *resume*.

10 Press ⎵Spacebar, and then complete the paragraph by typing **includes a Business Software Applications Specialist certificate from FPCC.** Compare your screen with Figure 2.32.

Figure 2.32

11 Press Enter. On the **Insert tab**, in the **Text group**, click the **Object button arrow**, and then click **Text from File**. From the files downloaded with this project, locate and **Insert** the file **w02B_Cover_Letter_Text**.

> Some of the words in the cover letter text display red squiggles and double blue underlines. You may also see brown dotted underlines. These indicate potential spelling, grammar, or writing style errors, and will be addressed before the end of this project.

12 Scroll as necessary to display the lower half of the letter on your screen, and be sure your insertion point is positioned in the blank paragraph at the end of the document.

13 Type **Sincerely,** as the complimentary closing, and then press Enter two times to leave space between the complimentary closing and the writer's identification.

> This allows space for the writer to sign the letter above his or her name.

14 Type **Jennifer Garcia** as the writer's identification, and then press Enter.

15 Type **Enclosure** to indicate that a document is included with the letter. **Save** 🖫 your document, and then compare your screen with Figure 2.33.

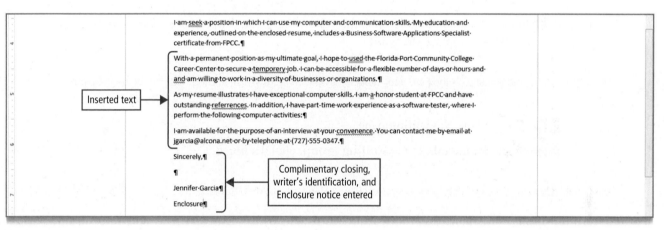

Figure 2.33

Activity 2.16 | Finding and Replacing Text

MOS
1.1.1, 2.1.1

Use the Find command to locate text in a document quickly. Use the Find and Replace command to make the same change, or to make more than one change at a time, in a document.

1 Press Ctrl + Home to position the insertion point at the beginning of the document.

> Because a find operation—or a find and replace operation—begins from the location of the insertion point and proceeds to the end of the document, it is good practice to position the insertion point at the beginning of the document before initiating the command.

2 On the **Home tab**, in the **Editing group**, click **Find**.

> The Navigation pane displays on the left side of the screen with a search box at the top of the pane.

 MAC TIP Display the menu, click Edit, point to Find, click Replace; use this navigation pane for Steps 3-5.

3 In the search box, type **ac** If necessary, scroll down slightly in your document to view the entire body text of the letter, and then compare your screen with Figure 2.34.

> In the document, the search letters *ac* are selected and highlighted in yellow for both words that begin with the letters *ac* and also for the word *contact*, which contains this letter combination. In the Navigation pane, the three instances are shown in context—*ac* displays in bold.

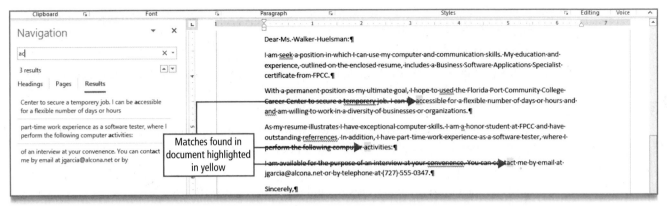

Figure 2.34

> **4** Click in the search box again, and type as necessary to display the word *accessible* in the search box.

> > One match for the search term displays in context in the Navigation pane and is highlighted in the document.

> **5** In the document, double-click the yellow highlighted word *accessible*, and then type **available** to replace the word.

MAC TIP Complete this step in the Find and Replace navigation pane; move to Step 7 (do not close the pane).

> **6** **Close** ☒ the **Navigation** pane.

> **7** On the **Home tab**, in the **Editing group**, click **Replace**.

MAC TIP Click the Settings icon, click Advanced Find & Replace, click the Replace tab.

> **8** In the **Find and Replace** dialog box, in the **Find what** box, replace the existing text by typing **FPCC** In the **Replace with** box, type **Florida Port Community College** and then compare your screen with Figure 2.35.

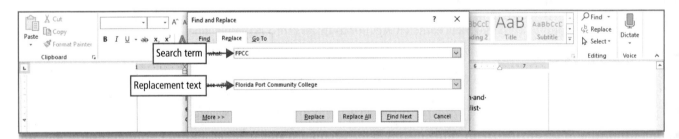

Figure 2.35

> **9** In the lower left corner of the dialog box, click **More** to expand the dialog box, and then under **Search Options**, select the **Match case** check box.

> > The acronym *FPCC* appears in the document two times. In a formal letter, the reader may not know what the acronym means, so you should include the full text instead of an acronym. In this instance, you must select the *Match case* check box so that the replaced text will match the case you typed in the Replace with box, and *not* display in all uppercase letters in the manner of *FPCC*.

MAC TIP Be sure All appears in the Search list box.

10 In the **Find and Replace** dialog box, click **Replace All** to replace both instances of *FPCC*. Click **OK** to close the message box.

11 In the **Find and Replace** dialog box, clear the **Match case** check box, click **Less**, and then **Close** the dialog box.

The Find and Replace dialog box opens with the settings used the last time it was open. Therefore, it is good practice to reset this dialog box to its default settings each time you use it.

MAC TIP   Close the Find & Replace pane.

12 **Save** your document.

Activity 2.17 | Selecting Text and Moving Text by Using Drag and Drop

By using Word's *drag-and-drop* feature, you can use the mouse to drag selected text from one location to another. This method is most useful when the text you are moving is on the same screen as the destination location.

1 Take a moment to study the table in Figure 2.36 to become familiar with the techniques you can use to select text in a document quickly.

Selecting Text in a Document	
To select this:	**Do this:**
A portion of text	Click to position the insertion point at the beginning of the text you want to select, hold down Shift, and then click at the end of the text you want to select. Alternatively, hold down the left mouse button and drag from the beginning to the end of the text you want to select.
A word	Double-click the word.
A sentence	Hold down Ctrl and click anywhere in the sentence. (Mac users: Hold down command ⌘)
A paragraph	Triple-click anywhere in the paragraph; or, move the pointer to the left of the line, into the margin area. When the ⟋ pointer displays, double-click.
A line	Move the pointer to the left of the line. When the ⟋ pointer displays, click one time.
One character at a time	Position the insertion point to the left of the first character, hold down Shift, and press ← or → as many times as desired.
A string of words	Position the insertion point to the left of the first word, hold down Shift and Ctrl, and then press ← or → as many times as desired. (Mac users: Hold down command ⌘. This will select the rest of the text in the line before or after the insertion point.)
Consecutive lines	Position the insertion point to the left of the first word, hold down Shift and press ↑ or ↓.
Consecutive paragraphs	Position the insertion point to the left of the first word, hold down Shift and Ctrl and press ↑ or ↓. (Mac users: Hold down command ⌘)
The entire document	Hold down Ctrl and press A. Alternatively, move the pointer to the left of any line in the document. When the ⟋ pointer displays, triple-click. (Mac users: Hold down command ⌘)

Figure 2.36

2 Be sure you can view the entire body of the letter on your screen. In the paragraph that begins *With a permanent position*, in the second line, locate and double-click *days*.

3 Point to the selected word to display the ⬚ pointer.

4 Drag to the right until the dotted vertical line that floats next to the pointer is positioned to the right of the word *hours* in the same line, as shown in Figure 2.37.

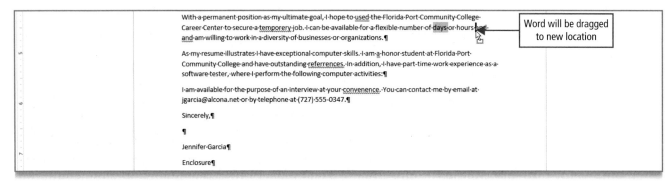

With·a·permanent·position·as·my·ultimate·goal,·I·hope·to·used·the·Florida·Port·Community·College·
Career·Center·to·secure·a·temporery·job.·I·can·be·available·for·a·flexible·number·of·days·or·hours·and·
and·am·willing·to·work·in·a·diversity·of·businesses·or·organizations.¶

As·my·resume·illustrates·I·have·exceptional·computer·skills.·I·am·a·honor·student·at·Florida·Port·
Community·College·and·have·outstanding·referrences.·In·addition,·I·have·part-time·work·experience·as·a·
software·tester,·where·I·perform·the·following·computer·activities:¶

I·am·available·for·the·purpose·of·an·interview·at·your·convenence.·You·can·contact·me·by·email·at·
jgarcia@alcona.net·or·by·telephone·at·(727)·555-0347.¶

Sincerely,¶

¶

Jennifer·Garcia¶

Enclosure¶

Word will be dragged to new location

Figure 2.37

5 Release the mouse button to move the text. Select the word *hours* and drag it to the left of the word *or*—the previous location of the word *days*. Click anywhere in the document to deselect the text.

6 Examine the text that you moved, and add or remove spaces as necessary.

7 Hold down Ctrl, and then in the paragraph that begins *I am available*, click anywhere in the first sentence to select the entire sentence.

⬚ **MAC TIP** Hold down command ⌘.

8 Release Ctrl. Drag the selected sentence to the end of the paragraph by positioning the small vertical line that floats with the pointer to the left of the paragraph mark. **Save** 💾 your document, and then compare your screen with Figure 2.38.

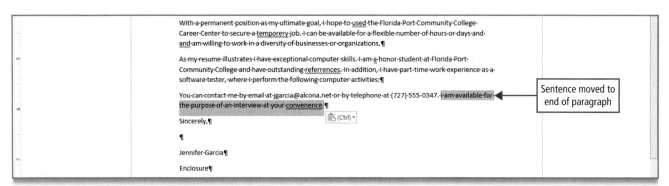

With·a·permanent·position·as·my·ultimate·goal,·I·hope·to·used·the·Florida·Port·Community·College·
Career·Center·to·secure·a·temporery·job.·I·can·be·available·for·a·flexible·number·of·hours·or·days·and·
and·am·willing·to·work·in·a·diversity·of·businesses·or·organizations.¶

As·my·resume·illustrates·I·have·exceptional·computer·skills.·I·am·a·honor·student·at·Florida·Port·
Community·College·and·have·outstanding·referrences.·In·addition,·I·have·part-time·work·experience·as·a·
software·tester,·where·I·perform·the·following·computer·activities:¶

You·can·contact·me·by·email·at·jgarcia@alcona.net·or·by·telephone·at·(727)·555-0347.·I·am·available·for·
the·purpose·of·an·interview·at·your·convenence.¶

Sincerely,¶

¶

Jennifer·Garcia¶

Enclosure¶

Sentence moved to end of paragraph

Figure 2.38

Activity 2.18 | Inserting a Table into a Document and Applying a Table Style

1 Locate the paragraph that begins *You can contact me*, and then click to position the insertion point at the beginning of the paragraph. Press Enter one time, and then press ↑ one time to position the insertion point in the new blank paragraph.

2 With the insertion point in the new blank paragraph, on the **Insert tab**, in the **Tables group**, click **Table**. In the **Table** grid, in the third row, click the second square to insert a 2x3 table.

3 In the first cell of the table, type **Microsoft Access** and then press Tab. Type **Test database queries** and then press Tab. Complete the table using the following information:

Microsoft Excel	Enter software test data
Microsoft Word	Create and mail form letters

4 On the **Table Tools Layout tab**, in the **Table group**, click **Select**, and then click **Select Table**.

5 On the **Table Tools Layout tab**, in the **Cell Size group**, click **AutoFit**, and then click **AutoFit Contents** to have Word choose the best column widths for the two columns based on the text you entered.

6 With the table still selected, under **Table Tools**, click the **Design tab**. In the **Table Styles group**, click **More** ⏷. Under **Plain Tables**, click the second style—**Table Grid Light**.

Use Table Styles to change the visual style of a table.

7 With the table still selected, on the **Home tab**, in the **Paragraph group**, click **Center** ☰ to center the table between the left and right margins. Click anywhere to deselect the table.

8 Select the blank paragraph under the table, and then on the **Layout tab**, in the **Paragraph group**, change the **Spacing After** to **0 pt**.

9 Save 🖫 and then compare your screen with Figure 2.39.

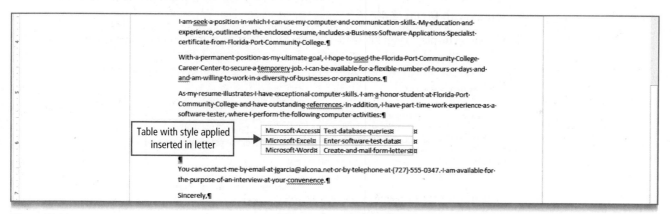

Figure 2.39

Objective 6 Use the Word Editor to Check Your Document

ALERT Activating Proofing

If you do not see any red squiggles or double blue underlines under words, the automatic spelling and/or grammar checking has been turned off on your system. To activate the spelling and grammar checking, display Backstage view, click Options, click Proofing, and then under *When correcting spelling in Microsoft Office programs*, select the first four check boxes. Under *When correcting spelling and grammar in Word*, select the first four check boxes, and then click the Writing Style arrow and click Grammar & Refinements. Under *Exceptions for*, clear both check boxes. To display the flagged items, click the Recheck Document button, and then close the dialog box.

GO! Learn How
Video W2-6

The best way to check your document is to use the Word **Editor**, which, according to Microsoft, is your digital writing assistant in Word. Editor flags misspellings, grammatical mistakes, and writing style issues as you type by marking red squiggles for spelling, blue double underlines for grammar—for example, the misuse of *their*, *there*, and *they're*—and brown dotted underlines for writing issues such as clarity and concise language.

Word will not flag the word *sign* as misspelled even though you intended to type *sing a song* rather than *sign a song*, because both are words contained within Word's dictionary. Your own knowledge and proofreading skills are still required, even when using a sophisticated word processing program like Word.

Activity 2.19 | Using the Word Editor to Check for Spelling, Grammar, and Writing Issues

There are two ways to respond to spelling, grammar, and writing items flagged by Word. You can right-click a flagged word or phrase, and then from the shortcut menu choose a correction or action. Or, you can launch Editor, which provides more options than the shortcut menus.

> **ALERT**   The Word Editor may vary in flagging items; your results may not match the screens and steps exactly but you will be able to make appropriate adjustments to the text.

1 Position the body of the letter on your screen, and then examine the text to locate the various items that Word has flagged as potential errors.

A list of grammar rules applied by a computer program like Word can never be exact, and a computer dictionary cannot contain all known words and proper names. Therefore, you will need to check any words flagged by Word, and you will also need to proofread for content errors.

2 In the lower left corner of your screen, in the status bar, locate and point to the ⬚ icon to display the ScreenTip *Word found proofing errors. Click or tap to correct them.* Compare your screen with Figure 2.40.

If this button displays, you know there are potential errors identified in the document.

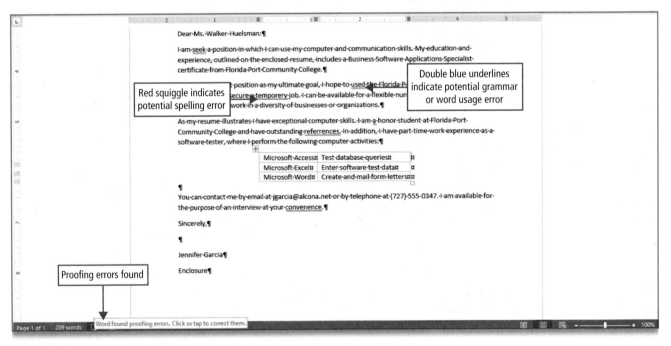

Figure 2.40

3 In the paragraph that begins *With a permanent*, in the second line, locate the word *temporery* with the red squiggle. Point to the word and right-click, and then click **temporary** to correct the spelling error.

> ⬚ **MAC TIP**   Hold down control and click the misspelled word to display the shortcut menu.

4 In the next line, locate the word *and* that displays with a red squiggle, point to the word and right-click, and then on the shortcut menu, click **Delete Repeated Word** to delete the duplicate word.

5 Press Ctrl + Home to move the insertion point to the beginning of the document. Click the **Review tab**, and then in the **Proofing group**, click **Check Document** (or yours may indicate *Spelling & Grammar*). If the proper name *Huelsman* is flagged, you can Ignore All.

Word's dictionary contains only very common proper names—unusual names like this may be flagged as a potential spelling error. If this is a name that you frequently type, consider adding it to the dictionary.

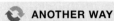 **ANOTHER WAY**   press F7 to start the Editor; Mac users, fn + F7 .

ALERT   **The Order of Flagged Items May Vary**

Your Editor pane might consolidate issues. If you see a Results button, click it, and proceed with correcting spelling and grammar and writing issues. The order of flagged items may differ from the Steps below.

6 Compare your screen with Figure 2.41.

The word *seek* is highlighted as a grammar error, and *seeking* is suggested.

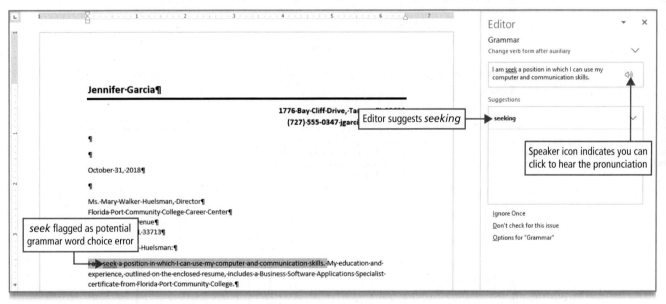

Figure 2.41

7 In the **Editor** pane, under **Suggestions**, click **seeking** to change to the correct usage.

The next marked word—a possible grammar error—displays.

MAC TIP   Click Change.

8 Compare your screen with Figure 2.42 to see the next flagged item.

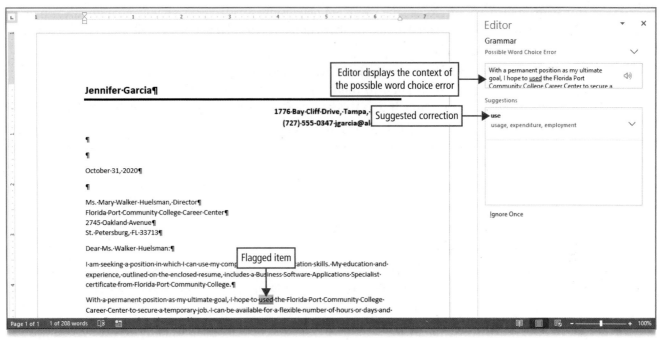

Figure 2.42

> **9** Under **Suggestions**, click **use** to change *used* to *use*. Compare your screen with Figure 2.43.
>
>> For the next flagged item, Word indicates a writing issue for clarity and conciseness. Indicating that you have an "ultimate goal" might be an overstatement—Word suggests using only "goal."

NOTE Depending on recent updates to Word, the order of corrections in the next steps may vary. Use the suggestions to make appropriate corrections until you reach Step 12.

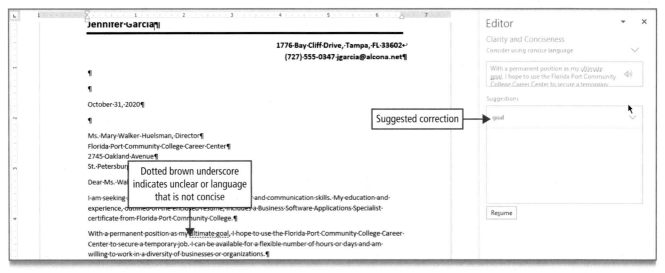

Figure 2.43

> **10** Under **Suggestions**, click **goal** to delete the word *ultimate*; or make this change manually.
>
> **11** Under **Suggestions**, click **references** to correct the spelling error, and then under **Suggestions**, click **an** to correct the grammar error. Click **convenience** to correct the spelling error.

NOTE If Word does not flag this on your system, edit your document to make this change.

12 To use more concise language, click **for** to replace the phrase *for the purpose of*, or if this is not flagged on your system, in the paragraph above *Sincerely*, delete the words *the purpose of*.

13 In the message box indicating the check is complete, click **OK**.

14 **Save** 🖫 your document. If necessary, Close the Editor pane.

Activity 2.20 | Using the Thesaurus

1.3.2

A *thesaurus* is a research tool that lists *synonyms*—words that have the same or similar meaning to the word you selected.

1 Scroll so that you can view the body of the letter. In the paragraph that begins *With a permanent*, in the last line, double-click to select the word *diversity*, and then in the **Proofing** group, click **Thesaurus**.

> The Thesaurus pane displays on the right with a list of synonyms; the list will vary in length depending on the selected word.

🔄 **ANOTHER WAY**   Right-click the word, on the shortcut menu, point to Synonyms, and then click Thesaurus.

2 In the **Thesaurus** pane, point to the word *variety*, and then click the arrow that displays. Click **Insert** to change *diversity* to *variety*.

🖥 **MAC TIP**   Hold down ctrl, click *variety*, click Insert.

3 In the paragraph that begins *As my resume*, double-click the word *exceptional*, and then on the ribbon, click **Thesaurus** again.

4 In the **Thesaurus** pane, point to *excellent*, click the **arrow**, and then click **Insert**. Compare your screen with Figure 2.44.

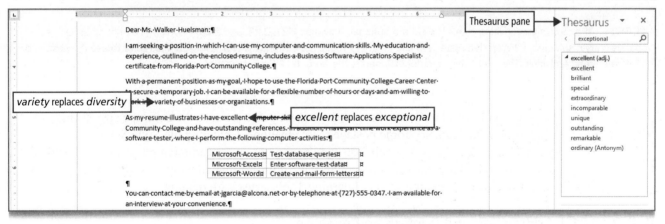

Figure 2.44

5 **Close** ☒ the **Thesaurus** pane.

6 Click the **File tab** to display **Backstage** view, and then on the **Info tab**, in the lower right portion of the screen, click **Show All Properties**.

🖥 **MAC TIP**   Display the menu bar, click File, click Properties, click the Summary tab. For Tags, use Keywords.

7 In the **Tags** box, type **cover letter** and in the **Subject** box, type your course name and section number. In the **Author** box, be sure your name is indicated and edit if necessary.

8 On the left, click **Save**. In the upper right corner of the Word window, click **Close** ⊠.

MAC TIP Click Save on the Quick Access Toolbar.

For Non-MyLab Submissions Determine What Your Instructor Requires for Submission
As directed by your instructor, submit your completed Word file.

---

9 In **MyLab IT**, locate and click the Grader Project **Word 2B Cover Letter**. In **step 3**, under **Upload Completed Assignment**, click **Choose File**. In the **Open** dialog box, navigate to your **Word Chapter 2 folder**, and then click your **Student_Word_2B_Cover_Letter** file one time to select it. In the lower right corner of the **Open** dialog box, click **Open**.

The name of your selected file displays above the Upload button.

10 To submit your file to **MyLab IT** for grading, click **Upload**, wait a moment for a green **Success!** message, and then in **step 4**, click the blue **Submit for Grading** button. Click **Close Assignment** to return to your list of **Course Materials**.

You have completed Project 2B **END**

Objective 7 | **Print an Envelope, Change a Style Set, Create a Word Template, and Use Learning Tools**

ALERT The remaining activities in this Project are optional. Activities 2.21, 2.22, and 2.23, in which you print an envelope, change a style set, create a Word template, and use Learning Tools, are optional. Check with your instructor to see if you should complete these Activities. These Activities are not included in the **MyLab IT** Grader system.

Student Training
Video W2-7

Word's command to Create Envelopes enables you to choose the envelope size, format the addresses, and add electronic postage to an envelope. Changing the Style Set is easily accomplished from the Design tab. You can create your own custom templates in Word, and you might also want to use one of Word's thousands of pre-formatted templates, for which you can search from Word's opening screen. Learning Tools assist with reading.

Activity 2.21 | **Addressing and Printing an Envelope**

Use Word's Envelopes command on the Mailings tab to format and print an envelope.

1 Display your **2B_Cover_Letter**, select the four lines that comprise the inside address.

2 On the **Mailings tab**, in the **Create group**, click **Envelopes** and notice that the selected text is filled in as the **Delivery address**.

3 Click in the **Return address** box.

MAC TIP Deselect *Use my address*.

4 Type **Jennifer Garcia** and press Enter. Type **1776 Bay Cliff Drive** and then press Enter. Type **Tampa, FL 33602**

5 In the lower portion of the **Envelopes and Labels** dialog box, click **Options**, and then compare your screen with Figure 2.45.

The default envelope size is a standard business envelope referred to as a Size 10.

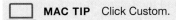 **MAC TIP** Click Custom.

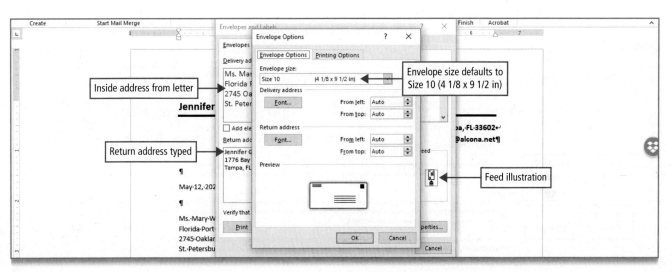

Figure 2.45

6 Click **OK** to close the **Envelope Options** dialog box. As shown under **Feed**, insert an envelope in your printer and then click **Print**.

Depending on the type and brand of printer you are using, your feed area may vary.

7 If necessary, **Close** ☒ the **Envelopes and Labels** dialog box. Leave your **2B_Cover_Letter** open for the next Activity.

Activity 2.22 | Changing a Style Set

1.2.2, 2.2.4

The Paragraph Spacing command offers various options for changing the style set so that you can set the line and paragraph spacing of your entire document. A gallery of predefined values displays; or you can create your own custom paragraph spacing.

1 With your **2B_Cover_Letter** displayed, click the **File tab**, on the left click **Save As**, click **Browse**, navigate to your **Word Chapter 2** folder, and then using your own name, save this document as **Lastname_Firstname_2B_Cover_Letter_No_Paragraph_Space**

2 On the **Home tab**, in the **Editing group**, click **Select**, and then click **Select All**.

3 On the **Design tab**, in the **Document Formatting group**, click **Paragraph Spacing**, and then under **Built-In**, click **No Paragraph Space**.

With no spacing after a paragraph, to use this style set, you will need to insert blank paragraphs to create appropriate space within your letter.

4 Click at the end of the dateline, and then press Enter four times to move the first line of the inside address to approximately two inches from the top of the paper.

5 Click after the ZIP code in the inside address and press Enter one time. Click at the end of the salutation and press Enter one time.

6 ▶ Click at the end of the first paragraph of body text and press [Enter] one time. Click at the end of the second paragraph of body text and press [Enter] one time.

7 ▶ Click after the colon above the table and press [Enter] one time. Click at the end of the last paragraph of body text and press [Enter] one time.

8 ▶ Click at the end of the closing and press [Enter] two times to leave three blank paragraphs between the closing and the writer's identification. Click after *Garcia* and press [Enter] one time to leave a blank paragraph between the writer's identification and the Enclosure notation. Compare your screen with Figure 2.46.

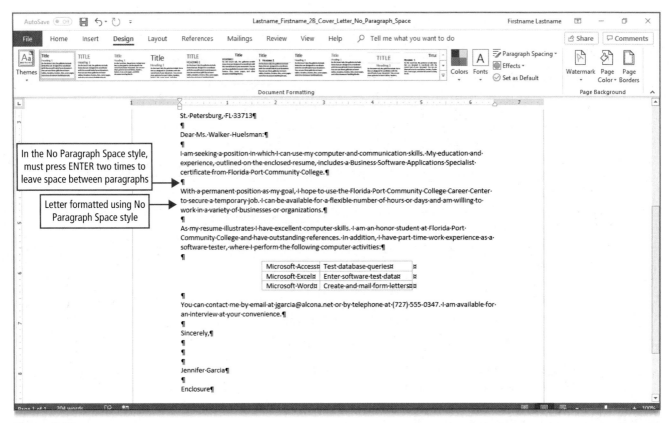

Figure 2.46

9 ▶ Save 💾 your document and in the upper right corner of the Word window, click **Close** ☒. Submit if directed to do so by your instructor.

Activity 2.23 | Creating a Word Template

A ***template*** is a file you use as a starting point for a *new* document. A template has a predefined document structure and defined settings, such as font, margins, and available styles. On Word's opening screen, you can select from among many different templates—or you can create your own custom template.

When you open a template as the starting point for a new document, the template file opens a copy of itself, unnamed, and then you use the structure—and possibly some content, such as headings—as the starting point for a new document.

All documents are based on a template. When you create a new blank document, it is based on Word's ***Normal template***, which serves as the starting point for all blank Word documents.

1 ▶ Start Word and click **Blank document**. Type **Jennifer Garcia** and then press [Enter].

2 ▸ Type **1776 Bay Cliff Drive, Tampa, FL 33602** hold down Shift and then press Enter.

3 ▸ Type **(727) 555-0347 jgarcia@alcona.net** and then press Enter. If the email address changes to blue text, right-click the email address, and then click **Remove Hyperlink**.

4 ▸ Select the first paragraph—*Jennifer Garcia*—and then on the mini toolbar, apply **Bold** B and change the **Font Size** to **16**.

5 ▸ Select the two address lines that form the second paragraph. On the mini toolbar, apply **Bold** B and change the **Font Size** to **12**.

6 ▸ With the two-line paragraph still selected, on the **Home tab**, in the **Paragraph group**, click **Align Right** ≡.

7 ▸ Click anywhere in the first paragraph—*Jennifer Garcia*. In the **Paragraph group**, click the **Borders button arrow** ⊞ ▾, and then at the bottom, click **Borders and Shading**.

8 ▸ In the **Borders and Shading** dialog box, on the **Borders tab**, under **Style**, be sure the first style—a single solid line—is selected.

9 ▸ Click the **Width arrow**, and then click **3 pt**. To the right, under **Preview**, click the bottom border of the diagram. Under **Apply to**, be sure *Paragraph* displays.

10 ▸ Click **OK** to display a 3 pt line below *Jennifer Garcia*, which extends from the left margin to the right margin.

11 ▸ Click the **File tab**, on the left click **Save As**, and then click **Browse** to display the **Save As** dialog box.

12 ▸ In the lower portion of the **Save As** dialog box, click the **Save as type arrow**, and then on the list click **Word Template**. At the top of the **Save As** dialog box, examine the path in the **address bar** as shown in Figure 2.47.

By default, Word stores template files that you create on the hard drive of your computer in your user folder, in a folder named Custom Office Templates. By doing so, the template is always available to you from this folder.

MAC TIP Click the File Format arrow.

Path to Custom Office Templates folder

Your name will differ

Figure 2.47

13 ▸ Click in the **File name** box, and then using your own name, type **Lastname_Firstname_2B_Letterhead_Template** Click **Save**.

MAC TIP Click in the Save As box.

14 ▸ In the upper right corner of the Word window, click **Close** ✕.

15 ▸ In **File Explorer**, navigate to the **Documents** folder on your hard drive, and then double-click to open the folder **Custom Office Templates**. Double-click your **Lastname_Firstname_2B_Letterhead_Template** document. Compare your screen with Figure 2.48.

Word opens a copy of your 2B_Letterhead_Template in the form of a new Word document. The title bar indicates *Document* followed by a number. You are not opening the original template file, and changes that you make to this new document will not affect the contents of your stored 2B_Letterhead_Template file. You can insert text into the document, and then save it with an appropriate name.

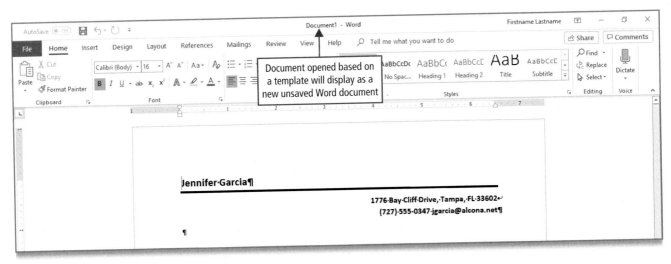

Figure 2.48

16 In the upper right corner of the Word window, click **Close** ⊠.

Activity 2.24 | Using Learning Tools and Read Aloud

Learning Tools are features in Word that add visual changes to assist with reading fluency and comprehension. You enable Learning Tools from the View tab, and depending on how you want to focus on your document while viewing it on your screen, you can enable various commands.

The *Page Color* command changes the color to make the text easy to scan and consume; for example, you can set the Page color to *Sepia* (pale yellow with print feel) or to *Inverse* (black background with white text).

The *Column Width* command changes the width of the line length to fit more or less text on each line. Options include Very Narrow, Narrow, Moderate, or Wide. The *Text Spacing* command increases spacing between words, characters, and lines.

The *Syllables* command shows breaks between syllables of words. If you are editing, you can type and make edits to your document and the syllable marks will appear in real time as you type.

The *Read Aloud* command reads text out loud and highlights each word as it is read. This command is available in both Word and Outlook. If you start typing while this feature is enabled, the narration will pause so you can make edits and then resume the narration. The Read Aloud command is also available on the Review tab so you can use it in any of Word's views.

1 Open your completed **2B_Cover_Letter** document, and then click to position your insertion point at the beginning of the paragraph that begins *I am seeking.*

2 Be sure that your computer speaker is on, and if you are in a college lab or public space, use headphones. On the **Review tab**, in the **Speech group**, click **Read Aloud** to hear a narration of the text, and notice that as each word is read aloud, it is highlighted.

3 Click **Read Aloud** again to stop the narration.

4 Click the **View tab**, and then in the **Immersive group**, click **Learning Tools**.

5 Click **Column Width**, and then click **Very Narrow**. Click **Page Color**, and then click **Sepia**. If necessary, click **Text Spacing**. Click **Syllables**, and then compare your screen with Figure 2.49.

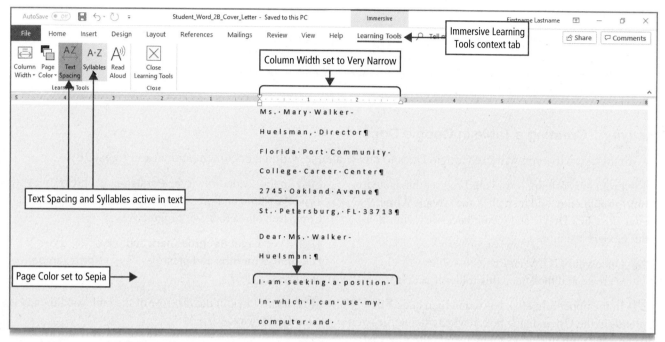

Figure 2.49

6 On the ribbon, click **Close Learning Tools**.

7 In the upper right corner of the Word window, click **Close** ☒.

You have completed the optional portion of this Project **END**

»»» GO! With Google Docs

Objective	Create a Table in Google Docs

> **ALERT** **Working with Web-Based Applications and Services**
>
> Computer programs and services on the web receive continuous updates and improvements, so the steps to complete this web-based Activity may differ from the ones shown. You can often look at the screens and the information presented to determine how to complete the Activity.
>
> If you do not already have a Google account, you will need to create one before you begin this Activity. Go to http://google.com and, in the upper right corner, click Sign In. On the Sign In screen, click Create Account. On the Create your Google Account page, complete the form, read and agree to the Terms of Service and Privacy Policy, and then click Next step. On the Welcome screen, click Get Started.

Activity | Creating a Table in Google Docs

In this Activity, you will use Google Docs to create a table within a document similar to Project 2B.

1 From the desktop, open your browser, navigate to **http://google.com**, and then click the **Google Apps** menu ▦. Click **Drive**, and then if necessary, sign in to your Google account.

2 Open your **GO! Web Projects** folder—or click New to create and then open this folder if necessary.

3 In the upper left, click **New**, and then click **File upload**. In the **Open** dialog box, navigate to the files you downloaded with this project, and then in the **File List**, double-click to open **w02_2B_Web**.

4 When the upload is complete, in the **Google Drive file list**, double-click the document to open it in Google Docs. If necessary, click Open with Google Docs.

5 Click in the document and then press Ctrl + End to move to the end of the document. Press Enter one time.

6 On the menu bar, click **Insert**, point to **Table**, and then insert a 3x4 table.

7 Type **Position** and press Tab. Type **Type** and press Tab. Type **Location** and press Tab.

8 In the second row type **Paralegal** and press Tab. Type **Part-time** and press Tab. Type **Tampa** and press Tab. Compare your screen with Figure A.

9 Type **Legal Records Clerk** and press Tab. Type **Full-time, 2 months** and press Tab. Type **North Tampa** and press Tab.

10 Right-click in the last row of the table, and then click **Delete row**.

11 Drag to select all the cells in the first row. On the toolbar, click the **Normal text button arrow** , and then click **Heading 2**. With the three column titles still selected, on the toolbar, locate and click **Center**.

12 Press Ctrl + Home to move to the top of the document, and then compare your screen with Figure B.

13 Submit the file as directed by your instructor. In the upper right, click your user name, and then click **Sign out**. **Close** your browser window. Your file is automatically saved in your Google Drive.

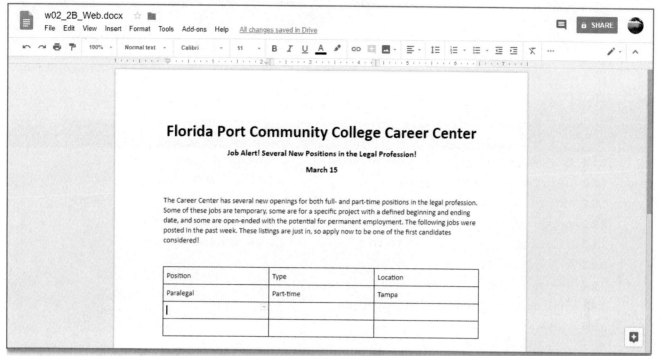

Figure A

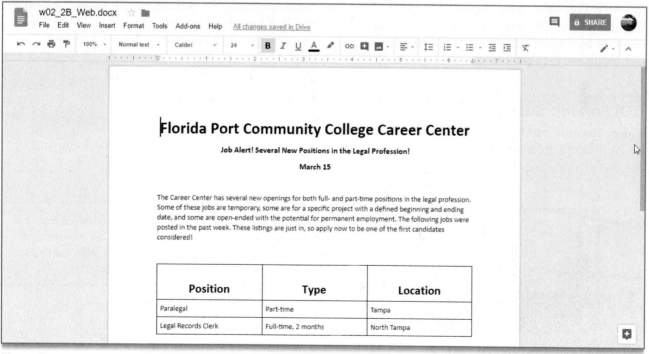

Figure B

wavebreakmedia/Shutterstock, Monkey Business Images/Fotolia, Ivanko80/Shutterstock, Monkey Business Images/Shutterstock

Microsoft Office Specialist (MOS) Skills in This Chapter	
Project 2A	**Project 2B**
1.1.4 Show and hide formatting symbols and hidden text	**1.1.1** Search for text
1.2.3 Insert and modify headers and footers	**1.2.2** Apply style sets
1.3.2 Modify basic document properties	**1.3.2** Modify basic document properties
2.2.2 Apply formatting by using Format Painter	**2.1.1** Find and replace text
3.1.3 Create tables by specifying rows and columns	**2.2.4** Apply built-in styles to text
3.2.3 Merge and split cells	
3.2.4 Resize tables, rows, and columns	
3.3.1 Format paragraphs as numbered and bulleted lists	
3.3.4 Increase and decrease list levels	

Build Your E-Portfolio

An E-Portfolio is a collection of evidence, stored electronically, that showcases what you have accomplished while completing your education. Collecting and then sharing your work products with potential employers reflects your academic and career goals. Your completed documents from the following projects are good examples to show what you have learned: 2G, 2K, and 2L.

GO! For Job Success

Video: Resume and Cover Letter Tips

Your instructor may assign this video to your class, and then ask you to think about, or discuss with your classmates, these questions:

g-stockstudio/Shutterstock

A cover letter should contain information that is different from but complimentary to the information than the facts on your resume and be tailored to the specific job you are applying for. Name two different things that you could mention in a cover letter.

Why should you avoid fancy layout techniques or elaborate templates for your resume document?

Why is creating and then including a LinkedIn page on your resume a good idea?

End of Chapter

Summary

Word tables enable you to present information in a logical and orderly format. Each cell in a Word table behaves like a document; as you type in a cell, wordwrap moves text to the next line.

A good source of information for resume formats is a Business Communications textbook. A simple two-column table created in Word is suitable to create an appropriate resume for a recent college graduate.

Instead of switching to old-fashioned single-spacing to create a letter, use Word's default settings and then apply Spacing after of 0 pt to all but the last line of the inside address.

Business letters follow a standard format and should always contain a dateline, an inside address, a salutation, body text, a complimentary closing, and the writer's identification.

GO! Learn It Online

Review the concepts, key terms, and MOS skills in this chapter by completing these online challenges, which you can find at **MyLab IT**.

Chapter Quiz: Answer matching and multiple choice questions to test what you learned in this chapter.

Lessons on the GO!: Learn how to use all the new apps and features as they are introduced by Microsoft.

MOS Prep Quiz: Answer questions to review the MOS skills that you practiced in this chapter.

GO! Collaborative Team Project (Available in Instructor Resource Center)

If your instructor assigns this project to your class, you can expect to work with one or more of your classmates—either in person or by using internet tools—to create work products similar to those that you created in this chapter. A team is a group of workers who work together to solve a problem, make a decision, or create a work product. Collaboration is when you work together with others as a team in an intellectual endeavor to complete a shared task or achieve a shared goal.

Monkey Business Images/Fotolia

Project Guide for Word Chapter 2

Your instructor will assign Projects from this list to ensure your learning and assess your knowledge.

		Project Guide for Word Chapter 2		
Project	**Apply Skills from These Chapter Objectives**	**Project Type**		**Project Location**
2A MyLab IT	Objectives 1-3 from Project 2A	**2A Instructional Project (Grader Project)** Guided instruction to learn the skills in Project A.	Instruction	In **MyLab IT** and in text
2B MyLab IT	Objectives 4-7 from Project 2B	**2B Instructional Project (Grader Project)** Guided instruction to learn the skills in Project B.	Instruction	In **MyLab IT** and in text
2C	Objectives 1-3 from Project 2A	**2C Skills Review (Scorecard Grading)** A guided review of the skills from Project 2A.	Review	In text
2D	Objectives 4-7 from Project 2B	**2D Skills Review (Scorecard Grading)** A guided review of the skills from Project 2B.	Review	In text
2E MyLab IT	Objectives 1-3 from Project 2A	**2E Mastery (Grader Project)** A demonstration of your mastery of the skills in Project 2A with extensive decision-making.	Mastery and Transfer of Learning	In **MyLab IT** and in text
2F MyLab IT	Objectives 4-7 from Project 2B	**2F Mastery (Grader Project)** A demonstration of your mastery of the skills in Project 2B with extensive decision-making.	Mastery and Transfer of Learning	In **MyLab IT** and in text
2G MyLab IT	Objectives 1 -7 from Projects 2A and 2B	**2G Mastery (Grader Project)** A demonstration of your mastery of the skills in Projects 2A and 2B with extensive decision-making.	Mastery and Transfer of Learning	In **MyLab IT** and in text
2H	Combination of Objectives from Projects 2A and 2B	**2H GO! Fix It (Scorecard Grading)** A demonstration of your mastery of the skills in Projects 2A and 2B by creating a correct result from a document that contains errors you must find.	Critical Thinking	IRC
2I	Combination of Objectives from Projects 2A and 2B	**2I GO! Make It (Scorecard Grading)** A demonstration of your mastery of the skills in Projects 2A and 2B by creating a result from a supplied picture.	Critical Thinking	IRC
2J	Combination of Objectives from Projects 2A and 2B	**2J GO! Solve It (Rubric Grading)** A demonstration of your mastery of the skills in Projects 2A and 2B, your decision-making skills, and your critical thinking skills. A task-specific rubric helps you self-assess your result.	Critical Thinking	IRC
2K	Combination of Objectives from Projects 2A and 2B	**2K GO! Solve It (Rubric Grading)** A demonstration of your mastery of the skills in Projects 2A and 2B, your decision-making skills, and your critical thinking skills. A task-specific rubric helps you self-assess your result.	Critical Thinking	In text
2L	Combination of Objectives from Projects 2A and 2B	**2L GO! Think (Rubric Grading)** A demonstration of your understanding of the Chapter concepts applied in a manner that you would outside of college. An analytic rubric helps you and your instructor grade the quality of your work by comparing it to the work an expert in the discipline would create.	Critical Thinking	In text
2M	Combination of Objectives from Projects 2A and 2B	**2M GO! Think (Rubric Grading)** A demonstration of your understanding of the Chapter concepts applied in a manner that you would outside of college. An analytic rubric helps you and your instructor grade the quality of your work by comparing it to the work an expert in the discipline would create.	Critical Thinking	IRC
2N	Combination of Objectives from Projects 2A and 2B	**2N You and GO! (Rubric Grading)** A demonstration of your understanding of the Chapter concepts applied in a manner that you would in a personal situation. An analytic rubric helps you and your instructor grade the quality of your work.	Critical Thinking	IRC
2O	Combination of Objectives from Projects 2A and 2B	**2O Collaborative Team Project for Word Chapter 2** A demonstration of your understanding of concepts and your ability to work collaboratively in a group role-playing assessment, requiring both collaboration and self-management.	Critical Thinking	IRC

Glossary

Glossary of Chapter Key Terms

AutoCorrect A feature that corrects common typing and spelling errors as you type, for example changing *teh* to *the*.

Body The text of a letter.

Cell The box at the intersection of a row and column in a Word table.

Cell margins The space inside a table cell between the text and the cell borders—top, bottom, left, and right.

Column Width A Learning Tools command that changes the width of the line length to fit more or less text on each line; options include Very Narrow, Narrow, Moderate, or Wide.

Complimentary closing A parting farewell in a business letter.

Cover letter A document that you send with your resume to provide additional information about your skills and experience.

Date & Time A command with which you can automatically insert the current date and time into a document in a variety of formats.

Dateline The first line in a business letter that contains the current date and which is positioned just below the letterhead if a letterhead is used.

Drag-and-drop A technique by which you can move, by dragging, selected text from one location in a document to another.

Editor A digital writing assistant in Word that flags misspellings, grammatical errors, and writing style issues.

Enclosures Additional documents included with a business letter.

Inside address The name and address of the person receiving the letter; always positioned below the date line.

Inverse A Page Color in Learning Tools that displays the text in white on a black background.

Learning Tools Features in Word that add visual changes to assist with reading fluency and comprehension.

Letterhead The personal or company information that displays at the top of a letter, and which commonly includes a name, address, and contact information.

Line break indicator A formatting mark in the shape of a bent arrow that indicates a manual line break.

LinkedIn A professional networking website that focuses on business and employment-oriented services and on which you can build and share your professional identify and connect with others in your field of interest.

Manual line break A line break that moves the text to the right of the insertion point to a new line while keeping the text in the same paragraph.

No Paragraph Space The built-in paragraph style—available from the Paragraph Spacing command—that inserts *no* extra space before or after a paragraph and uses line spacing of 1.

Normal template The template that serves as a basis for all Word documents.

Office Presentation Service A Word feature to present your Word document to others who can watch in a web browser.

One-click Row/Column Insertion A Word table feature with which you can insert a new row or column by pointing to the desired location and then clicking.

Page Color A Learning Tools command that changes the color of the page to make the text easy to scan and consume.

Read Aloud A Learning Tools command that reads text out loud and highlights each word as it is read; this command is available in both Word and Outlook.

Resume Assistant A feature in Word with which you can see suggestions from LinkedIn to help you update your resume.

Salutation The greeting line of a business letter.

Sepia A Page Color command in Learning Tools that shades the screen in pale yellow with a print feel.

Single spacing The common name for line spacing in which there is *no* extra space before or after a paragraph; uses line spacing of 1.

Skype A Microsoft product with which you can make voice calls, make video calls, transfer files, or send messages—including instant messages and text messages—over the Internet.

Style set A collection of character and paragraph formatting that is stored and named.

Subject line The optional line following the inside address in a business letter that states the purpose of the letter.

Syllables A Learning Tools command that shows breaks between syllables of words.

Synonyms Words with the same or similar meaning.

Table (Word) An arrangement of information organized into rows and columns.

Template An existing document that you use as a starting point for a new document; it opens a copy of itself, unnamed, and then you use the structure—and possibly some content, such as headings—as the starting point for a new document.

Text from File A command to insert text from another file into your document.

Text Spacing A Learning Tools command that increases the spacing between words, characters, and lines.

Thesaurus A research tool that provides a list of synonyms.

Writer's identification The name and title of the author of a letter placed near the bottom of the letter under the complimentary closing—also referred to as the *writer's signature block*.

Writer's signature block The name and title of the author of a letter placed near the bottom of the letter, under the complimentary closing—also referred to as the *writer's identification*.

Chapter Review

Apply 2A skills from these Objectives:

1. Create a Table for a Resume
2. Format a Table
3. Present a Word Document Online

In the following Skills Review, you will use a table to create a resume for Ashley Kent. Your completed resume will look similar to the one shown in Figure 2.50.

Project Files

For Project 2C, you will need the following files:

New blank Word document

w02C_Skills

w02C_Experience

You will save your document as:

Lastname_Firstname_2C_Student_Resume

Project Results

Ashley Kent

2212 Bramble Road
St. Petersburg, FL 33713
(727) 555-0237
ashleykent@alcona.net

OBJECTIVE — A computer programmer position in a small startup company that requires excellent computer programming skills, systems analysis experience, and knowledge of database design.

SKILLS

Computer Programming
- Advanced C/C++
- Java
- Ruby on Rails
- SQL

Leadership
- Secretary, Florida Port Community College Computer Club
- Vice President, Associated Students, Bay Hills High School

Additional Skills
- Microsoft Office
- Adobe Creative Suite
- Adobe Acrobat Pro

EXPERIENCE — **Database Designer** (part-time), Admissions and Records
Florida Port Community College, St. Petersburg, FL
September 2019 to present

Software Tester (part-time), Macro Games Inc., Tampa, FL
September 2016 to September 2019

EDUCATION — **Florida Port Community College**, Computer Science major
September 2020 to present

Graduate of Bay Hills High School
June 2019

Student_Word_2C_Student_Resume

Figure 2.50

(continues on next page)

Chapter Review

1 ▶ Start Word and display a blank document. Be sure that formatting marks and rulers display. **Save** the document in your **Word Chapter 2** folder, using your own name, as **Lastname_Firstname_2C_Student_Resume**

a. Add the file name to the footer, and then close the footer area. (Mac users: from your student data files, open Mac_w02C_Student_Resume and use this file instead of a new blank document. On the Header & Footer tab, in the Insert group, click Field. Under Categories, click Document Information. Under Field names, click FileName. Click OK.)

b. Click the **Insert tab**, and then in the **Tables group**, click **Table**. In the **Table** grid, in the fourth row, click the second square to insert a **2x4** table.

c. In the first cell of the table, type **Ashley Kent** and then press (Enter). Type the following text, pressing (Enter) after each line *except* the last line:

   2212 Bramble Road
   St. Petersburg, FL 33713
   (727) 555-0237
   ashleykent@alcona.net

d. Press (↓) to move to the first cell in the second row. Type **SKILLS** and then press (↓) to move to the first cell in the third row.

e. Type **EXPERIENCE** and then press (↓). Type **EDUCATION**

f. In the first cell, if the email address displays in blue, right-click the email address, and then on the shortcut menu, click **Remove Hyperlink**. **Save** your document.

2 ▶ Click in the cell to the right of *SKILLS*, and then type the following, pressing (Enter) after each line including the last line:

   Computer Programming
   Advanced C/C++
   Java
   Ruby on Rails
   SQL

a. With the insertion point in the new line at the end of the cell, click the **Insert tab**. In the **Text group**, click the **Object button arrow**, and then click **Text from File**.

b. Navigate to the files downloaded with this project, select **w02C_Skills**, and then click **Insert**. Press (Backspace) one time to remove the blank line.

c. Click in the cell to the right of *EXPERIENCE*, and then insert the file **w02C_Experience**. Press (Backspace) one time to remove the blank line.

d. Click in the cell to the right of *EDUCATION*, and then type the following four items, pressing (Enter) after all items *except* the last four items:

   Florida Port Community College, Computer Science major
   September 2020 to present
   Graduate of Bay Hills High School
   June 2019

3 ▶ Point to the upper left corner of the *SKILLS* cell, and then click the **Row Insertion** button. (Mac users: Point to the upper left corner of the cell, right-click, point to Insert, click Rows Above.)

   In the first cell of the new row, type **OBJECTIVE** and then press (Tab).

a. Type **A computer programmer position in a small startup company that requires excellent computer programming skills, systems analysis experience, and knowledge of database design.**

b. In any row, point to the vertical border between the two columns to display the (+) pointer. Drag the column border to the left to approximately **1.5 inches on the horizontal ruler**.

c. Under **Table Tools**, on the **Layout tab**, in the **Cell Size group**, click **AutoFit**, and then click **AutoFit Window** to be sure that your table stretches across the page within the margins.

d. In the **Alignment group**, click **Cell Margins**, and then increase the **Top** and **Bottom** cell margins to **0.04**. Click **OK**.

e. In the first row of the table, drag across both cells to select them. On the **Table Tools Layout tab**, in the **Merge group**, click **Merge Cells**. Right-click over the selected cell, and then on the mini toolbar, click **Center**.

f. In the top row, select the first paragraph of text— *Ashley Kent*. On the mini toolbar, increase the **Font Size** to **20** and apply **Bold**.

g. In the second row, point to the word *OBJECTIVE*, hold down the left mouse button, and then drag down to select the row headings in uppercase letters. On the mini toolbar, click **Bold**. **Save** your document.

(continues on next page)

Chapter Review

4 Click in the cell to the right of *OBJECTIVE*. On the **Layout tab**, in the **Paragraph group**, click the **Spacing After up spin arrow** three times to change the spacing to **18 pt**.

a. In the cell to the right of *SKILLS*, apply **Bold** to the words *Computer Programming*, *Leadership*, and *Additional Skills*. Then, under each bold heading in the cell, select the lines of text, and create a bulleted list.

b. In the first two bulleted lists, click in the last bullet item, and then on the **Layout tab**, in the **Paragraph group**, set the **Spacing After** to **12 pt**.

c. In the last bulleted list, click in the last bullet item, and then set the **Spacing After** to **18 pt**.

d. In the cell to the right of *EXPERIENCE*, apply **Bold** to *Database Designer* and *Software Tester*. Click in the line *September 2019 to present* and apply **Spacing After** of **12 pt**. Click in the line *September 2016 to September 2019* and apply **Spacing After** of **18 pt**.

e. In the cell to the right of *EDUCATION*, apply **Bold** to *Florida Port Community College* and *Graduate of Bay Hills High School*.

f. In the same cell, click in the line *September 2020 to present* and apply **Spacing After** of **12 pt**.

g. In the first row, click in the last line—*ashleykent@ alcona.net*—and then change the **Spacing After** to **18 pt**. Click in the first line—*Ashley Kent*—and set the **Spacing Before** to **30 pt** and the **Spacing After** to **6 pt**.

5 On the **Table Tools Layout tab**, in the **Table group**, click **Select**, and then click **Select Table**. On the **Table Tools Design tab**, in the **Borders group**, click the **Borders button arrow**, and then click **No Border**.

a. In the **Borders group**, click the **Borders button arrow** again, and then at the bottom of the gallery, click **Borders and Shading**. In the **Borders and Shading** dialog box, under **Setting**, click **Custom**. Under **Style**, scroll down slightly, and then click the style with two equal lines.

b. Click the **Width arrow**, and then click **1 1/2 pt**. Under **Preview**, click the top border of the preview box, and then click **OK**.

c. Click the **File tab** to display **Backstage** view, on the left click **Info**, and then in the lower right portion of the screen, click **Show All Properties**. In the **Tags** box, type **resume, table** and in the **Subject** box, type your course name and section number. In the **Author** box, be sure your name is indicated and edit if necessary. (Mac users: On the menu bar, click File, click Properties, click Summary tab. For Tags, use Keywords.)

d. On the left, click **Print** to display **Print Preview**.

e. On the left, click **Save**, and then if you want to do so, present your document online to a fellow classmate. If directed by your instructor to do so, submit your paper printout, your electronic image of your document that looks like a printed document, or your original Word file. Close Word.

You have completed Project 2C **END**

Chapter Review

Skills Review | Project 2D Cover Letter

Apply 2B skills from these Objectives:

4. Create a Letterhead for a Cover Letter
5. Create a Cover Letter and Correct and Reorganize Text
6. Use the Word Editor to Check Your Document
7. Print an Envelope, Change a Style Set, Create a Word Template, and Use Learning Tools

In the following Skills Review, you will create a cover letter with a letterhead to accompany a resume. Your completed document will look similar to Figure 2.51.

Project Files

For Project 2D, you will need the following files:

New blank Word document

w02D_Cover_Letter_Text

You will save your document as:

Lastname_Firstname_2D_Cover_Letter

Project Results

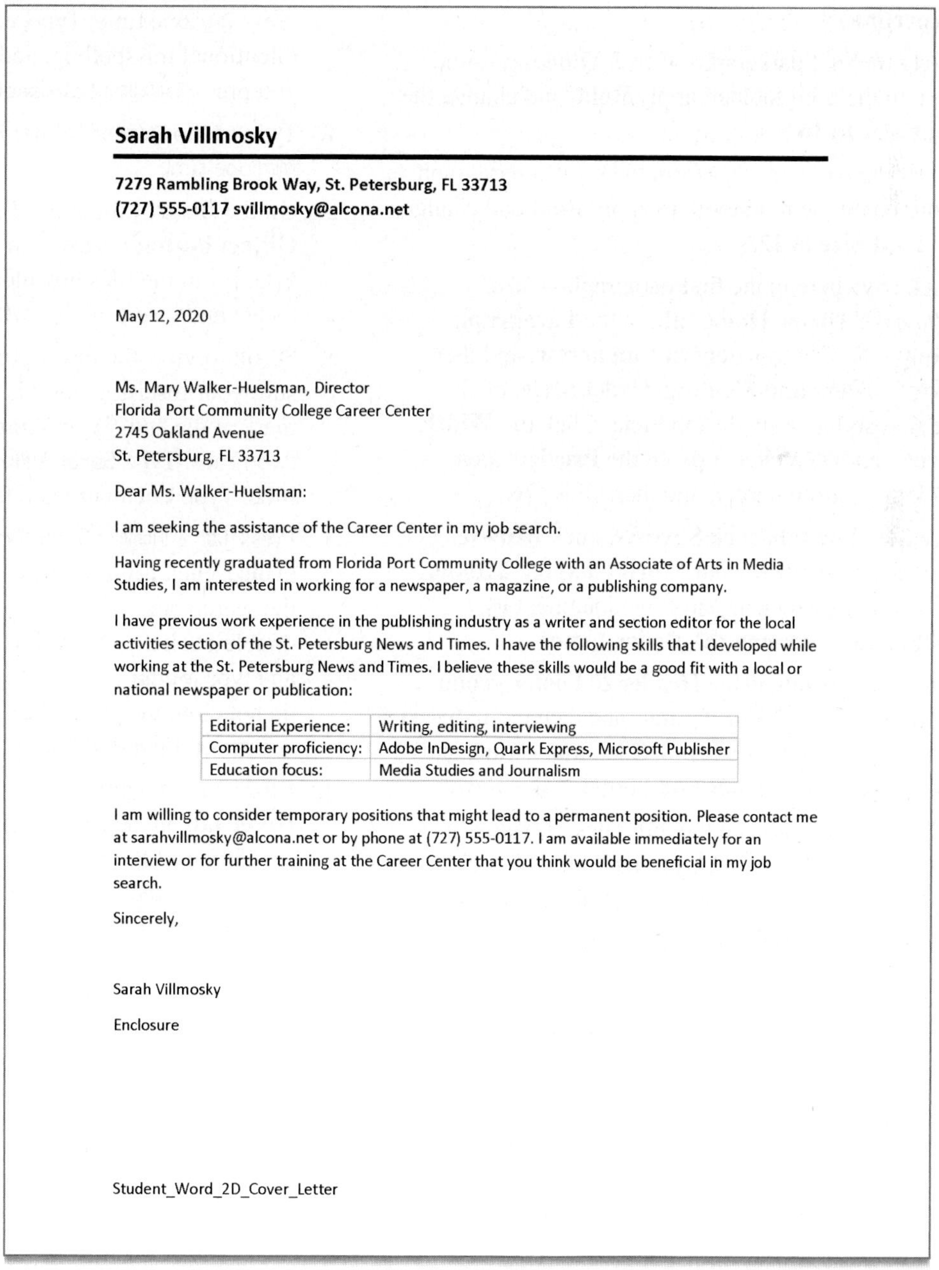

Sarah Villmosky

7279 Rambling Brook Way, St. Petersburg, FL 33713
(727) 555-0117 svillmosky@alcona.net

May 12, 2020

Ms. Mary Walker-Huelsman, Director
Florida Port Community College Career Center
2745 Oakland Avenue
St. Petersburg, FL 33713

Dear Ms. Walker-Huelsman:

I am seeking the assistance of the Career Center in my job search.

Having recently graduated from Florida Port Community College with an Associate of Arts in Media Studies, I am interested in working for a newspaper, a magazine, or a publishing company.

I have previous work experience in the publishing industry as a writer and section editor for the local activities section of the St. Petersburg News and Times. I have the following skills that I developed while working at the St. Petersburg News and Times. I believe these skills would be a good fit with a local or national newspaper or publication:

Editorial Experience:	Writing, editing, interviewing
Computer proficiency:	Adobe InDesign, Quark Express, Microsoft Publisher
Education focus:	Media Studies and Journalism

I am willing to consider temporary positions that might lead to a permanent position. Please contact me at sarahvillmosky@alcona.net or by phone at (727) 555-0117. I am available immediately for an interview or for further training at the Career Center that you think would be beneficial in my job search.

Sincerely,

Sarah Villmosky

Enclosure

Student_Word_2D_Cover_Letter

Figure 2.51

(continues on next page)

Chapter Review

1 ▶ Start Word and display a blank document; be sure that formatting marks and rulers display. (Mac users: from your student data files, open Mac_w02D_Cover_Letter and use this file instead of a new blank document.)

a. Type **Sarah Villmosky** and then press Enter. Type **7279 Rambling Brook Way, St. Petersburg, FL 33713** hold down Shift, and then press Enter to insert a manual line break.

b. Type **(727) 555-0117 svillmosky@alcona.net** and then press Enter. If the email address changes to blue text, right-click the address, and then click **Remove Hyperlink**.

c. Select the first paragraph—*Sarah Villmosky*—and then on the mini toolbar, apply **Bold**, and change the **Font Size** to **16**.

d. Select the two lines that form the second paragraph, and then on the mini toolbar, apply **Bold** and change the **Font Size** to **12**.

e. Click anywhere in the first paragraph—*Sarah Villmosky*. On the **Home tab**, in the **Paragraph group**, click the **Borders button arrow**, and then click **Borders and Shading**. Under **Style**, click the first style—a single solid line. Click the **Width arrow**, and then click **3 pt**. In the **Preview** area, click the bottom border, and then click **OK**.

f. Click the **File tab**, click **Save As**, click **Browse**, and then navigate to your **Word Chapter 2 folder**. Using your own name, save the document as **Lastname_Firstname_2D_Cover_Letter**

g. On the **Insert tab**, in the **Header & Footer group**, click **Footer**, click **Edit Footer**, and then in the **Insert group**, click **Document Info**. Click **File Name**, and then click **Close Header and Footer**. Click **Save**.

2 ▶ Click the **File tab**. On the left, click **Options**. On the left side of the **Word Options** dialog box, click **Proofing**, and then under **AutoCorrect options**, click the **AutoCorrect Options** button. (Mac users: On the menu bar, click Tools, click AutoCorrect.)

a. In the **AutoCorrect** dialog box, click the **AutoCorrect tab**. Under **Replace**, type the misspelled word **assistence** and under **With**, type **assistance** Click **Add**. If the entry already exists, click Replace instead, and then click Yes. Click **OK** two times to close the dialog boxes.

b. Press Ctrl + End, and then press Enter two times. On the **Insert tab**, in the **Text group**, click **Date & Time**, and then click the third date format. Click **OK**.

c. Press Enter two times. Type **Ms. Mary Walker-Huelsman, Director** and press Enter. Type **Florida Port Community College Career Center** and press Enter. Type **2745 Oakland Avenue** and press Enter. Type **St. Petersburg, FL 33713** and press Enter.

d. Select the first three lines of the inside address, and then on the **Layout tab**, in the **Paragraph group**, change the **Spacing After** to **0 pt**.

e. Click in the blank paragraph below the inside address. Type **Dear Ms. Walker-Huelsman:** and then press Enter one time. Type, exactly as shown with the intentional misspelling, and then watch *assistence* as you press Spacebar: **I am seeking the assistence**

f. Type **of the Career Center in my job search.** Press Enter one time.

g. On the **Insert tab**, in the **Text Group**, click the **Object button arrow**, and then click **Text from File**. From the files downloaded with this project, locate and insert the file **w02D_Cover_Letter_Text**.

h. Scroll to view the lower portion of the page, and be sure your insertion point is in the empty paragraph mark at the end. Type **Sincerely,** and then press Enter two times. Type **Sarah Villmosky** and press Enter one time. Type **Enclosure** and then **Save** your document.

i. Press Ctrl + Home. On the **Home tab**, in the **Editing group**, click **Find**. In the **Navigation** pane, click in the search box, and then type **Journalism** In the letter, double-click the yellow highlighted word *Journalism* and type **Media Studies** (Mac users, in the next step, do not close the pane; click the Settings icon, click Advanced Find & Replace, click the Replace tab.)

j. **Close** the **Navigation** pane, and then on the **Home tab**, in the **Editing group**, click **Replace**. In the **Find and Replace** dialog box, in the **Find what** box, replace the existing text by typing **SPNT** In the **Replace with** box, type **St. Petersburg News and Times** Click **More** to expand the dialog box, select the **Match case** check box, click **Replace All**, and then click **OK**. Clear the **Match case** check box, click **Less**, and then **Close** the **Find and Replace** dialog box.

k. In the paragraph that begins *I am available*, hold down Ctrl, and then click anywhere in the first sentence. Release Ctrl, and then drag the selected sentence to the end of the paragraph by positioning the small vertical line that floats with the insertion point to the left of the paragraph mark.

(continues on next page)

Chapter Review

3 Click at the beginning of the paragraph that begins *I am willing*, and then press [Enter] one time to insert a new blank paragraph. Press [↑] one time to position your insertion point in the new blank paragraph. On the **Insert tab**, in the **Tables group**, click **Table**. In the **Table grid**, in the third row, click the second square to insert a 2x3 table. Type the following information in the table:

Editorial experience:	Writing, editing, interviewing
Computer proficiency:	Adobe InDesign, QuarkXPress, Microsoft Publisher
Education focus:	Media Studies and Journalism

a. Click anywhere inside the table. On the **Table Tools Layout tab**, in the **Table group**, click **Select**, and then click **Select Table**. In the **Cell Size group**, click **AutoFit**, and then click **AutoFit Contents**.

b. With the table selected, on the **Design tab**, in the **Table Styles group**, click **More** [▾]. Under **Plain Tables**, click the second style—**Table Grid Light**.

c. With the table still selected, on the **Home tab**, in the **Paragraphs group**, click **Center**. Select the blank paragraph below the table, and then on the **Layout tab**, set the **Spacing After** to **0** pt. **Save** your document.

4 Press [Ctrl] + [Home]. On the **Review tab**, in the **Proofing group**, click **Check Document** (or *Spelling & Grammar*) to open the **Editor** pane. For the spelling of *Villmosky*, in the **Editor** pane, click **Ignore All**. If necessary, for the spelling of *Huelsman*, click **Ignore All**.

a. For the grammar error *a*, click **an**. (Mac users: Click Change.) For the spelling error *intrested*, click **interested**. Click **Delete Repeated Word** to delete the duplicated word *for*. Change *activitys* to **activities**. Change *benificial* to **beneficial**. Click **OK** when the check is complete.

b. In the paragraph that begins *I am willing*, in the third line, double-click the word *preparation*. In the **Proofing group**, click **Thesaurus**.

c. In the **Thesaurus** pane, point to *training*, click the **arrow**, and then click **Insert**. **Close** the **Thesaurus** pane. (Mac users: Hold down [Ctrl], click *training*, click Insert.)

d. Click **File tab**, on the left, click **Info**, and then in the lower right portion of the screen, click **Show All Properties**. In the **Tags** box, type **cover letter** and in the **Subject** box, type your course name and section number. (Mac users: Display the menu bar, click File, click Properties, click the Summary tab.)

e. In the **Author** box, be sure your name is indicated and edit if necessary. On the left, click **Save**. If directed by your instructor to do so, submit your paper printout, your electronic image of your document that looks like a printed document, or your original Word file. **Close** Word.

You have completed Project 2D **END**

Content-Based Assessments (Mastery and Transfer of Learning)

MyLab IT Grader

Mastering Word | **Project 2E Table of Job Listings**

Apply 2A skills from these Objectives:

1. Create a Table
2. Format a Table
3. Present a Word Document Online

In the following Mastering Word project, you will use a Word table to create an announcement for new job postings at the Career Center. Your completed document will look similar to Figure 2.52.

Project Files for MyLab IT Grader

1. In your **MyLab IT** course, locate and click **Word 2E Job Listings**, Download Materials, and then Download All Files.
2. Extract the zipped folder to your Word Chapter 2 folder. Close the Grader download screens.
3. Take a moment to open the downloaded **Word_2E_Job_Listings_Instructions**; note any recent updates to the book.

Project Results

Florida Port Community College Career Center

Job Alert! New Positions for Computer Science Majors!

April 11

Florida Port Community College Career Center has new jobs available for both part-time and full-time positions in Computer Science. Some of these jobs are temporary, some are for a specific project with a defined beginning and ending date, and some are open-ended with the potential for permanent employment. The following jobs were posted in the past week. These listings are just in, so apply now to be one of the first candidates considered!

For further information about any of these new jobs, or a complete listing of jobs that are available through the Career Center, please call Mary Walker-Huelsman at (727) 555-0030 or visit our website at www.fpcc.pro/careers.

New Computer Science Listings for the Week of April 11

POSITION	TYPE	LOCATION
Computer Engineer	Full-time, two months	Clearwater
Project Assistant	Full-time, three months	Coral Springs
Software Developer	Full-time, open-ended	Tampa
UI Designer	Part-time, two months	St. Petersburg

To help prepare yourself before applying for these jobs, we recommend that you review the following articles on our website at www.fpcc.pro/careers.

Topic	Article Title
Research	Working in Computer Science Fields
Interviewing	Interviewing in Startup Companies

Student_Word_2E_Job_Listings

Figure 2.52

For Non-MyLab Submissions

For Project 2E, you will need:
A new blank Word document
w02E_New_Jobs

In your Word Chapter 2 folder, save your document as:
Lastname_Firstname_2E_Job_Listings

After you have named and saved your document, on the next page, begin with Step 2. (Mac users: See MAC TIP in Activity 2.01 to change settings.)
After Step 11, save and submit your file as directed by your instructor.

(continues on next page)

Content-Based Assessments (Mastery and Transfer of Learning)

1 Navigate to your **Word Chapter 2 folder**, and then double-click the Word file you downloaded from **MyLab IT** that displays your name—**Student_Word_2E_Job_Listings**. If necessary, at the top, click **Enable Editing**. (Mac users: if you are not submitting your file in **MyLab IT**, from the student data files that accompany this project, open Mac_w02E_New_Jobs and use this file instead of a new blank document.)

2 Type **Florida Port Community College Career Center** and press Enter. Type **Job Alert! New Positions for Computer Science Majors!** and press Enter. Type **April 11** and press Enter. Insert the text from the file you downloaded with this project named **w02E_New_Jobs** by using the **Text from File** command.

3 At the top of the document, select and **Center** the three title lines. Select the title *Florida Port Community College Career Center*, change the **Font Size** to **20 pt** and apply **Bold**. Apply **Bold** to the second and third title lines. Locate the paragraph that begins *For further*, and then below that paragraph, position the insertion point in the second blank paragraph. **Insert** a three-column, four-row (**3x4**) table. Enter the following text into the table:

POSITION	TYPE	LOCATION
Computer Engineer	Full-time, two months	Clearwater
Software Developer	Full-time, open-ended	Tampa
UI Designer	Part-time, two months	St. Petersburg

4 In the table, point to the upper left corner of the cell *Software Developer* to display the **Row Insertion** button, and then click to insert a new row. In the new row, type the following information so that the job titles remain in alphabetic order: (Mac users: In your table, click where you want to add a row or column. To the right of the Table Design tab, click the Layout tab, and then use the commands in the Rows & Columns group.)

Project Assistant	Full-time, three months	Coral Springs

5 Select the entire table. From the **Table Tools Layout tab**, apply **AutoFit Contents**. With the table still selected, on the **Home tab**, **Center** the table between the left and right margins, and then add **6 pt Spacing Before** and **6 pt Spacing After**.

6 With the table still selected, remove all table borders, and then add a **Custom 1 pt** solid line top border and bottom border. Select all three cells in the first row, apply **Bold**, and then **Center** the text. Click anywhere in the first row, and then on the **Table Tools Layout tab**, in the **Rows & Columns group**, insert a row above. Merge the three cells in the new top row, and then type **New Computer Science Listings for the Week of April 11** Notice that the new row keeps the formatting of the row from which it was created.

7 Move to the end of the document, and then **Insert** a two-column, three-row (2x3) table. Enter the following text into the table:

Topic	Article Title
Research	Working in Computer Science Fields
Interviewing	Interviewing in Startup Companies

8 Select the entire table. On the **Layout tab**, in the **Cell Size group**, use the **AutoFit** button to **AutoFit Contents**. On the **Home tab**, **Center** the table. On the **Layout tab**, add **6 pt Spacing Before** and **6 pt Spacing After**.

9 With the table still selected, remove all table borders, and then add a **Custom 1 pt** solid line top border and bottom border. Select the cells in the first row, apply **Bold** and **Center**.

10 Insert the **File Name** in the footer. Display **Backstage** view, click **Info**, and then in the lower right portion of the screen, click **Show All Properties**. In the **Tags** box type **new listings, computer science** and in the **Subject** box type your course name and section number. In the **Author** box, be sure your name is indicated and edit if necessary. (Mac users: To insert the file name, on the Header & Footer tab, in the Insert group, click Field. Under Categories, click Document Information. Under Field names, click FileName. To show properties, on the menu bar click File, click Properties, click the Summary tab. For Tags, use Keywords.)

11 On the left, click **Save**. In the upper right corner of the Word window, click **Close** ☒.

12 In **MyLab IT**, locate and click the Grader Project **Word 2E Job Listings**. In **step 3**, under **Upload Completed Assignment**, click **Choose File**. In the **Open** dialog box, navigate to your **Word Chapter 2 folder**, and then click your **Student_Word_2E_Job_Listings** file one time to select it. In the lower right corner of the **Open** dialog box, click **Open**.

The name of your selected file displays above the Upload button.

13 To submit your file to **MyLab IT** for grading, click **Upload**, wait a moment for a green **Success!** message, and then in **step 4**, click the blue **Submit for Grading** button. Click **Close Assignment** to return to your list of **Course Materials**.

You have completed Project 2E | **END**

Content-Based Assessments (Mastery and Transfer of Learning)

MyLab IT Grader

Mastering Word | **Project 2F Career Tips Memo**

Apply 2B skills from these Objectives:

4. Create a Letterhead for a Cover Letter
5. Create a Cover Letter and Correct and Reorganize Text
6. Use the Word Editor to Check Your Document
7. Print an Envelope, Change a Style Set, Create a Word Template, and Use Learning Tools

In the following Mastering Word project, you will create a memo that includes job tips for students and graduates using the services of the Florida Port Community College Career Center. Your completed document will look similar to Figure 2.53.

Project Files for **MyLab IT Grader**

1. In your **MyLab IT** course, locate and click **Word 2F Career Tips**, Download Materials, and then Download All Files.
2. Extract the zipped folder to your Word Chapter 2 folder. Close the Grader download screens.
3. Take a moment to open the downloaded **Word_2F_Career_Tips_Instructions**; note any recent updates to the book.

Project Results

Florida Port Community College Career Center

Memo

DATE: January 12, 2021

TO: Florida Port Community College Students and Graduates

FROM: Mary Walker-Huelsman, Director

SUBJECT: Using the Career Center

Tips for Students and Recent Graduates of Florida Port Community College

It is no surprise that after you leave college, you will be entering one of the most competitive job markets on record. That doesn't mean it's impossible to get your dream job. It does, however, mean that it's critical that you know how to put your best self forward to job interviewers and that you highlight all your academic, personal, and professional achievements in a way that will help you stand out from the crowd. An Associate degree from Florida Port Community College is just the first step on your journey to getting the professional career that you want.

Give 100 Percent to Every Job

Treat every job as a career. Be willing to go beyond your assignment and complete tasks not delegated to you. Take the initiative to see ways to contribute to the company. Be willing to stay if there is unfinished work. You never know who you will meet on any job. Making a positive impression every time will give you a network of people who may help you down the road. Networking is an established means that professionals use to further their careers. You can always benefit from networking. You will distinguish yourself from potential competitors if you truly give 100 percent to each job. Always remember these job basics:

Job Item	Tip for Success
Time Management	Show up on time and don't hurry to leave
Attire	Dress appropriately for the job
Work Area	Keep your work area neat and organized

Use the Career Center

Here at the Career Center and on our website, we offer tips on how to write a stellar resume and a cover letter that puts your hard work up front and center. Have you volunteered somewhere? Have you participated at a club at school? Were you a TA or a tutor? Did you make the Dean's list or graduate with honors? These are the kinds of achievements interviewers want to see. Meet with your career guidance counselor and together, come up with a plan to find the jobs that you want and get the important interview.

Student_Word_2F_Career_Tips

Figure 2.53

For Non-MyLab Submissions

For Project 2F, you will need:
w02F_Career_Tips
w02F_Memo_Text

In your Word Chapter 2 folder, save your w02F_Career_Tips document as:
Lastname_Firstname_2F_Career_Tips

After you have named and saved your document, on the next page, begin with Step 2.

After Step 12, save and submit your file as directed by your instructor.

(continues on next page)

Content-Based Assessments (Mastery and Transfer of Learning)

Mastering Word: Project 2F Career Tips Memo (continued)

1 Navigate to your **Word Chapter 2 folder**, and then double-click the Word file you downloaded from **MyLab IT** that displays your name—**Student_Word_2F_Career_Tips**. If necessary, at the top, click **Enable Editing**.

2 Insert the **File Name** in the footer. If necessary, display formatting marks. By using the information below, complete the memo headings by positioning your insertion point to the left of the paragraph mark for each heading.

DATE:	January 12, 2021
TO:	Florida Port Community College Students and Graduates
FROM:	Mary Walker-Huelsman, Director
SUBJECT:	Using the CC

3 Position the insertion point in the blank paragraph below the memo heading. **Insert** the file **w02F_Memo_Text**, and then press Backspace one time to remove the blank line at the end of the inserted text.

4 Position the insertion point at the top of the document. From the **Review tab**, display the **Editor** pane. By clicking the suggested words in the **Editor**, correct *too* to **to**, *proffessionals* to **professionals**, *benifit* to **benefit**, *Deans* to **Dean's**, *guidence* to **guidance**, and *interveiw* to **interview**.

5 In the paragraph that begins *Treat every job*, in the second line, locate and double-click the word *donate*. (Mac users: Hold down control, click *donate* in the Thesaurus pane, and then click Insert "donate".) Use the **Thesaurus** to replace the word with *contribute*. In the last line of the same paragraph, right-click the word *fundamentals*, point to **Synonyms**, and then click *basics*. If necessary, close the Thesaurus pane.

6 In the paragraph that begins *An Associate degree*, move the first sentence to the end of the paragraph.

7 Below the paragraph that begins *Treat every job*, click in the blank paragraph, and then **Insert** a **2x4** table.

8 Type the following information in the table:

Job Item	Tip for Success
Time Management	Show up on time and don't hurry to leave
Attire	Dress appropriately for the job
Work Area	Keep your work area neat and organized

9 Select the entire table. **AutoFit Contents**, and then apply the **Grid Table 1 Light – Accent 1** table style. **Center** the table between the left and right margins.

10 Position the insertion point at the top of the document, and then by using the **Match case** option, replace all instances of *CC* with *Career Center*.

11 Display **Backstage** view, click **Info**, and then click **Show All Properties**. As the **Tags**, type **memo, job tips** (Note: Mac users use the Keywords box.) As the **Subject**, type your course name and section number. Be sure your name is indicated as the **Author**, and edit if necessary.

12 On the left, click **Save**. In the upper right corner of the Word window, click **Close** ⊠.

13 In **MyLab IT**, locate and click the Grader Project **Word 2F Career Tips**. In **step 3**, under **Upload Completed Assignment**, click **Choose File**. In the **Open** dialog box, navigate to your **Word Chapter 2 folder**, and then click your **Student_Word_2F_Career_Tips** file one time to select it. In the lower right corner of the **Open** dialog box, click **Open**.

The name of your selected file displays above the Upload button.

14 To submit your file to **MyLab IT** for grading, click **Upload**, wait a moment for a green **Success!** message, and then in **step 4**, click the blue **Submit for Grading** button. Click **Close Assignment** to return to your list of **Course Materials**.

You have completed Project 2F **END**

| **Mastering Word** | **Project 2G Application Letter and Resume** |

In the following Mastering Word project, you will create a cover letter and resume. Your completed documents will look similar to Figure 2.54.

Apply 2A and 2B skills from these Objectives:

1. Create a Table for a Resume
2. Format a Table
3. Present a Word Document Online
4. Create a Letterhead for a Cover Letter
5. Create a Cover Letter and Correct and Reorganize Text
6. Use the Word Editor to Check Your Document
7. Print an Envelope, Change a Style Set, Create a Word Template, and Use Learning Tools

Project Files for MyLab IT Grader

1. In your **MyLab IT** course, locate and click **Word 2G Letter and Resume**, Download Materials, and then Download All Files.
2. Extract the zipped folder to your Word Chapter 2 folder. Close the Grader download screens.
3. Take a moment to open the downloaded **Word_2G_Letter_and_Resume_Instructions**; note any recent updates to the book.

Project Results

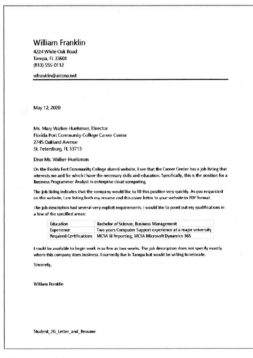

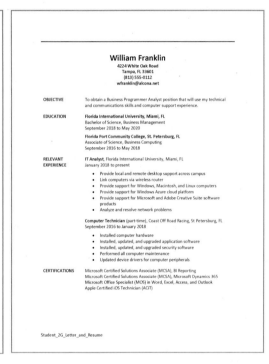

Figure 2.54

For Non-MyLab Submissions

For Project 2G, you will need:

w02G_Letter_and_Resume
w02G_Letter_Text

In your Word Chapter 2 folder, save your w02G_Letter_and_Resume document as:

Lastname_Firstname_2G_Letter_and_Resume

After you have named and saved your document, on the next page, begin with Step 2.
After Step 15, save and submit your file as directed by your instructor.

(continues on next page)

1 Navigate to your **Word Chapter 2 folder**, and then double-click the Word file you downloaded from **MyLab IT** that displays your name—**Student_ Word_2G_Letter_and_Resume**. If necessary, at the top, click **Enable Editing**.

2 Add the **File Name** to the footer. Be sure that rulers and formatting marks display. On **Page 1**, click in the blank paragraph below the letterhead, and then press Enter two times. Use the **Date & Time** command to insert the current date using the third format. Press Enter two times. Type **Ms. Mary Walker-Huelsman, Director** and press Enter. Type **Florida Port Community College Career Center** and press Enter. Type **2745 Oakland Avenue** and press Enter. Type **St. Petersburg, FL 33713** and press Enter. Select the first three lines of the inside address, and then set **Spacing After** to **0 pt**.

3 Click in the blank paragraph below the inside address. Type **Dear Ms. Walker-Huelsman:** and press Enter. **Insert** the text from the file **w02G_Letter_Text** and press Backspace one time to remove the blank line at the bottom of the inserted text.

4 Press Ctrl + Home to move to the top of the document. From the **Review tab**, display the **Editor** pane. Take appropriate action on each flagged item including removing the comma from the conjunction.

5 Press Ctrl + Home to move to the top of the document again, and then replace all instances of **posting** with **listing**

6 In the paragraph that begins *The job description*, use the Thesaurus pane or the Synonyms command on the shortcut menu to change *specific* to *explicit* and *credentials* to *qualifications*.

7 In the paragraph that begins *I currently live in Tampa* select the first sentence of the paragraph and drag it to the end of the same paragraph.

8 Click at the beginning of the paragraph that begins *I could be available*, press Enter to insert a new blank paragraph, and then press ↑ to position your insertion point in the new blank paragraph. **Insert** a **2x3** table, and then type the text shown in Table 1 at the bottom of the page.

9 Select the entire table. **AutoFit Contents**, and then apply the **Table Grid Light** table style—under **Plain Tables**, in the first row, the first style. **Center** the table between the left and right margins. Select the blank paragraph mark below the table and apply **Spacing After** of **0 pt**.

10 In the resume on **Page 2**, insert a new second row in the table. In the first cell of the new row, type **OBJECTIVE** and press Tab. Type **To obtain a Business Programmer Analyst position that will use my technical and communications skills and computer support experience.** Add **12 pt Spacing After** to the text you just typed and apply **Bold** to the word *OBJECVTIVE*. (Mac users: When inserting a row above in a table, the formatting style of the row below is applied. Deselect bold formatting as necessary.)

11 Select the entire resume table and apply **AutoFit Contents**. Remove the table borders, and then from the **Borders and Shading** dialog box, apply a **Custom** single solid line **1 1/2 pt** top border to the table.

12 In the first row of the resume table, select both cells and then **Merge Cells**. **Center** the five lines and apply **Bold**. In the first row, select *William Franklin* and change the **Font Size** to **20 pt** and add **24 pt Spacing Before**. Click in the email address at the bottom of the first row, and then add **24 pt Spacing After**.

13 In the cell to the right of *RELEVANT EXPERIENCE*, below the line that begins *January 2018*, apply bullets to the six lines that comprise the job duties. Create a similar bulleted list for the duties as a Computer Technician.

14 Display **Backstage** view, click **Info**, and then click **Show All Properties**. As the **Tags**, type **cover letter, resume** (Mac users; use Keywords.) As the **Subject**, type your course name and section number. Be sure your name is indicated as the **Author**, and edit if necessary.

Table 1

Education	Bachelor of Science, Business Management
Experience	Two years Computer Support experience at a major university
Required Certifications	MCSA BI Reporting, MCSA Microsoft Dynamics 365

(continues on next page)

Mastering Word: Project 2G Application Letter and Resume (continued)

15 On the left, click **Save**. In the upper right corner of the Word window, click **Close** ☒.

16 In **MyLab IT**, locate and click the Grader Project **Word 2G Letter and Resume**. In **step 3**, under **Upload Completed Assignment**, click **Choose File**. In the **Open** dialog box, navigate to your **Word Chapter 2 folder**, and then click your **Student_Word_2G_Letter_and_Resume** file one time to select it. In the lower right corner of the **Open** dialog box, click **Open**.

The name of your selected file displays above the Upload button.

17 To submit your file to **MyLab IT** for grading, click **Upload**, wait a moment for a green **Success!** message, and then in **step 4**, click the blue **Submit for Grading** button. Click **Close Assignment** to return to your list of **Course Materials**.

You have completed Project 2G | **END**

Apply a combination of the 2A and 2B skills.

GO! Fix It	**Project 2H New Jobs**	**IRC**
GO! Make It	**Project 2I Training**	**IRC**
GO! Solve It	**Project 2J Job Postings**	**IRC**
GO! Solve It	**Project 2K Agenda**	

Project Files

For Project 2K, you will need the following file:

Agenda template from Word's Online templates

You will save your document as:

Lastname_Firstname_2K_Agenda

Start Word, on the left click New, and then search for an online template using the search term **formal meeting agenda** Click the agenda and then click Create. Save the agenda in your Word Chapter 2 folder as **Lastname_Firstname_2K_Agenda** Use the following information to prepare an agenda for an FPCC Career Center meeting.

The meeting will be chaired by Mary Walker-Huelsman. It will be the monthly meeting of the Career Center's staff—Kevin Rau, Marilyn Kelly, André Randolph, Susan Nguyen, and Charles James. The meeting will be held on March 15 at 3:00 p.m. The old business agenda items (open issues) include 1) seeking more job listings related to the printing and food service industries; 2) expanding the alumni website, and 3) the addition of a part-time trainer. The new business agenda items will include 1) writing a grant so the center can serve more students and alumni; 2) expanding the training area with 20 additional workstations; 3) purchase of new computers for the training room; and 4) renewal of printing service contract.

Add the file name to the footer, add your name, your course name, the section number, and then add the keywords **agenda, monthly staff meeting** to the Properties area. Submit as directed.

		Performance Level		
		Exemplary: You consistently applied the relevant skills	**Proficient: You sometimes, but not always, applied the relevant skills**	**Developing: You rarely or never applied the relevant skills**
Performance Criteria	**Select an agenda template**	Agenda template is appropriate for the information provided for the meeting.	Agenda template is used, but does not fit the information provided.	No template is used for the agenda.
	Add appropriate information to the template	All information is inserted in the appropriate places.	All information is included, but not in the appropriate places.	Information is missing.
	Format template information	All text in the template is properly aligned and formatted.	All text is included, but alignment or formatting is inconsistent.	No additional formatting has been added.

You have completed Project 2K **END**

Rubric

The following outcomes-based assessments are *open-ended assessments*. That is, there is no specific correct result; your result will depend on your approach to the information provided. Make *Professional Quality* your goal. Use the following scoring rubric to guide you in *how* to approach the problem and then to evaluate *how well* your approach solves the problem.

The *criteria*—Software Mastery, Content, Format and Layout, and Process—represent the knowledge and skills you have gained that you can apply to solving the problem. The *levels of performance*—Professional Quality, Approaching Professional Quality, or Needs Quality Improvements—help you and your instructor evaluate your result.

	Your completed project is of Professional Quality if you:	Your completed project is Approaching Professional Quality if you:	Your completed project Needs Quality Improvements if you:
1-Software Mastery	Choose and apply the most appropriate skills, tools, and features and identify efficient methods to solve the problem.	Choose and apply some appropriate skills, tools, and features, but not in the most efficient manner.	Choose inappropriate skills, tools, or features, or are inefficient in solving the problem.
2-Content	Construct a solution that is clear and well organized, contains content that is accurate, appropriate to the audience and purpose, and is complete. Provide a solution that contains no errors of spelling, grammar, or style.	Construct a solution in which some components are unclear, poorly organized, inconsistent, or incomplete. Misjudge the needs of the audience. Have some errors in spelling, grammar, or style, but the errors do not detract from comprehension.	Construct a solution that is unclear, incomplete, or poorly organized, contains some inaccurate or inappropriate content, and contains many errors of spelling, grammar, or style. Do not solve the problem.
3-Format and Layout	Format and arrange all elements to communicate information and ideas, clarify function, illustrate relationships, and indicate relative importance.	Apply appropriate format and layout features to some elements, but not others. Overuse features, causing minor distraction.	Apply format and layout that does not communicate information or ideas clearly. Do not use format and layout features to clarify function, illustrate relationships, or indicate relative importance. Use available features excessively, causing distraction.
4-Process	Use an organized approach that integrates planning, development, self-assessment, revision, and reflection.	Demonstrate an organized approach in some areas, but not others; or, use an insufficient process of organization throughout.	Do not use an organized approach to solve the problem.

GO! Think	Project 2L Workshops

Apply a combination of the 2A and 2B skills.

Project Files

For Project 2L, you will need the following files:

New blank Word document

w02L_Workshop_Information

You will save your document as:

Lastname_Firstname_2L_Workshops

The Florida Port Community College Career Center offers a series of workshops for both students and alumni. Any eligible student or graduate can attend the workshops, and there is no fee. Currently, the Career Center offers a three-session workshop covering Excel and Word, a two-session workshop covering Business Communication, and a one-session workshop covering Creating a Resume.

Print the w02L_Workshop_Information file and use the information to complete this project. Create an announcement with a title, an introductory paragraph, and a table listing the workshops and the topics covered in each workshop. Use the file w02L_Workshop_Information for help with the topics covered in each workshop. Format the table cells appropriately. Add an appropriate footer and document properties. Save the document as **Lastname_Firstname_2L_Workshops** and submit it as directed.

	You have completed Project 2L	END

GO! Think	Project 2M Schedule	IRC

You and GO!	Project 2N Personal Resume	IRC

GO! Cumulative Team Project	Project 2O Bell Orchid Hotels	IRC

Creating Research Papers, Newsletters, and Merged Mailing Labels

3

WORD 2019

create jobs 51/Shutterstock

In This Chapter

 GO! To Work with Word

Microsoft Word provides many tools for creating complex documents. For example, Word has tools that enable you to create a research paper that includes citations, footnotes, and a bibliography, and to research information from other sources directly from within Word. You can also create multiple-column newsletters, format the nameplate at the top of the newsletter, use special character formatting to create distinctive title text, and add borders and shading to paragraphs to highlight important information.

In this chapter, you will edit and format a research paper, create a two-column newsletter, and optionally create a set of mailing labels to mail the newsletter to multiple recipients.

The projects in this chapter relate to **University Medical Center**, which is a patient-care and research institution serving the metropolitan area of Memphis, Tennessee. Because of its outstanding reputation in the medical community and around the world, University Medical Center can attract top physicians, scientists, and researchers in all fields of medicine and achieve a level of funding that allows it to build and operate state-of-the-art facilities. A program in biomedical research was recently added. Individuals throughout the eastern United States travel to University Medical Center for diagnosis and care.

Project Activities

In Activities 3.01 through 3.14, you will edit and format a research paper that contains an overview of a new area of study. This paper was created by Gerard Foster, a medical intern at University Medical Center, for distribution to his classmates studying various physiologic monitoring devices. Your completed document will look similar to Figure 3.1.

Project Files for MyLab IT Grader

1. In your storage location, create a folder named **Word Chapter 3**
2. In your **MyLab IT** course, locate and click **Word 3A Quantitative Technology**, Download Materials, and then Download All Files.
3. Extract the zipped folder to your Word Chapter 3 folder. Close the Grader download screens.
4. Take a moment to open the downloaded **Word_3A_Quantitative_Technology_Instructions**; note any recent updates to the book.

Project Results

GO! Project 3A
Where We're Going

Figure 3.1 Project 3A Quantitative Technology

For Non-MyLab Submissions

For Project 3A, you will need:
w03A_Quantitative_Technology

In your storage location, create a folder named **Word Chapter 3**
In your Word Chapter 3 folder, save your document as:
Lastname_Firstname_3A_Quantitative_Technology

After you have named and saved your document, on the next page, begin with Step 2.

Objective 1 Create a Research Paper

GO! Learn How
Video W3-1

When you write a research paper or a report for college or business, follow a format prescribed by one of the standard *style guides*—a manual that contains standards for the design and writing of documents. The two most commonly used styles for research papers are those created by the *Modern Language Association (MLA)* and the *American Psychological Association (APA)*; there are several others.

Activity 3.01 | Formatting the Spacing and First-Page Information for a Research Paper

2.2.3

When formatting the text for your research paper, refer to the standards for the style guide that you have chosen. In this Activity, you will create a research paper using the MLA style. The MLA style uses 1-inch margins, a 0.5" first line indent, and double spacing throughout the body of the document with no extra space above or below paragraphs.

1 Navigate to your **Word Chapter 3 folder**, and then double-click the Word file you downloaded from **MyLab IT** that displays your name—**Student_Word_3A_Quantitative_ Technology**. If necessary, at the top click **Enable Editing**.

2 On the **Review tab**, from the **Proofing group**, display the Word **Editor**, and then click **Ignore Once** for each instance of any flagged items—this will remove any red squiggles or other markings from your document. When complete, click **OK**, and if necessary, close the Editor pane.

> 🖥️ **MAC TIP** To display group names on the ribbon, display the menu, click Word, click Preferences, click View, select the Show group titles check box.

3 Press Ctrl + A to select all the text in the document. With the entire document selected, on the **Home tab**, in the **Paragraph group**, click **Line and Paragraph Spacing** ↕≡▾, and then change the line spacing to **2.0**. On the **Layout tab**, in the **Paragraph group**, change the **Spacing After** to **0 pt**.

> 🖥️ **MAC TIP** Press command ⌘ + A to select the entire document.

> 🔄 **ANOTHER WAY** On the Home tab, in the Editing group, click Select, and then click Select All to select the entire document.

4 Press Ctrl + Home to deselect and move to the top of the document. Press Enter one time to create a blank line at the top of the document, and then click to position the insertion point in the new blank paragraph. Type **Gerard Foster** and press Enter.

> 🖥️ **MAC TIP** Press command ⌘ + fn + ←.

5 Type **Dr. Hillary Kim** and press `Enter`. Type **Biomedical Research 617** and press `Enter`. Type **February 15, 2021** and press `Enter`.

6 Type **Quantified Self Movement Gains Momentum** and then press `Ctrl` + `E`, which is the keyboard shortcut to center a paragraph of text. Click **Save** 🖫, and then compare your screen with Figure 3.2.

> To create the document heading for a research paper, on the first line, type the report author. On the second line, type the person for whom the report is prepared—for example, your professor or supervisor. On the third line, type the name of the class or business. On the fourth line, type the date. On the fifth line, type the report title and center it.

🖥 **MAC TIP** Press `command ⌘` + `E` to center a paragraph.

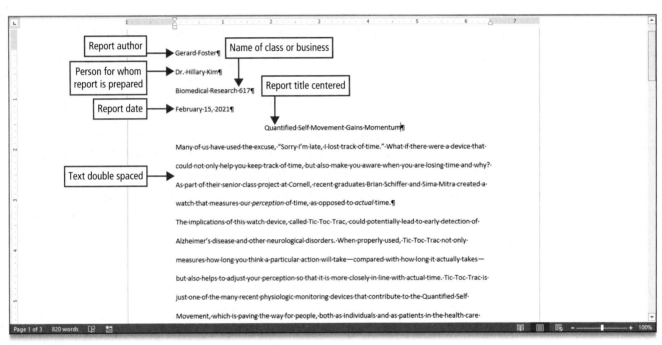

Figure 3.2

Activity 3.02 | Formatting the Page Numbering and Paragraph Indents for a Research Paper

MOS
2.2.3

1 On the **Insert tab**, in the **Header & Footer group**, click **Header**, and then at the bottom of the list, click **Edit Header**.

2 Type **Foster** and then press `Spacebar` one time.

> Recall that the text you insert into a header or footer displays on every page of a document. Within a header or footer, you can insert many types of information; for example, automatic page numbers, the date, the time, the file name, or pictures.

3 ▸ Under **Header and Footer Tools**, on the **Design tab**, in the **Header & Footer group**, click **Page Number**, and then point to **Current Position**. In the gallery, under **Simple**, click **Plain Number**. Compare your screen with Figure 3.3.

Word will automatically number the pages using this number format.

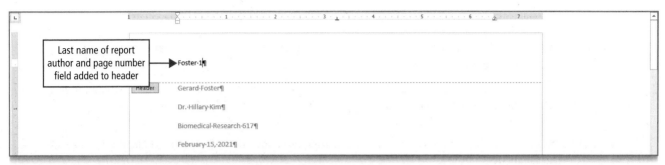

Last name of report author and page number field added to header ➔ Foster·1¶

Header
Gerard·Foster¶
Dr.·Hillary·Kim¶
Biomedical·Research·617¶
February·15,·2021¶

Figure 3.3

4 ▸ On the **Home tab**, in the **Paragraph group**, click **Align Right** . Double-click anywhere in the document to close the Header area.

💻 **MAC TIP**   Click Page Number; in the Alignment box, click Right, click OK.

5 ▸ Near the top of **Page 1**, locate the paragraph beginning *Many of us*, and then click to position the insertion point at the beginning of the paragraph. On the right of your screen, by moving the vertical scroll box, scroll down to view the end of the document, hold down Shift, and then click to the right of the last paragraph mark to select all of the text from the insertion point to the end of the document. Release Shift.

6 ▸ With the text selected, in the **Paragraph group**, click the **Dialog Box Launcher** button to display the **Paragraph** dialog box.

💻 **MAC TIP**   Click Line and Paragraph Spacing. Click Line Spacing Options to open the Paragraph dialog box.

7 ▸ On the **Indents and Spacing tab**, under **Indentation**, click the **Special arrow**, and then click **First line**. In the **By** box, be sure **0.5"** displays. Click **OK**. Compare your screen with Figure 3.4.

The MLA style uses 0.5-inch indents at the beginning of the first line of every paragraph. *Indenting*— moving the beginning of the first line of a paragraph to the right or left of the rest of the paragraph— provides visual cues to the reader to help divide the document text and make it easier to read.

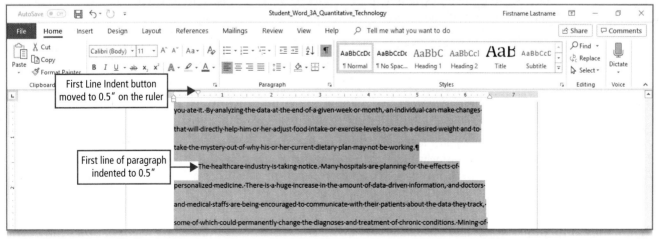

First Line Indent button moved to 0.5" on the ruler

First line of paragraph indented to 0.5"

you·ate·it.·By·analyzing·the·data·at·the·end·of·a·given·week·or·month,·an·individual·can·make·changes·that·will·directly·help·him·or·her·adjust·food·intake·or·exercise·levels·to·reach·a·desired·weight·and·to·take·the·mystery·out·of·why·his·or·her·current·dietary·plan·may·not·be·working.¶

The·healthcare·industry·is·taking·notice.·Many·hospitals·are·planning·for·the·effects·of·personalized·medicine.·There·is·a·huge·increase·in·the·amount·of·data-driven·information,·and·doctors·and·medical·staffs·are·being·encouraged·to·communicate·with·their·patients·about·the·data·they·track,·some·of·which·could·permanently·change·the·diagnoses·and·treatment·of·chronic·conditions.·Mining·of·

Figure 3.4

ANOTHER WAY On the ruler, point to the First Line Indent button ▽, and then drag the button to 0.5" on the horizontal ruler.

8 Press Ctrl + Home to deselect and move to the top of the document. On the **Insert tab**, in the **Header & Footer group**, click **Footer**, and then at the bottom of the list click **Edit Footer**.

9 In the **Insert group**, click **Document Info**, and then click **File Name**. On the ribbon, click **Close Header and Footer**.

The file name in the footer is *not* part of the research report format, but it is included in projects in this instruction so that you and your instructor can identify your work.

MAC TIP Click Field. In the Field dialog box, under Categories, click Document Information. Under Field names, click FileName.

10 Save 🖫 your document.

MORE KNOWLEDGE | **Suppressing the Page Number on the First Page of a Document**

Some style guidelines require that the page number and other header and footer information on the first page be hidden from view—*suppressed*. To hide the information contained in the header and footer areas on Page 1 of a document, double-click in the header or footer area. Then, under Header and Footer Tools, on the Design tab, in the Options group, select the Different First Page check box.

Objective 2 | **Insert Footnotes in a Research Paper**

GO! Learn How
Video W3-2

Within report text, numbers mark the location of ***notes***—information that expands on the topic being discussed but that does not fit well in the document text. The numbers refer to ***footnotes***—notes placed at the bottom of the page containing the note, or to ***endnotes***—notes placed at the end of a document or chapter.

Activity 3.03 | **Inserting Footnotes**

4.1.1

You can add footnotes as you type your document or after your document is complete. Word renumbers the footnotes automatically, so footnotes do not need to be entered in order, and if one footnote is removed, the remaining footnotes automatically renumber.

1 Scroll to view the upper portion of **Page 2**, and then locate the paragraph that begins *Accurate records*. In the third line of the paragraph, click to position the insertion point to the right of the period after *infancy*.

2 On the **References tab**, in the **Footnotes group**, click **Insert Footnote**.

Word creates space for a footnote in the footnote area at the bottom of the page and adds a footnote number to the text at the insertion point location. Footnote *1* displays in the footnote area, and the insertion point moves to the right of the number. A short black line is added just above the footnote area. You do not need to type the footnote number.

3 Type **The U.S. Department of Health & Human Services indicates that the widespread use of Health Information Technology will improve the quality of health care.**

This is an explanatory footnote; the footnote provides additional information that does not fit well in the body of the report.

4 Scroll to view the top of **Page 1**, and then locate the paragraph that begins *Many of us.* At the end of the paragraph, click to position the insertion point to the right of the period following *time.*

5 On the **References tab**, in the **Footnotes group**, click **Insert Footnote**. Type **Organizations such as airlines and the military could benefit because many employees are involved in time-sensitive operations.** Notice that the footnote you just added becomes the new footnote *1*. Click **Save** 🖫, and then compare your screen with Figure 3.5.

The first footnote that you typed, which is on Page 2 and begins *The U.S. Department of Health,* is renumbered as footnote *2*.

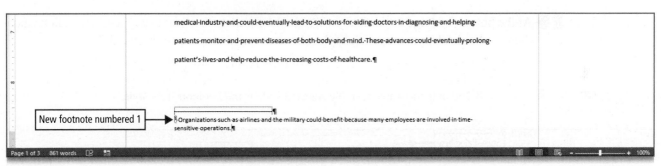

medical·industry·and·could·eventually·lead·to·solutions·for·aiding·doctors·in·diagnosing·and·helping·

patients·monitor·and·prevent·diseases·of·both·body·and·mind.·These·advances·could·eventually·prolong·

patient's·lives·and·help·reduce·the·increasing·costs·of·healthcare.¶

New footnote numbered 1 → §·Organizations·such·as·airlines·and·the·military·could·benefit·because·many·employees·are·involved·in·time-sensitive·operations.¶

Page 1 of 3   861 words

Figure 3.5

MORE KNOWLEDGE | **Using Symbols Rather Than Numbers for Notes**

Instead of using numbers to designate footnotes, you can use standard footnote symbols. The seven traditional symbols, available from the Footnote and Endnote dialog box, in order, are * (asterisk), † (dagger), ‡ (double dagger), § (section mark), || (parallels), ¶ (paragraph mark), and # (number or pound sign). This sequence can be continuous, which is the default setting, or it can begin anew with each page.

Activity 3.04 | Modifying a Footnote Style

4.1.2, 2.3.2 (Expert)

Microsoft Word contains built-in paragraph formats called *styles*—groups of formatting commands, such as font, font size, font color, paragraph alignment, and line spacing—that can be applied to a paragraph with one command.

The default style for footnote text is a single-spaced paragraph that uses a 10-point Calibri font and no paragraph indents. MLA style specifies double-spaced text in all areas of a research paper—including footnotes. According to the MLA style, first lines of footnotes must also be indented 0.5 inch and use the same font size as the report text.

1 Click the **Home tab**, and then in the **Paragraph group**, examine the font size and line spacing settings. Notice that the new footnote displays in 10 pt font size and is single-spaced, even though the font size of the document text is 11 pt and the text is double-spaced, as shown in Figure 3.6.

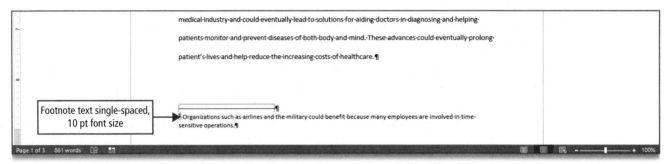

Figure 3.6

2 At the bottom of **Page 1**, point anywhere in the footnote text you just typed, right-click, and then on the shortcut menu, click **Style**. Compare your screen with Figure 3.7.

The Style dialog box displays, listing the styles currently in use in the document, in addition to some of the word processing elements that come with special built-in styles. Because you right-clicked in the footnote text, the selected style is the Footnote Text style.

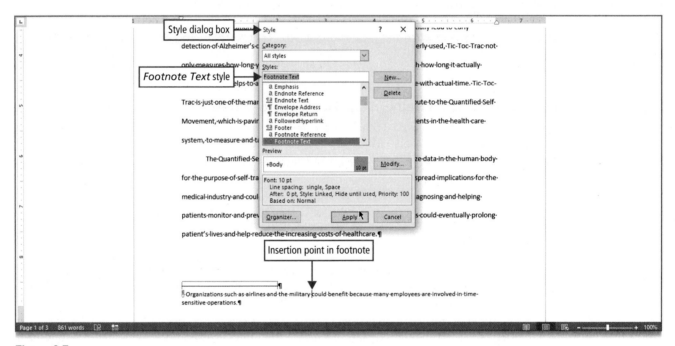

Figure 3.7

3 In the **Style** dialog box, click **Modify**, and then in the **Modify Style** dialog box, locate the small **Formatting** toolbar in the center of the dialog box. Click the **Font Size button arrow**, click **11**, and then compare your screen with Figure 3.8.

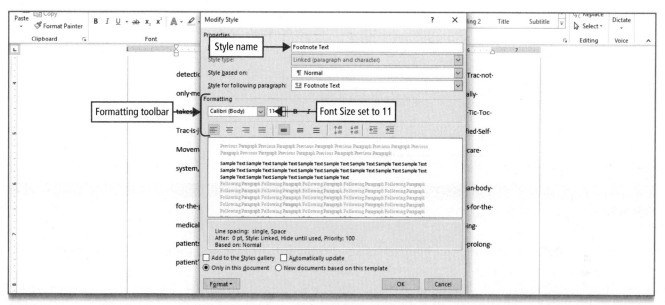

Figure 3.8

4 In the lower left corner of the dialog box, click **Format**, and then click **Paragraph**. In the **Paragraph** dialog box, on the **Indents and Spacing tab**, under **Indentation**, click the **Special arrow**, and then click **First line**.

5 Under **Spacing**, click the **Line spacing arrow**, and then click **Double**. Compare your dialog box with Figure 3.9.

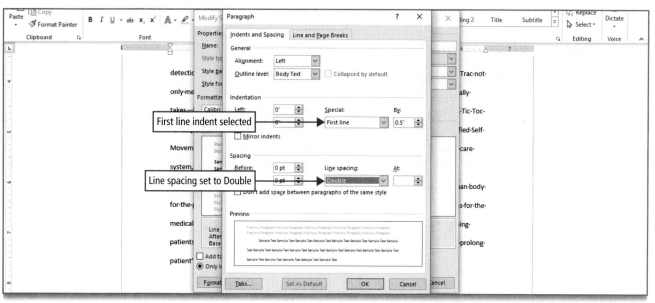

Figure 3.9

6 ▶ Click **OK** to close the **Paragraph** dialog box, click **OK** to close the **Modify Style** dialog box, and then click **Apply** to apply the new style and close the dialog box. Compare your screen with Figure 3.10.

Word formats your inserted footnotes with the modified Footnote Text paragraph style; any new footnotes that you insert will also use this format.

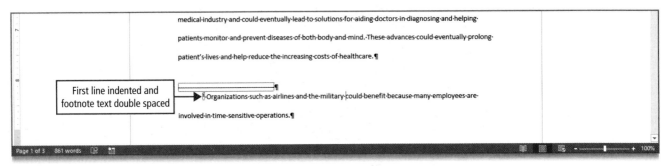

medical·industry·and·could·eventually·lead·to·solutions·for·aiding·doctors·in·diagnosing·and·helping·

patients·monitor·and·prevent·diseases·of·both·body·and·mind.·These·advances·could·eventually·prolong·

patient's·lives·and·help·reduce·the·increasing·costs·of·healthcare.¶

First line indented and footnote text double spaced → ⁸Organizations·such·as·airlines·and·the·military·could·benefit·because·many·employees·are·

involved·in·time-sensitive·operations.¶

Page 1 of 3   861 words

Figure 3.10

7 ▶ Scroll to view the bottom of **Page 2** to confirm that the new format was also applied to the second footnote, and then **Save** 🖫 your document.

Objective 3 — Create Citations and a Bibliography in a Research Paper

GO! Learn How
Video W3-3

Reports and research papers typically include information that you find in other sources, and these sources of information must be credited. When you use quotations from or detailed summaries of other people's work, you must specify the source of the information. A *citation* is a note inserted into the text of a report or research paper that refers the reader to a source in the *bibliography*. Create a bibliography at the end of a research paper to list the sources you have referenced. Such a list is typically titled *Works Cited* (in MLA style), *Bibliography*, *Sources*, or *References*.

Activity 3.05 | Adding Citations for a Book

4.1.3, 4.1.4

When writing a long research paper, you will likely reference numerous books, articles, and websites. Some of your research sources may be referenced many times, others only one time. References to sources within the text of your research paper are indicated in an *abbreviated* manner. However, as you enter a citation for the first time, you can also enter the *complete* information about the source. Then, when you have finished your paper, you will be able to automatically generate the list of sources that must be included at the end of your research paper.

1 ▶ On the **References tab**, in the **Citations & Bibliography group**, click the **Style button arrow**, and then click **MLA** to insert a reference using MLA bibliography style.

2 ▶ Scroll to view the middle of **Page 2**. In the paragraph that begins *Accurate records*, at the end of the paragraph, click to position the insertion point to the right of the quotation mark.

The citation in the document points to the full source information in the bibliography, which typically includes the name of the author, the full title of the work, the year of publication, and other publication information.

3 ⟩ Click **Insert Citation**, and then click **Add New Source**. Click the **Type of Source arrow**, and then click **Book**. Add the following information, and then compare your screen with Figure 3.11:

Author:	Sopol, Eric J.
Title:	The Creative Destruction of Medicine
Year:	2012
City:	New York
Publisher:	Basic Books
Medium	Print

MAC TIP The order of fields is Author, Title, City, Publisher, Year; there is no Medium field.

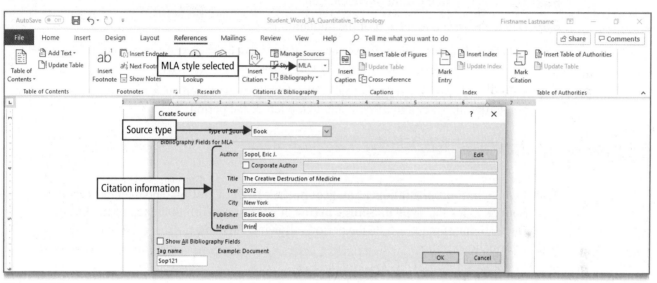

Figure 3.11

4 ⟩ Click **OK** to insert the citation. Point to *(Sopol)* and click one time to select the citation.

In the MLA style, citations that refer to items on the *Works Cited* page are placed in parentheses and are referred to as ***parenthetical references***—references that include the last name of the author or authors and the page number in the referenced source, which you add to the reference. No year is indicated, and there is no comma between the name and the page number. Both MLA and APA styles use parenthetical references for source citations rather than using footnotes.

5 ⟩ **Save** 🖫 the document.

NOTE   Citing Corporate Authors and Indicating the Medium

If the author of a document is only identified as the name of an organization, select the Corporate Author check box and type the name of the organization in the Corporate Author box.

In the 7th edition of the *MLA Handbook for Writers of Research Papers*, the category Medium was added and must be included for any item on the Works Cited page. Entries for this category can include Print, Web, Performance, and Photograph, among many others.

Activity 3.06 | Editing Citations

4.1.3

1 ⟩ In the lower right corner of the box that surrounds the selected reference, point to the small arrow to display the ScreenTip *Citation Options*. Click this **Citation Options arrow**, and then on the list of options, click **Edit Citation**.

2 In the **Edit Citation** dialog box, under **Add**, in the **Pages** box, type **5** to indicate that you are citing from page 5 of this source. Compare your screen with Figure 3.12.

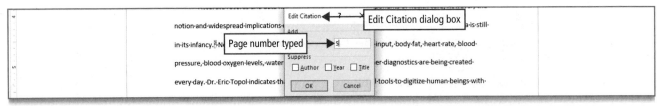

Figure 3.12

3 Click **OK** to display the page number of the citation. Click outside of the citation box to deselect it.

4 Type a period to the right of the citation.

5 Delete the period to the left of the quotation mark.

> In the MLA style, if the reference occurs at the end of a sentence, the parenthetical reference always displays to the left of the punctuation mark that ends the sentence.

6 Press Ctrl + End to move to the end of the document, and then click to position the insertion point after the letter *e* in *disease* and to the left of the period.

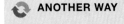 **MAC TIP** Press command ⌘ + fn + →.

7 In the **Citations & Bibliography group**, click **Insert Citation**, and then click **Add New Source**. Click the **Type of Source arrow**, if necessary scroll to the top of the list, click **Book**. Being sure to include the period following the name *Salzberg*, add the following information:

Author:	Glaser, John P., and Claudia Salzberg.
Title:	The Strategic Application of Information Technology in Health Care Organizations
Year:	2011
City:	San Francisco
Publisher:	Jossey-Bass
Medium:	Print

8 Click **OK**. Click the inserted citation to select it, click the **Citation Options arrow**, and then click **Edit Citation**.

ANOTHER WAY In the Create Source dialog box, if you prefer, you can enter each author name separately by using the Edit command to the right of the Author box. Initiate the command for each author of the work, and then Word will automatically format all the names properly and in the correct order in the Works Cited list.

9 In the **Edit Citation** dialog box, under **Add**, in the **Pages** box, type **28** to indicate that you are citing from page 28 of this source. Click **OK**.

10 On the **References tab**, in the **Citations & Bibliography group**, click **Manage Sources**, and then compare your screen with Figure 3.13.

> The Source Manager dialog box displays. Other citations on your computer might display in the Master List box. The citations for the current document display in the Current List box. Word

maintains the Master List so that if you use the same sources regularly, you can copy sources from your Master List to the current document. A preview of the bibliography entry also displays at the bottom of the dialog box.

MAC TIP   Click Citations, at the bottom of the pane, click Settings. Click Citation Source Manager. There is no preview.

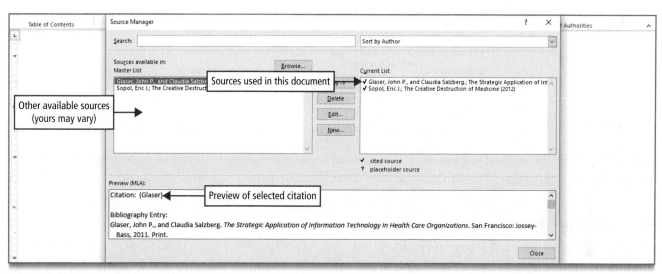

Figure 3.13

11 At the bottom of the **Source Manager** dialog box, click **Close**. Click anywhere in the document to deselect the parenthetical reference, and then **Save** 🖫 your document.

MORE KNOWLEDGE   **Word Formats the MLA Style for Two or More Authors Automatically**

According to MLA Style, to cite a book by two or more authors, reverse only the name of the first author and place a period after the name of the last author. In this example, you typed the exact MLA style, however, if you type *John P. Glaser; Claudia Salzberg* Word will automatically format the Works Cited page properly, inserting all necessary punctuation and putting the names in the proper order.

Activity 3.07 | Adding Citations for a Website

4.1.4

1 In the lower portion of **Page 2**, in the paragraph that begins *Doctors have long urged*, in the third line, click to position the insertion point after the *s* in *States* and to the left of the period.

2 In the **Citations & Bibliography group**, click **Insert Citation**, and then click **Add New Source**. Click the **Type of Source arrow**, scroll down as necessary, and then click **Web site**. Type the following information (Mac users: there is no Medium field.):

Author:	**Ogden, Cynthia L.**
Name of Web Page:	**NCHS Data Brief Number 82**
Year:	**2012**
Month:	**January**
Day:	**15**
Year Accessed:	**2021**
Month Accessed:	**January**
Day Accessed:	**17**
Medium	**Web**

3 ▶ Click **OK**. Save 🖫, and then compare your screen with Figure 3.14.

A parenthetical reference is added. Because the cited webpage has no page numbers, only the author name is used in the parenthetical reference.

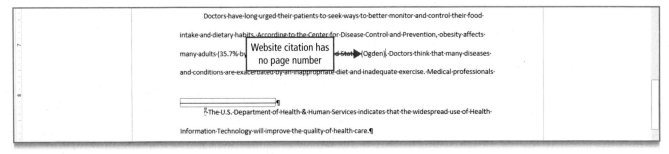

Doctors·have·long·urged·their·patients·to·seek·ways·to·better·monitor·and·control·their·food·

intake·and·dietary·habits.·According·to·the·Center·for·Disease·Control·and·Prevention,·obesity·affects·

many·adults·(35.7%·by···········d·Stat▶(Ogden).·Doctors·think·that·many·diseases·

and·conditions·are·exacerbated·by·an·inappropriate·diet·and·inadequate·exercise.·Medical·professionals·

The·U.S.·Department·of·Health·&·Human·Services·indicates·that·the·widespread·use·of·Health·

Information·Technology·will·improve·the·quality·of·health·care.¶

> Website citation has no page number

Figure 3.14

MORE KNOWLEDGE **Including URLs of Web Sources**

With the 7th edition of the *MLA Handbook for Writers of Research Papers*, including the URL of Web sources is recommended only when the reader would have difficulty finding the source without it or if your instructor requires it. Otherwise, readers will likely find the resource by using search tools. If you include the URL, enclose it in angle brackets and end with a period.

Activity 3.08 | Inserting Page Breaks

MOS
2.3.2

Your bibliography must begin on a new page, so at the bottom of the last page of your report, you must insert a manual page break to start a new page.

1 ▶ Press **Ctrl** + **End** to move the insertion point to the end of the document.

If there is a footnote on the last page of your research paper, the insertion point will display at the end of the final paragraph, but above the footnote—a footnote is always associated with the page that contains the footnote.

2 ▶ Press **Ctrl** + **Enter** to insert a manual page break.

A ***manual page break*** forces a page to end at the insertion point location, and then places any subsequent text at the top of the next page. Recall that the new paragraph retains the formatting of the previous paragraph, so in this instance the first line is indented.

A ***page break indicator***, which shows where a manual page break is inserted, displays at the bottom of Page 3.

3 ▶ On the **Home tab**, in the **Paragraph group**, click the **Dialog Box Launcher** button 🔲 to display the **Paragraph** dialog box.

4 ▶ On the **Indents and Spacing tab**, under **Indentation**, click the **Special arrow**, and then if necessary, click **(none)**. Click **OK**, and then Save 🖫 your document.

ANOTHER WAY On the ruler, point to the First Line Indent button 🔻, and then drag the button to 0" on the horizontal ruler.

Activity 3.09 | Creating a Reference Page

MOS
4.1.4, 4.2.3

At the end of a report or research paper, include a list of each source referenced. *Works Cited* is the reference page heading used in the MLA style guidelines. Other styles may refer to this page as a *Bibliography* (Business Style) or *References* (APA Style). Always display this information on a separate page.

1 With the insertion point blinking in the first paragraph of **Page 4**, on the **References tab**, in the **Citations & Bibliography group**, in the **Style** box, be sure *MLA* displays.

2 In the **Citations & Bibliography group**, click **Bibliography**, and then near the bottom of the list, click **Works Cited**.

3 Select the paragraph *Works Cited*. On the **Home tab**, in the **Font group**, change the **Font** to **Calibri**, and then change the **Font Size** to **11**. Click the **Font Color arrow** ⬛▾, and then in the second column, click the first color. With the text *Works Cited* still selected, in the **Paragraph group**, click **Center** ☰.

4 Click to the left of *Works Cited* and then drag down to select the title *Works Cited* and the three citations. On the **Layout tab**, in the **Paragraph group**, click the **Dialog Box Launcher** button ⬑, and then in the **Paragraph** dialog box, change the **Spacing Before** to **0 pt**, change the **Spacing After** to **0 pt**, and then set the **Line spacing** to **Double**. Click **OK**.

> 🖥 **MAC TIP**   Click the Line and Paragraph Spacing button, click Line Spacing Options.

The bibliography entries that you created display as a field, which is indicated by the gray shading. This field links to the Source Manager for the citations. The references display alphabetically by the author's last name.

The entries display according to MLA guidelines; the text is double-spaced, and each entry uses a *hanging indent*—the first line of each entry extends 0.5 inch to the left of the remaining lines of the entry.

5 At the bottom of **Page 4**, click in the last blank paragraph to deselect the text, and then compare your screen with Figure 3.15. **Save** 💾 your document.

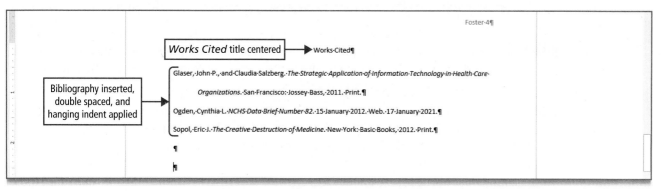

Figure 3.15

Activity 3.10 | Managing and Modifying Sources for a Document

Use the Source Manager to organize the sources cited in your document. For example, in the Source Manager dialog box, you can copy sources from the master list to the current list, delete a source, edit a source, or search for a source. You can also display a preview of how your citations will appear in your document.

1 On the **References tab**, in the **Citations & Bibliography group**, click **Manage Sources**.

> **MAC TIP** On the References tab, click Citations, click the settings button in the bottom right corner of the Citations pane. Click Citation Source Manager. Click the reference for Sopol, click Edit, edit the name *Sopol* to *Topol*. Click OK, click Close. On Page 2, click the Topol reference, click the arrow, click Update Citations and Bibliography. Then move to the Activity 3.11.

2 On the left, in the **Master List**, click the entry for *Sopol, Eric J.* and then between the **Master List** and the **Current List**, click **Edit**.

The name of this source should be *Topol* instead of *Sopol*.

3 In the **Edit Source** dialog box, in the **Author** box, delete *S* and type **T**

4 Click **OK**. When the message box indicates *This source exists in your master list and current document. Do you want to update both lists with these changes?* click **Yes**. Compare your screen with Figure 3.16.

In the lower portion of the Source Manager dialog box, a preview of the corrected entry displays.

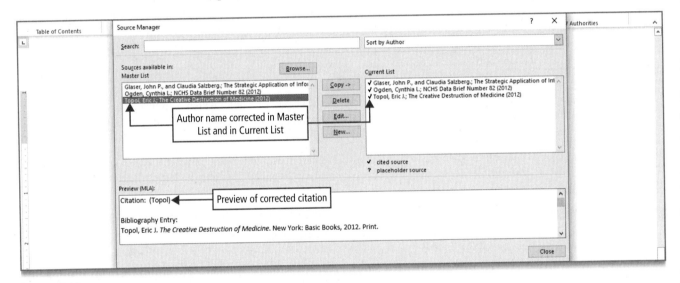

Figure 3.16

5 In the lower right corner, click **Close**. On your **Works Cited page**, notice that the author name is *not* corrected. Scroll to view the lower portion of **Page 2** and notice that the author name *is* corrected and the citation is selected.

6 On the selected citation *(Topol 5)*, click the **Citation Options arrow**, and then click **Update Citations and Bibliography**. Scroll to view your **Works Cited page** and notice that this action updates the Works Cited page with the corrected name but also changes the line spacing of the citations.

Editing a source in Source Manager updates only the sources in the document; to update the Works Cited page, use the Update Citations and Bibliography command on the citation.

7 On the *Works Cited* page, drag to select the three citations, and then from the **Home tab**, redisplay the **Paragraph** dialog box. Reset the **Spacing Before** and **Spacing After** to **0 pt** and the **Line spacing** to **Double**. Click **OK**. Click **Save**.

Activity 3.11 | Using the Navigation Pane to Go to a Specific Page

MOS
1.1.1, 1.1.3

In a multipage document, use the Navigation pane to move to a specific page or to find specific objects in the document.

1 Press `Ctrl` + `Home` to move to the top of the document. Click the **View tab**, and then in the **Show group**, select the **Navigation Pane** check box.

📃 **MAC TIP**   At the top of the Navigation pane, click the Find and Replace icon (magnifying glass). Click the Settings button, click Advanced Find & Replace, and then click the Go To tab. Under Go to what, select Footnote.

2 In the **Navigation** pane, on the right end of the **Search document** box, click the **Search for more things arrow**, and then compare your screen with Figure 3.17.

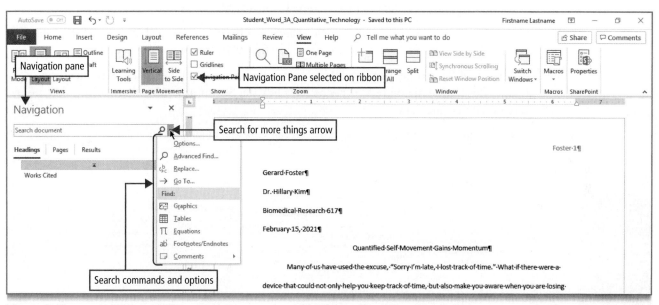

Figure 3.17

3 Under **Find**, click **Footnotes/Endnotes**. Notice that the first numbered footnote is selected.

4 In the **Navigation** pane, to the right of *Result 1 of 2*, click the ▼ arrow to move to the next numbered footnote.

5 Click the **Search for more things arrow** again, and then click **Go To**. In the **Find and Replace** dialog box, under **Go to what**, be sure **Page** is selected, and then in the **Enter page number** box, type **4**

6 Click **Go To**, and then click **Close**. Notice that **Page 4** displays.

The Navigation pane is useful when you need to navigate to find various elements, especially in a very long document.

7 In the **Navigation pane**, click **Pages**, and notice that you can view thumbnail images of your document's pages.

Here you can scroll quickly through the pages of a long document.

8 **Close** ⊠ the **Navigation** pane.

Activity 3.12 │ Managing Document Properties

MOS
1.3.2

For a research paper, you may want to add additional document properties.

1 Press `Ctrl` + `Home` to return to the top of your document. From the **File tab**, display **Backstage** view, click **Info**, and then in the lower right corner of the screen, click **Show All Properties**.

2 As the document **Title**, type **Quantified Self Movement Gains Momentum** and then as the **Tags**, type **quantified self, research paper**

3 Click in the **Comments** box and type **draft copy of report for class** and then in the **Categories** box, type **biomedical research**

4 In the **Subject** box, type your course name and section number. In the **Company** box, select and delete any existing text, and then type **University Medical Center**

5 Click in the **Manager** box and type **Dr. Hillary Kim** If necessary, click outside of the Manager box to close it. Be sure your name displays as the **Author** and edit if necessary.

6 At the top of the **Properties** list, click the text *Properties*, and then click **Advanced Properties**. In the dialog box, if necessary click the **Summary tab**, and then compare your screen with Figure 3.18.

In the Advanced Properties dialog box, you can view and modify additional document properties.

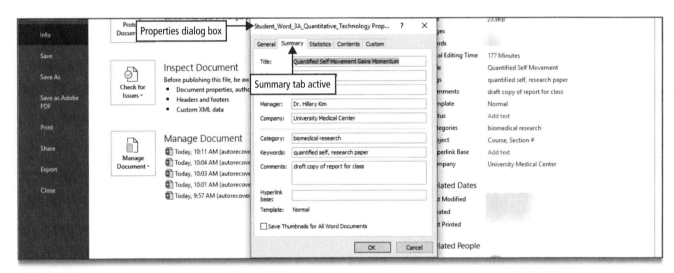

Figure 3.18

7 Click the **Statistics tab**.

The document statistics show the number of revisions made to the document, the last time the document was edited, and the number of paragraphs, lines, words, and characters in the document. Additional information categories are available by clicking the Custom tab.

8 **Close** ⌧ the dialog box. On the left, click **Save** to save and return to your document.

Activity 3.13 | **Using Smart Lookup, Researcher, Text Highlighting, Cover Pages, and Side to Side Page Movement**

Smart Lookup is a Word feature with which you can get information about text you select. Smart Lookup can show definitions, images, and results from various online sources.

Researcher is a Word feature that helps you find topics and reliable sources for your research paper. For sources that you select, citation information is available.

Text Highlight Color is a Word command with which you can apply a highlight color to selected text.

1 Scroll to view **Page 2** of your document, and then in the paragraph that begins *Accurate records*, in the fifth line of the paragraph, locate and select *Dr. Eric Topol*.

2 With *Dr. Eric Topol* selected, on the **References tab**, in the **Research group**, click **Smart Lookup**. Compare your screen with Figure 3.19.

> The Smart Lookup pane displays on the right. Here you can see that Dr. Topol is an American cardiologist, geneticist, and digital medicine researcher.

NOTE You may have to enable Office intelligent services to use Smart Lookup and Researcher. To do so, click the File tab, on the left click Options, in the Word Options dialog box, on the left click General, and then under Office intelligent services, select the Enable services check box.

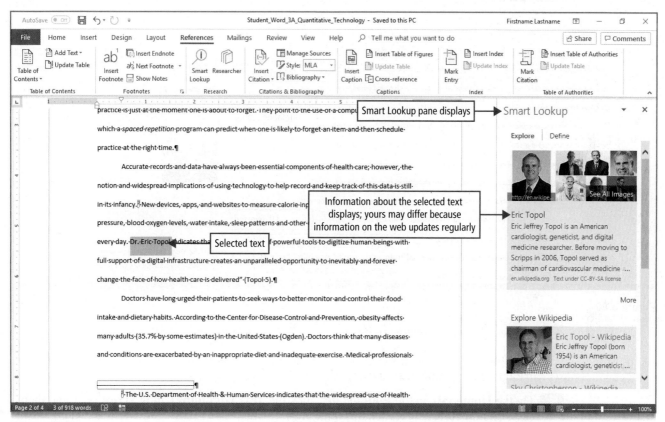

Figure 3.19

3 In the **Smart Lookup pane**, scroll down and then click the **blue text** for any of the additional informational sources about Dr. Topol; for example, his Wikipedia page, information about the Scripps Genomic Health Initiative, Dr. Topol's faculty page at The Scripps Research Institute, or the page related to the book cited in your research paper—*The Creative Destruction of Medicine*.

> Smart Lookup enables you to search for information about a topic from within Word without having to open a browser and begin a new search.

4 **Close** ⊠ your browser window, and then **Close** ⊠ the **Smart Lookup pane**.

5 On the **References tab**, in the **Research group**, click **Researcher** to display the **Researcher pane** on the right.

6 With the insertion point blinking in the search box, type, including the quotation marks, **"quantified self"** and then press `Enter`. Under **Top sources for "quantified self"** click **Journals**. Compare your screen with Figure 3.20.

Here you can search for scholarly journal articles about a topic from within Word. You can scroll down and find links to many articles related to the topic *quantified self*.

When searching for a phrase or a concept that contains two or more words, use quotation marks so that the search engine conducts the search on the entire phrase. The search engine in Researcher is Microsoft's Bing.

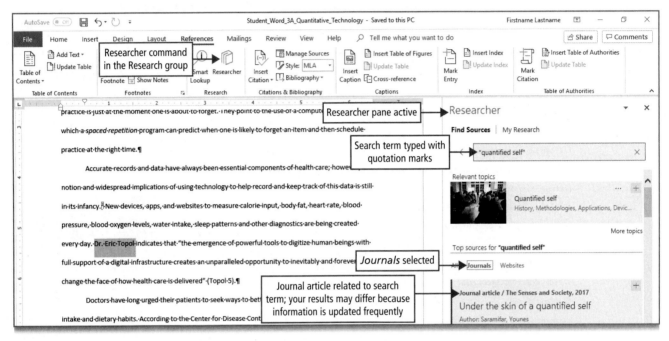

Figure 3.20

7 Close ☒ the **Researcher pane**.

8 On **Page 2**, in the paragraph that begins *Gary Wolf, who along*, in the first line of the paragraph, select the text *Quantified Self*.

9 On the **Home tab**, in the **Font group**, click the **Text Highlight Color arrow** and then click **Bright Green** as shown in Figure 3.21.

This highlighting will serve as a reminder to conduct additional research about the topic *quantified self* by using the Researcher feature in Word.

🖥 **MAC TIP** On the Home tab, in the Font group, click the Highlight arrow.

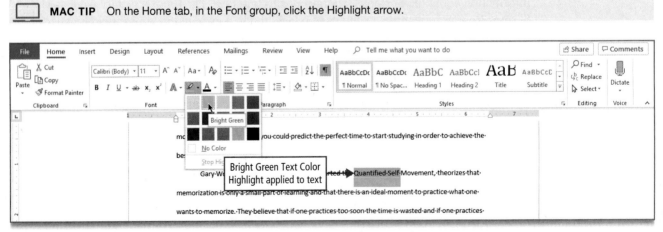

Figure 3.21

10 On the **View tab**, in the **Page Movement group**, click **Side to Side**, and then click the horizontal scroll arrows to slide pages left or right

The *Side to Side* command enables you to see whole pages by sliding each page from right to left or left to right. This is convenient when you have multiple pages and you want to see how the pages look side by side. Depending on your screen size and screen resolution, there may be variations in how the Side to Side view displays on your computer.

11 On the **View tab**, in the **Page Movement group**, click **Vertical** to return to the default setting.

Vertical is the default Page Movement setting, meaning you can use the vertical scroll arrows to move the pages up or down on your screen.

12 On the **Insert tab**, in the **Pages group**, click **Cover Page**, and then in the gallery, click **Banded**—or select any other cover page design. Press Ctrl + Home to see the cover page.

Academic research papers do not typically include a stylized cover page. In business organizations, or for informal college term papers, adding a cover page is appropriate. Here you can choose from many styles that are pre-built, and you can further customize those with different fonts and colors.

13 On the Quick Access toolbar, click **Undo** ↺ —you will not include a cover page for this project.

14 Click **Save** 🖫.

<table>
<tr><td>Objective 4</td><td>Use Read Mode, PDF Reflow, and Save Documents in Alternative File Formats</td></tr>
</table>

GO! Learn How
Video W3-4

Read Mode optimizes the view of the Word screen for the times when you are *reading* Word documents on the screen and not creating or editing them. Microsoft's research indicates that two-thirds of user sessions in Word contain no editing—meaning that people are simply reading the Word document on the screen. The Column Layout feature of Read Mode reflows the document to fit the size of the device you are reading so that the text is as easy to read on a tablet device as it is to read on a standard desktop computer screen. The Object Zoom feature of Read Mode resizes graphics to fit the screen you are using, but you can click or tap to zoom in on the graphic.

PDF Reflow enables you to import PDF files into Word so that you can transform a PDF into a fully editable Word document. This is useful if you have lost the original Word file or if someone sends you a PDF that you would like to modify. PDF Reflow is not intended to act as a viewer for PDF files—for that you will still want to use a PDF reader such as Adobe Reader. In Windows 10, the Microsoft Edge browser also serves as a PDF reader.

Activity 3.14 | Using Read Mode, PDF Reflow, and Saving Documents in Alternative File Formats

MOS
1.3.1

1 Press Ctrl + Home to move to the top of your document. On the **View tab**, in the **Views group**, click **Read Mode**, and notice that Read Mode keeps footnotes displayed on the page associated with the footnote.

Read Mode displays differently for different screen sizes and screen resolution settings; if you have a different resolution setting, your screens may differ slightly than those shown here.

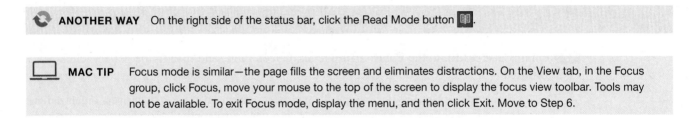

ANOTHER WAY   On the right side of the status bar, click the Read Mode button 📖.

MAC TIP   Focus mode is similar—the page fills the screen and eliminates distractions. On the View tab, in the Focus group, click Focus, move your mouse to the top of the screen to display the focus view toolbar. Tools may not be available. To exit Focus mode, display the menu, and then click Exit. Move to Step 6.

2 In the upper left corner, click **Tools**.

You can use these tools to find something within the document or use Smart Lookup to conduct an internet search.

3 Click **Find**, and then in the **Search** box, type **Topol** Notice that Word displays the first page where the search term displays and highlights the term in yellow. Compare your screen with Figure 3.22.

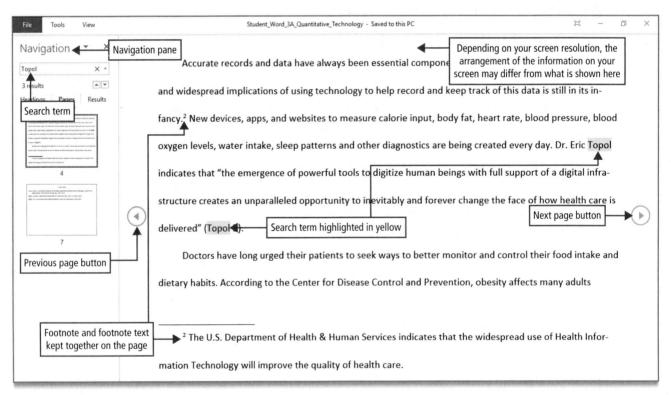

Figure 3.22

4 In the upper left corner, click **View**, and then take a moment to study the table in Figure 3.23.

View Commands in Read Mode	
View Command	**Action**
Edit Document	Return to Print Layout view to continue editing the document.
Navigation Pane	Search for specific text or click a heading or page to move to that location.
Show Comments	See comments, if any, within the document.
Column Width	Change the display of the document to fit more or less text on each line.
Page Color	Change the colors used to show the document to make it easier to read. Some readers prefer a sepia (brownish-gray) shading as the background or a black background with white text.
Layout	Read in different layouts. Select Column Layout, which is the default, or Paper Layout, which mimics the 8.5 x 11 format but without the ribbon.
A–Z Syllables	Show the breaks between the syllables.
A–Z Text Spacing	Increase spacing between words, characters, and lines.
Read Aloud	Read text out loud and highlight each word as it's read.

Figure 3.23

5 On the **View** menu, click **Edit Document** to return to **Print Layout** view. **Close** ☒ the **Navigation** pane.

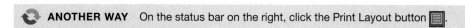 **ANOTHER WAY** On the status bar on the right, click the Print Layout button 📄.

6 **Save** 💾 your document. In the upper right corner of the Word window, click **Close** ☒.

 For Non-MyLab Submissions Determine What Your Instructor Requires for Submission
As directed by your instructor, submit your completed Word document.

7 In **MyLab IT**, locate and click the Grader Project **Word 3A Quantitative Technology**. In **step 3**, under **Upload Completed Assignment**, click **Choose File**. In the **Open** dialog box, navigate to your **Word Chapter 3 folder**, and then click your **Student_Word_3A_ Quantitative_Technology** file one time to select it. In the lower right corner of the **Open** dialog box, click **Open**.

The name of your selected file displays above the Upload button.

8 To submit your file to **MyLab IT** for grading, click **Upload**, wait a moment for a green **Success!** message, and then in **step 4**, click the blue **Submit for Grading** button. Click **Close Assignment** to return to your list of **Course Materials**.

You have completed Project 3A | **END**

ALERT   The Remaining Steps in this Activity are Optional

The remaining steps in the Activity are optional and are not included in the **MyLab IT** Grader system for this project. Your instructor may want you to complete these steps; or you may want to practice these steps on your own to see how PDF Reflow works and to see how to save Word documents in alternative file formats.

9 Start Word, and then on the left, click **Open**.

Recall that PDF Reflow enables you to import PDF files into Word so that you can transform a PDF into a fully editable Word document.

You can save a Word document in many different file formats, and there are times when you will want to do this. For example, you can save a Word document as a PDF or as a Plain Text file, which is a simple file consisting of lines of text with no formatting that almost any computer can open and display. Files saved in this file format will have the file name extension of .txt.

10 Click **Browse**, and then in the **Open** dialog box, navigate to the files you downloaded with this project. Click **w03A_PDF_optional**.

NOTE   **Locating Your w03A_PDF_optional File**

Your instructor can provide this file to you from the Instructor Resource Center, or you can download the student data files from www.pearsonhighered.com/go.

11 In the lower right corner, click **Open**. When a message indicates that *Word will now convert the PDF to an editable Word document . . .*, click **OK**.

12 If necessary, click **Enable Editing**, click **OK** again, and then compare your screen with Figure 3.24.

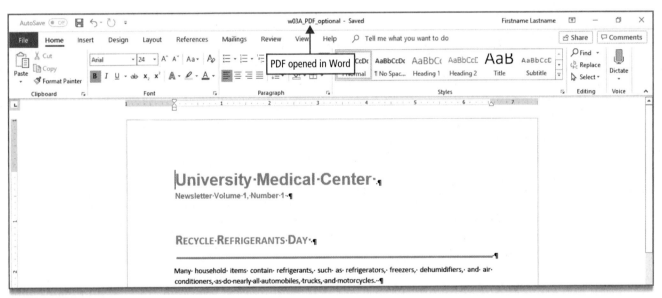

Figure 3.24

13 Click the **File tab**, and then on the left click **Save As**. Click **Browse**, and then navigate to your **Word Chapter 3** folder. In the **File name** box, using your own name, type **Lastname_Firstname_3A_Alt_File_Format** and then click the **Save as type arrow**.

14 On the **Save as type** list, notice the many file types you can use to save a Word document. Then, on the list, click **Plain Text**, and click **Save**. In the **File Conversion** dialog box, click **OK**.

15 **Close** ⊠ Word. Submit your Plain Text file if directed to do so by your instructor.

You have completed the optional portion of Project 3A   **END**

Objective	Use the Research Bar in Google Docs

Activity | Using the Research Bar in Google Docs

Google Docs provides a research tool that you can use to find studies and academic papers on many topics. You can narrow your search results by selecting "Scholar" from the drop-down menu in the search bar. After you find the study, you can insert it as a citation or a footnote. You can also choose to use the MLA, APA, or Chicago citation formatting.

1 From the desktop, open your browser, navigate to **http://google.com**, and then click the **Google Apps** menu ▦. Click **Drive**, and then if necessary, sign in to your Google account.

2 Open your **GO! Web Projects** folder—or click New to create and then open this folder if necessary.

3 In the upper left corner, click **New**, and then click **File upload**. In the **Open** dialog box, navigate to the files you downloaded for this chapter, and then in the **File List**, double-click to open **w03_3A_Web**.

4 Point to the uploaded file **w03_3A_Web**, and then right-click. On the shortcut menu, scroll as necessary, and then click **Rename**. Using your own last name and first name, type **Lastname_Firstname_WD_3A_Web** and then click **OK** to rename the file.

5 Point to the file in the file list, right-click, on the shortcut menu point to **Open with**, and then click **Google Docs**.

6 Press [Ctrl] + [End] to move to the end of the document, and then press [Enter] one time. Type **There are many studies related to the quantified self movement conducted by Melanie Swan, who is interested in crowdsourced health research.**

7 On the menu bar, click **Tools**, and then click **Explore** to open the **Explore pane** on the right.

8 At the top of the **Explore pane**, click in the search box, and then—being sure to include the quotation marks and uppercase letters as indicated—type **"quantified self" AND "Melanie Swan"** Press [Enter].

9 *Point* to the first item in the list and point to the quotation marks that display to the right; compare your screen with Figure A.

»» **GO!** With Google continues on next page

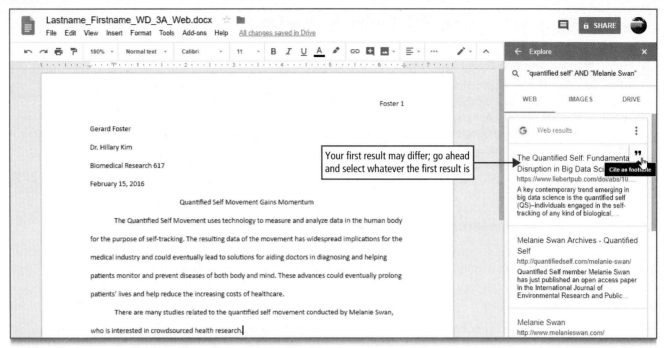

Figure A

10 Click **Cite as footnote**. Notice that a footnote number is inserted at the end of the sentence. Scroll down to view the bottom of the page, and then compare your screen with Figure B.

11 Submit the file as directed by your instructor. In the upper right, click your user name or picture, and then click **Sign out**. **Close** your browser window. Your file is automatically saved in your Google Drive.

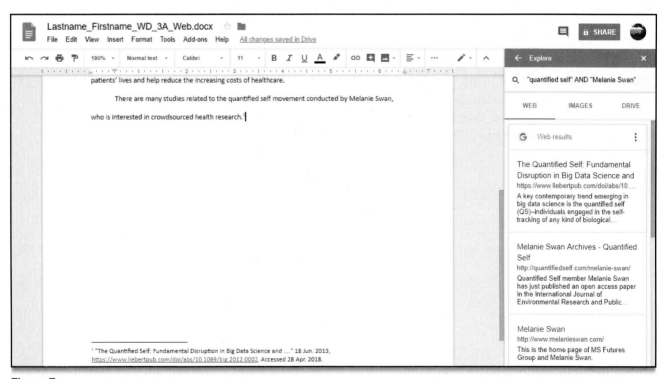

Figure B

Newsletter with Optional Mailing Labels

Project Activities

In Activities 3.15 through 3.29, you will edit a newsletter that University Medical Center is sending to the board of directors; optionally, you can create the necessary mailing labels. Your completed documents will look similar to Figure 3.25.

Project Files for MyLab IT Grader

1. In your **MyLab IT** course, locate and click **Word 3B Environment Newsletter**, Download Materials, and then Download All Files.
2. Extract the zipped folder to your Word Chapter 3 folder. Close the Grader download screens.
3. Take a moment to open the downloaded **Word_3B_Environment_Newsletter_Instructions**; note any recent updates to the book.

Project Results

GO! Project 3B
Where We're Going

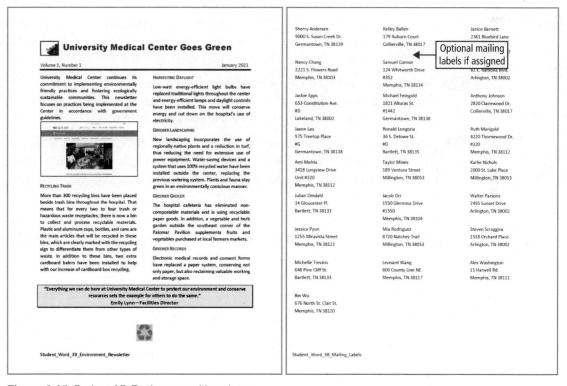

Figure 3.25 Project 3B Environment Newsletter

For Non-MyLab Submissions

For Project 3B, you will need:
w03B_Environment_Newsletter
w03B_Recycle_Symbol
w03B_Recycling
w03B_Addresses (optional if labels assigned)

In your Word Chapter 3 folder, save your document as:
Lastname_Firstname_3B_Environment_Newsletter
Lastname_Firstname_3B_Mailing_Labels (optional if labels assigned)

After you have named and saved your document, on the next page, begin with Step 2.

Objective 5 | Format a Multiple-Column Newsletter

ALERT Because Office 365 is a cloud-based subscription service that receives continuous updates, you may encounter some variations in what appears on your screen and what is shown in this instruction. Microsoft Office 365 is fully installed on your PC or Mac; no internet access is necessary to create or edit documents. When you *are* connected to the internet, you will receive monthly upgrades and new features, so you always have the latest versions of Office apps as soon as they are available. Your subscription gives you continuous free access to the latest innovations and refinements.

GO! Learn How
Video W3-5

A *newsletter* is a periodical that communicates news and information to a specific group. Newsletters, as well as all newspapers and most magazines, use multiple columns for articles because text in narrower columns is easier to read than text that stretches across a page.

You can create a newsletter in Word by changing a single column of text into two or more columns. If a column does not end where you want it to, you can end the column at a location of your choice by inserting a *manual column break*—an artificial end to a column to balance columns or to provide space for the insertion of other objects.

Activity 3.15 | Changing One Column of Text to Two Columns

2.3.1, 2.3.2

Newsletters are usually two or three columns wide. When using 8.5 × 11-inch paper in portrait orientation, avoid creating four or more columns because they are so narrow that word spacing looks awkward, often resulting in one long word on a line by itself.

1 Navigate to your **Word Chapter 3 folder**, and then double-click the Word file you downloaded from **MyLab IT** that displays your name—**Student_Word_3B_Environment_Newsletter**. If necessary, at the top click **Enable Editing**.

2 On the **Insert tab**, in the **Header & Footer group**, click **Footer**, and then at the bottom click **Edit Footer**. On the **Header & Footer Tools Design tab**, in the **Insert group**, click **Document Info**, and then click **File Name** to insert the file name in the footer. On the ribbon, click **Close Header and Footer**.

3 Select the first two paragraphs—the title and the Volume information and date. On the mini toolbar, click the **Font Color button arrow** $\boxed{\underline{A}\cdot}$, and then under **Theme Colors**, in the fifth column, click the last color.

MAC TIP Use ribbon commands.

4 With the text still selected, on the **Home tab**, in the **Paragraph group**, click the **Borders button arrow** $\boxed{\boxplus\cdot}$, and then at the bottom, click **Borders and Shading**.

5 In the **Borders and Shading** dialog box, on the **Borders tab**, click the **Color arrow**, and then under **Theme Colors**, in the fifth column, click the last color.

6 Click the **Width arrow**, and then click **3 pt**. In the **Preview** box at the right, point to the *bottom* border of the preview and click one time. Compare your screen with Figure 3.26.

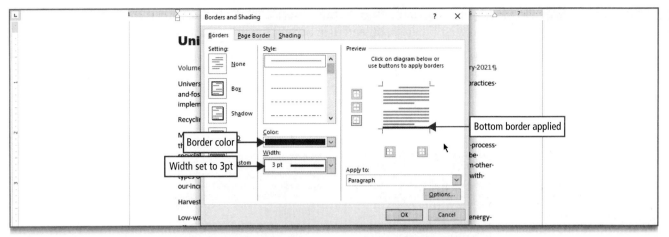
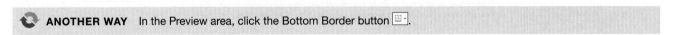

Figure 3.26

🔄 **ANOTHER WAY**   In the Preview area, click the Bottom Border button ⊞▾.

7 In the **Borders and Shading** dialog box, click **OK**.

The line visually defines the newsletter's ***nameplate***—the banner on the front page of a newsletter that identifies the publication.

8 Below the Volume information, click at the beginning of the paragraph that begins *University Medical Center continues*. By using the vertical scroll box, scroll to view the lower portion of the document, hold down Shift, and then click after the paragraph mark at the end of the paragraph that begins *Electronic medical records* to select all of the text between the insertion point and the sentence ending with the word *space*. Be sure that the paragraph mark is included in the selection. Compare your screen with Figure 3.27.

Use Shift to define a selection that may be difficult to select by dragging.

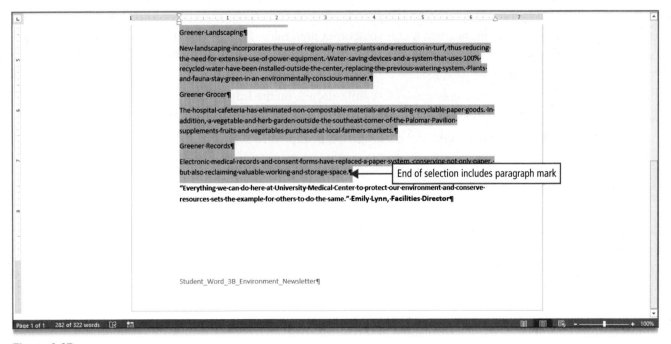

Figure 3.27

9 ▶ On the **Layout tab**, in the **Page Setup group**, click **Columns**, and then click **Two**. Compare your screen with Figure 3.28, and then **Save** 🖫 your newsletter.

Word divides the selected text into two columns and inserts a ***section break*** at the end of the selection, dividing the one-column section of the document from the two-column section of the document. A ***section*** is a portion of a document that can be formatted differently from the rest of the document. A section break marks the end of one section and the beginning of another section.

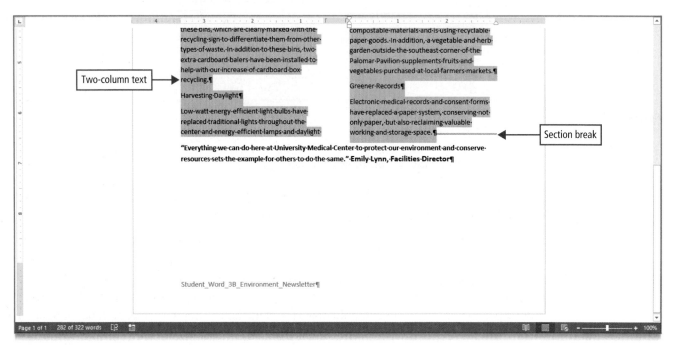

Figure 3.28

Activity 3.16 │ Formatting Multiple Columns

2.3.1

The uneven right margin of a single page-width column is easy to read. When you create narrow columns, justified text is sometimes preferable. Depending on the design and layout of your newsletter, you might decide to reduce extra space between paragraphs and between columns to improve the readability of the document.

1 ▶ With the two columns of text still selected, on the **Layout tab**, in the **Paragraph group**, click the **Spacing After down spin arrow** one time to change the spacing after to **6 pt**.

2 ▶ On the **Home tab**, in the **Paragraph group**, click **Justify** ☰.

3 Click anywhere in the document to deselect the text, compare your screen with Figure 3.29, and then **Save** 🖫.

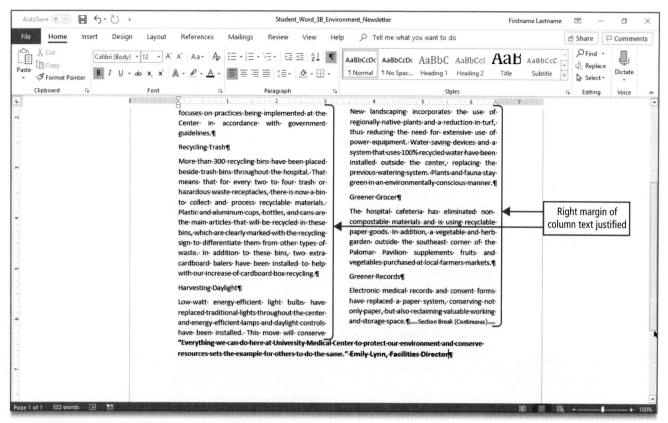

Figure 3.29

Activity 3.17 │ Inserting a Column Break

1 Near the bottom of the first column, click to position the insertion point at the beginning of the line *Harvesting Daylight*.

2 On the **Layout tab**, in the **Page Setup group**, click **Breaks**. Under **Page Breaks**, click **Column**, and then if necessary, scroll to view the bottom of the first column.

A column break displays at the bottom of the first column; text to the right of the column break moves to the top of the next column.

3 Compare your screen with Figure 3.30, and then **Save** 🖫.

A *column break indicator*—a dotted line containing the words *Column Break*—displays at the bottom of the column.

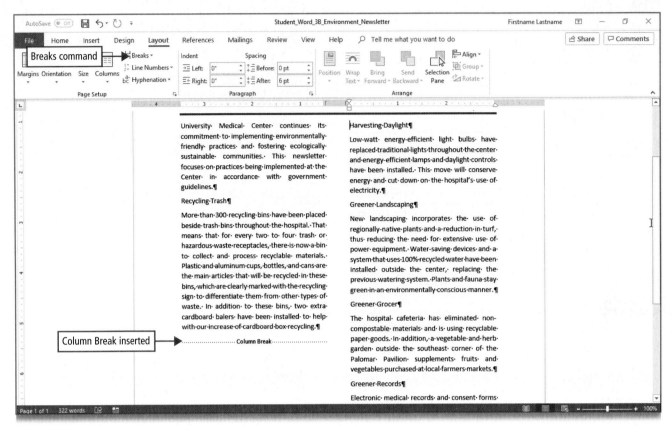

Figure 3.30

Activity 3.18 | Inserting a Picture

Pictures can make your newsletter visually appealing and more interesting.

1 Press Ctrl + End to move to the end of the document.

2 On the **Insert tab**, in the **Illustrations group**, click **Pictures**. Navigate to your **Word Chapter 3** folder, and then double-click the file **w03B_Recycle_Symbol** to insert the image at the insertion point. If a blue message regarding *Automatic Alt Text* displays, click Got it. Compare your screen with Figure 3.31.

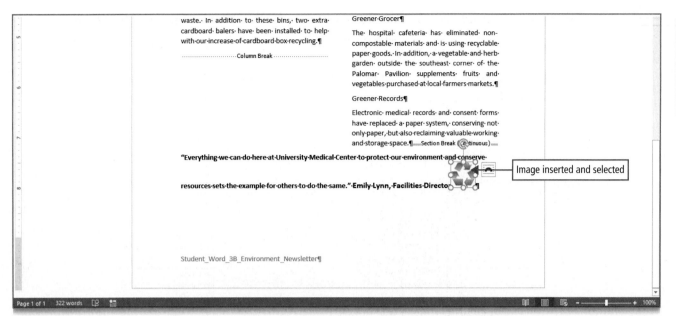

Figure 3.31

> 3 ▸ With the image selected, on the **Picture Tools Format tab**, in the **Size group**, click in the **Height** box. If necessary, type **0.5** and then press Enter.

> 4 ▸ On the **Picture Tools Format tab**, in the **Arrange group**, click **Wrap Text**, and then click **Square**. In the **Arrange group**, click **Position**, and then at the bottom of the gallery, click **More Layout Options**. Compare your screen with Figure 3.32.

🖥 **MAC TIP** On the Picture Format tab, in the Arrange group, click the Wrap Text button, and then click Square.

🔄 **ANOTHER WAY** To the right of the picture, click the Layout Options button, and then click Square.

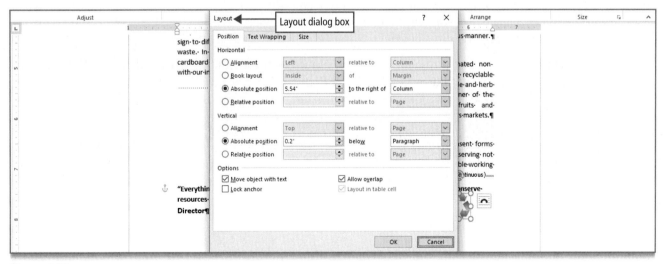

Figure 3.32

5 In the **Layout** dialog box, on the **Position tab**, under **Horizontal**, click the **Alignment** option button. Click the **Alignment arrow**, and then click **Centered**. Click the **relative to arrow** and then click **Page**.

6 Under **Vertical**, click the **Alignment** option button. Click the **Alignment arrow**, and then click **Bottom**. Click the **relative to arrow**, and then click **Margin**. Compare your screen with Figure 3.33.

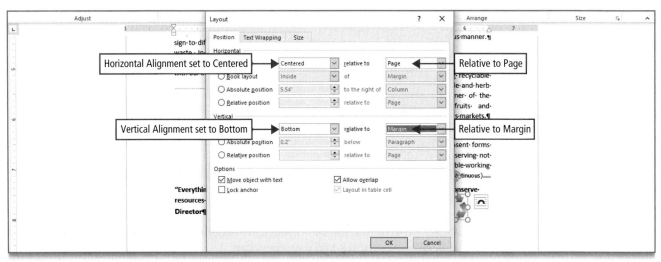

Figure 3.33

7 Click **OK**, scroll to the bottom of the page, and then notice that the recycle image is centered in the lower portion of your document. **Save** the document.

ANOTHER WAY   Drag the image to visually position the image.

Activity 3.19 | Cropping a Picture and Resizing a Picture by Scaling

5.1.2, 5.4.1

In this Activity, you will insert a picture and edit the picture by cropping and scaling. When you *crop* a picture, you remove unwanted or unnecessary areas of the picture. When you *scale* a picture, you resize it to a percentage of its size.

1 Press Ctrl + Home to move to the top of the document. On the **Insert tab**, in the **Illustrations group**, click **Pictures**. In the **Insert Picture** dialog box, navigate to the files you downloaded with this project, and then double-click **w03B_Recycling** to insert it.

2 With the picture selected, on the **Picture Tools Format tab**, in the **Size group**, click the upper portion of the **Crop** button to display crop handles around the picture. Compare your screen with Figure 3.34.

Crop handles are used like sizing handles to define unwanted areas of the picture.

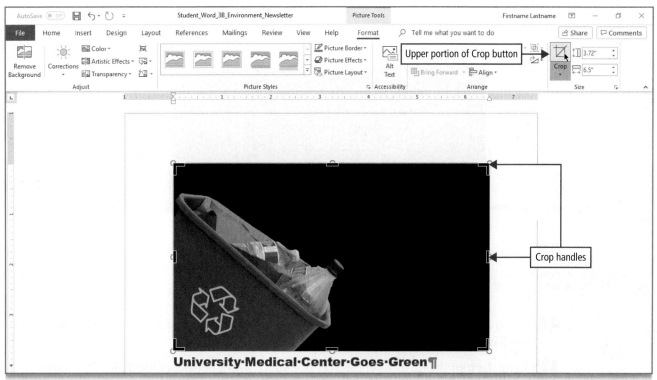

Figure 3.34

3 Point to the center right crop handle to display the ⊢ pointer. Compare your screen with Figure 3.35.

Use the *crop pointer* to crop areas of a picture.

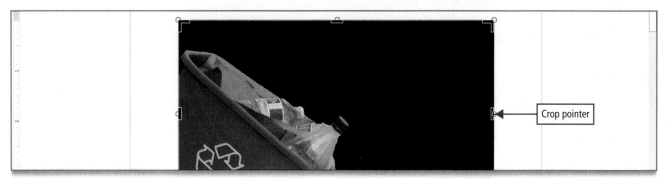

Figure 3.35

4 With the crop pointer displayed, hold down the left mouse button and drag to the left to approximately **5 inches on the horizontal ruler**, and then release the mouse button. Compare your screen with Figure 3.36.

The portion of the image to be removed displays in gray.

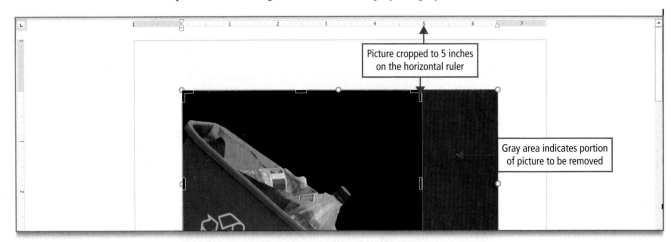

Figure 3.36

5 Click anywhere in the document outside of the image to apply the crop.

ANOTHER WAY Click the upper portion of the Crop button to apply the crop.

6 Click to select the picture again. On the **Picture Tools Format tab**, in the **Size group**, click the **Dialog Box Launcher** button.

7 In the **Layout** dialog box, on the **Size tab**, in the lower portion of the dialog box under **Scale**, be sure that the **Lock aspect ratio** and **Relative to original picture size** check boxes are selected. Under **Scale**, select the percentage number in the **Height box**, type **10** and then press Tab. Compare your screen with Figure 3.37.

When *Lock aspect ratio* is selected, the height and width of the picture are sized proportionately and only one scale value is necessary. The second value—in this instance Width—adjusts proportionately. When *Relative to original picture size* is selected, the scale is applied as a percentage of the original picture size.

MAC TIP In the Arrange group, click Wrap Text, click More Layout Options, and then click the Size tab.

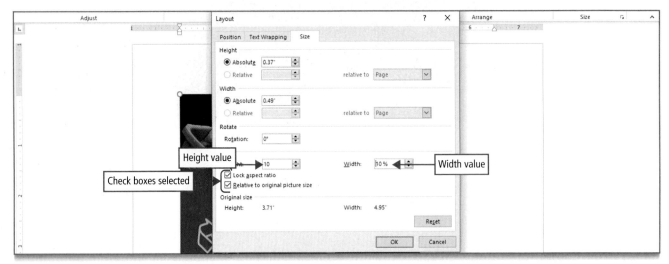

Figure 3.37

8 In the **Layout** dialog box, click the **Text Wrapping tab**. Under **Wrapping style**, click **Square**.

9 Click the **Position tab**, and then under **Horizontal**, click the **Alignment** option button. Be sure that the **Alignment** indicates **Left** and **relative to Column**. Under **Vertical**, click the **Alignment** option button, and then change the alignment to **Top relative to Margin**. Click **OK**, and then compare your screen with Figure 3.38.

Picture aligned and resized

Figure 3.38

Activity 3.20 | Setting Transparent Color and Recoloring a Picture

MOS
5.2.3

You can make one color in a picture transparent using the Set Transparent Color command. When you *recolor* a picture, you change all the colors in the picture to shades of a single color.

1 On the **View tab**, in the **Zoom group**, click **Zoom**, and then click **200%**. Click **OK**. Drag the scroll boxes as necessary so that you can view the recycle bin picture at the top of the document.

2 If necessary, select the recycle bin picture. Click the **Picture Tools Format tab**. In the **Adjust group**, click **Color**, and then below the gallery, click **Set Transparent Color**. Move the pointer into the document to display the ✐ pointer.

3 Point anywhere in the black background of the recycle bin picture, and then click to apply the transparent color to the background. Compare your screen with Figure 3.39.

Transparent color applied to black background

Figure 3.39

4 Press `Ctrl` + `End` to move to the end of your document, and then select the picture of the recycle symbol. Click the **Picture Tools Format tab**, and then in the **Adjust group**, click **Color** to display a gallery of recoloring options. Under **Recolor**, point to one of the Recolor options that are blue, for example the one shown in Figure 3.40.

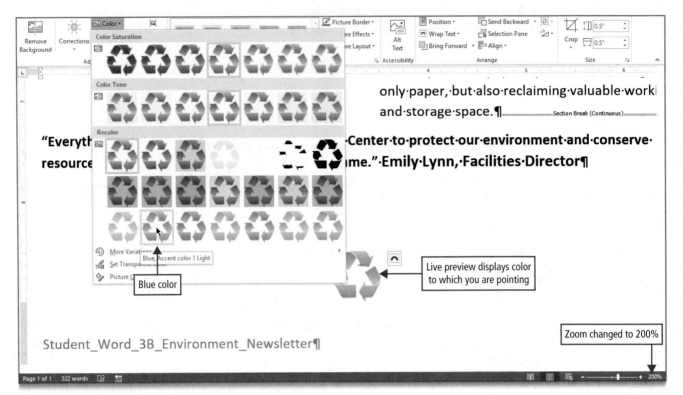

Figure 3.40

5 Click the blue recolor option to apply it, or select any of the blue options, and then **Save** 💾 the document.

Activity 3.21 | Adjusting the Brightness and Contrast of a Picture

5.2.4

Brightness is the relative lightness of a picture. *Contrast* is the difference between the darkest and lightest area of a picture.

1 If necessary, select the recycle symbol. On the **Format tab**, in the **Adjust group**, click **Corrections**. Under **Brightness/Contrast**, point to several of the options to view the effect that the settings have on the picture.

📱 **MAC TIP**   Live Preview while pointing to options is not available.

2 Under **Brightness/Contrast**, use the ScreenTips to locate the setting **Brightness: -40% Contrast: +40%** as shown in Figure 3.41.

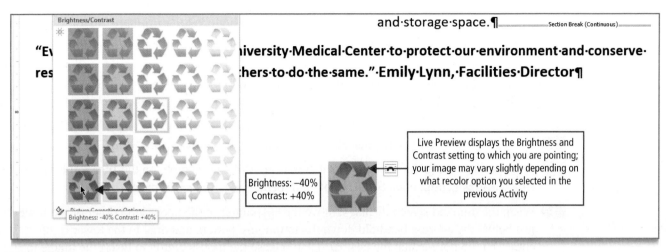

Figure 3.41

3 Click to apply **Brightness: -40% Contrast: +40%** to the recycle image.

4 On the **View tab**, in the **Zoom group**, click **100%**, if necessary, click **OK**, and then **Save** 🔲 your document.

Activity 3.22 | Applying a Border to a Picture and Flipping a Picture

MOS
5.2.4

The *flip* commands create a reverse image of a picture or object.

1 Press Ctrl + Home to move to the top of the document, and then select the picture of the recycle bin. Click the **Picture Tools Format tab**, and then in the **Picture Styles group**, click the **Picture Border button**. Under **Theme Colors**, in the fourth column, click the first color.

2 Click **Picture Border** again, and then point to **Weight**. Click **1 1/2 pt** to change the thickness of the border.

3 On the **Format tab**, in the **Arrange group**, click **Rotate Objects** ⬜, and then click **Flip Horizontal**. Click anywhere in the document to deselect the picture. **Save** 🔲, and then compare your screen with Figure 3.42.

Figure 3.42

Activity 3.23 | Inserting and Formatting a Screen Clipping

5.1.5

A *screenshot* is an image of an active window on your computer that you can paste into a document. Screenshots are especially useful when you want to insert an image of a website into your Word document. You can also insert a screenshot by using *Screen Clipping*, a tool with which you can take a quick snapshot of part of the screen, and then add it to your document.

1 In the paragraph that begins *University Medical Center continues*, click after the period at the end of the paragraph. Start your web browser, and then navigate to the site **www.data.gov/ecosystems/** (If this website is not available, go to another section of the data.gov site or go to www.epa.gov.)

2 From the taskbar, redisplay your **3B_Environment_Newsletter** document.

3 With the insertion point sill positioned at the end of the paragraph, on the **Insert tab**, in the **Illustrations group**, click **Screenshot**, and then click **Screen Clipping**.

4 When the dimmed screen displays, move the ⊞ pointer to the upper left corner of the screen just below the address bar, hold down the left mouse button, and drag to the lower right corner but do not include the taskbar. Then release the mouse button to insert the image in your document. Compare your screen with Figure 3.43.

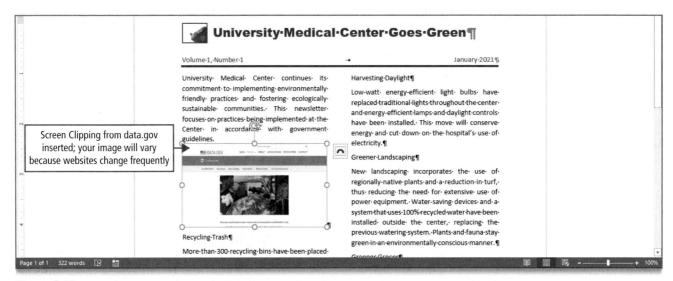

Figure 3.43

5 With the inserted screenshot selected, on the **Format tab**, in the **Picture Styles group**, click **Picture Border**, and then under **Theme Colors**, in the second column, click the first color.

6 Save 🖫 the document.

| MORE KNOWLEDGE | Inserting a Link in a Document |

You can create a link in your document for quick access to webpages and files. To insert a link in a document, first position the insertion point where you want the link to appear. On the Insert tab, in the Links group, click Hyperlink. In the Insert Hyperlink dialog box, in the Text to display box, type the text that will display in the document as a blue hyperlink. At the bottom, in the Address box, type the URL and then click OK.

Special text and paragraph formatting is useful to emphasize text, and it makes your newsletter look more professional. For example, you can place a border around one or more paragraphs or add shading to a paragraph. When adding shading, use light colors; dark shading can make the text difficult to read.

Activity 3.24 | Applying the Small Caps Font Effect

2.2.1

For headlines and titles, *small caps* is an attractive font effect. The effect changes lowercase letters to uppercase letters, but with the height of lowercase letters.

1 Under the screenshot, select the paragraph *Recycling Trash* including the paragraph mark.

2 Right-click the selected text, and then on the shortcut menu, click **Font** to display the **Font** dialog box. Click the **Font color arrow**, and then in the fifth column, click the last color.

3 Under **Font style**, click **Bold**. Under **Effects**, select the **Small caps** check box. Compare your screen with Figure 3.44.

The Font dialog box provides more options than are available on the ribbon and enables you to make several changes at the same time. In the Preview box, the text displays with the selected formatting options applied.

MAC TIP Display the menu bar, click Format, click Font, under Effects, select the Small caps check box; or, right-click over the selected text and click Font to display the Font dialog box.

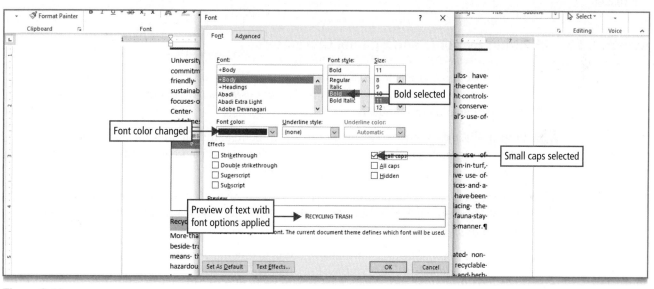

Figure 3.44

4 Click **OK**. With the text still selected, point to the text and right-click, and then on the mini toolbar, double-click **Format Painter** so that you can apply the selected format multiple times. Then, in the second column, with the pointer, select each of the heading paragraphs—*Harvesting Daylight*, *Greener Landscaping*, *Greener Grocer*, and *Greener Records*—to apply the same formats. Press Esc to turn off Format Painter.

MAC TIP On the Home tab, in the Clipboard group, double-click the Format Painter icon.

5 In the first column, below the screenshot, notice that the space between the *Recycling Trash* subheading and the screenshot is fairly small. Click anywhere in the *Recycling Trash* subheading, and then on the **Layout tab**, in the **Paragraph group**, click the **Before up spin arrow** two times to set the **Spacing Before** to **12 pt**.

6 Compare your screen with Figure 3.45, and then **Save** 💾 your document.

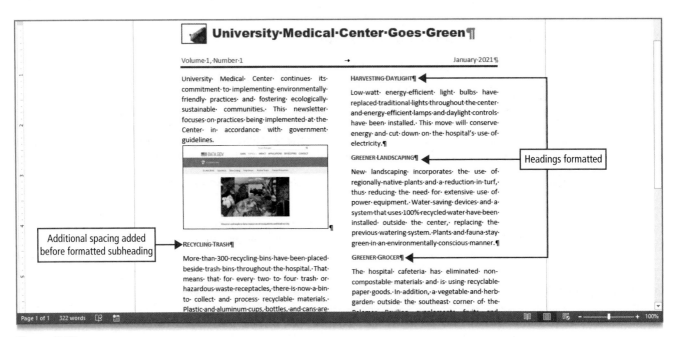

Figure 3.45

Activity 3.25 | Inserting Symbols and Special Characters

MOS
2.1.2

You can insert symbols and special characters in a Word document, including copyright symbols, trademark symbols, and em dashes. An ***em dash*** is a punctuation symbol used to indicate an explanation or emphasis.

1 Press Ctrl + End to move to the end of the document, and then after the name *Emily Lynn* delete the comma and the space that separates her name from her job title—*Facilities Director*.

2 With the insertion point positioned before the *F* in *Facilities*, on the **Insert tab**, in the **Symbols group**, click **Symbol**. Below the gallery, click **More Symbols** to display the **Symbol** dialog box.

Here you can choose the symbol that you want to insert in your document.

3 In the **Symbol** dialog box, click the **Special Characters tab**. Scroll the list to view the types of special characters that you can insert; notice that some of the characters can be inserted using a Shortcut key.

4 Click **Em Dash**, and then in the lower right portion of the dialog box, click **Insert**. If necessary, drag the title bar of the Symbol window up or to the side, and then compare your screen with Figure 3.46.

An em dash displays between the name *Lynn* and the word *Facilities*.

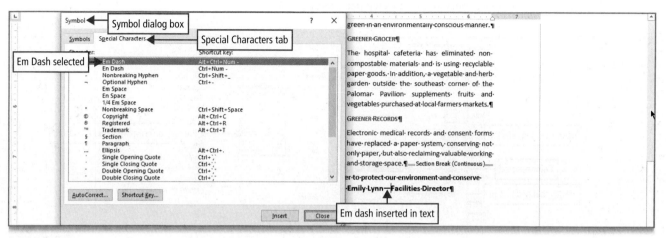

Figure 3.46

5 In the **Symbol** dialog box, click **Close**, and then **Save** your document.

Activity 3.26 | Adding Borders and Shading to a Paragraph

Paragraph borders provide strong visual cues to the reader. You can use paragraph shading with or without borders; however, combined with a border, light shading can be very effective in drawing the reader's eye to specific text.

1 At the end of the document, being sure to include the paragraph mark at the end, select the two lines of bold text that begin *"Everything we can do*.

The recycle picture may also be selected because it is anchored to the paragraph.

2 On the **Home tab**, in the **Paragraph group**, click the **Borders button arrow**, and then click **Borders and Shading**.

3 In the **Borders and Shading** dialog box, be sure the **Borders tab** is selected. Under **Setting**, click **Shadow**. Click the **Color arrow**, and then in the fifth column, click the last color. Click the **Width arrow**, and then click **1 pt**. Compare your screen with Figure 3.47.

In the lower right portion of the Borders and Shading dialog box, the *Apply to* box indicates *Paragraph*. The *Apply to* box directs where the border will be applied—in this instance, the border will be applied to the selected paragraph.

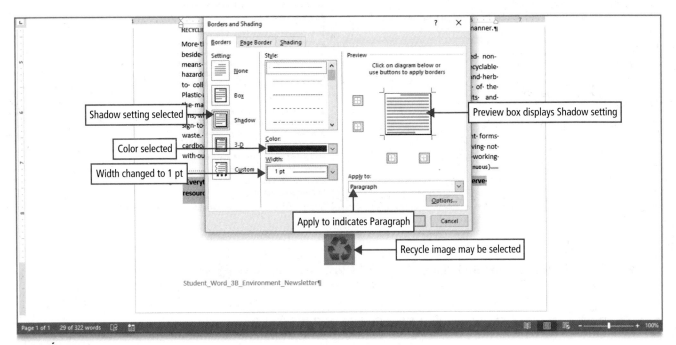

Figure 3.47

NOTE   Adding Simple Borders to Text

You can add simple borders from the Borders button gallery, located in the Paragraph group. This button offers less control over the border appearance, however, because the line thickness and color applied will match the most recently used on the computer at which you are working. The Borders and Shading dialog box enables you to make your own custom selections.

---

4 At the top of the **Borders and Shading** dialog box, click the **Shading tab**.

5 Click the **Fill arrow**, and then in the fifth column, click the second color. Notice that the shading change is reflected in the Preview area on the right side of the dialog box.

6 Click **OK**. On the **Home tab**, in the **Paragraph group**, click **Center** ☰.

7 Click anywhere in the document to deselect, and then compare your screen with Figure 3.48.

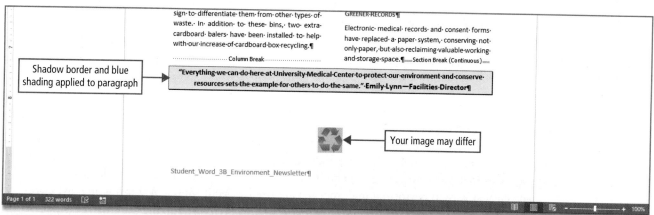

sign· to· differentiate· them· from· other· types· of· waste.· In· addition· to· these· bins,· two· extra· cardboard· balers· have· been· installed· to· help· with·our·increase·of·cardboard·box·recycling.¶

GREENER·RECORDS¶

Electronic· medical· records· and· consent· forms· have· replaced· a· paper· system,· conserving· not· only·paper,·but·also·reclaiming·valuable·working· and·storage·space.¶══Section Break (Continuous)══

Shadow border and blue shading applied to paragraph

·······················Column Break························

"Everything·we·can·do·here·at·University·Medical·Center·to·protect·our·environment·and·conserve· resources·sets·the·example·for·others·to·do·the·same."·Emily·Lynn—Facilities·Director¶

Your image may differ

Student_Word_3B_Environment_Newsletter¶

Page 1 of 1   322 words   100%

Figure 3.48

8 In the shaded paragraph, in the second line, click in front of the *E* in the name *Emily*. Hold down Shift and then press Enter.

Holding down Shift while pressing Enter inserts a ***manual line break***, which moves the text to the right of the insertion point to a new line while keeping the text in the same paragraph. A ***line break indicator***, in the shape of a bent arrow, indicates a manual line break.

9 Press Ctrl + Home to move the insertion point to the top of the document. Click the **File tab** to display **Backstage** view, and then on the left click **Info**. On the right, at the bottom of the **Properties** list, click **Show All Properties**.

10 On the list of **Properties**, click to the right of **Tags**, and then type **newsletter, January**

11 Click to the right of **Subject**, and then type your course name and section number. Under **Related People**, be sure that your name displays as the author. If necessary, right-click the author name, click Edit Property, type your name, and click OK.

12 On the left, click **Save**. In the upper right corner of the Word window, click **Close** ☒.

For Non-MyLab Submissions Determine What Your Instructor Requires for Submission
As directed by your instructor, submit your completed Word document.

---

13 In **MyLab IT**, locate and click the Grader Project **Word 3B Environment Newsletter**. In **step 3**, under **Upload Completed Assignment**, click **Choose File**. In the **Open** dialog box, navigate to your **Word Chapter 3 folder**, and then click your **Student_Word_3B_ Environment_Newsletter** file one time to select it. In the lower right corner of the **Open** dialog box, click **Open**.

The name of your selected file displays above the Upload button.

14 To submit your file to **MyLab IT** for grading, click **Upload**, wait a moment for a green **Success!** message, and then in **step 4**, click the blue **Submit for Grading** button. Click **Close Assignment** to return to your list of **Course Materials**.

You have completed Project 3B **END**

GO! Learn How
Video W3-7

Word's *mail merge* feature joins a *main document* and a *data source* to create customized letters or labels. The main document contains the text or formatting that remains constant. For labels, the main document contains the formatting for a specific label size. The data source contains information including the names and addresses of the individuals for whom the labels are being created. Names and addresses in a data source might come from an Excel worksheet or an Access database.

The easiest way to perform a mail merge is to use the Mail Merge Wizard, which asks you questions and, based on your answers, walks you step by step through the mail merge process.

Activity 3.27 | Starting the Mail Merge Wizard

4.3.1
(Expert)

In this Activity, you will open the data source for the mail merge, which is an Excel worksheet containing names and addresses.

1 Start Word and display a new blank document. Display formatting marks and rulers. Using your own name, **Save** the document in your **Word Chapter 3** folder as **Lastname_Firstname_Word_3B_Mailing_Labels**

2 Click the **Mailings tab**. In the **Start Mail Merge group**, click **Start Mail Merge**, and then click **Step-by-Step Mail Merge Wizard** to display the **Mail Merge** pane on the right.

3 In the **Mail Merge** pane, under **Select document type**, click **Labels**. At the bottom of the **Mail Merge** pane, click **Next: Starting document** to display Step 2 of 6.

4 Under **Select starting document**, be sure **Change document layout** is selected, and then under **Change document layout**, click **Label options**.

5 In the **Label Options** dialog box, under **Printer information**, click the **Tray arrow**, and then if necessary, click Default tray (Automatically Select)—the exact wording may vary depending on your printer, but select the *Default* or *Automatic* option so that you can print the labels on regular paper rather than manually inserting labels in the printer.

6 Under **Label information**, click the **Label vendors arrow**, and then click **Avery US Letter**. Under **Product number**, scroll about halfway down the list, and then click **5160 Address Labels**. Compare your screen with Figure 3.49.

The Avery 5160 address label is a commonly used label. The precut sheets contain three columns of 10 labels each—for a total of 30 labels per sheet.

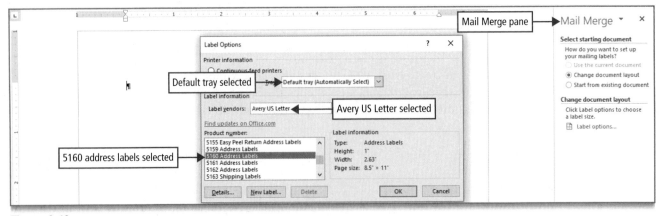

Figure 3.49

7 At the bottom of the **Label Options** dialog box, click **OK**. If a message box displays, click OK to set up the labels. If the gridlines that define each label do not display, on the Table Tools Layout tab, in the Table group, click View Gridlines.

8 At the bottom of the **Mail Merge** pane, click **Next: Select recipients**. In the **Mail Merge** pane, under **Select recipients**, be sure the **Use an existing list** option button is selected. Under **Use an existing list**, click **Browse**.

> The label page is set up with three columns and ten rows. Here, in Step 3 of the Mail Merge Wizard, you must identify the recipients—the data source. For your recipient data source, you can choose to use an existing list—for example, a list of names and addresses that you have in an Access database, an Excel worksheet, or your Outlook contacts list. If you do not have an existing data source, you can create a new list at this point in the wizard.

9 In the **Select Data Source** dialog box, navigate to the files you downloaded with this chapter, click one time to select the Excel file **w03B_Addresses**, and then click **Open** to display the **Select Table** dialog box. Compare your screen with Figure 3.50.

> In the Select Table dialog box, the sheet name of the Excel workbook is selected, and at the bottom the check box for *First row of data contains column headers* is selected.

> Each row of information in the Excel worksheet that contains data for one person is referred to as a *record*. The column headings—for example, *Last Name* and *First Name*—are referred to as *fields*.

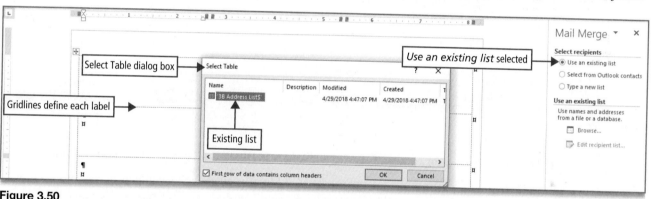

Figure 3.50

10 In the **Select Table** dialog box, click **OK**, and then compare your screen with Figure 3.51.

> The Mail Merge Recipients dialog box displays. Here you can perform various actions on the list; for example, you can sort, filter, find duplicates in, locate a specific recipient, or validate addresses.

> You can also select the path in the Data Source to enable editing to add additional recipients to the list.

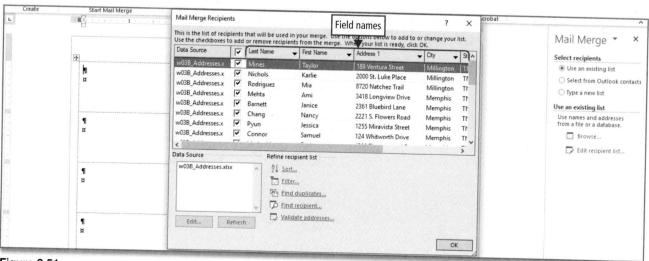

Figure 3.51

11 In the lower right corner of the **Mail Merge Recipients** dialog box, click **OK**.

The labels in the Word document display, and *<<Next Record>>* displays in each label cell.

Activity 3.28 | Completing the Mail Merge

4.3.2
(Expert),
4.3.4
(Expert)

1 At the bottom of the **Mail Merge** pane, click **Next: Arrange your labels**.

2 Under **Arrange your labels**, click **Address block**. In the **Insert Address Block** dialog box, under **Specify address elements**, examine the various formats for names. If necessary, under *Insert recipient's name in this format*, select the *Joshua Randall Jr.* format. Compare your dialog box with Figure 3.52.

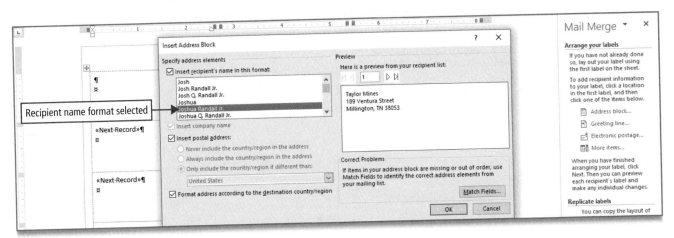

Figure 3.52

3 In the lower right corner of the **Insert Address Block** dialog box, click **Match Fields**.

If your field names are descriptive, the Mail Merge program will identify them correctly, as is the case with most of the information in the *Required for Address Block* section. However, the Address 2 field is unmatched—in the source file, this column is named *Unit*.

4 Click the **Address 2 arrow**, and then from the list of available fields, click **Unit** to match the Mail Merge field with the field in your data source.

5 At the bottom of the **Match Fields** dialog box, click **OK**. At the bottom of the **Insert Address Block** dialog box, click **OK**.

6 In the **Mail Merge** pane, under **Replicate labels**, click **Update all labels** to insert an address block in each label space for each subsequent record.

7 At the bottom of the **Mail Merge** pane, click **Next: Preview your labels**. Notice that for addresses with four lines, the last line of the address is cut off.

8 Press Ctrl + A to select all of the label text, click the **Layout tab**, and then in the **Paragraph group**, click in the **Spacing Before** box. Type **3** and press Enter to adjust the spacing in your label.

9 Click in any label to deselect, and notice that 4-line addresses are no longer cut off. Compare your screen with Figure 3.53.

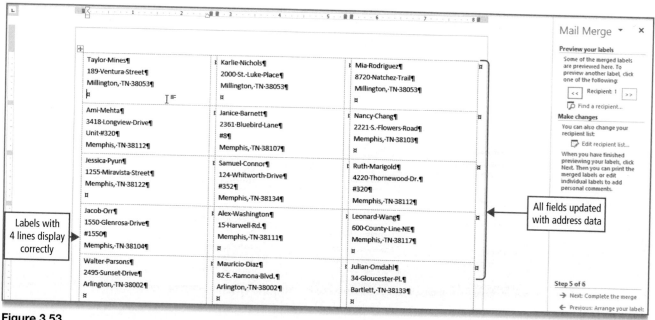

Figure 3.53

10 At the bottom of the **Mail Merge** pane, click **Next: Complete the merge**.

Step 6 of the Mail Merge displays. At this point, you can print or edit your labels, although this is done more easily in the document window.

11 **Save** 🖫 your labels, and then on the right, **Close** ☒ the **Mail Merge** pane.

Activity 3.29 | Previewing and Printing Mail Merge Results

MOS
4.3.3
(Expert)

If you discover that you need to make further changes to your labels, you can still make them even though the Mail Merge task pane is closed.

1 Add the file name to the footer, close the footer area, and then move to the top of Page 2. Click anywhere in the empty table row, and then click the **Table Tools Layout tab**. In the **Rows & Columns group**, click **Delete**, and then click **Delete Rows**.

Adding footer text to a label sheet replaces the last row of labels on a page with the footer text and moves the last row of labels to the top of the next page. In this instance, a blank second page is created, which you can delete by deleting the blank row.

2 Notice that the labels do not display in alphabetical order. Click the **Mailings tab**, and then in the **Start Mail Merge group**, click **Edit Recipient List** to display the list of names and addresses.

3 In the **Mail Merge Recipients** dialog box, click the **Last Name** field heading, and notice that the names are sorted alphabetically by the recipient's last name.

Mailing labels are often sorted by either last name or by ZIP Code.

4 Click the **Last Name** field heading again, and then notice that the last names are sorted in descending order. Click the **Last Name** field one more time to return to ascending order, and then click **OK**. Press Ctrl + Home, and then compare your screen with Figure 3.54.

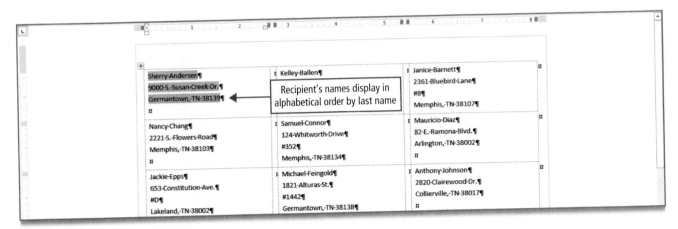

Figure 3.54

5 From the **File tab**, display **Backstage** view, on the left click **Info**, and in the lower right, click **Show All Properties**. On the list of **Properties**, click to the right of **Tags**, and then type **labels**

6 Click to the right of **Subject**, and then type your course name and section number. Be sure that your name displays as the author. If necessary, right-click the author name, click Edit Property, type your name, and click OK.

7 On the left, click **Save**. In the upper right corner of the Word window, click **Close** ⊠. If directed by your instructor to do so, submit your Lastname_Firstname_3B_Mailing_Labels file as a paper printout, an electronic image of your document that looks like a printed document, or your completed Word file.

If you print, the labels will print on whatever paper is in the printer; unless you have preformatted labels available, the labels will print on a sheet of paper. Printing the labels on plain paper enables you to proofread the labels before you print them on more expensive label sheets.

You have completed the optional portion of this project **END**

Objective | Format a Newsletter in Google Docs

ALERT   **Working with Web-Based Applications and Services**

Computer programs and services on the web receive continuous updates and improvements, so the steps to complete this web-based Activity may differ from the ones shown. You can often look at the screens and the information presented to determine how to complete the Activity.

If you do not already have a Google account, you will need to create one before you begin this Activity. Go to http://google.com and, in the upper right corner, click Sign In. On the Sign In screen, click Create Account. On the Create your Google Account page, complete the form, read and agree to the Terms of Service and Privacy Policy, and then click Next step. On the Welcome screen, click Get Started.

Activity | Formatting a Two-Column Newsletter in Google Docs

In this Activity, you will use Google Docs to edit a newsletter similar to the one you edited in Project 3B.

1 From the desktop, open your browser, navigate to **http://google.com**, and then click the **Google Apps** menu ▦. Click **Drive**, and then if necessary, sign in to your Google account.

2 Open your **GO! Web Projects** folder—or click New to create and then open this folder if necessary.

3 On the left, click **New**, and then click **File upload**. In the **Open** dialog box, navigate to the files you downloaded for this chapter, and then in the **File List**, double-click to open **w03_3B_Web**.

4 Point to the uploaded file **w03_3B_Web**, and then right-click. On the shortcut menu, scroll as necessary, and then click **Rename**. Using your own last name and first name, type **Lastname_Firstname_WD_3B_Web** and then click **OK** to rename the file.

5 Right-click the file you just renamed, point to **Open with**, and then click **Google Docs**.

6 Drag to select the newsletter title—*University Medical Center Goes Green*. On the toolbar, click the **Font size arrow**, and then click **18**. With the newsletter title still selected, on the toolbar, click the **Text color button** Ａ, and then in the second row, click the third from last color—**blue**.

Apply the same **Font Color** to the five subheadings—*Recycling Trash, Harvesting Daylight, Greener Landscaping, Greener Grocer,* and *Greener Records.*

7 Press Ctrl + End to move to the end of the document, and then press Enter. On the menu bar, click **Insert**, point to **Image**, and then click **Upload from computer**. In the **Open** dialog box, navigate to the files downloaded with this chapter, and then double-click **w03B_Recycle_Symbol**.

8 Select the image and then on the toolbar, click **Center** ☰.

9 Click at the beginning of the paragraph heading *Recycling Trash*, and then drag down to select the text for the five articles—ending with the period after the word *space*.

10 With the five headings and their accompanying paragraphs selected, on the toolbar, click **Format**. Point to **Columns**, and then click the second option—text with two columns. Click anywhere to deselect, and then compare your screen with Figure A.

11 Submit the file as directed by your instructor. In the upper right, click your user name, and then click **Sign out**. **Close** your browser window. Your file is automatically saved in your Google Drive.

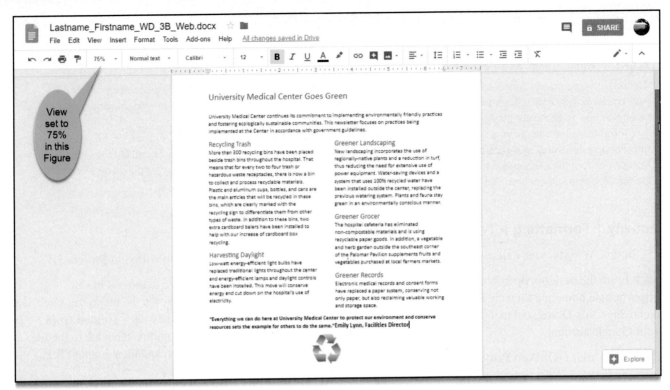

Figure A

wavebreakmedia/Shutterstock, Monkey Business Images/Fotolia, Ivanko80/Shutterstock, Monkey Business Images/Shutterstock

3
WORD

Microsoft Office Specialist (MOS) Skills in This Chapter

Project A	Project B
1.1.1 Search for text	**2.1.2** Insert symbols and special characters
1.1.3 Move to specific locations and objects in a document	**2.2.1** Apply text effects
1.3.1 Save documents in alternative file formats	**2.3.2** Insert page, section, and column breaks
1.3.2 Modify basic document properties	**4.3.1** (Expert) Manage recipient lists
2.2.3 Set line and paragraph spacing and indentation	**4.3.2** (Expert) Insert merged fields
2.3.1 Format text in multiple columns	**4.3.3** (Expert) Preview merge results
2.3.2 Insert page, section, and column breaks	**4.3.4** (Expert) Create merged documents, labels, and envelopes
2.3.2 (Expert) Modify existing styles	**5.1.2** Insert pictures
4.1.1 Insert footnotes and endnotes	**5.1.5** Insert screenshots and screen clippings
4.1.2 Modify footnote and endnote properties	**5.2.3** Remove picture backgrounds
4.1.3 Create and modify bibliography citation sources	**5.2.4** Format graphic elements
4.1.4 Insert citations for bibliographies	**5.4.1** Position objects
4.2.3 Insert bibliographies	**5.4.2** Wrap text around objects

Build Your E-Portfolio

An E-Portfolio is a collection of evidence, stored electronically, that showcases what you have accomplished while completing your education. Collecting and then sharing your work products with potential employers reflects your academic and career goals. Your completed documents from the following projects are good examples to show what you have learned: 3G, 3K, and 3L.

Go! For Job Success

Video: Interview Walkthru

Your instructor may assign this video to your class, and then ask you to think about, or discuss with your classmates, these questions:

g-stockstudio/ Shutterstock

> What kind of information should you gather before going to a job interview?

> What items should you take with you to an interview?

> What things will the interviewer be noticing about you to determine if you are prepared for the interview?

End of Chapter

Summary

Word assists you in formatting a research paper for college or business by providing built-in styles and formats for the most commonly used footnote and citation styles for research papers—MLA and APA.

Word helps you create the bibliography for your research paper by recording all of your citations in the Source Manager, and then generating the bibliography—in MLA, called Works Cited—for you.

Newsletters are often used by organizations to communicate information to a specific group. A newsletter can be formatted in two columns with a nameplate at the top that identifies the publication.

The Mail Merge Wizard enables you to easily merge a main document and a data source to create customized letters or labels. The data source can be a Word table, Excel spreadsheet, or Access database.

GO! Learn It Online

Review the concepts, key terms, and MOS skills in this chapter by completing these online challenges, which you can find at **MyLab IT**.

Chapter Quiz: Answer matching and multiple choice questions to test what you learned in this chapter.

Lessons on the GO!: Learn how to use all the new apps and features as they are introduced by Microsoft.

MOS Prep Quiz: Answer questions to review the MOS skills that you practiced in this chapter.

GO! Collaborative Team Project (Available in Instructor Resource Center)

If your instructor assigns this project to your class, you can expect to work with one or more of your classmates—either in person or by using internet tools—to create work products similar to those that you created in this chapter. A team is a group of workers who work together to solve a problem, make a decision, or create a work product. Collaboration is when you work together with others as a team in an intellectual endeavor to complete a shared task or achieve a shared goal.

Monkey Business Images/Fotolia

Project Guide for Word Chapter 3

Your instructor may assign one or more of these projects to help you review the chapter and assess your mastery and understanding of its contents.

Project	Apply Skills from These Chapter Objectives	Project Type	Project Location
3A **MyLab IT**	Objectives 1-4 from Project 3A	**3A Instructional Project (Grader Project)** **Instruction** Guided instruction to learn the skills in Project A.	In **MyLab IT** and in text
3B **MyLab IT**	Objectives 5-7 from Project 3B	**3B Instructional Project (Grader Project)** **Instruction** Guided instruction to learn the skills in Project B.	In **MyLab IT** and in text
3C	Objectives 1-4 from Project 3A	**3C Skills Review** **Review** A guided review of the skills from Project 3A. In text	In text
3D	Objectives 5-7 from Project 3B	**3D Skills Review Review** **Review** A guided review of the skills from Project 3B.	In text
3E **MyLab IT**	Objectives 1-4 from Project 3A	**3E Mastery (Grader Project)** **Mastery and Transfer of Learning** A demonstration of your mastery of the skills in Project 3A with extensive decision-making.	In **MyLab IT** and in text
3F **MyLab IT**	Objectives 5-7 from Project 3B	**3F Mastery (Grader Project)** **Mastery and Transfer of Learning** A demonstration of your mastery of the skills in Project 3B with extensive decision-making.	In **MyLab IT** and in text
3G **MyLab IT**	Objectives 1-7 from Projects 3A and 3B	**3G Mastery (Grader Project)** **Mastery and Transfer of Learning** A demonstration of your mastery of the skills in Projects 3A and 3B with extensive decision-making.	In **MyLab IT** and in text
3H	Combination of Objectives from Projects 3A and 3B	**3H GO! Fix It (Scorecard Grading** **Critical Thinking** A demonstration of your mastery of the skills in Projects 3A and 3B by creating a correct result from a document that contains errors you must find.	Online
3I	Combination of Objectives from Projects 3A and 3B	**3I GO! Make It (Scorecard Grading** **Critical Thinking** A demonstration of your mastery of the skills in Projects 3A and 3B by creating a result from a supplied picture.	Online
3J	Combination of Objectives from Projects 3A and 3B	**3J GO! Solve It (Rubric Grading)** **Critical Thinking** A demonstration of your mastery of the skills in Projects 3A and 3B, your decision-making skills, and your critical thinking skills. A task-specific rubric helps you self-assess your result.	Online
3K	Combination of Objectives from Projects 3A and 3B	**3K GO! Solve It (Rubric Grading)** **Critical Thinking** A demonstration of your mastery of the skills in Projects 3A and 3B, your decision-making skills, and your critical thinking skills. A task-specific rubric helps you self-assess your result.	In text
3L	Combination of Objectives from Projects 3A and 3B	**3L GO! Think (Rubric Grading)** **Critical Thinking** A demonstration of your understanding of the Chapter concepts applied in a manner that you would outside of college. An analytic rubric helps you and your instructor grade the quality of your work by comparing it to the work an expert in the discipline would create.	In text
3M	Combination of Objectives from Projects 3A and 3B	**3M GO! Think (Rubric Grading)** **Critical Thinking** A demonstration of your understanding of the Chapter concepts applied in a manner that you would outside of college. An analytic rubric helps you and your instructor grade the quality of your work by comparing it to the work an expert in the discipline would create.	IRC
3N	Combination of Objectives from Projects 3A and 3B	**3N You and GO! (Rubric Grading)** **Critical Thinking** A demonstration of your understanding of the Chapter concepts applied in a manner that you would in a personal situation. An analytic rubric helps you and your instructor grade the quality of your work.	IRC
3O	Combination of Objectives from Projects 3A and 3B	**3O Cumulative Team Project for Word Chapter 3** **Critical Thinking** A demonstration of your understanding of concepts and your ability to work collaboratively in a group role-playing assessment, requiring both collaboration and self-management.	IRC
Capstone Project for Word Chapters 1-3	Combination of Objectives from Projects 1A, 1B, 2A, 2B, 3A, and 3B	**Word Capstone (Grader Project)** **Mastery and Transfer of Learning** A demonstration of your mastery of the skills in Chapters 1-3 with extensive decision making.	In **MyLab IT**

Glossary

Glossary of Chapter Key Terms

American Psychological Association (APA) One of two commonly used style guides for formatting research papers.

Bibliography A list of cited works in a report or research paper; also referred to as Works Cited, Sources, or References, depending upon the report style.

Brightness The relative lightness of a picture.

Citation A note inserted into the text of a research paper that refers the reader to a source in the bibliography.

Column break indicator A dotted line containing the words *Column Break* that displays at the bottom of the column.

Contrast The difference between the darkest and lightest area of a picture.

Crop A command that removes unwanted or unnecessary areas of a picture.

Crop handles Handles used to define unwanted areas of a picture.

Crop pointer The pointer used to crop areas of a picture.

Data source A document that contains a list of variable information, such as names and addresses, that you merge with a main document to create customized form letters or labels.

Em dash A punctuation symbol that indicates an explanation or emphasis.

Endnote In a research paper, a note placed at the end of a document or chapter.

Fields In a mail merge, the column headings in the data source.

Flip A command that creates a reverse image of a picture or object.

Footnote In a research paper, a note placed at the bottom of the page.

Hanging indent An indent style in which the first line of a paragraph extends to the left of the remaining lines and that is commonly used for bibliographic entries.

Indenting Moving the beginning of the first line of a paragraph to the right or left of the rest of the paragraph to provide visual cues to the reader to help divide the document text and make it easier to read.

Line break indicator A non-printing character in the shape of a bent arrow that indicates a manual line break.

Mail merge A feature that joins a main document and a data source to create customized letters or labels.

Main document In a mail merge, the document that contains the text or formatting that remains constant.

Manual column break An artificial end to a column to balance columns or to provide space for the insertion of other objects.

Manual line break A break that moves text to the right of the insertion point to a new line while keeping the text in the same paragraph.

Manual page break The action of forcing a page to end and placing subsequent text at the top of the next page.

Modern Language Association (MLA) One of two commonly used style guides for formatting research papers.

Nameplate The banner on the front page of a newsletter that identifies the publication.

Newsletter A periodical that communicates news and information to a specific group.

Note In a research paper, information that expands on the topic, but that does not fit well in the document text.

Page break indicator A dotted line with the text *Page Break* that indicates where a manual page break was inserted.

Parenthetical references References that include the last name of the author or authors, and the page number in the referenced source.

PDF Reflow The ability to import PDF files into Word so that you can transform a PDF back into a fully editable Word document.

Read Mode A view in Word that optimizes the Word screen for the times when you are reading Word documents on the screen and not creating or editing them.

Recolor A feature that enables you to change all colors in the picture to shades of a single color.

Record Each row of information that contains data for one person.

Researcher A Word feature that helps you find topics and reliable sources for a research paper; for sources that you select, citation information is available.

Scale A command that resizes a picture to a percentage of its size.

Screen Clipping A tool with which you can take a quick snapshot of part of a screen, and then add it to your document.

Screenshot An image of an active window on your computer that you can paste into a document.

Section A portion of a document that can be formatted differently from the rest of the document.

Section break A double dotted line that indicates the end of one section and the beginning of another section.

Side to Side A Page Movement setting that enables you to see whole pages by sliding each page from right to left or left to right.

Small caps A font effect that changes lowercase letters to uppercase letters, but with the height of lowercase letters.

Smart Lookup A Word feature with which you can get more information about text you select; shows definitions, images, and results from various online sources.

Style A group of formatting commands, such as font, font size, font color, paragraph alignment, and line spacing, that you can apply to a paragraph with one command.

Style guide A manual that contains standards for the design and writing of documents.

Suppress A Word feature that hides header and footer information, including the page number, on the first page of a document.

Text Highlight Color A Word command with which you can apply a highlight color to selected text.

Works Cited In the MLA style, a list of cited works placed at the end of a research paper or report.

Chapter Review

Apply 3A skills from these Objectives:

1. Create a Research Paper
2. Insert Footnotes in a Research Paper
3. Create Citations and a Bibliography in a Research Paper
4. Use Read Mode, PDF Reflow, and Save Documents in Alternate Formats

In the following Skills Review, you will edit and format a research paper that contains information about the effects of diet and exercise. This paper was created by Rachel Holder, a medical intern at University Medical Center, for distribution to her classmates studying physiology. Your completed document will look similar to the one shown in Figure 3.55.

Project Files

For Project 3C, you will need the following file:

w03C_Diet_Exercise

You will save your document as:

Lastname_Firstname_3C_Diet_Exercise

Project Results

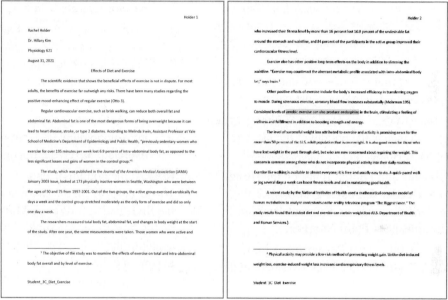

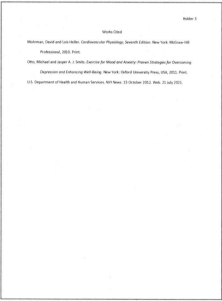

Figure 3.55

(continues on next page)

Chapter Review

1 Start Word. On Word's opening screen, on the left, click **Open**. Navigate to the files downloaded with this project, and then locate and open the document **w03C_Diet_Exercise**. Display the formatting marks and rulers. **Save** the file in your **Word Chapter 3** folder as Lastname_Firstname_3C_Diet_Exercise

a. Press Ctrl + A to select all the text. On the **Home tab**, in the **Paragraph group**, click **Line and Paragraph Spacing**, and then change the line spacing to **2.0**. On the **Layout tab**, change the **Spacing After** to **0 pt**.

b. Press Ctrl + Home, press Enter to create a blank line at the top of the document, and then click to position the insertion point in the new blank line. Type **Rachel Holder** and press Enter. Type **Dr. Hillary Kim** and press Enter. Type **Physiology 621** and press Enter. Type **August 31, 2021** and press Enter.

c. Type **Effects of Diet and Exercise** and then press Ctrl + E to center the title you just typed.

2 On the **Insert tab**, in the **Header & Footer group**, click **Header**, and then at the bottom of the list, click **Edit Header**. Type **Holder** and then press Spacebar.

a. Under **Header and Footer Tools**, on the **Design tab**, in the **Header & Footer group**, click **Page Number**, and then point to **Current Position**. Under **Simple**, click **Plain Number**.

b. On the **Home tab**, in the **Paragraph group**, click **Align Right**. Double-click anywhere in the document to close the Header area.

c. Near the top of **Page 1**, locate the paragraph beginning *The scientific evidence*, and then click to position the insertion point at the beginning of that paragraph. Scroll to the end of the document, hold down Shift, and then click to the right of the last paragraph mark to select all of the text from the insertion point to the end of the document.

d. On the **Home tab**, in the **Paragraph group**, click the **Dialog Box Launcher** button. In the **Paragraph** dialog box, on the **Indents and Spacing tab**, under **Indentation**, click the **Special arrow**, and then click **First line**. Click **OK**.

e. On the **Insert tab**, in the **Header & Footer group**, click **Footer**, and then click **Edit Footer**. In the **Insert group**, click **Document Info**, and then click **File Name**. Click **Close Header and Footer**.

3 Scroll to view the top of **Page 2**, locate the paragraph that begins *Exercise also has*, and then at the end of that paragraph, click to position the insertion point to the right of the period following *Irwin*. On the **References tab**, in the **Footnotes group**, click **Insert Footnote**.

a. As the footnote text, type **Physical activity may provide a low-risk method of preventing weight gain. Unlike diet-induced weight loss, exercise-induced weight loss increases cardiorespiratory fitness levels.**

b. In the upper portion of **Page 1**, locate the paragraph that begins *Regular cardiovascular exercise*. Click to position the insertion point at the end of the paragraph and insert a footnote.

c. As the footnote text, type **The objective of the study was to examine the effects of exercise on total and intra-abdominal body fat overall and by level of exercise. Save** your document.

4 At the bottom of **Page 1**, right-click in the footnote you just typed. On the shortcut menu, click **Style**. In the **Style** dialog box, click **Modify**. In the **Modify Style** dialog box, locate the small **Formatting** toolbar in the center of the dialog box, click the **Font Size button arrow**, and then click **11**.

a. In the lower left corner of the dialog box, click **Format**, and then click **Paragraph**. In the **Paragraph** dialog box, under **Indentation**, click the **Special arrow**, and then click **First line**. Under **Spacing**, click the **Line spacing arrow**, and then click **Double**.

b. Click **OK** to close the **Paragraph** dialog box, click **OK** to close the **Modify Style** dialog box, and then click **Apply** to apply the new style. **Save** your document.

5 Scroll to view the top of **Page 1**, and then in the paragraph that begins *The scientific evidence*, click to position the insertion point to the left of the period at the end of the paragraph.

(continues on next page)

Chapter Review

Skills Review: Project 3C Diet and Exercise Report (continued)

a. On the **References tab**, in the **Citations & Bibliography group**, click the **Style button arrow**, and then click **MLA** to insert a reference using MLA style. Click **Insert Citation**, and then click **Add New Source**. Click the **Type of Source arrow**, scroll as necessary to locate and click **Book**, and then add the following information: (Mac users: there is no Medium field; the order of the fields differs slightly.)

Author	Otto, Michael and Jasper A. J. Smits.
Title	Exercise for Mood and Anxiety: Proven Strategies for Overcoming Depression and Enhancing Well-Being
Year	2011
City	New York
Publisher	Oxford University Press, USA
Medium	Print

b. Click **OK** to insert the citation. In the paragraph, click to select the citation, click the **Citation Options arrow**, and then click **Edit Citation**. In the **Edit Citation** dialog box, under **Add**, in the **Pages** box, type **3** and then click **OK**.

c. On the upper portion of **Page 2**, in the paragraph that begins *Other positive effects*, in the second line, click to position the insertion point to the left of the period following *substantially*. In the **Citations & Bibliography group**, click **Insert Citation**, and then click **Add New Source**. Click the **Type of Source arrow**, click **Book**, and then add the following information: (Mac users: There is no Medium field; order of the fields differs slightly.)

Author	Lohrman, David and Lois Heller.
Title	Cardiovascular Physiology, Seventh Edition
Year	2010
City	New York
Publisher	McGraw-Hill Professional
Medium	Print

d. Click **OK**. Click to select the citation in the paragraph, click the **Citation Options arrow**, and then click **Edit Citation**. In the **Edit Citation** dialog box, under **Add**, in the **Pages** box, type **195** and then click **OK**.

6 Press Ctrl + End to move to the end of the last paragraph in the document. Click to the left of the period following *loss*. In the **Citations & Bibliography group**, click **Insert Citation**, and then click **Add New Source**. Click the **Type of Source arrow**, click **Web site**, and then select the **Corporate Author** check box. Add the following information: (Mac users: There is no Medium field; the order of the fields differs slightly.)

Corporate Author	U.S. Department of Health and Human Services
Name of Web Page	NIH News
Year	2012
Month	October
Day	15
Year Accessed	2021
Month Accessed	July
Day Accessed	21
Medium	Web

a. Click **OK**. Press Ctrl + End to move the insertion point to the end of the document. Press Ctrl + Enter to insert a manual page break. On the **Home tab**, in the **Paragraph group**, click the **Dialog Box Launcher** button. In the **Paragraph** dialog box, on the **Indents and Spacing tab**, under **Indentation**, click the **Special arrow**, and then click **(none)**. Click **OK**. (Mac users: To display the Paragraph dialog box, on the Home tab, in the Paragraph group, click the Line and Paragraph Spacing button, click Line Spacing Options.)

b. On the **References tab**, in the **Citations & Bibliography group**, be sure **MLA** displays in the **Style** box. In the **Citations & Bibliography group**, click **Bibliography**, and then at the bottom, click **Works Cited**.

c. Select the paragraph *Works Cited*. On the **Home tab**, in the **Font group**, change the **Font** to **Calibri**, and then change the **Font Size** to **11**. Click the **Font Color arrow**, and then in the second column, click the first color. With the text *Works Cited* still selected, in the **Paragraph group**, click **Center**.

d. Click to the left of *Works Cited* and then drag down to select the the title *Works Cited* and the three citations. Display the **Paragraph** dialog box, change the **Spacing Before** to **0 pt**, change the **Spacing After** to **0 pt**, and then set **Line spacing** to **Double**. Click **OK**. **Save** your document.

(continues on next page)

Chapter Review

7 On the **References tab**, in the **Citations & Bibliography group**, click **Manage Sources**. On the left, on the **Master List**, click the entry for *Lohrman, David*, and then click **Edit**. In the **Edit Source** dialog box, in the **Author** box, change the *L* in *Lohrman* to **M** Click **OK**, click **Yes**, and then click **Close**.

(Mac users: On the References tab, click Citations, click the Settings button in the bottom right corner of the Citations pane. Click Citation Source Manager. Click the reference for Lohrman, click Edit, edit the name *Lohrman* to *Mohrman*. Click OK, and then click Close. On Page 2 of the document, click the *Lohrman* reference, click the arrow, and then click Update Citations and Bibliography. Move to step b.)

   a. On **Page 2**, in the paragraph that begins *Other positive effects*, in the third line, on the selected citation, click the **Citation Options arrow**, and then click **Update Citations and Bibliography**.

   b. On the *Works Cited* page, drag to select the three citations, and then from the **Home tab**, redisplay the **Paragraph** dialog box. Reset the **Spacing Before** and **Spacing After** to **0 pt** and the **Line spacing** to **Double**. Click **OK**.

   c. From the **File tab**, display **Backstage** view, on the left click **Info**, and then in the lower right, click **Show All Properties**. Add the following information:

Title	Diet and Exercise
Tags	weight loss, exercise, diet
Comments	Draft copy of report for class
Categories	biomedical research
Company	University Medical Center
Manager	Dr. Hillary Kim

   d. Click outside of the **Manager** box to close it. In the **Subject** box, type your course name and section number. Be sure that your name displays as the Author and edit if necessary. On the left, click **Save** to redisplay your document.

8 On **Page 1**, in the paragraph that begins *Regular cardiovascular*, in the third line, select the text *Melinda Irwin*. On the **References tab**, in the **Research group**, click **Smart Lookup**. In the **Smart Lookup** pane, scroll down to view the results—you will likely see Dr. Irwin's page in the Public Health department at Yale University. If you want to do so, click this link to see more of Dr. Irwin's research.

   a. **Close** the **Smart Lookup** pane. On the **References tab**, in the **Research group**, click **Researcher**. In the **Researcher** pane, in the search box, type— being sure to include the quotation marks and uppercase letters as indicated—**"aerobic exercise" AND "endorphins"** and then press Enter.

   b. Under **Top sources**, click **Websites**, and notice the websites you can visit regarding this topic.

   c. On **Page 2** of your research paper, in the paragraph that begins *Other positive effects*, in the third line, select the text *aerobic exercise can also produce endorphins*. With the text selected, on the **Home tab**, in the **Font group**, click the **Text Highlight Color arrow**, and then apply **Yellow** highlighting.

   d. **Close** the **Researcher** pane.

   e. Press Ctrl + Home to move to the top of your document. On the **View tab**, in the **Views group**, click **Read Mode**. In the upper left, click **Tools**, click **Find**, and then in the search box, type **Yale** and notice that the text you searched for is highlighted in the document.

   f. In the upper left, click **View**, and then click **Edit Document** to return to Print Layout view. **Close** the **Navigation** pane. **Save** your document, and view the Print Preview. If directed by your instructor to do so, submit your paper printout, your electronic image of your document that looks like a printed document, or your Word file. **Close** Word.

You have completed Project 3C | END

Chapter Review

Skills Review   Project 3D Career Newsletter

Apply 3B skills from these Objectives:

5. Format a Multiple-Column Newsletter
6. Use Special Character and Paragraph Formatting
7. Create Mailing Labels Using Mail Merge

In the following Skills Review, you will format a newsletter regarding professional development opportunities offered by University Medical Center, and you will create mailing labels for staff interested in these opportunities. Your completed document will look similar to Figure 3.56.

Project Files

For Project 3D, you will need the following files:

New blank Word document
w03D_Career_Newsletter
w03D_Career_Sign (optional)
w03D_Medical_Symbol
w03D_Addresses

You will save your documents as:

Lastname_Firstname_3D_Career_Newsletter
Lastname_Firstname_3D_Mailing_Labels

Project Results

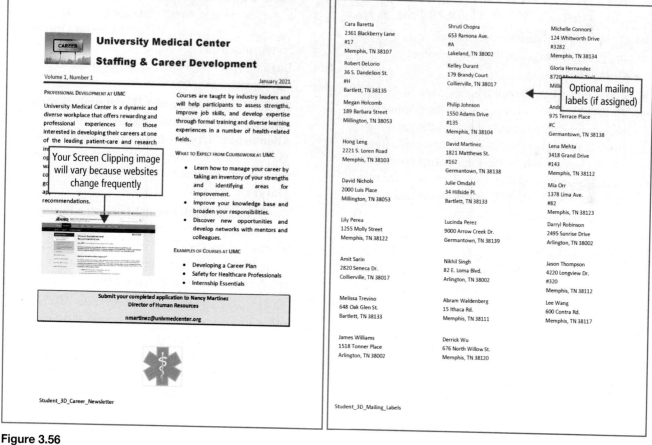

Figure 3.56

(continues on next page)

Chapter Review

1 ▶ Start Word. On Word's opening screen, on the left click **Open**. Navigate to the files you downloaded with this project, and then locate and open **w03D_Career_Newsletter**. Using your own name, **Save** the file in your **Word Chapter 3** folder as **Lastname_Firstname_3D_Career_Newsletter** and then add the file name to the footer.

a. Select the first two lines of the document. On the mini toolbar, change the **Font** to **Arial Black** and the **Font Size** to **18**. Select the first three lines of the document. Click the **Font Color button arrow**, and then under **Theme Colors**, in the fifth column, click the last color.

b. With the text still selected, on the **Home tab**, in the **Paragraph group**, click the **Borders button arrow**, and then at the bottom, click **Borders and Shading**. In the **Borders and Shading** dialog box, on the **Borders tab**, click the **Color arrow**, and then under **Theme Colors**, in the fifth column, click the last color.

c. Click the **Width arrow**, and then click **3 pt**. In the **Preview** box, click the bottom border. Click **OK**.

d. Click at the beginning of the paragraph that begins *Professional Development*. Scroll the document, hold down (Shift), and then click after the paragraph mark at the end of the *Internship Essentials* line. On the **Layout tab**, in the **Page Setup group**, click **Columns**, and then click **Two**. With the two columns of text selected, on the **Home tab**, in the **Paragraph group**, click **Justify**.

e. In the first column, click at the beginning of the paragraph that begins *Courses are taught*. On the **Layout tab**, in the **Page Setup group**, click **Breaks**. Under **Page Breaks**, click **Column**.

2 ▶ Press (Ctrl) + (Home). On the **Insert tab**, in the **Illustrations group**, click **Pictures**. From the files downloaded with this project, insert the file **w03D_Career_Sign**.

a. With the image selected, on the **Format tab**, in the **Size group**, click the **Dialog Box Launcher** button. In the **Layout** dialog box, on the **Size tab**, under **Scale**, be sure the **Lock aspect ratio** and **Relative to original picture size** check boxes are selected. Select the number in the **Height box**, type **15** and then press (Tab).

b. In the **Layout** dialog box, click the **Text Wrapping tab**. Under **Wrapping style**, click **Square**.

c. Click the **Position tab**, and then under **Horizontal**, click the **Alignment** option button. Be sure that the **Alignment** indicates **Left** and **relative to Column**. Under **Vertical**, click the **Alignment** option button, and then change the alignment to **Top relative to Margin**. Click **OK**. Compare the picture size and placement with Figure 3.56 and adjust the size of the image if necessary. **Save** your newsletter.

3 ▶ Press (Ctrl) + (End) to move to the end of the document. On the **Insert tab**, in the **Illustrations group**, click **Pictures**, and then from your student data files, insert the picture **w03D_Medical_Symbol**.

a. With the image selected, on the **Picture Tools Format tab**, in the **Adjust group**, click **Color**, and then under **Recolor**, in the last row, click one of the paler images such as blue or gray or purple.

b. With the picture selected, on the **Picture Tools Format tab**, in the **Size group**, click in the **Height** box. If necessary, type **1** and then press (Enter). To the right of the picture, click the **Layout Options** button, and then click **Square**. At the bottom of the **Layout Options gallery**, click **See more** to display the **Layout** dialog box.

c. On the **Position tab**, under **Horizontal**, click the **Alignment** option button, and then change the **Alignment** to **Centered relative to Page**. Under **Vertical**, click the **Alignment** option button, and then change **Alignment** to **Bottom relative to Margin**. Click **OK**.

d. On the **Picture Tools Format tab**, in the **Picture Styles group**, click the **Picture Border button**. Under **Theme Colors**, in the fifth column, click the second color. Click the **Picture Border button arrow** again, and then point to **Weight**. Click **1 pt**.

4 ▶ In the paragraph that begins *University Medical Center is a dynamic*, click after the period at the end of the paragraph, and then press (Enter) one time. With the insertion point in the new blank paragraph, open your web browser, and then navigate to **www.ahrq.gov/clinic/**

a. From the taskbar, redisplay your **3D_Career_Newletter** document. With the insertion point positioned in the new blank paragraph, on the **Insert tab**, in the **Illustrations group**, click **Screenshot**. Click **Screen Clipping**, position the ⊞ pointer in the upper left corner of the website—below the address bar—and then drag down to the lower right corner—do not include the taskbar.

(continues on next page)

Chapter Review

b. Select the subheading *Professional Development at UMC* including the paragraph mark. Right-click the selected text, and then on the shortcut menu, click **Font**. In the **Font** dialog box, click the **Font color arrow**, and then in the fifth column, click the last color. Under **Font style**, click **Bold**, and then under **Effects**, select **Small caps**. Click **OK**.

c. With the text still selected, right-click, and then on the mini toolbar, double-click **Format Painter**. In the second column, with the ▲I pointer, select each of the subheadings—*What to Expect from Coursework at UMC* and *Examples of Courses at UMC*. Press [Esc] to turn off Format Painter.

5 Press [Ctrl] + [End] to move to the end of the document, and then select the two lines of bold text—the graphic will also be selected. On the **Home tab**, in the **Paragraph group**, click the **Borders button arrow**, and then click **Borders and Shading**.

a. In the **Borders and Shading** dialog box, on the **Borders tab**, under **Setting**, click **Shadow**. Click the **Color arrow**, and then in the fifth column, click the last color. Click the **Width arrow**, and then click **1 pt**.

b. In the **Borders and Shading** dialog box, click the **Shading tab**. Click the **Fill arrow**, and then in the fifth column, click the second color. Click **OK**. On the **Home tab**, in the **Paragraph group**, click **Center**. In the shaded paragraph, click in front of the *D* in the word *Director*. Hold down [Shift] and then press [Enter].

c. Press [Ctrl] + [Home], and then click the **File tab**. On the left, click **Info**, and then at the bottom right, click **Show All Properties**. Click to the right of **Tags**, and then type **newsletter, careers** Click to the right of **Subject**, and then type your course name and section number. Under **Related People**, if necessary, type your name in the Author box. Display the **Print Preview** and make any necessary corrections. **Save** the document; close Word and close your browser window. Submit this file as directed by your instructor.

6 (NOTE: The remainder of this Project, which is the creation of mailing labels, is optional. Complete only if assigned by your instructor.)

Start Word and display a new blank document. **Save** the document in your **Word Chapter 3** folder as **Lastname_Firstname_3D_Mailing_Labels**

a. Click the **Mailings tab**. In the **Start Mail Merge group**, click **Start Mail Merge**, and then click **Step-by-Step Mail Merge Wizard**. In the **Mail Merge** pane, under **Select document type**, click **Labels**. At the bottom of the **Mail Merge** pane, click **Next: Starting document**.

b. Under **Select starting document**, under **Change document layout**, click **Label options**. In the **Label Options** dialog box, under **Printer information**, be sure that the **Default tray** is selected.

c. Under **Label information**, click the **Label vendors arrow**, and then click **Avery US Letter**. Under **Product number**, scroll about halfway down the list, and then click **5160 Address Labels**. At the bottom of the **Label Options** dialog box, click **OK**. At the bottom of the **Mail Merge** pane, click **Next: Select recipients**.

d. In the **Mail Merge** pane, under **Select recipients**, under **Use an existing list**, click **Browse**. In the **Select Data Source** dialog box, navigate to the files downloaded for this project, click the Excel file **w03D_Addresses** one time to select it, and then click **Open** to display the **Select Table** dialog box. Click **OK**.

7 In the lower left portion of the **Mail Merge Recipients** dialog box, in the **Data Source** box, click the file name *w03D_Addresses*. Then, at the bottom of the **Mail Merge Recipients** dialog box, click **Edit**. In the lower left corner of the displayed **Edit Data Source** dialog box, click **New Entry**. In the blank record—the blue shaded row at the bottom of the list—type the following, pressing [Tab] to move from field to field:

First Name	Mia
Last Name	Orr
Address 1	1378 Lima Ave.
Unit	#82
City	Memphis
State	TN
ZIP Code	38123

a. In the lower right corner of the **Edit Data Source** dialog box, click **OK**, and then in the displayed message, click **Yes**. At the bottom of the **Mail Merge Recipients** dialog box, click **OK**.

b. At the bottom of the **Mail Merge** pane, click **Next: Arrange your labels**. Under **Arrange your labels**, click **Address block**. In the lower right corner of the **Insert Address Block** dialog box, click **Match Fields**.

(continues on next page)

Chapter Review

c. Click the **Address 2 arrow**, and then from the list of available fields, click **Unit**. Click **OK** two times.

d. In the **Mail Merge** pane, under **Replicate labels**, click **Update all labels**. At the bottom of the **Mail Merge** pane, click **Next: Preview your labels**. Press Ctrl + A to select all of the label text, click the **Layout tab**, and then in the **Paragraph group**, click in the **Spacing Before** box. Type **3** and press Enter. At the bottom of the **Mail Merge** pane, click **Next: Complete the merge**.

e. Click the **Mailings tab**, and then in the **Start Mail Merge group**, click **Edit Recipient List** to display the list of names and addresses. In the **Mail Merge Recipients** dialog box, click the **Last Name** field heading to sort the names. Click **OK**. **Close** the **Mail Merge** pane.

f. Scroll the document and then click anywhere in the empty table row at the bottom. Click the **Table Tools Layout tab**. In the **Rows & Columns group**, click **Delete**, and then click **Delete Rows**. Add the file name to the footer, close the footer area, and then in Backstage view, display **Show All Properties**. As the **Tags**, type **labels** and as the **Subject**, type your course name and section number. Be sure your name displays as the **Author**, and then **Save** your file.

g. If directed by your instructor to do so, submit your paper printout, your electronic image of your document, or your original Word files. **Close** Word.

You have completed Project 3D **END**

Content-Based Assessments (Mastery and Transfer of Learning)

MyLab IT Grader	Mastering Word	Project 3E Skin Protection Report

Apply 3A skills from these Objectives:

1. Create a Research Paper
2. Insert Footnotes in a Research Paper
3. Create Citations and a Bibliography in a Research Paper
4. Use Read Mode, PDF Reflow, and Save Documents in Alternate Formats

In the following Mastering Word project, you will edit and format a research paper that contains information about skin protection and the use of sunblocks and sunscreens. This paper was created by Rachel Holder, a medical intern at University Medical Center, for distribution to her classmates studying dermatology. Your completed document will look similar to the one shown in Figure 3.57.

Project Files for MyLab IT Grader

1. In your **MyLab IT** course, locate and click **Word 3E Skin Protection**, Download Materials, and then Download All Files.
2. Extract the zipped folder to your Word Chapter 3 folder. Close the Grader download screens.
3. Take a moment to open the downloaded **Word_3E_Skin_Protection_Instructions** document; note any recent updates to the book.

Project Results

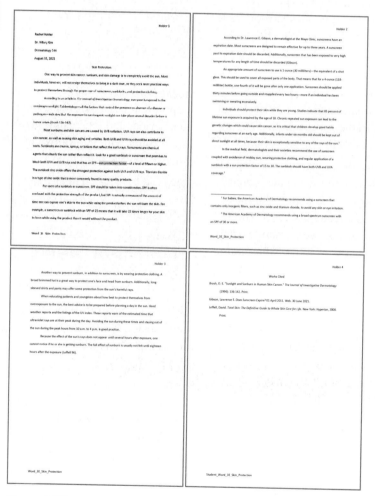

Figure 3.57

(continues on next page)

For Non-MyLab Submissions

For Project 3E, you will need:
w03E_Skin_Protection

In your Word Chapter 3 folder, save your document as:
Lastname_Firstname_3E_Skin_Protection

After you have named and saved your document, on the next page, begin with Step 2.

After Step 17, save and submit your file as directed by your instructor.

Content-Based Assessments (Mastery and Transfer of Learning)

1 Navigate to your **Word Chapter 3 folder**, and then double-click the Word file you downloaded from **MyLab IT** that displays your name—**Student_ Word_3E_Skin_Protection**. If necessary, at the top, click **Enable Editing**.

2 Select all the text, change the **Line Spacing** to **2.0**, and then change the **Spacing After** to **0 pt**.

3 At the top of the document, insert a new blank paragraph, and then in the new blank paragraph, type **Rachel Holder** and press Enter. Type **Dr. Hillary Kim** and press Enter. Type **Dermatology 544** and press Enter. Type **August 31, 2021** and press Enter.

4 In the new blank paragraph, type **Skin Protection** Center the title *Skin Protection*. Insert a header, type **Holder** and then press Spacebar one time. Display the **Page Number** gallery, and then in the **Current Position**, add the **Plain Number** style (Mac users, in the Header & Footer group, click Page Number, on the menu click Page Number; under Alignment, be sure Right is selected.)

5 Apply **Align Right** formatting to the header. Insert a footer with the file name. To the paragraph that begins *One way to prevent*, apply a **First line** indent of **0.5**.

6 On **Page 2**, at the end of the paragraph that begins *In the medical field*, immediately following the period at the end of the paragraph, insert a footnote with the following text (one footnote is already inserted): **The American Academy of Dermatology recommends using a broad spectrum sunscreen with an SPF of 30 or more.** Be sure to type the period at the end of the footnote.

7 Modify the **Footnote Text** style so that the **Font Size** is **11**, there is a **First line indent** of **0.5"**, and the spacing is **Double**. Then, apply the style.

8 On **Page 1**, at the end of the paragraph that begins *According to an article*, click to the left of the period. Using **MLA** format, insert a citation for a **Journal Article** with the following information: (Note: Mac users, select Article in a journal. Fill in only the fields indicated; there is no Medium field.)

Author	Brash, D. E.
Title	Sunlight and Sunburn in Human Skin Cancer
Journal Name	The Journal of Investigative Dermatology
Year	1996
Pages	136-142
Medium	Print

9 In the report, select the citation you just created, display the **Citation Options**, and then edit the citation to include **Pages 136-142**

10 At the top of **Page 2**, at the end of the paragraph that begins *According to Dr. Lawrence*, click to the left of the period, and then insert a citation for a **Web site** with the following information: (Mac users: there is no Medium field.)

Author	Gibson, Lawrence E.
Name of Web Page	Does Sunscreen Expire?
Year	2011
Month	April
Day	01
Year Accessed	2021
Month Accessed	June
Day Accessed	30
Medium	Web

11 On **Page 3**, at the end of the last paragraph of the report that begins *Because the effect*, click to the left of the period, and then using MLA format, insert a citation for a **Book** with the following information: (Mac users: there is no Medium field.)

Author	Leffell, David.
Title	Total Skin: The Definitive Guide to Whole Skin Care for Life
Year	2000
City	New York
Publisher	Hyperion
Medium	Print

12 In the report, select the citation you just created, display the **Citation Options**, and then edit the citation to include **Page 96**

13 Move to the end of the document, and then insert a manual page break to create a new page. On the new **Page 4**, display the **Paragraph** dialog box, and then change the **Indentation** under **Special** to **(none)**.

14 On the **References tab**, click **Bibliography**, and at the bottom click **Works Cited**. Select the paragraph *Works Cited*, change the **Font** to **Calibri**, change the **Font Size** to **11**. Display the **Font Color** gallery, and then in the second column, click the first color. Then center the *Works Cited* title.

(continues on next page)

Content-Based Assessments (Mastery and Transfer of Learning)

Mastering Word: Project 3E Skin Protection Report (continued)

15 Click to the left of *Works Cited* and then drag down to select *Works Cited* and the three citations. Display the **Paragraph** dialog box, change the **Spacing Before** to **0 pt**, change the **Spacing After** to **0 pt**, and set the **Line spacing** to **Double**.

16 Move to the top of your document. From the **References tab**, open **Researcher**, and then—including the quotation marks—search for **"sun protection factor"** and press [Enter]. Under **Top sources**, click **Journals**, and notice the extensive number of journal articles on this topic. **Close** the **Researcher pane**, and then on **Page 1**, in the paragraph that begins *Most sunburns*, in the fifth line, select the text *sun protection factor*. To the selected text, apply **Yellow Text Highlight Color**.

17 **Save** 🖫 your document. In the upper right corner of the Word window, click **Close** ⊠.

18 In **MyLab IT**, locate and click the Grader Project **Word 3E Skin Protection**. In **step 3**, under **Upload Completed Assignment**, click **Choose File**. In the **Open** dialog box, navigate to your **Word Chapter 3 folder**, and then click your **Student_Word_3E_Skin_Protection** file one time to select it. In the lower right corner of the **Open** dialog box, click **Open**.

The name of your selected file displays above the Upload button.

19 To submit your file to **MyLab IT** for grading, click **Upload**, wait a moment for a green **Success!** message, and then in **step 4**, click the blue **Submit for Grading** button. Click **Close Assignment** to return to your list of **Course Materials**.

You have completed Project 3E | END

MyLab IT Grader | **Mastering Word** **Project 3F Dogs Newsletter and Mailing Labels**

Apply 3B skills from these Objectives:

5. Format a Multiple-Column Newsletter
6. Use Special Character and Paragraph Formatting
7. Create Mailing Labels Using Mail Merge

In the following Mastering Word project, you will format a newsletter with information about the therapy dogs handled by volunteers at the University Medical Center. As an optional activity, you can create mailing labels so the newsletter can be sent to the volunteer staff. Your completed documents will look similar to Figure 3.58.

Project Files for **MyLab IT Grader**

1. In your **MyLab IT** course, locate and click **Word 3F Dogs Newsletter**, Download Materials, and then Download All Files.
2. Extract the zipped folder to your Word Chapter 3 folder. Close the Grader download screens.
3. Take a moment to open the downloaded **Word_3F_Dogs_Newsletter_Instructions**; note any recent updates to the book.

Project Results

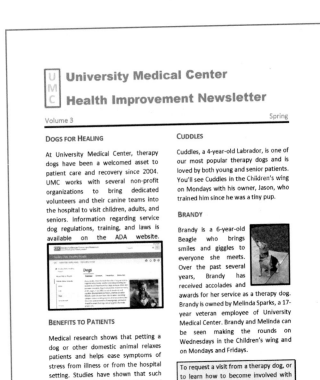

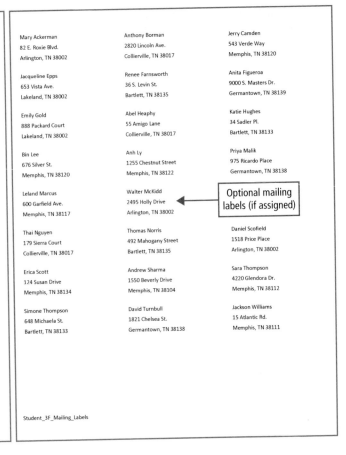

Optional mailing labels (if assigned)

Figure 3.58

For Non-MyLab Submissions

For Project 3E, you will need:

w03F_Dogs_Newsletter

w03F_Dog

w03F_Logo

w03F_Addresses (Optional: For use only if you are completing the Mailing Labels portion of this project)

After you have named and saved your document, on the next page, begin with Step 2.

After Step 10, save and submit your file as directed by your instructor.

In your Word Chapter 3 folder, save your document as:

Lastname_Firstname_3F_Dogs_Newsletter

(continues on next page)

Content-Based Assessments (Mastery and Transfer of Learning)

Mastering Word: Project 3F Dogs Newsletter and Mailing Labels (continued)

1 Navigate to your **Word Chapter 3 folder**, and then double-click the Word file you downloaded from **MyLab IT** that displays your name—**Student_Word_3F_Dogs_Newsletter**. If necessary, at the top, click **Enable Editing**.

2 Add the **File Name** to the footer of your document. Select the first three paragraphs of the document that form the newsletter's nameplate, and then from the **Font Color** gallery, in the seventh column, click the fifth color. With the text still selected, display the **Borders and Shading** dialog box. Apply a **3 pt** bottom border, and as the border color, click the **Color arrow**, and then in the second column, click the first color.

3 Click at the beginning of the newsletter title *University Medical Center*. From your downloaded files, insert the picture **w03F_Logo**. If necessary, change the image **Height** to 1" Change the **Brightness/Contrast** to **Brightness: 0% (Normal) Contrast: +40%**. Change the **Text Wrapping** to **Square**. Change the **Horizontal Alignment** of the image to **Left relative** to **Margin** and the **Vertical Alignment** to **Top relative** to **Margin**.

4 Starting with the paragraph that begins *Dogs for Healing*, select all of the text from that point to the end of the document. Change the **Spacing After** to **10 pt** Format the selected text in two columns, and then apply **Justify** alignment. Insert a **Column** break before the subheading *Cuddles*.

5 Click at the beginning of the sentence that begins with *Brandy is a 6-year-old Beagle*. From the files downloaded with this project, insert the picture **w03F_Dog**. Rotate the picture using **Flip Horizontal**. Change the picture **Width** to **1**"

6 Set the wrapping style of the picture to **Square**. Change the **Horizontal Alignment** to **Right relative** to **Margin** and the **Vertical Alignment** to **Top relative** to **Line**. Apply a **Picture Border** using the first color in the second column and change the **Weight** to **2 1/4 pt**. **Save** your file.

7 Open your web browser and if necessary, maximize the window. Navigate to **https://www.cdc.gov/healthypets/pets/dogs.html** If the website is not available, choose another page on the www.cdc.gov website. From the taskbar, redisplay your **3F_Dogs_Newsletter**, click at the end of the paragraph below the *Dogs for Healing* subheading. Insert a **Screen Clipping** of the website—do not include the address bar at the top or the taskbar at the bottom. To the screenclipping, apply a **Picture Border** using the first color in the second column, and set the **Weight** to **3 pt**.

8 Select the subheading *Dogs for Healing* including the paragraph mark. By using the **Font** dialog box, change the **Size** to **16**, apply **Bold**, and apply the **Small caps** effect. Click the **Font color arrow**, and then in the seventh column, click the last color. Apply the same formatting to the subheadings *Benefits to Patients*, *Cuddles*, and *Brandy*.

9 Select the last paragraph in the newsletter including the paragraph mark, and then from the **Borders and Shading** dialog box, apply a **1 pt Shadow** border using the first color in the second column. From the **Shading tab**, apply a **Fill color**—in the seventh column, click the second color.

10 **Save** your document. In the upper right corner of the Word window, click **Close**.

11 In **MyLab IT**, locate and click the Grader Project **Word 3F Dogs Newsletter**. In **step 3**, under **Upload Completed Assignment**, click **Choose File**. In the **Open** dialog box, navigate to your **Word Chapter 3 folder**, and then click your **Student_Word_3F_Dogs_Newsletter** file one time to select it. In the lower right corner of the **Open** dialog box, click **Open**.

The name of your selected file displays above the Upload button.

12 To submit your file to **MyLab IT** for grading, click **Upload**, wait a moment for a green **Success!** message, and then in **step 4**, click the blue **Submit for Grading** button. Click **Close Assignment** to return to your list of **Course Materials**.

You have completed Project 3F | **END**

Content-Based Assessments (Mastery and Transfer of Learning)

ALERT   Optional Bonus Project to Produce Mailing Labels

Your instructor may ask you to complete this optional bonus project to produce mailing labels. Check with your instructor to see if you should complete the mailing labels. This project is not included in the **MyLab IT** Grader system. Your instructor can provide you the file w03F_Addresses, or you can download the file from www.pearsonhighered.com/go

1 Start Word and display a new blank document. **Save** the document in your **Word Chapter 3** folder as **Lastname_Firstname_3F_Mailing_Labels**

2 Start the **Step-by-Step Mail Merge Wizard** and as the document type create **Labels**. Move to the next step of the Mail Merge wizard. Click **Label options**, be sure that the **Default tray** is selected and that the label vendor is **Avery US Letter**. As the **Product number**, click **5160 Address Labels**. Move to the next step of the Mail Merge wizard, and then click **Use an existing list**. Click **Browse**, navigate to your downloaded files, click the Excel file **w03F_Addresses**, click **Open**, and then click **OK** two times.

3 Move to the next step of the Mail Merge Wizard, and then click **Address block**. Click **OK**, and then **Update all labels**. Move to the next step of the Mail Merge Wizard to preview the labels. Then **Complete the merge**. Delete the last two rows from the bottom of the table, and then add the file name to the footer.

4 **Save** your file. As directed by your instructor, print or submit electronically.

You have completed the optional portion of this project | **END**

Content-Based Assessments (Mastery and Transfer of Learning)

MyLab IT Grader	Mastering Word	Project 3G Research Paper, Newsletter, and Mailing Labels

Apply 3A and 3B skills from these Objectives:

1. Create a Research Paper
2. Insert Footnotes in a Research Paper
3. Create Citations and a Bibliography in a Research Paper
4. Use Read Mode, PDF Reflow, and Save Documents in Alternate Formats
5. Format a Multiple-Column Newsletter
6. Use Special Character and Paragraph Formatting
7. Create Mailing Labels Using Mail Merge

In the following Mastering Word project, you will edit and format a research paper and a newsletter. Optionally, you will create mailing labels. Your completed documents will look similar to Figure 3.59.

Project Files for MyLab IT Grader

1. In your **MyLab IT** course, locate and click **Word 3G Newsletter and Research Paper**, Download Materials, and then Download All Files.
2. Extract the zipped folder to your Word Chapter 3 folder. Close the Grader download screens.
3. Take a moment to open the downloaded **Word_3G_Newsletter_and_Research_Paper_ Instructions**; note any recent updates to the book.

Project Results

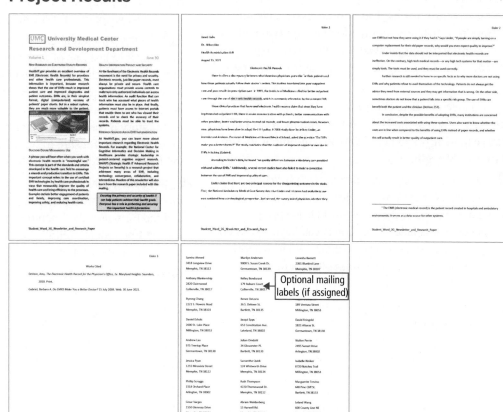

Figure 3.59

For Non-MyLab Submissions

For Project 3G, you will need:

w03G_Newsletter_and_Research_Paper

w03G_Logo

w03G_Addresses (Optional: For use only if you are completing the Mailing Labels portion of this project)

In your Word Chapter 3 folder, save your document as:

Lastname_Firstname_3G_Newsletter_and_Research_Paper

After you have named and saved your document, on the next page, begin with Step 2.

After step 18, save and submit your file as directed by your instructor.

(continues on next page)

1 Navigate to your **Word Chapter 3 folder**, and then double-click the Word file you downloaded from **MyLab IT** that displays your name—**Student_Word_3G_Newsletter_and_Research_Paper**. If necessary, at the top, click **Enable Editing**.

2 Add the **File Name** to the footer. Scroll down to **Page 2**, which is the first page of the research paper. Click anywhere on the page, and then because this is a separate section, add the **File Name** to the footer again so that it appears in both sections of the document. Press Ctrl + Home to move back to the top of the newsletter on **Page 1**. On **Page 1**, click at the beginning of the newsletter title. From your downloaded files, insert the picture **w03G_Logo**. If necessary, change the **Height** to **0.4"** Recolor the logo by applying a blue recolor option in a light shade. To the logo image, apply a **Picture Border** using the second color in the first column.

3 Change the **Text Wrapping** of the logo image to **Square**. Change the **Horizontal Alignment** to **Left** relative to **Margin** and the **Vertical Alignment** to **Top** relative to **Margin**.

4 Starting with the subheading paragraph *New Research on Electronic Health Records*, select all of the text from that point to the end of the page—include the paragraph mark but do not include the Section Break in your selection. Format the selected text in two columns, and then apply **Justify** alignment. Insert a **Column** break before the subheading *Health Information Privacy and Security*.

5 Open your web browser, and then navigate to **www.healthit.gov** Redisplay your document, and then click at the end of the paragraph below the *New Research on Electronic Health Records* subheading. Insert a **Screen Clipping** of the website—do not include the address bar or the taskbar. To the inserted screenshot, apply a **Picture Border** using the first color in the second column, and change the **Weight** to **1 pt**, If necessary, set the **Height** of the screen clipping to **1.5"**.

6 Select the subheading *New Research on Electronic Health Records* including the paragraph mark. From the **Font** dialog box, apply **Bold** and **Small caps**. Click the **Font color arrow**, and then in the fourth column, click the first color. Apply the same formatting to the subheadings *Doctors Define Meaningful Use*, *Health Information Privacy and Security* and *Research Sources Aid in EHR Implementation*. Select the *Doctors Define Meaningful Use* subheading and then change the **Spacing Before** to **18 pt**.

7 Select the last paragraph in the newsletter—the text in bold italic that begins *Ensuring the privacy* including the paragraph mark but not the Section Break lines. From the **Borders and Shading** dialog box, apply a **1 pt Shadow** border and as the **Color**, in the second column click the first color. On the **Shading tab**, click the **Fill arrow**, and then in the fourth column, click the second color. **Center** the paragraph text. **Save** your document.

8 On **Page 2**, beginning with *Janet Eisler*, select all of the text on the page but not the Page Break line. With the text on **Page 2** selected, change the **Line Spacing** to **2.0**, and then change the **Spacing After** to **0 pt**.

9 To the paragraph that begins *There is often a discrepancy*, apply a **First line** indent of **0.5** inches.

10 In the paragraph that begins *Linder claims that*, in the next to last line of text, after the period at the end of the sentence that ends *if they had it*, insert a footnote with the following text: **The EMR (electronic medical record) is the patient record created in hospitals and ambulatory environments; it serves as a data source for other systems.** Be sure to type the period at the end of the footnote text.

11 Right-click anywhere in the footnote text, and then modify the **Footnote Text** style to set the **Font Size** to **11** and the format of the Footnote Text paragraph to include a **First line** indent of **0.5"** and **Double** spacing. Apply the new style to the footnote text.

12 On the first page of the research paper, at the end of the paragraph that begins *Those clinical practices*, click to the left of the period, and then using **MLA** format, insert a citation for a **Web site** with the following information: (Mac users, there is no Medium field.)

Author	Gabriel, Barbara A.
Name of Web Page	Do EMRS Make You a Better Doctor?
Year	2008
Month	July
Day	15
Year Accessed	2021
Month Accessed	June
Day Accessed	30
Medium	Web

(continues on next page)

Content-Based Assessments (Mastery and Transfer of Learning)

13 On the second page of the research paper, at the end of the paragraph that begins *Further research*, click to the left of the period, and then using **MLA** format, insert a citation for a **Book** with the following information: (Mac users, there is no Medium field.)

Author	DeVore, Amy.
Title	The Electronic Health Record for the Physician's Office, 1e
Year	2010
City	Maryland Heights
Publisher	Saunders
Medium	Print

14 In the report, select the citation you just created, display the **Citation Options**, and then edit the citation to include **Pages 253**

15 From the **References tab**, open **Researcher**, and then—including the quotation marks—search for **"electronic health records"** and press Enter. Under **Top sources**, click **Journals**, and notice the extensive number of journal articles on this topic. **Close** the **Researcher pane**, and then on the first page of the research paper, in the paragraph that begins *There is often a discrepancy*, in the fourth line, select the text *electronic health records*. To the selected text, apply **Yellow Text Highlight Color**.

16 On the last page of the research paper click in the blank paragraph. On the **References tab**, click **Bibliography**, and then at the bottom of the list, click **Works Cited**.

17 Select the paragraph *Works Cited*, and then change the font to **Calibri**, change the font size to **11**, and then change the font color to **Black, Text 1**. Center the text *Works Cited*.

18 Click to the left of the title *Works Cited*, and then drag down to select the title *Works Cited* and the two citations. From the **Paragraph** dialog box, change the **Spacing Before** to **0 pt**, change the **Spacing After** to **0 pt**, and set the **Line spacing** to **Double**. Move to the top of your document and **Save**.

19 In **MyLab IT**, locate and click the Grader Project **Word 3G Newsletter and Research Paper**. In **step 3**, under **Upload Completed Assignment**, click **Choose File**. In the **Open** dialog box, navigate to your **Word Chapter 3 folder**, and then click your **Student_Word_3G_Newsletter_and_Research_Paper** file one time to select it. In the lower right corner of the **Open** dialog box, click **Open**.

The name of your selected file displays above the Upload button.

20 To submit your file to **MyLab IT** for grading, click **Upload**, wait a moment for a green **Success!** message, and then in **step 4**, click the blue **Submit for Grading** button. Click **Close Assignment** to return to your list of **Course Materials**.

You have completed Project 3G **END**

ALERT   **Optional Bonus Project to Produce Mailing Labels**

Your instructor may ask you to complete this optional bonus project to produce mailing labels. Check with your instructor to see if you should complete the mailing labels. This project is not included in the **MyLab IT** Grader system. Your instructor can provide you the file w03G_Addresses, or you can download the file from www.pearsonhighered.com/go

1 Start Word and display a new blank document. **Save** the document in your **Word Chapter 3** folder as **Lastname_Firstname_3G_Mailing_Labels**

2 Start the **Step-by-Step Mail Merge Wizard** and as the document type create **Labels**. Move to the next step of the Mail Merge wizard. Click **Label options**, be sure that the **Default tray** is selected and that the label vendor is **Avery US Letter**. As the **Product number**, click **5160 Address Labels**. Move to the next step of the Mail Merge wizard, and then click **Use an existing list**. Click **Browse**, navigate to your downloaded student data files, click the Excel file **w03G_Addresses**, click **Open**, and then click **OK** two times.

3 Move to the next step of the Mail Merge Wizard, and then click **Address block**. Click **OK**, and then **Update all labels**. Move to the next step of the Mail Merge Wizard to preview the labels. Then **Complete the merge**. Delete the last two rows from the bottom of the table, and then add the file name to the footer.

4 **Save** your file. As directed by your instructor, print or submit electronically.

You have completed the optional portion of this project   **END**

Content-Based Assessments (Critical Thinking)

GO! Fix It	Project 3H Hospital Materials	IRC
GO! Make It	Project 3I Health Newsletter	IRC
GO! Solve It	Project 3J Colds and Flu	IRC
GO! Solve It	Project 3K Cycling Newsletter	

Apply a combination of the 3A and 3B skills

Project Files

For Project 3K, you will need the following files:

w03K_Cycling_Newsletter
w03K_Bicycle

You will save your document as:

Lastname_Firstname_3K_Cycling_Newsletter

The University Medical Center Emergency Department publishes a monthly newsletter focusing on safety and injury prevention. The topic for the current newsletter is bicycle safety. From your student data files, open **w03K_Cycling_Newsletter**, add the file name to the footer, and then save the file in your Word Chapter 3 folder as **Lastname_Firstname_3K_Cycling_Newsletter**

Using the techniques that you practiced in this chapter, format the document in two-column, newsletter format. Format the newsletter heading so that it is clearly separate from the body of the newsletter and is easily identified as the heading. Insert column breaks as necessary and apply appropriate formatting to subheadings. Insert and format the bicycle picture, and insert a Screen Clipping of a relevant website. Apply a border and shading to the last paragraph so that it is formatted attractively.

Add your name, your course name and section number, and the keywords **safety, newsletter** to the Properties area. Submit as directed.

		Performance Level		
		Exemplary: You consistently applied the relevant skills	**Proficient: You sometimes, but not always, applied the relevant skills**	**Developing: You rarely or never applied the relevant skills**
Performance Criteria	**Format newsletter heading**	The nameplate is formatted attractively and in a manner that clearly indicates that it is the nameplate.	The nameplate includes some formatting but is not clearly separated from the body of the newsletter.	The newsletter does not include a nameplate.
	Insert and format picture	The image is sized and positioned appropriately.	The image is inserted but is formatted or positioned poorly.	No image is included.
	Border and shading added to a paragraph	The last paragraph displays an attractive border with shading that enables the reader to read the text.	A border or shading is displayed but not both; or the shading is too dark to enable the reader to easily read the text.	No border or shading is added to a paragraph.
	Insert a screenshot	A screenshot is inserted in one of the columns; the screenshot is related to the content of the article.	A screenshot is inserted in the document but does not relate to the content of the article.	No screenshot is inserted.

You have completed Project 3K | END

Rubric

The following outcomes-based assessments are *open-ended assessments*. That is, there is no specific correct result; your result will depend on your approach to the information provided. Make *Professional Quality* your goal. Use the following scoring rubric to guide you in *how* to approach the problem and then to evaluate *how well* your approach solves the problem.

The *criteria*—Software Mastery, Content, Format and Layout, and Process—represent the knowledge and skills you have gained that you can apply to solving the problem. The *levels of performance*—Professional Quality, Approaching Professional Quality, or Needs Quality Improvements—help you and your instructor evaluate your result

	Your completed project is of Professional Quality if you:	Your completed project is Approaching Professional Quality if you:	Your completed project Needs Quality Improvements if you:
1-Software Mastery	Choose and apply the most appropriate skills, tools, and features and identify efficient methods to solve the problem.	Choose and apply some appropriate skills, tools, and features, but not in the most efficient manner.	Choose inappropriate skills, tools, or features, or are inefficient in solving the problem.
2-Content	Construct a solution that is clear and well organized, contains content that is accurate, appropriate to the audience and purpose, and is complete. Provide a solution that contains no errors of spelling, grammar, or style.	Construct a solution in which some components are unclear, poorly organized, inconsistent, or incomplete. Misjudge the needs of the audience. Have some errors in spelling, grammar, or style, but the errors do not detract from comprehension.	Construct a solution that is unclear, incomplete, or poorly organized, contains some inaccurate or inappropriate content, and contains many errors of spelling, grammar, or style. Do not solve the problem.
3-Format and Layout	Format and arrange all elements to communicate information and ideas, clarify function, illustrate relationships, and indicate relative importance.	Apply appropriate format and layout features to some elements, but not others. Overuse features, causing minor distraction.	Apply format and layout that does not communicate information or ideas clearly. Do not use format and layout features to clarify function, illustrate relationships, or indicate relative importance. Use available features excessively, causing distraction.
4-Process	Use an organized approach that integrates planning, development, self-assessment, revision, and reflection.	Demonstrate an organized approach in some areas, but not others; or, use an insufficient process of organization throughout.	Do not use an organized approach to solve the problem.

Content-Based Assessments (Critical Thinking)

GO! Think	Project 3L Influenza Report

Apply a combination of the 3A and 3B skills.

Project Files

For Project 3L, you will need the following file:

New blank Word document

You will save your document as:

Lastname_Firstname_3L_Influenza

As part of the ongoing research conducted by University Medical Center in the area of community health and contagious diseases, Dr. Hillary Kim has asked Sarah Stanger to create a report on influenza—how it spreads and how it can be prevented in the community.

Create a new file and save it as **Lastname_Firstname_3L_Influenza** Create the report in MLA format. The report should include at least two footnotes, at least two citations, and should include a *Works Cited* page.

The report should contain an introduction and information about what influenza is, how it spreads, and how it can be prevented. A good place to start is at http://health.nih.gov/topic/influenza.

Add the file name to the footer. Add appropriate information to the Document Properties and submit it as directed.

	You have completed Project 3L	END

GO! Think	Project 3M Volunteer Newsletter	IRC

You and GO!	Project 3N College Newsletter	IRC

GO! Cumulative Team Project	Project 3O Bell Orchid Hotels	IRC

Using Styles and Creating Multilevel Lists and Charts

PROJECT 4A

Outcomes
Edit a handout using styles and arrange text into an organized list.

Objectives

1. Apply and Modify Styles
2. Create New Styles
3. Manage Styles
4. Create a Multilevel List

PROJECT 4B

Outcomes
Change a style set and create and format a chart.

Objectives

5. Change the Style Set of a Document and Apply a Template
6. Insert a Chart and Enter Data into a Chart
7. Change a Chart Type
8. Format a Chart

Parkol/Shutterstock

In This Chapter

GO! to Work with Word

In this chapter, you will apply styles, create multilevel lists, attach a template to a document, and display numerical data in charts. The theme and style set features provide a simple way to coordinate colors, fonts, and effects used in a document. For example, if you publish a monthly newsletter, you can apply styles to article headings and modify lists to ensure that all editions of the newsletter maintain a consistent and professional look. Charts display numerical data in a visual format. Formatting chart elements adds interest and assists the reader in interpreting the displayed data.

The projects in this chapter relate to **Costa Rican Treks**, a tour company named for the small country in Central America with a diverse ecosystem. Costa Rican Treks offers exciting but affordable adventure tours for individuals and groups. Travelers go off the beaten path to explore amazing remote places in this scenic country. If you prefer to experience the heart of Costa Rica on the water, try the kayaking or rafting tours. Costa Rican Treks also offers hiking and Jeep tours. Whatever you prefer—mountain, sea, volcano—our trained guides are experts in the history, geography, culture, and flora and fauna of Costa Rica.

PROJECT

4A Customer Handout

MyLab IT
Project 4A Grader for Instruction
Project 4A Simulation for Training and Review

Project Activities

In Activities 4.01 through 4.11, you will create a handout for Costa Rican Treks customers who are interested in scuba diving tours. You will use styles and multilevel list formats so that the document is attractive and easy to read. Your completed document will look similar to Figure 4.1.

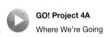

Project Files for MyLab IT Grader

1. In your storage location, create a folder named **Word Chapter 4**.
2. In your **MyLab IT** course, locate and click **Word 4A Customer Handout**, Download Materials, and then Download All Files.
3. Extract the zipped folder to your Word Chapter 4 folder. Close the Grader download screens.
4. Take a moment to open the downloaded **Word_4A_Customer_Handout_Instructions**; note any recent updates to the book.

Project Results

GO! Project 4A
Where We're Going

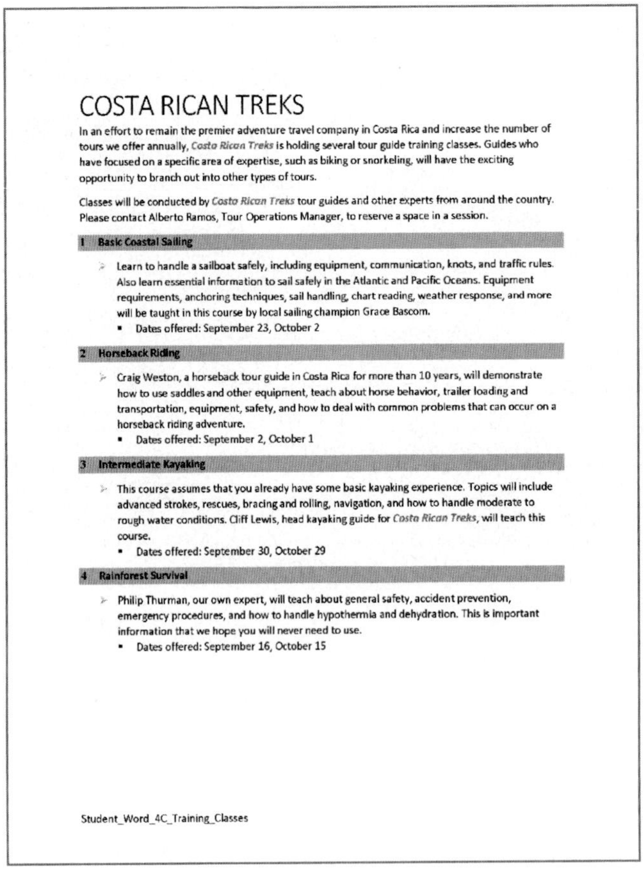

COSTA RICAN TREKS

In an effort to remain the premier adventure travel company in Costa Rica and increase the number of tours we offer annually, *Costa Rican Treks* is holding several tour guide training classes. Guides who have focused on a specific area of expertise, such as biking or snorkeling, will have the exciting opportunity to branch out into other types of tours.

Classes will be conducted by *Costa Rican Treks* tour guides and other experts from around the country. Please contact Alberto Ramos, Tour Operations Manager, to reserve a space in a session.

1 Basic Coastal Sailing

- Learn to handle a sailboat safely, including equipment, communication, knots, and traffic rules. Also learn essential information to sail safely in the Atlantic and Pacific Oceans. Equipment requirements, anchoring techniques, sail handling, chart reading, weather response, and more will be taught in this course by local sailing champion Grace Bascom.
  - Dates offered: September 23, October 2

2 Horseback Riding

- Craig Weston, a horseback tour guide in Costa Rica for more than 10 years, will demonstrate how to use saddles and other equipment, teach about horse behavior, trailer loading and transportation, equipment, safety, and how to deal with common problems that can occur on a horseback riding adventure.
  - Dates offered: September 2, October 1

3 Intermediate Kayaking

- This course assumes that you already have some basic kayaking experience. Topics will include advanced strokes, rescues, bracing and rolling, navigation, and how to handle moderate to rough water conditions. Cliff Lewis, head kayaking guide for *Costa Rican Treks*, will teach this course.
  - Dates offered: September 30, October 29

4 Rainforest Survival

- Philip Thurman, our own expert, will teach about general safety, accident prevention, emergency procedures, and how to handle hypothermia and dehydration. This is important information that we hope you will never need to use.
  - Dates offered: September 16, October 15

Student_Word_4C_Training_Classes

Figure 4.1 Project 4A Customer Handout

For Non-MyLab Submissions
For Project 4A, you will need:
w04A_Customer_Handout

In your storage location, create a folder named **Word Chapter 4**
In your Word Chapter 4 folder, save your document as:
Lastname_Firstname_4A_Customer_Handout

After you have named and saved your document, on the next page, begin with Step 2.

GO! Learn How
Video W4-1

A *style* is a group of formatting commands, such as font, font size, font color, paragraph alignment, and line spacing. Using styles to format text has several advantages over using *direct formatting*—the process of applying each format separately; for example, bold, then font size, then font color, and so on. Styles are faster to apply, result in a consistent look, and can be automatically updated in all instances in a document, which can be especially useful in long documents.

Activity 4.01   Applying Styles to Paragraphs

MOS
2.2.4

Styles that are grouped together comprise a *style set*. A style set is a group of styles that are designed to work together. Specific styles—for example, *Title* or *Heading 1*—that display in the Styles gallery on the ribbon can be applied to any selected text.

1 Navigate to your **Word Chapter 4 folder**, and then double-click the Word file you downloaded from **MyLab IT** that displays your name—**Student_Word_4A_Customer_Handout**.

2 Scroll to the bottom of **Page 1**, right-click in the footer area, and then click **Edit Footer**. On the ribbon, under **Header & Footer Tools**, on the **Design tab**, in the **Insert group**, click **Document Info**, and then click **File Name**. **Close** the footer area. If necessary, display the rulers and formatting marks.

MAC TIP   To display group names on the ribbon, display the menu, click Word, click Preferences, click View, select the Show group titles check box.

3 Press Ctrl + Home to move to the top of the document.

MAC TIP   Press command ⌘ + fn + ←.

4 On the **Home tab**, in the **Styles group**, notice that the **Normal** style is selected—outlined in blue. Compare your screen with Figure 4.2.

The *Normal* style is the default style in Word for a new blank document. Normal style formatting includes the Calibri font, 11 point font size, line spacing at 1.08, and 8 pt spacing after a paragraph.

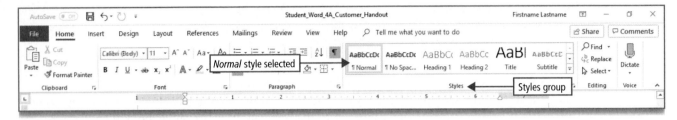

Figure 4.2

5 Including the paragraph mark, select the first paragraph, which forms the title of the document—*Costa Rican Treks*. On the **Home tab**, in the **Styles group**, click the **More** button to display the Styles gallery. Point to the style named **Title**, and then compare your screen with Figure 4.3.

Live Preview displays how the text will look with the Title style applied.

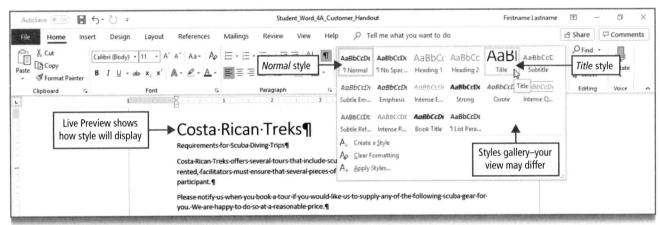

Figure 4.3

6 Click **Title**, and then click anywhere in the document to deselect the title.

The Title style includes the 28 point Calibri Light font, single line spacing and 0 pt spacing after the paragraph.

7 ▶ Select the second paragraph, which begins *Requirements for*, and is the subtitle of the document. In the **Styles group**, click **More** ⌄, and then in the gallery, click **Subtitle**.

The Subtitle style includes a Black, Text 1, Lighter 35% font color and expanding of the text by 0.75 pt.

8 ▶ Select the third and fourth paragraphs, beginning with *Costa Rican Treks offers* and ending with the text *at a reasonable price*. In the **Styles group**, click **More** ⌄, and then in the gallery, click **Emphasis**. Click anywhere to deselect the text, and then compare your screen with Figure 4.4.

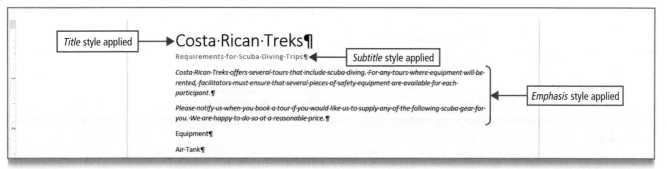

Figure 4.4

9 ▶ **Save** 🖫 your document.

Activity 4.02 | Modifying Existing Style Attributes

You are not limited to the exact formatting of a style—you can change it to suit your needs. For example, you might like the formatting of a style with the exception of the font size. If you plan to use a customized style repeatedly in a document, it's a good idea to modify the style to look exactly the way you want it. You can either save the modified style as a new style or you can update the existing style to match the new formatting.

1 ▶ Select the heading *Equipment*. Using the technique you practiced, apply the **Heading 1** style.

The Heading 1 style includes the 16 point Calibri Light font, an Accent 1 font color, 12 pt spacing before the paragraph and 0 pt spacing after the paragraph.
A small black square displays to the left of the paragraph indicating that the Heading 1 style also includes the ***Keep with next*** and ***Keep lines together*** formatting—Word commands that keep a heading with its first paragraph of text together on the page, or prevent a single line from displaying by itself at the bottom of a page or at the top of a page.

2 ▶ With the paragraph selected, change the **Font Size** to **18**.

3 ▶ On the mini toolbar, click **Styles**. In the **Styles** gallery, right-click **Heading 1**, and then compare your screen with Figure 4.5.

⌨ **MAC TIP** On the Home tab, display the Styles gallery, and then press ⌐control⌐ and click the Heading 1 style.

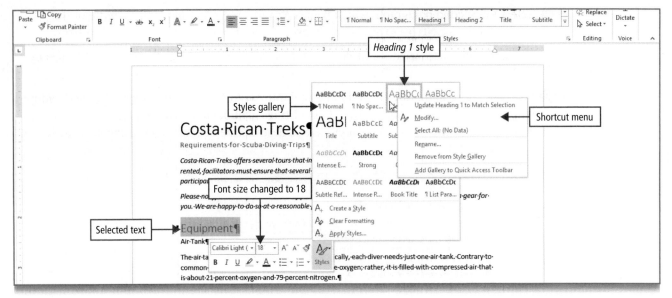

Figure 4.5

4 From the shortcut menu, click **Update Heading 1 to Match Selection**, and then click anywhere to deselect the text.

> By updating the heading style, you ensure that the next time you apply the Heading 1 style in *this* document, it will retain these new formats. In this manner, you can customize a style. The changes to the Heading 1 style are stored *only* in this document and will not affect the Heading 1 style in any other documents.

5 Scroll down to view the lower portion of **Page 1**, and then select the heading *Attire*. On the **Home tab**, in the **Styles** group, click **Heading 1**, and notice that the *modified* **Heading 1** style is applied to the paragraph. Click anywhere in the document to deselect the text. **Save** your document.

Activity 4.03 | Changing the Document Theme

1.3.2

Recall that a theme is a predefined combination of colors, fonts, and effects; the *Office* theme is the default theme applied to new blank documents. Styles use the font scheme, color scheme, and effects associated with the current theme. If you change the theme, the styles adopt the fonts, colors, and effects of the new theme.

1 Press Ctrl + Home. Click the **Design tab**, and then in the **Document Formatting group**, click **Themes**. In the gallery, point to the various themes and notice the changes in your document.

> Live Preview enables you to see the effects a theme has on text with styles applied.

2 Click **Facet**, and then compare your screen with Figure 4.6.

> The Facet theme's fonts, colors, and effects display in the document. All the styles will now use the Facet theme.

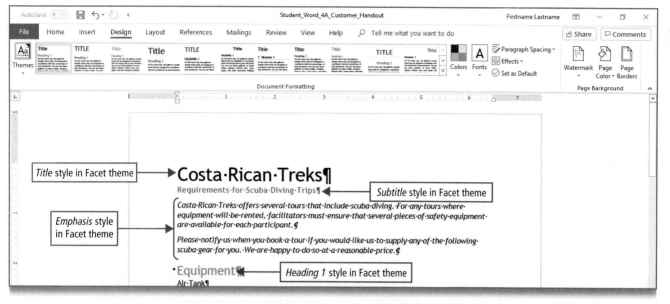

Figure 4.6

3 Select the subtitle, which begins *Requirements for*. Change the **Font Size** to **14** and apply **Bold** ⬚B.

> In this handout, this emphasis on the subtitle is useful. Because there are no other subtitles and you will not be applying this style again in this document, it is not necessary to modify the actual style.

4 With the subtitle still selected, on the **Home tab**, in the **Font group**, click **Change Case** ⬚Aa▾, and then from the list, click **UPPERCASE**.

> The *Change Case* feature allows you to quickly change the capitalization of characters. In the selection, all characters now display in uppercase letters.

5 Select the third and fourth paragraphs, beginning with *Costa Rican Treks offers* and ending with the text *at a reasonable price*. Change the **Font Size** to **12**, and then on the **Home tab**, in the **Styles** gallery, right-click **Emphasis**, and then click **Update Emphasis to Match Selection**. Click anywhere to deselect the text. **Save** ⬚ your document.

Objective 2 Create New Styles

GO! Learn How
Video W4-2

You can create a new style based on formats that you specify. For example, if you frequently use a 12 point Verdana font with bold emphasis and double spacing, you can create a style to apply those settings to a paragraph with a single click, instead of using multiple steps each time you want that specific formatting. Any new styles that you create are stored with the document and are available any time that the document is open.

Activity 4.04 | Creating Custom Styles and Assigning Shortcut Keys

You can assign a shortcut key to a style, which allows you to apply the style using the keyboard instead of clicking the style in the Styles gallery.

1 Select the paragraph that begins *Examples: Aluminum*, and then change the **Font Size** to **12**, click **Bold** ⬚B, and then click **Italic** ⬚I.

2 With the paragraph still selected, on the **Home tab**, in the **Styles group**, click the **More** button ⊡. In the lower portion of the gallery, click **Create a Style**.

3 In the **Create New Style from Formatting** dialog box, in the **Name** box, type **Examples** and then compare your screen with Figure 4.7.

> Select a name for your new style that will remind you of the type of text to which the style applies. A preview of the style displays in the Paragraph style preview box.

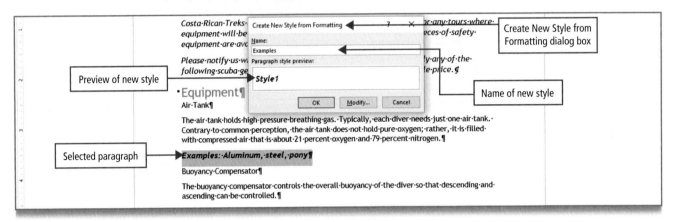

Figure 4.7

4 At the bottom of the dialog box, click **Modify**.

5 In the **Create New Style from Formatting** dialog box, at the bottom left, click **Format**, and then click **Shortcut key**.

6 In the **Customize Keyboard** dialog box, with the insertion point in the **Press new shortcut key** box, press Alt + E. Compare your screen with Figure 4.8.

> The Commands box indicates that the shortcut key will be assigned to the Examples style. The text *Alt+E* indicates the keys that have been pressed. A message indicates that the shortcut key is currently unassigned.

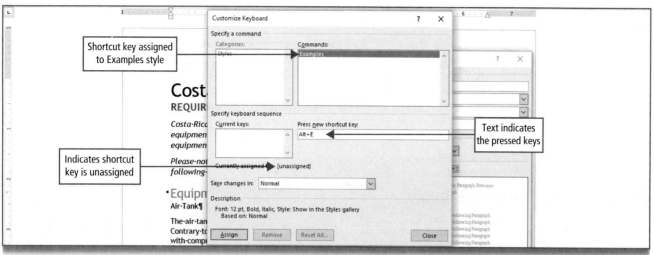

Figure 4.8

7 In the **Customize Keyboard** dialog box, click **Assign**. Click **Close**, and then in the **Create New Style from Formatting** dialog box, click **OK**.

The *Examples* style is added to the available styles for this document and displays in the Styles gallery. The shortcut key Alt + E is assigned to the *Examples* style.

8 Scroll down as necessary and select the paragraph that begins *Examples: Wings*. Press Alt + E to apply the new style *Examples*.

MAC TIP Press control + E to apply the style to the Examples: Wings paragraph.

9 Using the technique you just practiced, select the four remaining paragraphs that begin *Examples:*, and then apply the **Examples** style. Be sure to apply the style to the *Examples:* paragraph on Page 2. Click anywhere on **Page 1** to deselect the text, and then compare your screen with Figure 4.9.

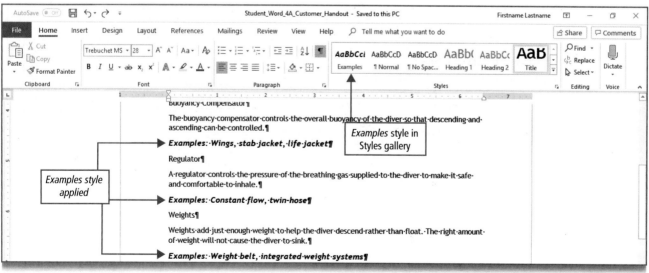

Figure 4.9

10 **Save** your document.

Objective 3 | Manage Styles

GO! Learn How
Video W4-3

You can accomplish most of the tasks related to applying, modifying, and creating styles easily by using the Styles gallery. However, if you create and modify many styles in a document, you will find it useful to work in the *Styles pane*. The Styles pane displays a list of styles and contains tools to manage styles. Additionally, by viewing available styles in the Styles pane, you can see the exact details of all the formatting that is included with each style.

Activity 4.05 | Customizing Settings for Existing Styles

1 Press Ctrl + Home, and then click anywhere in the title *Costa Rican Treks*. On the **Home tab**, in the lower right corner of the **Styles** group, click the **Dialog Box Launcher** to display the **Styles** pane. If the Styles pane displays in the middle of your screen, in the Styles pane, double-click to the right of Styles to snap the Styles pane to the right side of the Word window. Compare your screen with Figure 4.10.

The Styles pane displays the same group of available styles found in the Styles gallery, including the new *Examples* style that you created.

MAC TIP On the Home tab, in the Styles group, click Styles Pane.

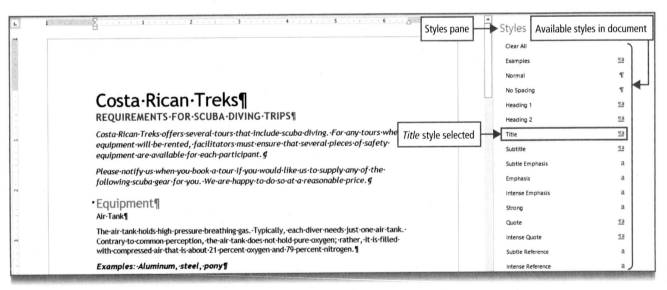

Figure 4.10

2 In the **Styles** pane, point to **Title** to display a ScreenTip with the details of the formats associated with the style. In the **ScreenTip**, under **Style**, notice that *Style Linked* is indicated.

3 Move your mouse pointer into the document to close the ScreenTip. In the **Styles** pane, examine the symbols to the right of each style, as shown in Figure 4.11.

A *character style*, indicated by the symbol **a**, contains formatting characteristics that you apply to text—for example, font name, font size, font color, bold emphasis, and so on.

A *paragraph style*, indicated by the symbol ¶, includes everything that a character style contains, plus all aspects of a paragraph's appearance—for example, text alignment, tab stops, line spacing, and borders.

A *linked style*, indicated by the symbol ¶a, behaves as either a character style or a paragraph style, depending on what you select.

List styles, which apply formats to a list, and *table styles*, which apply a consistent look to the borders, shading, and so on of a table, are also available but do not display here.

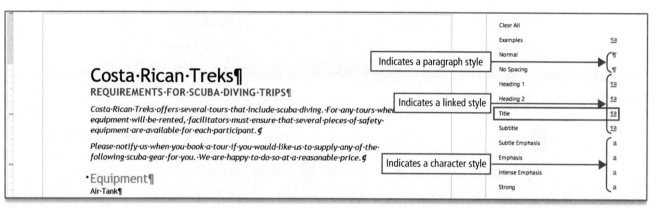

Figure 4.11

4 In the **Styles** pane, point to **Heading 1**, and then click the **arrow** to display a list of commands. Compare your screen with Figure 4.12.

ANOTHER WAY In the Styles gallery, right-click Heading 1.

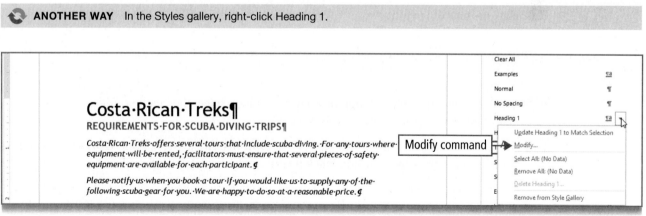

Figure 4.12

5 From the displayed list, click **Modify**. In the **Modify Style** dialog box, under **Formatting**, click **Underline** ⊍. Click the **Font Color arrow**, and then in the eighth column, point to the fifth color. Compare your screen with Figure 4.13.

The Modify command allows you to make changes to the selected style.

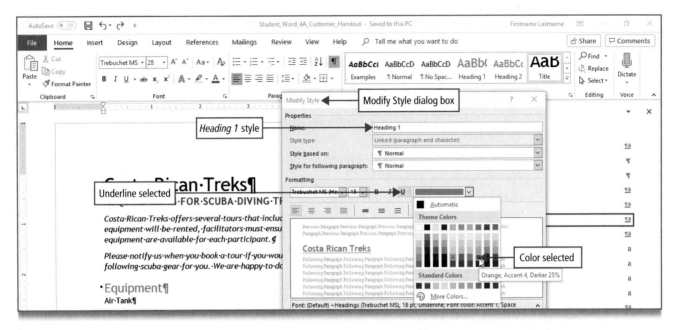

Figure 4.13

6 ▶ Click to change the color, and then click **OK** to close the Modify Styles dialog box. Scroll as necessary, and then notice that both headings—*Equipment* and *Attire*—are underlined and display in an orange font color. **Save** 🖫 your document.

MORE KNOWLEDGE **Using Styles in Other Documents**

By default, styles that you create are stored in the current document only. However, you can make the style available in other documents. To do so, in the Modify Styles dialog box, select the New documents based on this template option button, which deselects the Only in this document option button.

Activity 4.06 | Viewing Style Formats

⌨️ **MAC TIP** Skip this Activity and continue with Activity 4.07.

1 ▶ Scroll to view the upper portion of **Page 1**, and then select the heading *Equipment*. Notice that in the Styles pane *Heading 1* is selected.

2 ▶ At the bottom right of the **Styles** pane, click **Options**. In the **Style Pane Options** dialog box, in the **Select styles to show** box, click the **arrow** to display specific selection styles.

The selected option—in this case, the default option *Recommended*—determines the styles that display in the Styles pane. The Recommended option causes the most commonly used styles to display.

3 ▶ At the bottom of the **Style Pane Options** dialog box, click **Cancel** to close the dialog box.

4 ▶ Near the bottom of the **Styles** pane, select the **Show Preview** check box.

The *Show Preview* feature causes a visual representation of each style to display in the Styles pane.

5 ▶ Clear the **Show Preview** check box.

6 At the bottom of the **Styles** pane, click **Style Inspector** 📖. In the **Style Inspector** pane, notice the name of the style applied to the selected text displays.

The *Style Inspector* pane displays the name of the style with formats applied and contains paragraph-level and text-level formatting options that allow you to modify the style or reset to default formats.

7 At the bottom of the **Style Inspector** pane, click **Reveal Formatting** 📖 to display the **Reveal Formatting** pane. If the Reveal Formatting button does not display, drag the lower edge of the Style Inspector pane down until the button displays. If necessary, drag the Styles pane to the left until it is docked. Compare your screen with Figure 4.14.

The *Reveal Formatting* pane displays the formatted selection—in this case, *Equipment*—and displays a complete description of the formats applied to the selection.

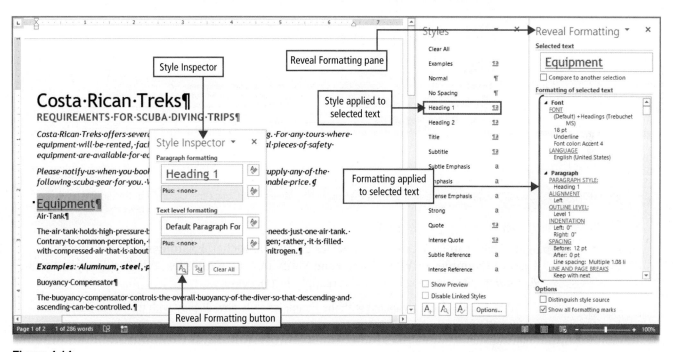

Figure 4.14

8 **Close** ✕ the Style Inspector pane, the Reveal Formatting pane, and the Styles pane. **Save** 💾 your document.

Activity 4.07 | Clearing Existing Formats

MOS
2.2.4

There may be instances where you wish to remove all formatting from existing text—for example, when you create a multilevel list.

1 Scroll to view the upper portion of **Page 1**, and then select the paragraph that begins *Examples: Aluminum*. On the **Home tab**, in the **Font group**, click **Clear All Formatting** 📖. Compare your screen with Figure 4.15.

The Clear All Formatting command removes all formatting of the applied style from the selected text. Text returns to the *Normal* style formatting for the current theme.

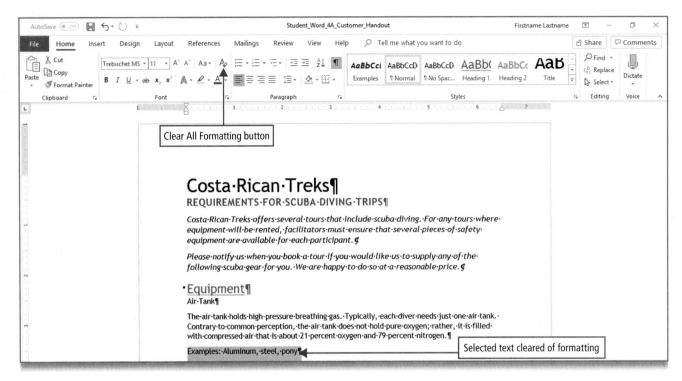

Figure 4.15

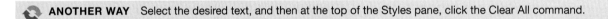

ANOTHER WAY   Select the desired text, and then at the top of the Styles pane, click the Clear All command.

2 With the text still selected, in the **Styles group**, right-click **Examples**, and then click **Update Examples to Match Selection**. Verify that the **Examples** style is still applied to the *Examples: Aluminum* selection and reapply it if necessary.

All instances of text formatted with the Examples style now display with the Normal style formatting.

3 **Save** 🖫 your document.

Activity 4.08 | Removing a Style

If a style that you created is no longer needed, you can remove it from the Styles gallery.

1 In the **Styles group**, right-click **Examples**, and then click **Remove from Style Gallery**.

The Examples style is removed from the Styles gallery. The style is no longer needed because all the paragraphs that are examples of scuba gear will be included in a multilevel list. Although the Examples style is removed from the Styles gallery, it is not deleted from the document.

2 **Save** 🖫 your document.

MORE KNOWLEDGE   **Removing Built-in Styles**

Built-in styles are predefined in Word whenever you open a new document. Although you can remove a built-in style from a single document, the built-in style is not deleted from the Word program; the built-in style will be available in all other documents.

Objective 4 | Create a Multilevel List

GO! Learn How
Video W4-4

When a document includes a list of items, you can format the items as a bulleted list, as a numbered list, or as a *multilevel list*. Use a multilevel list when you want to add a visual hierarchical structure to the items in the list.

Activity 4.09 | Creating a Multilevel List with Bullets and Modifying List Indentation

MOS
3.3.4

1 On **Page 1**, scroll to position the heading *Equipment* near the top of your screen. Beginning with the paragraph *Air Tank*, select the 12 paragraphs between the headings *Equipment* and *Attire*.

2 On the **Home tab**, in the **Paragraph group**, click **Multilevel List** to display the gallery. Under **List Library**, point to the ❖, ➤, ■ (bullet) style, which is the multilevel bullet list style. Compare your screen with Figure 4.16.

Word provides several built-in styles for multilevel lists. You can customize any style.

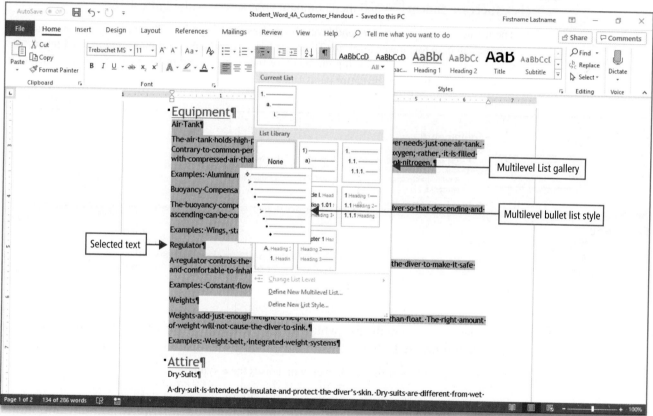

Figure 4.16

3 ▶ Click the **multilevel bullet list** style. Compare your screen with Figure 4.17.

All the items in the list display at the first level; the items are not visually indented to show different levels.

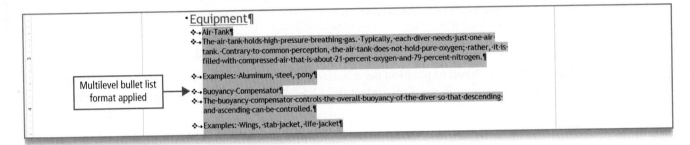

Figure 4.17

4 ▶ Click anywhere in the second list item, which begins *The air tank*. In the **Paragraph group**, click **Increase Indent** 📑, and then compare your screen with Figure 4.18.

The list item displays at the second level which uses the ➢ symbol. The Increase Indent command demotes an item to a lower level; the Decrease Indent command promotes an item to a higher level. To change the list level using the Increase Indent command or Decrease Indent command, it is not necessary to select the entire paragraph.

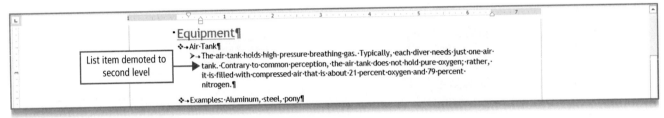

Figure 4.18

🔁 **ANOTHER WAY**   Select the item, and press ⎯Tab⎯ to demote the item or press ⎯Shift⎯ + ⎯Tab⎯ to promote it.

5 ▶ Click in the third item in the list, which begins *Examples: Aluminum*. In the **Paragraph group**, click **Increase Indent** 📑 two times, and then compare your screen with Figure 4.19.

The list item displays at the third level, which uses the ■ symbol.

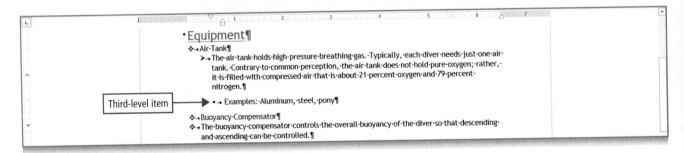

Figure 4.19

6 Using the technique you just practiced, continue setting levels for the remainder of the multilevel list as follows: Apply the second-level indent for the descriptive paragraphs that begin *The buoyancy*, *A regulator*, and *Weights add*. Apply the third-level indent for the paragraphs that begin *Examples*.

7 Compare your screen with Figure 4.20. If necessary, adjust your list by clicking Increase Indent or Decrease Indent so that your list matches the one shown in Figure 4.20.

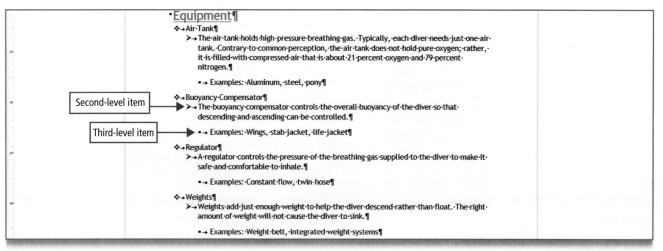

Figure 4.20

8 **Save** 🖫 your document.

MORE KNOWLEDGE **Selecting List Items**

To select several items in a document that are *contiguous*—adjacent to one another—click the first item, hold down Shift, and then click the last item. To select several items that are *noncontiguous*—not adjacent to one another—hold down Ctrl, and then click each item. After items are selected, you can format all the selected items at one time.

Activity 4.10 | Modifying the Numbering and Formatting in a Multilevel List Style

3.3.2 and 3.3.3

1 Select the entire multilevel list. Click **Multilevel List** 📜. At the bottom of the gallery, click **Define New List Style**.

In the Define New List Style dialog box, you can select formatting options for each level in your list. By default, the dialog box displays formatting options starting with the *1st level*.

2 Under **Properties**, in the **Name** box, type **Equipment List** Under **Formatting**, in the small toolbar above the preview area, to the right of *Bullet:* ❖, click the **Numbering Style arrow**.

3 In the list, scroll to the top of the list, and then click the **1, 2, 3** style. Click the **Font Color arrow**, which currently displays black, and then in the eighth column, click the fifth color. Compare your screen with Figure 4.21.

The numbering style and font color change will be applied only to first-level items. The style changes are visible in the preview area.

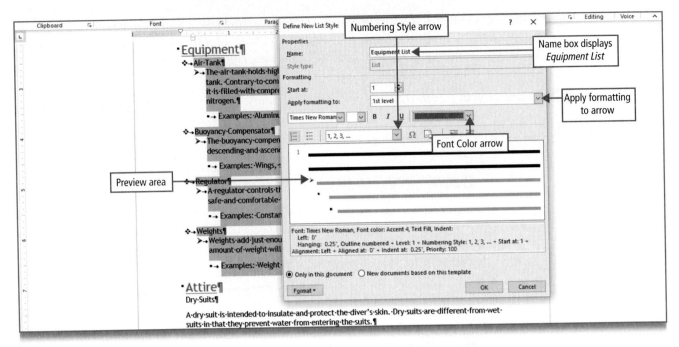

Figure 4.21

4 ▸ Under **Formatting**, click the **Apply formatting to arrow**, and then click **2nd level**. Click the **Font Color arrow**, and then in the eighth column, click the first color to change the bullet color for the second-level items.

5 ▸ Click the **Apply formatting to arrow**, and then click **3rd level**. Change the **Font Color**—in the eighth column click the first color. Click **Insert Symbol** 🔲. In the **Symbol** dialog box, be sure Wingdings displays. If necessary, click the Font arrow, and then click Wingdings. At the bottom of the **Symbol** dialog box, in the **Character code** box, select the existing text, type **170** and then compare your screen with Figure 4.22.

The ◆ symbol, represented by the character code 170 is selected.

🖵 **MAC TIP**   Visually locate the symbol indicated in Figure 4.22. The symbol on the Mac displays in black.

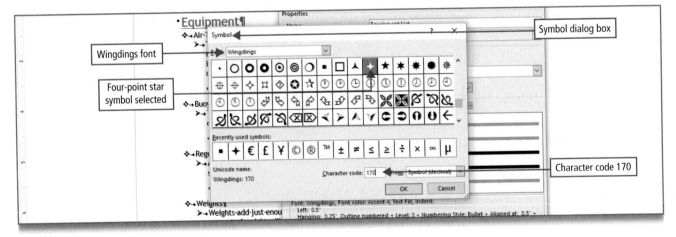

Figure 4.22

🔄 **ANOTHER WAY**   If you do not know the character code, in the Symbol dialog box, locate and click the desired symbol.

6 Click **OK** to apply the selected symbol and close the Symbol dialog box.

Third-level items will display with the ◆ symbol and orange font color.

7 In the **Define New List Style** dialog box, notice the preview of your changes, and then click **OK** to close the dialog box. Click anywhere to deselect the text, and then compare your screen with Figure 4.23.

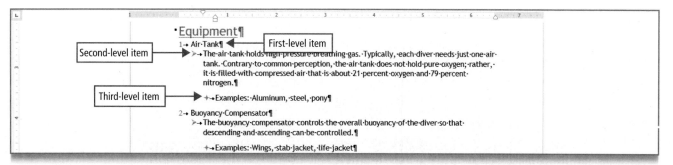

Figure 4.23

8 Select the entire list. With all 12 paragraphs selected, click the **Layout tab**, and then in the **Paragraph group**, click the **Spacing After down spin arrow** to **6 pt**. Save 🖫 your changes.

Activity 4.11 | Applying the Current List Style and Changing the List Levels

After you define a new list style, you can apply the style to other similar items in your document.

1 Scroll to display the heading *Attire* and all remaining paragraphs in the document. Beginning with the paragraph *Dry Suits*, select the remaining paragraphs of the document.

2 Click the **Home tab**, and then in the **Paragraph group**, click **Multilevel List** 🔽. In the gallery, under **List Styles**, point to the list style that you created to display the ScreenTip *Equipment List*, and then click the **Equipment List** style. Compare your screen with Figure 4.24.

Each paragraph is formatted as a first-level item.

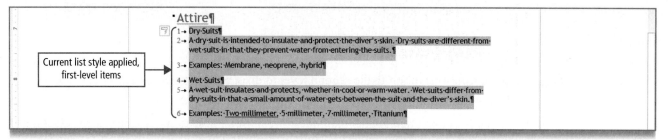

Figure 4.24

3 Under the *Attire* heading, select the paragraph that begins *A dry suit*. Hold down `Ctrl` and select the paragraph that begins *A wet suit*. Click **Multilevel List** ⟦☰▾⟧, and then click **Change List Level**. Compare your screen with Figure 4.25.

Hold down `Ctrl` to select nonadjacent text. All available list levels display for the selected paragraphs. You can increase or decrease the list level for selected items in a list by assigning the desired level.

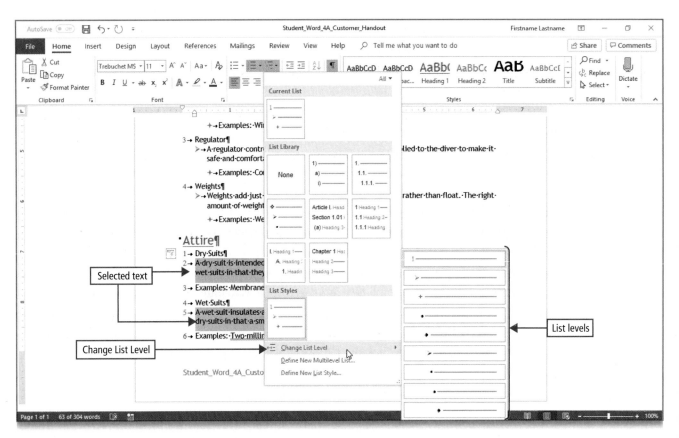

Figure 4.25

4 From the levels list, point to the second level to display the ScreenTip **Level 2**. Click the **Level 2** list level.

5 Select the paragraph that begins *Examples: Membrane*, hold down `Ctrl`, and then select the paragraph that begins *Examples: Two millimeter*. Using the technique you just practiced, assign the third list level that displays the symbol ✦ —**Level 3**.

6 Select the entire list. With all six paragraphs selected, click the **Layout tab**, and then in the **Paragraph group**, click the **Spacing After down spin arrow** to **6 pt**. Deselect the text, and then compare your screen with Figure 4.26.

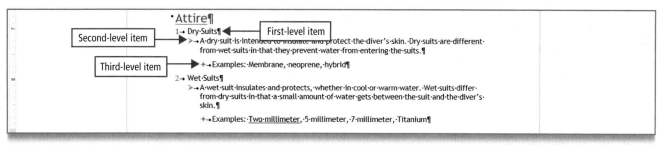

Figure 4.26

7 Display the document **Properties**. In the **Tags** box, type **scuba diving** and then in the **Subject** box, type your course name and section number. If necessary, edit the author name to display your name.

8 On the left, click **Print** to display **Print Preview**. If necessary, return to the document and make any necessary changes. **Save** your document and **Close** Word.

For Non-MyLab Submissions Determine What Your Instructor Requires
As directed by your instructor, submit your completed Word file.

9 In **MyLab IT**, locate and click the Grader Project **Word 4A Customer Handout**. In **step 3**, under **Upload Completed Assignment**, click **Choose File**. In the **Open** dialog box, navigate to your **Word Chapter 4 folder**, and then click your **Student_Word_4A_ Customer_Handout** file one time to select it. In the lower right corner of the **Open** dialog box, click **Open**.

The name of your selected file displays above the Upload button.

10 To submit your file to **MyLab IT** for grading, click **Upload**, wait a moment for a green **Success!** message, and then in **step 4**, click the blue **Submit for Grading** button. Click **Close Assignment** to return to your list of **Course Materials**.

You have completed Project 4A | END

Planning Memo with a Chart

Project Activities

In Activities 4.12 through 4.23, you will edit a memo to all the company tour guides regarding an upcoming planning session for the types of tours the company will offer in the coming year. The group will discuss information gathered from customer research to provide an appropriate mix of tour types that will appeal to a wide audience. You will add a chart to illustrate plans for tour types in the coming year. Your completed document will look similar to Figure 4.27.

 ## Project Files for MyLab IT Grader

1. In your **MyLab IT** course, locate and click **Word 4B Planning Memo**, Download Materials, and then Download All Files.
2. Extract the zipped folder to your Word Chapter 4 folder. Close the Grader download screens.
3. Take a moment to open the downloaded **Word_4B_Planning_Memo_Instructions**; note any recent updates to the book.

Project Results

GO! Project 4B

Where We're Going

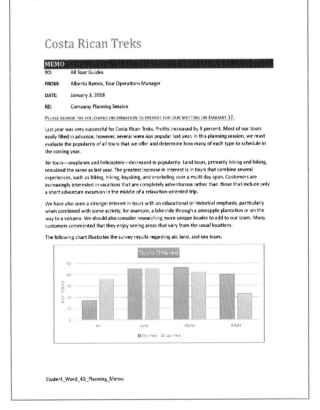

Figure 4.27 Project 4B Planning Memo

For Non-MyLab Submissions

For Project 4B, you will need:

w04B_Planning_Memo
w04B_Custom_Styles

In your Word Chapter 4 folder, save your document as:

Lastname_Firstname_4B_Planning_Memo

After you have named and saved your document, on the next page, begin with Step 2.

GO! Learn How
Video W4-5

Recall that a style set is a group of styles that is designed to work together. A style set is useful when you want to change the look of all the styles in a document in one step rather than modifying individual styles. You can modify the document using a built-in style set or by attaching a template.

Activity 4.12 | Formatting a Memo

A *memo*, also referred to as a *memorandum*, is a written message to someone working in the same organization. Among organizations, memo formats vary, and there are many acceptable memo formats. Always consult trusted references or the preferences set by your organization when deciding on the proper formats for your professional memos.

1 Navigate to your **Word Chapter 4 folder**, and then double-click the Word file you downloaded from **MyLab IT** that displays your name—**Student_Word_4B_Planning_Memo**.

2 Select the first paragraph of the document—*Costa Rican Treks*. On the **Home tab**, in the **Styles group**, click **Title**.

3 Select the second paragraph, the heading *MEMO*, and then apply the **Heading 1** style.

4 Select the text *TO:*—include the colon—hold down Ctrl, and then select the text *FROM:*, *DATE:*, and *RE:*. Apply **Bold** B to these four memo headings.

MAC TIP   Hold down command ⌘ to select nonadjacent text.

5 Select the paragraph that begins *Please review*. In the **Styles** group, click **More**. In the gallery, use the ScreenTips to locate and then click **Intense Reference**. Click anywhere to deselect the text. **Save** your document. Compare your screen with Figure 4.28.

Figure 4.28

Activity 4.13 | Changing the Style Set of a Document

MOS
1.2.2

By changing a style set, you can apply a group of styles to a document in one step.

1 Click the **Design tab**. In the **Document Formatting group**, click the **More** button ⯆. Point to the last style, and then compare your screen with Figure 4.29.

All available style sets display in the Style Set gallery. The style set currently applied to a document displays under This Document.

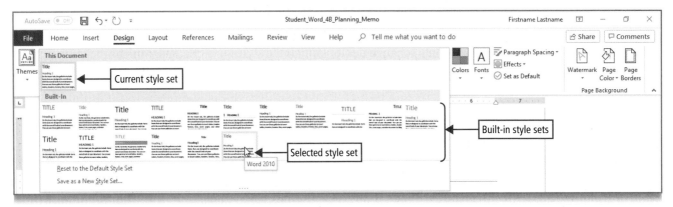

Figure 4.29

2 Click the last style set, and then compare your screen with Figure 4.30.

The selected style set includes different before and after paragraph spacing and applied styles such as Title, Heading 1, and Intense Reference also display a different format.

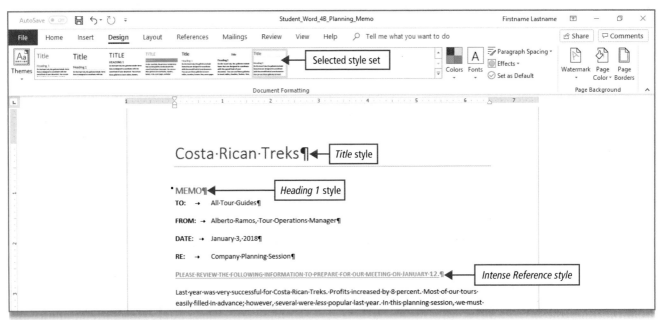

Figure 4.30

3 On the **Design tab**, in the **Document Formatting group**, click the **More** button ⯆. Below the gallery, click **Reset to the Default Style Set** to return the document to its original formatting.

Activity 4.14 | Changing the Paragraph Spacing of a Document

MOS
2.2.3

Each style set reflects the font scheme and color scheme of the current theme, including the paragraph spacing formats. Built-in paragraph spacing formats allow you to change the paragraph spacing and line spacing for an entire document in one step.

1 On the **Design tab**, in the **Document Formatting group**, click **Paragraph Spacing**. Compare your screen with Figure 4.31, and then take a moment to study the table shown in Figure 4.32.

Word provides six built-in styles for paragraph spacing.

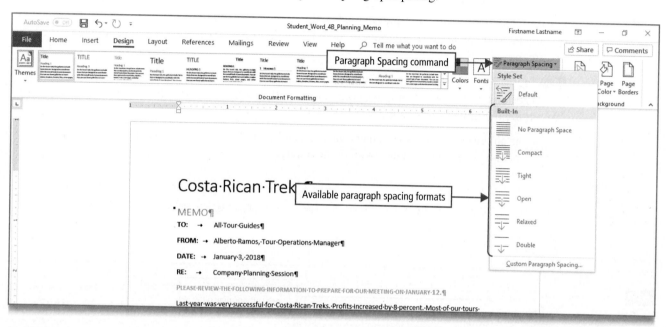

Figure 4.31

Paragraph Spacing Formats

Option	Spacing Before	Spacing After	Line Spacing
No paragraph spacing	0 pt	0 pt	1
Compact	0 pt	4 pt	1
Tight	0 pt	6 pt	1.15
Open	0 pt	10 pt	1.15
Relaxed	0 pt	6 pt	1.5
Double	0 pt	8 pt	2

Figure 4.32

2 In the gallery, point to **Open**. Notice that the ScreenTip describes the paragraph spacing format and that Live Preview displays how the document would look with this paragraph spacing format applied. Click **Open**.

3 Save 🖫 your document.

Activity 4.15 | Customizing the Ribbon and Attaching a Template to a Document

Word Options form a collection of settings that you can change to customize Word. In this Activity, you will customize the ribbon and attach a template. Recall that a template is an existing document—for example, the Normal template—that you use as a starting point for a new document. You can apply a template to an existing document to change the appearance of the document.

1 Press Ctrl + Home. Click the **File tab**, and then on the left, click **Options** to display the **Word Options** dialog box. Compare your screen with Figure 4.33, and then take a few moments to study the table in Figure 4.34.

In an organizational environment such as a college or business, you may not have access or permission to change some or all of the settings.

⬜ **MAC TIP** On the menu, click Word, click Preferences, click Ribbon & Toolbar. Skip to Step 3.

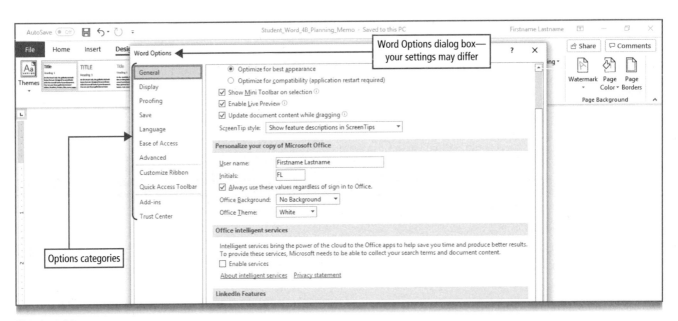

Figure 4.33

Word Options	
Category	**Options to:**
General	Set up Word for your personal way of working—for example, changing the Office Background—and personalize Word with your name and initials.
Display	Control the way content displays pages on the screen and when it prints.
Proofing	Control how Word corrects and formats your text—for example, how AutoCorrect and spell checker perform.
Save	Specify where you want to save your Word documents by default and set the AutoRecover time for saving information.
Language	Set the default language and add additional languages for editing documents.
Ease of Access	Make Word more accessible
Advanced	Control advanced features, including editing and printing options.
Customize Ribbon	Add commands to existing tabs, create new tabs, and set up your own keyboard shortcuts.
Quick Access Toolbar	Customize the Quick Access Toolbar by adding commands.
Add-Ins	View and manage add-in programs that come with the Word software or ones that you add to Word.
Trust Center	Control privacy and security when working with files from other sources or when you share files with others.

Figure 4.34

2 In the **Word Options** dialog box, on the left, click **Customize Ribbon**.

The Word Options dialog box displays a list of popular commands on the left and main tabs display on the right. Under Main Tabs, the checkmarks to the left of the tab names indicate tabs that are currently available on the ribbon.

3 In the **Word Options** dialog box, in the **Main Tabs** list, select the **Developer** check box. Compare your screen with Figure 4.35.

The Developer tab extends the capabilities of Word—including commands for using existing templates.

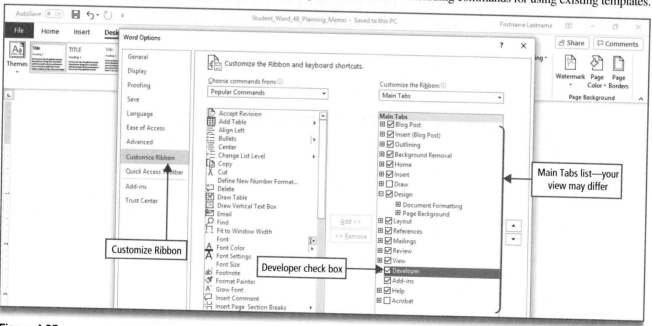

Figure 4.35

4 Click **OK** to close the **Word Options** dialog box.

The Developer tab displays on the ribbon to the right of the View tab.

5 Click the **Developer tab**, and then in the **Templates group**, click **Document Template**.

MAC TIP On the Developer tab, click Word Add-ins.

6 In the **Templates and Add-ins** dialog box, to the right of the **Document template** box, click **Attach** to display the **Attach Template** dialog box.

7 In the **Attach Template** dialog box, navigate to the files you downloaded for this project, click **w04B_Custom_Styles**, and then click **Open**.

The file w04B_Custom_Styles is a Word template that contains styles created by the marketing director to be used in all Costa Rican Treks documents.

8 In the **Templates and Add-ins** dialog box, to the left of **Automatically update document styles**, select the check box, and then compare your screen with Figure 4.36.

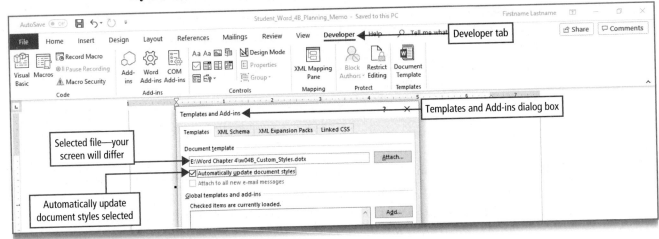

Figure 4.36

9 In the **Templates and Add-ins** dialog box, click **OK**. Compare your screen with Figure 4.37.

All styles contained in the w04B_Custom_Styles template are applied to your document.

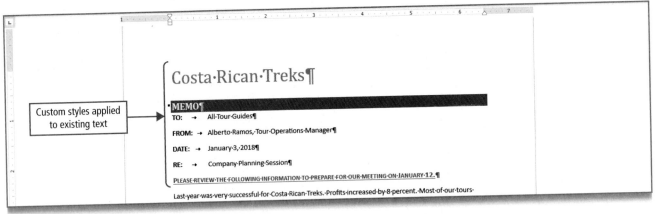

Figure 4.37

10 Right-click the **Developer tab**, and then from the shortcut menu, click **Customize the Ribbon**. Under **Main Tabs**, clear the **Developer** check box, and then click **OK**. Save 🖫 your document.

The Developer tab no longer displays on the ribbon.

MAC TIP On the menu, click Word, click Preferences, click Ribbon & Toolbar, clear the Developer check box, click Save, and then close the dialog box.

Objective 6 | Insert a Chart and Enter Data into a Chart

GO! Learn How
Video W4-6

A ***chart*** is a visual representation of ***numerical data***—numbers that represent facts. Word provides the same chart tools that are available in Excel. The data for a chart that you create in Word is stored in a worksheet, and the worksheet is saved with the Word document. Charts make numbers easier for the reader to understand.

Activity 4.16 | Inserting a Chart

1 Press Ctrl + End to move the insertion point to the end of the document.

> **MAC TIP** Press command ⌘ + fn + → to move to the end of the document.

2 Click the **Insert tab**, and then in the **Illustrations group**, click **Chart** to display the **Insert Chart** dialog box. Take a moment to examine the chart types described in the table shown in Figure 4.38.

The available chart types display on the left side of the Insert Chart dialog box. The most commonly used chart types are column, bar, pie, line, and area.

Commonly Used Chart Types Available in Word	
Chart Type	**Purpose of Chart**
Column, Bar	Show comparison among related data
Pie	Show proportion of parts to a whole
Line, Area	Show trends over time

Figure 4.38

> **MAC TIP** Point to Column, click Clustered Bar, and then skip the remaining steps in this Activity and continue with the next Activity.

3 On the left side of the **Insert Chart** dialog box, click **Bar**. In the right pane, at the top, click the first style—**Clustered Bar**. Compare your screen with Figure 4.39.

A bar chart is a good choice because this data will *compare* the number of tours offered in two different years. A ***bar chart*** shows a comparison among related data.

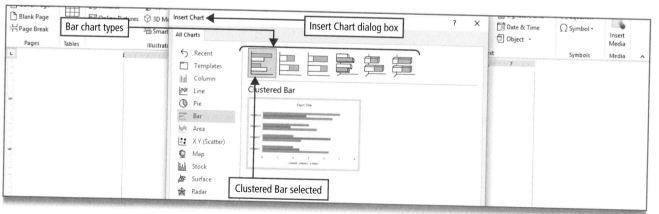

Figure 4.39

4 Click **OK** to insert the chart in your document and open the related *Chart in Microsoft Word* worksheet. Compare your screen with Figure 4.40.

The chart displays on Page 2 of your Word document. Sample data displays in the worksheet.

The process of inserting a chart in your document in this manner is referred to as ***embedding***—the object, in this case a chart, becomes part of the Word document. When you edit the data in the worksheet, the chart in your Word document updates automatically.

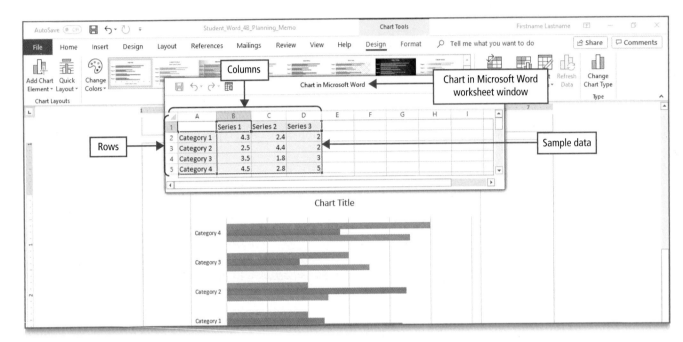

Figure 4.40

Activity 4.17 | Entering Chart Data

You can replace the sample data in the worksheet with specific tour data for your chart.

1 In the **Chart in Microsoft Word** worksheet, point to the small box where **column B** and **row 1** intersect—referred to as cell **B1**—and click. Compare your screen with Figure 4.41.

A ***cell*** is the location where a row and column intersect. The cells are named by their column and row headings. For example, cell B1, containing the text *Series 1*, is in column B and row 1.

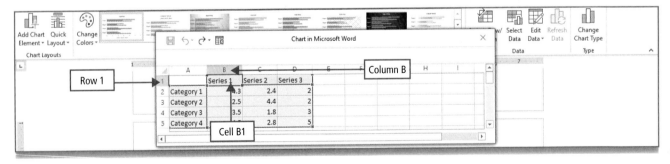

Figure 4.41

2 With cell **B1** selected, type **This Year** and then press [Tab]. With cell **C1** selected, type **Last Year** and then press [Tab] two times to move to cell **A2**—which displays the text *Category 1*.

3 With cell **A2** selected, type **Air** and then press ⌨Tab to move to cell **B2**. Type **17** and then press ⌨Tab. In cell **C2,** type **36** and then press ⌨Tab two times to move to **row 3**.

> As you enter data in the worksheet, the chart is automatically updated in the Word document. When entering a large amount of data in a cell, it may not fully display. If necessary, the data worksheet or chart can be modified to display the data completely.

4 Without changing any values in column D—Series 3, type the following data in columns A, B, and C. After typing *10* in C5, press ⌨Tab to select cell D5.

	This Year	Last Year
Air	17	36
Land	45	45
Water	46	42
Multi	35	10

5 Compare your screen with Figure 4.42.

> The red lines and shading for cells B1 through D1 indicate data headings. The purple lines and shading for cells A2 through A5 indicate category headings. The blue line—the *data range border*—surrounds the cells containing numerical data that display in the chart. The group of cells with red, purple, and blue shading is referred to as the *chart data range*—the range of data that will be used to create the chart.

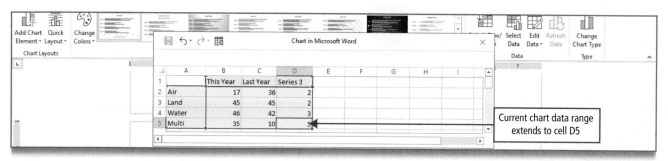

Figure 4.42

6 In the **Chart in Microsoft Word** worksheet, point to the lower right corner of the blue border to display the 🔲 pointer, and then drag to the left to select only cells **A1** through **C5**. Compare your screen with Figure 4.43.

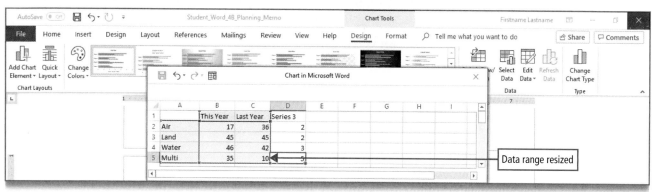

Figure 4.43

🖥 **MAC TIP** Click any cell in the worksheet so that D5 is not active. Then point to the lower right corner of D5 and drag to left so that cells A1 through C5 are selected.

7 Release the mouse button to change the selected range of data used in the chart. In the upper right corner of the worksheet window, click **Close** ⊠. Click the chart border to select the chart. **Save** 🖫 your Word document, and then compare your screen with Figure 4.44.

The *chart area* refers to the entire chart and all its elements. The categories—the tour type names—display along the left side of the chart on the *category axis*. The scale—based on the numerical data—displays along the lower edge of the chart on the *value axis*.

Data markers, the bars in your chart, are the shapes representing each of the cells that contain data, referred to as the *data points*. A *data series* consists of related data points represented by a unique color. For example, this chart has two data series—*This Year* and *Last Year*. The *legend* identifies the colors assigned to each data series or category.

With the chart selected, the Chart Tools display on the ribbon and include two additional tabs—Design and Format—to provide commands with which you can modify and format chart elements.

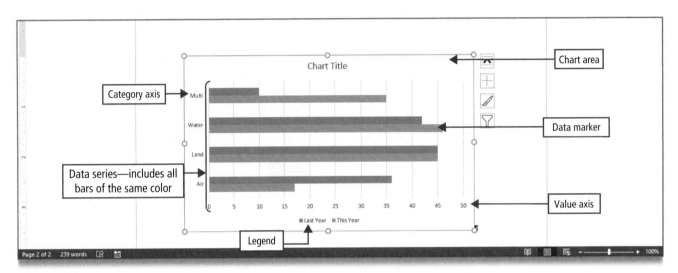

Figure 4.44

Activity 4.18 | Editing Chart Data

You can edit data points to update a chart.

1 Be sure your chart is selected; if necessary, click the chart border to select it. On the ribbon, under **Chart Tools**, click the **Design tab**, and then in the **Data group**, click the upper portion of the **Edit Data** button to redisplay the embedded Chart in Microsoft Word worksheet.

2 In the **Chart in Microsoft Word** worksheet, click cell **B5**. Type **40** and then click cell **C5**. Type **23** and then press Enter.

Word automatically updates the chart to reflect these data point changes.

👆 **BY TOUCH** Double-tap a cell, and then type the number.

3 **Close** ⊠ the worksheet, and then **Save** 🖫 your Word document. Compare your screen with Figure 4.45.

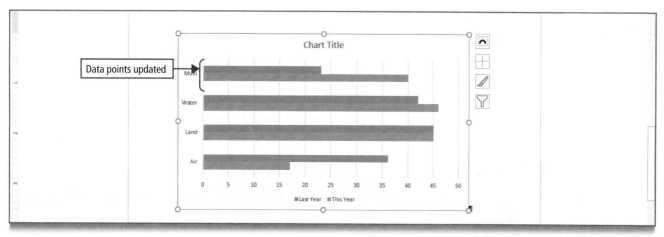

Figure 4.45

Objective 7 | Change a Chart Type

GO! Learn How

Video W4-7

A chart commonly shows one of three types of relationships—a comparison among data, the proportion of parts to a whole, or trends over time. You may decide to alter the chart type—for example, change a bar chart to a column chart—so that the chart displays more attractively in the document.

Activity 4.19 | Changing the Chart Type

The data in the tour types chart compares tour numbers for two years and is appropriately represented by a bar chart. A *column chart*, which shows a comparison among related data, is also appropriate to compare data.

1 With the chart selected, on the **Chart Tools Design tab**, in the **Type group**, click **Change Chart Type**.

2 In the **Change Chart Type** dialog box, on the left, click **Column**, and then in the right pane, at the top, click the first chart type—**Clustered Column**. Click **OK**, and then compare your screen with Figure 4.46.

The category names display on the horizontal axis; the number scale displays on the vertical axis.

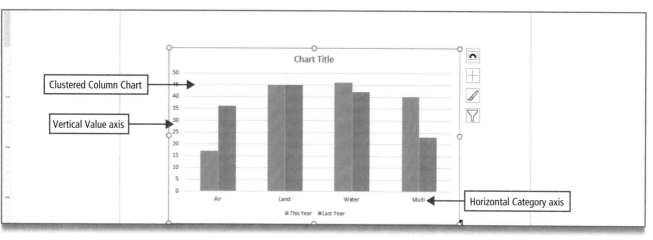

Figure 4.46

3 **Save** your document.

Activity 4.20 | Adding Chart Elements

Add chart elements to help the reader understand the data in your chart. For example, you can add a title to the chart and to individual axes, or add **data labels**, which display the value represented by each data marker.

1 Four buttons—*Layout Options*, *Chart Elements*, *Chart Styles*, and *Chart Filters*—display to the right of the chart. Take a moment to read the descriptions of each button in the table in Figure 4.47.

Available Chart Buttons		
Chart Button	**Icon**	**Purpose**
Layout Options	⌐	To set how a chart interacts with the text around it
Chart Elements	+	To add, remove, or change chart elements—such as a chart title, legend, gridlines, and data labels
Chart Styles	✎	To apply a style and color scheme to a chart
Chart Filters	▼	To define what data points and names display on a chart

Figure 4.47

2 Click **Chart Elements** [+], and then select the **Axis Titles** check box. To the right of **Axis Titles**, click the arrow, and then clear the **Primary Horizontal** check box to remove the primary horizontal title text box from the chart. Compare your screen with Figure 4.48.

By default, when you select Axis Titles, both the primary horizontal axis title and primary vertical axis title text boxes display in the chart. In this case, because the legend identifies the categories, the primary horizontal axis title is not needed.

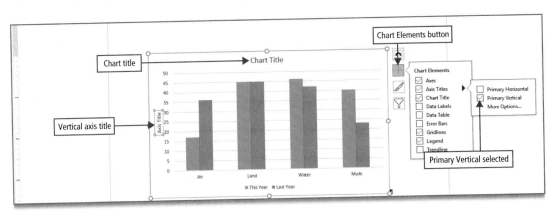

Figure 4.48

⌨ **MAC TIP**   On the Chart Design tab, in the Chart Layouts group, click Add Chart Element. Point to Axis Titles, click Primary Vertical.

3 To the left of the vertical axis, select the text *Axis Title*. Type **# of Tours** and notice that the text displays vertically in the text box. Click outside the axis title to deselect the title.

4 Above the chart, click the text box that displays *Chart Title*, and then replace the chart title text with **Tours Offered**

5 Click in an empty corner of the chart to deselect the title text box. **Save** 🖫 your document.

Objective 8 | Format a Chart

GO! Learn How
Video W4-8

You can format a chart to change the appearance of chart elements.

Activity 4.21 | Applying a Chart Style and Changing the Chart Color

A ***chart style*** refers to the overall visual look of a chart, including graphic effects, colors, and backgrounds. For example, you can have flat or beveled columns, colors that are solid or transparent, and backgrounds that are dark or light.

1 To the right of the chart, click **Chart Styles** 🖉. With **Style** selected, scroll down and click the fifth style—**Style 5**.

🖥 **MAC TIP**   On the Chart Design tab, in the Chart Styles group, click Style 5.

---

2 At the top of the **Chart Styles** list, click **Color**. Under **Monochromatic**, in the sixth row, click the green color scheme. Compare your screen with Figure 4.49.

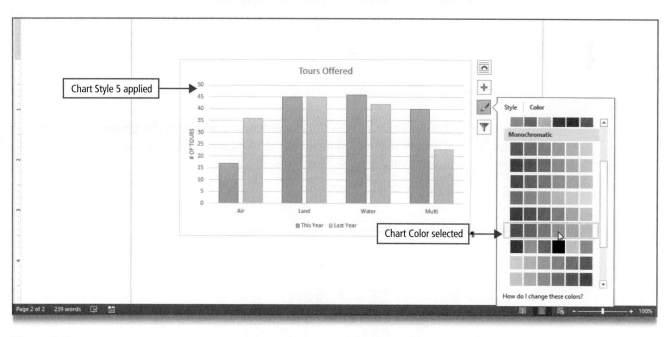

Figure 4.49

🖥 **MAC TIP**   On the Chart Design tab, in the Chart Styles group, click Change Colors to display the Color Gallery.

---

3 Click in the document to close the **Chart Styles** list, and then **Save** 🖫 your document.

Activity 4.22 | Formatting Chart Elements

Individual chart elements can also be formatted to enhance the appearance of the chart.

1 Select the chart title. On the **Chart Tools Format tab**, in the **Shape Styles group**, click the **More** button. In the gallery, in the fifth row, click the last style. Click in an empty corner of the chart to deselect the chart title, and then compare your screen with Figure 4.50.

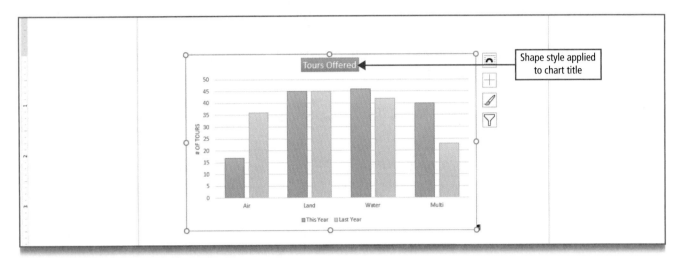

Figure 4.50

2 Click the border of the chart. On the **Format tab**, in the **Shape Styles group**, click **Shape Outline**, and then in the last column, click the first color. Deselect the chart, and then compare your screen with Figure 4.51.

A green border surrounds the entire chart.

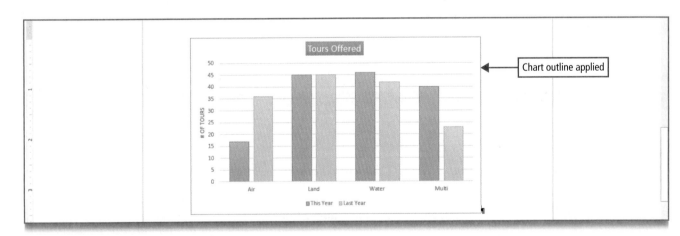

Figure 4.51

3 Save your document.

Activity 4.23 | Resizing and Positioning a Chart

You can resize and position both the chart and individual chart elements. You can also position the chart on the page relative to the left and right margins.

1 Click the chart to select it. To the right of the chart, click **Layout Options** ⌃. Near the bottom of the gallery, click **See more** to display the **Layout** dialog box.

When you insert a chart, the default text wrapping setting is In Line with Text. Use the Layout dialog box to change the position, text wrapping, and size of a chart.

> **MAC TIP** Click Format, click Arrange, click Wrap Text, and then click More Layout Options.

2 In the **Layout** dialog box, click the **Size tab**, and then under **Height**, click the **Absolute down spin arrow** to **2.7**. Click **OK** to close the dialog box.

When you change the position, text wrapping, or size of a chart, the chart may display differently in the document. In this case, the chart displays at the bottom of Page 1.

3 With the chart selected, on the **Home tab**, in the **Paragraph group**, click **Center** ☰. Compare your screen with Figure 4.52.

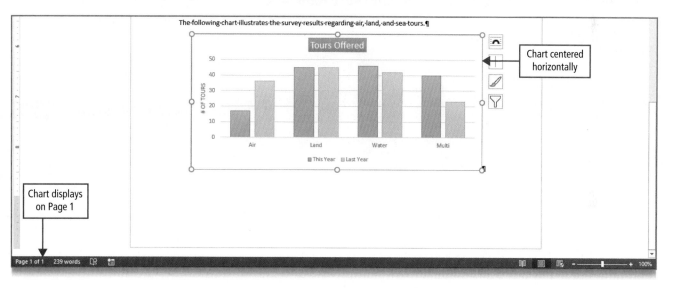

The-following-chart-illustrates-the-survey-results-regarding-air,-land,-and-sea-tours.¶

> Chart centered horizontally

> Chart displays on Page 1

Page 1 of 1   239 words

Figure 4.52

> **ANOTHER WAY** On the Format tab, in the Arrange group, you can modify the text wrapping and alignment of the chart; and in the Size group, you can change the size.

4 Press Ctrl + Home, and then **Insert** the **File Name** in the footer. Display the document **Properties**. In the **Tags** box, type **tours data** and in the **Subject** box, type your course name and section number. If necessary, edit the author name to display your name.

5 Display the **Print Preview**. If necessary, return to the document and make any necessary changes. **Save**  your document and then **Close** Word.

> **For Non-MyLab Submissions Determine What Your Instructor Requires**
> As directed by your instructor, submit your completed Word file.

6 In **MyLab IT**, locate and click the Grader Project **Word 4B Planning Memo**. In step 3, under **Upload Completed Assignment**, click **Choose File**. In the **Open** dialog box, navigate to your **Word Chapter 4** folder, and then click your **Student_Word_4B_Planning_Memo** file one time to select it. In the lower right corner of the **Open** dialog box, click **Open**.

The name of your selected file displays above the Upload button.

7 To submit your file to **MyLab IT** for grading, click **Upload**, wait a moment for a green **Success!** message, and then in **step 4**, click the blue **Submit for Grading** button. Click **Close Assignment** to return to your list of **Course Materials**.

MORE KNOWLEDGE **Saving a Chart Template as a Template**

Right-click the border of the chart, and then from the shortcut menu, click Save as Template. Then, save the chart in the location in which you are saving your templates. The chart template will be saved with the file extension .crtx.

You have completed Project 4B **END**

4
WORD

Microsoft Office Specialist (MOS) Skills in This Chapter	
Project 4A	**Project 4B**
2.2.4 Apply built-in styles to text	1.2.2 Apply document style sets
3.3.2 Change bullet characters and number formats for a list level	2.2.3 Set line and paragraph spacing and indentation
3.3.3 Define a custom bullet character and number format	
3.3.4 Increase and decrease list levels	

Build Your E-Portfolio

An E-Portfolio is a collection of evidence, stored electronically, that showcases what you have accomplished while completing your education. Collecting and then sharing your work products with potential employers reflects your academic and career goals. Your completed documents from the following projects are good examples to show what you have learned: 4G, 4K, and 4L.

GO! For Job Success

Discussion: Big Data

Your instructor may assign these questions to your class, and then ask you to think about them or discuss them with your classmates:

"Big data" describes information that a company has that is so massive in the number of records that it is difficult to analyze using standard database techniques. It often refers to information that a company collects in the course of doing business that is not usually used for any other purpose than to process transactions. An example is airline ticket sales: The information airlines collect in a ticket sale includes names, addresses, travel preferences, destinations, credit cards, seating preferences, etc. Analyzing this information could result in information that would be useful in updating flight schedules, changing seat layouts, and marketing plans.

g-stockstudio/ Shutterstock

What are some other industries that collect large amounts of data about customers during the course of a normal transaction?

What other industries would benefit from data such as that collected during an airline ticket sale?

Do you think it is ethical for businesses to sell the information they collect to other businesses?

End of Chapter

Summary

Use built-in and customized theme and style features to coordinate colors, fonts, effects, and other formatting elements. Apply themes and styles to maintain a consistent and professional appearance in documents.

A multilevel list displays information in an organized, hierarchical structure. You can create and save a custom multilevel list style, and apply it to other lists within the same document or in other documents.

A custom theme that is saved as a Word template can be attached to other documents. This is a quick and easy method to change the appearance of an existing document and provide consistency among related documents.

Because a chart displays numbers in a visual format, readers can easily understand the data. Add and format chart elements to enhance the chart's appearance.

GO! Learn It Online

Review the concepts, key terms, and MOS skills in this chapter by completing these online challenges, which you can find at **MyLab IT**.

Chapter Quiz: Answer matching and multiple-choice questions to test what you learned in this chapter.

Crossword Puzzle: Spell out the words that match the numbered clues, and put them in the puzzle squares.

MOS Prep Quiz: Answer questions to review the MOS skills that you practiced in this chapter.

Project Guide for Word Chapter 4

Your instructor will assign Projects from this list to ensure your learning and assess your knowledge.

Project	Apply Skills from These Chapter Objectives	Project Type		Project Location
4A **MyLab IT**	Objectives 1–4 from Project 4A	**4A Instructional Project (Grader Project)** Guided instruction to learn the skills in Project 4A.	**Instruction**	In **MyLab IT** and in text
4B **MyLab IT**	Objectives 5–8 from Project 4B	**4B Instructional Project (Grader Project)** Guided instruction to learn the skills in Project 4B.	**Instruction**	In **MyLab IT** and in text
4C	Objectives 1–4 from Project 4A	**4C Skills Review (Scorecard Grading)** A guided review of the skills from Project 4A.	**Review**	In text
4D	Objectives 5–8 from Project 4B	**4D Skills Review (Scorecard Grading)** A guided review of the skills from Project 4B.	**Review**	In text
4E **MyLab IT**	Objectives 1–4 from Project 4A	**4E Mastery (Grader Project)** **Mastery and Transfer of Learning** A demonstration of your mastery of the skills in Project 4A with extensive decision making.		In **MyLab IT** and in text
4F **MyLab IT**	Objectives 5–8 from Project 4B	**4F Mastery (Grader Project)** **Mastery and Transfer of Learning** A demonstration of your mastery of the skills in Project 4B with extensive decision making.		In **MyLab IT** and in text
4G **MyLab IT**	Objectives 1–8 from Projects 4A and 4B	**4G Mastery (Grader Project)** **Mastery and Transfer of Learning** A demonstration of your mastery of the skills in Projects 4A and 4B with extensive decision making.		In **MyLab IT** and in text
4H	Objectives from Projects 4A and 4B	**4H GO! Fix It (Scorecard Grading)** **Critical Thinking** A demonstration of your mastery of the skills in Projects 4A and 4B by creating a correct result from a document that contains errors you must find.		IRC
4I	Objectives from Projects 4A and 4B	**4I GO! Make It (Scorecard Grading)** **Critical Thinking** A demonstration of your mastery of the skills in Projects 4A and 4B by creating a result from a supplied picture.		IRC
4J	Objectives from Projects 4A and 4B	**4J GO! Solve It (Rubric Grading)** **Critical Thinking** A demonstration of your mastery of the skills in Projects 4A and 4B, your decision-making skills, and your critical thinking skills. A task-specific rubric helps you self-assess your result.		IRC
4K	Objectives from Projects 4A and 4B	**4K GO! Solve It (Rubric Grading)** **Critical Thinking** A demonstration of your mastery of the skills in Projects 4A and 4B, your decision-making skills, and your critical thinking skills. A task-specific rubric helps you self-assess your result.		In text
4L	Objectives from Projects 4A and 4B	**4L GO! Think (Rubric Grading)** **Critical Thinking** A demonstration of your understanding of the chapter concepts applied in a manner that you would outside of college. An analytic rubric helps you and your instructor grade the quality of your work by comparing it to the work an expert in the discipline would create.		In text
4M	Objectives from Projects 4A and 4B	**4M GO! Think (Rubric Grading)** **Critical Thinking** A demonstration of your understanding of the chapter concepts applied in a manner that you would outside of college. An analytic rubric helps you and your instructor grade the quality of your work by comparing it to the work an expert in the discipline would create.		IRC
4N	Objectives from Projects 4A and 4B	**4N You and GO! (Rubric Grading)** **Critical Thinking** A demonstration of your understanding of the chapter concepts applied in a manner that you would in a personal situation. An analytic rubric helps you and your instructor grade the quality of your work.		IRC

Glossary

Glossary of Chapter Key Terms

Bar chart A chart type that shows a comparison among related data.

Category axis The area of the chart that identifies the categories of data.

Cell The intersection of a column and row.

Change Case A formatting command that allows you to quickly change the capitalization of selected text.

Character style A style, indicated by the symbol **a**, that contains formatting characteristics that you apply to text, such as font name, font size, font color, bold emphasis, and so on.

Chart A visual representation of numerical data.

Chart area The entire chart and all its elements.

Chart data range The group of cells with red, purple, and blue shading that is used to create a chart.

Chart Elements A Word feature that displays commands to add, remove, or change chart elements, such as the title, legend, gridlines, and data labels.

Chart Filters A Word feature that displays commands to define what data points and names display on a chart.

Chart style The overall visual look of a chart in terms of its graphic effects, colors, and backgrounds.

Chart Styles A Word feature that displays commands to apply a style and color scheme to a chart.

Column chart A chart type that shows a comparison among related data.

Contiguous Items that are adjacent to one another.

Data labels The part of a chart that displays the value represented by each data marker.

Data markers The shapes in a chart representing each of the cells that contain data.

Data points The cells that contain numerical data used in a chart.

Data range border The blue line that surrounds the cells containing numerical data that display in the chart.

Data series In a chart, related data points represented by a unique color.

Direct formatting The process of applying each format separately, for example bold, then font size, then font color, and so on.

Embedding The process of inserting an object, such as a chart, into a Word document so that it becomes part of the document.

Keep lines together A formatting feature that prevents a single line from displaying by itself at the bottom of a page or at the top of a page.

Keep with next A formatting feature that keeps a heading with its first paragraph of text together on the page.

Layout Options A Word feature that displays commands to control the manner in which text wraps around a chart or other object.

Legend The part of a chart that identifies the colors assigned to each data series or category.

Linked style A style, indicated by the symbol **a** ¶, that behaves as either a character style or a paragraph style, depending on what you select.

List style A style that applies a format to a list.

Memorandum (Memo) A written message sent to someone working in the same organization.

Multilevel list A list in which the items display in a visual hierarchical structure.

Noncontiguous Items that are not adjacent to one another.

Normal The default style in Word for new documents and which includes default styles and customizations that determine the basic look of a document; for example, it includes the Calibri font, 11-pt font size, line spacing at 1.08, and 8-pt spacing after a paragraph.

Numerical data Numbers that represent facts.

Paragraph style A style, indicated by ¶, that includes everything that a character style contains, plus all aspects of a paragraph's appearance; for example, text alignment, tab stops, line spacing, and borders.

Reveal Formatting A pane that displays the formatted selection and includes a complete description of formats applied.

Show Preview A formatting feature that displays a visual representation of each style in the Styles pane.

Style A group of formatting commands, such as font, font size, font color, paragraph alignment, and line spacing, that can be applied to selected text with one command.

Style Inspector A pane that displays the name of the selected style with formats applied and contains paragraph- and text-level formatting options.

Style set A group of styles that are designed to work together.

Styles pane A pane that displays a list of styles and contains tools to manage styles.

Table style A style that applies a consistent look to borders, shading, and so on of a table.

Value axis The area of a chart that displays a numerical scale based on the numerical data in a chart.

Word Options A collection of settings that you can change to customize Word.

Chapter Review

In the following Skills Review, you will add styles and a multilevel list format to a document that describes training classes for Costa Rican Treks tour guides. Your completed document will look similar to Figure 4.53.

Apply 4A skills from these Objectives:

1. Apply and Modify Styles
2. Create New Styles
3. Manage Styles
4. Create a Multilevel List

Project Files

For Project 4C, you will need the following file:

w04C_Training_Classes

You will save your document as:

Lastname_Firstname_4C_Training_Classes

Project Results

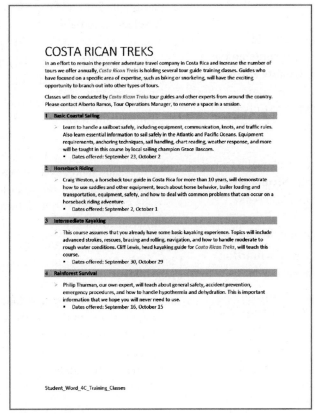

Figure 4.53

(continues on next page)

Chapter Review

1 ▶ Start Word. Navigate to the student data files that accompany this chapter, and then open the file **w04C_Training_Classes**. **Save** the document in your **Word Chapter 4** folder as **Lastname_Firstname_4C_Training_Classes** and then **Insert** a **Footer** with the **File Name**.

a. Select the first paragraph—*Costa Rican Treks*. On the **Home tab**, in the **Styles group**, click **Title**.

b. In the second paragraph, in the second line, select the text **Costa Rican Treks**. Display the **Styles** gallery, and then click **Strong**. In the **Font group**, click the **Font Color arrow**, and then in the sixth column, click the first color.

c. With the text *Costa Rican Treks* still selected, display the **Styles** gallery, right-click **Strong**, and then from the shortcut menu, click **Update Strong to Match Selection**. (Mac users, on the Home tab, display the Styles gallery, press control, click the Strong style, click Update Strong to Match Selection.)

d. In the third paragraph, in the first line, select the text *Costa Rican Treks*, and then apply the **Strong** style. In the eleventh paragraph that begins *This course*, in the third line, select *Costa Rican Treks*—do not include the comma—and then apply the **Strong** style.

2 ▶ On the **Design tab**, in the **Document Formatting group**, click **Themes**, and then click **Retrospect**.

a. Select the title of the document—*Costa Rican Treks*. Click the **Home tab**. In the **Font group**, click **Change Case**, and then click **UPPERCASE**.

b. Including the paragraph mark, select the fourth paragraph *Basic Coastal Sailing*, and then apply **Bold**. In the **Paragraph group**, click the **Shading button arrow**, and then in the ninth column, click the first color.

c. With the paragraph still selected, display the **Styles** gallery, and then click **Create a Style**. (Mac users, on the Home tab, in the Styles group, click Style Pane, and then click New Style.)

d. In the **Name** box, type **Class Title** and then click **OK**.

e. Scroll down as necessary, select the paragraph *Horseback Riding*, and then apply the **Class Title** style.

f. Using the same technique, apply the **Class Title** style to the paragraphs *Intermediate Kayaking* and *Rainforest Survival*.

3 ▶ Press Ctrl + Home. In the **Styles group**, click the **Dialog Box Launcher**. (Mac users, on the Home tab, in the Styles group, click Style Pane.)

a. In the **Styles** pane, point to **Strong**, click the **arrow**, and then click **Modify**.

b. In the **Modify Style** dialog box, under **Formatting**, click **Italic**. Click **OK** to close the dialog box and update all instances of the *Strong* style. **Close** the **Styles** pane.

4 ▶ Click to position the insertion point to the left of the paragraph *Basic Coastal Sailing*, and then from this point, select all remaining text in the document.

a. On the **Home tab**, in the **Paragraph group**, click **Multilevel List**. Under **List Library**, locate and then click the ❖, ➤, ■ (bullet) style.

b. Click in the first paragraph following *Basic Coastal Sailing*, and then in the **Paragraph group**, click **Increase Indent**. Click in the second paragraph following *Basic Coastal Sailing*, which begins *Dates*, and then click **Increase Indent** two times. Under *Horseback Riding*, *Intermediate Kayaking*, and *Rainforest Survival*, format the paragraphs in the same manner.

5 ▶ Select the entire multilevel list. Click **Multilevel List**. At the bottom of the gallery, click **Define New List Style**.

a. Name the style **Training Class** and then under **Formatting**, in the **Apply formatting to** box, be sure *1st level* displays. In the small toolbar above the preview area, click the **Numbering Style arrow**, in the list, scroll up to locate and then click the **1, 2, 3** style.

b. Under **Formatting**, click the **Apply formatting to arrow**, and then click **2nd level**. Click the **Font Color arrow**, and then in the ninth column, click the first color. Click **OK** to close the dialog box.

c. Display the document **Properties**. In the **Tags** box, type **training classes** and then in the Subject box, type your course name and section number. If necessary, edit the author name to display your name.

d. **Save** and **Close** your document and submit as directed by your instructor.

You have completed Project 4C | END

Chapter Review

Skills Review | **Project 4D Strategy Session**

Apply 4B skills from these Objectives:

5. Change the Style Set of a Document and Apply a Template
6. Insert a Chart and Enter Data into a Chart
7. Change a Chart Type
8. Format a Chart

In the following Skills Review, you will create a memo for Maria Tornio, President of Costa Rican Treks, which details the company's financial performance and provides strategies for the upcoming year. Your completed document will look similar to Figure 4.54.

Project Files

For Project 4D, you will need the following files:

w04D_Strategy_Session

w04D_Memo_Styles

You will save your document as:

Lastname_Firstname_4D_Strategy_Session

Project Results

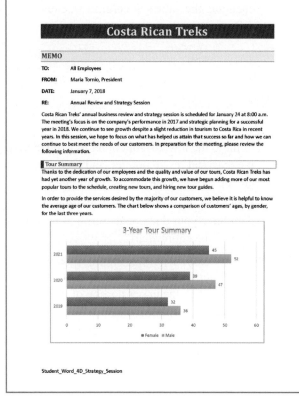

Figure 4.54

(continues on next page)

Chapter Review

1 ▶ Start Word. Navigate to the student data files that accompany this chapter, and then open the file **w04D_ Strategy_Session**. **Save** the document in your **Word Chapter 4** folder as **Lastname_Firstname_4D_Strategy_ Session** and then **Insert** a **Footer** with the **File Name**. **Close** the footer area.

a. Select the first paragraph—*Costa Rican Treks*. On the **Home tab**, in the **Styles** group, apply the **Title** style. Select the second paragraph—*MEMO*, display the **Styles** gallery, and then click **Heading 1**.

b. Select the memo heading TO:—include the colon—hold down [Ctrl] and then select the memo headings FROM:, DATE:, and RE:. On the **Home tab**, in the **Font group**, click **Bold**. (Mac users, hold down [command ⌘]).

c. Select the paragraph *Tour Summary*, press and hold [Ctrl], and then select the paragraphs *Local Industry Assessment* and *Customer Feedback*. Apply the **Heading 2** style.

d. On the **Design tab**, in the **Document Formatting group**, click **Paragraph Spacing**, and then click **Open**.

2 ▶ Click the **File tab**, and then click **Options**. In the **Word Options** dialog box, click **Customize Ribbon**. In the **Main Tabs** list, select the **Developer** check box, and then click **OK**. (Mac users, on the menu, click Word, click Preferences, click Ribbon & Toolbar, click Developer, and then click Save.)

a. On the **Developer tab**, in the **Templates group**, click **Document Template**. (Mac users, on the Developer tab, click Word Add-Ins).

b. In the **Templates and Add-ins** dialog box, click **Attach**. In the **Attach Template** dialog box, navigate to your student files, click **w04D_ Memo_Styles**, and then click **Open**. Select the **Automatically update document styles** check box, and then click **OK**.

c. On the **File tab**, click **Options**. In the **Word Options** dialog box, click **Customize Ribbon**. In the **Main Tabs** list, click to deselect the **Developer** check box, and then click **OK**. (Mac users, on the menu, click Word, click Preferences, click Ribbon & Toolbar, deselect Developer, and then click Save.)

d. On **Page 1**, below *Tour Summary*, locate the paragraph that begins *In order to provide*. Position the insertion point at the end of the paragraph, and then press [Enter].

3 ▶ Click the **Insert tab**, and then in the **Illustrations group**, click **Chart**.

a. On the left side of the **Insert Chart** dialog box, be sure **Column** is selected. At the top of the right pane, click the first chart type—**Clustered Column**—and then click **OK**.

b. In the **Chart in Microsoft Word** worksheet, click cell **B1**, type **Male** and then press [Tab]. With cell **C1** selected, type **Female** and then click cell **A2**.

c. With cell **A2** selected, type **2019** and then press [Tab]. In cell **B2**, type **36**, press [Tab], and then in cell **C2**, type **32** Press [Tab] two times to move to **row 3**.

d. Using the technique you just practiced, and without changing the values in **column D**, enter the following data:

	Male	Female
2019	36	32
2020	47	39
2021	52	43

e. Point to the lower right corner of cell **D5** to display the diagonal resize pointer, and then drag to the left and up to select only cells **A1** through **C4**.

f. **Close** the Chart in Microsoft Word worksheet, and then **Save** your document. Scroll as necessary to display the entire chart.

4 ▶ If necessary, click in an empty area of the chart to select it. Under **Chart Tools**, on the **Design tab**, in the **Data group**, click the upper portion of the **Edit Data** button to redisplay the worksheet.

a. In the worksheet, click cell **C4**, type **45** press [Enter], and then **Close** the worksheet.

b. With the chart selected, under **Chart Tools**, on the **Design tab**, in the **Type group**, click **Change Chart Type**.

c. In the **Change Chart Type** dialog box, on the left, click **Bar**, and then on the right, at the top, click the first chart type—**Clustered Bar**. Click **OK**. (Mac users, point to Column, and then under 2-D bar, click Clustered Bar.)

(continues on next page)

Chapter Review

5 Select the text *Chart Title*, and then type **3-Year Tour Summary**

a. Click in an empty area of the chart, and then to the right of the chart, click **Chart Elements**. Select the **Data Labels** check box. (Mac users, on the Chart Design tab, in the Chart Layouts group, click Add Chart Element, point to Data Labels, and click Outside End.)

b. Click **Chart Styles**. Scroll down, and then click the fifth style—**Style 5**. At the top of the list, click **Color**, and then under **Colorful**, click the fourth color scheme. (Mac users, use the Chart Design options on the ribbon to change the style and color.)

c. Select the chart title. Click the **Format tab**, and then in the **WordArt Styles group**, click the **More** button. In the gallery, in the second row, click the second style. Click in an empty corner area of the chart. On the **Format tab**, in the **Shape Styles group**, click **Shape Outline**, and then in the last column, click the first color.

d. Click **Layout Options**, and then click **See more**. In the **Layout** dialog box, click the **Size tab** and under **Height**, click the **Absolute down spin arrow** to **3.3"** Click **OK** to close the dialog box. (Mac users, on the Format tab, click Arrange, click Wrap Text, and then click More Layout options.)

e. With the chart selected, on the **Home tab**, in the **Paragraph group**, click **Center**.

f. Display the document **Properties**. In the **Tags** box, type **strategy session** and in the **Subject** box, type your course name and section number. If necessary, edit the author name to display your name.

g. **Save** and **Close** your document, and then submit as directed by your instructor.

You have completed Project 4D | **END**

MyLab IT Grader

Apply 4A skills from these Objectives:

1. Apply and Modify Styles
2. Create New Styles
3. Manage Styles
4. Create a Multilevel List

Mastering Word Project 4E Trip Tips

In the following Mastering Word project, you will create a handout that details tips for tour participants for Alberto Ramos, Tour Operations Manager of Costa Rican Treks. Your completed document will look similar to Figure 4.55.

Project Files for MyLab IT Grader

1. In your **MyLab IT** course, locate and click **Word 4E Trip Tips**, Download Materials, and then Download All Files.
2. Extract the zipped folder to your Word Chapter 4 folder. Close the Grader download screens.
3. Take a moment to open the downloaded **Word_4E_Trip_Tips_Instructions**; note any recent updates to the book.

Project Results

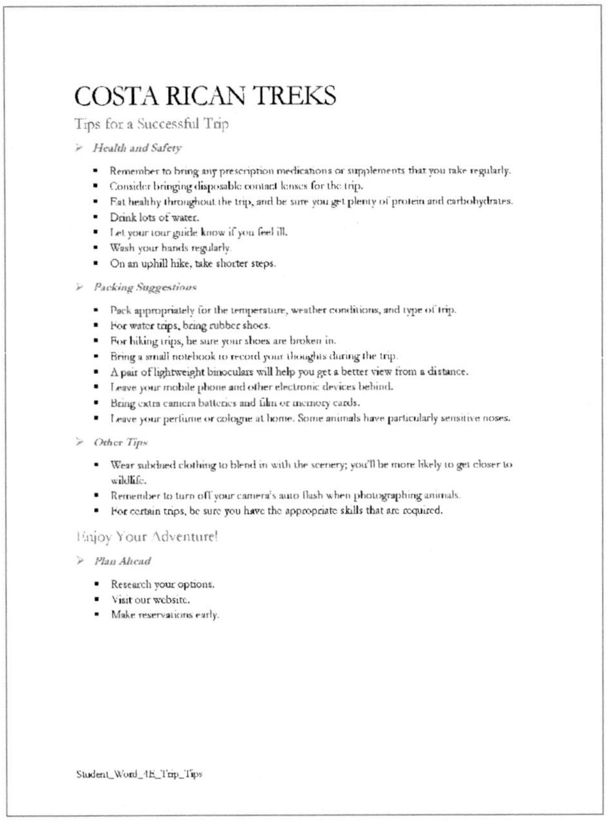

COSTA RICAN TREKS

Tips for a Successful Trip

- *Health and Safety*
  - Remember to bring any prescription medications or supplements that you take regularly.
  - Consider bringing disposable contact lenses for the trip.
  - Eat healthy throughout the trip, and be sure you get plenty of protein and carbohydrates.
  - Drink lots of water.
  - Let your tour guide know if you feel ill.
  - Wash your hands regularly.
  - On an uphill hike, take shorter steps.
- *Packing Suggestions*
  - Pack appropriately for the temperature, weather conditions, and type of trip.
  - For water trips, bring rubber shoes.
  - For hiking trips, be sure your shoes are broken in.
  - Bring a small notebook to record your thoughts during the trip.
  - A pair of lightweight binoculars will help you get a better view from a distance.
  - Leave your mobile phone and other electronic devices behind.
  - Bring extra camera batteries and film or memory cards.
  - Leave your perfume or cologne at home. Some animals have particularly sensitive noses.
- *Other Tips*
  - Wear subdued clothing to blend in with the scenery; you'll be more likely to get closer to wildlife.
  - Remember to turn off your camera's auto flash when photographing animals.
  - For certain trips, be sure you have the appropriate skills that are required.

Enjoy Your Adventure!

- *Plan Ahead*
  - Research your options.
  - Visit our website.
  - Make reservations early.

Student_Word_4E_Trip_Tips

Figure 4.55

For Non-MyLab Submissions

For Project 4E, you will need:
w04E_Trip_Tips

In your Word Chapter 4 folder, save your document as:
Lastname_Firstname_4E_Trip_Tips

After you have named and saved your document, on the next page, begin with Step 2.
After Step 13, save and submit your file as directed by your instructor.

(continues on next page)

1 Navigate to your **Word Chapter 4 folder**, and then double-click the Word file you downloaded from **MyLab IT** that displays your name—**Student_Word_4E_Trip_Tips**.

2 Select the first paragraph—*Costa Rican Treks*. Apply the **Title** style, and then change the case to **UPPERCASE**.

3 Select the second paragraph that begins *Tips for*, and then apply the **Heading 2** style. Change the **Font Size** to **16**, and then change the **Spacing After** to **6 pt**.

4 With the second paragraph selected, update the **Heading 2** style to match the selection. Near the bottom of **Page 1**, select the paragraph *Enjoy Your Adventure!* Apply the **Heading 2** style.

5 Change the document **Theme** to **Organic**.

6 Near the top of **Page 1**, select the third paragraph, *Health and Safety*. Apply **Italic**, and then change the **Font Color**—in the seventh column, apply the first color. With the text selected, create a new style, and then name the new style **Tip Heading** (Mac users, verify that the style is applied to the selection and if not, in the Styles gallery, click Tip Heading.)

7 Apply the **Tip Heading** style to the paragraphs *Packing Suggestions*, *Other Tips*, and *Plan Ahead*. **Modify** the **Tip Heading** style by applying **Bold**.

8 Select the block of text beginning with *Health and Safety* and ending with *that are required* near the bottom of **Page 1**. Apply a **Multilevel List** with the ❖, ➢, ■ style.

9 Select the paragraphs below each *Tip Heading* paragraph, and then increase the indent one time.

10 Select the entire list, and then display the **Define New List Style** dialog box. Name the style **Tips List** and change the **1st level** to **Bullet:** ➢ Display the font color palette, and then in the fifth column, click the first color. Set the **2nd level** by inserting a symbol using the **WingDings character code 167**—the **small filled square**. (Mac users, there are two filled squares. Be sure to choose the smaller filled square).

11 At the bottom of **Page 1**, beginning with *Plan Ahead*, select the last four paragraphs. Apply the **Tips List** multilevel list style. Select the last three paragraphs, and then increase the indent one time.

12 Insert the **File Name** in the **Footer**. Display the document **Properties**. In the **Tags** box, type **trip tips list** and then in the **Subject** box, type your course name and section number. If necessary, edit the author name to display your name.

13 Display the **Print Preview**. If necessary, return to the document and make any necessary changes. **Save** your document, and then **Close** Word.

14 In **MyLab IT**, locate and click the Grader Project **Word 4E Trip Tips**. In step 3, under **Upload Completed Assignment**, click **Choose File**. In the **Open** dialog box, navigate to your **Word Chapter 4** folder, and then click your **Student_Word_4E_Trip_Tips** file one time to select it. In the lower right corner of the **Open** dialog box, click **Open**.

The name of your selected file displays above the Upload button.

15 To submit your file to **MyLab IT** for grading, click **Upload**, wait a moment for a green **Success!** message, and then in step 4, click the blue **Submit for Grading** button. Click **Close Assignment** to return to your list of **Course Materials**.

You have completed Project 4E **END**

Mastering Word | **Project 4F Hiking FAQ**

Apply 4B skills from these Objectives:

5. Change the Style Set of a Document and Apply a Template
6. Insert a Chart and Enter Data into a Chart
7. Change a Chart Type
8. Format a Chart

In the following Mastering Word project, you will create a document that provides frequently asked questions and includes a chart about hiking trips offered by Costa Rican Treks. Your completed document will look similar to Figure 4.56.

Project Files for **MyLab IT** Grader

1. In your **MyLab IT** course, locate and click **Word 4F Hiking FAQ**, Download Materials, and then Download All Files.
2. Extract the zipped folder to your Word Chapter 4 folder. Close the Grader download screens.
3. Take a moment to open the downloaded **Word_4F_Hiking_FAQ_Instructions**; note any recent updates to the book.

Project Results

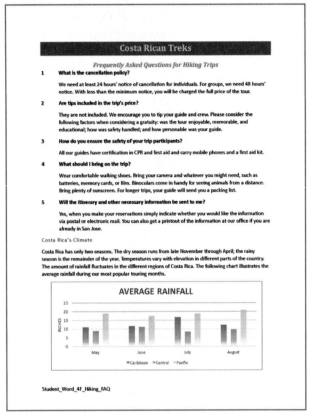

Figure 4.56

For Non-MyLab Submissions

For Project 4F, you will need:

w04F_Hiking_FAQ

w04F_Hiking_Styles

In your Word Chapter 4 folder, save your document as:

Lastname_Firstname_4F_Hiking_FAQ

After you have named and saved your document, on the next page, begin with Step 2.

After Step 12, save and submit your file as directed by your instructor.

(continues on next page)

Content-Based Assessments (Mastery and Transfer of Learning)

1 Navigate to your **Word Chapter 4 folder**, and then double-click the Word file you downloaded from **MyLab IT** that displays your name—**Student_Word_4F_Hiking_FAQ**.

2 Format the first paragraph *Costa Rican Treks* with the **Heading 1** style, and then change the **Font Size** to **18**. Select the second paragraph, and then apply the **Heading 2** style.

3 Select the paragraph *Costa Rica's Climate*, and then apply the **Subtitle** style.

4 Change the **Paragraph Spacing** style to **Compact**.

5 Select all the numbered paragraphs, and then apply **Bold**. For each single paragraph following a numbered paragraph, increase the indent one time.

6 Customize the ribbon to display the **Developer tab**. Display the **Templates and Add-ins** dialog box. From the files you downloaded for this project, attach the file **w04F_Hiking_Styles**, and then select the option to **Automatically update document styles**. Remove the **Developer tab** from the ribbon.

7 Move the insertion point to the end of the document, and then press Enter. **Insert** a **Clustered Column** chart, and then beginning in cell **B1**, type the following data in the Chart in Microsoft Word worksheet, pressing Tab to move from one cell to the next.

	Caribbean	Central	Pacific
May	11	8.9	18.9
June	11.7	11.3	17.5
July	16.8	8.5	18.9
August	12.3	9.8	20.9

8 Close the worksheet. Change the chart title to **Average Rainfall** and then display a **Primary Vertical Axis Title** with the title **Inches**

9 Change the **Chart Style** to **Style 9**, and then change the chart **Color** scheme—under **Monochromatic**, apply the second color scheme. Select the chart border, and then change the chart **Shape Outline**—in the sixth column, apply the first color.

10 Display the **Layout** dialog box, and then change the **Absolute Height** of the chart to **2.4"**. **Center** the chart horizontally on the page. Insert the **File Name** in the footer.

11 Display the document **Properties**. In the **Tags** box, type **FAQ** and then in the **Subject** box, type your course name and section number. If necessary, edit the author name to display your name.

12 Display the **Print Preview**. If necessary, return to the document and make any necessary changes. **Save** your document, and then **Close** Word.

13 In **MyLab IT**, locate and click the Grader Project **Word 4F Hiking FAQ**. In step 3, under **Upload Completed Assignment**, click **Choose File**. In the **Open** dialog box, navigate to your **Word Chapter 4** folder, and then click your **Student_Word_4F_Hiking_FAQ** file one time to select it. In the lower right corner of the **Open** dialog box, click **Open**.

The name of your selected file displays above the Upload button.

14 To submit your file to **MyLab IT** for grading, click **Upload**, wait a moment for a green **Success!** message, and then in step 4, click the blue **Submit for Grading** button. Click **Close Assignment** to return to your list of **Course Materials**.

You have completed Project 4F `END`

Mastering Word　Project 4G Expense Reduction

Apply 4A and 4B skills from these Objectives:

1. Apply and Modify Styles
2. Create New Styles
3. Manage Styles
4. Create a Multilevel List
5. Change the Style Set of a Document and Apply a Template
6. Insert a Chart and Enter Data into a Chart
7. Change a Chart Type
8. Format a Chart

In the following Mastering Word project, you will create a memo that includes ideas for reducing expenses for Paulo Alvarez, Vice President of Finance for Costa Rican Treks. Your completed document will look similar to Figure 4.57.

Project Files for MyLab IT Grader

1. In your **MyLab IT** course, locate and click **Word 4G Expense Reduction**, Download Materials, and then Download All Files.
2. Extract the zipped folder to your Word Chapter 4 folder. Close the Grader download screens.
3. Take a moment to open the downloaded **Word_4G_Expense_Reduction_Instructions**; note any recent updates to the book.

Project Results

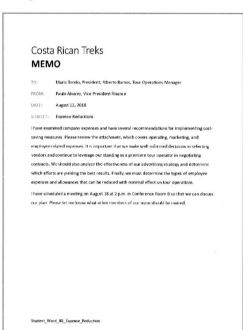

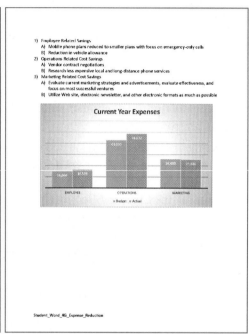

Figure 4.57

For Non-MyLab Submissions

For Project 4G, you will need:　　　　　　　　　　　　In your Word Chapter 4 folder, save your document as:

w04G_Expense_Reduction　　　　　　　　　　　　**Lastname_Firstname_4G_Expense_Reduction**

After you have named and saved your document, on the next page, begin with Step 2.

After Step 12, save and submit your file as directed by your instructor.

(continues on next page)

Content-Based Assessments (Mastery and Transfer of Learning)

1 Navigate to your **Word Chapter 4 folder**, and then double-click the Word file you downloaded from **MyLab IT** that displays your name—**Student_Word_4G_Expense_Reduction**.

2 Apply the **Title** style to the first paragraph. Apply the **Strong** style to the second paragraph—*Memo*. With *Memo* selected, change the **Font Size** to **26**, and then change the text to **UPPERCASE**.

3 Select the text *TO:*—include the colon, but do not include the formatting marks—and then apply **Bold** and change the **Font Color**—in the sixth column, click the first color. Save the selection as a new style with the name **Memo Heading** (Mac users, click the Style type arrow. Click Linked (paragraph and character), and then click OK. If necessary, apply the style to the TO: heading.)

4 Apply the **Memo Heading** style to the memo headings *FROM:*, *DATE:*, and *SUBJECT:*.

5 Change the **Paragraph Spacing** style to **Relaxed**. On **Page 1**, beginning with the heading *TO:*, change the **Font Size** of all the remaining text in the document to **12**. Be sure to include the text and blank paragraphs on page 2.

6 Select the text on **Page 2** (do not include the blank paragraphs), and then apply a **Multilevel List**—in the first row, apply the second style—**1), a), i)**. For the paragraphs beginning *Mobile phone*, *Reduction*, *Vendor*, *Research*, *Evaluate*, and *Utilize*, **Increase Indent** one time.

7 Select the entire list, and then display the **Define New List Style** dialog box. Name the style **Reduction List** and then change the **2nd level** letter style to **A, B, C**.

8 Press `Ctrl` + `End` to move to the end of the document. Insert a **Clustered Column** chart and type the following chart data in columns A, B, and C:

	Budget	Actual
Employee	15,000	16,525
Operations	43,000	48,632
Marketing	26,000	25,480

9 Select the chart data range so that it only includes **A1** through **C4**, and then **Close** the worksheet. (Mac users, you may need to select the range in two steps: drag to select columns A:C, and then drag to select rows 1:4.) Apply the **Style 4** chart style. Format the chart **Shape Outline**—in the fifth column, apply the first color.

10 Change the **Chart Title** to **Current Year Expenses** and then deselect the title and **Center** the chart horizontally on the page.

11 Insert the **File Name** in the footer. Display the document **Properties**. In the **Tags** box, type **expenses** and then in the **Subject** box, type your course name and section number. If necessary, edit the author name to display your name.

12 Display the **Print Preview**. If necessary, return to the document and make any necessary changes. **Save** your document, and then **Close** Word.

13 In **MyLab IT**, locate and click the Grader Project **Word 4G Expense Reduction**. In step 3, under **Upload Completed Assignment**, click **Choose File**. In the **Open** dialog box, navigate to your **Word Chapter 4** folder, and then click your **Student_Word_4G_Expense_Reduction** file one time to select it. In the lower right corner of the **Open** dialog box, click **Open**.

The name of your selected file displays above the Upload button.

14 To submit your file to **MyLab IT** for grading, click **Upload**, wait a moment for a green **Success!** message, and then in step 4, click the blue **Submit for Grading** button. Click **Close Assignment** to return to your list of **Course Materials**.

You have completed Project 4G | **END**

Content-Based Assessments (Critical Thinking)

Project Files

For Project 4K, you will need the following file:

w04K_Custom_Adventure

You will save your document as:

Lastname_Firstname_4K_Custom_Adventure

Open the file **w04K_Custom_Adventure** and save it in your **Word Chapter 4** folder as **Lastname_Firstname_4K_Custom_Adventure** Change the theme, and apply existing styles to the first two and last two paragraphs of the document. Create a new style for *Choose a Region*, and apply the new style to *Choose Your Favorite Activities* and *Develop Your Skills*. Define a multilevel list style and apply the style to all lists in the document. Adjust paragraph and text formats to display the information appropriately in a one-page document. Include the file name in the footer, add appropriate document properties, and submit as directed by your instructor.

		Performance Level		
		Exemplary: You consistently applied the relevant skills	**Proficient: You sometimes, but not always, applied the relevant skills**	**Developing: You rarely or never applied the relevant skills**
Performance Criteria	**Change theme and apply existing styles**	All existing styles are applied correctly using an appropriate theme.	Existing styles are applied correctly but an appropriate theme is not used.	One or more styles are not applied correctly.
	Create a new style	A new style is created and applied correctly.	A new style is created but not applied correctly.	A new style is not created.
	Create a multilevel list	A multilevel list style is created and applied correctly.	A multilevel list style is applied correctly but the default style is used.	A multilevel list style is not applied correctly.
	Format attractively and appropriately	Document formatting is attractive and appropriate.	The document is adequately formatted but is unattractive or difficult to read.	The document is formatted inadequately.

You have completed Project 4K | END

Outcomes-Based Assessments (Critical Thinking)

Rubric

The following outcomes-based assessments are open-ended assessments. That is, there is no specific correct result; your result will depend on your approach to the information provided. Make *Professional Quality* your goal. Use the following scoring rubric to guide you in how to approach the problem and then to evaluate how well your approach solves the problem.

The *criteria*—Software Mastery, Content, Format and Layout, and Process—represent the knowledge and skills you have gained that you can apply to solving the problem. The *levels of performance*—Professional Quality, Approaching Professional Quality, or Needs Quality Improvements—help you and your instructor evaluate your result.

	Your completed project is of Professional Quality if you:	Your completed project is Approaching Professional Quality if you:	Your completed project Needs Quality Improvements if you:
1-Software Mastery	Choose and apply the most appropriate skills, tools, and features and identify efficient methods to solve the problem.	Choose and apply some appropriate skills, tools, and features, but not in the most efficient manner.	Choose inappropriate skills, tools, or features, or are inefficient in solving the problem.
2-Content	Construct a solution that is clear and well organized, contains content that is accurate, appropriate to the audience and purpose, and is complete. Provide a solution that contains no errors of spelling, grammar, or style.	Construct a solution in which some components are unclear, poorly organized, inconsistent, or incomplete. Misjudge the needs of the audience. Have some errors in spelling, grammar, or style, but the errors do not detract from comprehension.	Construct a solution that is unclear, incomplete, or poorly organized, contains some inaccurate or inappropriate content, and contains many errors of spelling, grammar, or style. Do not solve the problem.
3-Format and Layout	Format and arrange all elements to communicate information and ideas, clarify function, illustrate relationships, and indicate relative importance.	Apply appropriate format and layout features to some elements, but not others. Overuse features, causing minor distraction.	Apply format and layout that does not communicate information or ideas clearly. Do not use format and layout features to clarify function, illustrate relationships, or indicate relative importance. Use available features excessively, causing distraction.
4-Process	Use an organized approach that integrates planning, development, self-assessment, revision, and reflection.	Demonstrate an organized approach in some areas, but not others; or, use an insufficient process of organization throughout.	Do not use an organized approach to solve the problem.

Outcomes-Based Assessments (Critical Thinking)

Apply a combination of the 4A and 4B skills.

| GO! Think | Project 4L Training |

Project Files

For Project 4L, you will need the following file:
New blank Word document
You will save your file as:
Lastname_Firstname_4L_Training

Alberto Ramos, Tour Operations Manager, wants to send a memo to all tour guides concerning the following upcoming training opportunities.

Date	Training	Location	Length
June 6	Horseback Riding	Barbille Stables	4 hours
June 17	Orienteering	Manuel Antonio Park	8 hours
June 29	Basic Coastal Sailing	Playa Hermosa	6 hours
July 7	White Water Rafting	Pacuare River	5 hours

Using this information, create a memo inviting tour guides to attend as many training sessions as possible. Include a custom multilevel list for the four training sessions. Insert a chart to compare class length. Format the entire memo in a manner that is professional and easy to read and understand. Save the document as **Lastname_Firstname_4L_Training** Insert the file name in the footer and add appropriate document properties. Submit as directed by your instructor.

You have completed Project 4L | END

| GO! Think | Project 4M Waterfalls Handout | IRC |
| You and GO! | Project 4N Cover Letter | IRC |

Using Advanced Table Features and Advanced Editing Tools

5
WORD 2019

JGI/Jamie Grill/Shutterstock

In This Chapter

GO! to Work with Word

In this chapter, you will use Word's advanced table features. A table provides a convenient way to organize text. Formatting a table makes data easier to read and provides a professional appearance. You can create and apply custom table styles, merge and split cells, and change the way text displays within the cells. The Organizer feature enables you to copy custom styles from one document to another. In this chapter, you will also use Word's advanced editing tools such as the advanced Find and Replace options.

The projects in this chapter relate to **Chesterfield Creations**, a manufacturer of high-quality leather and fabric accessories for men and women. Products include wallets, belts, handbags, key chains, backpacks, business cases, laptop sleeves, and travel bags. The Toronto-based company distributes its products to department stores and specialty shops throughout the United States and Canada. Chesterfield Creations also has a website from which over 60 percent of its products are sold. The company pays shipping costs for both delivery and returns and bases its operating philosophy on exceptional customer service.

PROJECT 5A Product Summary

MyLab IT
Project 5A Grader for Instruction
Project 5A Simulation for Training and Review

Project Activities

In Activities 5.01 through 5.13, you will create, modify, and format tables containing new product information to produce a document that will be distributed to the Chesterfield Creations sales team. Chesterfield Creations is introducing new products for the spring season. Amara Malik, Marketing Vice President, has asked you to create a document that summarizes the new product lines. Your completed document will look similar to Figure 5.1.

Project Files for **MyLab IT Grader**

1. In your storage location, create a folder named **Word Chapter 5**.
2. In your **MyLab IT** course, locate and click **Word 5A Product Summary**, click Download Materials, and then click Download All Files.
3. Extract the zipped folder to your Word Chapter 5 folder. Close the Grader download screens.
4. Take a moment to open the downloaded **Word_5A_Product_Summary_Instructions;** note any recent updates to the book.

Project Results

GO! Project 5A
Where We're Going

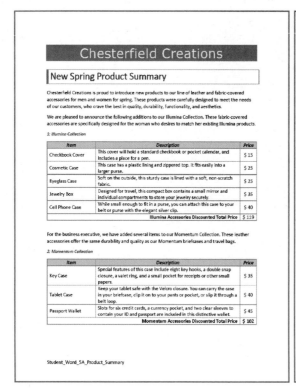
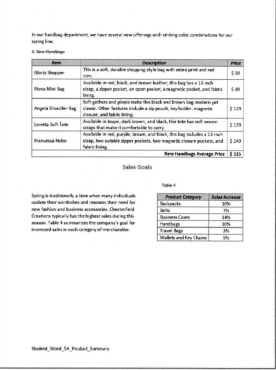

Figure 5.1 Project 5A Product Summary

For Non-MyLab Submissions

For Project 5A, you will need the following files:

w05A_Product_Summary
w05A_Chesterfield_Document_Styles

In your storage location, create a folder named **Word Chapter 5**
In your Word Chapter 5 folder, save w05A_Product_Summary as:
Lastname_Firstname_5A_Product_Summary

After you have named and saved your document, on the next page, begin with Step 2.

Objective 1 | Create and Apply a Custom Table Style

GO! Learn How
Video W5-1

A *style* is a group of formatting commands—such as font, font size, and font color—that can be applied with a single command. Styles in an existing document can be copied to another document.

You can create a *table style* and apply it to any table you create to give your tables a consistent format. A table style can include formatting for the entire table and for specific table elements such as rows and columns. You can use the *Split Table* feature to divide an existing table into two tables in which the selected row—where the insertion point is located—becomes the first row of the second table.

Activity 5.01 | Copy a Style from a Template to a Document by Using the Style Organizer

MOS
Expert 2.3.3

Chesterfield Creations has a Word template that stores several common document styles used in their corporate communications, and employees routinely copy styles from this template to create new corporate documents.

To copy a style from another document or from a template, use the *Organizer*—a dialog box where you can modify a document by copying styles stored in another document or template.

1 Navigate to your **Word Chapter 5** folder, and then double-click the Word file you downloaded from **MyLab IT** that displays your name—**Student_Word_5A_Product_Summary**. If necessary, at the top click **Enable Editing**.

2 If necessary, display the rulers and formatting marks. If any words are flagged as spelling or grammar errors, right-click, and then click **Ignore All**.

3 Press Ctrl + Home to be sure you are at the top of the document. On the **Home tab**, in the **Styles group**, *point to* but do not click, **Heading 1**. Notice that Live Preview displays the first paragraph of the document in the default blue text and font size for the Heading 1 style.

MAC TIP Press command ⌘ + fn + ←. Preview may not display.

4 *Point to*, but do not click, the **Title** style. Notice that Live Preview displays the first paragraph of the document in the default black text and font size for the Title style.

5 On the **Home tab**, in the **Styles group**, click the **Dialog Box Launcher** ⟓, in the displayed dialog box, point to the title *Styles*, and then double-click to snap the **Styles** pane to the right side of your screen. At the bottom of the **Styles** pane, click the third button, **Manage Styles** ⟰.

6 In the **Manage Styles** dialog box, in the lower left corner, click **Import/Export** to display the **Organizer Styles** pane. Compare your screen with Figure 5.2.

MAC TIP Display the menu bar, click Tools, click Templates and Add-ins. In the Templates and Add-ins box, click Organizer. Move to Step 8.

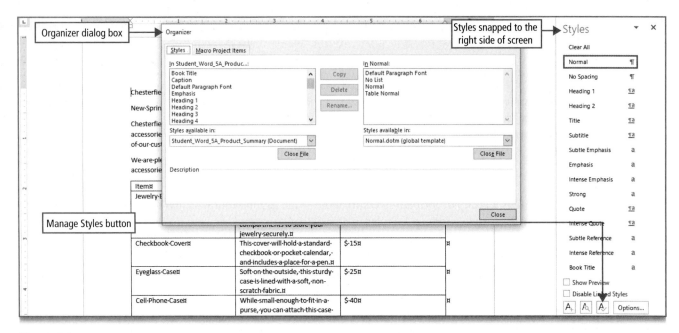

Figure 5.2

> **7** On the **left side** of the **Organizer** dialog box, in the **Styles available in:** box, be sure your *Student_Word_5A_Product_Summary (Document)* displays.

> **8** On the **right side** of the dialog box, under the **Styles available in:** box, click **Close File**, and notice that the button changes to an **Open File** button.

>> This action closes the default template from which you can copy styles and displays the Open File command so you can select a different template or document from which you can copy styles into your displayed document.

> **9** Click **Open File**, navigate to the files downloaded with this project, click one time to select the file **w05A_Chesterfield_Document_Styles**, and then in the lower right corner, click **Open**. Compare your screen with Figure 5.3.

>> This action places the styles contained in the *w05A_Chesterfield_Document_Styles (Template)* into the Organizer so that you can use those styles in your 5A_Product_Summary document.

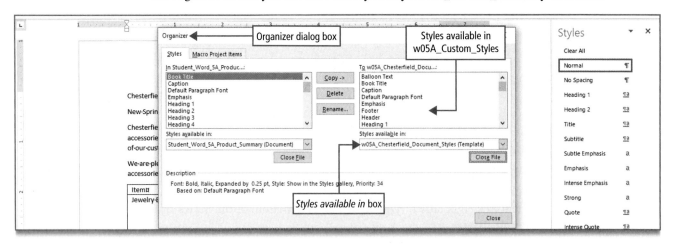

Figure 5.3

> **10** In the upper right portion of the dialog box, in the upper box, scroll down, and then click **Heading 2**. Hold down Ctrl, scroll down, and then click **Title**.

>> Two styles are selected. Use this technique to select one or more styles to copy to another document.

⬜ **MAC TIP** Hold down command ⌘ while scrolling.

11 In the center of the **Organizer** dialog box, locate the **Copy** button, and notice that it displays a left-pointing arrow. With the two styles selected on the left, click **Copy**. When a message displays asking if you want to overwrite the existing style entry Heading 2, click **Yes to All**.

> This action copies the Heading 2 and Title styles from the w05A_Chesterfield_Document_Styles template file to your 5A_Product_Summary document so that you will be able to use these styles in your document.

12 In the lower right corner, click **Close** to close the dialog box. With your **5A_Product_Summary** document displayed, if necessary, on the right, **Close** ☒ the **Styles** pane.

13 On the **Home tab**, in the **Styles group**, *point to* but do not click, **Title**. Compare your screen with Figure 5.4.

> Live Preview displays how the document title would look if the new Title style is applied. The new Heading 2 and Title styles are copied to your *5A_Product_Summary* document. These two styles, both of which display green formatting, are now available to you in this document to apply.

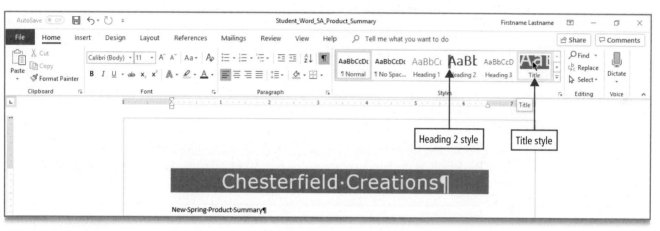

Figure 5.4

14 Select the first paragraph of the document—the company name *Chesterfield Creations*. On the **Home tab**, in the **Styles group**, click **Title**.

15 Select the second paragraph that begins *New Spring*, and then in the **Styles group**, click **Heading 2**. Click anywhere in the third paragraph, and then compare your screen with Figure 5.5.

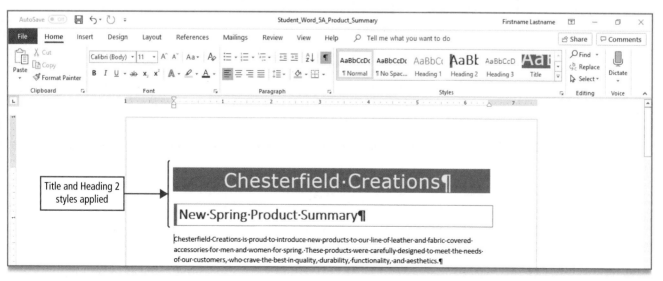

Figure 5.5

Activity 5.02 | Creating a Table Style and Splitting a Table

3.2.5

When you create a table style, you can apply formats—for example, colored borders—to the entire table. You can also add special formats to individual parts of the table—for example, bold emphasis and shading—to specific cells.

If you must format many tables using the same custom style, you will save time by first creating a table style containing all the elements that you want, and then applying that style to all your tables. Using the same attractive table style for all the tables in a document provides a professional and uniform appearance.

1 On the **Home tab**, in the **Styles group**, click the **Dialog Box Launcher** ⬚ to display the **Styles** pane.

> **MAC TIP** In the Styles group, click the Styles Pane button. In the next step, look near the top of the Styles pane.

2 At the bottom of the **Styles** pane, click the first button, **New Style** Ⓐ. In the **Create New Style from Formatting** dialog box, under **Properties**, in the **Name** box, type **Chesterfield Creations** Click the **Style type arrow**, and then click **Table**.

> A sample table displays in the preview area. Use the Create New Style from Formatting dialog box to create a new style to apply a set of formats to a table.

3 Under **Formatting**, click the **Border button arrow** ⊞ ▾, and then click **All Borders**. Click the **Line Weight arrow** ½ pt ───── ▾, and then click **1 pt**. Click the **Border Color arrow** ▾, and then under **Theme Colors**, in the last column, click the fifth color. Compare your screen with Figure 5.6.

> Under *Formatting*, in the *Apply formatting to* box, the formatting will be applied to the whole table. By default, at the bottom of the dialog box, Word indicates that this style is available only in this document.

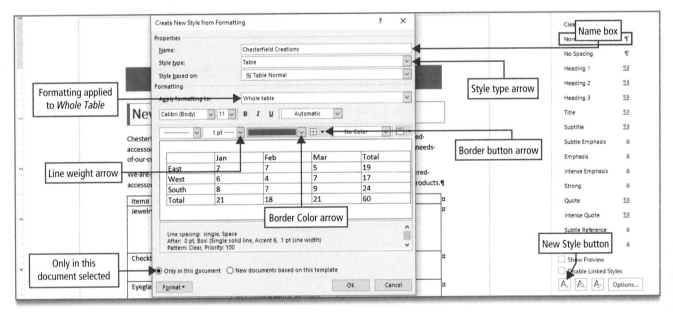

Figure 5.6

4 Click **OK** to close the dialog box, and then **Close** ✕ the **Styles** pane.

5 Scroll down as necessary to view the first table in your document. In the seventh row of the first table, click to position the insertion point in the first cell, which contains the text *Item*. On the ribbon, click the **Table Tools Layout tab**, and then in the **Merge group**, click **Split Table**.

> The original table splits into two separate tables and a new blank paragraph displays above the second table.

6 If necessary, click to position the insertion point in the blank paragraph above the second table, and then press [Enter] one time. Type **For the business executive, we have added several items to our Momentum Collection. These leather accessories offer the same durability and quality as our Momentum briefcases and travel bags.**

BY TOUCH Tap in the blank paragraph, and then on the taskbar, tap the Touch Keyboard button. Tap the appropriate keys to type the text, and then on the Touch Keyboard, tap the X button.

7 Save 🖫 your document.

MORE KNOWLEDGE **Creating a Custom Table Style from the Table Styles Gallery**

If the insertion point is in an existing table, you can create a custom table style from the Table Styles gallery. Under Table Tools, on the Design tab, in the Table Styles group, click More, and then click New Table Style to display the Create New Style from Formatting dialog box.

Activity 5.03 | Applying and Modifying a Table Style

You can apply a table style to an existing table. Additionally, you can modify an existing style or make formatting changes after a style has been applied to a table.

1 Scroll as necessary to view the first table in the document, and then click in the top left cell, which contains the text *Item*.

You can apply a table style when the insertion point is positioned anywhere within a table.

2 Click the **Table Tools Design tab**, and then in the **Table Styles group**, click **More** 🔽.

3 In the **Table Styles** gallery, under **Custom**, point to the style. Notice that the ScreenTip—*Chesterfield Creations*—displays.

4 Click the **Chesterfield Creations** style to apply the table style to the table. Compare your screen with Figure 5.7.

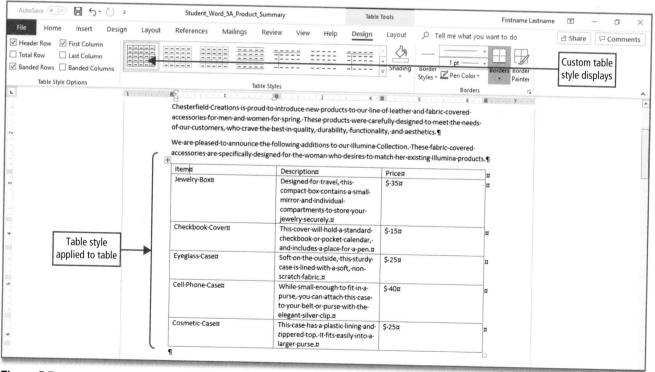

Figure 5.7

5 Scroll as necessary, and then click to position the insertion point anywhere in the second table of the document—the table spans two pages. On the **Table Tools Design tab**, in the **Table Styles group**, click **More** ⊡, and then under **Custom**, click the **Chesterfield Creations** style.

On the ribbon, in the Table Styles group, at the left, the *Chesterfield Creations* table style displays.

6 On the ribbon, in the **Table Styles** gallery, right-click the **Chesterfield Creations** style. A shortcut menu displays commands for working with styles as described in the table in Figure 5.8.

Table Style Commands	
Command	**Description**
Apply (and Clear Formatting)	Table style applied; text formatting reverts to Normal style.
Apply and Maintain Formatting	Table style applied, including text formatting.
New Table Style	Create a new, custom table style.
Modify Table Style	Edit the table style.
Delete Table Style	Remove the style from the Table Styles gallery.
Set as Default	Style is used as the default for all tables created in the document.
Add Gallery to Quick Access Toolbar	Table Styles gallery is added to the Quick Access Toolbar.

Figure 5.8

7 On the shortcut menu, click **Modify Table Style**. In the **Modify Style** dialog box, under **Formatting**, click the **Apply formatting to arrow**, and then click **Header row**.

You can apply formatting to specific table elements. In the *Chesterfield Creations* style, you want to change formats that apply only to the *header row*—the first row of a table containing column titles.

8 Click **Bold** **B**, and then click the **Fill Color arrow** ⌄. Under **Theme Colors**, in the last column, click the fourth color. Compare your screen with Figure 5.9.

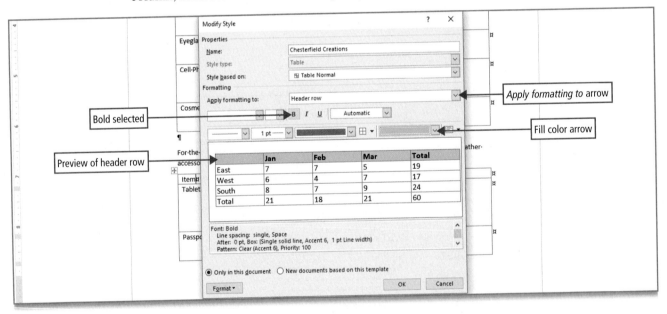

Figure 5.9

9 Click **OK** to close the dialog box, and then press Ctrl + Home. On the **View tab**, in the **Zoom group**, click **Multiple Pages**. Compare your screen with Figure 5.10.

The additional formatting is applied to the header rows in the first and second tables. *Multiple Pages* is a zoom setting that decreases the magnification to display several pages of a document.

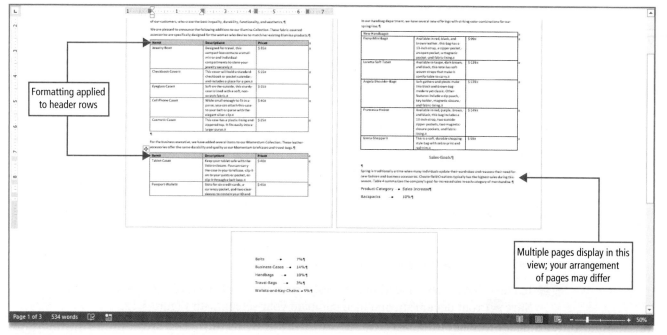

Formatting applied to header rows

Multiple pages display in this view; your arrangement of pages may differ

Figure 5.10

10 On the **View tab**, in the **Zoom group**, click **100%**, and then **Save** your document.

MORE KNOWLEDGE | **Repeating Header Rows**

When a table is large enough to cause part of the table to display on a second page, the header row of the table can be repeated on the second page. To do so, with the insertion point in the header row, on the Layout tab, in the Table group, click the Properties button. In the Table Properties dialog box, click the Row tab, and then under Options, click *Repeat as header row at the top of each page*.

Objective 2 | **Format Cells in a Word Table**

GO! Learn How
Video W5-2

Special formatting features that are unavailable for use with paragraph text are available in tables. For example, you can combine or divide cells and adjust the positioning of text.

Activity 5.04 | **Merging and Splitting Cells**

MOS
3.2.3

You can *split* cells to change the structure of a table. Merging is the process of combining two or more adjacent cells into one cell so that the text spans multiple columns or rows. Splitting divides selected cells into multiple cells with a specified number of rows and columns. In this Activity, you will split cells to add column titles to a header row.

1 Scroll to view the third table of your document—on **Page 2**—and then in the first row, in the first cell, click to position the insertion point to the right of the text *New Handbags*.

2 Click the **Table Tools Layout tab**, and then in the **Merge group**, click **Split Cells**. In the **Split Cells** dialog box, click the **Number of columns up spin arrow** to set the number to **3**. If necessary, click the **Number of rows down spin arrow** to set the number to **1**. Compare your screen with Figure 5.11.

Because you want this header row to match the header rows in the other two product tables, you will split the cell into multiple cells and add column titles.

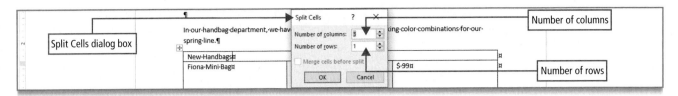

Figure 5.11

3 ▶ Click **OK** to close the dialog box. Notice that the selected cell is split into three cells.

When splitting a cell that contains text, the text is automatically moved to the top left cell created by the split. When you change the structure of a table, some formatting features may be removed.

4 ▶ In the first cell of the header row, select the existing text *New Handbags*, and then type **Item** Press Tab to move to the second cell of the header row, and then type **Description** Press Tab, and then in the last cell of the header row type **Price** Click the **Table Tools Design tab**, and then in the **Table Styles group**, click **More** ⊡.

5 ▶ In the **Table Styles** gallery, under **Custom**, click your **Chesterfield Creations** style. **Save** 🖫 your document, and then compare your screen with Figure 5.12.

Figure 5.12

MORE KNOWLEDGE **Splitting Multiple Cells**

You can modify the number of rows or columns for any group of adjacent cells in a table. Select the cells you want to modify, and then on the Layout tab, in the Merge group, click the Split Cells button. In the Split Cells dialog box, change the number of columns or rows to the desired values.

Activity 5.05 | **Positioning Text within Cells**

Within a cell, you can align text horizontally—left, center, or right. Within a cell, you can also align text vertically—top, center, or bottom. The default setting is to align text at the top left of a cell. Changing cell alignments often makes a table easier to read and look more symmetrical.

1 ▶ Press Ctrl + Home to move to the top **Page 1**. In the first table, in the left margin, point to the header row to display the 𝄃 pointer, and then click one time to select the header row.

2 ▶ Click the **Table Tools Layout tab**, and then in the **Alignment group**, click **Align Center** ▤.

Within each cell, the text in the header row is centered horizontally and vertically.

3 ▶ Below the header row, drag to select all the cells in the first and second columns, and then in the **Alignment group**, click **Align Center Left** ▤.

The selected text is left aligned and centered vertically within the cells.

4 Below the header row, drag to select all the cells in the third column, and then in the **Alignment group**, click **Align Center** ▣. Click anywhere in the table to deselect the text, and then compare your screen with Figure 5.13.

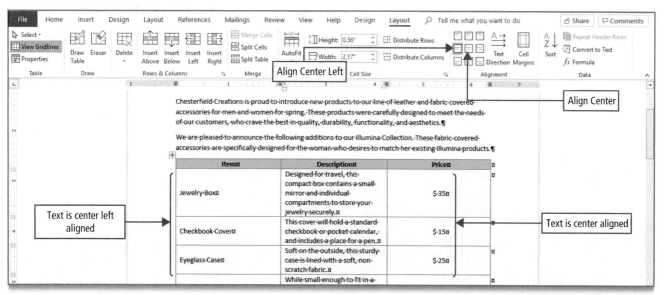

Figure 5.13

5 Using the techniques you just practiced, format the **header row** in the second and third tables in the document to match the formatting of the header row in the first table—**Align Center** ▣. In the second and third tables, apply **Align Center Left** ▣ to the first and second columns below the header row, and then apply **Align Center** ▣ to the text in the third column below the header row. **Save** ▣ your document.

Objective 3 | Use Advanced Table Features

GO! Learn How
Video W5-3

Word tables have some capabilities similar to those in an Excel spreadsheet; for example, sorting data and performing simple calculations. **Sorting** is the action of ordering data, usually in alphabetical or numeric order. Additionally, you can convert existing text to a table format and resize tables in several ways.

Activity 5.06 | Sorting Tables by Category

In this Activity, you will sort the data in the three product tables by price and item to make it easier for the sales team to reference specific items.

1 Press Ctrl + Home to display **Page 1**, and then click to position the insertion point anywhere in the first table.

Recall that in a table, you can sort data in **ascending** order—from the smallest to the largest number or alphabetically from A to Z; or, you can sort data in **descending** order—from the largest to the smallest number or alphabetically from Z to A. Regardless of the columns that are selected in the sort operation, all cells in each row move together to keep the data intact.

2 On the **Table Tools Layout tab**, in the **Data group**, click **Sort**.

The Sort dialog box displays. Here you can sort alphabetically, by number, or by date. The Sort feature can be applied to entire tables, to selected data within tables, to paragraphs, or to body text that is separated by characters such as tabs or commas. You can sort information using a maximum of three columns.

3 In the **Sort** dialog box, under **Sort by**, click the **Sort by arrow**. Notice that your three headings display on the list, and then click **Price**. Compare your screen with Figure 5.14.

> This action will sort the data in the table by the product's price. When a table has a header row, Word displays each column's header text in the *Sort by* list. By default, the Header row option is selected at the bottom left of the Sort dialog box. If a table does not have a header row, select the No header row option button. Without a header row, the sort options for a table will display as *Column 1*, *Column 2*, and so on.

> Because the Price column contains numbers, the Type box displays *Number*. When working in tables, the Using box displays the default *Paragraphs*.

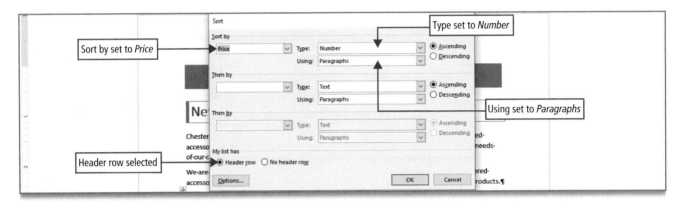

Figure 5.14

4 Under **Then by**, click the first **Then by arrow**, and then click **Item**. Notice that the **Type** box displays *Text*.

> You must designate the columns in the order that you want them sorted. Word will first sort the data by price in ascending order. If two or more items have the same price, Word will arrange those items in alphabetical order by Item name.

5 Click **OK** to close the dialog box and notice that the two items with the same price of *$25* are listed in alphabetical order by Item name. Click anywhere outside of the table to deselect the table, and then compare your screen with Figure 5.15.

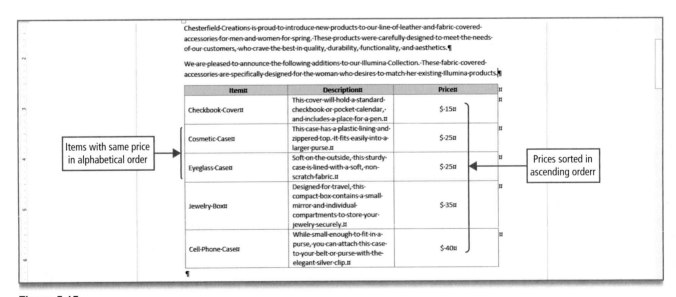

Figure 5.15

6 Scroll to view the bottom of **Page 1**, and then click to position the insertion point anywhere in the second table of the document. On the **Table Tools Layout tab**, in the **Data group**, click **Sort**.

> The Sort by box displays *Price*, and the Then by box displays *Item*. In the Sort dialog box, Word retains the last sort options used in a document.

7 Click **OK** and notice that the table is sorted similarly to the first table.

8 On **Page 2**, click to position the insertion point anywhere in the third table of the document. On the **Table Tools Layout tab**, click the **Sort** button, and then click **OK**. Notice that the table is sorted in the same manner as the previous two tables.

9 **Save** 🖫 your document.

Activity 5.07 | Converting Text to a Table and Modifying Fonts within a Table

3.1.1

To improve the appearance of a document, you can convert existing text, such as a list of information, to a table. In this Activity, you will convert text to a table and then apply the same table style that you have applied to the other tables in the document.

1 Scroll to view the bottom of **Page 2** and the top of **Page 3**.

2 Beginning with the paragraph that begins *Product Category*, drag down to select all the remaining text in the document. Be sure to include the text on *Page 3*—you should have seven paragraphs selected.

3 On the **Insert tab**, in the **Tables group**, click **Table**, and then at the bottom click **Convert Text to Table** to display the **Convert Text to Table** dialog box. Compare your screen with Figure 5.16.

> Word uses characters such as tabs, commas, or hyphens to determine the number of columns. The selected text consists of seven paragraphs—or rows—with each paragraph containing a single tab. By default, Word uses the tab formatting mark to separate each paragraph into two parts—forming the two columns of the table. Under the *Separate text at* section of the dialog box, you can define the character Word uses to separate the text into columns. You can also change the number of columns or rows, based on the text you are converting.

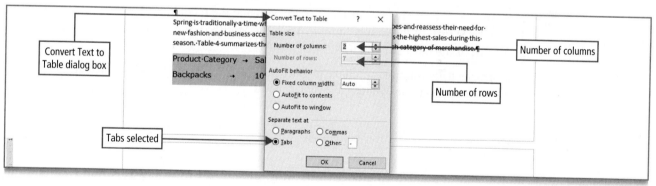

Figure 5.16

4 Click **OK** to close the dialog box.

> Word creates a table that contains two columns and seven rows. The table displays across two pages.

5 With the table selected, on the **Home tab**, in the **Font group**, click the **Font arrow** [Calibri (Body) ▾], and then click **Calibri (Body)**.

6 **Save** 🖫 your document.

Activity 5.08 | Setting Table Column Widths and Resizing Columns by Using AutoFit

3.2.4

Word provides several methods for resizing a table. The *AutoFit* command automatically adjusts column widths or the width of the entire table. The *AutoFit Contents* command resizes the column widths to accommodate the maximum field size. You can change a row height or column width by dragging a border or by designating specific width and height settings. In this Activity, to improve the overall appearance of the document, you will modify column widths.

1 Press Ctrl + Home to move to the top of **Page 1**. In the first table in the document, point to the top border of the first column—*Item*—and when the ⬇ pointer displays, click one time to select the entire column.

2 On the **Table Tools Layout tab**, in the **Cell Size group**, click the **Width down spin arrow** as many times as necessary to set width of the column to **1.5"**. Using the same technique, select the second column in the table—*Description*—and then in the **Cell Size group**, click the **Width up spin arrow** as many times as necessary to set the column width to **4.5"**.

3 Select the last column in the table—*Price*—and then using the techniques you just practiced, set the width of the column to **0.5"**. Compare your screen with Figure 5.17.

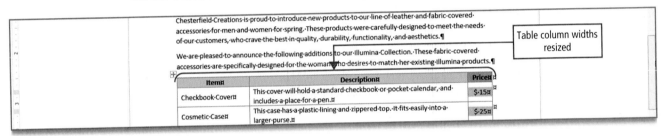

Figure 5.17

4 In the second and third tables of the document, using the techniques you just practiced, change the **Width** of the first column to **1.5"**, the **Width** of the second column to **4.5"**, and the **Width** of the third column to **0.5"**.

By making these adjustments, all the product tables have the same structure—the first, second, and third column widths in all three tables are identical.

ANOTHER WAY Type directly in the Width or Height boxes.

5 At the bottom of **Page 1**, below the second table, click to position the insertion point to the left of the paragraph that begins *In our handbag department*, and then press Ctrl + Enter to insert a page break.

MAC TIP Press command ⌘ + Enter.

6 At the bottom of **Page 2**, click to position your insertion point anywhere in the last table of the document—the table you created by converting text to a table. On the **Table Tools Layout tab**, in the **Cell Size group**, click **AutoFit**, and then click **AutoFit Contents**. Compare your screen with Figure 5.18.

The AutoFit Contents command resizes a table by changing the column widths to fit the existing data. In this table, the widths of both columns were decreased.

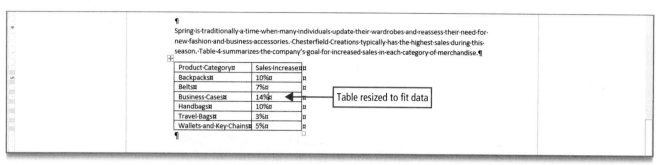

Figure 5.18

7 Click to position the insertion point anywhere in the table, and then on the **Table Tools Design tab**, in the **Table Styles group**, click **More** ⬛. In the **Table Styles** gallery, under **Custom**, click **Chesterfield Creations**.

8 Select the **header row**, and then on the **Table Tools Layout tab**, in the **Alignment group**, click **Align Center** ▣. Select the remaining cells in the second column, and then click **Align Center** ▣. **Save** ▣ your document.

MORE KNOWLEDGE **Using the Sizing Handle**

At the lower right of a table, drag the sizing handle to change the entire table to the desired size.

Activity 5.09 | **Using Formulas in Tables and Creating Custom Field Formats**

Expert 4.1.1

To perform simple calculations, you can insert a *formula* in a Word table. A formula is a mathematical expression that contains *functions*, operators, constants, and properties, and returns a value to a cell. A function is a predefined formula that performs calculations by using specific values in a particular order. Word includes a limited number of built-in functions—for example, SUM and AVERAGE.

1 Press [Ctrl] + [Home] to move to the top of **Page 1**, scroll as necessary to view all of the first table, and then click anywhere in the first table of the document. Point to the bottom left corner of the table to display the **One-Click Row/Column Insertion** button ⊕. Compare your screen with Figure 5.19.

The One-Click Row/Column Insertion button provides a quick method to insert a row or column in a table.

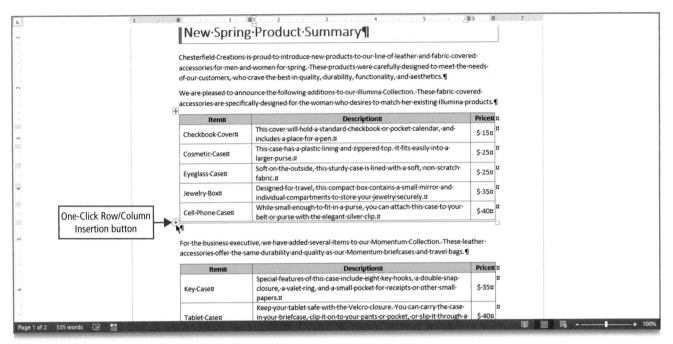

Figure 5.19

> **2** ▶ Click the **One-Click Row/Column Insertion** button ⊕ to insert a new row at the bottom of the table.

🖥 **MAC TIP** Use ribbon commands in the Rows & Columns group.

🔄 **ANOTHER WAY** On the Layout tab, in the Rows & Columns group, click Insert Below.

> **3** ▶ In the new row, select the first two cells, and then on the **Table Tools Layout tab**, in the **Merge group**, click **Merge Cells**. In the merged cell, type **Illumina Accessories Total Price** Select the text you just typed, and then apply **Bold** B. On the **Table Tools Layout tab**, in the **Alignment group**, click **Align Center Right** 🔲. Press Tab to move to the last cell in the table. Compare your screen with Figure 5.20.

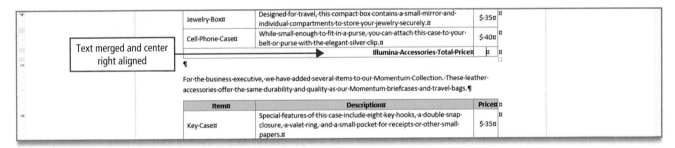

Figure 5.20

> **4** ▶ On the **Table Tools Layout tab**, in the **Data group**, click **Formula**. In the **Formula** dialog box, under **Number format**, click the **Number format arrow**, and then click **#,##0**—the first option. Click to position the insertion point to the left of the characters displayed in the **Number format** text, and then type **$** Compare your screen with Figure 5.21.

🖥 **MAC TIP** Delete the second format that displays in the box.

> The Formula dialog box contains the default formula =SUM(ABOVE). All formulas begin with an equal sign =. This formula includes the SUM function and calculates the total of the numbers in all of the cells above the current cell—up to the first empty cell or a cell that contains text—and places the result in the current cell. You can specify a special number format—in this instance a whole number preceded by a dollar sign.

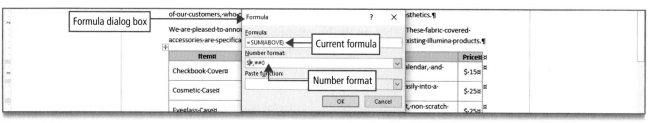

Figure 5.21

> 5 ▸ Click **OK** to close the dialog box. Notice that *$ 140* displays in the active cell, so a customer buying each piece of the Illumina series would pay *$ 140* for the entire set of accessories.

> A formula is a type of *field*—a placeholder for data. The displayed number is a formula field representing the value calculated by the formula.

> 6 ▸ Select the inserted formula result, and then apply **Bold** B.

> 7 ▸ Position the insertion point anywhere in the second table. Point to the lower left border of the table, and then click the **One-Click Row/Column Insertion** button. In the new row, select the first two cells, and then on the **Table Tools Layout tab**, in the **Merge group**, click **Merge Cells**. In the merged cell, type **Momentum Accessories Total Price** and then select the text you just typed. Apply **Bold** B and **Align Center Right** ▤. Press Tab.

🖥 **MAC TIP** Use ribbon commands in the Rows & Columns group.

> 8 ▸ On the **Table Tools Layout tab**, in the **Data group**, click **Formula**. In the **Formula** dialog box, under **Number format**, click the **Number format arrow**, and then click **#,##0**. Click to position the insertion point to the left of the characters in the **Number format** text, and then type **$** Click **OK**. Compare your screen with Figure 5.22.

> A customer buying each piece of the Momentum series would pay *$120* for the entire set of accessories.

🖥 **MAC TIP** Select $#,##0. Click OK and delete characters as necessary to display $#,##0

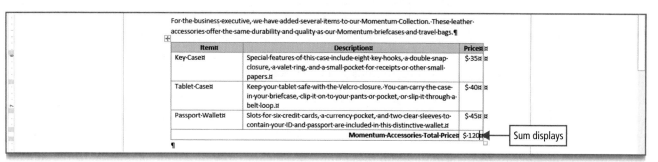

Figure 5.22

> 9 ▸ Select *$ 120* and apply **Bold** B.

> 10 ▸ In the third table of the document, use the technique you just practiced to insert a new row at the bottom of the table. Select the first two cells and merge them. In the merged cell, type **New Handbags Average Price** and then apply **Bold** B and **Align Center Right** ▤.

11 Press `Tab` to position the insertion point in the last cell of the table, and then click **Formula**. In the **Formula** dialog box, in the **Formula** box, delete the existing text, and then type **=** Under **Paste function**, click the **Paste function arrow**, and then click **AVERAGE**. In the **Formula** box, notice that *=AVERAGE* displays followed by *( )*. With the insertion point between the left and right parentheses, type **ABOVE**

> You can use the Paste function box to specify a built-in function—such as AVERAGE, PRODUCT, MIN (the minimum value in a list), or MAX (the maximum value in a list). By typing *ABOVE*, the calculation includes all of the values listed above the current cell in the table. You are using the AVERAGE function to calculate the average price of the new handbags.

12 In the **Formula** dialog box, under **Number format**, click the **Number format arrow**, and then click **#,##0**. Click to position the insertion point to the left of the **Number format** text, and then type **$** Compare your screen with Figure 5.23.

🖥️ **MAC TIP** Select $#,##0. Click OK and delete characters as necessary to display $#,##0

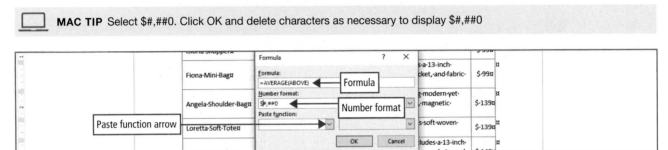

Figure 5.23

13 Click **OK** to close the **Formula** dialog box. Select the inserted formula result, and then apply **Bold** `B`. **Save** `💾` your document.

> The average price of the five handbags—*$ 117*—displays in the active cell.

MORE KNOWLEDGE | **Inserting Rows and Columns in a Table**

To insert a new row in an existing table, point to the left of the border between two existing rows, and then click the One-Click Row/Column Insertion button. To insert a new column, point above the border between two existing columns, and then click the One-Click Row/Column Insertion button. To insert a column at the extreme right of the table, point to the top right corner of the table, and then click the One-Click Row/Column Insertion button.

Activity 5.10 | Updating Formula Fields in Tables

You can edit an existing formula in a table. Additionally, if you change a value in a table, you must manually update the field containing the formula.

1 On **Page 1**, in the first table, in the last row, click to position the insertion point to the left of the word *Total*, type **Discounted** and then press `Spacebar`.

2 Press `Tab` to select the cell containing the formula, right-click over the selected cell, and then on the shortcut menu, click **Edit Field**. In the **Field** dialog box, under **Field properties**, click **Formula**.

3 In the **Formula** dialog box, in the **Formula** box, be sure the insertion point displays to the right of the formula *=SUM(ABOVE)*, and then type ***.85** Compare your screen with Figure 5.24.

> Formulas are not restricted to the built-in functions. You can also create your own. Customers purchasing the entire Illumina collection of accessories receive a 15 percent discount. The modified formula reflects this discounted price. The total price is multiplied by 85 percent (.85), representing 100 percent minus the 15 percent discount.

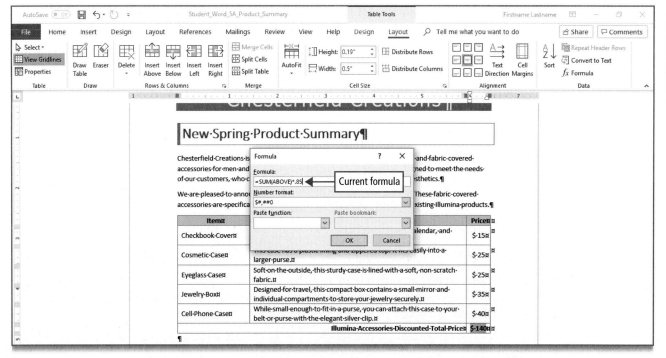

Figure 5.24

4 Click **OK**, and notice that a new, lower price—*$ 119*—displays in the active cell.

5 In the second table, in the last row, click to position the insertion point to the left of the word *Total*, type **Discounted** and then press `Spacebar`.

6 Press `Tab`, right-click over the selected cell, and then on the shortcut menu, click **Edit Field**. In the **Field** dialog box, under **Field properties**, click the **Formula** button.

> 🖥 **MAC TIP** Use commands on the Table Layout tab.

7 In the **Formula** dialog box, in the **Formula** box, if necessary click to position the insertion point to the right of the displayed formula *=SUM(ABOVE)*, and then type ***.85** Click **OK**.

The discounted total for the Momentum collection of accessories—*$ 102*—displays in the active cell.

8 In the third table, in the last column, below the **header row**, click in the third cell—the price of the Angela Shoulder Bag. Select only the number *139*, and then type **129**

Unlike Excel, when you change a value that is used in a formula, the resulting calculation is not automatically updated.

9 In the bottom right cell of the table, select the formula result. Right-click the selection, and then on the shortcut menu, click **Update Field**.

The value *$ 115* displays in the active cell and represents a formula field. If a number used in the calculation is changed, you must use the Update Field command to recalculate the value.

10 **Save** 🖫 your document.

NOTE Summing Rows

The default formula is =SUM(ABOVE), assuming the cell above the selected cell contains a number. If there is a number in the cell to the left of the selected cell and no number in the cell above, the default is =SUM(LEFT). If you want to sum the entire range, avoid leaving a cell empty within a range. If there is no value, then enter a 0.

Activity 5.11 | Adding Captions, Excluding Labels from Captions, and Setting Caption Positions

Expert 3.4.1,
Expert 3.4.2

Captions are labels that you can add to Word objects such as a picture or table. As you add captions to objects within a document, Word automatically numbers the captions sequentially. It is good practice to add a caption to each table in a document to make it easier to refer to specific tables in the body text.

1 On **Page 1**, click to position the insertion point anywhere in the first table. On the **References tab**, in the **Captions group**, click **Insert Caption**.

> Because the object selected is a table, in the Caption box, the default caption *Table 1* displays. Word automatically numbers objects sequentially. If the selected object is not a table, you can change the object type by clicking the Label arrow in the Caption dialog box.

2 In the **Caption** dialog box, select the **Exclude label from caption** check box.

> The label *Table* is removed, and only the number *1* displays in the Caption box.

3 In the **Caption** box, to the right of *1,* type a colon : press ⌨Spacebar, and then type **Illumina Collection** If necessary, under **Options**, click the **Position arrow**, and then click **Above selected item**. Compare your screen with Figure 5.25.

> You can adjust the position of a caption to display above or below the document element. In this instance, the caption is set to display above the table.

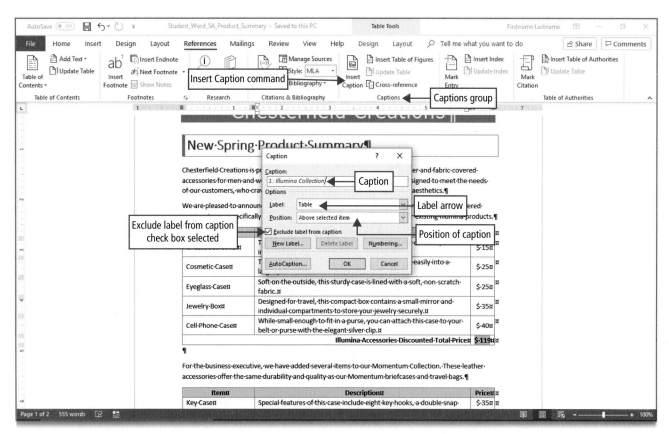

Figure 5.25

4 Click **OK** to close the **Caption** dialog box. Notice that the caption displays above the table.

5 Using the technique you just practiced, add captions to the second and third tables. For the second table caption, insert the caption **2: Momentum Collection** above the table. For the third table, insert the caption **3: New Handbags** above the table.

6 **Save** 🖫 your document.

<table>
<tr><td>**Objective 4**</td><td>**Modify Table Properties**</td></tr>
</table>

GO! Learn How

Video W5-4

Tables, like all other Word objects, have properties that you can alter. For example, you can change how text wraps around tables and define cell spacing. Modify table properties to improve the overall appearance of your document.

Activity 5.12 | Moving a Table and Wrapping Text Around Tables

If you have a long document with several tables and body text, you can apply text wrapping to have the text flow around the table. This can create a shorter document and improve the overall readability of the document.

1 Press Ctrl + End to move to the bottom of **Page 2**, and then scroll up slightly to view the text above the 2-column table.

MAC TIP command ⌘ + fn + →

2 Point to the upper left corner of the table to display the **table move handle** ⊞ and the ⌖ pointer, hold down the left mouse button, and then drag the table up and to the right until the top border of the table is aligned with the top of the paragraph that begins *Spring is* and the right border is at approximately **6.5" on the horizontal ruler**. Compare your screen with Figure 5.26. If your table position does not match the figure, on the Quick Access Toolbar click Undo ↶ and begin again.

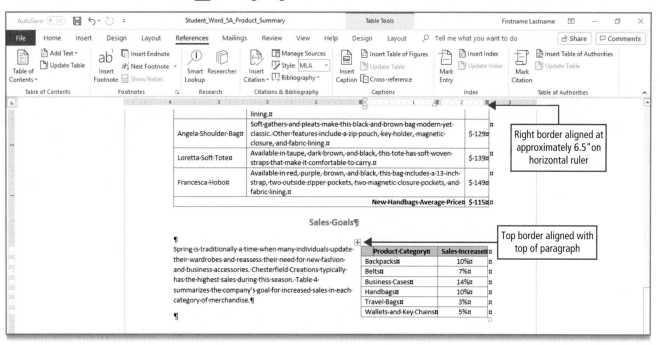

Figure 5.26

3 Click to position the insertion point anywhere in the table. On the **Table Tools Layout tab**, in the **Table group**, click **Properties**. In the **Table Properties** dialog box, on the **Table tab**, under **Text wrapping**, be sure **Around** is selected, and then click the **Positioning** button.

4 In the **Table Positioning** dialog box, under **Distance from surrounding text**, click the **Left up spin arrow** as necessary to set the distance to **0.5"**. Compare your screen with Figure 5.27.

You can define how close existing text displays in relation to the top, bottom, left, or right of a table. By changing the Left box value to 0.5, the text will display one-half inch from the left border of the table.

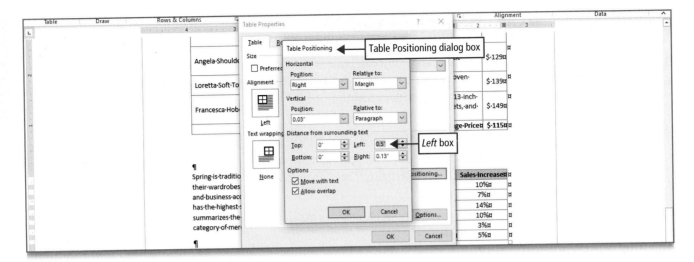

Figure 5.27

5 ▶ Click **OK** two times to close the dialog boxes.

Activity 5.13 | Changing Caption Formats

1 ▶ With the insertion point in the table, on the **References tab**, in the **Captions group**, click **Insert Caption**. In the **Caption** dialog box, clear the **Exclude label from caption** check box. With *Table 4* displayed in the **Caption** box and *Above selected item* displayed in the **Position** box, click **OK** to close the dialog box and insert the caption at the left margin.

2 ▶ Select the caption. Change the **Font Size** to **10** and apply **Bold** B. Click the **Font Color** A ▾ arrow, and then in the last column, click the last color.

3 ▶ With the caption selected, on the **Home tab**, in the **Paragraph group**, click the **Dialog Launcher** button ⌐, and then at the bottom of the **Paragraph** dialog box, click **Tabs**. In the **Tabs** dialog box, under **Tab stop position**, type **4** and then click **Set** and click **OK**. Click to the left of the caption, and then press Tab. Compare your screen with Figure 5.28.

You can format a caption just as you would format body text. In this instance, you format the caption to display above the table and coordinate with the color scheme of the table.

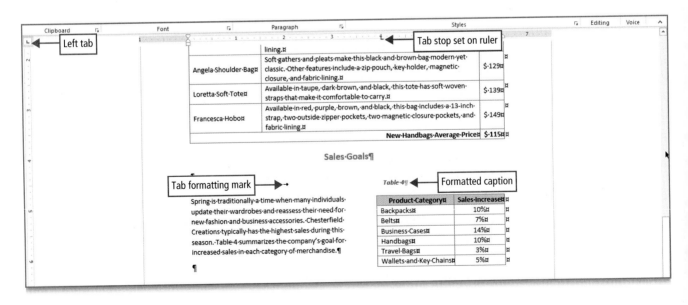

Figure 5.28

4 Select the caption *Table 4*. On the **Home tab**, in the **Styles group**, click **More** ⊡, and then in the **Styles** gallery, click **Create a Style**.

5 In the **Create New Style from Formatting** dialog box, in the **Name** box, type **Table Caption** and then click **OK**.

6 Press [Ctrl] + [Home]. Select the first table caption, on the ribbon, in the **Styles group**, click **More** ⊡, and then near the top of the gallery, click the **Table Caption** style.

7 By using the same technique, apply the **Table Caption** style to the remaining two captions in the document.

8 Press [Ctrl] + [Home].

9 From the **Insert tab**, use the techniques you have practiced to insert the **File Name** in the footer.

10 Click the **File tab** to display **Backstage** view and display the **Info tab**. On the right, at the bottom of the **Properties** list, click **Show All Properties**. As the **Tags**, type **product summary, tables** In the **Subject** box, type your course name and section number. If necessary, edit the author name to display your name.

11 On the left, click **Save** to save your document and return to the Word window. In the upper right corner of the Word window, click **Close** ☒.

> **For Non-MyLab Submissions Determine What Your Instructor Requires for Submission**
> As directed by your instructor, submit your completed Word file.

12 In **MyLab IT**, locate and click the Grader Project **Word 5A Product Summary**. In **step 3**, under **Upload Completed Assignment**, click **Choose File**. In the **Open** dialog box, navigate to your **Word Chapter 5 folder**, and then click your **Student_Word_5A_Product_Summary** file one time to select it. In the lower right corner of the **Open** dialog box, click **Open**.

The name of your selected file displays above the Upload button.

13 To submit your file to **MyLab IT** for grading, click **Upload**, wait a moment for a green **Success!** message, and then in **step 4**, click the blue **Submit for Grading** button. Click **Close Assignment** to return to your list of **Course Materials**.

You have completed Project 5A | **END**

Project Activities

In Activities 5.14 through 5.24, you will examine Word settings, translate text, insert an equation, and use find and replace options to create a draft version of an FAQ list. Nanci Scholtz, Vice President of Online Marketing for Chesterfield Creations, is compiling a list of Frequently Asked Questions, or FAQs, to share with customers who shop from the company's online site. She plans to include the information in a separate webpage on the company's website. Your completed document will look similar to Figure 5.29.

Project Files for MyLab IT Grader

1. In your **MyLab IT** course, locate and click **Word 5B FAQ List**, Download Materials, and then Download All Files.
2. Extract the zipped folder to your Word Chapter 5 folder. Close the Grader download screens.
3. Take a moment to open the downloaded **Word_5B_FAQ_List_Instructions**; note any recent updates to the book.

Project Results

GO! Project 5B
Where We're Going

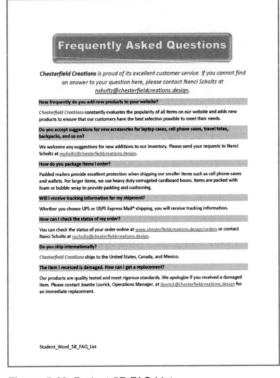

Figure 5.29 Project 5B FAQ List

For Non-MyLab Submissions

For Project 5B, you will need the following files:
w05B_FAQ_List
w05B_Image
w05B For _Packaging

In your Word Chapter 5 folder, save your document as:
Lastname_Firstname_5B_FAQ_List

Open w05B_FAQ_List, save it in your Word Chapter 5 folder as **Lastname_Firstname_5B_FAQ_List** and then on the next page, begin with Step 2

Objective 5 | Manage Document Versions

GO! Learn How

Video W5-5

When you install Microsoft Office, default settings are created for many features. For example, when working on an unsaved document, Word saves a temporary version every ten minutes. This amount of time can be adjusted to suit your needs. Recall that Word settings are modified in the Word Options dialog box.

Activity 5.14 | Changing the AutoSave Frequency

In this Activity, you will change the save frequency for the *AutoRecover* option, which helps prevent losing unsaved changes by automatically creating a backup version of the current document.

1 Navigate to your **Word Chapter 5 folder**, and then double-click the Word file you downloaded from **MyLab IT** that displays your name—**Student_Word_5B_FAQ_List**. If necessary, at the top click **Enable Editing**.

2 Be sure your document displays in **Print Layout** view. At the bottom of **Page 1**, right-click in the footer area, and then click **Edit Footer**. On the ribbon, in the **Insert group**, click **Document Info**, and then click **File Name**. **Close** the footer area.

MAC TIP On the Header & Footer tab, in the Insert group, click Field. In the Field dialog box, under Categories, click Document Information. Under Field names, click FileName.

3 Click the **File tab**, and then on the left click **Options** to display the **Word Options** dialog box.

MAC TIP Display the menu bar, click Word, click Preferences; in the Output and Sharing section, click Save.

4 In the **Word Options** dialog box, on the left, click **Save**. Under **Save documents**, verify that the *Save AutoRecover information every* check box and the *Keep the last autosaved version if I close without saving* check box are selected. To the right of **Save AutoRecover information every** click the **down spin arrow** as many times as necessary to set the minutes to **1**, and then compare your screen with Figure 5.30.

For purposes of this instruction, Word will save a version of this document every minute. The AutoRecover file location box displays the location where the temporary versions are stored.

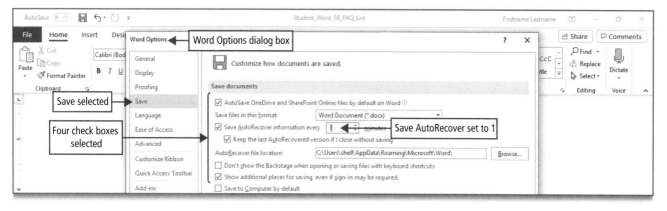

Figure 5.30

5 In the lower right corner, click **OK** to save the change you made and to close the **Word Options** dialog box.

MAC TIP Click the Close button.

Activity 5.15 | Zooming from the View Tab

By changing the way in which documents display on your screen, you make your editing tasks easier and more efficient. For example, you can display multiple pages of a long document or increase the zoom level to make reading easier or to examine specific text more closely.

1 ▶ Press Ctrl + Home, and then click at the end of the first paragraph—*FAQ*. Press Enter one time to insert a new blank paragraph.

2 ▶ Type **Chesterfield Creations is proud of its excellent customer service. If you cannot find an answer to your question here, please contact Nanci Scholtz at nscholtz@chesterfieldcreations.design.**

3 ▶ Select the text *nscholtz@chesterfieldcreations.design* and on the **Insert tab**, click **Link**. Then click **OK** to add a hyperlink to this text.

4 ▶ Click the **View tab**, and then in the **Zoom group**, click **Zoom**. In the **Zoom** dialog box, under **Zoom to**, click the **200%** option button, and then compare your screen with Figure 5.31.

In the Zoom dialog box, you can select from among several pre-set zoom levels, select a specific number of pages to view at one time, or use the Percent box to indicate a specific zoom level.

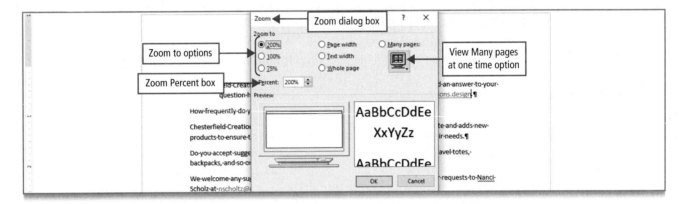

Figure 5.31

🔄 **ANOTHER WAY**   Use the Zoom slider at the right end of the status bar to change the Zoom percentage.

5 ▶ Click **OK** and notice that the document displays in a magnified view.

6 ▶ Scroll as necessary, and then in the paragraph that begins *We welcome*, notice that the email address has an error in the company name—chesterfi*le*d instead of chesterfi*el*d. Select the letters *le* and then type **el**

A magnified view is useful when you must make a close inspection of characters—for example, when typing email addresses or scientific formulas.

7 ▶ On the **View tab**, in the **Zoom group**, click **Multiple Pages** to display both **Page 1** and **Page 2** on your screen.

The Multiple Pages zoom setting decreases the magnification. Although the displayed text is smaller, you have an overall view of the page arrangement.

8 ▶ On the **View tab**, in the **Zoom group**, click **100%** to return to the default zoom setting.

Activity 5.16 | Managing Document Versions

Expert 1.1.2

You can examine an older version of your current document that was automatically saved—for example, to check the wording of a paragraph.

MAC TIP Move to Activity 5.17. On a Mac, to find and recover a previous version of a Word document, open the document, click File, click Revert To, click Browse All Versions. Find the latest version you have saved and click Restore.

1 Click the **File tab**, and then on the left, if necessary, click **Info**. To the right of the **Manage Document** box, take a moment to review the list.

> The list displays the most recently saved versions of the current document. Recall that you changed the AutoSave frequency to 1 minute. Several versions may display depending on the amount of time it has taken you to reach this Step in the Project.

2 Click the **Manage Document** button, and then click **Recover Unsaved Documents** to display the **Open** dialog box.

> In the Open dialog box, the *UnsavedFiles* folder displays the file names of old documents that have never been saved. From this dialog box, you can select the file you want to display. Note: This folder may be empty on your computer.

3 In the lower right corner, click **Cancel** to close the **Open** dialog box. Click the **File tab**. To the right of the **Manage Document** button, at the bottom of the list, click the last file name to display the oldest version of the current document. Compare your screen with Figure 5.32.

> A temporary, autosaved version of the current document opens as a Read-Only document. A message bar displays indicating that a newer version is available. You can replace a current document with a previous version by clicking the Restore button on the message bar.

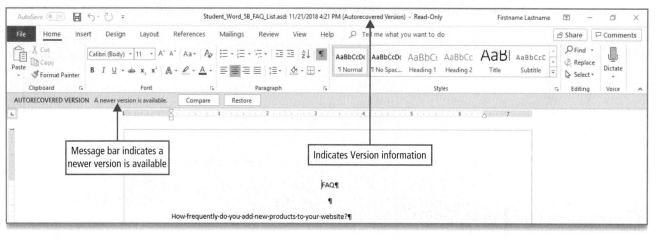

Figure 5.32

4 In the upper right corner, click **Close** ✕. In the **Microsoft Word** message box, click **Don't Save**.

> All recent versions of the current document display in the Manage Document list.

5 At the bottom of the **Manage Document** list, right-click the last file name, and then on the shortcut menu, click **Delete This Version**. In the message box, click **Yes** to confirm the deletion.

> The oldest version of the current document is deleted.

6 On the left, click **Options**, and then in the **Word Options** dialog box, on the left click **Save**. Reset the **Save AutoRecover information every** information back to 10 minutes by clicking the up spin arrow as many times as necessary to set the minutes to **10**, and then click **OK** to close the **Word Options** dialog box and restore the default setting. **Save** 🖫 your document.

GO! Learn How
Video W5-6

As you are writing, you may want to gather material—for example, text or pictures related to your topic. This supporting information may be located in another document or on the internet. Recall that you can use the Clipboard to collect a group of graphics or selected text blocks and then paste them into a document.

Activity 5.17 | Collecting Images and Text from Multiple Documents

In this Activity, you will copy images and text from two different documents and then paste them into your current document.

1 ▶ Press Ctrl + Home. On the **Home tab**, in the lower right corner of the **Clipboard group**, click the **Dialog Box Launcher** ⌐ to display the **Clipboard** pane. If necessary, at the top of the pane, click **Clear All** to delete anything currently on the Clipboard.

> **MAC TIP** The Mac Clipboard can hold only one item; follow the MAC TIPS to complete this Activity. To view the Clipboard, open Finder, on the Finder toolbar, click Edit. Click Show Clipboard. When Clipboard is open, your Word document is not active. Close the Clipboard.

2 ▶ Be sure that only your **Student_5B_FAQ_List** document and the **Clipboard** display; if necessary, close any other open windows. Click the **File tab**, on the left click **Open**, click **Browse**, and then in the **Open** dialog box, from the files downloaded for this Project, locate and open the file **w05B_Image**. If necessary, in the **Clipboard group**, click the **Dialog Box Launcher** ⌐ to display the pane.

> **MAC TIP** Disregard any reference to the Clipboard display or Clipboard pane.

3 ▶ With the **w05B_Image** document displayed, click the **Frequently Asked Questions** graphic one time to select it. On the **Home tab**, in the **Clipboard group**, click **Copy**. Compare your screen with Figure 5.33.

The image in your w05B_Image document displays on the Clipboard pane—or yours may display *(preview not available)*.

> **MAC TIP** Go to Step 1 in Activity 5.18; paste the image; return to Step 5 in this Activity.

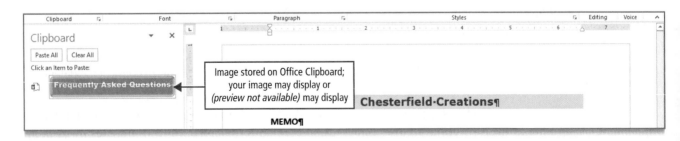

Figure 5.33

4 Close ⊠ the **w05B_Image** file.

5 From the files downloaded with this Project, open the file **w05B_Packaging**. If necessary, on the **Home tab**, in the **Clipboard group**, click the **Dialog Box Launcher** 🔲 to display the **Clipboard** pane. Without selecting the paragraph mark at the end, select the entire paragraph that begins *Padded mailers*, and then **Copy** the selection to the Clipboard. Compare your screen with Figure 5.34.

The first few lines of the copied text display on the Clipboard. When copying multiple items to the Clipboard, the most recently copied item displays at the top of the list.

⌨ **MAC TIP** Go to Step 2 in Activity 5.18 and paste as instructed.

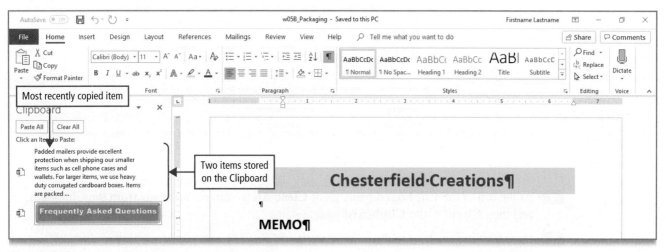

Figure 5.34

6 Close ⊠ the **w05B_Packaging** document.

Activity 5.18 │ Pasting Information from the Clipboard Pane

After you have collected text items or images on the Clipboard, you can paste them into a document in any order.

1 Press Ctrl + Home. Press Delete three times to delete the text *FAQ*; do not delete the paragraph mark. In the **Clipboard** pane, click the graphic *Frequently Asked Questions*.

The graphic is inserted in the blank paragraph.

2 Locate the sixth text paragraph of the document, which begins *Will I receive*. Click to position the insertion point to the left of the paragraph, press Enter one time, and then press ↑ one time. In the new paragraph, type **How do you package the items I order?** and then press Enter.

3 In the **Clipboard** pane, click the text entry that begins *Padded mailers* to paste the entire block of text at the insertion point. Compare your screen with Figure 5.35.

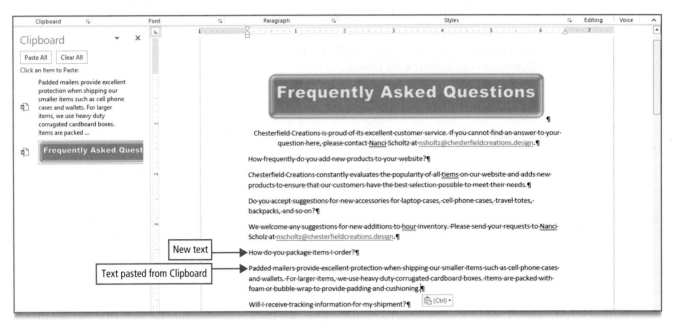

Figure 5.35

4 At the top of the **Clipboard** pane, click **Clear All** to remove all items from the Clipboard, and then **Close** ☒ the **Clipboard** pane.

5 Press ⌃Ctrl + Home. Locate the paragraph that begins *How frequently*, and then select the entire paragraph, including the paragraph mark. Press and hold ⌃Ctrl, and then select the next question—the paragraph that begins *Do you accept.*

6 Continue to hold down ⌃Ctrl, and then select all the remaining paragraphs that end in a question mark, scrolling down with the scroll bar or the **Vertical Scrollbar down arrow** ▾ as necessary to move through the document.

ALERT   Do Not Scroll with Your Mouse Wheel

When holding down ⌃Ctrl, on some mouse devices, using the mouse wheel zooms your view rather than scrolling. For this Activity, scroll by using the scroll bar on the right edge of the window.

---

7 With all the questions selected, apply **Bold** B. On the **Home tab**, in the **Paragraph group**, click the **Shading arrow** ⬙ ▾, and then in the eighth column, click the first color.

8 Click anywhere to deselect the text, scroll through the document to be sure you have shaded each question; there are a total of 12 shaded questions. Then scroll so that the *Frequently Asked Questions* graphic displays at the top of your screen.

9 Under the graphic, select the paragraph that begins *Chesterfield Creations is proud*. To the selected paragraph, apply **Italic**. Display the **Font Color** gallery, and then in the last column click the last color. Change the **Font Size** to **14**. Click anywhere to deselect the paragraph, and then compare your screen with Figure 5.36.

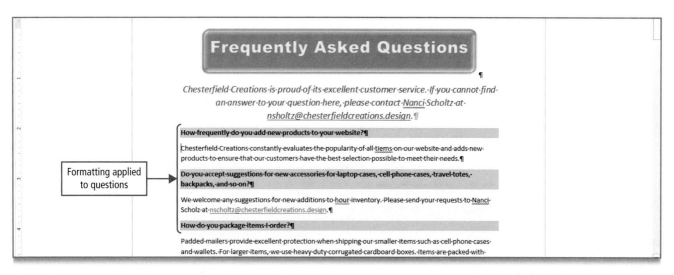

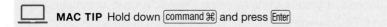

Figure 5.36

10 Scroll to view the bottom of **Page 1**. Click to position your insertion point to the left of the paragraph that begins *I would like a refund*, hold down Ctrl, and then press Enter to insert a page break so that the question and answer do not break across two pages.

 MAC TIP Hold down command ⌘ and press Enter

11 **Save** 💾 your document.

Objective 7 | Translate Text and Insert Equations

GO! Learn How
Video W5-7

While composing a document, you can insert special characters such as trademark symbols, translate text into a different language, and enter simple or complex equations in a document.

Activity 5.19 | Inserting Special Characters

MOS
2.1.2

1 On **Page 1**, locate the paragraph that begins *Whether you choose*, and then click to position the insertion point immediately to the right of *Express Mail*. Click the **Insert tab**. In the **Symbols group**, click **Symbol**, and then on the list, click **More Symbols**.

Here you will find characters that are not available on your keyboard.

 MAC TIP Click Advanced Symbol; move the dialog box so you can view your text.

2 ▶ In the **Symbol** dialog box, click the **Special Characters tab**, and then click the symbol ®—**Registered**. Notice the keyboard shortcut—Alt+Ctrl+R—displays to the right of the symbol.

The *federal registration symbol*—®—indicates that a patent or trademark has been registered with the United States Patent and Trademark Office. Here, the symbol applies to the term *Express Mail*.

MAC TIP No keyboard shortcut provided.

3 ▶ In the lower right corner of the dialog box, click **Insert** to insert the symbol to the right of *Mail*, and then click **Close**. Compare your screen with Figure 5.37.

Figure 5.37

Activity 5.20 | Translating Text

You can translate a word or phrase into a different language. Because Chesterfield Creations has customers outside of the United States, the FAQ will include text for Spanish-speaking and French-speaking customers that can eventually be linked to FAQ pages written in those languages. In this Activity, you will add Spanish and French text to the FAQ list.

1 ▶ Press Ctrl + End to move to the end of your document, press Enter one time to insert another blank paragraph, and then type **FAQ: Spanish**

2 ▶ Select the text *Spanish*. Click the **Review tab**. In the **Language group**, click **Translate**, and then click **Translate Selection**.

3 ▶ If a message displays regarding **Intelligent Services**, click **Turn on** to display the **Translator** pane on the right. Compare your screen with Figure 5.38.

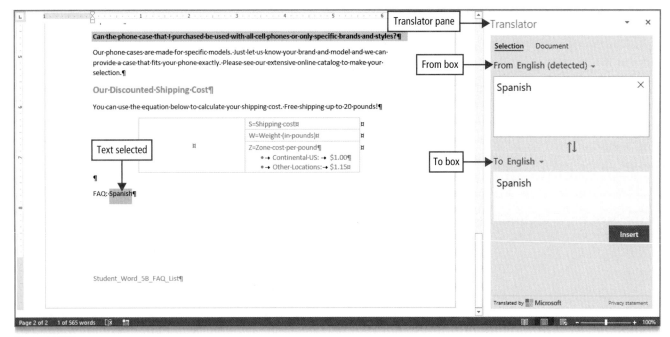

Figure 5.38

4 In the lower portion of the **Translator** pane, in the **To** box, click the ▾ **arrow**.

5 Scroll as necessary on the displayed list, and then click **Spanish**. In the lower right corner, click **Insert**. Compare your screen with Figure 5.39.

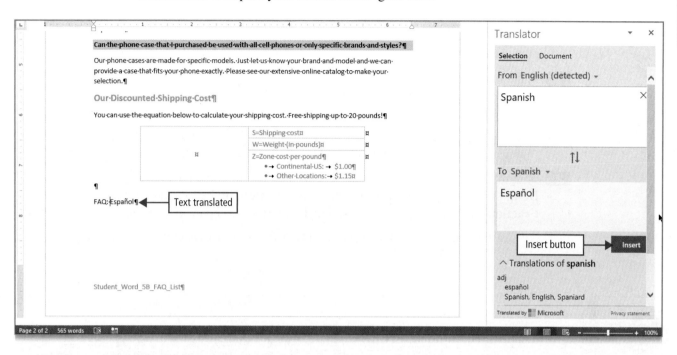

Figure 5.39

6 Position the insertion point at the end of the paragraph. Press Enter one time, type **FAQ:** and then press Spacebar.

7 Type **French** and then select the text *French* that you just typed.

8 In the lower portion of the **Translator** pane, in the **To** box, click the ▾ **arrow**.

9 Scroll as necessary on the displayed list, and then click **French**. In the lower right corner, click **Insert**. Compare your screen with Figure 5.40.

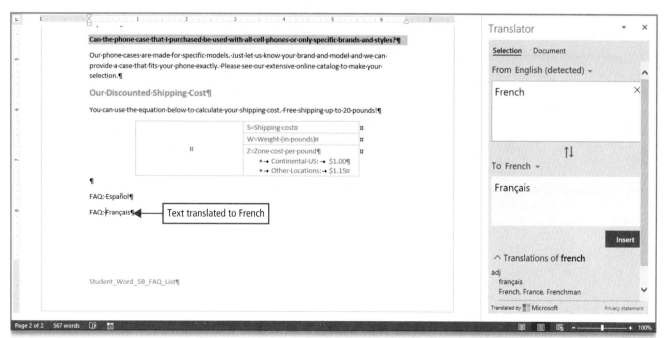

Figure 5.40

10 Close ☒ the **Translator** pane.

11 Select both paragraphs that begin *FAQ*. Change the **Font Size** to **14**, and apply **Bold** ☐.

Ms. Scholtz will develop specific FAQs in both languages here.

Activity 5.21 | Inserting Equations

In this Activity, you will insert an equation to help customers calculate shipping costs.

1 In the lower portion of **Page 2**, click in the large left cell of the table. Click the **Insert tab**, and then in the **Symbols group**, click the **Equation arrow**. In the list, take a moment to view the **Built-In** equations, and then at the bottom of the list, click **Insert New Equation**.

An equation placeholder displays in the table cell. On the ribbon, the Equation Tools Design tab displays, which includes built-in formulas and components you can modify to meet your needs.

2 With the equation placeholder selected, type **S=** On the ribbon, on the **Equation Tools Design tab**, in the **Structures group**, click **Fraction**. In the **Fraction** gallery, under **Fraction**, click the first format—**Stacked Fraction**. Compare your screen with Figure 5.41.

A fraction with a top and bottom placeholder displays to the right of the text you just typed.

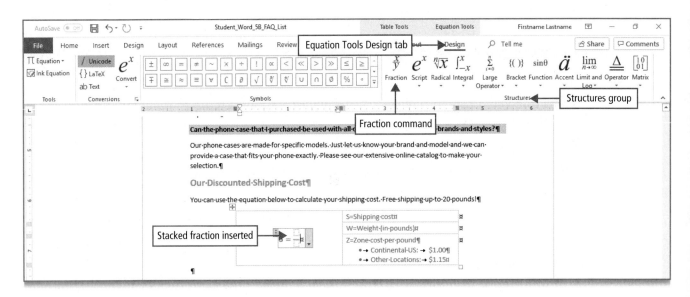

Figure 5.41

3 In the fraction, click the top placeholder, and then type **W-20** Click the bottom placeholder, and then type **2** Click to the right of the fraction, type ***Z** and then compare your screen with Figure 5.42.

The *variables*—letters that represent values—in the equation are described in the second cell of the table. In this equation, the customer will pay a reduced shipping cost based on the weight and destination, and if the weight is 20 pounds or less, the customer pays no shipping cost.

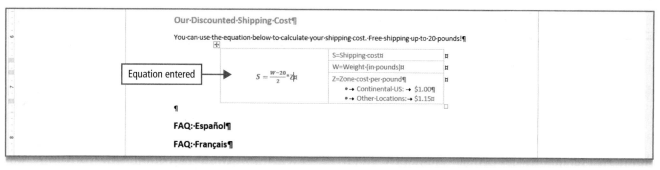

Figure 5.42

> **4** Select the entire equation, and then on the **Home tab**, change the **Font Size** to **14**. **Save** 💾 your document.

Objective 8   Use Advanced Find and Replace Options

From the Find and Replace dialog box, you can locate occurrences of words that sound the same although spelled differently, find phrases that are capitalized in exactly the same way, and find different forms of a word—such as *work*, *worked*, and *working*.

Activity 5.22 │ Using Find and Replace to Change Text Formatting

GO! Learn How
Video W5-8

2.1.1,
Expert 2.1.2

You can change the formatting of a word or phrase that is repeated throughout a document by using the Find and Replace dialog box. In this Activity, you will change the formatting of the company name that appears numerous times in the FAQ list.

> **1** Press Ctrl + Home to move to the top of the document. On the **Home tab**, in the **Editing group**, click **Replace** to display the **Find and Replace** dialog box.

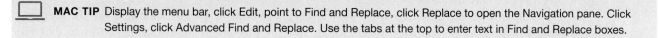

MAC TIP Display the menu bar, click Edit, point to Find and Replace, click Replace to open the Navigation pane. Click Settings, click Advanced Find and Replace. Use the tabs at the top to enter text in Find and Replace boxes.

> **2** In the **Find what** box, type **Chesterfield Creations** and then in the **Replace with** box, type the exact same text **Chesterfield Creations**

> **3** Below the **Replace with** box, click **More** to expand this dialog box.

The More button exposes advanced settings with which you can refine this command. At the bottom of the expanded dialog box, the Format button provides additional options for text, paragraph, tab, and style formats. The Special button provides options for location or replacing special characters.

> **4** Near the bottom of the **Find and Replace** dialog box, under **Replace**, click **Format**, and then on the list, click **Font**.

5 In the **Replace Font** dialog box, under **Font style**, click **Bold Italic**. Click the **Font color arrow**, and then in the last column, click the fifth color. Compare your screen with Figure 5.43.

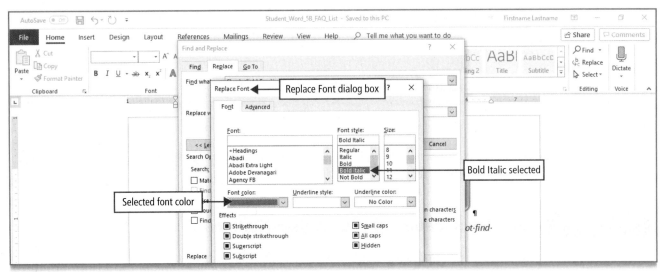

Figure 5.43

6 Click **OK** to close the **Replace Font** dialog box, and then in the middle of the **Find and Replace** dialog box, click **Replace All**. When a Microsoft Word message displays indicating that you have made *4* replacements, click **OK**. Leave the expanded dialog box displayed.

This action finds each instance of the text *Chesterfield Creations*, and then replaces the font format with bold italic in the green color that you selected.

Activity 5.23 | Using Wildcards to Find and Replace Text

Expert 2.1.1

Use a *wildcard* in the Find and Replace dialog box when you are not certain of the exact term you want to find. A wildcard is a special character such as * or ? that you insert with a *Find what* term. For example, searching a document for the term b*k could find *blink*, *book*, *brick*, or any other word in the document that begins with b and ends with k.

Using a wildcard can save time when you do not know the specific characters in the search term. In this Activity, you will use a wildcard to search for email and webpage addresses that may be spelled incorrectly.

1 In the **Find and Replace** dialog box, in the **Find what** box, delete the existing text, and then type **Sc*z**

2 Press `Tab` to move to and select the text in the **Replace with** box. Type **Scholtz** and then at the bottom of the **Find and Replace** dialog box, click **No Formatting** to remove the formatting settings from the previous Activity.

3 Under **Search Options**, select the **Use wildcards** check box. Compare your screen with Figure 5.44.

The name *Scholtz* may have been spelled incorrectly. By using the Find command to locate each instance that begins with *S* and ends with *z*, you can find, and then verify, the correct spelling of this name in every instance.

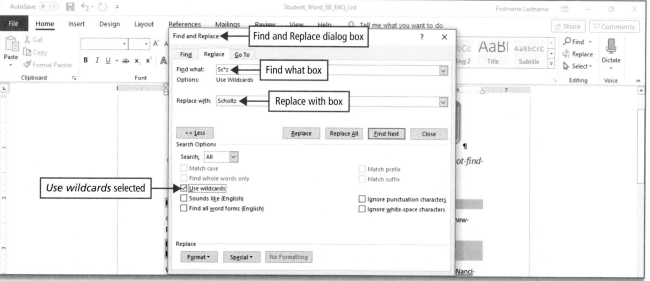

Figure 5.44

4 In the **Find and Replace** dialog box, click **Less** so that the dialog box is smaller, and then drag the title bar of the **Find and Replace** dialog box to the upper left corner of your screen so that it is not blocking your view of the document. Click **Find Next**. Notice that the first instance of the text *Scholtz* is selected in the document.

This instance is spelled correctly—no changes are required.

5 In the **Find and Replace** dialog box, click **Find Next** again, and notice that in this occurrence the name is not spelled correctly.

6 Click **Replace**, and then compare your screen with Figure 5.45.

The misspelling is corrected, and Word selects the next occurrence of text that begins with *Sc* and ends with *z*.

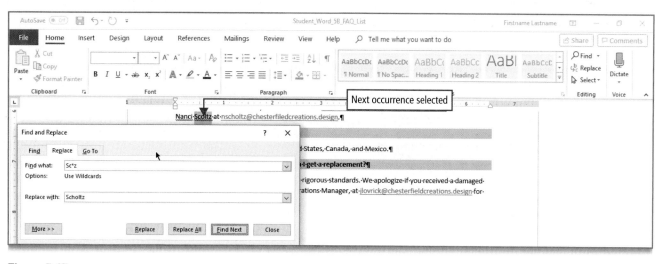

Figure 5.45

7 ▶ The selected text *Scoltz* is incorrect; click **Replace** to correct the error and move to the next occurrence.

8 ▶ The selected text *Scholtz* is spelled correctly. Click **Find Next** to move to the next occurrence.

A Microsoft Word message box indicates that you have searched the entire document.

9 ▶ In the message box, click **OK**.

10 In the **Find and Replace** dialog box, click **More**, clear the **Use wildcards** check box, and then click **Less** to restore the dialog box to its default settings. **Close** ☒ the **Find and Replace** dialog box, and then **Save** ▤ the document.

Activity 5.24 | Using Editor to Check a Document

1 ▶ Press ⌃ + ⌂. On the **Review tab**, in the **Proofing group**, click **Check Document** (yours may indicate Spelling & Grammar). If necessary, click the **Review All Results** button at the top of the pane. Compare your screen with Figure 5.46.

The Editor pane displays on the right, indicating the first suggested error—Nanci. It is good practice to position the insertion point at the beginning of the document when checking the entire document for errors in spelling, grammar, and writing style.

🖥 **MAC TIP** A Spelling and Grammar dialog box may display.

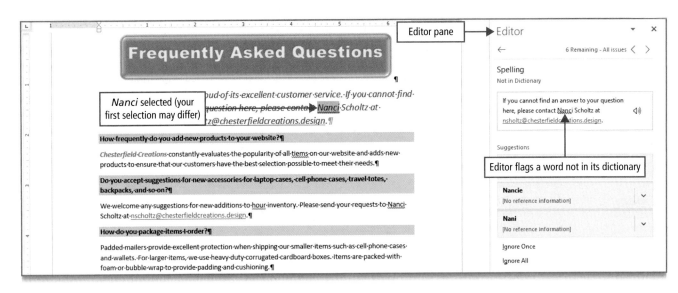

Figure 5.46

ALERT   Selections May Differ

Flagged errors depend on the Proofing settings in the Word Options dialog box or on the actions of others who might have used the computer at which you are working. Not all of the potential errors listed in this Activity may appear in your check using the Editor. Your document may also display errors not indicated here. If you encounter flagged words or phrases that are not included here, take appropriate action.

2 If *Nanci* is indicated as a spelling error, in the **Editor** pane, click **Ignore All**.

All occurrences of *Nanci* are ignored.

3 If *Scholtz* is indicated as a spelling error, click **Ignore All**.

All occurrences of *Scholtz* are ignored.

4 Correct *tiems* to **items**.

5 If the email address *nscholtz@chesterfieldcreations.design* is flagged, click **Ignore All**.

6 For the word choice error *hour*, in the **Editor** pane, click *our*.

In this instance, Word identified *hour* as a word that is spelled correctly but used in the wrong context.

7 If necessary, click **Ignore All** to ignore the proper names *Josette* and *Lovrick* and the email address *jlovrick@chesterfieldcreations.design*.

8 Continue, and if necessary, click **Ignore** for the foreign words.

A Microsoft Word message box indicates that the spelling and grammar check is complete.

9 Click **OK** to close the message box **Close** ⊠ the **Editor** pane. Press Ctrl + Home.

10 Click the **File tab**, if necessary, on the left click **Info**, and then click **Show All Properties**. In the **Tags** box, type **faq list** In the **Subject** box, type your course name and section number. If necessary, edit the author name to display your name.

MAC TIP Display the menu bar, click File, click Properties, click the Summary tab.

---

11 On the left, click **Save** to save your document and return to the Word window.

12 In the upper right corner of the Word window, click **Close** ⊠.

For Non-MyLab Submissions Determine What Your Instructor Requires for Submission
As directed by your instructor, submit your completed Word document.

---

13 In **MyLab IT**, locate and click the Grader Project **Word 5B FAQ List**. In **step 3**, under **Upload Completed Assignment**, click **Choose File**. In the **Open** dialog box, navigate to your **Word Chapter 5 folder**, and then click your **Student_Word_5B_FAQ_List** file one time to select it. In the lower right corner of the **Open** dialog box, click **Open**.

The name of your selected file displays above the Upload button.

14 To submit your file to **MyLab IT** for grading, click **Upload**, wait a moment for a green **Success!** message, and then in **step 4**, click the blue **Submit for Grading** button. Click **Close Assignment** to return to your list of **Course Materials**.

You have completed Project 5B **END**

»» GO! To Work

Microsoft Office Specialist (MOS) Skills in This Chapter

Project 5A		Project 5B	
3.1.1	Convert text to tables	1.1.1	Search for text
3.2.1	Sort table data	2.1.1	Find and replace text
3.2.3	Merge and split cells	2.1.2	Insert symbols and special characters
3.2.4	Resize tables, rows, and columns	2.1.1	**Expert:** Find and replace text by using wildcards and special characters
3.2.5	Split tables	2.1.2	**Expert:** Find and replace formatting and styles
1.1.2	**Expert:** Manage document versions		
2.3.3	**Expert:** Copy styles to other documents and templates		
3.4.2	**Expert:** Configure caption properties		
3.4.1	**Expert:** Insert figure and table captions		
4.1.1	**Expert:** Add custom fields		

Build Your E-Portfolio

An E-Portfolio is a collection of evidence, stored electronically, that showcases what you have accomplished while completing your education. Collecting and then sharing your work products with potential employers reflects your academic and career goals. Your completed documents from the following projects are good examples to show what you have learned: 5G, 5K, and 5L.

GO! For Job Success

Discussion: 3D Printing

Your instructor may assign this discussion to your class, and then ask you to think about, or discuss with your classmates, these quesions:

3D printing is a manufacturing process where three-dimensional objects are created from a digital file. You are familiar with laser printers that read digital files, like a Word document, and place ink on paper. 3D "printers" are machines that lay down layers of materials based on instructions from a digital file. The result is an object, like a part for an automobile, instead of a document.

g-stockstudio/ Shutterstock

> What are some industries that could benefit from trying out completely new products by using a 3D printer without having to build new manufacturing plants?

> What are some medical devices that could be improved by being made specifically for you or a friend or family member by using a 3D printer?

> If a 3D printer could be sent into space and receive instructions from earth, what are some objects it could create that would help scientists understand space objects?

End of Chapter

Summary

Creating and applying a table style standardizes the appearance of multiple tables in a document. The style can include formatting for the entire table and for specific elements—such as rows and columns.

Word has advanced tools that enable you to present table data efficiently and attractively—such as changing alignment within cells, merging and splitting cells, sorting data, and changing text direction.

Use the Manage Document Versions feature to locate and examine an older version of your current document that was automatically saved. View the list on the Info tab in Backstage view.

The Word Translate feature enables you to translate either a selection of text or create a translated copy of your document. This feature is also available in PowerPoint, OneNote, and Excel.

GO! Learn It Online

Review the concepts, key terms, and MOS skills in this chapter by completing these online challenges, which you can find at **MyLab IT**.

Chapter Quiz: Answer matching and multiple choice questions to test what you learned in this chapter.

Lessons on the GO!: Learn how to use all the new apps and features as they are introduced by Microsoft.

MOS Prep Quiz: Answer questions to review the MOS skills that you practiced in this chapter.

Your instructor will assign Projects from this list to ensure your learning and assess your knowledge.

		Project Guide for Word Chapter 5		
Project	**Apply Skills from These Chapter Objectives**	**Project Type**		**Project Location**
5A MyLab IT	Objectives 1–4 from Project 5A	**5A Instructional Project (Grader Project)** Guided instruction to learn the skills in Project 5A.	Instruction	In **MyLab IT** and in text
5B MyLab IT	Objectives 5–8 from Project 5B	**5B Instructional Project (Grader Project)** Guided instruction to learn the skills in Project 5B.	Instruction	In **MyLab IT** and in text
5C	Objectives 1–4 from Project 5A	**5C Skills Review (Scorecard Grading)** A guided review of the skills from Project 5A.	Review	In text
5D	Objectives 5–8 from Project 5B	**5D Skills Review (Scorecard Grading)** A guided review of the skills from Project 5B.	Review	In text
5E MyLab IT	Objectives 1–4 from Project 5A	**5E Mastery (Grader Project)** A demonstration of your mastery of the skills in Project 5A with extensive decision-making.	Mastery and Transfer of Learning	In **MyLab IT** and in text
5F MyLab IT	Objectives 5–8 from Project 5B	**5F Mastery (Grader Project)** A demonstration of your mastery of the skills in Project 5B with extensive decision-making.	Mastery and Transfer of Learning	In **MyLab IT** and in text
5G MyLab IT	Objectives 1–8 from Projects 5A and 5B	**5G Mastery (Grader Project)** A demonstration of your mastery of the skills in Projects 5A and 5B with extensive decision-making.	Mastery and Transfer of Learning	In **MyLab IT** and in text
5H	Combination of Objectives from Projects 5A and 5B	**5H GO! Fix It (Scorecard Grading)** A demonstration of your mastery of the skills in Projects 5A and 5B by creating a correct result from a document that contains errors you must find.	Critical Thinking	IRC
5I	Combination of Objectives from Projects 5A and 5B	**5I GO! Make It (Scorecard Grading)** A demonstration of your mastery of the skills in Projects 5A and 5B by creating a result from a supplied picture.	Critical Thinking	IRC
5J	Combination of Objectives from Projects 5A and 5B	**5J GO! Solve It (Rubric Grading)** A demonstration of your mastery of the skills in Projects 5A and 5B, your decision-making skills, and your critical thinking skills. A task-specific rubric helps you self-assess your result.	Critical Thinking	IRC
5K	Combination of Objectives from Projects 5A and 5B	**5K GO! Solve It (Rubric Grading)** A demonstration of your mastery of the skills in Projects 5A and 5B, your decision-making skills, and your critical thinking skills. A task-specific rubric helps you self-assess your result.	Critical Thinking	In text
5L	Combination of Objectives from Projects 5A and 5B	**5L GO! Think (Rubric Grading)** A demonstration of your understanding of the Chapter concepts applied in a manner that you would outside of college. An analytic rubric helps you and your instructor grade the quality of your work by comparing it to the work an expert in the discipline would create.	Critical Thinking	In text
5M	Combination of Objectives from Projects 5A and 5B	**5M GO! Think (Rubric Grading)** A demonstration of your understanding of the Chapter concepts applied in a manner that you would outside of college. An analytic rubric helps you and your instructor grade the quality of your work by comparing it to the work an expert in the discipline would create.	Critical Thinking	IRC
5N	Combination of Objectives from Projects 5A and 5B	**5N You and GO! (Rubric Grading)** A demonstration of your understanding of the Chapter concepts applied in a manner that you would in a personal situation. An analytic rubric helps you and your instructor grade the quality of your work.	Critical Thinking	IRC

Glossary

Glossary of Chapter Key Terms

Ascending The order of text sorted alphabetically from A to Z or numbers sorted from the smallest to the largest.

AutoFit A table feature that automatically adjusts column widths or the width of the entire table.

AutoFit Contents A table feature that resizes the column widths to accommodate the maximum field size.

AutoRecover A feature that helps prevent losing unsaved changes by automatically creating a backup version of the current document.

Caption A label that is added to a Word object and numbered sequentially.

Descending The order of text sorted alphabetically from Z to A or numbers sorted from the largest to the smallest.

Federal registration symbol The symbol ® that indicates that a patent or trademark is registered with the United States Patent and Trademark Office.

Field A placeholder for data.

Formula A mathematical expression that contains functions, operators, constants, and properties, and returns a value to a cell.

Function A predefined formula that performs calculations by using specific values in a particular order.

Header row The first row of a table containing column titles.

Merge A table feature that combines two or more adjacent cells into one cell so that the text spans multiple columns or rows.

Multiple Pages A zoom setting that decreases the magnification to display several pages of a document.

Organizer A dialog box where you can modify a document by using styles stored in another document or template.

Sorting The action of ordering data, usually in alphabetical or numeric order.

Split A table feature that divides selected cells into multiple cells with a specified number of rows and columns.

Split Table A table feature that divides an existing table into two tables in which the selected row—where the insertion point is located—becomes the first row of the second table.

Style A group of formatting commands—such as font, font size, and font color—that can be applied with a single command.

Table style A style that includes formatting for the entire table and specific table elements, such as rows and columns.

Variable In an equation, a letter that represents a value.

Wildcard A special character such as * or ? that is used to search for an unknown term.

Chapter Review

Skills Review	Project 5C Sales Conference

Apply 5A skills from these Objectives:

1. Create and Apply a Custom Table Style
2. Format Cells in a Word Table
3. Use Advanced Table Features
4. Modify Table Properties

In the following Skills Review, you will format tables and insert formulas to create a memo regarding a conference for sales managers at Chesterfield Creations. Your completed document will look similar to Figure 5.47.

Project Files

For Project 5C, you will need the following files:

w05C_Sales_Conference

w05C_Sales_Styles

You will save your file as:

Lastname_Firstname_5C_Sales_Conference

Project Results

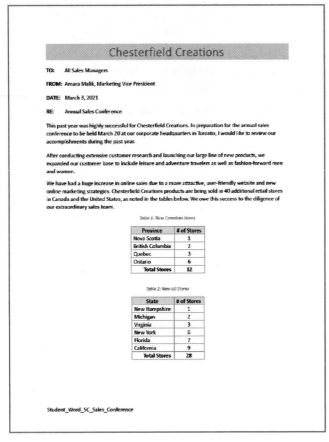

Figure 5.47

(continues on next page)

Chapter Review

Skills Review: Project 5C Sales Conference (continued)

1 **Start** Word. From the files downloaded for this chapter, open the file **w05C_Sales_Conference**. Save the document in your **Word Chapter 5** folder, using your own name, as **Lastname_Firstname_5C_Sales_Conference** Insert the file name in the footer. Display the rulers and formatting marks. If any words are flagged as spelling errors, **Ignore All**.

a. On the **Home tab**, in the **Styles group**, click the **Dialog Box Launcher** button. If necessary, double-click the title *Styles* to snap the pane to the right side of your screen. (Mac users: On the menu bar, click Tools, click Templates and Add-ins, click Organizer, move to Step d.)

b. At the bottom of the **Styles pane**, click the third button—**Manage Styles**.

c. In the lower left corner of the **Manage Styles** dialog box, click **Import/Export** to display the **Organizer** dialog box.

d. On the left side of the **Organizer** dialog box, be sure the name of your *Lastname_Firstname_5C_Sales_Conference* file displays. On the right side of the **Organizer**, click the **Close File** button. Click the **Open File** button, navigate to the files you downloaded for this chapter, click one time to select the file **w05C_Sales_Styles**, and then click **Open**.

e. On the right side of the **Organizer**, scroll as necessary, select **Heading 2**, press and hold Ctrl, and then select **Title**. In the middle of the **Organizer** dialog box, **Copy**. **Close** the **Organizer**. **Save** your document.

2 Select the first paragraph—*Chesterfield Creations*, and then apply the **Title** style.

a. At the bottom of the **Styles** pane, click the first button—**New Style**. In the **Create New Style from Formatting** dialog box, under **Properties**, in the **Name** box, type **Sales Conference** Click the **Style type arrow**, and then click **Table**. (Mac users: In the Styles group, click the Styles Pane button; click New Style.)

b. Under **Formatting**, click the **Borders button arrow**, and then click **All Borders**. Click the **Line Weight arrow**, and then click **1 pt**. Click the **Border Color arrow**, and then in the sixth column, click the first color.

c. Under **Formatting**, click the **Apply formatting to arrow**, and then click **Header row**. Click the **Fill Color arrow**, and then in the sixth column, click the third color. Click **OK**. **Close** the **Styles** pane.

d. In the sixth row of the table, click in the first cell that contains the text *State*. On the **Table Tools Layout tab**, in the **Merge group**, click **Split Table**.

3 In the first table, click in the first cell. Click the **Table Tools Design tab**. In the **Table Styles group**, click the **More** button, and then click the orange **Sales Conference** table style. In a similar manner, click in the first cell in the second table, and then apply the **Sales Conference** table style.

a. On the **Table Tools Design tab**, in the **Table Styles group**, right-click the **Sales Conference** table style, and then click **Modify Table Style**. Click the **Apply formatting to arrow**, and then click **Header row**. Apply **Bold**, and then click **OK**.

b. In the first table, position the insertion point to the right of *Province*. On the **Table Tools Layout tab**, in the **Merge group**, click **Split Cells**, and then click **OK**. In the first row, click in the second cell, and type **# of Stores**

c. Select the **header row**, and then on the **Table Tools Layout tab**, in the **Alignment group**, click **Align Center**. In the first column, select all cells below the header row, and then click **Align Center Left**. In the second column, select all cells below the header row, and then click **Align Center**.

d. In the second table, position the insertion point to the right of *State*. On the **Table Tools Layout tab**, in the **Merge group**, click **Split Cells**, and then click **OK**. In the first row, click in the second cell, and type **# of Stores**

e. Select the **header row**, and then on the **Table Tools Layout tab**, in the **Alignment group**, click **Align Center**. In the first column, select all cells below the header row, and then click **Align Center Left**. In the second column, select all cells below the header row, and then click **Align Center**.

4 Click anywhere in the first table, and then on the **Table Tools Layout tab**, in the **Data group**, click **Sort**. Click the **Sort by arrow**, click **# of Stores**, and then click **OK**. Click anywhere in the second table, and then in the **Data group**, click **Sort**. In the **Sort** dialog box, click the **Sort by arrow**, click **# of Stores**, and then click **OK**.

(continues on next page)

Chapter Review

5 Near the bottom of **Page 1**, select the paragraph *Conference Information,* and then apply the **Heading 2** style.

a. On **Page 2**, locate the paragraph that begins *Topic,* and then beginning with this paragraph, select the six paragraphs at the end of the document.

b. On the **Insert tab**, in the **Tables group**, click **Table**, and then click **Convert Text to Table**. Click **OK** to close the dialog box.

6 Click to position your insertion point anywhere in the table you inserted. On the **Table Tools Design tab**, in the **Table Styles group**, click the **Sales Conference** table style.

a. On the **Table Tools Layout tab**, in the **Cell Size group**, click **AutoFit**, and then click **AutoFit Contents**.

b. Select the **header row**, and then in the **Alignment group**, click **Align Center**. Select the remaining cells in the table, and then click **Align Center Left**.

7 On **Page 1**, in the first table, in the last row, click to position the insertion point in the first cell—the cell containing *Ontario*. On the **Table Tools Layout tab**, in the **Cell Size group**, click **AutoFit**, and then click **AutoFit Contents**. Point to the bottom left corner of the table, and then click the **One-Click Row/Column Insertion** button. (Mac users: Use ribbon commands to insert a new row.)

a. In the new last row of the table, click in the first cell, and then type **Total Stores** Select the text, and apply **Bold**. In the **Alignment group**, click **Align Center Right**. Press [Tab], and then in the **Data group**, click **Formula**.

b. In the **Formula** dialog box, with *=SUM(ABOVE)* displayed, click the **Number format arrow**, and then click **0**. Click **OK**. Select the inserted formula result and apply **Bold**.

8 In the second table, in the last row, click to position the insertion point in the first cell—the cell containing the text *California*. On the **Table Tools Layout tab**, in the **Cell Size group**, click **AutoFit**, and then click **AutoFit Contents**. Point to the bottom left corner of the table, and then click the **One-Click Row/Column Insertion** button.

a. In the new last row, click in the first cell, and then type **Total Stores** Select the text, and apply **Bold**. In the **Alignment group**, click **Align Center Right**. Press [Tab], and then in the **Data group**, click **Formula**.

b. In the **Formula** dialog box, with *=SUM(ABOVE)* displayed, click the **Number format arrow**, and then click **0**. Click **OK**. Select the inserted formula result, and apply **Bold**.

c. In the first table, in the second column, click in the fifth cell. Select *5*, and then type **6** In the last cell of the table, select *11*, right-click the selection, and then click **Update Field**.

d. In the second table, in the second column, click in the sixth cell. Select *8*, and then type **7** In the last cell of the table, select *29*, right-click the selection, and then click **Update Field**.

9 Click to position the insertion point anywhere in the first table. On the **References tab**, in the **Captions group**, click **Insert Caption**. In the **Caption** dialog box, with the insertion point to the right of *Table 1*, type a colon **:** and press [Spacebar]. Type **New Canadian Stores** If necessary, under **Options**, click the **Position arrow**, and then click **Above selected item**. Click **OK**.

a. Click to position the insertion point anywhere in the second table. In the **Captions group**, click **Insert Caption**. In the **Caption** dialog box, with the insertion point to the right of *Table 2*, type a colon **:** and then press [Spacebar]. Type **New US Stores** If necessary, under **Options**, click the **Position arrow**, and then click **Above selected item**. Click **OK**.

b. On **Page 2**, click to position the insertion point anywhere in the last table. On the **Table Tools Layout tab**, in the **Table group**, click **Properties**. In the **Table Properties** dialog box, if necessary, under **Text wrapping**, click **Around**, and then click **Positioning**.

c. In the **Table Positioning** dialog box, under **Distance from surrounding text**, click the **Left up spin arrow** as necessary to set the measurement to **0.5"**. Click **OK** two times to close the dialog boxes. Point to the **Table Move Handle**, and then drag the table up and to the right until the top border is even with the first line of the last paragraph and the right border is aligned with the right margin. Refer to Figure 5.47.

d. Click anywhere in the table. On the **References tab**, in the **Captions group**, click **Insert Caption**. In the **Caption** dialog box, with *Table 3* displayed, click **OK**. Select the caption, and then on the **Home tab**, in the **Paragraph group**, click **Align Right**. In the last paragraph of the document, select the text *Listed below are*, and then to replace the selected text, type **Table 3 lists**

(continues on next page)

Chapter Review

10 On **Page 1**, click to position the insertion point anywhere in the first table. On the **Table Tools Layout tab**, in the **Table group**, click **Properties**. In the **Table Properties** dialog box, under **Alignment**, click **Center**, and then click **OK**. Click to position the insertion point anywhere in the second table. In the **Table group**, click **Properties**. In the **Table Properties** dialog box, under **Alignment**, click **Center**, and then click **OK**. Select the captions for *Table 1* and *Table 2*, and then press Ctrl + E to center the captions over the tables.

11 Press Ctrl + Home. Click the **File tab**, and then click **Show All Properties**. As the **Tags**, type **sales conference** In the **Subject** box, type your course name and section number. If necessary, edit the author name to display your name.

12 On the left, click **Save** to save your document and return to the Word window. In the upper right corner of the Word window, click **Close**. Submit your file as directed by your instructor.

You have completed Project 5C | END

Skills Review | **Project 5D Outdoor Accessories**

Apply 5B skills from these Objectives:

5. Manage Document Versions
6. Collect and Paste Images and Text
7. Translate Text and Insert Equations
8. Use Advanced Find and Replace Options

In the following Skills Review, you will create a document for Aarushi Mehta, Design Director at Chesterfield Creations, which details new outdoor accessories sold by the company. Your completed document will look similar to Figure 5.48.

Project Files

For Project 5D, you will need the following files:

w05D_Outdoor_Accessories

w05D_Product_Images

w05D_Product_Info

You will save your file as:

Lastname_Firstname_5D_Outdoor Accessories

Project Results

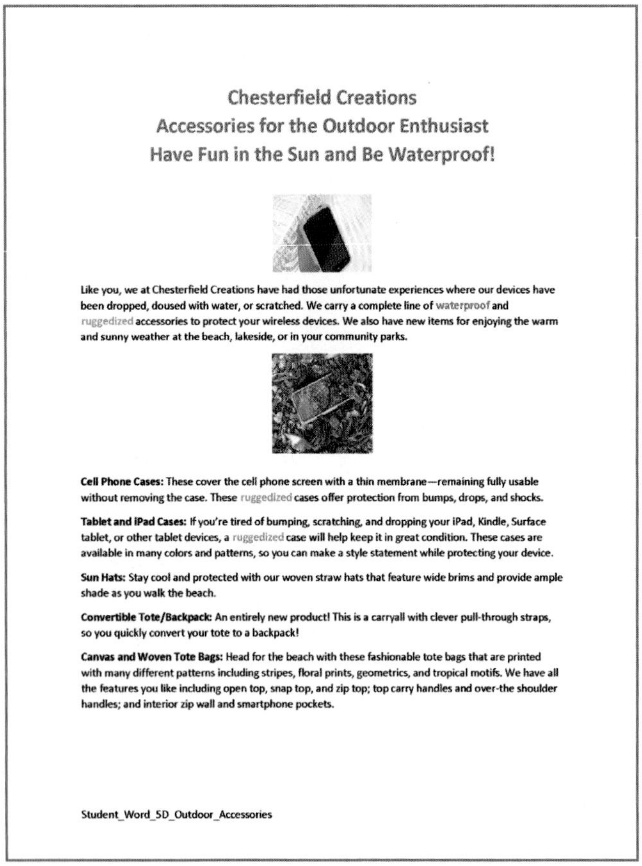

Chesterfield Creations
Accessories for the Outdoor Enthusiast
Have Fun in the Sun and Be Waterproof!

Like you, we at Chesterfield Creations have had those unfortunate experiences where our devices have been dropped, doused with water, or scratched. We carry a complete line of waterproof and ruggedized accessories to protect your wireless devices. We also have new items for enjoying the warm and sunny weather at the beach, lakeside, or in your community parks.

Cell Phone Cases: These cover the cell phone screen with a thin membrane—remaining fully usable without removing the case. These ruggedized cases offer protection from bumps, drops, and shocks.

Tablet and iPad Cases: If you're tired of bumping, scratching, and dropping your iPad, Kindle, Surface tablet, or other tablet devices, a ruggedized case will help keep it in great condition. These cases are available in many colors and patterns, so you can make a style statement while protecting your device.

Sun Hats: Stay cool and protected with our woven straw hats that feature wide brims and provide ample shade as you walk the beach.

Convertible Tote/Backpack: An entirely new product! This is a carryall with clever pull-through straps, so you quickly convert your tote to a backpack!

Canvas and Woven Tote Bags: Head for the beach with these fashionable tote bags that are printed with many different patterns including stripes, floral prints, geometrics, and tropical motifs. We have all the features you like including open top, snap top, and zip top; top carry handles and over-the-shoulder handles; and interior zip wall and smartphone pockets.

Student_Word_5D_Outdoor_Accessories

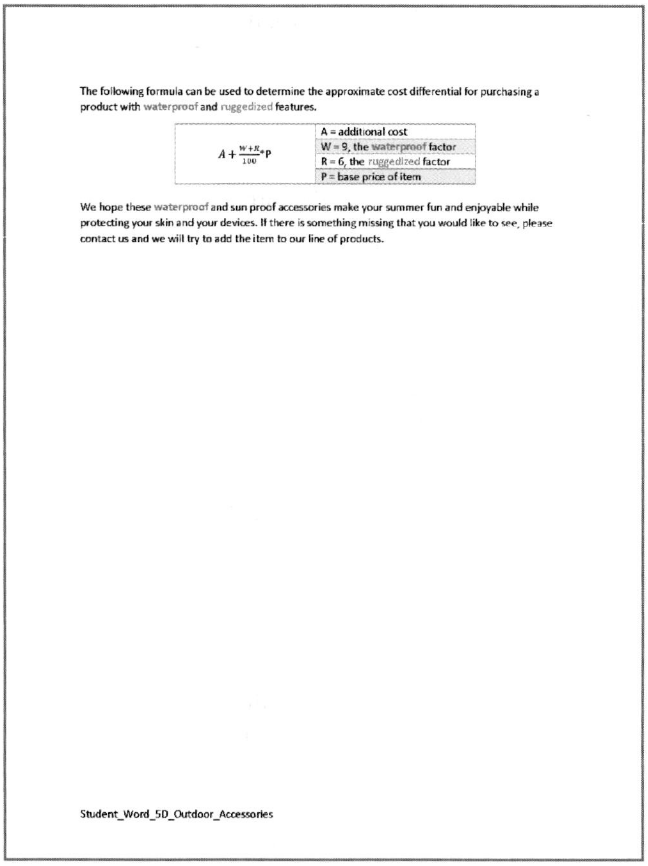

The following formula can be used to determine the approximate cost differential for purchasing a product with waterproof and ruggedized features.

$$A + \frac{W+R}{100} \cdot P$$

A = additional cost	
W = 9, the waterproof factor	
R = 6, the ruggedized factor	
P = base price of item	

We hope these waterproof and sun proof accessories make your summer fun and enjoyable while protecting your skin and your devices. If there is something missing that you would like to see, please contact us and we will try to add the item to our line of products.

Student_Word_5D_Outdoor_Accessories

Figure 5.48

(continues on next page)

Chapter Review

1 From the files you downloaded for this project, open the file **w05D_Outdoor_Accessories**. Click the **File tab**, click **Save As**, click **Browse**, navigate to your **Word Chapter 5** folder, and then using your own name, save the document as **Lastname_Firstname_5D_Outdoor_Accessories**

a. Right-click in the footer area, and then click **Edit Footer**. On the ribbon, on the **Header & Footer Tools Design tab**, in the **Insert group**, click **Document Info**, and then click **File Name**. **Close** the footer area.

b. Click the **View tab**. In the **Zoom group**, click **Zoom**. In the **Zoom** dialog box, under **Zoom to**, click **200%**, and then click **OK**. In the first row of the table, click to position the insertion point to the left of *cost*, and then press (Backspace) to remove the extra space. On the **View tab**, in the **Zoom group**, click **100%**.

c. Select the first three paragraphs. Change the **Font Size** to **20**, apply **Bold**, click the **Font Color arrow**, and then in the sixth column, click the fifth color. Press (Ctrl) + (E) to center the three paragraphs.

d. Click the **Home tab**, and then in the **Clipboard group**, click the **Dialog Box Launcher** to display the **Clipboard** pane. If necessary, at the top of the pane, click **Clear All** to delete any items on the Clipboard. (Mac users: The Mac clipboard holds only one item. To complete, navigate to the files downloaded with this project, open w05D_Product_Images, open w05D_Product_Info, on the File tab, point to Open Recent, select your Lastname_Firstname_5D_Outdoor_Accessories file; move to Step 2. Using the instructions in 2a-c, copy and paste images navigating to the file you need by using Open Recent.)

e. From the files downloaded with this project, open **w05D_Product_Images**. Point to the first graphic—a cell phone in water—right-click, and then click **Copy**. Using the same technique, **Copy** the second graphic—a cell phone on the ground. **Close** the **w05D_Product_Images** file.

f. From the files downloaded with this project, open **w05D_Product_Info**. Press (Ctrl) + (A) to select all of the text, right-click the selected text, click **Copy**, and then **Close** the **w05D_Product_Info** file.

2 Above the paragraph that begins *Like you*, position the insertion point in the blank paragraph. In the **Clipboard** pane, click the **phone in water** graphic, and then press (Ctrl) + (E).

a. Click to position the insertion point at the end of the paragraph that begins *Like you*, and then press (Enter) one time. In the **Clipboard** pane, click the **phone on the ground** graphic, and then press (Ctrl) + (E).

b. Click to position the insertion point to the left of the paragraph that begins *The following formula*. In the **Clipboard** pane, click the text entry that begins *Cell Phone Cases* to paste the entire block of text at the insertion point. In the **Clipboard** pane, click **Clear All**, and then **Close** the **Clipboard** pane.

c. In the paragraph that begins *Cell Phone Cases*, click to position the insertion point to the right of the word *membrane*. Click the **Insert tab**. In the **Symbols group**, click **Symbol**, and then click **More Symbols**. In the **Symbol** dialog box, click the **Special Characters tab**, and then click the first character—**Em Dash**. Click **Insert**, and then **Close** the **Symbol** dialog box. Type **remaining** and then **Save** your document.

3 Near the bottom of **Page 1**, click to the left of the paragraph that begins *The following formula*, and then press (Ctrl) + (Enter)

a. On **Page 2**, click in the left cell of the table, and then on the **Insert tab**, in the **Symbols group**, click **Equation**. In the inserted equation placeholder, type **A=** Under **Equation Tools**, on the **Design tab**, in the **Structures group**, click **Fraction**, and then click the first format—**Stacked Fraction**.

b. In the fraction, click in the top placeholder, and then type **W+R** Click in the bottom placeholder, and then type **100** Click to position the insertion point to the right of the fraction and to the left of the end-of-cell marker, and then type ***P** **Save** your document.

(continues on next page)

Chapter Review

4 Press Ctrl + Home. Click the **Home tab**, and then in the **Editing group**, click **Replace**. In the **Find and Replace** dialog box, in the **Find what** box, type **waterproof** and then in the **Replace with** box, type the same text **waterproof**

a. Below the **Replace with** box, click **More**. Under **Search Options**, select the **Match case** check box. At the bottom, under **Replace**, click **Format**, and then on the list, click **Font**.

b. In the **Replace Font** dialog box, under **Font style**, click **Bold**. Click the **Font color arrow**, and then in the next to last column, click the first color.

c. Click **OK** to close the **Find Font** dialog box, and then in the **Find and Replace** dialog box, click **Replace All**. When a **Microsoft Word** message box displays indicating that you have made 4 replacements, click **OK**. Close the **Find** and **Replace** dialog box.

d. **Press** Ctrl + Home, and then redisplay the **Find and Replace** dialog box. Using the same technique, replace all instances of *ruggedized* and select **Match case**. Be sure to clear the formatting for the **Find what** box. For the replaced text, change the **Font style** to **Bold**. Display the **Font Color** gallery, and then in the sixth column, click the first color. When a **Microsoft Word** message box displays indicating that you have made 5 replacements, click **OK**.

e. In the **Find and Replace** dialog box, **Delete** the text in the **Find what** box, and then clear the **Match case** check box. **Delete** the text in the **Replace with** box, click **No Formatting**, and then click **Less**. **Close** the **Find and Replace** dialog box.

5 Press Ctrl + Home. Click the **Review tab**, and then in the **Proofing group**, check your document for spelling and grammar.

a. If necessary, click the Results. For any grammar errors, select the suggestion. Click **Ignore Once** for any other errors. When a message indicates that the spelling and grammar check is complete, click **OK** to close the dialog box. **Close** the pane on the right.

b. Click the **File tab**, and then click the **Info tab**, click **Show All Properties**. In the **Tags** box, type **waterproof, ruggedized** In the **Subject** box, type your course name and section number. If necessary, edit the author name to display your name. On the left, click **Save**. **Close** Word, and then submit your **Word_5D_Outdoor_Accessories** file to your instructor as directed.

You have completed Project 5D **END**

Mastering Word   Project 5E Travel Bags

Apply **5A** skills from these Objectives:

1. Create and Apply a Custom Table Style
2. Format Cells in a Word Table
3. Use Advanced Table Features
4. Modify Table Properties

In the following Mastering Word project, you will create a memo to all Chesterfield Creations sales managers announcing the Flair Collection of travel bags. Your completed document will look similar to Figure 5.49.

Project Files for MyLab IT Grader

1. In your **MyLab IT** course, locate and click **Word 5E Travel Bags**, Download Materials, and then Download All Files.
2. Extract the zipped folder to your Word Chapter 5 folder. Close the Grader download screens.
3. Take a moment to open the downloaded **Word_5E_Travel_Bags_Instructions** document; note any recent updates to the book.

Project Results

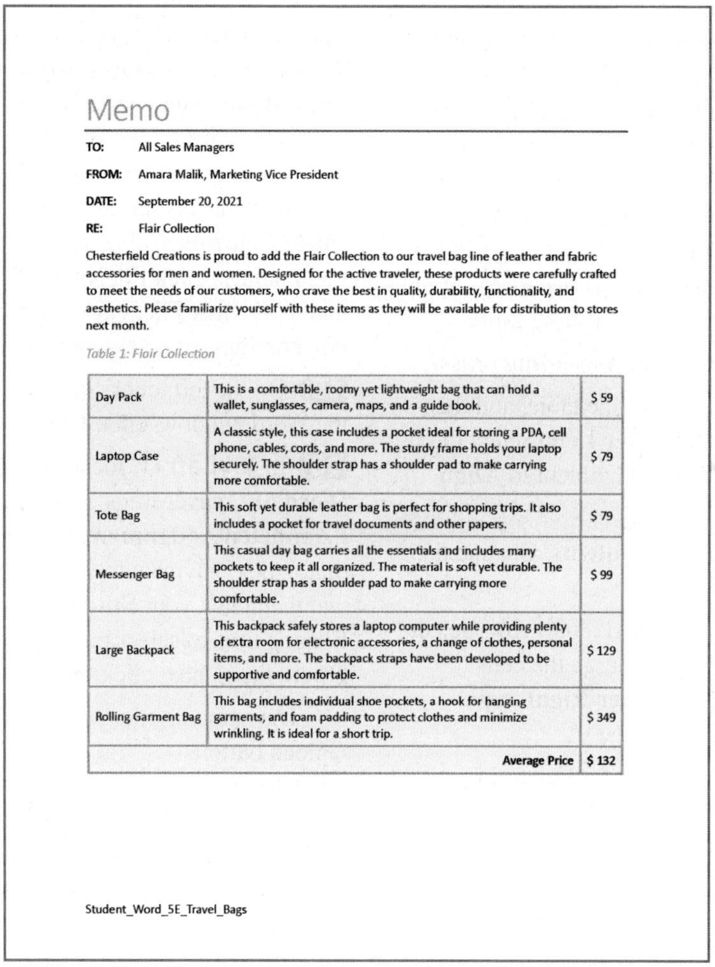

Memo

TO:	All Sales Managers
FROM:	Amara Malik, Marketing Vice President
DATE:	September 20, 2021
RE:	Flair Collection

Chesterfield Creations is proud to add the Flair Collection to our travel bag line of leather and fabric accessories for men and women. Designed for the active traveler, these products were carefully crafted to meet the needs of our customers, who crave the best in quality, durability, functionality, and aesthetics. Please familiarize yourself with these items as they will be available for distribution to stores next month.

Table 1: Flair Collection

Day Pack	This is a comfortable, roomy yet lightweight bag that can hold a wallet, sunglasses, camera, maps, and a guide book.	$ 59
Laptop Case	A classic style, this case includes a pocket ideal for storing a PDA, cell phone, cables, cords, and more. The sturdy frame holds your laptop securely. The shoulder strap has a shoulder pad to make carrying more comfortable.	$ 79
Tote Bag	This soft yet durable leather bag is perfect for shopping trips. It also includes a pocket for travel documents and other papers.	$ 79
Messenger Bag	This casual day bag carries all the essentials and includes many pockets to keep it all organized. The material is soft yet durable. The shoulder strap has a shoulder pad to make carrying more comfortable.	$ 99
Large Backpack	This backpack safely stores a laptop computer while providing plenty of extra room for electronic accessories, a change of clothes, personal items, and more. The backpack straps have been developed to be supportive and comfortable.	$ 129
Rolling Garment Bag	This bag includes individual shoe pockets, a hook for hanging garments, and foam padding to protect clothes and minimize wrinkling. It is ideal for a short trip.	$ 349
	Average Price	$ 132

Student_Word_5E_Travel_Bags

Figure 5.49

(continues on next page)

For Non-MyLab Submissions

For Project 5E, you will need:
w05E_Travel_Bags

In your Word Chapter 5 folder, save your document as:
Lastname_Firstname_5E_Travel_Bags

After you have named and saved your document, on the next page, begin with Step 2.
After Step 15, save and submit your file as directed by your instructor.

Mastering Word: Project 5E Travel Bags (continued)

1 Navigate to your **Word Chapter 5 folder**, and then double-click the Word file you downloaded from **MyLab IT** that displays your name—**Student_Word_5E_Travel_Bags**. If necessary, at the top, click **Enable Editing**.

2 Select the first paragraph—*Memo*—and then apply the **Title** style.

3 Select the paragraph that begins *Rolling Garment Bag* and the remaining five paragraphs in the document. Convert the selected text to a table with 3 columns and 6 rows.

4 Display the **Styles** pane, and then at the bottom, click **New Style** to display the **Create New Style from Formatting** dialog box. (Mac users: On the Home tab, click the Styles Pane.).

5 Name the style **Flair Collection** Set the **Style type** to **Table**. Set the borders to **All Borders** and change the **Line Weight** to **1 ½pt**. Display the **Border Color** gallery, and then in the eighth column, click the next to last color. Display the **Fill Color** gallery, and then in the eighth column, click the second color. If necessary, apply the **Flair Collection** table style to the **Whole table**

6 Sort the table by **Column 3** in **Ascending** order.

7 Select the first two columns of the table, and then change the alignment to **Align Center Left**. Select the third column, and then change the alignment to **Align Center**.

8 Resize the table to **AutoFit Contents**. Change the width of the second column to **4.5"**.

9 At the bottom of the table, insert a new row. Select the first and second cells, and then merge the cells. Change the alignment to **Align Center Right**, type **Average Price** and then apply **Bold**.

10 In the last cell of the table, insert a **Formula**. Change the formula to **=AVERAGE(ABOVE)** Set the **Number format** to **#,##0** and then to the left of the number format, type **$** Click **OK**. Select the displayed value and apply **Bold**. (Mac users: Delete the second format that displays in the box.)

11 Display the **Table Properties** dialog box, and then change the table alignment to **Center**.

12 Display the **Caption** dialog box, and then modify the text as necessary to display the caption above the table as *Table 1:* **Flair Collection** In the document, select the caption, change the **Font Size** to **12**. Display the **Font Color** gallery, and then in the eighth column, click the next to last color.

13 Click anywhere in the table, and then on the **Table Tools Layout tab**, in the **Alignment group**, set the **Top and Bottom** cell margins to **0.05"**.

14 Insert the **File Name** in the footer. Click the **File tab** to display **Backstage** view, and then in the lower right portion of the screen, click **Show All Properties**. In the **Tags** box type **travel bag announcement** and in the **Subject** box type your course name and section number. In the **Author** box, be sure your name is indicated and edit if necessary. (Mac users: To insert the file name, on the Header & Footer tab, in the Insert group, click Field. Under Categories, click Document Information. Under Field names, click FileName. To show properties, on the menu bar click File, click Properties, click the Summary tab. For Tags, use Keywords.)

15 On the left, click **Save**. In the upper right corner of the Word window, click **Close** ☒.

16 In **MyLab IT**, locate and click the Grader Project **Word 5E Travel Bags**. In **step 3**, under **Upload Completed Assignment**, click **Choose File**. In the **Open** dialog box, navigate to your **Word Chapter 5 folder**, and then click your **Student_Word_5E_Travel_Bags** file one time to select it. In the lower right corner of the **Open** dialog box, click **Open**.

The name of your selected file displays above the Upload button.

17 To submit your file to **MyLab IT** for grading, click **Upload**, wait a moment for a green **Success!** message, and then in **step 4**, click the blue **Submit for Grading** button. Click **Close Assignment** to return to your list of **Course Materials**.

You have completed Project 5E | **END**

| MyLab IT Grader | Mastering Word | Project 5F Sale Flyer |

In the following Mastering Word project, you will create a flyer for Nanci Scholtz, Marketing Vice President, to announce a Fall sales event with discounts on smartphone and tablet accessories. Your completed document will look similar to Figure 5.50.

Apply 5B skills from these Objectives:

5. Manage Document Versions
6. Collect and Paste Images and Text
7. Translate Text and Insert Equations
8. Use Advanced Find and Replace Options

Project Files for MyLab IT Grader

1. In your **MyLab IT** course, locate and click **Word 5F Sale Flyer**, Download Materials, and then Download All Files.
2. Extract the zipped folder to your Word Chapter 5 folder. Close the Grader download screens.
3. Take a moment to open the downloaded **Word_5F_Sale_Flyer_Instructions**; note any recent updates to the book.

Project Results

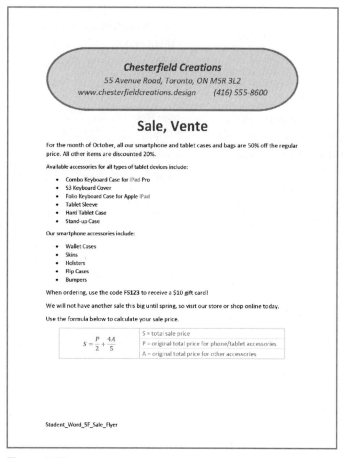

Figure 5.50

For Project 5F, you will need: In your Word Chapter 5 folder, save your document as:

w05F_Sale_Flyer   **Lastname_Firstname_5F_Sale_Flyer**

w05F_Sale_List

After you have named and saved your document, on the next page, begin with Step 2.

After Step 10, save and submit your file as directed by your instructor.

(continues on next page)

1 Navigate to your **Word Chapter 5 folder**, and then double-click the Word file you downloaded from **MyLab IT** that displays your name—**Student_Word_5F_Sale_Flyer**. If necessary, at the top, click **Enable Editing**.

2 Insert the file name in the footer.

3 Using **Zoom** as necessary, in the table cell that contains the text $S = total\ sale\ price$, position the insertion point to the left of the equal sign, and then delete the extra space.

4 Display the **Clipboard** pane, if necessary click **Clear All**, and then save, but do not close, the current document. From the files you downloaded for this project, open the document **w05F_Sale_List**. Click the outer edge of the graphic to select it, and then **Copy** the **Chesterfield Creations** graphic to the Clipboard. Beginning with the text *Available accessories*, select the remaining text in the document, and then **Copy** the selection to the Clipboard. **Close** the **w05F_Sale_List** file. Position the insertion point at the beginning of the document—in the blank paragraph—and then paste the Chesterfield Creations graphic. (Mac users: The Mac clipboard holds only one item. To complete, navigate to the files downloaded with this project, open w05_Sale_List. On the File tab, point to Open Recent, select your Student_5F_Sale_Flyer file. Using the instructions in Steps 4-5, copy and paste the graphic and text as instructed.)

5 Position the insertion point in the blank paragraph following the paragraph that begins *For the month*. **Paste** the text that begins *Available accessories*. Below the pasted text, delete the blank paragraph. Clear the Clipboard, and then close the **Clipboard** pane.

6 At the top of the document, select the text *SALE*. Translate the selected text to **French** and click **Insert**. To the left of the word *Vente*, type **Sale,** and then press Spacebar one time. **Close** the **Translator** pane.

7 In the first cell of the table, insert an **Equation** placeholder. In the placeholder, type **S=** Insert a **Stacked Fraction**, type **+** and then insert a second **Stacked Fraction**. In the first fraction, in the top placeholder, type **P** and then in the bottom placeholder, type **2** In the second fraction, in the top placeholder, type **4A** and then in the bottom placeholder, type **5**

8 Position the insertion point at the beginning of the document. By using the **Find and Replace** dialog box, change the formatting of all occurrences of **iPad** to include bold emphasis and from the color gallery, in the eighth column, apply the fifth color. Click **Replace All** to make 2 replacements. Change the **Replace with** box to **No Formatting**, and then **Close** the **Find and Replace** dialog box.

9 Display the document properties. Be sure your name displays in the Author box. As the **Subject**, type your course name and section number. As the **Tags**, type **sale flyer** On the left, click **Save**. (Mac users: click OK.)

10 In the upper right corner of the Word window, click **Close** ✕.

11 In **MyLab IT**, locate and click the Grader Project **Word 5F Sale Flyer**. In **step 3**, under **Upload Completed Assignment**, click **Choose File**. In the **Open** dialog box, navigate to your **Word Chapter 5 folder**, and then click your **Student_Word_5F_Sale_Flyer** file one time to select it. In the lower right corner of the **Open** dialog box, click **Open**.

The name of your selected file displays above the Upload button.

12 To submit your file to **MyLab IT** for grading, click **Upload**, wait a moment for a green **Success!** message, and then in **step 4**, click the blue **Submit for Grading** button. Click **Close Assignment** to return to your list of **Course Materials**.

You have completed Project 5F **END**

MyLab IT Grader

Mastering Word   **Project 5G Gift Special**

Apply 5A and 5B skills from these Objectives:

1. Create and Apply a Custom Table Style
2. Format Cells in a Word Table
3. Use Advanced Table Features
4. Modify Table Properties
5. Manage Document Versions
6. Collect and Paste Images and Text
7. Translate Text and Insert Equations
8. Use Advanced Find and Replace Options

In the following Mastering Word project, you will create a flyer that provides descriptions of new products available for gift giving at Chesterfield Creations. Your completed document will look similar to Figure 5.51.

Project Files for MyLab IT Grader

1. In your Course Materials, locate and click **Word 5G Gift Special**, Download Materials, and then Download All Files.
2. Extract the zipped folder to your Word Chapter 5 folder. Close the Grader download screens.
3. Take a moment to open the downloaded **Word_5G_Gift_Special_Instructions**; note any recent updates to the book.

Project Results

NEW GIFT IDEAS FOR THE BUSINESS PROFESSIONAL

Just in time for the gift-giving season, Chesterfield Creations is pleased to add three computer bags to our Mainline Collection designed for the business professional. These bags offer the same durability and quality as our other business bags but with an updated style and added functionality to carry all the gadgets you need. Sale price available until December 31—25% off!

Item	Description	Price
Compact Bag	Special features include a pocket for items such as tickets and other travel information, and the most comfortable shoulder strap on the market. The *computer sleeve* has extra padding for the ultimate protection.	$ 149
Streamlined Tote	Available in a choice of five colors, the front pocket provides ample storage for tickets and other documents, metal feet protect the bag from dirty surfaces, extra padding in the *computer sleeve* stores your laptop securely, and the removable pouch can hold personal items.	$ 199
Large Tote	Similar to our other computer totes, this item has plenty of extra room for notebooks, pens, presentation information, personal items, and electronic accessories.	$ 209
	Average Price	$ 186
Prix de vente/Sale Price		
$S = P*.75$		

Chesterfield Creations
55 Avenue Road, Toronto, ON M5R 3L2
www.chesterfieldcreations.design   (416) 555-8600

Student_Word_5G_Gift_Special

Figure 5.51

For Non-MyLab Submissions

For Project 5G, you will need:
w05G_Gift_Special
w05G_Information

In your Word Chapter 5 folder, save your document as:
Lastname_Firstname_5G_Gift_Special

After you have named and saved your document, on the next page, begin with Step 2.

After step 20, save and submit your file as directed by your instructor.

(continues on next page)

Mastering Word: Project 5G Gift Special (continued)

1 Navigate to your **Word Chapter 5 folder**, and then double-click the Word file you downloaded from **MyLab IT** that displays your name—**Student_Word_5G_Gift_Special**. If necessary, at the top, click **Enable Editing**.

2 Insert the **File Name** in the footer. Select the first paragraph, and then apply the **Heading 1** style.

3 Starting with the paragraph that begins *Compact Bag*, select the last three paragraphs of the document, change the **Font Size** to **14**, and then with the text still selected, **Convert Text to Table** with three columns and three rows.

4 On the **Home tab,** in the **Styles group**, click the **Dialog Box Launcher** button. Point to the word **Styles** and double-click to snap the **Styles pane** to the right, and then at the bottom of the pane, click the **New Style** button. (Mac users: On the Home tab, click Styles Pane.)

5 In the **Create New Style from Formatting** dialog box, create a new style named **Gift** and then set the **Style type** to **Table**. Apply the style to **All Borders**. Set the **Line Weight** to **1 ½ pt**, and then set the **Border Color**— in the last column, click the last color. Change the **Fill Color**—in the last column, click the second color. Apply the **Gift** style to the **Whole table**. **Close** the **Styles** pane.

6 Click in the first cell of the table. On the **Table Tools Layout tab**, in the **Table group**, click **Select**, and then click **Select Column**. In the **Cell Size group**, change the column **Width** to **1.2"**. Change the second column **Width** to **4.5"**, and the third column **Width** to **0.7"**. Position the insertion point anywhere in the first row, and then click **Insert Above**.

7 In the first cell of the new row, type **Item** and then press **Tab**. Type **Description** Press **Tab** and then type **Price** Select the **header row** you just created, apply **Bold**, and then in the **Alignment group**, click **Align Center**.

8 Click anywhere in the second row of the table. In the **Table group**, click **Select**, and then click **Select Row**. Change the row **Height** to **1.5"**. Change the height of **row 3** to **1.8"** and change the height of **row 4** to **1.4"**.

9 In the first column, select all the cells below the header row. Apply **Bold**. On the **Table Tools Layout tab**, in the **Alignment group**, click **Align Center**, and then in the same group, click **Text Direction** two times. In the second column, select all the cells below the header row, and then click **Align Center Left**. In the last column, select all the cells below the header row, and click **Align Center**.

10 Point to the lower left corner of the table, and then click the **One-Click Row/Column Insertion** button. In the last row, change the **Height** to **0.4"**.

11 In the last row, select the first and second cells, and then **Merge Cells**. Click **Text Direction** one time, and then click **Align Center Right**. Type **Average Price** and then apply **Bold**.

12 In the last cell of the table, insert the **Formula**: **=AVERAGE(ABOVE)** Change the **Number format** to **#,##0**, to the left of the number format, type **$** and then click **OK**. Select the displayed value, and then apply **Bold**. (Mac users: Delete the second format that displays in the box.)

13 Point to the lower left corner of the table, and then click the **One-Click Row/Column Insertion** button. Merge the two cells in the new row.

14 With the alignment set to **Align Center**, type **Sale Price** and press **Enter**.

15 Insert an equation placeholder, and then type **S=P*.75**

16 Without selecting the paragraph mark, select the text *Sale Price*, and then translate it to **French**. Click to place the insertion point to the left of *S* in *Sale*. Type **/** and then press **←** one time. In the **Translator** pane, click **Insert**. **Close** the **Translator** pane.

17 **Save** your document but do not close it. Display the **Clipboard** pane, and then if necessary, click **Clear All**. From the files downloaded with this project, open the Word document **w05G_Information**. Click the right edge of the graphic to select it, and then **Copy** it to the **Clipboard**. Select the paragraph of text that begins *Just in time*, and then **Copy** it to the **Clipboard**. **Close** the **w05G_Information** document. Click in the blank paragraph at the end of your **Student_5G_Gift_Special** document, press **Enter** one time, and then from the **Clipboard** pane, paste the graphic. At the top of the document, click in the blank paragraph below the heading, and then paste the paragraph of text. Delete the empty paragraph below the pasted text. (Mac users: From your files open w05G_Information; on the File tab, point to Open Recent and select your Student_5G_Gift_Special file. Follow the steps in Step 17 to copy and paste the graphic and text.)

(continues on next page)

Content-Based Assessments (Mastery and Transfer of Learning)

Mastering Word: Project 5G Gift Special (continued)

18 **Close** the **Clipboard pane**, and then move to the top of your document. Replace all instances of *computer sleeve* with the same text but formatted with **Bold Italic** and a font color—in the sixth column, click the next to last color. After the 2 replacements are made, return the **Find and Replace** dialog box to its original settings.

19 Display the document properties. Be sure your name displays in the Author box. As the **Subject**, type your course name and section number. As the **Tags**, type **gift sale** On the left, click **Save**.

20 In the upper right corner of the Word window, click **Close** X.

21 In **MyLab IT**, locate and click the Grader Project **Word 5G Gift Special**. In **step 3**, under **Upload Completed Assignment**, click **Choose File**. In the **Open** dialog box, navigate to your **Word Chapter 5 folder**, and then click your **Student_Word_5G_Gift_Special** file one time to select it. In the lower right corner of the **Open** dialog box, click **Open**.

The name of your selected file displays above the Upload button.

22 To submit your file to **MyLab IT** for grading, click **Upload**, wait a moment for a green **Success!** message, and then in **step 4**, click the blue **Submit for Grading** button. Click **Close Assignment** to return to your list of **Course Materials**.

You have completed Project 5G | END

GO! Fix It	Project 5H Safety Program	IRC
GO! Make It	Project 5I Screen Protectors	IRC
GO! Solve It	Project 5J Planning Committee	IRC
GO! Solve It	Project 5K Wallet Collection	

Project Files

For Project 5K, you will need the following file:

w05K_Wallet_Collection

You will save your file as:

Lastname_Firstname_5K_Wallet_Collection

From your student data files, open the file **w05K_Wallet_Collection** and save it to your **Word Chapter 5** folder as **Lastname_Firstname_5K_Wallet_Collection** Using the information for the specific wallets, convert the text to a table. Insert a header row, add appropriate column headings, and then sort the table by price and item name. Create a formula to display the average price of the items. Create and apply a table style. Adjust paragraph, text, table, and cell formats to display attractively in a one-page document. Insert the file name in the footer and add appropriate document properties. Submit your document as directed by your instructor.

		Performance Level		
		Exemplary: You consistently applied the relevant skills	**Proficient: You sometimes, but not always, applied the relevant skills**	**Developing: You rarely or never applied the relevant skills**
Performance Criteria	**Convert text to table**	All appropriate text is displayed in a table.	At least one item of text is not displayed in a table.	No text is displayed in a table.
	Sort the table	The data in the table is sorted by both price and item name.	The data in the table is sorted only by price or item name.	The data in the table is not sorted.
	Create a formula	The average price is calculated using a formula and displays in a new row.	The average price displays in a new row, but a formula is not used.	The average price does not display in a new row.
	Create and apply a table style	A new table style is created and applied to the table.	A table style is applied to the table, but it is a built-in style—not new.	No table style is applied to the table.
	Format the document	All items in the document are formatted appropriately.	At least one item in the document is not formatted appropriately.	No items in the document are formatted.

You have completed Project 5K | END

Outcomes-Based Assessments (Critical Thinking)

Rubric

The following outcomes-based assessments are open-ended assessments. That is, there is no specific correct result; your result will depend on your approach to the information provided. Make *Professional Quality* your goal. Use the following scoring rubric to guide you in *how* to approach the problem and then to evaluate *how well* your approach solves the problem.

The *criteria*—Software Mastery, Content, Format and Layout, and Process—represent the knowledge and skills you have gained that you can apply to solving the problem. The *levels of performance*—Professional Quality, Approaching Professional Quality, or Needs Quality Improvements—help you and your instructor evaluate your result.

	Your completed project is of Professional Quality if you:	Your completed project is Approaching Professional Quality if you:	Your completed project Needs Quality Improvements if you:
1-Software Mastery	Choose and apply the most appropriate skills, tools, and features and identify efficient methods to solve the problem.	Choose and apply some appropriate skills, tools, and features, but not in the most efficient manner.	Choose inappropriate skills, tools, or features, or are inefficient in solving the problem.
2-Content	Construct a solution that is clear and well organized, contains content that is accurate, appropriate to the audience and purpose, and is complete. Provide a solution that contains no errors of spelling, grammar, or style.	Construct a solution in which some components are unclear, poorly organized, inconsistent, or incomplete. Misjudge the needs of the audience. Have some errors in spelling, grammar, or style, but the errors do not detract from comprehension.	Construct a solution that is unclear, incomplete, or poorly organized, contains some inaccurate or inappropriate content, and contains many errors of spelling, grammar, or style. Do not solve the problem.
3-Format and Layout	Format and arrange all elements to communicate information and ideas, clarify function, illustrate relationships, and indicate relative importance.	Apply appropriate format and layout features to some elements, but not others. Overuse features, causing minor distraction.	Apply format and layout that does not communicate information or ideas clearly. Do not use format and layout features to clarify function, illustrate relationships, or indicate relative importance. Use available features excessively, causing distraction.
4-Process	Use an organized approach that integrates planning, development, self-assessment, revision, and reflection.	Demonstrate an organized approach in some areas, but not others; or, use an insufficient process of organization throughout.	Do not use an organized approach to solve the problem.

Outcomes-Based Assessments (Critical Thinking)

Apply a combination of the 5A and 5B skills.

GO! Think	Project 5L Company Picnic

Project Files

For Project 5L, you will need the following file:

New blank Word document

You will save your file as:

Lastname_Firstname_5L_Company_Picnic

Every year, Chesterfield Creations holds a picnic for employees and their families. This year the picnic will be held on June 16 from 10 a.m. to 4 p.m. at High Park in Toronto. Lunch and snacks are provided. There will be music and an assortment of games for young and old. In addition, other park activities are available for a fee—such as pony rides and miniature golf.

Using this information, create a flyer to distribute to employees as an email attachment. Create a document that explains the picnic and lists the schedule of events in a table format. Insert a second table that lists fees for specific activities. Use a formula to provide the total cost for these events. Create a table style and apply it to both tables. Format the flyer, including table and cell properties, so that it is attractive and easy to read. Save the file as **Lastname_Firstname_5L_Company_Picnic** Insert the file name in the footer and add appropriate document properties. Submit the document as directed by your instructor.

You have completed Project 5L | **END**

GO! Think	Project 5M Employee Newsletter	IRC
You and GO!	Project 5N Personal Budget	IRC

Building Documents from Reusable Content and Revising Documents Using Markup Tools

6

WORD 2019

PROJECT 6A

Outcomes
Create reusable content and construct a document with building blocks and theme templates.

Objectives
1. Create Custom Building Blocks
2. Create and Save a Theme Template
3. Create a Document by Using Building Blocks

PROJECT 6B

Outcomes
Collaborate with others to edit, review, and finalize a document.

Objectives
4. Use Comments in a Document
5. Track Changes in a Document
6. View Side by Side, Compare, and Combine Documents

GaudiLab/Shutterstock

In This Chapter

 GO! To Work with Word

In this chapter you will work with building blocks—objects that can be reused in multiple documents. You will customize predefined building blocks and create your own reusable content. You will create a theme—by defining the colors, fonts, and effects—to give documents a customized appearance. You will build a new document from the custom building blocks and theme. Word includes features to review revisions and comments made in a document. This makes it easy to work with a team to collaborate on documents. You will insert comments, track changes, review changes made by others, and then accept or reject those changes.

The projects in this chapter relate to **Mountain View Public Library**, which serves the Claremont, Tennessee, community at three locations—the Main library, the East Branch, and the West Branch. The library's extensive collection includes books, audio books, music CDs, video DVDs, magazines, and newspapers—for all ages. The Mountain View Public Library also provides sophisticated online and technology services, youth programs, and frequent appearances by both local and nationally known authors. The citizens of Claremont support the Mountain View Public Library with local taxes, donations, and special events fees.

PROJECT 6A

Newsletter with Reusable Content and Custom Theme

MyLab IT block top right

MyLab IT
Project 6A Grader for Instruction
Project 6A Simulation for Training and Review

Project Activities

In Activities 6.01 through 6.12, you will assist Ami Sanjay, Director of Library Services at Mountain View Public Library, in designing a custom look for documents that the library produces by creating a custom theme and building blocks for content that can be reused. Your completed document will look similar to Figure 6.1.

Project Files for **MyLab IT Grader**

1. In your storage location, create a folder named **Word Chapter 6**.
2. In your **MyLab IT** course, locate and click **Word 6A February Newsletter**, Download Materials, and then Download All Files.
3. Extract the zipped folder to your Word Chapter 6 folder. Close the Grader download screens.
4. Take a moment to open the downloaded **Word_6A_February_Newsletter_Instructions**; note any recent updates to the book.

Project Results

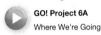

GO! Project 6A
Where We're Going

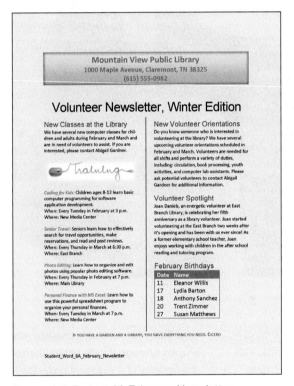

Figure 6.1 Project 6A February Newsletter

For Non-MyLab Submissions

For Project 6A, you will need:
w06A_February_Newsletter
w06A_Training
w06A_Building_Blocks

In your storage location, create a folder named Word Chapter 6
In your Word Chapter 6 folder, save your documents as:
Lastname_Firstname_6A_February_Newsletter
Lastname_Firstname_6A_Building_Blocks

Complete Activities 6.01 through 6.07 and save files as instructed in your book. For Activity 6.01, open w06A_Building_Blocks from your student data files. In Activity 6.08, step 1, open w06A_February_Newsletter, save the file as Lastname_Firstname_6A_February_Newsletter and then continue with step 2.

Objective 1 | Create Custom Building Blocks

ALERT Because Office 365 is a cloud-based subscription service that receives continuous updates, you may encounter some variations in what appears on your screen and what is shown in this instruction. Microsoft Office 365 is fully installed on your PC or Mac; no internet access is necessary to create or edit documents. When you *are* connected to the internet, you will receive monthly upgrades and new features, so you always have the latest versions of Office apps as soon as they are available. Your subscription gives you continuous free access to the latest innovations and refinements.

GO! Learn How
Video W6-1

Building blocks are reusable pieces of content or other document parts—for example, headers, footers, page number formats—that are stored in galleries. The Headers gallery, the Footers gallery, the Page Numbers gallery, and the Bibliographies gallery, some of which you have already used, are all examples of building block galleries. You can also create your own building blocks for content that you use frequently.

ALERT **Completing This Project in One Working Session**

If you are working in a school lab, plan to complete Project 6A in one working session. Building blocks are stored on the computer at which you are working. Thus, in a school lab, if you close Word before completing the project, the building blocks might be deleted and will not be available for your use—you will have to re-create them. On your own computer, you can close Word, and the building blocks will remain until you purposely delete them.

Activity 6.01 | Formatting a Text Box

Recall that a *text box* is a movable, resizable container for text or graphics. In this Activity, you will format a text box that the library can use for any documents requiring the library's contact information.

1 Navigate to your **Word Chapter 6 folder**, and then from the files you downloaded from **MyLab IT**, double-click **w06A_Building_Blocks**. If necessary, display the formatting marks. Save the file as **Lastname_Firstname_6A_Building_Blocks**

2 Click the outer edge of the text box to select it. On the **Format tab**, in the **Shape Styles group**, click **More** ⃞. In the **Shape Styles** gallery, in the fourth row, click the fifth style. Compare your screen with Figure 6.2.

MAC TIP To display group names on the ribbon, display the menu, click Word, click Preferences, click View, select the Show group titles check box.

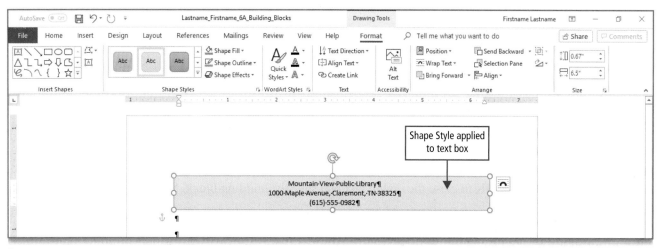

Shape Style applied to text box

Mountain·View·Public·Library¶
1000·Maple·Avenue,·Claremont,·TN·38325¶
(615)·555-0982¶

Figure 6.2

3 ▶ On the **Format tab**, in the **Shape Styles group**, click **Shape Effects**. Point to **Shadow**, and then under **Inner**, in the second row, click the second style.

4 ▶ In the text box, select the first paragraph, change the **Font Size** to **20**, and then apply **Bold** ☐B☐. Select the second and third paragraphs, change the **Font Size** to **16**, and then apply **Bold** ☐B☐. Notice the height of the text box automatically adjusts to accommodate the text.

5 ▶ Click the outer edge of the text box so that none of the text is selected, but that the text box itself is selected and displays sizing handles. Compare your screen with Figure 6.3 and then **Save** ☐☐ your document.

Figure 6.3

Activity 6.02 | Adding a Building Block to a Gallery

☐ **MAC TIP**   If this feature is not available on your system, skip this Activity.

1 ▶ With the text box selected, on the **Insert tab**, in the **Text group**, click **Text Box**, and then click **Save Selection to Text Box Gallery**. In the **Create New Building Block** dialog box, in the **Name** box, type **Library Information** Notice that the **Gallery** box displays *Text Boxes*.

By selecting the Text Boxes gallery, this building block will display in the gallery of other text box building blocks.

2 ▶ In the **Description** box, type **Library contact information for publications** and then compare your screen with Figure 6.4.

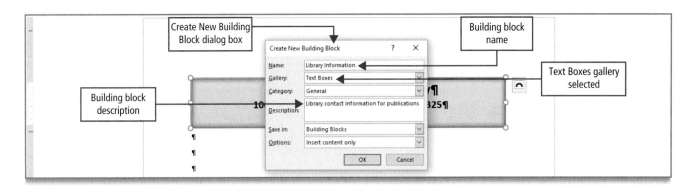

Figure 6.4

3 ▶ Click **OK** to close the dialog box and save the building block. **Save** ☐☐ your document.

ALERT   **Saving Building Blocks**

Building blocks that you create in a gallery are saved on the computer at which you are working.

Activity 6.03 | Using the Building Blocks Organizer to View and Edit Building Blocks

MAC TIP If this feature is not available on your system, skip this Activity.

MOS
Expert 3.1.2

The *Building Blocks Organizer* enables you to view—in a single location—all of the available building blocks from all galleries.

1 On the **Insert tab**, in the **Text group**, click **Explore Quick Parts** 📄 ▾.

Quick Parts are the reusable pieces of content that are available to insert into a document, including building blocks, document properties, and fields.

2 From the list, click **Building Blocks Organizer**. In the **Building Blocks Organizer** dialog box, in the upper left corner, click **Name** to sort the building blocks alphabetically by name.

Here you can view all of the building blocks available in Word. In this dialog box, you can also delete a building block, edit its properties—for example, change the name, description, or gallery location—or select and insert it into a document.

3 Using the scroll bar in the center of the **Building Blocks Organizer** dialog box, scroll down until you see your building block that begins *Library*, and then click to select it. Compare your screen with Figure 6.5.

In the preview area on the right, notice that under the preview of the building block, the name and description that you entered displays.

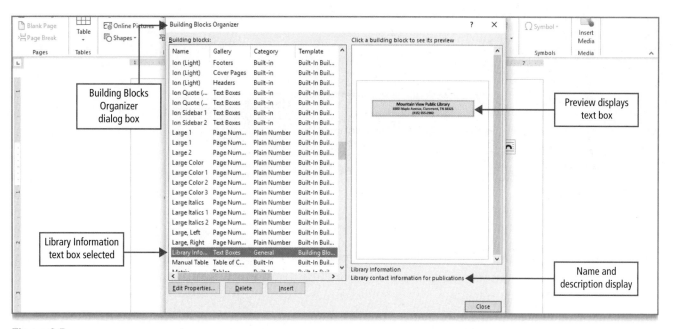

Figure 6.5

4 In the **Building Blocks Organizer** dialog box, click **Edit Properties**.

5 Be sure *Building Blocks* is selected in the *Save in* list, and then in the **Modify Building Block** dialog box, click in the **Description** box.

6 In the **Description** box, select the word *contact*, and then press Delete.

You can edit building block properties in the Modify Building Block dialog box. In this case, you are changing the description of the text box building block.

7 In the **Modify Building Block** dialog box, click **OK**. In the **Microsoft Word** message box, when asked if you want to redefine the building block entry, click **Yes**. In the lower right corner of the **Building Blocks Organizer** dialog box, click **Close**, and then **Save** 💾 your document.

Activity 6.04 | Saving a Custom Building Block as a Quick Table

Quick Tables are tables that are stored as building blocks. Word includes many predesigned Quick Tables, and you can also create your own tables and save them as Quick Tables in the Quick Tables gallery. In this Activity, you will modify an existing Quick Table and then save it as a new building block.

1 Below the text box, position the insertion point in the second blank paragraph. On the **Insert tab**, in the **Tables group**, click **Table**, and then at the bottom of the list, point to **Quick Tables**. In the **Quick Tables** gallery, scroll down to locate **Tabular List**, as shown in Figure 6.6.

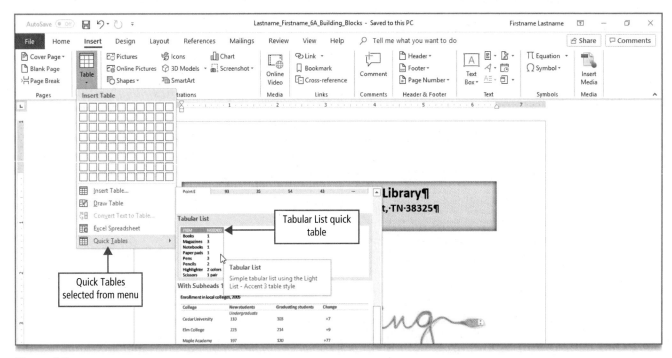

Figure 6.6

MAC TIP   In the second blank paragraph below the text box, insert a table with 2 columns and 8 rows. In the first cell, type Date and then press Tab. Type Name and then AutoFit both columns. Apply the List Table 3 – Accent 3 table style. Save the document and then skip the remainder of this Activity.

---

2 Click **Tabular List**. In the first row of the table, click in the first cell, select the text **ITEM**, and then type **Date** to replace the text

3 Press Tab to move to the second cell, and with **NEEDED** selected, type **Name**

4 Select all the remaining cells of the table, and then press Delete to delete the text. Compare your screen with Figure 6.7.

Because this table will be used as a building block to enter birthday information, the sample text is not needed.

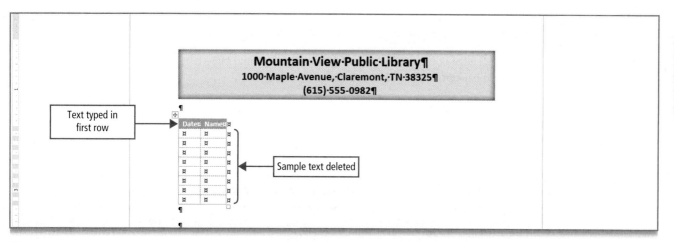

Figure 6.7

5 Click in the table, point slightly outside of the upper left corner of the table, and then click the **table move handle** ⊞ to select the entire table.

6 With the table selected, on the **Insert tab**, in the **Tables group**, click **Table**. In the displayed list, point to **Quick Tables**, and then at the bottom of the list, click **Save Selection to Quick Tables Gallery**.

7 In the **Create New Building Block** dialog box, in the **Name** box, type **Birthday Table** and then click in the **Description** box. Type **Use for staff birthdays in publications** and then compare your screen with Figure 6.8.

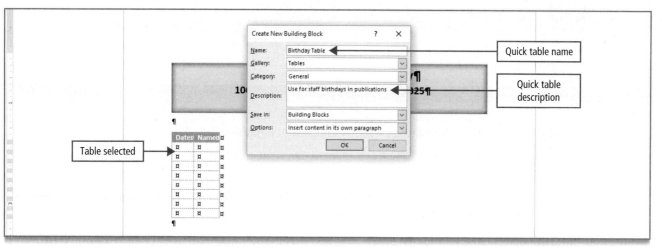

Figure 6.8

8 Click **OK** to save the table in the **Quick Tables** gallery. **Save** 🖫 your document.

Activity 6.05 | Saving a Picture and an AutoText Entry as Quick Parts

In this Activity, you will modify an image and save it as a building block so that it can be used in any document that includes information about library computer classes.

1 Select the **Training picture**. On the **Format tab**, in the **Picture Styles group**, click **Picture Effects**. Point to **Soft Edges**, and then click **10 point**.

> The soft edge does not display on the white background but when the image is inserted on a colored background it will be apparent.

🖥 **MAC TIP** Skip steps 2–4.

---

2 With the picture selected, on the **Insert tab**, in the **Text group**, click **Explore Quick Parts** 📄 ▾. From the list, click **Save Selection to Quick Part Gallery**.

> By choosing the Save Selection to Quick Part Gallery command, building blocks that you create are saved in the Quick Parts gallery and assigned to the General category. However, you can save the building block in any of the other relevant galleries or create your own custom gallery. You can also create your own category if you want to do so.

3 In the **Create New Building Block** dialog box, in the **Name** box, type **Training Image** and then click in the **Description** box. Type **Library training image** and then compare your screen with Figure 6.9.

> You can create and then select any content and save it as a building block in this manner.

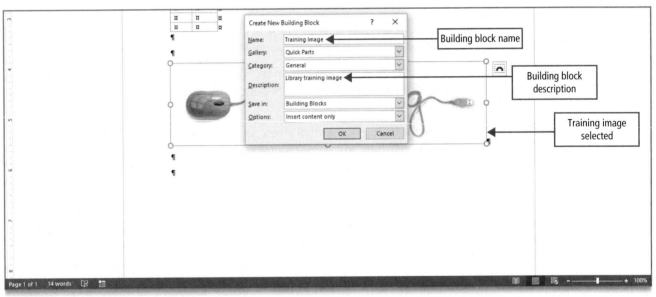

Figure 6.9

4 Click **OK** to close the dialog box and save the building block.

> Your new building block is saved; you can insert it in a document by selecting it from the Quick Parts gallery.

5 Press Ctrl + End to move to the end of the document. Type **If you have a garden and a library, you have everything you need. Cicero**

6 Select the text you just typed. On the **Insert tab**, in the **Text group**, click **Explore Quick Parts** 📄 ▾. From the list, click **AutoText**, and then click **Save Selection to AutoText Gallery**.

7 In the **Create New Building Block** dialog box, in the **Name** box, type **Quote** and then in the **Description** box, type **Quote for newsletter**

8 Verify that the **Gallery** displays **AutoText**. Click the **Save in box arrow**, and then click **Building Blocks**. Compare your screen with Figure 6.10.

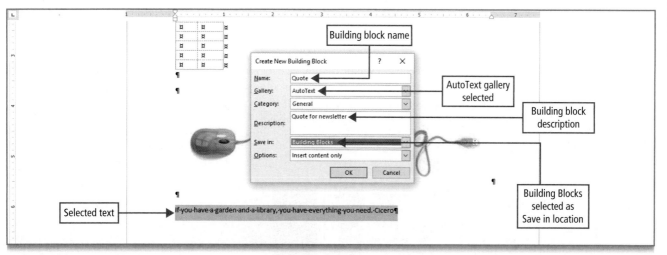

Building block name

Create New Building Block

Name: Quote
Gallery: AutoText ← AutoText gallery selected
Category: General
Description: Quote for newsletter ← Building block description
Save in: Building Blocks ← Building Blocks selected as Save in location
Options: Insert content only

Selected text → If·you·have·a·garden·and·a·library,·you·have·everything·you·need.·Cicero¶

Figure 6.10

9 Click **OK** to close the dialog box, and then press Ctrl + Home. **Save** 💾 your document. On the **File tab**, click **Close** to close the document and leave Word open.

Objective 2 | Create and Save a Theme Template

GO! Learn How
Video W6-2

Recall that a ***theme*** is a predefined combination of colors, fonts, and line and fill effects that look good together and is applied to an entire document by a single selection. Word comes with a group of predefined themes—the default theme is named *Office*. You can also create your own theme by selecting any combination of colors, fonts, and effects, which, when saved, creates a ***theme template***. A theme template, which stores a set of colors, fonts, and effects—lines and fill effects—can be shared with other Office programs, such as Excel and PowerPoint.

Activity 6.06 | Creating Custom Theme Colors and Theme Fonts

💻 **MAC TIP** Skip Activities 6.06 and 6.07 and continue with Activity 6.08.

Expert
3.2.1, 3.2.2

1 Press Ctrl + N to display a new blank document.

2 On the **Design tab**, in the **Document Formatting group**, click **Themes**. In the **Themes** gallery, click **Organic**.

3 On the **Design tab**, in the **Document Formatting group**, click **Colors**. In the **Theme Colors** gallery, take a moment to examine the various color schemes, scrolling as necessary, and then at the bottom of the list, click **Customize Colors**.

4 In the **Create New Theme Colors** dialog box, click the **Text/Background – Dark 1 arrow**, and then under **Theme Colors**, in the seventh column, click the first color. Using the same technique, change **Accent 1**—in the eighth column, click the first color. Change **Accent 4**—in the seventh column, click the fourth color. In the **Name** box, delete the existing text. Type **Newsletter Colors** and then compare your screen with Figure 6.11.

A set of theme colors contains four text/background colors, six accent colors, and two hyperlink colors. You can select a new color for any category and save the combination of colors with a new name. In this case, you are changing the colors for the Text/Background – Dark 1, Accent 1, and Accent 4 categories, and saving the color combination with the name Newsletter Colors. The Sample box displays both the original and modified theme color schemes.

Figure 6.11

5 Click **Save** to close the **Create New Theme Colors** dialog box. In the **Document Formatting group**, click **Fonts**, and then at the bottom of the list, click **Customize Fonts**.

Theme fonts contain a heading font—the upper font—and a body text font—the lower font. You can use an existing set of Built-In fonts for your new theme, or define new sets of fonts.

6 In the **Create New Theme Fonts** dialog box, click the **Heading font arrow**, scroll as necessary to locate and then click **Arial**. Click the **Body font arrow**, scroll as necessary, and then click **Calibri**. In the **Name** box, delete the existing text, and then type **Newsletter Fonts**

The custom Theme Fonts—Newsletter Fonts—includes the Arial heading font and the Calibri body text font.

7 Click **Save** to close the **Create New Theme Fonts** dialog box.

Activity 6.07 | Saving a Custom Theme Template

Expert
3.2.3

To use your custom theme in other Microsoft Office files, you can save it as a theme template.

1 In the **Document Formatting group**, click **Themes**, and then at the bottom of the **Themes** gallery, click **Save Current Theme** to display the **Save Current Theme** dialog box. Compare your screen with Figure 6.12.

By default, saving a new theme displays the Templates folder, which includes the Document Themes folder, containing separate folders for Theme Colors, Theme Effects, and Theme Fonts. The Save as type box specifies the file type *Office Theme*.

If you save your theme in the Templates folder, it is available to the Office programs on the computer at which you are working. In a college or organization, you may not have permission to update this folder, but on your own computer, you can save your themes here if you want to do so.

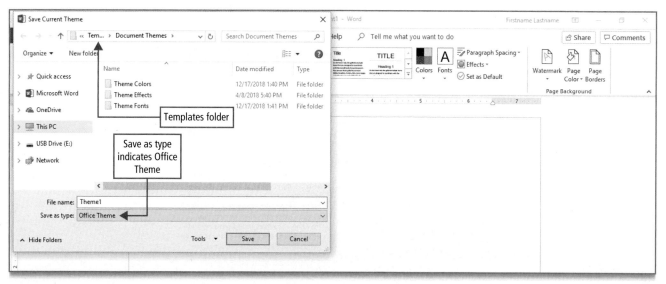

Figure 6.12

> **2** In the **Save Current Theme** dialog box, navigate to your **Word Chapter 6** folder. In the **File name** box, type **Lastname_Firstname_6A_Library_Theme** and then click **Save**.

> **3** Click the **File tab**, and then click **Close**. Do not save changes. Keep Word open for the next activity.

Objective 3 | Create a Document by Using Building Blocks

GO! Learn How
Video W6-3

One of the benefits of creating building blocks and theme templates is that they can be used repeatedly to create individual documents. The building blocks ensure consistency in format and structure, and the theme template provides consistency in colors, fonts, and effects.

Activity 6.08 | Applying a Custom Theme and a Page Color

1.2.4

In this Activity, you will apply a theme template and format text in columns.

> **1** From the files you downloaded with this project, open the file **Student_Word_6A_ February_Newsletter**. (If you are *not* submitting your project for grading in **MyLab IT**, from your student data files, open the file w06A_February_Newsletter and save the file as Lastname_Firstname_6A_February_Newsletter.)

> This document contains a newsletter formatted in two columns with several styles applied.

> **2** Insert a **Footer** with the **File Name**. **Close** the footer area. If necessary, display the rulers and formatting marks.

> **3** On the **Design tab**, in the **Document Formatting group**, click **Themes**, and then click **Browse for Themes**. In the **Choose Theme or Themed Document** dialog box, navigate to your **Word Chapter 6** folder, and then click your file **Lastname_Firstname_6A_Library_ Theme**. Compare your screen with Figure 6.13.

☐ **MAC TIP** From the files you downloaded with this project, apply the Mac_6A_Library_Theme file.

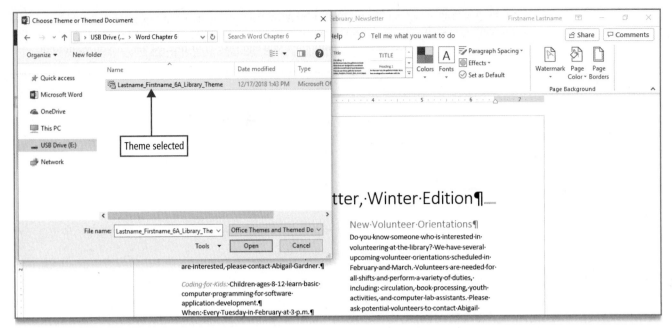

Figure 6.13

> **4** Click **Open** to apply the theme and notice that the text with the heading styles applied is formatted with the color of the custom theme that you created.

> **5** On the **Design tab**, in the **Page Background group**, click **Page Color**. In the last column, click the second color. Compare your screen with Figure 6.14.

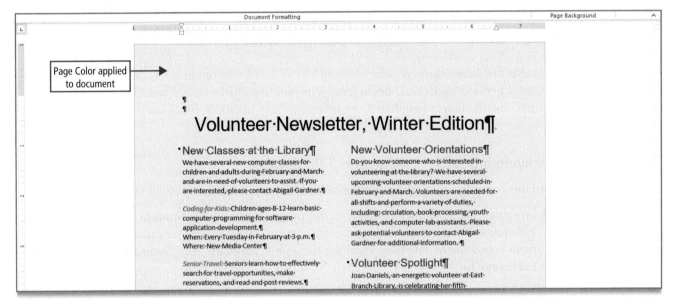

Figure 6.14

> **6** Click anywhere in the two-column area of the document. On the **Layout tab**, in the **Page Setup group**, click the **Columns arrow**, and then click **More Columns** to display the **Columns** dialog box.

> You can modify column formats in the Columns dialog box. For example, you can change the number of columns, the width of the columns, the spacing after columns, and insert a line to separate the columns.

7 In the **Columns** dialog box, above the **Preview** area, click the **Line between** check box so that it is selected, and then click **OK** to insert a line between the two columns of the newsletter. Compare your screen with Figure 6.15, and then **Save** 🖫 your document.

Figure 6.15

Activity 6.09 | Inserting Quick Parts

In this Activity, you will insert the text box and picture Quick Parts that you created.

1 Press `Ctrl` + `Home`. On the **Insert tab**, in the **Text group**, click **Text Box**. To the right of the **Text Box** gallery, drag the vertical scroll box to the bottom of the gallery, and then under **General**, click the **Library Information** building block.

The theme colors of your custom theme are applied to the building block.

> 🖥 **MAC TIP** Open your Lastname_Firstname_6A_Building_Blocks file. Select the text box and then copy and paste the text box at the top of your newsletter document. Leave your 6A_Building_Blocks file open.

2 In the first column, click at the end of the paragraph that begins *We have several new* and then press `Enter`.

3 On the **Insert tab**, in the **Text group**, click **Explore Quick Parts** 🗒 ▾, and notice that your *Training Image* building block displays. Compare your screen with Figure 6.16.

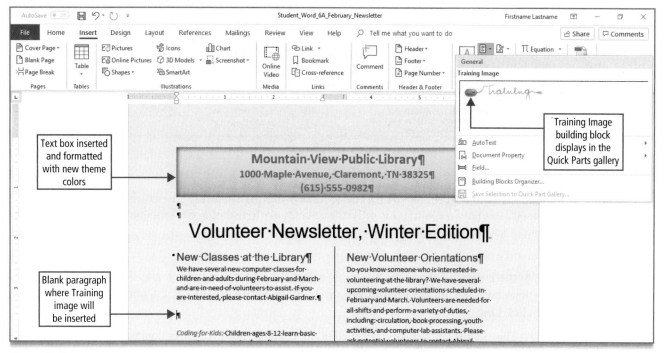

Figure 6.16

4 Under **General**, click the **Training Image** building block to insert it, and then **Save** 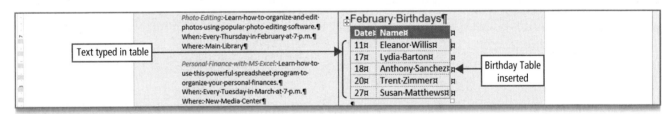 your document.

Activity 6.10 | Inserting a Quick Table and an AutoText Quick Part

In this Activity, you will complete the newsletter by inserting the Quick Table and the AutoText that you created.

1 In the second column, click in the blank paragraph below *February Birthdays*. On the **Insert tab**, in the **Tables group**, click **Table**, point to **Quick Tables**, scroll to the bottom of the list, and then under **General**, click **Birthday Table**.

2 In the second row of the table, click in the first cell. Type **11** and then press Tab. Type **Eleanor Willis** and then press Tab. Use the same technique to type the following text in the table.

17	**Lydia Barton**
18	**Anthony Sanchez**
20	**Trent Zimmer**
27	**Susan Matthews**

3 Select the empty rows in the table. On the **Table Tools Layout tab**, in the **Rows & Columns group**, click the **Delete arrow**, and then click **Delete Rows**. Click the **table move handle** ⊞ to select the entire table, and then change the **Font Size** to **14**. Click outside the table so that it is not selected, and then compare your screen with Figure 6.17.

Figure 6.17

4 At the bottom of the second column, select the blank paragraph mark. With the paragraph mark selected, on the **Layout tab**, in the **Page Setup group**, click **Columns**, and then click **One**.

The existing text remains formatted in two columns; however, the bottom of the document returns to one column—full page width.

5 ▶ With the paragraph mark selected, on the **Insert tab**, in the **Text group**, click **Explore Quick Parts** 📄 ▾, point to **AutoText**, and then click **Quote**.

 MAC TIP   To insert the AutoText entry, type Quote and then when the ScreenTip displays, press [Enter].

6 ▶ Select the inserted text. On the **Home Tab**, in the **Styles group**, click **More** ▾, and then click **Intense Reference**. In the **Paragraph group**, click **Center** ☰, and then deselect the text. Compare your screen with Figure 6.18.

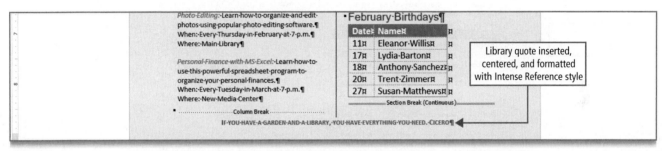

Figure 6.18

7 ▶ If a second page displays in the document, select any blank paragraphs on the second page and press [Delete]. **Save** 💾 your document.

Activity 6.11 │ Manually Hyphenating a Document

MOS
2.2.1

1 ▶ Press [Ctrl] + [Home]. On the **Layout tab**, in the **Page Setup group**, click **Hyphenation**, and then click **Manual** to display the **Manual Hyphenation: English (United States)** dialog box.

Hyphenation is a tool in Word that controls how words are split between two lines. By selecting Manual, you can control which words are hyphenated.

2 ▶ In the **Manual Hyphenation: English (United States)** dialog box, in the **Hyphenate at** box, with *chil-dren* displayed, click **Yes** to accept the hyphenated word. If additional words display in the **Hyphenate at** box, click **Cancel**.

3 ▶ When a message displays indicating that the hyphenation is complete, click **OK**. **Save** 💾 your document.

Activity 6.12 │ Deleting Custom Building Blocks, Theme Colors, and Theme Fonts

MOS
Expert
3.1.2

You can delete user-created building blocks, theme colors, and theme fonts if they are no longer needed. If you are sharing a computer with others, you must restore Word to its default settings. In this activity, you will delete the building blocks, theme colors, and theme fonts that you created.

 MAC TIP   Skip steps 1–6.

1 On the **Insert tab**, in the **Text group**, click **Explore Quick Parts** 📄 ▾. Right-click the **Training Image** building block, and then click **Organize and Delete**. Compare your screen with Figure 6.19.

> The Training Image building block is selected in the Building Blocks Organizer dialog box. A preview of the building block displays on the right. The name and description of the building block displays below the preview.

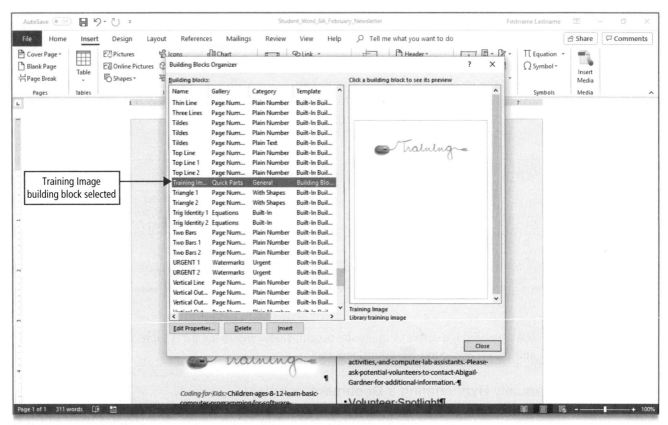

Figure 6.19

2 Click **Delete**. When a message displays to confirm the deletion, click **Yes**.

MORE KNOWLEDGE **Deleting Building Blocks**

To delete a building block, you must have an open document so that the Quick Parts command is active.

---

3 In the **Building Blocks Organizer** dialog box, in the upper left corner, click **Name** to sort the building blocks alphabetically by name.

4 By using the scroll bar in the center of the **Building Blocks Organizer** dialog box, scroll down until you see your building block that begins *Birthday*, and then click to select it. Click **Delete**, and then click **Yes** to confirm the deletion.

5 Using the same technique, scroll to locate your building block *Library Information*, and then **Delete** it. **Delete** the **Quote** building block. **Close** the **Building Blocks Organizer** dialog box.

6 On the **Design tab**, in the **Document Formatting group**, click **Colors**. At the top of the **Theme Colors** gallery, right-click **Newsletter Colors**, and then click **Delete**. When a message displays to confirm the deletion, click **Yes**. Using the same technique, display the **Theme Fonts** gallery, and then **Delete** the **Newsletter Fonts**.

> Because the theme—including the custom theme colors and theme fonts—has been saved, you no longer need the Newsletter Colors and Newsletter Fonts to display in the respective lists.

7 Display the document **Properties**. In the **Tags** box, type **library newsletter** and in the **Subject** box, type your course name and section number. If necessary, edit the author name to display your name. **Save** your document and **Close** Word.

For Non-MyLab Submissions Determine What Your Instructor Requires

As directed by your instructor, submit your completed Word file.

---

8 In **MyLab IT**, locate and click the Grader Project **Word 6A February Newsletter**. In **step 3**, under **Upload Completed Assignment**, click **Choose File**. In the **Open** dialog box, navigate to your **Word Chapter 6 folder**, and then click your **Student_Word_6A_ February_Newsletter** file one time to select it. In the lower right corner of the **Open** dialog box, click **Open**.

The name of your selected file displays above the Upload button.

9 To submit your file to **MyLab IT** for grading, click **Upload**, wait a moment for a green **Success!** message, and then in **step 4**, click the blue **Submit for Grading** button. Click **Close Assignment** to return to your list of **Course Materials**.

MORE KNOWLEDGE **Printing Page Backgrounds**

To print the background color or fill effect of a document, display the Word Options dialog box, select Display, and under Printing Options, select the Print background colors and images check box. Click OK.

You have completed Project 6A **END**

Events Schedule with Tracked Changes

Project Activities

In Activities 6.13 through 6.22, you will assist Abigail Gardner, Director of Programs and Youth Services, in using the markup tools in Word to add comments and make changes to a schedule of events. You will accept or reject each change, and then compare and combine your document with another draft version to create a final document. Your completed document will look similar to Figure 6.20.

 Project Files for MyLab IT Grader

1. In your **MyLab IT** course, locate and click **Word 6B Events Schedule**, Download Materials, and then Download All Files.
2. Extract the zipped folder to your Word Chapter 6 folder. Close the Grader download screens.
3. Take a moment to open the downloaded **Word_6B_Events_Schedule_Instructions**; note any recent updates to the book.

Project Results

GO! Project 6B
Where We're Going

Mountain View Public Library

Children's Department

September Events

Mountain View Public Library offers many special events to area children at our three branches. Attending one of these activities is a wonderful way to promote a love of reading that will last a lifetime.

Meet the Author

This month's author is Isabelle Saunders, author of *Splendid Dreams*. She will read her story, answer questions, and sign copies of her book. Ms. Saunders will appear at the Main Library on September 23 at 7:00 p.m. All ages are welcome to attend.

Toddler Story Time

Toddler story time is geared toward children who are 2-3 years old. Composed of stories and songs, and usually geared toward the seasons, it is a wonderful opportunity to foster a love of reading. This event is held at the Main Library on Mondays at 10:00 a.m., the East Branch on Wednesdays at 10:30 a.m., and the West Branch on Fridays at 9:30 a.m.

Preschool Story Time

Preschool story time is designed for children ages 3-5. This is a great setting for children to learn to sit and listen as the librarian reads several books. Children are encouraged to respond to questions about each book. The youngsters are assisted in selecting and checking out other books by the featured authors. Preschool story time is held at 1:00 p.m. at the Main Library on Mondays.

Baby Story Time

Specifically designed for children under 2 years old, baby story time provides an opportunity for your child to hear several stories and participate in songs and finger plays. Additional time is provided to play with toys, listen to music, and for you to interact with other parents. This one-hour program is held at the Main Library on Tuesdays at 9:30 a.m., the East Branch on Thursdays at 10:30 a.m., and the West Branch on Fridays at 2:30 p.m.

Story and Craft

This month's story and craft time will be held at the West Branch at 4:00 p.m. on September 16. The theme will be butterflies. Children ages 5-12 are welcome to attend. To reserve your place, please call Abigail Gardner at (615) 555-0982 to register.

Animal Adventures

Safari Steve from Wildlife Friends will bring in many small animals for children to look at, touch, and learn about. This event is suitable for families and will be held at the Main Library at 7:00 p.m. on September 24.

Student_Word_6B_Schedule_Combined

Internet Safety

This seminar is geared for teenagers, ages 13-17. It will cover a variety of techniques for maintaining safety while on the Internet. This event will be held at the East Branch location at 7:30 p.m. on September 25.

Seek and Find at the Library

Led by librarian Annette Liebig, this session explains how to find a specific book, magazine, audio book, CD, DVD, or other items at the library. Appropriate for children ages 8 and up, this seminar will be held at 7:00 p.m. on September 27 at our West Branch location.

Student_Word_6B_Schedule_Combined

Figure 6.20 Project 6B Events Schedule

For Non-MyLab Submissions

For Project 6B, you will need:
w06B_Events_Schedule
w06B_Schedule_Revisions

In your Word Chapter 6 folder, save your document as:
Lastname_Firstname_6B_Events_Schedule
Lastname_Firstname_6B_Schedule_Combined

After you have named and saved your document, on the next page, begin with step 2.

ALERT Because Office 365 is a cloud-based subscription service that receives continuous updates, you may encounter some variations in what appears on your screen and what is shown in this instruction. Microsoft Office 365 is fully installed on your PC or Mac; no internet access is necessary to create or edit documents. When you *are* connected to the internet, you will receive monthly upgrades and new features, so you always have the latest versions of Office apps as soon as they are available. Your subscription gives you continuous free access to the latest innovations and refinements.

GO! Learn How
Video W6-4

Building a final document often involves more than one person. One person usually drafts the original and becomes the document ***author***—or *owner*—and then others add their portions of text and comment on, or propose changes to, the text of others. A ***reviewer*** is someone who reviews and marks changes on a document.

A ***comment*** is a note that an author or reviewer adds to a document. Comments are a good way to communicate when more than one person is involved with the writing, reviewing, and editing process. Comments are like sticky notes attached to the document—they can be viewed and read by others but are not part of the document text.

Activity 6.13 | Inserting and Replying to Comments

MOS
6.1.1, 6.1.2

For the library's monthly schedule of events, Abigail Gardner has created a draft document; edits and comments have been added by others. In this Activity, you will insert a comment to suggest confirming a scheduled guest.

1 Navigate to your **Word Chapter 6 folder**, and then double-click the Word file you downloaded from **MyLab IT** that displays your name—**Student_Word_6B_Events_Schedule**.

2 Insert the file name in the footer, and then close the footer area. If necessary, display the rulers and formatting marks.

3 Click the **Review tab**. In the **Comments group**, verify that **Show Comments** is *not* selected. In the **Tracking group**, verify that **Simple Markup** displays as shown in Figure 6.21. If a different markup style displays, click the arrow, and then click Simple Markup.

In *Simple Markup* view, *revisions*—changes made to a document—are indicated by vertical red lines in the left margin, and comments that have been made are indicated by icons in the right margin.

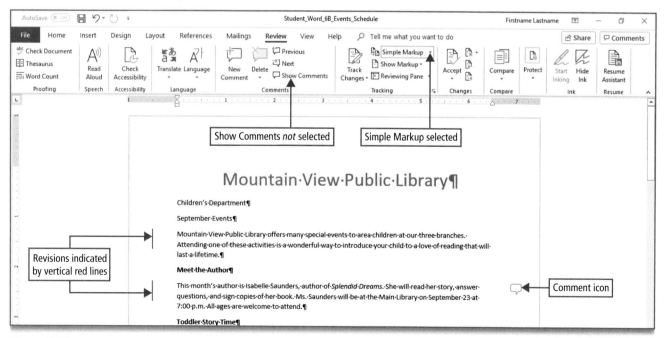

Figure 6.21

4 If necessary, press Ctrl + Home. On the **Review tab**, in the **Comments group**, click **Show Comments** so that it is selected. Compare your screen with Figure 6.22.

The comments display in *balloons* in the nonprinting *markup area*. A balloon is the outlined shape in which a comment or formatting change displays. The markup area is the space to the right or left of the document where comments and also formatting changes—for example, applying italic—display. Each comment includes the name of the reviewer who made the comment. Each reviewer's comments are identified by a distinct color.

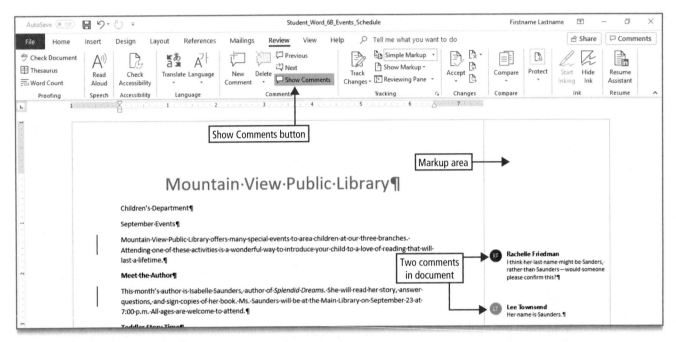

Figure 6.22

5 On the **Review tab**, in the **Tracking group**, click the **Dialog Box Launcher** ⬚. In the **Track Changes Options** dialog box, click **Change User Name**.

MAC TIP Skip steps 5–7.

ALERT Changing the User Name and Initials

In a school lab or organization, you may not be able to change the user name and initials, so make a note of the name and initials currently displayed so that you can identify your revisions in this document.

6 If you are able to do so, in the **User name** box, delete any existing text, and then type your own first and last names. In the **Initials** box, delete any existing text, and then type your initials. Below the **Initials** box, select the **Always use these values regardless of sign in to Office** check box. Compare your screen with Figure 6.23. If you are unable to make this change, move to step 7.

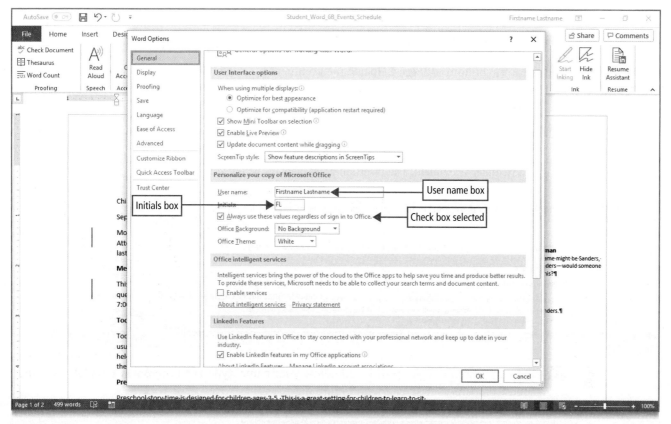

Figure 6.23

7 Click **OK** two times to close the dialog boxes.

8 On **Page 1**, select the fifth paragraph *Meet the Author*. On the **Review tab**, in the **Comments group**, click **New Comment**, and notice that a new comment balloon displays in the markup area with the user name configured on your computer. Type **Check with Barry Smith to confirm.** Compare your screen with Figure 6.24.

You can insert a comment at a specific location in a document or to selected text, such as an entire paragraph. Your name—or the name configured for the computer at which you are working—displays at the beginning of the comment.

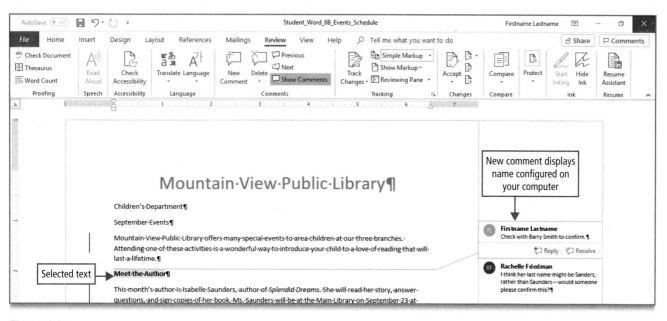

Figure 6.24

9 ▶ Near the bottom of **Page 1**, locate the comment by Rachelle Friedman that begins *Should we mention*. Point to the comment and notice that shaded text displays in the document indicating where the comment was inserted.

10 ▶ In the Rachelle Friedman comment, click **Reply**. Compare your screen with Figure 6.25.

Your name is inserted below the comment. It is indented, indicating that this is a *reply* to Rachelle Friedman's comment. The insertion point displays below your name.

MAC TIP   The Reply button is located in the upper right corner of the comment balloon.

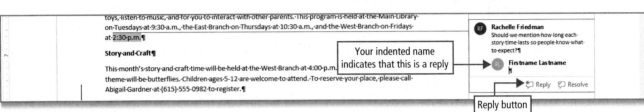

Figure 6.25

11 ▶ With the insertion point positioned below your name, type **The program is scheduled for one hour.** Compare your screen with Figure 6.26.

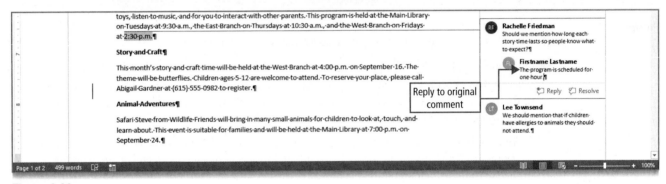

Figure 6.26

12 ▶ Save your document.

Activity 6.14 │ Editing and Deleting Comments

Typically, comments are temporary. One person inserts a comment, another person answers the question or revises the text based on the comment—and then the comments are removed before the document is final. In this Activity, you will replace text in your comment and delete comments.

1 ▶ Click the comment you inserted referencing *Barry Smith*—the first comment in the document. Select the text *Barry Smith*, type **Caroline Otto** and then adjust spacing as necessary.

In this manner, you can edit your comments.

2 ▶ Immediately below your comment, click the comment created by Rachelle Friedman, which begins *I think her last name*, and notice the following comment created by *Lee Townsend*. Compare your screen with Figure 6.27.

Because the question asked by Rachelle Friedman has been answered by Lee Townsend, both comments can be deleted.

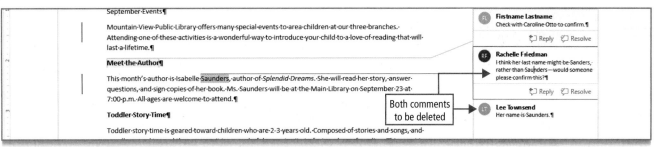

Figure 6.27

> **3** With your insertion point positioned in the comment by *Rachelle Friedman*, on the **Review tab**, in the **Comments group**, click the upper portion of the **Delete** button to delete the comment.

> **4** Point to the comment by *Lee Townsend*, right-click, and then from the shortcut menu, click **Delete Comment**.
>
>   Use either technique to delete a comment.

> **5** In the **Comments group**, click **Next**. In the markup area, notice that the comment by *Rachelle Friedman* is selected. Compare your screen with Figure 6.28.
>
>   In the Comments group, you can use the Next and Previous buttons in this manner to navigate through the comments in a document.

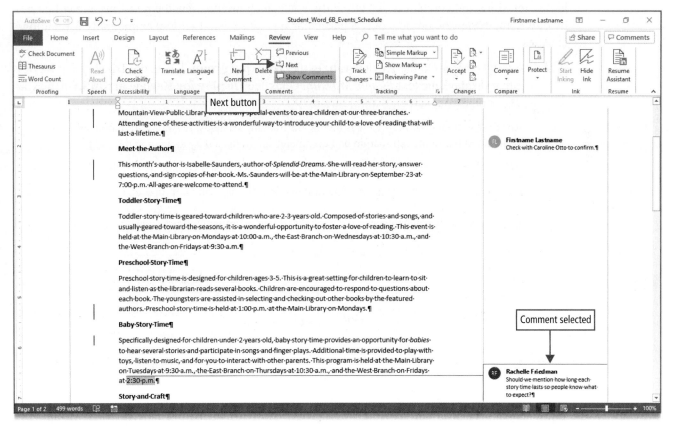

Figure 6.28

> **6** In the **Comments group**, click **Next** two times to select the comment by Lee Townsend that begins *We should mention*, and then use any technique you have practiced to **Delete** the comment.

> **7** Save 💾 your document.

Objective 5 Track Changes in a Document

GO! Learn How
Video W6-5

When you turn on the *Track Changes* feature, it makes a record of—*tracks*—the changes made to a document. As you revise the document with your changes, Word uses markup to visually indicate insertions, deletions, comments, formatting changes, and content that has moved.

Each reviewer's revisions and comments display in a different color. This is useful if, for example, you want to quickly scan only for edits made by your supervisor or only for edits made by a coworker. After the document has been reviewed by the appropriate individuals, you can locate the changes and accept or reject the revisions on a case-by-case basis or globally in the entire document.

Activity 6.15 | Viewing All Tracked Changes in a Document and Setting Tracking and Markup Options

After one or more reviewers have made revisions and inserted comments, you can view the revisions in various ways. You can display the document in its original or final form, showing or hiding revisions and comments. Additionally, you can choose to view the revisions and comments by only some reviewers or view only a particular type of revision—for example, only formatting changes.

1 Press Ctrl + Home. On the **Review tab**, in the **Tracking group**, locate the **Display for Review** box that displays the text *Simple Markup*. Click the **Display for Review arrow** to display a list. Compare your screen with Figure 6.29.

Recall that *Simple Markup* view is a view for tracking changes; revisions are indicated by a vertical red bar in the left margin and comments are indicated by an icon in the right margin.

All Markup view displays the document with all revisions and comments visible.

No Markup view displays the document in its final form—with all proposed changes included and comments hidden.

Original view displays the original, unchanged document with all revisions and comments hidden.

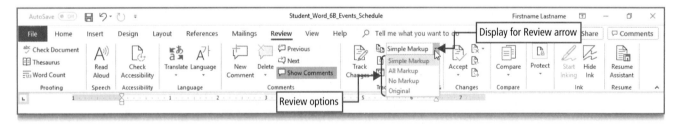

Figure 6.29

2 On the list, click **No Markup**. Notice that all comments and indicated changes are hidden. The document displays with all proposed changes included.

When you are editing a document in which you are proposing changes, this view is useful because the revisions of others or the markup of your own revisions is not distracting.

3 In the **Tracking group**, click the **Display for Review arrow**, and then from the list, click **All Markup**. Compare your screen with Figure 6.30.

At the stage where you, the document owner, must decide which revisions to accept or reject, you will find this view to be the most useful. The document displays with revisions—changes are shown as *markup*. Markup refers to the formatting Word uses to denote the revisions visually. For example, when a reviewer changes text, the original text displays with strikethrough formatting by default. When a reviewer inserts new text, the new text is underlined. A *vertical change bar* displays in the left margin next to each line of text that contains a revision. In All Markup view, the vertical change bar displays in black; in Simple Markup view, it displays in red. In All Markup view, shaded text indicates where a comment has been inserted.

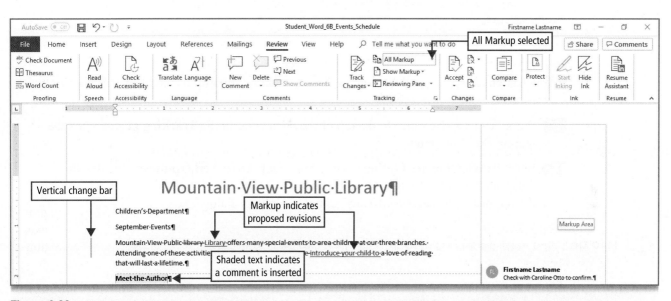

Figure 6.30

🖐️ **BY TOUCH**   Tap any vertical change bar to toggle between Simple Markup view and All Markup view.

4 In the **Tracking group**, click **Show Markup**, and then point to **Specific People** to see the name of each individual who proposed changes to this document. Compare your screen with Figure 6.31.

Here you can turn off the display of revisions by one or more reviewers. For example, you might want to view only the revisions proposed by a supervisor—before you consider the revisions proposed by others—by clearing the check box for all reviewers except the supervisor. In the Show Markup list, you can also determine which changes display by deselecting one or more of the options. *Ink* refers to marks made directly on a document by using a stylus on a Tablet PC.

⌨️ **MAC TIP**   On the Review tab, in the Tracking group, click Markup Options, and then point to Reviewers.

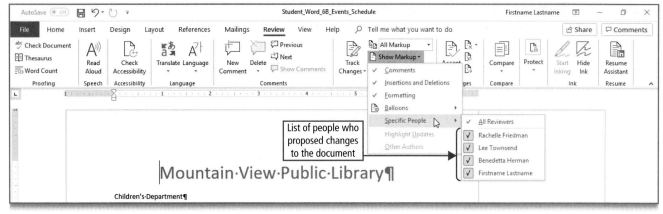

Figure 6.31

5 Click anywhere in the document to close the **Show Markup** list and leave all revision types by all reviewers displayed.

6 Press Ctrl + Home to move to the top of the document. In the **Tracking group**, click the **Dialog Box Launcher**.

7 In the **Track Changes Options** dialog box, click **Advanced Options** to display **the Advanced Track Changes Options** dialog box. The table shown in Figure 6.32 describes the options in the Advanced Track Changes Options dialog box.

MAC TIP In the Tracking group, click Markup Options, and then click Preferences.

Settings in the Advanced Track Changes Options Dialog Box	
Option	**Settings you can adjust**
Insertions, Deletions, Changed Lines, Comments	Specify the format and color of inserted text, deleted text, changed lines, and comments. By default, inserted text is underlined, deleted text displays with strikethrough formatting, and the vertical change bar indicating changes displays on the outside border—left margin. Click an arrow to select a different format and click the Color arrow to select a different color. The default, by author, indicates that Word will assign a different color to each person who inserts comments or tracks changes.
Moved from, Moved to	Specify the format of moved text. The default is green with double strikethrough in the moved content and a double underline below the content in its new location. To turn off this feature, clear the Track moves check box.
Inserted cells, Deleted cells	Specify the color that will display in a table if cells are inserted, deleted, merged, or split.
Track formatting markup area	Specify the location and width of the markup area. By default the location is at the right margin and the preferred width for balloons is set to 3.7". You can also control the display of connecting lines to text.

Figure 6.32

8 In the **Advanced Track Changes Options** dialog box, locate and verify that the Track formatting check box is selected. Below the check box, select the value in the **Preferred width** box, type **3** and then click **OK**.

This action will cause the markup area to display with a width of 3 inches.

9 Click **OK** again, and then **Save** 🖫 your document.

Use the Advanced Track Changes Options dialog box in this manner to set Track Changes to display the way that works best for you.

Activity 6.16 | Using the Reviewing Pane

The *Reviewing Pane*, which displays in a separate scrollable window, shows all of the changes and comments that currently display in your document. In this activity you will use the Reviewing Pane to view a summary of all changes and comments in the document.

1 On the **Review tab**, in the **Tracking group**, click the **Reviewing Pane arrow**. From the list, click **Reviewing Pane Vertical**, and then compare your screen with Figure 6.33.

The Reviewing Pane displays at the left of the document. Optionally, you can display the Reviewing Pane horizontally at the bottom of the document window. The summary section at the top of the Reviewing Pane displays the number of revisions that remain in your document.

MAC TIP   Click Reviewing to display the Reviewing pane.

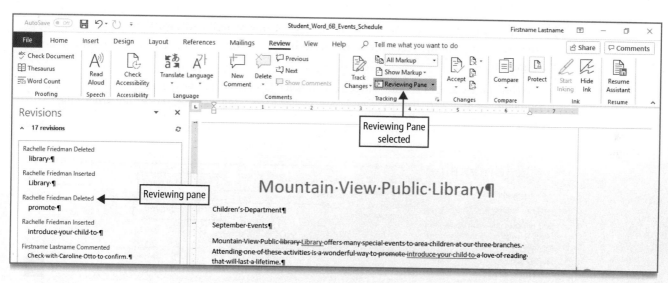

Figure 6.33

2 Take a moment to read the entries in the **Reviewing Pane**.

In the Reviewing Pane, you can view each type of revision, view the name of the reviewer associated with each item, and read long comments that do not display in the comments in the markup area. The Reviewing Pane is also useful for ensuring that all tracked changes have been *removed* from your document when it is ready for final distribution.

3 At the top of the **Reviewing Pane**, click **Close** ☒.

ALERT   Completing the Remainder of This Project in One Working Session

Plan to complete the remaining activities in this project in one working session. For purposes of instruction, some revisions in documents must be made within a restricted time frame. If you must take a break, save the document, and then close Word. When you return to complete the project, reopen your 6B_Events_Schedule file. If you are sharing a computer, be sure the user name and initials are the same as in the previous activities.

Activity 6.17 | Tracking Changes and Locking Tracking to Restrict Editing

6.2.1, 6.2.4

The Track Changes feature is turned off by default; you must turn on the feature each time you want to begin tracking changes in a document.

> **1** Press Ctrl + Home, if necessary, to move to the top of the document. On the **Review tab**, in the **Tracking group**, click the upper portion of the **Track Changes** button to enable tracking. Notice that the button displays in blue to indicate that the feature is turned on.

MAC TIP In the Tracking group click Track Changes to turn the slider to ON. Skip steps 2–4.

> **2** In the **Tracking group**, click the **Track Changes arrow**, and then click **Lock Tracking**.

The *Lock Tracking* feature prevents reviewers from turning off Track Changes and making changes that are not visible in markup.

> **3** In the **Lock Tracking** dialog box, in the **Enter password (optional)** box, type **1234** and then press Tab. In the **Reenter to confirm** box, type **1234** and then compare your screen with Figure 6.34.

The Track Changes feature will remain turned on, regardless of who edits the document—the author or reviewers. The password only applies to tracking changes; it does not protect the document.

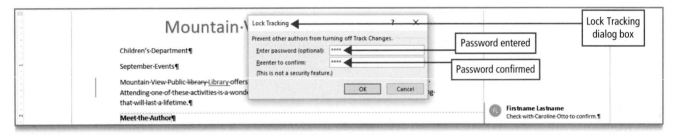

Figure 6.34

> **4** Click **OK** to close the **Lock Tracking** dialog box. Notice that the Track Changes button no longer displays in blue.

> **5** Select the second and third paragraphs in the document—*Children's Department* and *September Events*. Change the **Font Size** to **20**, apply **Bold** B, and then **Center** ☰ the selection. Compare your screen with Figure 6.35.

As you make each change, the markup displays in the markup area, and the vertical change bar displays to the left of the paragraph. The types of changes—formatted text and center alignment—are indicated in the balloons in the markup area and lines point to the location of the revisions.

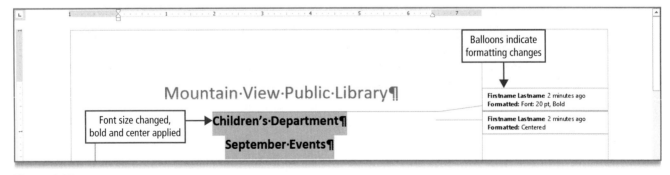

Figure 6.35

6 Locate the paragraph below *Baby Story Time* that begins *Specifically designed*. In the third line, click to position the insertion point to the left of *program*, type **one-hour** and then press Spacebar.

The inserted text is underlined and displays with your designated color.

7 Point to the inserted text, and then compare your screen with Figure 6.36.

A ScreenTip displays, showing the revision that was made, which reviewer made the change, and the date and time of the change.

Figure 6.36

8 In the markup area, read the comment that begins *Should we mention*. Use any technique you practiced to **Delete** the comment. **Save** your document.

Having responded to this suggestion by inserting appropriate text, you can delete the comment. When developing important documents, having others review the document can improve its content and appearance.

MORE KNOWLEDGE **Sharing a Document Using OneDrive**

Use the Share command to allow reviewers to insert comments or edit a document that has been saved to OneDrive. To share a saved document, open the document. Click the File tab, click Share, and then click Save to Cloud. Click the OneDrive folder to which you want to save the file, and then click Save.

Activity 6.18 | Accepting or Rejecting Changes in a Document

MOS
6.2.2, 6.2.3

After all reviewers have made their proposed revisions and added their comments, the document owner must decide which changes to accept and incorporate into the document and which changes to reject. Unlike revisions, it is not possible to accept or reject comments; instead, the document owner reads the comments, takes appropriate action or makes a decision, and then deletes each comment. In this Activity, you will accept and reject changes to create a final document.

1 Press Ctrl + Home.

When reviewing comments and changes in a document, it is good practice to start at the beginning of the document to be sure you do not miss any comments or revisions.

2 On the **Review tab**, in the **Tracking group**, click the **Track Changes arrow**, and then click **Lock Tracking**. In the **Unlock Tracking** dialog box, in the Password box, type **1234**, and then click **OK**.

Because you are finalizing the changes in a document, it is necessary to unlock tracking. After entering the password, you have unlocked tracking. In the Tracking group, the Track Changes button displays in blue, which indicates that the feature is turned on.

 MAC TIP Skip step 2.

3 On the **Review tab**, in the **Changes group**, click **Next Change** 📄. Notice that the second and third paragraphs in the document are selected.

In the Changes group, the Next Change button and the Previous Change button enable you to navigate from one revision or comment to the next or previous one.

4 In the **Changes group**, click the **Accept arrow**—the lower portion of the Accept button, and then click **Accept This Change**.

The text formatting is accepted for the selection, the related balloon no longer displays in the markup area, and the two paragraphs are still selected. When reviewing a document, changes can be accepted or rejected individually, or all at one time.

5 In the **Changes group**, click the upper portion of the **Accept** button to accept the alignment change and move to the next revision.

The centering change is applied to both paragraphs and the word *library* is selected.

🔄 **ANOTHER WAY**   Right-click the selection, and then click Accept.

---

6 In the next paragraph, point to the strikethrough text *library* and notice that the ScreenTip indicates that Rachelle Friedman deleted *library*. Then, point to the underline directly below *Library* to display a ScreenTip. Compare your screen with Figure 6.37.

When a reviewer replaces text—for example, when Rachelle replaced *library* with *Library*—the inserted text displays with an underline and in the color designated for the reviewer. The original text displays with strikethrough formatting.

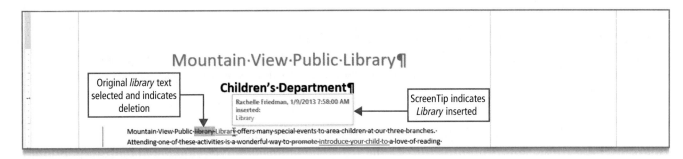

Figure 6.37

7 In the **Changes group**, click **Accept** two times to accept the deletion of *library* and the insertion of *Library*.

The next change, the deletion of *promote*, is selected.

8 With the suggested deletion—*promote*—selected, in the **Changes group**, click **Reject**, and then point to the selected text *introduce your child to*, to display a ScreenTip. Compare your screen with Figure 6.38.

The original text *promote* is reinserted in the sentence. As the document owner, you decide which proposed revisions to accept; you are not required to accept every change in a document.

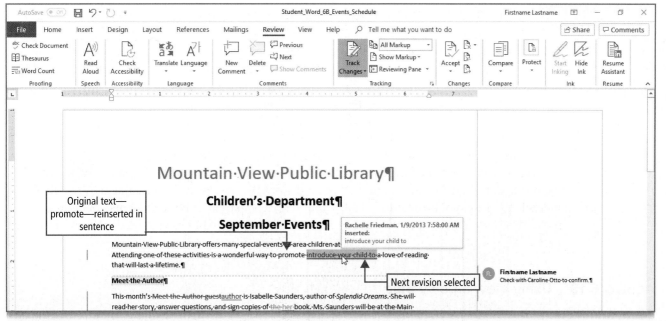

Figure 6.38

9 Click **Reject** again to reject the insertion of *introduce your child to* and to select the next change.

10 In the **Changes group**, click the **Accept arrow**. From the list, click **Accept All Changes and Stop Tracking**.

All remaining changes in the document are accepted and Track Changes is turned off.

11 Press Ctrl + Home, verify that the remaining comment displays, and then compare your screen with Figure 6.39.

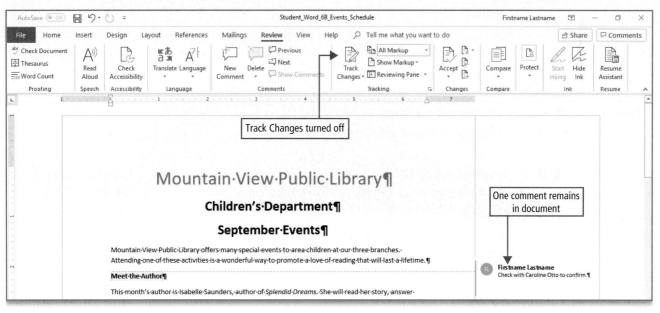

Figure 6.39

12 **Save** 🖫 your document; leave it open for the next activity.

Objective 6 | View Side by Side, Compare, and Combine Documents

GO! Learn How
Video W6-6

It is not always possible for reviewers to make their comments and edits on a single Word file. Each reviewer might edit a copy of the file, and then the document owner must gather all of the files and combine all the revisions into a single final document. One method to examine the changes is to use the ***View Side by Side*** command. Using the View Side by Side command displays two open documents, in separate windows, next to each other on your screen.

Word has two other features, ***Compare*** and ***Combine***, which enable you to view revisions in two documents and determine which changes to accept and which ones to reject. Compare is useful when reviewing differences between an original document and the latest version of the document. When using Compare, Word indicates that all revisions were made by the same individual. The Combine feature enables you to review two different documents containing revisions—both based on an original document—and the individuals who made the revisions are identified.

Activity 6.19 | Using View Side by Side

Abigail Garner has received another copy of the original file, which contains revisions and comments from two additional reviewers—Angie Harper and Natalia Ricci. In this Activity, you will use View Side by Side to compare the new document with the version you finalized in the previous activity.

1 With your file **Student_Word_6B_Events_Schedule** open and the insertion point at the top of the document, **Open** from the files you downloaded with this project **w06B_Schedule_Revisions**.

> **MAC TIP**   Skip steps 2–4.

2 On the **View tab**, in the **Window group**, click **View Side by Side** to display both documents.

> This view enables you to see whether there have been any major changes to the original document that should be discussed by the reviewers before making revisions. Both documents contain the same basic text.

> **ALERT**   **Why Doesn't the Entire Window Display?**
> Depending upon your screen resolution, the entire window may not display.

3 In the **w06B_Schedule_Revisions** document, if necessary, drag the horizontal scroll bar to the right so that you can see the markup area. Notice that both documents scroll. Compare your screen with Figure 6.40. Depending on your screen resolution, your view may differ.

> Edits and comments made by Angie Harper and Natalia Ricci display in the w06B_Schedule_ Revisions file. When View Side by Side is active, ***synchronous scrolling***—both documents scroll simultaneously—is turned on by default.

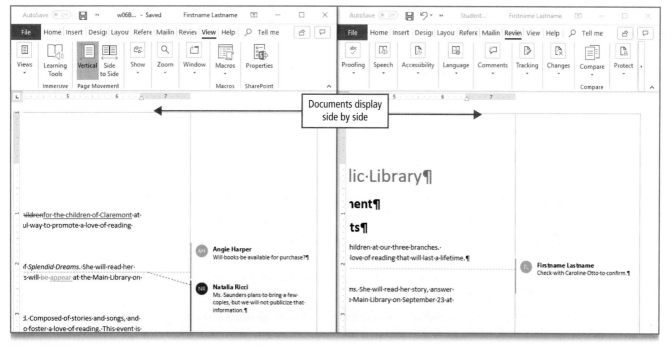

Figure 6.40

---

4 In the **w06B_Schedule_Revisions** document, in the **Window group**, click **View Side by Side** 🔲 to restore program windows to their original size.

5 In the **w06B_Schedule_Revisions** document, select the first paragraph, and then apply the **Heading 1** style.

6 Display the **Save As** dialog box, and then **Save** the file in your **Word Chapter 6 folder** as Lastname_Firstname_6B_Schedule_Revisions

7 **Close** ✖ the **Lastname_Firstname_6B_Schedule_Revisions** document. Notice your **Student_Word_6B_Events_Schedule** document displays.

8 Press Ctrl + W to close your **Student_Word_6B_Events_Schedule**, without closing Word.

Activity 6.20 | Combining Documents and Resolving Multi-Document Style Conflicts

MOS
Expert
1.1.3

In this Activity, you will combine the document containing revisions and comments by Angie Harper and Natalia Ricci with your finalized version of the events schedule. Then, you will accept or reject the additional revisions to create a final document ready for distribution to the public.

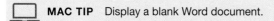

MAC TIP   Display a blank Word document.

---

1 On the **Review tab**, in the **Compare group**, click **Compare**. From the list, click **Combine** to display the **Combine Documents** dialog box.

When using the Combine feature, it is not necessary to have an open document.

2 In the **Combine Documents** dialog box, click the **Original document arrow**, and then click **Browse**. In the **Open** dialog box, navigate to your **Word Chapter 6** folder, select the file **Lastname_Firstname_6B_Schedule_Revisions**, and then click **Open**.

Recall that this file includes revisions and comments from two additional reviewers. *Original document* usually refers to a document without revisions or, in this case, the document that you have not yet reviewed. The file also includes the formatting change you made to the first paragraph.

 ANOTHER WAY To the right of the **Original document** box, click **Browse**.

3 Under **Original document**, in the **Label unmarked changes with** box, if your name does not display, delete the existing text, and then type your first and last names.

4 Click the **Revised document arrow**, and then click **Browse**. Navigate to your **Word Chapter 6** folder, select **Student_Word_6B_Events_Schedule**, and then click **Open**. (If you are not submitting the file in **MyLab IT**, select your Lastname_Firstname_6B_Events_Schedule file.)

Revised document refers to the latest version of the document—in this case, the document where you accepted and rejected changes.

5 Under **Revised document**, in the **Label unmarked changes with** box, if your name does not display, delete the existing text, and then type your first and last names.

6 In the **Combine Documents** dialog box, click **More**, and then under **Show changes in**, be sure the **New document** option is selected. Compare your screen with Figure 6.41.

The More button expands the dialog box to display additional settings. By selecting the New document option, all changes in both files display in a new document.

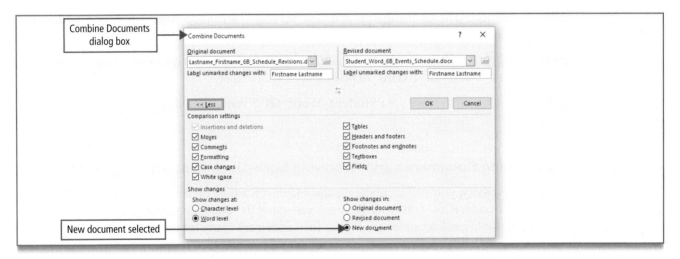

Figure 6.41

7 In the **Combine Documents** dialog box, click **Less**, and then click **OK**. In the message box indicating that Word can only store one style of formatting changes in the final merged document, under **Keep formatting changes**, select **The other document (Student_Word_6B_Events_Schedule)** option button.

When combining two documents, style conflicts can exist when formatting changes are made to the same text in different versions of the document in the same time frame. In this case, the conflict exists because both files contain a formatting change applied to the first paragraph. The message box allows you to select the document that contains the formatting change you want to display in the combined document.

8 In the message box, click **Continue with Merge**. Compare your screen with Figure 6.42.

The Tri-Pane Review Panel displays with the combined document in the left pane, the original document in the top right pane, and the revised document in the bottom right pane. The Reviewing Pane displays to the left of your screen, indicating all accepted changes in your Lastname_Firstname_6B_Events_Schedule file with your user name.

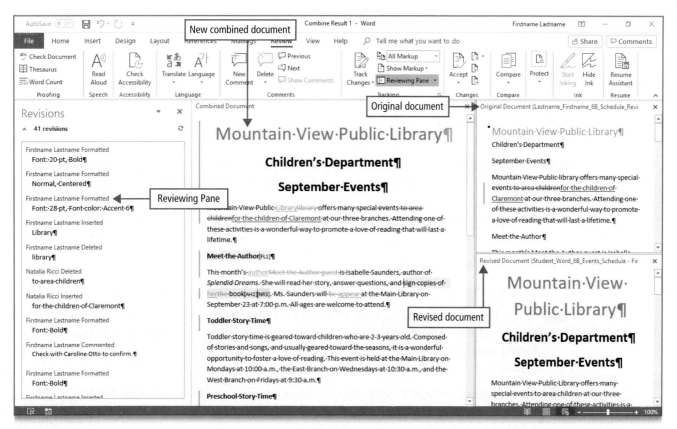

Figure 6.42

ALERT   Should Both Documents Display?

If only the combined document displays, in the Compare group, click Compare, click Show Source Documents, and then click Show Both. If the Reviewing Pane does not display, in the Tracking group, click the Reviewing Pane arrow, and then click Reviewing Pane Vertical.

MAC TIP   Only the combined document will display.

---

9 If necessary, click to position the insertion point at the beginning of the **Combined Document**. **Save** the document in your **Word Chapter 6** folder as **Lastname_Firstname_6B_Schedule_Combined**

Activity 6.21 │ Accepting and Rejecting Changes in a Combined Document

1 With the **Lastname_Firstname_6B_Schedule_Combined** document active, on the **Review tab**, in the **Comments group**, click the **Delete arrow**, and then click **Delete All Comments in Document**. If necessary, press Ctrl + Home.

2 In the **Changes group**, click **Next Change**, and then click **Accept** to accept the first change. Continue to click **Accept** until the revision *to area children* is selected. Compare your screen with Figure 6.43.

Figure 6.43

Mountain·View·Public·Library¶

Children's·Department¶

September·Events¶

3 On the **Review tab**, in the **Changes group**, with the revision *to area children* selected, click **Reject** two times.

4 In the **Changes group**, click the **Accept arrow**, and then click **Accept All Changes and Stop Tracking**. In the **Reviewing Pane**, notice that no further revisions or comments remain.

5 On the right of your screen, **Close** ☒ the two panes—the original and revised documents. **Close** ☒ the **Reviewing Pane**, press ⌃Ctrl + Home, and then **Save** 🖫 your changes.

Because all remaining revisions in the document are accepted, there is no longer a need to view the original or revised documents.

Activity 6.22 | Restoring Default Settings

In this Activity, you will reset the width of the markup area and finalize the document.

1 In the **Tracking group**, click the **Dialog Box Launcher** 🗗, and then click **Advanced Options**. In the **Advanced Track Changes Options** dialog box, below the **Track formatting** check box, select the value in the **Preferred width** box. Type **3.7** and then click **OK** two times to close the dialog boxes.

2 At the bottom of **Page 1**, right-click in the footer area, and then click **Edit Footer**. Right-click the file name, and then click **Update Field** to apply the correct file name in the footer. **Close** the footer area.

3 Display the document **Properties**. In the **Tags** box, type **final events schedule** and then in the **Subject** box, type your course name and section number. If necessary, edit the author name to display your name, and then **Save** and **Close** your document.

For Non-MyLab Submissions Determine What Your Instructor Requires
As directed by your instructor, submit your completed Word file.

4 In **MyLab IT**, locate and click the Grader Project **Word 6B Events Schedule**. In step 3, under **Upload Completed Assignment**, click **Choose File**. In the **Open** dialog box, navigate to your **Word Chapter 6** folder, and then click your **Lastname_Firstname_6B_Schedule_Combined** file one time to select it. In the lower right corner of the **Open** dialog box, click **Open**.

The name of your selected file displays above the Upload button.

5 To submit your file to **MyLab IT** for grading, click **Upload**, wait a moment for a green **Success!** message, and then in **step 4**, click the blue **Submit for Grading** button. Click **Close Assignment** to return to your list of **Course Materials**.

You have completed Project 6B **END**

Microsoft Office Specialist (MOS) Skills in This Chapter	
Project 6A	**Project 6B**
1.2.4 Format page background elements	**6.1.1** Add comments
Expert 2.2.1 Configure hyphenation and line numbers	**6.1.2** Review and reply to comments
Expert 3.1.1 Create QuickParts	**6.1.3** Resolve comments
Expert 3.1.2 Manage building blocks	**6.1.4** Delete comments
Expert 3.2.1 Create custom color sets	**6.2.1** Track changes
Expert 3.2.2 Create custom font sets	**6.2.2** Review tracked changes
Expert 3.2.3 Create custom themes	**6.2.3** Accept and reject tracked changes
	6.2.4 Lock and unlock change tracking
	Expert 1.1.4 Compare and combine multiple documents

Build Your E-Portfolio

An E-Portfolio is a collection of evidence, stored electronically, that showcases what you have accomplished while completing your education. Collecting and then sharing your work products with potential employers reflects your academic and career goals. Your completed documents from the following projects are good examples to show what you have learned: 6G, 6K, and 6L.

GO! For Job Success

The Internet of Things

Physical objects can be embedded with electronics and software that allow connectivity and data exchange with manufacturers, operators, and each other. These connected objects make up The Internet of Things. Examples include cars that send data on fuel efficiency to the manufacturer and devices that remind patients to take medications and report medical information to their doctors.

Amazon has introduced the Dash Button, which allows customers to order refills of household supplies simply by pressing the button when the item runs low, no computer or Amazon app required. One area where the Internet of Things has huge potential is in sensors that can create an alert when there is danger, such as sensors in a bridge that can signal when the structure is weakening.

g-stockstudio/ Shutterstock

> If you owned a business, what are some ways that the Internet of Things could increase energy efficiency?

> What are some items in your household that would be convenient to reorder with the push of a button?

> What is another example of when danger could be averted by sensors inside a "thing"?

End of Chapter

Summary

Inserting building blocks—such as text boxes, pictures, Quick Tables, and AutoText—can save time and provide consistency in your documents. Use built-in document elements or create your own building blocks.

A theme template, defined by colors, fonts, and effects, enhances the appearance of a document. Attach a theme template to multiple documents to create documents that have a coordinated appearance.

The Track Changes feature enables a group of individuals to work together on a document. Reviewers can insert comments; reply to comments made by others; insert, edit, delete, and move text; and format documents.

The author of the document can accept or reject revisions. The author can compare two different versions of a document that has been revised using the Track Changes feature or combine them in a new document.

GO! Learn It Online

Review the concepts, key terms, and MOS skills in this chapter by completing these online challenges, which you can find at **MyLab IT**.

Chapter Quiz: Answer matching and multiple choice questions to test what you learned in this chapter.

Lessons on the GO!: Learn how to use all the new apps and features as they are introduced by Microsoft.

MOS Prep Quiz: Answer questions to review the MOS skills that you practiced in this chapter.

Project Guide for Word Chapter 6

Your instructor will assign Projects from this list to ensure your learning and assess your knowledge.

Project	Apply Skills from These Chapter Objectives	Project Type		Project Location
6A MyLab IT	Objectives 1–3 from Project 6A	**6A Instructional Project (Grader Project)** Guided instruction to learn the skills in Project 6A.	**Instruction**	In MyLab IT and in text
6B MyLab IT	Objectives 4–6 from Project 6B	**6B Instructional Project (Grader Project)** Guided instruction to learn the skills in Project 6B.	**Instruction**	In MyLab IT and in text
6C	Objectives 1–3 from Project 6A	**6C Skills Review (Scorecard Grading)** A guided review of the skills from Project 6A.	**Review**	In text
6D	Objectives 4–6 from Project 6B	**6D Skills Review (Scorecard Grading)** A guided review of the skills from Project 6B.	**Review**	In text
6E MyLab IT	Objectives 1–3 from Project 6A	**6E Mastery (Grader Project)** A demonstration of your mastery of the skills in Project 6A with extensive decision making.	**Mastery and Transfer of Learning**	In MyLab IT and in text
6F MyLab IT	Objectives 4–6 from Project 6B	**6F Mastery (Grader Project)** A demonstration of your mastery of the skills in Project 6B with extensive decision making.	**Mastery and Transfer of Learning**	In MyLab IT and in text
6G MyLab IT	Objectives 1–6 from Project 6A and 6B	**6G Mastery (Grader Project)** A demonstration of your mastery of the skills in Projects 6A and 6B with extensive decision making.	**Mastery and Transfer of Learning**	In MyLab IT and in text
6H	Combination of Objectives from Projects 6A and 6B	**6H GO! Fix It (Scorecard Grading)** A demonstration of your mastery of the skills in Projects 6A and 6B by creating a correct result from a document that contains errors you must find.	**Critical Thinking**	IRC
6I	Combination of Objectives from Projects 6A and 6B	**6I GO! Make It (Scorecard Grading)** A demonstration of your mastery of the skills in Projects 6A and 6B by creating a result from a supplied picture.	**Critical Thinking**	IRC
6J	Combination of Objectives from Projects 6A and 6B	**6J GO! Solve It (Rubric Grading)** A demonstration of your mastery of the skills in Projects 6A and 6B, your decision-making skills, and your critical thinking skills. A task-specific rubric helps you self-assess your result.	**Critical Thinking**	IRC
6K	Combination of Objectives from Projects 6A and 6B	**6K GO! Solve It (Rubric Grading)** A demonstration of your mastery of the skills in Projects 6A and 6B, your decision-making skills, and your critical thinking skills. A task-specific rubric helps you self-assess your result.	**Critical Thinking**	In text
6L	Combination of Objectives from Projects 6A and 6B	**6L GO! Think (Rubric Grading)** A demonstration of your understanding of the chapter concepts applied in a manner that you would outside of college. An analytic rubric helps you and your instructor grade the quality of your work by comparing it to the work an expert in the discipline would create.	**Critical Thinking**	In text
6M	Combination of Objectives from Projects 6A and 6B	**6M GO! Think (Rubric Grading)** A demonstration of your understanding of the chapter concepts applied in a manner that you would outside of college. An analytic rubric helps you and your instructor grade the quality of your work by comparing it to the work an expert in the discipline would create.	**Critical Thinking**	IRC
6N	Combination of Objectives from Projects 6A and 6B	**6N You and GO! (Rubric Grading)** A demonstration of your understanding of the chapter concepts applied in a manner that you would in a personal situation. An analytic rubric helps you and your instructor grade the quality of your work.	**Critical Thinking**	IRC
Capstone Project for Word Chapters 4-6	Combination of Objectives from Chapters 4-6	A demonstration of your mastery of the skills in Chapters 4-6 with extensive decision making. **(Grader Project)**		In MyLab IT and IRC

Glossary

Glossary of Chapter Key Terms

All Markup A Track Changes view that displays the document with all revisions and comments visible.

Author The owner, or creator, of the original document.

Balloon The outline shape in which a comment or formatting change displays.

Building blocks Reusable pieces of content or other document parts—for example, headers, footers, and page number formats—that are stored in galleries.

Building Blocks Organizer A feature that enables you to view—in a single location—all of the available building blocks from all the different galleries.

Combine A Track Changes feature that allows you to review two different documents containing revisions, both based on an original document.

Comment A note that an author or reviewer adds to a document.

Compare A Track Changes feature that enables you to review differences between an original document and the latest version of the document.

Hyphenation A tool in Word that controls how words are split between two lines.

Ink Revision marks made directly on a document by using a stylus on a Tablet PC.

Lock Tracking A feature that prevents reviewers from turning off Track Changes and making changes that are not visible in markup.

Markup The formatting Word uses to denote a document's revisions visually.

Markup area The space to the right or left of a document where comments and formatting changes display in balloons.

No Markup A Track Changes view that displays the document in its final form—with all proposed changes included and comments hidden.

Original A Track Changes view that displays the original, unchanged document with all revisions and comments hidden.

Quick Parts Reusable pieces of content that are available to insert into a document, including building blocks, document properties, and fields.

Quick Tables Tables that are stored as building blocks.

Reviewer An individual who reviews and marks changes on a document.

Reviewing Pane A separate scrollable window that shows all of the changes and comments that currently display in a document.

Revisions Changes made to a document.

Simple Markup The default Track Changes view that indicates revisions by vertical red lines in the left margin and displays comment icons in the right margin.

Synchronous scrolling The setting that causes two documents to scroll simultaneously.

Text box A movable, resizable container for text or graphics.

Theme A predesigned set of colors, fonts, and line and fill effects that look good together and is applied to an entire document by a single selection.

Theme template A stored, user-defined set of colors, fonts, and effects that can be shared with other Office programs.

Track Changes A feature that makes a record of the changes made to a document.

Vertical change bar A line that displays in the left margin next to each line of text that contains a revision.

View Side by Side A view that displays two open documents, in separate windows, next to each other on the screen.

Chapter Review

| Skills Review | Project 6C Literacy Program |

In the following Skills Review, you will create and save building blocks and create a theme to be used in a flyer seeking volunteers for Mountain View Public Library's Adult Literacy Program. Your completed document will look similar to Figure 6.44.

Apply 6A skills from these Objectives:

1. Create Custom Building Blocks
2. Create and Save a Theme Template
3. Create a Document by Using Building Blocks

Project Files

For Project 6C, you will need the following files:

New blank Word document
w06C_Literacy_Program
w06C_Literacy_Blocks
w06C_Literacy_Image

You will save your files as:

Lastname_Firstname_6C_Literacy_Blocks
Lastname_Firstname_6C_Literacy_Program
Lastname_Firstname_6C_Literacy_Theme

Project Results

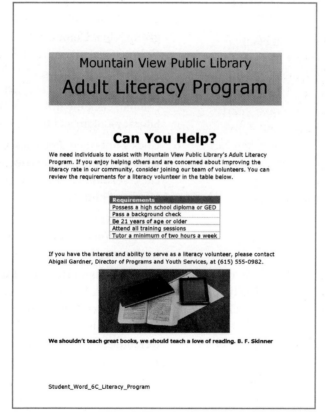

Figure 6.44

(continues on next page)

Chapter Review

1 Start Word. From your student data files, open **w06C_Literacy_Blocks** and if necessary, display the ruler and formatting marks. **Save** the file in your **Word Chapter 6** folder as **Lastname_Firstname_6C_Literacy_Blocks**

a. Select the text box at the top of the page. On the **Format tab**, in the **Shape Styles group**, click **More**. In the fourth row, click the third style.

b. Select the first line of text, and then change the **Font Size** to **24**. Select the second line of text, and then change the **Font Size** to **36**.

c. Click the outside edge of the text box to select it. On the **Insert tab**, in the **Text group**, click **Text Box**, and then click **Save Selection to Text Box Gallery**. In the **Name** box, type **Literacy Heading** and then click in the **Description** box. Type **Use as the heading for literacy documents** and then click **OK**. (Mac users, skip this step.)

2 Position the insertion point in the second blank paragraph below the text box. On the **Insert tab**, in the **Tables group**, click **Table**, point to **Quick Tables**, scroll down, and then click **Tabular List**. (Mac users, in the second blank paragraph below the text box, insert a table with 1 column and 8 rows. In the first cell, type Requirements and then AutoFit the column. Skip step 2a.)

a. Select the text **ITEM**, and then type **Requirements** Press Tab. Right-click, on the mini toolbar click **Delete**, and then click **Delete Columns**. Select the text in all the remaining cells of the table, and then press Delete.

b. Position the insertion point in the first cell of the table. Under **Table Tools**, on the **Design tab**, in the **Table Styles group**, click **More**. In the **Table Styles** gallery, under **List Tables**, in the fourth row, click the third style.

c. Point slightly outside of the upper left corner of the table, and then click the **table move handle** to select the entire table. On the **Insert tab**, in the **Tables group**, click **Table**. Point to **Quick Tables**, and then at the bottom of the gallery, click **Save Selection to Quick Tables Gallery**. In the **Name** box, type **Job Information** and then click in the **Description** box. Type **Use for listing job requirements** and then click **OK**. (Mac users, skip this step.)

d. Press Ctrl + End. Type **We shouldn't teach great books; we should teach a love of reading. B. F. Skinner**

e. Select the text you just typed. On the **Insert tab**, in the **Text group**, click **Explore Quick Parts**, click **AutoText**, and then click **Save Selection to AutoText Gallery**. In the **Create New Building Block** dialog box, in the **Name** box, type **Literacy** and then in the **Description** box, type **Quote for program** Click the **Save in arrow**, and then click **Building Blocks**. Click **OK**. (Mac users, select the text you typed. On the menu—not the ribbon—click Insert, point to AutoText, and then click New. Type Literacy and then click OK.)

f. **Save** your changes. Click the **File tab**, and then click **Close** to close the document but leave Word open.

3 Press Ctrl + N to display a new blank document. (Mac users, skip this step and skip steps 3a-3e. Continue with step 4.)

a. On the **Design tab**, in the **Document Formatting group**, click **Colors**, and then click **Customize Colors**. Click the **Accent 2 arrow**, and then under **Theme Colors**, in the last column, click the first color. Click the **Accent 3 arrow**, and then in the last column, click the fifth color. In the Name box, type **Literacy Colors** and then click Save.

b. Click **Fonts**, and then click **Customize Fonts**. Click the **Body font arrow**, scroll down, and then click **Verdana. Save** the theme fonts with the name **Literacy Fonts**

c. Click **Themes**, and then click **Save Current Theme**. In your **Word Chapter 6** folder, **Save** the theme as **Lastname_Firstname_6C_Literacy_Theme**

d. On the **Design tab**, in the **Document Formatting group**, click **Colors**, right-click **Literacy Colors**, and then click **Delete**. When a message displays to confirm the deletion, click **Yes**. Using the same technique, click **Fonts**, and then **Delete** the **Literacy Fonts**.

e. Click the **File tab**, and then **Close** the document without saving changes, but leave Word open.

4 From your student data files, open **w06C_Literacy_Program**. **Save** the file in your **Word Chapter 6** folder as **Lastname_Firstname_6C_Literacy_Program** and then insert the file name in the footer. Display rulers and formatting marks, if necessary.

(continues on next page)

Chapter Review

Skills Review: Project 6C Literacy Program (continued)

a. On the **Design tab**, in the **Document Formatting group**, click **Themes**, and then click **Browse for Themes**. In your **Word Chapter 6** folder, select your **Lastname_Firstname_6C_Literacy_Theme** file, and then click **Open** to apply the theme. (Mac users, from your student data files, apply the Mac_6C_Program_Theme file.)

b. With the insertion point at the top of the document, press Enter, and then position the insertion point in the first blank paragraph. On the **Insert tab**, in the **Text group**, click **Text Box**. Scroll to the bottom of the gallery, and then under **General**, click your **Literacy Heading** building block. (Mac users, open your Lastname_Firstname_6C_Literacy_Blocks file. Select the text box and then copy and paste the text box at the top of your document. Leave the building blocks file open.)

c. At the end of the paragraph that ends *in the table below*, position the insertion point after the period, and then press Enter two times.

5 On the **Insert tab**, in the **Tables group**, click **Table**, point to **Quick Tables**, scroll to the bottom of the gallery, and then under **General**, click **Job Information**. (Mac users, in your Lastname_Firstname_6C_Literacy_Blocks document, copy the table and then paste it in your newsletter document. Close the building blocks document.)

a. Position the insertion point in the second row of the table. Type the following text in the table, pressing Tab after each line to move to the next row:

Possess a high school diploma or GED

Pass a background check

Be 21 years of age or older

Attend all training sessions

Tutor a minimum of two hours a week

b. Select the empty rows of the table. On the **Table Tools Layout tab**, in the **Rows & Columns group** click **Delete**, and then click **Delete Rows**. Point slightly outside of the upper left corner of the table, and then click the **table move handle** to select the entire table. **Center** the table on the page.

6 Press Ctrl + End, press Enter, and then on the **Home tab**, in the **Paragraph group**, click **Center**. On the **Insert tab**, in the **Illustrations group**, click **Pictures**. In the **Insert Picture** dialog box, navigate to your student data files, select the file **w06C_Literacy_Image**, and then click **Insert**.

a. Position the insertion point to the right of the picture, and then press Enter. On the **Insert tab**, in the **Text group**, click **Explore Quick Parts**, click **AutoText**, and then click **Literacy**. (Mac users, to insert the AutoText entry, type Quote and then when the ScreenTip displays, press Enter.)

b. Select the inserted text, change the **Font Size** to **10**, and then apply **Bold**. If necessary, at the end of the document, delete the blank paragraph.

c. Press Ctrl + Home. Display the document **Properties**. In the **Tags** box, type literacy program, volunteers and in the **Subject** box, type your course name and section number. If necessary, edit the author name to display your name, and then **Save** the document.

d. On the **Insert tab**, in the **Text group**, click **Explore Quick Parts**, and then click **Building Blocks Organizer**. In the **Building Blocks Organizer** dialog box, in the upper left corner, click **Name** to sort the building blocks alphabetically by name. Locate your building block **Job Information**, click to select it, click **Delete**, and then click **Yes** to confirm the deletion. Using the same technique, scroll to locate and then **Delete** your building blocks **Literacy Heading** and **Literacy**. **Close** the dialog box. (Mac users, skip this step.)

7 **Save** and **Close** your document and submit as directed by your instructor. If a message displays regarding changes to building blocks, click **Save** to accept the changes.

You have completed Project 6C | **END**

Chapter Review

Apply 6B skills from these Objectives:

4. Use Comments in a Document
5. Track Changes in a Document
6. View Side by Side, Compare, and Combine Documents

In the following Skills Review, you will edit a user guide for Mountain View Public Library by creating and deleting comments, inserting text, applying formatting, and accepting changes made by others. Your completed document will look similar to Figure 6.45.

Project Files

For Project 6D, you will need the following files:

w06D_User_Guide

w06D_Reviewed_Guide

You will save your files as:

Lastname_Firstname_6D_User_Guide

Lastname_Firstname_6D_Combined_Guide

Project Results

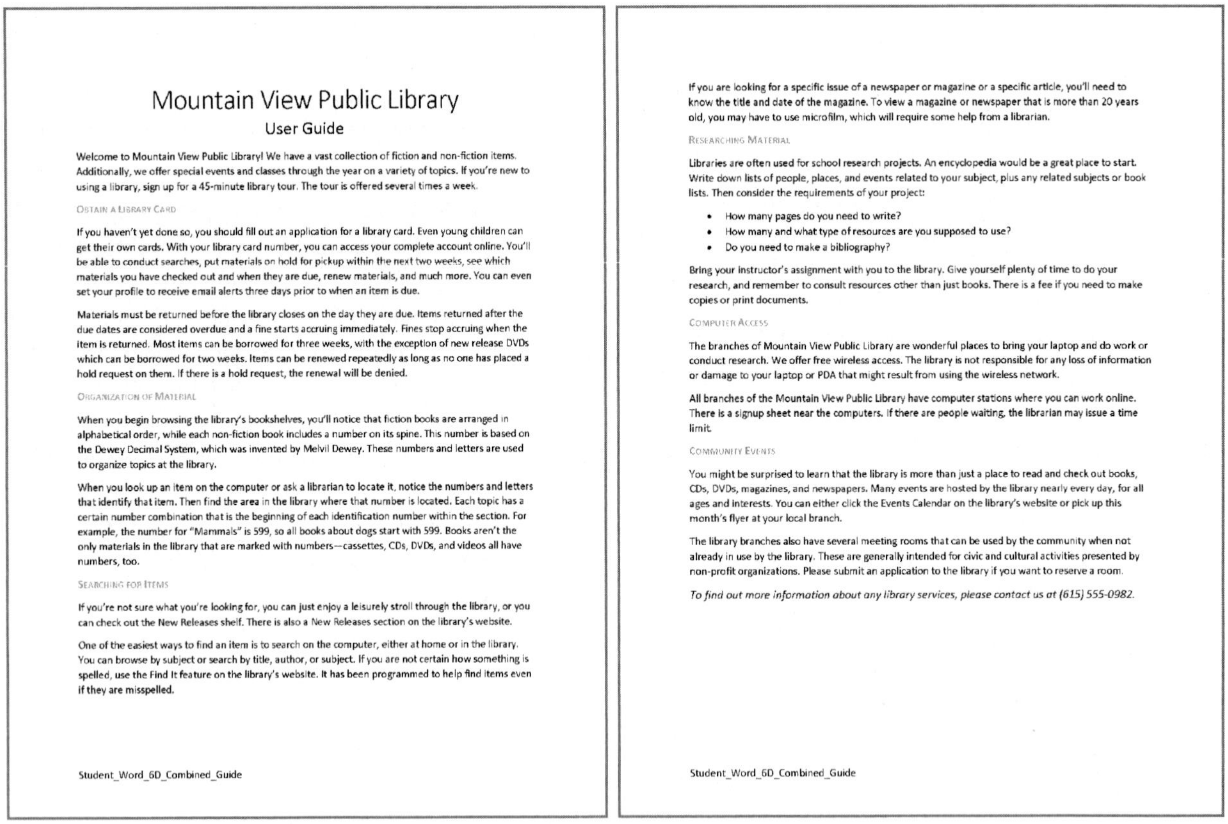

Figure 6.45

(continues on next page)

Chapter Review

1 **Start** Word. Navigate to your student files and open the file **w06D_User_Guide**. **Save** the document in your **Word Chapter 6** folder as **Lastname_Firstname_6D_User_Guide** and then insert the file name in the footer. (Mac users, skip step 1a.)

a. On the **Review tab**, in the **Tracking group**, click the **Dialog Box Launcher**. In the **Track Changes Options** dialog box, click **Change User Name**. If you are able to do so, in the **User name** box, delete any existing text, and then type your own first and last names. In the **Initials** box, delete any existing text, and then type your initials. Below the **Initials** box, select the **Always use these values regardless of sign in to Office** check box. Click **OK** two times.

b. On the **Review tab**, in the **Tracking group**, click the **Display for Review arrow**, and then click **All Markup**. In the paragraph beginning *Materials must be*, select the text **DVDs which can be borrowed for two weeks**. On the **Review tab**, in the **Comments group**, click **New Comment**. In the comment, type **Check with Angie Harper to confirm that it is two weeks.**

c. Press [Ctrl] + [Home]. Click to position the insertion point in the *Benedetta Herman* comment that begins *I thought*, and then in the **Comments group**, click **Delete**. Using the same technique, delete the *Caroline Marina* comment that begins *We offer*.

d. Locate your comment, and then replace *Angie Harper* with **Caroline Marina**

2 To enable tracking, in the **Tracking group**, click **Track Changes**. Select the first paragraph—the title—and then apply **Center**. Select the second paragraph—*User Guide*—change the **Font Size** to **18** and then apply **Center**.

a. In the paragraph that begins *When you begin browsing*, in the third line, replace the text *Melville* with **Melvil** and then if necessary, delete the related *Benedetta Herman* comment.

b. On **Page 2**, in the paragraph that begins *The branches of*, in the second line, delete the sentence *We have many comfortable desks and chairs*.

c. Press [Ctrl] + [End]. Press [Enter], and then type **To find out more information about any library services, please contact us at (615) 555-0982.** Select the text you just typed, change the **Font Size** to **12**, and apply **Italic**. Delete the *Benedetta Herman* comment that begins *Please add*.

d. Press [Ctrl] + [Home]. On the **Review tab**, in the **Changes group**, click the **Accept arrow**, and then click **Accept All Changes and Stop Tracking**.

e. **Save** your document. Click the **File tab**, and then **Close** the document but leave Word open.

3 On the **Review tab**, in the **Compare group**, click **Compare**, and then click **Combine**. In the **Combine Documents** dialog box, click the **Original document arrow**, and then click **Browse**. Navigate to your student files, select the file **w06D_Reviewed_Guide**, and then click **Open**.

a. Click the **Revised document arrow**, and then click **Browse**. Navigate to your **Word Chapter 6** folder, select the file **Lastname_Firstname_6D_User_Guide**, and then click **Open**.

b. In the **Combine Documents** dialog box, click **More**, and then under **Show changes in**, select the **New document** option, if necessary. Click **Less**, and then click **OK**. If necessary, on the right of your screen, close the Original Document Pane and the Revised Document Pane, and then on the left, close the Reviewing Pane. (Mac users, only the combined document will display.)

c. With the insertion point positioned at the beginning of the **Combined Document**, click **Save**, and then save the document in your **Word Chapter 6** folder as **Lastname_Firstname_6D_Combined_Guide**

4 On the **Review tab**, in the **Changes group**, click the **Accept arrow**, and then click **Accept All Changes and Stop Tracking**.

a. On **Page 2**, locate the *Angie Harper* comment. Select the two sentences that begin *Be aware*, and end *wireless device*. **Delete** the two sentences.

b. On the **Review tab**, in the **Comments group**, click the **Delete arrow**, and then click **Delete All Comments in Document**.

5 Right-click in the footer area, and then click **Edit Footer**. Right-click the existing text, and then from the shortcut menu, click **Update Field**. If the field does not display, insert the file name field. **Close** the footer area.

a. Press [Ctrl] + [Home]. Display the document **Properties**. In the **Tags** box, type **user guide** and in the **Subject** box, type your course name and section number. If necessary, edit the author name to display your name.

b. **Save** and **Close** your document and submit as directed by your instructor.

You have completed Project 6D | END

| **Mastering Word** **Project 6E Seminar Agenda**

Apply 6A skills from these Objectives:

1. Create Custom Building Blocks
2. Create and Save a Theme Template
3. Create a Document by Using Building Blocks

In the following Mastering Word project, you will create and save building blocks and create a theme for an agenda for Mountain View Public Library's seminar on Public Libraries and the Internet. Your completed documents will look similar to Figure 6.46.

Project Files for MyLab IT Grader

1. In your **MyLab IT** course, locate and click **Word 6E Seminar Agenda**, Download Materials, and then Download All Files.
2. Extract the zipped folder to your Word Chapter 6 folder. Close the Grader download screens.
3. Take a moment to open the downloaded **Word_6E_Seminar_Agenda_Instructions**; note any recent updates to the book.

Project Results

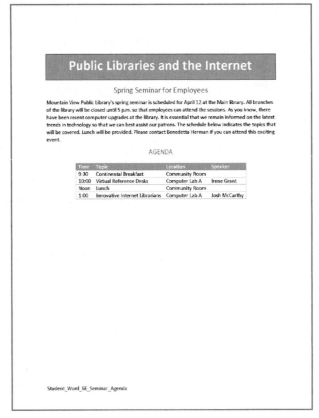

Figure 6.46

For Non-MyLab Submissions

For Project 6E, you will need:

w06E_Seminar Agenda

w06E_Seminar_Blocks

In your Word Chapter 6 folder, save your documents as:

Lastname_Firstname_6E_Seminar_Agenda

Lastname_Firstname_6E_Seminar_Blocks

Lastname_Firstname_6E_Seminar_Theme

Begin the project with step 1. In step 9 open w06E_Seminar_Agenda, and then save the file as Lastname_Firstname_6E_Seminar_Agenda. After step 17, save and submit your file as directed by your instructor.

(continues on next page)

Content-Based Assessments (Mastery and Transfer of Learning)

1 Navigate to your **Word Chapter 6 folder**, and then double-click the Word file **w06E_Seminar_Blocks**. Save the file as **Lastname_Firstname_6E_Seminar Blocks**.

2 To the text box, apply a shape style—in the second row, click the third style. In the text box, change the text **Font Size** to **28** and then apply **Bold** and **Center**.

3 Select and then save the text box in the Text Box gallery with the name **Internet Seminar** and the description **Use in Internet Seminar documents** (Mac users, skip this step.)

4 Click in the second blank paragraph below the text box, display the **Quick Tables** gallery, and then insert a **Double Table**. Above the table, delete the text *The Greek Alphabet* and then delete the last two columns and the last eight rows. Delete all of the text in the table. (Mac users, insert a table with 4 columns and 5 rows.)

5 In the first cell of the table, type **Time** and then press Tab. Type **Topic** and then press Tab. Type **Location** and then press Tab. Type **Speaker** and then display the **Table Style** gallery. Under **List Tables**, in the fourth row, apply the third style.

6 Save the table in the **Quick Tables** gallery with the name **Seminar Schedule** and the description **Use for seminar schedules** (Mac users, skip this step.)

7 **Save** your changes, and then **Close** the document but leave Word open.

8 Start a new blank document. Display the **Create New Theme Colors** dialog box. Change **Accent 1**—in the tenth column, click the fifth color. Change **Accent 2**—in the tenth column, click the first color. Change the **Name** to **Internet Colors** and then save the current theme in your **Word Chapter 6** folder as **Lastname_Firstname_6E_Seminar_Theme Close** your theme file but leave Word open. Do not save changes. (Mac users, skip this step).

9 From the files you downloaded with this project, **Open** the file **Student_Word_6E_Seminar_Agenda**, and then insert the file name in the footer. In the first blank paragraph, display the **Text Box** gallery, and then insert your **Internet Seminar** text box. (Mac users, open your Lastname_Firstname_6E_Seminar_Blocks file. Copy and paste the text box at the top of your document.)

10 Apply your **Lastname_Firstname_6E_Seminar_Theme** to the document. (Mac users, from the files for this project, apply Mac_6E_Seminar_Theme.)

11 Select the text *Spring Seminar for Employees*, apply the **Heading 1** style, and then apply **Center**. Change the **Spacing After** to **6 pt**. Select the text *AGENDA*, apply the **Heading 2** style, apply **Center**, and then change the **Spacing After** to **12 pt**.

12 Position the insertion point in the blank paragraph following *AGENDA*, and then insert your **Seminar Schedule** quick table. (Mac users, from your Lastname_Firstname_6E_Seminar_Blocks file, copy and paste the table in the blank paragraph following Agenda.)

13 In the table, enter the text shown in Table 1 below.

14 Select the table, and then **AutoFit** the table to contents. **Center** the table on the page.

15 Display the file properties. In the **Tags** box, type **seminar, agenda** and in the **Subject** box, type your course name and section number. If necessary, edit the author name to display your name. **Save** the document.

16 Display the **Building Blocks Organizer** dialog box, and then **Delete** your building blocks **Internet Seminar** and **Seminar Schedule**. Close the **Building Blocks Organizer** dialog box. Display the **Theme Colors** list, and then **Delete** the **Internet Colors**. (Mac users, skip this step.)

17 **Close** Word. When a message displays regarding changes to building blocks, click **Save** to accept the changes.

Table 1

Time	Topic	Location	Speaker
9:30	Continental Breakfast	Community Room	
10:00	Virtual Reference Desks	Computer Lab A	Irene Grant
Noon	Lunch	Community Room	
1:00	Innovative Internet Librarians	Computer Lab A	Josh McCarthy

(Return to step 14)

(continues on next page)

Mastering Word: Project 6E Seminar Agenda (continued)

18 In your **MyLab IT course**, locate and click the Grader Project **Word 6E Seminar Agenda**. In step 3, under **Upload Completed Assignment**, click **Choose File**. In the **Open** dialog box, navigate to your **Word Chapter 6** folder, and then click your **Student_ Word_6E_Seminar_Agenda** file one time to select it. In the lower right corner of the **Open** dialog box, click **Open**.

The name of your selected file displays above the Upload button.

19 To submit your file to **MyLab IT** for grading, click **Upload**, wait a moment for a green **Success!** message, and then in step 4, click the blue **Submit for Grading** button. Click **Close Assignment** to return to your list of **Course Materials**.

You have completed Project 6E **END**

| MyLab IT Grader | Mastering Word | Project 6F Library Classes |

Apply 6B skills from these Objectives:

4. Use Comments in a Document
5. Track Changes in a Document
6. View Side by Side, Compare, and Combine Documents

In the following Mastering Word project, you will edit a user guide for Mountain View Public Library by creating and deleting comments, inserting text, applying formatting, and accepting changes made by others. Your completed document will look similar to Figure 6.47.

Project Files for MyLab IT Grader

1. In your **MyLab IT** course, locate and click **Word 6F Library Classes**, Download Materials, and then Download All Files.
2. Extract the zipped folder to your Word Chapter 6 folder. Close the Grader download screens.
3. Take a moment to open the downloaded **Word_6F_Library_Classes_Instructions**; note any recent updates to the book.

Project Results

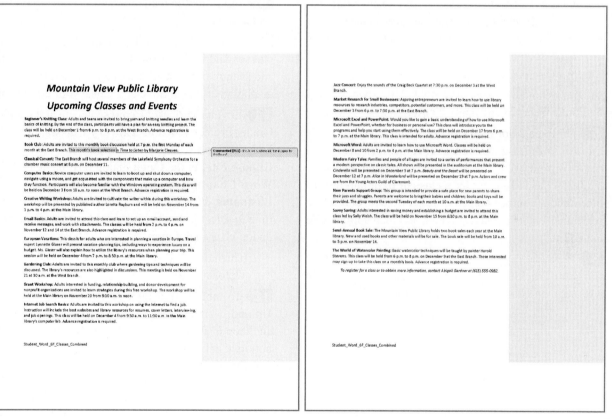

Figure 6.47

For Non-MyLab Submissions

For Project 6F, you will need:

w06F_Library_Classes
w06F_Classes_Reviewed

In your Word Chapter 6 folder, save your documents as:

Lastname_Firstname_6F_Library_Classes
Lastname_Firstname_6F_Classes_Combined

Open w06F_Library_Classes and then save the file as Lastname_Firstname_6F_Library_Classes. On the next page, begin with step 2. After step 10, save and submit your file as directed by your instructor.

(continues on next page)

Content-Based Assessments (Mastery and Transfer of Learning)

1 Navigate to your **Word Chapter 6 folder**, and then double-click the Word file you downloaded from **MyLab IT** that displays your name—**Student_Word_6F_Library_Classes**.

2 On the **Review tab**, in the **Tracking group**, display the **Track Changes Options** dialog box, and then click **Change User Name**. Under **Personalize your copy of Microsoft Office**, type your name in the **User name** box, and then type your initials in the **Initials** box, if necessary. Immediately below **Initials**, be sure the check box is selected. (Mac users, skip this step.)

3 In the **Tracking group**, change **Display for Review** to **All Markup**. In the *Book Club* paragraph, select the text *This month's book selection.* Insert a new comment with the text **Should we purchase additional copies for the library?** Delete the *Abigail Gardner* and the *Caroline Marina* comments regarding spelling.

4 Turn on **Track Changes**. Select the first two paragraphs, and then apply the **Book Title** style. Change the **Font Size** to **28** and apply **Center**.

5 On **Page 2**, locate the paragraph that begins *Microsoft Word*. **Delete** the text *101*, and then press [Ctrl] + [End] to move to the end of the document. Press [Enter], and then type **To register for a class or to obtain more information, contact Abigail Gardner at (615) 555-0982.** Select the sentence you just typed, and then apply **Italic** and **Center**.

6 Press [Ctrl] + [Home], and then **Accept All Changes and Stop Tracking**. **Save** your document, click the **File tab**, and then **Close** the document but leave Word open.

7 Display the **Combine Documents** dialog box. For the **Original document**, from the files you downloaded for this project, select the file **w06F_Classes_Reviewed**. For the **Revised document**, in your **Word Chapter 6** folder, select the file **Student_Word_6F_Library_Classes**. (If you are not submitting your files in **MyLab IT**, select your Lastname_Firstname_6F_Library_Classes file.) Verify that the **New document** option is selected and then click **OK**.

8 **Save** the combined document in your **Word Chapter 6** folder as **Lastname_Firstname_6F_Classes_Combined** and if necessary, close all open panes. **Accept All Changes and Stop Tracking**.

9 Insert the file name in the footer, and then **Close** the footer area.

10 Display the properties. In the **Tags** box, type **library classes** and in the **Subject** box, type your course name and section number. If necessary, edit the author name to display your name. **Save** and **Close** your document.

11 In your **MyLab IT course**, locate and click the Grader Project **Word 6F Library Classes**. In step 3, under **Upload Completed Assignment**, click **Choose File**. In the **Open** dialog box, navigate to your **Word Chapter 6** folder, and then click your **Lastname_Firstname_6F_Classes_Combined** file one time to select it. In the lower right corner of the **Open** dialog box, click **Open**.

The name of your selected file displays above the Upload button.

12 To submit your file to **MyLab IT** for grading, click **Upload**, wait a moment for a green **Success!** message, and then in step 4, click the blue **Submit for Grading** button. Click **Close Assignment** to return to your list of **Course Materials**.

You have completed Project 6F END

Mastering Word | **Project 6G Website Flyer**

Apply 6A and 6B skills from these Objectives:

1. Create Custom Building Blocks
2. Create and Save a Theme Template
3. Create a Document by Using Building Blocks
4. Use Comments in a Document
5. Track Changes in a Document
6. View Side by Side, Compare, and Combine Documents

In the following Mastering Word project, you will create a document to announce the launch of Mountain View Public Library's new website by creating and inserting building blocks, creating a custom theme, inserting text, applying formatting, and accepting changes made by others. Your completed document will look similar to Figure 6.48.

Project Files for MyLab IT Grader

1. In your **MyLab IT** course, locate and click **Word 6G Website Flyer**, Download Materials, and then Download All Files.
2. Extract the zipped folder to your Word Chapter 6 folder. Close the Grader download screens.
3. Take a moment to open the downloaded **Word_6G_Website_Flyer_Instructions**; note any recent updates to the book.

Project Results

Figure 6.48

For Non-MyLab Submissions
For Project 6G, you will need:
w06G_Website_Flyer

In your Word Chapter 6 folder, save your document as:
Lastname_Firstname_6G_Website_Flyer
Lastname_Firstname_6G_Website_Blocks
Lastname_Firstname_6G_Website_Theme

Begin the project with step 1. In step 11, open w06G_Website_Flyer, and then save the file as Lastname_Firstname_6G_Website_Flyer. After step 18, save and submit your file as directed by your instructor.

(continues on next page)

Mastering Word: Project 6G Website Flyer (continued)

1 **Start** Word, and then display a new document. Save the document in your **Word Chapter 6** folder as **Lastname_Firstname_6G_Website_Blocks** and be sure rulers and formatting marks display.

2 Display the **Quick Tables** gallery, and then insert a **Tabular List**. In the first cell, replace the text **ITEM** with **Location** and then press Tab. Replace the text **NEEDED** with **Day** and then delete all remaining text in the table. (Mac users, insert a table with 2 columns and 8 rows. In the first table cell, type Location, press Tab, and then type Day.)

3 Insert a third column in the table to the right of the *Day* column. In the first cell of the third column, type **Time** and then apply a **Table Style**—under **List Tables**, in the third row, click the third style.

4 **Save** the table in the **Quick Tables** gallery with the name **Training Schedule** and the **Description Use to display schedules for training** (Mac users, skip this step.)

5 Press Ctrl + End. Press Enter two times, and then type **The Internet is becoming the town square for the global village of tomorrow. Bill Gates** and then save the quote in the **AutoText** gallery with the name **Internet Quote** and the **Description Use in website documents** Change the **Save in** location to **Building Blocks**. (Mac users, select the text you typed. Click the Insert *menu*, point to AutoText, and then click New. Type Internet_Quote and then click OK.)

6 **Save** your changes. Click the **File tab**, and then **Close** the document but leave Word open.

7 Display a new blank document. Display the **Create New Theme Colors** dialog box, change **Accent 2**—in the ninth column, click the fifth color, and then save the theme colors with the name **Website Colors** (Mac users, skip this step.)

8 Display the **Create New Theme Fonts** dialog box, change the **Body font** to **Verdana**, and then save the theme fonts with the name **Website Fonts** (Mac users, skip this step.)

9 Save the current theme in your **Word Chapter 6** folder as **Lastname_Firstname_6G_Website_Theme** (Mac users, skip this step.)

10 **Delete** the **Website Colors** and **Website Fonts**. **Close** the document without saving changes but leave Word open. (Mac users, skip this step.)

11 From the files you downloaded with this project, open the file **Student_Word_6G_Website_Flyer**. Insert a footer with the file name. Apply your custom theme—**Lastname_Firstname_6G_Website_Theme**. (Mac users, apply the downloaded theme file—Mac_6G_Website_Theme.)

12 Select the first two paragraphs of the document. Change the **Font Size** to **22**, change the **Font Color**—in the ninth column, click the first color, and then apply **Bold** and **Center**.

13 Press Ctrl + End, and then insert the **Training Schedule** Quick Table. (Mac users, open your Lastname_Firstname_6G_Website_Blocks file, and then copy and paste the table at the end of your document.)

14 Beginning in the first cell of the second row, type the following text in the table.

East Branch	Tuesday	2 p.m.
Main Library	Monday	9 a.m.
West Branch	Friday	3 p.m.

15 Delete all empty rows in the table. Select the table, and then **AutoFit Contents**. **Center** the table horizontally in the document.

16 Press Ctrl + End, and then press Enter. Insert the **Internet Quote** AutoText. Select the inserted text, change the **Font Size** to **9**, change the **Font Color**—in the ninth column, click the first color; and then apply **Bold** and **Center**. If necessary, at the end of the document, delete the blank paragraph.

17 Press Ctrl + Home, and then **Accept All Changes**. Select the entire document and change the **Line Spacing** to **1.5**. On the **Layout tab**, click **Margins**, and then click **Custom Margins**. Change the **Top** and **Bottom** margins to **0.5** and then click **OK**.

18 Display the document properties. In the **Tags** box, type **website flyer** and then in the **Subject** box, type your course name and section number. If necessary, edit the author name to display your name. **Save** your document. **Delete** the **Training Schedule** and **Internet Quote** building blocks. **Close** Word and if prompted, save changes.

(continues on next page)

19 In your **MyLab IT course**, locate and click the Grader Project **Word 6G Website Flyer**. In step 3, under **Upload Completed Assignment**, click **Choose File**. In the **Open** dialog box, navigate to your **Word Chapter 6** folder, and then click your **Student_Word_6G_Website_Flyer** file one time to select it. In the lower right corner of the **Open** dialog box, click **Open**.

The name of your selected file displays above the Upload button.

20 To submit your file to **MyLab IT** for grading, click **Upload**, wait a moment for a green **Success!** message, and then in step 4, click the blue **Submit for Grading** button. Click **Close Assignment** to return to your list of **Course Materials**.

You have completed Project 6G **END**

Content-Based Assessments (Critical Thinking)

Apply a combination of the 6A and 6B skills.

GO! Fix It	**Project 6H Internship Memo**	IRC
GO! Make It	**Project 6I Request Form**	IRC
GO! Solve It	**Project 6J Employee Newsletter**	IRC
GO! Solve It	**Project 6K Library Rules**	

Project Files

For Project 6K, you will need the following files:

New blank Word document

w06K_Library_Rules

You will save your files as:

Lastname_Firstname_6K_Rules_Blocks

Lastname_Firstname_6K_Library_Rules

Display a new blank document and save it in your **Word Chapter 6** folder as **Lastname_Firstname_6K_Rules_Blocks** Insert a text box that includes the **text Mountain View Public Library** on the first line and **Library Rules** on the second line. Format the text box and the text, and then save the text box as a building block. Save and close the file but leave Word open.

From your student files, open the document **w06K_Library_Rules**. Accept all changes. Save the file to your **Word Chapter 6** folder as **Lastname_Firstname_6K_Library_Rules**. Modify the theme colors and format the text to improve readability. Insert the building block you created. Adjust the building block and text to create an attractive, one-page document. Insert the file name in the footer and add appropriate document properties. Submit the document as directed.

		Performance Level	
		Exemplary: You consistently applied the relevant skills	**Proficient: You sometimes, but not always, applied the relevant skills**	**Developing: You rarely or never applied the relevant skills**
Performance Criteria	**Create a text box building block**	A text box containing the correct information is saved as a building block.	A text box is saved as a building block but contains incorrect information.	No text box is saved as a building block.
	Accept changes	All changes are accepted.	Some changes are accepted but others are not.	No changes are accepted.
	Modify theme colors and format text	The theme colors are modified and the text is formatted attractively.	The theme colors are not modified or the text is not formatted attractively.	The theme colors are not modified and the text is not formatted.
	Insert building blocks	The building block is inserted and positioned appropriately.	The building block is not positioned inappropriately.	The building block is not inserted.

You have completed Project 6K END

Outcomes-Based Assessments (Critical Thinking)

Rubric

The following outcomes-based assessments are open-ended assessments. That is, there is no specific correct result; your result will depend on your approach to the information provided. Make *Professional Quality* your goal. Use the following scoring rubric to guide you in *how* to approach the problem and then to evaluate *how well* your approach solves the problem.

The *criteria*—Software Mastery, Content, Format and Layout, and Process—represent the knowledge and skills you have gained that you can apply to solving the problem. The *levels of performance*—Professional Quality, Approaching Professional Quality, or Needs Quality Improvements—help you and your instructor evaluate your result.

	Your completed project is of Professional Quality if you:	Your completed project is Approaching Professional Quality if you:	Your completed project Needs Quality Improvements if you:
1-Software Mastery	Choose and apply the most appropriate skills, tools, and features and identify efficient methods to solve the problem.	Choose and apply some appropriate skills, tools, and features, but not in the most efficient manner.	Choose inappropriate skills, tools, or features, or are inefficient in solving the problem.
2-Content	Construct a solution that is clear and well organized, contains content that is accurate, appropriate to the audience and purpose, and is complete. Provide a solution that contains no errors of spelling, grammar, or style.	Construct a solution in which some components are unclear, poorly organized, inconsistent, or incomplete. Misjudge the needs of the audience. Have some errors in spelling, grammar, or style, but the errors do not detract from comprehension.	Construct a solution that is unclear, incomplete, or poorly organized, contains some inaccurate or inappropriate content, and contains many errors of spelling, grammar, or style. Do not solve the problem.
3-Format and Layout	Format and arrange all elements to communicate information and ideas, clarify function, illustrate relationships, and indicate relative importance.	Apply appropriate format and layout features to some elements, but not others. Overuse features, causing minor distraction.	Apply format and layout that does not communicate information or ideas clearly. Do not use format and layout features to clarify function, illustrate relationships, or indicate relative importance. Use available features excessively, causing distraction.
4-Process	Use an organized approach that integrates planning, development, self-assessment, revision, and reflection.	Demonstrate an organized approach in some areas, but not others; or, use an insufficient process of organization throughout.	Do not use an organized approach to solve the problem.

Apply a combination of the 6A and 6B skills.

GO! Think | **Project 6L Fundraising Flyer**

Project Files

For Project 6L, you will need the following file:

New blank Word document

You will save your files as:

Lastname_Firstname_6L_Fundraising_Flyer

The Mountain View Public Library is conducting a fundraising campaign with a goal of $200,000 needed to upgrade the computer lab at the Main library and fund library programs. Donations can be sent to 1000 Maple Avenue, Claremont, TN 38325. Benedetta Herman, Director of Library Services, is chairing the fundraising committee and can be reached at (615) 555-0982. Donor levels include:

Type of Recognition	Amount of Gift
Bronze Book Club	$ 100 or more
Silver Book Club	$ 500 or more
Gold Book Club	$ 1,000 or more

Create a document that includes a text box containing the name and address of the library and an appropriate quotation. Save both objects as building blocks. Create a flyer explaining the campaign and how donors will be acknowledged. Customize the theme, add appropriate text, and insert your building blocks. Include a Quick Table to display the recognition types. Format the flyer in a professional manner. Save the file as **Lastname_Firstname_6L_Fundraising_Flyer** and insert the file name in the footer and appropriate properties. Submit the document as directed.

You have completed Project 6L | **END**

GO! Think | **Project 6M Reading Certificate** | **IRC**

You and GO! | **Project 6N Personal Calendar** | **IRC**

Creating Word Macros and Modifying Document Components

PROJECT 7A

Outcomes
In a Word document, create, edit, and run macros.

Objectives
1. Create Macros
2. Run Macros
3. Edit a Macro in the Visual Basic Editor
4. Use a Built-in Word Macro

PROJECT 7B

Outcomes
Modify the document layout and format graphic and text elements.

Objectives
5. Modify the Layout of a Document
6. Format Graphic and Text Elements in a Word Document

Lucky Business/Shutterstock

In This Chapter

 GO! to Work with Word

In this chapter, you will create and run macros and use the Visual Basic Editor. A macro enables you to improve your efficiency by performing a series of tasks in a single action. Additionally, you will learn how to customize Word in a variety of ways—for example, change the paper size, apply advanced formatting features to text, and modify graphic and text elements—to create a professional-looking document that meets your exact specifications.

The projects in this chapter relate to **Magical Park Corporation**, which operates 15 regional theme parks across the United States, Mexico, and Canada. Park types include traditional theme parks, water parks, and wildlife adventure parks. This year the company will launch three of its new "Imagination Parks" where attractions combine fun and the discovery of math and science information, and where teens and adults enjoy the free Friday night concerts. Magical Park Corporation also operates family-friendly resort hotels on many of their properties that include exceptional pools and championship golf courses.

Project Activities

In Activities 7.01 through 7.09, you will assist Sharon Reynolds, Human Resources Director for Magical Park, in automating Word tasks by creating macros that will be executed with a single click or a keyboard shortcut. These actions include inserting a specific footer, adding a formatted heading, inserting the current date in a header, and adjusting indentation in a bulleted list. Your completed document will look similar to Figure 7.1.

Project Files for **MyLab IT Grader**

1. In your storage location, create a folder named **Word Chapter 7**.
2. In your **MyLab IT** course, locate and click **Word 7A Expo Flyer**, Download Materials, and then Download All Files.
3. Extract the zipped folder to your Word Chapter 7 folder. Close the Grader download screens.
4. Take a moment to open the downloaded **Word_7A_Expo_Flyer_Instructions**; note any recent updates to the book.

Project Results

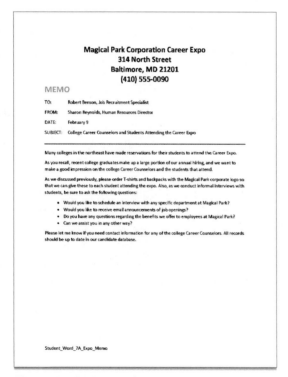

Figure 7.1 Project 7A Career Expo Flyer

For Non-MyLab Submissions
For Project 7A, you will need:
w07A_Expo_Flyer
w07A_Expo_Memo

In your storage location, create a folder named **Word Chapter 7**
In your Word Chapter 7 folder, save your documents as:
Lastname_Firstname_7A_Expo_Flyer (optional to submit)
Lastname_Firstname_7A_Expo_Memo

After you have named and saved your w07A_Expo_Flyer document, on the next page, begin with Step 2.

Objective 1   Create Macros

GO! Learn How
Video W7-1

A *macro* is set of commands and instructions that you group as a single command to accomplish a task automatically. When using Word, all macros are created in a programming language called *Visual Basic for Applications*, or *VBA*. You can use a macro to save time when performing routine editing and formatting, to combine several repetitive steps into one step, to make an option in a dialog box more accessible, or to automate a complex series of tasks. For example, you could create a macro that performs the steps to produce a customized header, and then you could insert the header into multiple documents without having to re-create the formatting steps for each document.

Activity 7.01 | Saving a Macro-Enabled Document

MOS
Expert 1.1.5

When you create, save, and use macros in a document, you must save the document as a Word Macro-Enabled Template (.dotm) or as a Word Macro-Enabled Document (.docm). Saving a document as either a Word document (.docx) or Word Template (.dotx) will cause any macros to be removed.

1 ▸ Navigate to your **Word Chapter 7 folder**, and then double-click the Word file you downloaded from **MyLab IT** that displays your name—**Student_Word_7A_Expo_Flyer**. If necessary, at the top click **Enable Editing**.

2 ▸ From the **File tab**, display the **Save As** dialog box. In the lower portion of the dialog box, click the **Save as type arrow**, and then on the list, click **Word Macro-Enabled Document**. Compare your screen with Figure 7.2.

⌷   **MAC TIP**   On the menu bar, click File, Save As, click the File Format arrow.

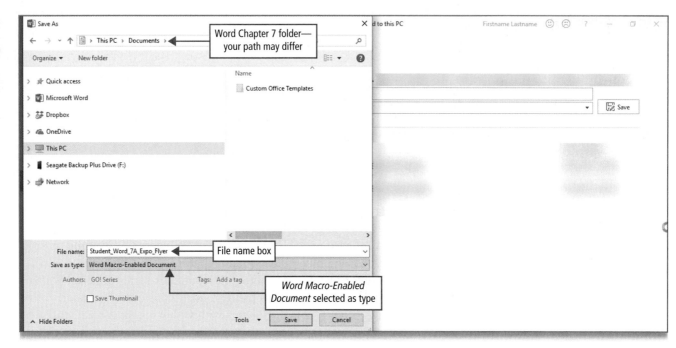

Figure 7.2

3 Click **Save**.

By saving your file as a macro-enabled document, new macros and changes to existing macros are automatically saved.

Activity 7.02 | Changing Macro Security Settings

MOS
Expert
1.1.17

When you create your own macros, you can trust the source. However, macros written by others may pose a potential security risk. Because a macro is written in a programming language, files can be erased or damaged by inserting unauthorized code. This unauthorized code is called a **macro virus**. To protect systems from this type of virus, organizations commonly set their security programs to disable macros automatically or block any email attachment that contains a macro. Because the staff of Magical Park uses macros to automate some of their tasks, you will adjust the security level in Word to allow macros to run.

1 Click the **File tab**, on the left click **Options**, and then in the **Word Options** dialog box, on the left, click **Customize Ribbon**.

On the right, Main Tabs that display on the ribbon are indicated with a checkmark.

💻 **MAC TIP** Display the menu bar, click Word, click Preferences, then click Ribbon & Toolbar.

---

2 On the right, in the **Main Tabs** list, locate and then select the **Developer** check box. Compare your screen with Figure 7.3.

The Developer tab extends the capabilities of Word—including commands for inserting content controls and creating macros.

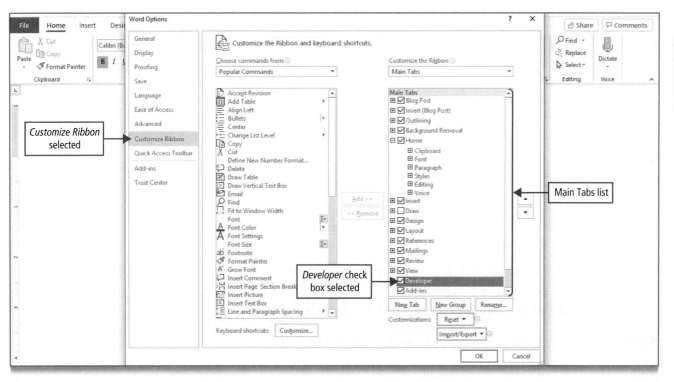

Figure 7.3

3 Click **OK** to close the Word Options dialog box. Notice that the **Developer tab** displays on the ribbon.

4 Click the **Developer tab**, and then in the **Code group**, click **Macro Security**. Compare your screen with Figure 7.4, and then take a few moments to study the table in Figure 7.5 to examine macro security settings.

Macro Settings display in the Trust Center dialog box. Your selected option may differ.

MAC TIP   On the menu bar, click Word, click Preferences, click Security.

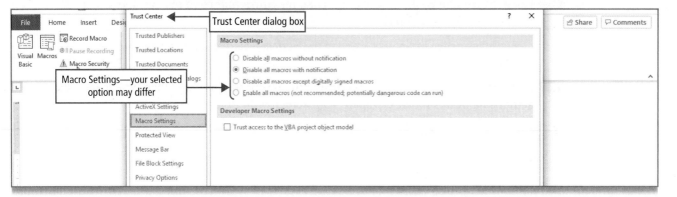

Figure 7.4

Macro Settings	
Setting	**Description**
Disable all macros without notification	Macros will not run in a document, and no notification message will display.
Disable all macros with notification	Macros will not run in a document, but a notification message will display with an option to run macros.
Disable all macros except digitally signed macros	Macros that have a valid digital signature and have been confirmed by Microsoft will be allowed to run.
Enable all macros	All macros will run. This option is a high security risk.

Figure 7.5

5 In the **Trust Center** dialog box, under **Macro Settings**, if necessary, click the **Disable all macros with notification** option button.

By selecting this macro setting, opening a document that has a macro attached causes a security warning to display and gives you the option to disable the macro.

6 Click **OK** to close the **Trust Center** dialog box.

Activity 7.03 | Recording a Keyboard-Activated Macro

Expert 1.1.5
Expert 4.2.1
Expert 4.2.2

The process of creating a macro while performing specific actions in a document is called *recording* a macro. Before you record a macro, the first thing you should do is plan the exact steps you will perform, and it is a good idea to write down those steps. For example, if you want to apply bold formatting and a specific Text Effect style during the recording of a macro, review the steps required to achieve this formatting before you begin recording the macro. Then you can record the macro by completing all of the steps. In this Activity, you will create a macro that will insert the file name in the footer.

1 On the **Developer tab**, in the **Code group**, click **Record Macro**.

2 In the **Record Macro** dialog box, in the **Macro name** box, type **Footer**

Each macro must be given a unique name. It is a good idea to name the macro with a descriptive name to help you recall the function of the macro. If you reuse a name, the new macro will replace the original macro. Macro names cannot contain spaces; however, you can use underscores to improve readability.

3 Under **Store macro in**, if necessary, click the **Store macro in arrow**, and select *All Documents (Normal.dotm)*.

By default, the macro will be saved in the Normal macro-enabled template so that it can be used in other documents.

4 In the **Description** box, click to position the insertion point, and then type **Inserts the author's name in a footer** Compare your screen with Figure 7.6.

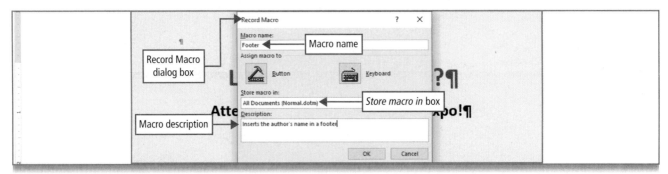

Figure 7.6

5 Under **Assign macro to**, click the **Keyboard** icon.

You can assign a button or a shortcut key to a macro. By clicking the *Keyboard* icon, you can assign a shortcut key that, when pressed, will cause the macro to run—also referred to as executing the macro.

6 In the **Customize Keyboard** dialog box, with the insertion point in the **Press new shortcut key** box, press and hold [Alt] and [Ctrl], and then press [B].

Alt+Ctrl+B displays in the *Press new shortcut key* box. If the shortcut key you choose is already in use, you should select another combination so that the original shortcut is not replaced. If the combination of keys is already in use, it will display next to *Currently assigned to*.

7 In the lower left corner of the dialog box, click **Assign**. Compare your screen with Figure 7.7.

Alt+Ctrl+B displays in the *Current keys* box. This keyboard sequence is assigned to the macro that is selected in the *Commands* box—your *Footer* macro. The macro name displays as *Normal.NewMacros.Footer* to indicate that the macro is user-created and stored in the Normal template.

🖥 **MAC TIP** The Current keys box indicates [option] + [control] + [B].

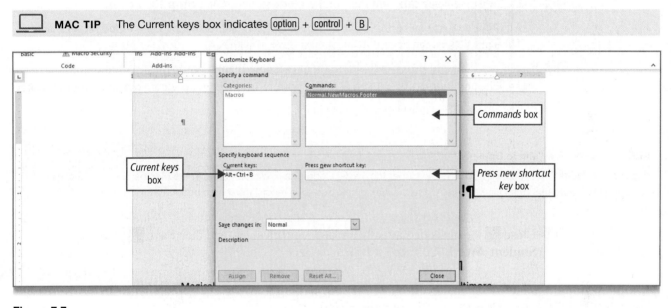

Figure 7.7

8 Near the bottom of the **Customize Keyboard** dialog box, click **Close**. Point anywhere in the document, and notice that the pointer changes to a 🖱 pointer. Compare your screen with Figure 7.8.

The 🖱 pointer indicates that you are now in recording mode. Any actions that you make will be recorded as part of the macro until you turn off the recording of the macro. Be sure to take your time as you perform each action so that extra steps are not recorded as part of the macro.

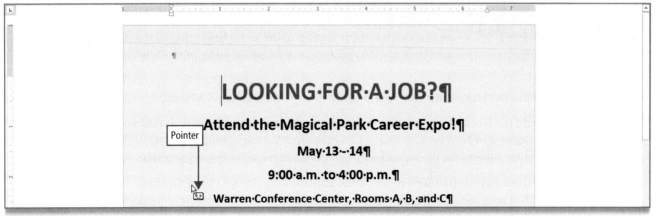

Figure 7.8

9 On the ribbon, click the **Insert tab**. In the **Header & Footer group**, click **Footer**, and then click **Edit Footer**.

10 With the insertion point in the footer, using your own name, type **Firstname Lastname** and then compare your screen with Figure 7.9.

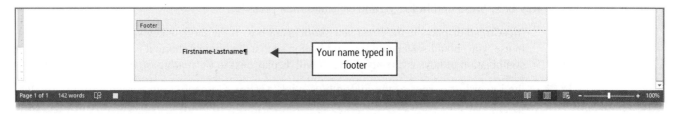

Firstname·Lastname¶   ← Your name typed in footer

Page 1 of 1   142 words

Figure 7.9

11 In the **Close group**, click **Close Header and Footer**.

12 Click the **Developer tab**, and then in the **Code group**, click **Stop Recording**.

All of the actions you performed in Steps 9 through 11 are recorded as part of the *Footer* macro. The same actions can be repeated by pressing Alt + Ctrl + B.

13 To test your macro, press Ctrl + N to display a new blank document. Press and hold Alt + Ctrl, and then press B. Scroll to the bottom of the page to view your name in the footer.

The macro runs—inserting your name in the footer.

ALERT   What If My Macro Doesn't Work?

If your macro doesn't work properly, on the Developer tab, in the Code group, click Macros. In the Macros dialog box, click the name of your macro, and then click Delete. Close the dialog box, and then record the macro again.

---

14 **Close** ✕ the blank document without saving changes, and then **Save** 🖫 your **Student_Word_7A_Expo_Flyer** document.

MORE KNOWLEDGE   Pausing While Recording a Macro

When recording a macro, you can temporarily suspend the recording if you need to perform other actions, and then resume the recording. To pause the recording, in the Code group, click Pause Recording. When you are ready to continue, click Resume Recorder.

Activity 7.04 | Recording a Button-Activated Macro

MOS
Expert 1.1.5
Expert 1.1.6
Expert 4.2.1
Expert 4.2.2

You can assign a macro to a command button that displays on the Quick Access Toolbar or on the ribbon. In this Activity, you will create a macro to insert a heading and assign it to a button.

1 Press Ctrl + Home to position the insertion point at the beginning of the document. Press Enter one time, and then click to position the insertion point in the new first paragraph of the document.

2 On the **Developer tab**, in the **Code group**, click **Record Macro**.

3 In the **Record Macro** dialog box, in the **Macro name box**, type **Heading** In the **Store macro in** box, be sure that *All Documents (Normal.dotm)* displays. In the **Description** box, type **Inserts the name, address, and phone number for the organization**

4 Under **Assign macro to**, click the **Button** icon. In the **Word Options** dialog box, in the left pane be sure **Quick Access Toolbar** is selected. To the right, under **Choose commands from**, click **Normal.NewMacros.Heading**—the name Word uses for your *Heading* macro.

5 In the middle of the dialog box, click **Add**. Compare your screen with Figure 7.10.

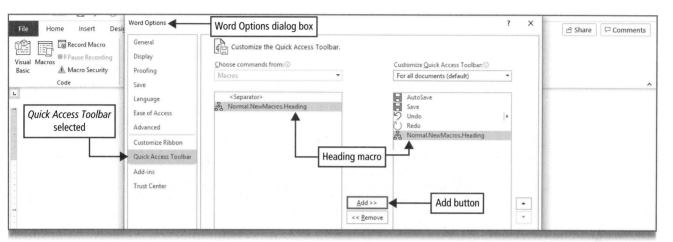

Figure 7.10

6 On the right side of the **Word Options** dialog box, click **Normal.NewMacros.Heading**. Below the list of commands, click **Modify**.

7 In the **Modify Button** dialog box, under **Symbol**, in the first row, click the third symbol—a blue circle containing a blue *i*. In the **Display name** box, notice that the macro name displays. Compare your screen with Figure 7.11.

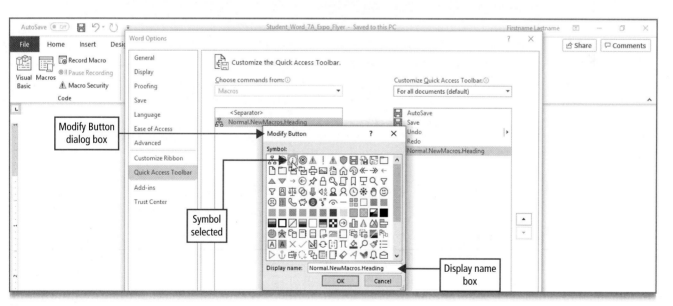

Figure 7.11

8 Click **OK**. In the list of Quick Access Toolbar commands, notice that the selected symbol displays to the left of *Normal.NewMacros.Heading*. Click **OK** to close the **Word Options** dialog box. Notice that the 🔲 pointer displays in the document and the *Heading* button (blue circle) displays on the Quick Access Toolbar.

9 Type the following text, pressing [Enter] after each of the first *three* lines.

Magical Park Career Expo

314 North Street

Baltimore, MD 21201

(410) 555-0090

10 With the insertion point to the right of the phone number, press [Ctrl] + [Shift] + [Home] to select all four lines.

> When you are recording a macro, you must use the keyboard to select text—you cannot drag.

MAC TIP With the insertion point to the right of the phone number, hold down SHIFT and then click to the left of *Magical* to select all 4 lines.

---

11 With all four lines selected, click the **Home tab**. In the **Styles group**, change the style to **No Spacing**, change the **Font Size** to **18**, apply **Bold** [B], and then click **Center** [≡].

12 Click the **Developer tab**, and then in the **Code group**, click **Stop Recording**. Compare your screen with Figure 7.12.

> All of the text you typed and formatted is saved as part of the macro.

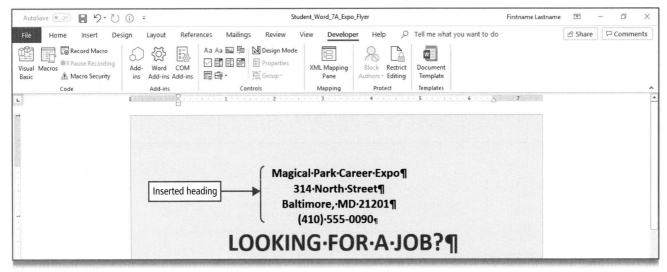

Figure 7.12

13 Press [Ctrl] + [Home], and then **Save** [💾] your document.

Activity 7.05 | Creating a Macro That Runs Automatically

MOS
Expert 1.1.5

You can create a macro that runs automatically based on the occurrence of a specific event—for example, when you open a Word document or exit Word. In this Activity, you will create a macro to insert the date and time in the header when you close a document.

MAC TIP You can create the macro, however, the macro may not run on the memo document.

---

1 ► On the **Developer tab**, in the **Code group**, click **Record Macro**.

2 ► In the **Record Macro** dialog box, in the **Macro name** box, type **AutoClose** Click the **Store macro in arrow**, and then click the name of your **7A_Expo_Flyer (document)**. Compare your screen with Figure 7.13 and then take a few moments to study the table in Figure 7.14 to examine the categories of automatic macros.

> *AutoClose* is a reserved word understood by Microsoft Word. When the term is used as a macro name, the macro will automatically run when the document is closed. Therefore, you do not need to assign a keystroke or button to the macro.

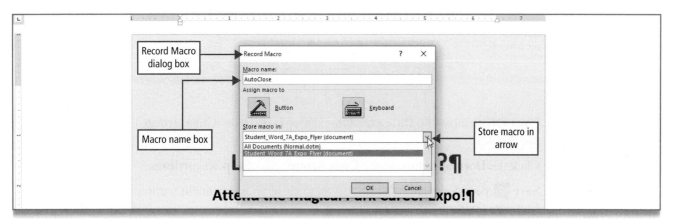

Figure 7.13

Automatic Macros	
Macro	**Description**
AutoExec	Runs when Word starts.
AutoOpen	Runs each time a document is opened.
AutoNew	Runs each time a new document is created.
AutoClose	Runs each time a document is closed.
AutoExit	Runs whenever you exit Word.

Figure 7.14

ALERT   Should The Macro Be Saved In The Normal Template?

Be careful to save this macro in your document rather than in the Normal.dotm template. If you save the macro in the Normal.dotm template on your computer, the macro will run every time *any* document is closed.

3 ► Click **OK** to start recording mode.

4 ► Click the **Insert tab**. In the **Header & Footer group**, click **Header**, and then on the list, click **Edit Header**.

5 ► Press Ctrl + A, and then press Delete.

> Any existing text is selected and then deleted. Because this macro will insert the current date and time whenever the document is closed, you want to be sure that any existing content is deleted.

6 ► On the **Header & Footer Tools Design tab**, in the **Insert group**, click **Date & Time**.

7 In the **Date and Time** dialog box, on the list, click the thirteenth format—with the date and time displayed in seconds. Compare your screen with Figure 7.15.

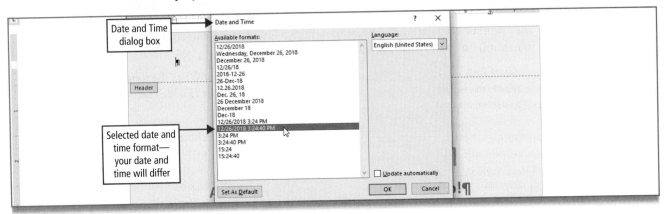

Figure 7.15

8 Click **OK** to close the **Date and Time** dialog box. In the **Close group**, click **Close Header and Footer**.

9 Click the **Developer tab**. In the **Code group**, click **Stop Recording**.

10 Save 🖫 your document. Press `Ctrl` + `W` to close your document without closing Word. Compare your screen with Figure 7.16.

When you close your document, the *AutoClose* macro runs—inserting the current date and time in the header. Because this change is made while closing the document, a Microsoft Word message box displays prompting you to save your changes.

🖥 **MAC TIP** Press `command ⌘` + `W`.

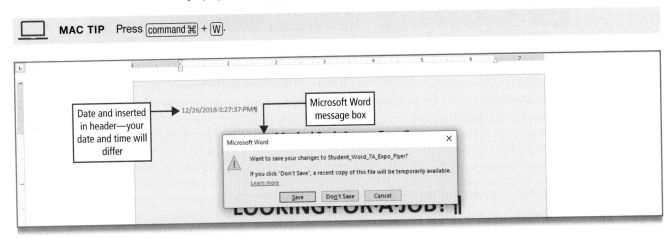

Figure 7.16

11 In the Microsoft Word message box, click **Save** to save your changes and close the document.

Objective 2 | **Run Macros**

GO! Learn How
Video W7-2

After you record a macro, you can reuse it so that you can work more efficiently. Recall that a macro is a series of commands and instructions that you group together as a single command to accomplish a task automatically. This method of "bundling" steps into a macro will save you time on many tasks.

Activity 7.06 | **Running a Macro**

Expert 1.1.5

1 Click the **File tab**, on the left click **Open**, and then click **Browse**. In the **Open** dialog box, navigate to the files you downloaded with this project, and then open the file **w07A_Expo_Memo**.

2 Click the **File tab**, on the left click **Save As**, click **Browse**, and then in the **Save As** dialog box, navigate to your **Word Chapter 7** folder. In the lower portion of the dialog box, click the **Save as type arrow**, and then on the list, click **Word Macro-Enabled Document**.

3 In the **File name** box, using your own name, type **Lastname_Firstname_7A_Expo_Memo** and then click **Save**. If any words are flagged as spelling errors, right-click the word, and then click Ignore All.

NOTE

This is the file you will submit for grading.

4 Select the second paragraph—*MEMO*. On the **Home tab**, in the **Font group**, click **Text Effects and Typography** [A▾], and then in the second row, click the fifth effect.

5 Click to position the insertion point in the empty paragraph at the top of the document, and then on the **Quick Access Toolbar**, click the button assigned to your **Heading** macro—the blue circle containing a blue *i*. Click anywhere in the document to cancel the selection, and then compare your screen with Figure 7.17.

MAC TIP Use the keyboard shortcut you created by pressing [option] + [control] + [H]. If necessary, format the heading as shown in the figure (bold, 18 pt. font, centered).

The Heading macro is executed and the heading information is inserted in your document. Recall that although you created the *Heading* macro in your *7A_Expo_Flyer* document, the macro was saved in the Normal template on your system, allowing it to be available to other documents.

Figure 7.17

6 Press and hold [Alt] + [Ctrl], and then press [B]. If necessary, scroll to the bottom of the page to view the footer.

The *Footer* macro runs—inserting your name in the footer.

7 Press [Ctrl] + [Home], and then **Save** [💾] your document.

Objective 3   **Edit a Macro in the Visual Basic Editor**

GO! Learn How
Video W7-3

One way to edit macros is by using the ***Visual Basic Editor***. The Visual Basic Editor enables you to view the programming code for existing macros. You can use the Visual Basic Editor either to edit a macro or to create a new macro. The capability of VBA is extensive; you can use it to create complex macros.

Activity 7.07 | Editing a Macro in the Visual Basic Editor

Expert 4.2.3

1 Locate the first paragraph of the document, and notice that it contains the text *Magical Park Career Expo.*

2 Click the **Developer tab**, and then in the **Code group**, click **Macros**. In the **Macros** dialog box, select the **Heading** macro, and then click **Edit**. If necessary, maximize the *Normal – [NewMacros (Code)]* window. Compare your screen with Figure 7.18.

The Visual Basic Editor displays the code associated with the *Footer* and *Heading* macros. A macro *procedure*—a block of programming code that performs one or more tasks—begins with the term *Sub* and ends with the term *End Sub*. The name following the word *Sub* indicates the name of the procedure. The description that you typed when you created the *Heading* macro displays as a *comment*. A comment is a line of text that is used solely for documentation—for example, the name of the individual who wrote the macro or the purpose of the macro. A comment is preceded by a single quotation mark, displays in green text, and is ignored when the macro runs.

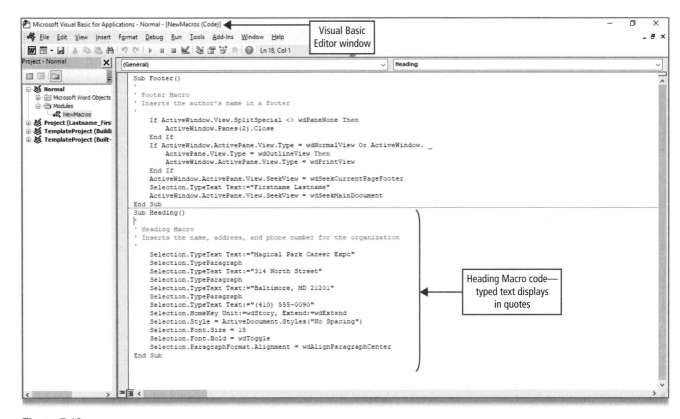

Figure 7.18

ALERT **Why Does My Visual Basic Editor Display Differently?**

Depending on how the Visual Basic Editor was last used, different panes may be displayed. For purposes of this instruction, the only panes that are required are the Project pane on the left and the Code pane on the right.

3 In the pane on the right, locate the text *Magical Park Career Expo*. Click to position the insertion point to the left of *Career*, type **Corporation** and then press Spacebar. Compare your screen with Figure 7.19.

> You are editing the macro so that when it runs the full name of the organization displays.

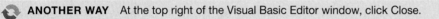

```
' Heading Macro
' Inserts the name, address, and phone number for the organization
'
    Selection.TypeText Text:="Magical Park Corporation Career Expo"        Edited text
    Selection.TypeParagraph
    Selection.TypeText Text:="314 North Street"
    Selection.TypeParagraph
    Selection.TypeText Text:="Baltimore, MD 21201"
    Selection.TypeParagraph
    Selection.TypeText Text:="(410) 555-0090"
    Selection.HomeKey Unit:=wdStory, Extend:=wdExtend
    Selection.Style = ActiveDocument.Styles("No Spacing")
    Selection.Font.Size = 18
    Selection.Font.Bold = wdToggle
    Selection.ParagraphFormat.Alignment = wdAlignParagraphCenter
End Sub
```

Figure 7.19

4 On the menu bar, click **File**, and then on the list, click **Close and Return to Microsoft Word**.

MAC TIP   Display the menu bar, click Word, click Close and Return to Microsoft Word.

ANOTHER WAY   At the top right of the Visual Basic Editor window, click Close.

---

5 In your **Lastname_Firstname_7A_Expo_Memo** document delete the heading—the first four paragraphs.

6 Press Enter one time to create a blank paragraph above the word *MEMO*, and then click to place your insertion point in that blank paragraph.

7 On the **Quick Access Toolbar**, click the button assigned to your **Heading** macro, and then compare your screen with Figure 7.20.

> The edited text displays in the heading.

Figure 7.20

8 Click anywhere in the document to cancel the selection, and then **Save** your document.

GO! Learn How

Video W7-4

Word has dozens of macros that are already built in and available in each document. For example, there are built-in macros to check for Accessibility, to bring objects to the front, to delete hyperlinks, and to format a picture.

Activity 7.08 | **Using a Built-in Word Macro**

In this Activity, you will use a macro that enables you to adjust the size of the indents for a bulleted list.

1 Locate and select the four bulleted paragraphs.

2 On the **Developer tab**, in the **Code group**, click **Macros**. In the **Macros** dialog box, click the **Macros in arrow**, and then click **Word commands**. Under **Macro name**, scroll as necessary, and then on the list, click **AdjustListIndents**—macro names are in alphabetical order.

> A list of available Word commands (macros) displays. The Description area explains what a selected command will do. The *AdjustListIndents* built-in macro modifies the indenting of a bulleted or numbered list.

3 In the **Macros** dialog box, click **Run**. In the **Adjust List Indents** dialog box, click the **Bullet position up spin arrow** to **0.4"**. Click the **Text indent up spin arrow** to **0.6"**. Compare your screen with Figure 7.21.

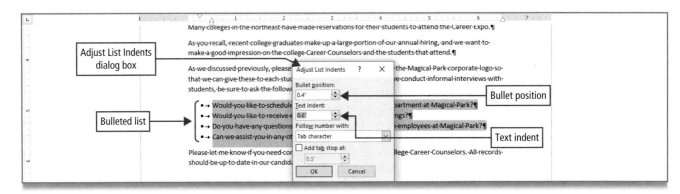

Figure 7.21

4 Click **OK**, and notice that the indentation of the bulleted list has changed.

5 Click **Save** 🖫. Press Ctrl + Home.

6 Click the **File tab**, display the **Info tab**, and then click **Show All Properties**. In the **Tags** box, type **macros** In the **Subject** box, type your course name and section number. If necessary, edit the author name to display your name.

7 On the left, click **Print** to view the Print Preview.

8 On the left, click the **Save As tab**, click **Browse**, and then in the **Save As** dialog box, navigate to your **Word Chapter 7** folder.

9 In the **File name** box, type **Lastname_Firstname_7A_Expo_Memo_Word_Document** Click the **Save as type arrow**, and then click **Word Document**. Click **Save**.

Because you cannot submit a macro-enabled document for grading, you must re-save your document as a Word document for submission.

10 **Close** your document and close Word.

For Non-MyLab Submissions   **Determine What Your Instructor Requires for Submission**

As directed by your instructor, submit your completed Lastname_Firstname_7A_Expo_Memo Word document.

---

11 In **MyLab IT**, locate and click the Grader Project **Word 7A Expo Flyer**. In **step 3**, under **Upload Completed Assignment**, click **Choose File**. In the **Open** dialog box, navigate to your **Word Chapter 7 folder**, and then click your **Student_7A_Expo_Memo** file one time to select it. In the lower right corner of the **Open** dialog box, click **Open**.

The name of your selected file displays above the Upload button.

12 To submit your file to **MyLab IT** for grading, click **Upload**, wait a moment for a green **Success!** message, and then in **step 4**, click the blue **Submit for Grading** button. Click **Close Assignment** to return to your list of **Course Materials**.

Activity 7.09 | Restoring Default Settings

Because you will not need the macros you created in the Normal template after completing this project, you will delete them and restore the default settings you changed.

1 If necessary, open Word and display a blank document. Click the **Developer tab**, and then in the **Code group**, click **Macros**. In the **Macros** dialog box, in the **Macros in** box, click the arrow and then click **All active templates and documents**. Under **Macro name**, click **Footer**, and then click **Delete**. In the **Microsoft Word** dialog box, click **Yes** to confirm the deletion.

MAC TIP   Click the minus (-) symbol to delete the macro.

2 By using the same technique, delete the **Heading** macro.

You are not deleting the *AutoClose* macro because it is stored only in the document.

3 Click **Close** to close the **Macros** dialog box.

4 Click the **File tab**, and then click **Options**. In the **Word Options** dialog box, click **Customize Ribbon**. Under **Main Tabs**, clear the **Developer** check box.

MAC TIP   To deselect the Developer tab, display the menu bar, click Word, Preferences, Ribbon & Toolbar, and then clear the Developer check box.

5 On the left side of the **Word Options** dialog box, click **Quick Access Toolbar**. On the right side, under **Customize Quick Access Toolbar**, click **Normal.NewMacros.Heading**. In the middle of the window, click **Remove**, and then click **OK**.

MAC TIP   It is not necessary to remove anything from the Quick Access Toolbar.

6 **Close** ☒ Word.

You have completed Project 7A   **END**

Project Activities

In Activities 7.10 through 7.17, you will create a brochure for visitors to the theme parks operated by Magical Park Corporation. To customize the document, you will change the paper size, format text, and edit graphics. Your completed file will look similar to Figure 7.22.

Project Files for MyLab IT Grader

1. In your **MyLab IT** course, locate and click **Word 7B Park Brochure**, Download Materials, and then Download All Files.
2. Extract the zipped folder to your Word Chapter 7 folder. Close the Grader download screens.
3. Take a moment to open the downloaded **Word_7B_Park_Brochure_Instructions**; note any recent updates to the book.

Project Results

GO! Project 7B
Where We're Going

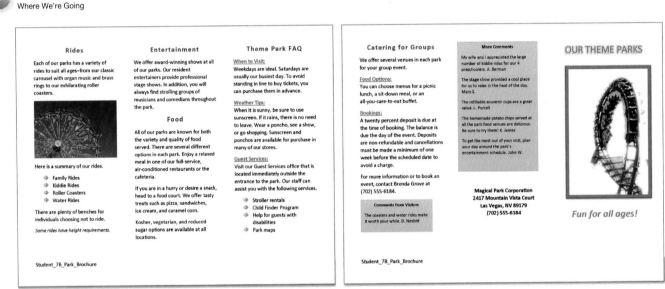

Figure 7.22 Project 7B Park Brochure

For Non-MyLab Submissions

For Project 7B, you will need:

w07B_Park_Brochure
w07B_Wheel
w07B_Coaster
w07B_Comments
w07B_Brochure_Bullet

In your Word Chapter 7 folder, save w07B_Park_Brochure as:
Lastname_Firstname_7B_Park_Brochure

After you have named and saved your document, on the next page, begin with Step 2.

ALERT   Because Office 365 is a cloud-based subscription service that receives continuous updates, you may encounter some variations in what appears on your screen and what is shown in this instruction. Microsoft Office 365 is fully installed on your PC or Mac; no internet access is necessary to create or edit documents. When you *are* connected to the internet, you will receive monthly upgrades and new features, so you always have the latest versions of Office apps as soon as they are available. Your subscription gives you continuous free access to the latest innovations and refinements.

GO! Learn How
Video W7-5

Word provides many features to format and display text in an attractive manner, such as changing the spacing between characters and controlling the display of phrases where the individual components should not be split between two lines. Additionally, the paper size can be changed to produce the desired result—in this instance, a small brochure.

Activity 7.10 | Changing Paper Size

1.2.1, 2.3.1, 2.3.2

1 Navigate to your **Word Chapter 7 folder**, and then double-click the Word file you downloaded from **MyLab IT** that displays your name—**Student_Word_7B_Park_Brochure**. If necessary, at the top click **Enable Editing**.

2 Insert the file name in the footer and display rulers and formatting marks. If any words are flagged as spelling errors, click **Ignore All**.

3 Click the **Layout tab**. In the **Page Setup group**, click **Orientation**, and then click **Landscape**.

4 In the **Page Setup group**, click **Margins**, and then click **Narrow**. In the **Page Setup group**, click **Columns**, and then click **Three**.

5 On **Page 1**, in the first column, position the insertion point to the left of the paragraph *Entertainment*. In the **Page Setup group**, click **Breaks**, and then under **Page Breaks**, click **Column**. In the second column, position the insertion point to the left of the paragraph *Theme Park FAQ*. In the **Page Setup group**, click **Breaks**, and then under **Page Breaks**, click **Column**.

6 In the third column, position the insertion point to the left of the paragraph *Catering for Groups*, and then press `Ctrl` + `Enter` to create a new page. Scroll up as necessary, and then notice the column and page breaks display as shown in Figure 7.23.

🖥 **MAC TIP**   Press `command ⌘` + `enter`.

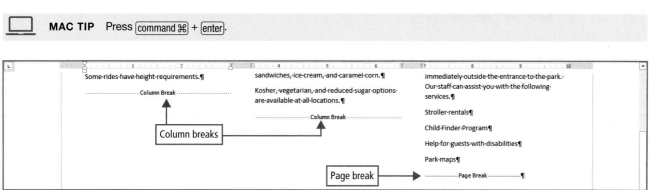

Figure 7.23

7 On **Page 2**, position the insertion point to the left of the paragraph *Magical Park Corporation*. In the **Page Setup group**, click **Breaks**, and then under **Page Breaks**, click **Column**. In the second column, position the insertion point in the last blank paragraph of the document, and then using the technique you practiced, insert a **Column** break.

8 Press `Ctrl` + `Home`. In the **Page Setup group**, click **Size**, and then at the bottom of the displayed list, click **More Paper Sizes**.

ANOTHER WAY Click the dialog box launcher to display the Page Setup dialog box, and then click the Paper tab.

9 In the **Page Setup** dialog box, with the **Paper tab** displayed, under **Paper size,** click the **Paper size arrow**, which displays *Letter*, scroll as necessary, and then click **Custom size**. Use the spin box arrows in the **Width** and **Height** boxes to set the **Width** to **9"** and the **Height** to **7"** and then compare your screen with Figure 7.24.

You can change the paper size to accommodate any type of document. In this case, the brochure requires a custom paper size.

MAC TIP Display the menu bar, click File, click Page Setup, click the Paper Size arrow, click Manage Custom Sizes. Enter the Width and Height sizes; click OK two times. Change the Orientation back to Landscape if necessary.

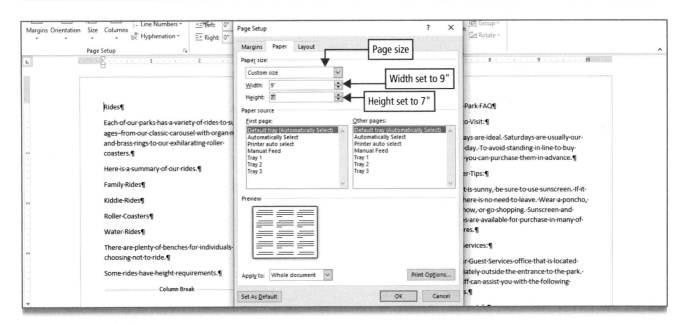

Figure 7.24

10 Click **OK** to close the **Page Setup** dialog box.

11 Save 💾 your changes.

Activity 7.11 | Changing Character Spacing

2.2.2, 3.3.1

You will format the text in the brochure by changing font sizes and applying styles. You will also change the ***character spacing*** for selected text to improve the appearance or readability of the brochure. Character spacing is a Word feature that enables you to change the default spacing constraints between characters.

You can manually set spacing options or use ***kerning*** to have Word automatically modify space between characters in selected text. Kerning automatically adjusts the spacing between pairs of characters, with a specified minimum point size, so that words and letters appear equally spaced.

1 In the first column, select the first paragraph—*Rides*. Change the **Font Size** to **14**, apply **Bold** B, click the **Font Color arrow** A·, and then in the last column, click the last color. **Center** the selected paragraph.

2 With the paragraph *Rides* selected, on the **Home tab**, in the **Font group**, click the **Dialog Box Launcher** ⌐.

3 ▸ In the **Font** dialog box, click the **Advanced tab**. Under **Character Spacing**, click the **Spacing arrow**, and then click **Expanded**. Click the **By spin box up arrow** as necessary to set **1.2 pt**. Compare your screen with Figure 7.25, and then take a moment to study the character spacing settings in Figure 7.26.

There are several different features that enable you to modify the character spacing. By changing the spacing to Expanded by 1.2 pt, the space between the characters is increased slightly. A preview of the character spacing displays in the Preview area of the Fonts dialog box.

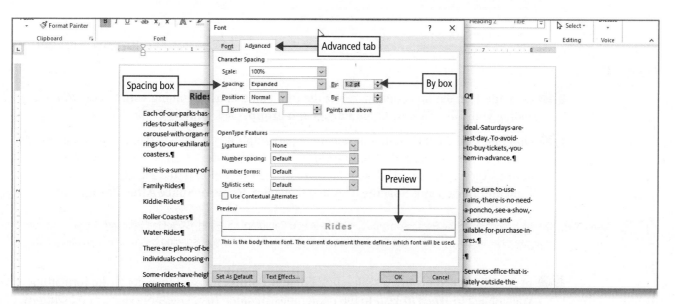

Figure 7.25

Character Spacing Settings	
Setting	**Description**
Scale	Expands or compresses text horizontally as a percentage of the current size.
Spacing	Expands or compresses spacing between characters by a specified number of points.
Position	Raises or lowers the location of text in relation to the current vertical location.
Kerning for fonts	Automatically adjusts the spacing between pairs of characters, with a specified minimum point size, so that words and letters appear equally spaced.
By	Specifies the number of points that should be used to space characters.

Figure 7.26

4 Click **OK** to close the **Font** dialog box. In the **Clipboard group**, double-click **Format Painter** to turn it on. Select each of the following paragraphs to apply the same formatting you applied to *Rides*: *Entertainment*, *Food*, *Theme Park FAQ*, and *Catering for Groups*—some text has moved to **Page 3**. In the **Clipboard group**, click **Format Painter** to turn it off. Press Ctrl + Home and then compare your screen with Figure 7.27.

Figure 7.27

5 On **Page 1**, in the first column, select the four paragraphs beginning with *Family Rides* and ending with *Water Rides*. In the **Paragraph group**, click **Bullets**.

6 On **Page 1**, in the third column, select the paragraph *When to Visit*, being sure to include the colon and paragraph mark. Apply **Bold** and **Underline**, click the **Font Color arrow**, and then in the last column, click the fifth color. In the **Paragraph group**, click **Line and Paragraph Spacing**, and then click **Remove Space After Paragraph**.

🖥 **MAC TIP** On the Home tab, in the Paragraph group, click Line and Paragraph spacing. Click Line Spacing Options. Change Spacing After to 0 pt.; you can use this technique when instructed to adjust spacing before or after a paragraph.

7 In the **Clipboard group**, double-click **Format Painter**, and then apply the formatting you applied to *When to Visit* to the paragraphs *Weather Tips*, *Guest Services*, *Food Options*, and *Bookings*. In the **Clipboard group**, click **Format Painter** to turn it off.

8 On **Page 1**, at the bottom of the third column, select the four paragraphs beginning with *Stroller rentals* and ending with *Park maps*. In the **Paragraph group**, click **Bullets**. Click to position the insertion point anywhere in the paragraph *Park maps*. In the **Paragraph group**, click **Line and Paragraph Spacing**, and then click **Remove Space After Paragraph**.

9 At the bottom of **Page 1**, in the first column, select the paragraph that begins *Some rides*. Change the **Font Size** to **10**, and then apply **Italic**. Deselect the text, and then compare your screen with Figure 7.28.

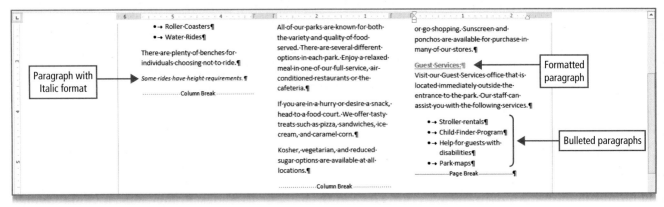

Figure 7.28

10 **Save** your document.

Activity 7.12 | Inserting Nonbreaking Hyphens and Nonbreaking Spaces

2.1.2

Recall that word wrap automatically moves text from the right edge of a paragraph to the beginning of the next line as necessary to fit within the margins. You can insert a ***nonbreaking hyphen*** to prevent a hyphenated word or phrase from being displayed on two lines.

Similarly, you can insert a ***nonbreaking space*** to keep two or more words together so that both words will wrap even if only the second word would normally wrap to the next line. For example, inserting nonbreaking spaces in a date will keep the entire date—month, day, and year—on the same line. Inserting a nonbreaking hyphen will keep a hyphenated surname—such as Huelsman-Walker—on the same line.

1 On **Page 1**, in the second column, in the paragraph that begins *All of our*, locate the phrase *air-conditioned*. Select the hyphen, on the **Insert tab**, in the **Symbols group**, click **Symbol**, and then click **More Symbols**. In the **Symbols** dialog box, click the **Special Characters tab**, click **Nonbreaking Hyphen**, click **Insert**, and then click **Close**. Notice the entire term *air-conditioned* displays on the same line. Compare your screen with Figure 7.29.

You can improve the readability of a document by inserting a nonbreaking hyphen.

MAC TIP On the Insert tab, in the Symbols group, click Advanced Symbol.

ANOTHER WAY Press Ctrl + Shift + - to insert a nonbreaking hyphen.

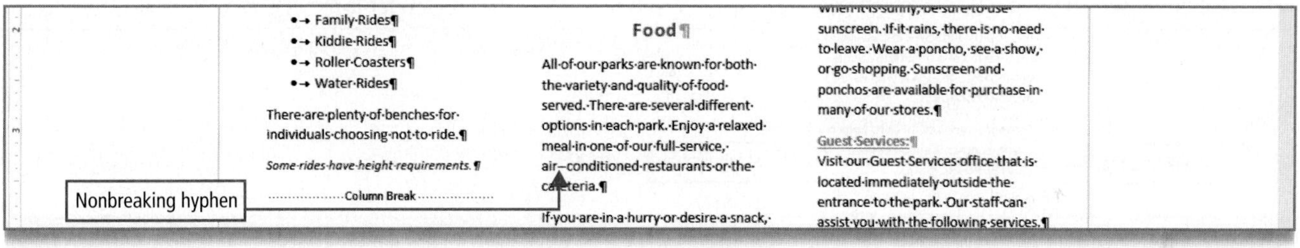

Figure 7.29

2 On **Page 2**, in the first column, in the fourth paragraph, locate the phrase *all-you-care-to-eat*. Select the hyphen between *all* and *you* and then by using the technique you just practiced or the keyboard shortcut Ctrl + Shift + -, insert a non-breaking hyphen. In a similar manner, insert nonbreaking hyphens to replace each of the remaining three hyphens in the phrase.

If you have a hyphenated term that contains multiple hyphens, it is good practice to replace all hyphens with nonbreaking hyphens. If preceding text or other elements are modified, this will ensure that the text will always display on a single line.

MAC TIP Use command ⌘ + shift + - as the keyboard shortcut for a nonbreaking hyphen.

---

3 On **Page 1**, in the second column, in the fifth paragraph, locate the term *ice cream*. Select the space following *ice*. On the **Insert tab**, in the **Symbols group**, click **Symbol**, and then click **More Symbols**. In the **Symbols** dialog box, click the **Special Characters tab**, click **Nonbreaking Space**, click **Insert**, and then click **Close**. Compare your screen with Figure 7.30.

The term *ice cream* displays on one line. A small raised circle, which is the formatting mark for a nonbreaking space, displays between the two words.

Figure 7.30

4 In the last line of the same paragraph, by using the technique you just practiced, replace the space between *caramel* and *corn* with a nonbreaking space.

5 On **Page 2**, in the first column, in the last paragraph, locate the phone number. By using the techniques you just practiced, replace the space with a nonbreaking space, and then replace the hyphen with a nonbreaking hyphen. Compare your screen with Figure 7.31.

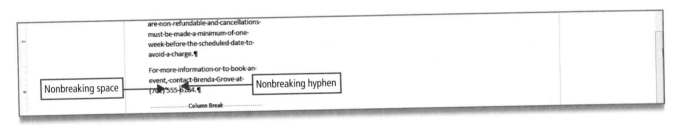

Figure 7.31

6 **Save** your document.

Objective 6 Format Graphic and Text Elements in a Word Document

GO! Learn How
Video W7-5

Inserting and formatting graphics and text can enhance the appearance of a document. Word provides many features to modify graphic and text elements.

Activity 7.13 | Viewing Document Gridlines

Document gridlines—nonprinting horizontal and vertical lines—assist you in aligning graphics and other elements.

1 On **Page 2**, in the third column, click to position the insertion point in the blank paragraph. Click the **View tab**, and then in the **Show group**, select the **Gridlines** check box. Compare your screen with Figure 7.32.

The gridlines display only within the margins of the document.

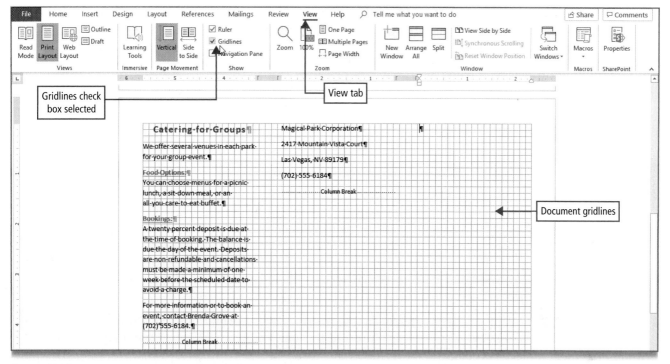

Figure 7.32

Activity 7.14 | Linking Text Boxes

5.1.6, 5.3.1

Recall that text boxes are movable, resizable containers for text or graphics. Word includes a feature to link two or more text boxes. When text boxes are linked, if the first text box cannot hold all the inserted text, the text will automatically flow into the next linked text box. In this Activity, you will use gridlines to position text boxes, link two text boxes, and then insert text from an existing file.

1 On **Page 2**, in the first column, click to position the insertion point at the end of the last paragraph. Click the **Insert tab**. In the **Text group**, click **Text Box**, and then click **Draw Text Box**. Using the gridlines, position the ⊞ pointer at the left margin two gridlines below the last paragraph, drag to the right **18** squares, drag down **7** squares, and then release the mouse button. If necessary resize the text box so that the right border aligns at approximately 2 inches on the horizontal ruler and the bottom border aligns at approximately 0.75 inch on the lower portion of the vertical ruler. Compare your screen with Figure 7.33.

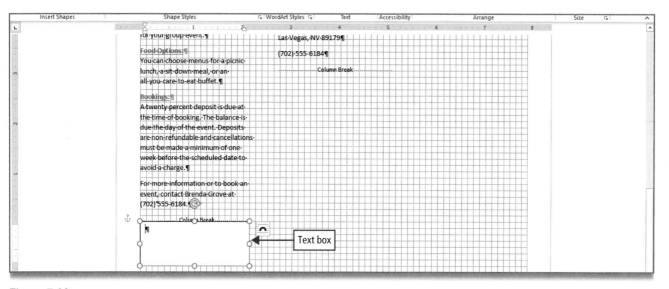

Figure 7.33

2 Click anywhere to the right of the text box to deselect it. On **Page 2**, in the second column, select the four paragraphs, and then apply **Bold** B. Center the selected paragraphs. Click the **Home tab**. In the **Paragraph group**, click **Line and Paragraph Spacing** ↕☰▾, and then click **Remove Space After Paragraph**.

3 In the second column, position the insertion point to the left of the first paragraph, and then press [Enter] two times.

4 In the second column, place the insertion point in the first blank paragraph that you just inserted. Click the **Insert tab**. In the **Text group**, click **Text Box**, and then click **Draw Text Box**.

5 Using the gridlines and existing text as a guide, position the ⊞ pointer at the top margin three gridlines to the left of *Magical*. Drag to the right **18** squares until the border is three gridlines to the right of *Corporation*, drag down until the bottom of the text box is aligned with the line below the text *avoid a charge* (in the first column), and then release the mouse button. If necessary, resize the text box so that the right border aligns at approximately 2 inches on the horizontal ruler and the bottom border aligns at approximately 3.5 inches on the vertical ruler.

6 With the text box selected, on the **Drawing Tools Format tab**, in the **Arrange group**, click **Wrap Text**, and then click **Top and Bottom**. Compare your screen with Figure 7.34.

Top and Bottom text wrapping causes the four paragraphs of text and the two blank paragraphs above them to be moved below the text box.

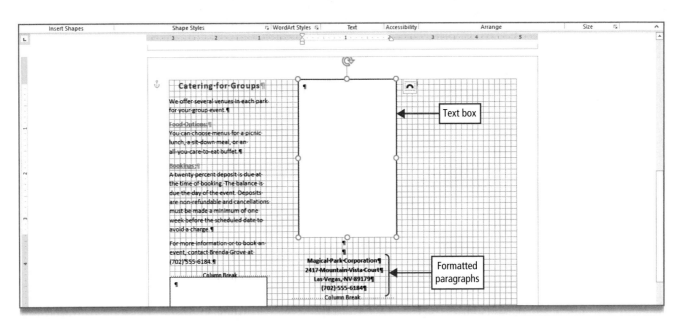

Figure 7.34

7 At the bottom of the first column, click in the text box to select it. On the **Drawing Tools Format tab**, in the **Text group**, click **Create Link**.

8 Move the pointer into a blank area of the document, and notice that the ⛾ pointer displays.

The upright pitcher indicates that the first text box is ready to be linked to another text box.

⌐⌐ **MAC TIP** The pointer displays as a link rather than a pitcher.

9 Move your pointer into the text box in the second column, and notice that the 🍶 pointer displays. Compare your screen with Figure 7.35.

> The pouring pitcher indicates that you can link the second text box to the first text box.

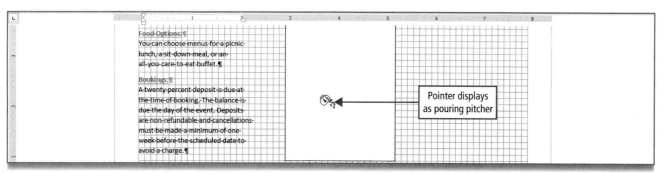

Figure 7.35

10 With the 🍶 pointer displayed, click in the second text box to create a link.

11 If necessary, click to position the insertion point in the first text box. Click the **Insert tab**. In the **Text group**, click the **Object button arrow** 🔲 ⋅, and then click **Text from File**. Navigate to the files you downloaded for this project, select the file **w07B_Comments**, and then click **Insert**. Compare your screen with Figure 7.36.

> The first two paragraphs of text display in the first text box and the remaining text displays in the second text box.

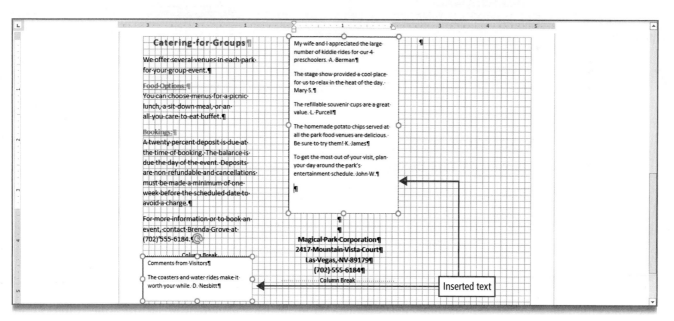

Figure 7.36

12 In the first text box, select the first paragraph—*Comments from Visitors*—and then apply **Bold** B and **Center** the paragraph.

13 In the second text box, click to position the insertion point to the left of the first paragraph. Press Enter one time, press ↑, and then type **More Comments** Select the text you just typed, apply **Bold** B, and **Center** the paragraph.

14 Click the **Drawing Tools Format tab**, and then in the **Shape Styles group**, click **More** ▾. In the **Shape Styles** gallery, in the fourth row, click the last style. Apply the same Shape Style to the other text box. Compare your screen with Figure 7.37.

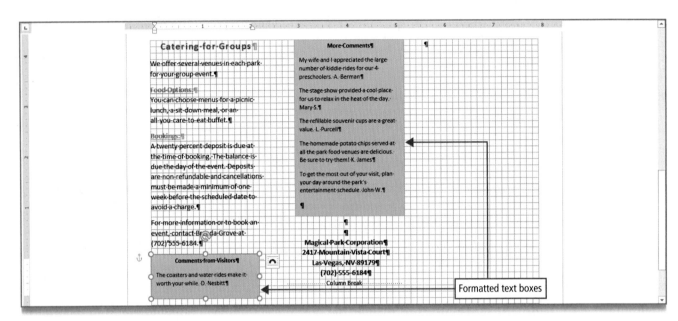

Figure 7.37

15 Click the **View tab**, and then in the **Show group**, clear the **Gridlines** check box to hide the gridlines. **Save** 💾 your document.

> **MORE KNOWLEDGE** | **Unlinking Text Boxes**
>
> To unlink text boxes, click in the first linked text box, and then on the Format tab, in the Text group, click Break Link.

Activity 7.15 | Modifying Text Effects

2.2.1

You can modify the built-in text effects in Word in a variety of ways—for example, by changing the weight and color of the outline and by altering the type of reflection.

1 On **Page 2**, position the insertion point in the blank paragraph at the top of the third column, and then type **OUR THEME PARKS**

2 Press Enter two times, and then type **Fun for all ages!** Select the paragraph you just typed, change the **Font Size** to **20**, apply **Italic** I, and **Center** the paragraph.

3 With *Fun for all ages!* still selected, click the **Home tab**, and then in the **Font group**, click **Text Effects and Typography** Ⓐ ▾. In the **Text Effects** gallery, in the first row, click the fifth effect. With the text still selected, click **Text Effects and Typography** Ⓐ ▾ again, point to **Outline**, and then under **Theme Colors**, in the last column, click the fifth color. In the **Font group**, click the **Font Color button arrow** Ⓐ ▾, and then in the last column, click the fourth color. Click anywhere to deselect the text, and then compare your screen with Figure 7.38.

> The theme allows you to choose a consistent color scheme to create a professional-looking document.

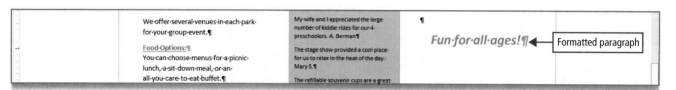

Figure 7.38

4 In the third column, select the first paragraph—*OUR THEME PARKS*. Change the **Font Size** to **20**, apply **Bold** Ⓑ, and then **Center** the paragraph.

5 With the paragraph still selected, on the **Home tab**, in the **Font group**, click **Text Effects and Typography** Ⓐ ▾, and then in the second row, click the second effect. Click **Text Effects and Typography** Ⓐ ▾ again, point to **Glow**, and then under **Glow Variations**, in the third row, click the last glow variation.

6 In the **Font group**, click the **Font Color button arrow** Ⓐ ▾, and then in the last column, click the fifth color. Deselect the text, and then compare your screen with Figure 7.39.

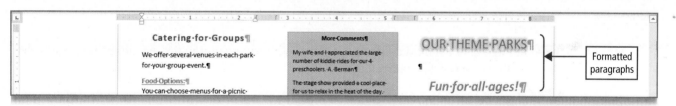

Figure 7.39

7 **Save** 🖫 your document.

Activity 7.16 | Applying Artistic Effects to Pictures

MOS

5.1.2, 5.2.1,
5.2.2, 5.2.4

You can change the appearance of a picture by applying an ***artistic effect***—a filter that you apply to an image to create a special effect.

1 On **Page 1**, in the first column, position the insertion point at the end of the second paragraph, and then press Enter one time.

2 Click the **Insert tab**, and then in the **Illustrations group**, click **Pictures**. In the **Insert Picture** dialog box, navigate to the files you downloaded with this project, select the file **w07B_Wheel**, and then click **Insert**.

🖵 **MAC TIP** Click Pictures, then click Picture from File. Use this technique whenever you insert a picture.

3 On the **Picture Tools Format tab**, in the **Adjust group**, click **Artistic Effects**. Point to several effects.

Live preview enables you to see how each effect will modify the picture.

4 In the **Artistic Effects** gallery, in the fourth row, click the last effect. Compare your screen with Figure 7.40.

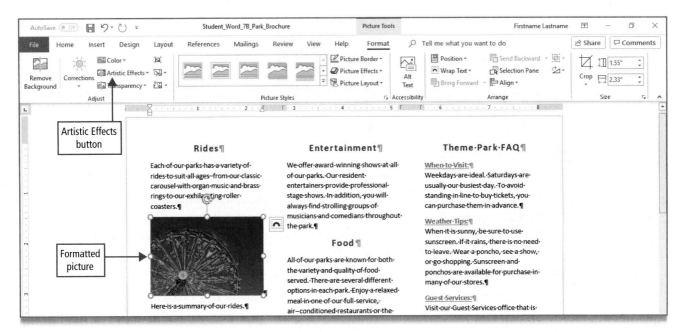

Figure 7.40

5 On **Page 2**, in the third column, position the insertion point in the second, blank paragraph, and then **Center** the blank paragraph.

6 Click the **Insert tab**, and then in the **Illustrations group**, click **Pictures**. In the **Insert Picture** dialog box, navigate to the files you downloaded with this project, select the file **w07B_Coaster**, and then click **Insert**.

7 In the **Adjust group**, click **Artistic Effects**, and then in the second row, click the fourth effect.

8 On the **Picture Tools Format tab**, in the **Picture Styles group**, click **More** ⏷, and then click the first picture style. In the **Picture Styles group**, click the **Picture Border** ◲ and then in the last column, click the fifth color. Compare your screen with Figure 7.41.

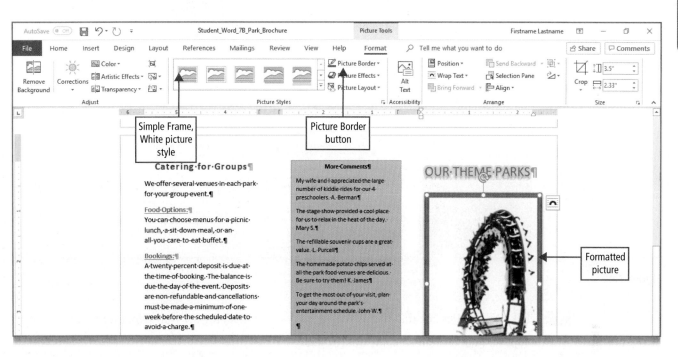

Figure 7.41

9 **Save** 🖫 your changes.

Activity 7.17 | Using a Picture as a Bullet

In this Activity, you will use a picture to replace the bullets in the document.

1 On **Page 1**, in the first column select the four bulleted paragraphs. Click the **Home tab**, in the **Paragraph group**, click the **Bullets button arrow** ⊞▾, and then click **Define New Bullet**.

2 In the **Define New Bullet** dialog box, under **Bullet character**, click **Picture**.

3 In the **Insert Pictures** dialog box, to the right of **From a file**, click **Browse**.

 MAC TIP When Finder displays, navigate to the files you downloaded with this project, and then click w07_Brochure_Bullet.

4 In the **Insert Picture** dialog box, navigate to the files you downloaded with this project, select the file **w07B_Brochure_Bullet**, and then click **Insert**. Compare your screen with Figure 7.42.

> The picture—a combination of yellow, blue, and green arrows—displays as a bullet in the Preview area of the Define New Bullet dialog box.

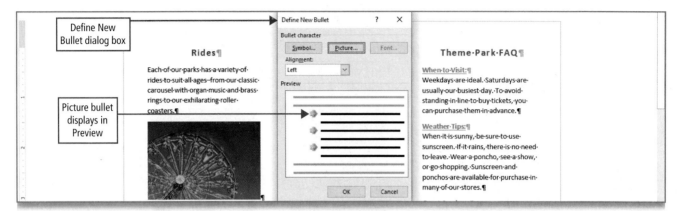

Figure 7.42

5 Click **OK**, and notice that the picture displays as bullets for the four paragraphs.

> The new bullet is stored in the Bullet Library.

6 On **Page 1**, in the third column, select the four bulleted paragraphs. In the **Paragraph group**, click the **Bullets button arrow** [≡ ▾], and then compare your screen with Figure 7.43.

> The new picture bullet displays under Recently Used Bullets, Bullet Library, and Document Bullets.

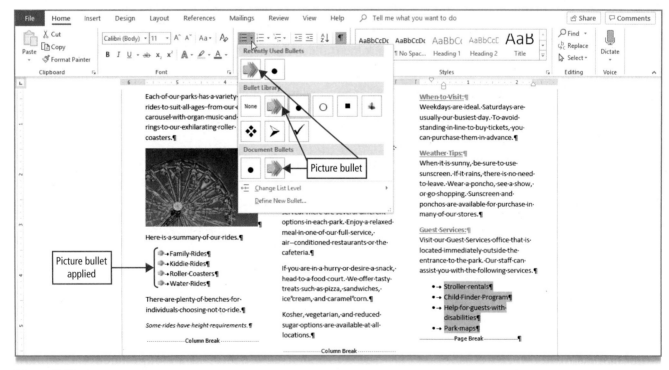

Figure 7.43

7 Under **Recently Used Bullets**, click the new picture bullet to apply the bullet to the selected paragraphs. Click anywhere to deselect the paragraphs, and then compare your screen with Figure 7.44.

Figure 7.44

8 Press Ctrl + Home. In Backstage view, click the **Info tab**, and then click **Show All Properties**. In the **Tags** box, type **brochure, graphics** In the **Subject** box, type your course name and section number. If necessary, edit the author name to display your name. On the left, click **Save** to save your document and return to the Word window.

9 On the **Home tab**, in the **Paragraph group**, click the **Bullets button arrow**. In the **Bullets** gallery, under **Bullet Library**, right-click the picture bullet, and then on the shortcut menu, click **Remove**.

10 In the upper right corner of the Word window, click **Close** ⊠.

For Non-MyLab Submissions   Determine What Your Instructor Requires for Submission
As directed by your instructor, submit your completed Word document.

11 In **MyLab IT**, locate and click the Grader Project **Word 7B Park Brochure**. In **step 3**, under **Upload Completed Assignment**, click **Choose File**. In the **Open** dialog box, navigate to your **Word Chapter 7 folder**, and then click your **Student_Word_7B_Park_Brochure** file one time to select it. In the lower right corner of the **Open** dialog box, click **Open**.

The name of your selected file displays above the Upload button.

12 To submit your file to **MyLab IT** for grading, click **Upload**, wait a moment for a green **Success!** message, and then in **step 4**, click the blue **Submit for Grading** button. Click **Close Assignment** to return to your list of **Course Materials**.

You have completed Project 7B **END**

»» GO! To Work

wavebreakmedia/Shutterstock, Monkey Business Images/Fotolia, Ivanko80/Shutterstock, Monkey Business Images/Shutterstock

Microsoft Office Specialist (MOS) Skills in This Chapter	
Project 7A	**Project 7B**
1.1.5 Expert: Enable macros in a document	**1.2.1** Set up document pages
1.1.6 Expert: Customize the Quick Access Toolbar	**2.1.1** Insert symbols and special characters
1.1.7 Expert: Display hidden ribbon tabs	**2.2.1** Apply text effects
4.2.1 Expert: Record simple macros	**2.2.2** Apply formatting by using Format Painter
4.2.2 Expert: Name simple macros	**2.3.1** Format text in multiple columns
4.2.3 Expert: Edit simple macros	**2.3.2** Insert page, section, and column breaks
	3.3.1 Format paragraphs as numbered and bulleted lists
	3.3.2 Change bullet characters and number formats
	3.3.3 Define custom bullet characters and number formats
	5.1.2 Insert Pictures
	5.1.6 Insert text boxes
	5.2.1 Apply artistic effects
	5.2.2 Apply picture effects and picture styles
	5.2.4 Format graphic elements
	5.3.1 Add and modify text in text boxes

Build Your E-Portfolio

An E-Portfolio is a collection of evidence, stored electronically, that showcases what you have accomplished while completing your education. Collecting and then sharing your work products with potential employers reflects your academic and career goals. Your completed documents from the following projects are good examples to show what you have learned: 7G, 7K, and 7L.

GO! For Job Success

Discussion: Cyber Hacking

Your instructor may assign these questions to your class, and then ask you to think about them or discuss them with your classmates:

The US Homeland Security Department describes cyber incidents (hacking) as actions where there is an attempt to gain unauthorized access to a system or its data, unwanted disruption to service, unauthorized use of a system, or change to a system without the owner's permission. As companies store and process more and more data at centralized, offsite "cloud" data centers, the opportunities for criminals to hack data are growing. Cyber security is an important part of every organization's information systems protocols, and many companies now employ a senior executive with the title Chief Information Security Officer.

g-stockstudio/ Shutterstock

> What cyber incidents have you heard of in the news over the last year?

> What precautions have you taken with your personal data to prevent a hack?

> What would you do if you learned that an organization you do business with, such as your bank or college, had been the subject of a cyber incident?

End of Chapter

Summary

A macro—a set of commands and instructions that can be applied in a single action—helps you work more efficiently. You can use built-in macros or create your own macros by recording actions or typing code.

Visual Basic for Applications, or VBA, is a programming language you can use to create macros. In the Visual Basic Editor, you can edit the code in an existing macro or type your own procedure to create a new macro.

Create specialized documents by changing the paper size and the margins. Modify how text displays by changing the character spacing and using nonbreaking hyphens and nonbreaking spaces where appropriate.

Select a theme to maintain a consistent color scheme and create a professional-looking document. You can enhance a document by linking text boxes, applying artistic effects, and using a picture as a bullet.

GO! Learn It Online

Review the concepts, key terms, and MOS skills in this chapter by completing these online challenges, which you can find at **MyLab IT**.

Chapter Quiz: Answer matching and multiple choice questions to test what you learned in this chapter.

Lessons on the GO!: Learn how to use all the new apps and features as they are introduced by Microsoft.

MOS Prep Quiz: Answer questions to review the MOS skills that you practiced in this chapter.

Project Guide for Word Chapter 7

Your instructor will assign Projects from this list to ensure your learning and assess your knowledge.

	Project Guide for Word Chapter 7		
Project	**Apply Skills from These Chapter Objectives**	**Project Type**	**Project Location**
7A MyLab IT	Objectives 1–4 from Project 7A	**7A Instructional Project (Grader Project)** **Instruction** Guided instruction to learn the skills in Project 7A.	In **MyLab IT** and in text
7B MyLab IT	Objectives 5–6 from Project 7B	**7B Instructional Project (Grader Project)** **Instruction** Guided instruction to learn the skills in Project 7B.	In **MyLab IT** and in text
7C	Objectives 1–4 from Project 7A	**7C Skills Review (Scorecard Grading)** **Review** A guided review of the skills from Project 7A.	In text
7D	Objectives 5–6 from Project 7B	**7D Skills Review (Scorecard Grading)** **Review** A guided review of the skills from Project 7B.	In text
7E MyLab IT	Objectives 1–4 from Project 7A	**7E Mastery (Grader Project)** **Mastery and Transfer of Learning** A demonstration of your mastery of the skills in Project 7A with extensive decision making.	In **MyLab IT** and in text
7F MyLab IT	Objectives 5–6 from Project 7B	**7F Mastery (Grader Project)** **Mastery and Transfer of Learning** A demonstration of your mastery of the skills in Project 7B with extensive decision making.	In **MyLab IT** and in text
7G MyLab IT	Objectives 1–6 from Projects 7A and 7B	**7G Mastery (Grader Project)** **Mastery and Transfer of Learning** A demonstration of your mastery of the skills in Projects 7A and 7B with extensive decision making.	In **MyLab IT** and in text
7H	Combination of Objectives from Projects 7A and 7B	**7H GO! Fix It (Scorecard Grading)** **Critical Thinking** A demonstration of your mastery of the skills in Projects 7A and 7B by creating a correct result from a document that contains errors you must find.	IRC
7I	Combination of Objectives from Projects 7A and 7B	**7I GO! Make It (Scorecard Grading)** **Critical Thinking** A demonstration of your mastery of the skills in Projects 7A and 7B by creating a result from a supplied picture.	IRC
7J	Combination of Objectives from Projects 7A and 7B	**7J GO! Solve It (Rubric Grading)** **Critical Thinking** A demonstration of your mastery of the skills in Projects 7A and 7B, your decision-making skills, and your critical thinking skills. A task-specific rubric helps you self-assess your result.	IRC
7K	Combination of Objectives from Projects 7A and 7B	**7K GO! Solve It (Rubric Grading)** **Critical Thinking** A demonstration of your mastery of the skills in Projects 7A and 7B, your decision-making skills, and your critical thinking skills. A task-specific rubric helps you self-assess your result.	In text
7L	Combination of Objectives from Projects 7A and 7B	**7L GO! Think (Rubric Grading)** **Critical Thinking** A demonstration of your understanding of the Chapter concepts applied in a manner that you would outside of college. An analytic rubric helps you and your instructor grade the quality of your work by comparing it to the work an expert in the discipline would create.	In text
7M	Combination of Objectives from Projects 7A and 7B	**7M GO! Think (Rubric Grading)** **Critical Thinking** A demonstration of your understanding of the Chapter concepts applied in a manner that you would outside of college. An analytic rubric helps you and your instructor grade the quality of your work by comparing it to the work an expert in the discipline would create.	IRC
7N	Combination of Objectives from Projects 7A and 7B	**7N You and GO! (Rubric Grading)** **Critical Thinking** A demonstration of your understanding of the Chapter concepts applied in a manner that you would in a personal situation. An analytic rubric helps you and your instructor grade the quality of your work.	IRC

Glossary

Glossary of Chapter Key Terms

AdjustListIndents A built-in macro used to modify the indenting of a bulleted or numbered list.

Artistic effect A filter that is applied to an image to create a special effect.

AutoClose A macro that will automatically run when closing a document.

Character spacing A Word feature that enables you to change the default spacing constraints between characters.

Comment In a macro procedure, a line of text that is used solely for documentation.

Document gridlines Nonprinting horizontal and vertical lines used to assist in aligning graphics and other elements in a document.

Kerning A character spacing option that automatically adjusts the spacing between pairs of characters, with a specified minimum point size, so that words and letters appear equally spaced.

Layout The placement and arrangement of the text and graphic elements on a slide.

Macro A set of commands and instructions that can be grouped as a single command to accomplish a task automatically.

Macro virus A macro that causes files to be erased or damaged by inserting unauthorized code.

Nonbreaking hyphen A formatting mark that prevents a hyphenated word or phrase from being displayed on two lines.

Nonbreaking space A formatting mark that keeps two words together so that both words will wrap even if only the second word would normally wrap to the next line.

Procedure A block of programming code that performs one or more tasks.

Recording The process of creating a macro while performing specific actions in a document.

VBA The abbreviation for Visual Basic for Applications—a programming language used to create macros.

Visual Basic Editor An editor that enables you to view and edit existing macro code or create a new macro.

Visual Basic for Applications (VBA) A programming language used to create macros.

Chapter Review

Apply 7A skills from these Objectives:

1. Create Macros
2. Run Macros
3. Edit a Macro in the Visual Basic Editor
4. Use a Built-in Word Macro

In the following project, you will create macros to improve your efficiency in editing a letter and press release that explains the scheduled career expos conducted by Magical Park Corporation. Your completed documents will look similar to Figure 7.45.

Project Files

For Project 7C, you will need the following files:

w07C_Expo_Schedule

w07C_Press_Release

You will save your files as:

Lastname_Firstname_7C_Expo_Schedule (Macro-Enabled Word Document)

Lastname_Firstname_7C_Press_Release (Macro-Enabled Word Document)

Project Results

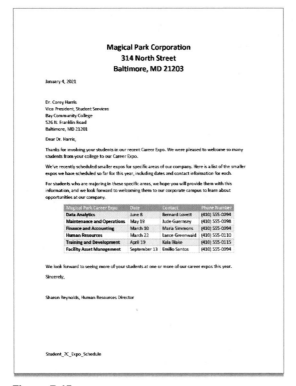
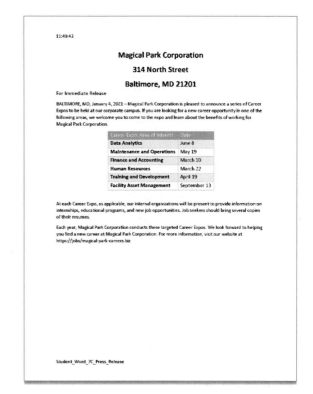

Figure 7.45

(continues on next page)

Chapter Review

Skills Review: Project 7C Expo Schedule (continued)

1 From the files you downloaded for this project, locate and open the file **w07C_Expo_Schedule**. Display the **Save As** dialog box, and then navigate to your **Word Chapter 7** folder. In the lower portion of the dialog box, click the **Save as type arrow**, and then from the list, click **Word Macro-Enabled Document**. In the **File name** box, using your own name, type **Lastname_Firstname_7C_Expo_Schedule** and then click **Save**.

a. Insert the file name in the footer.

b. Click the **File tab** to display Backstage view, and then on the left click **Options**. In the **Word Options** dialog box, on the left, click **Customize Ribbon**. (Mac users: Display the menu bar, click Preferences, Ribbon & Toolbar.)

c. In the **Main Tabs** list, locate and then select the **Developer** check box. Click **OK** to close the **Word Options** dialog box.

d. Click the **Developer tab**, and then in the **Code group**, click **Macro Security**. If necessary, in the **Trust Center** dialog box, under **Macro Settings**, select **Disable all macros with notification**. Click **OK** to close the dialog box. **Save** your document. (Mac users: Display the menu bar, click Word, Preferences, Security & Privacy.)

2 Press Ctrl + Home. On the **Developer tab**, in the **Code group**, click **Record Macro**.

a. In the **Record Macro** dialog box, in the **Macro name** box, type **Heading** Be sure the **Store macro in** box displays **All Documents (Normal.dotm)**.

b. In the **Description** box, click to position the insertion point, and then type **Inserts the organization's name and address**

c. Under **Assign macro to**, click **Keyboard**. In the **Customize Keyboard** dialog box, with the insertion point in the **Press new shortcut key** box, press and hold Alt + Ctrl, and then press G. Click **Assign**, and then click **Close**. (Mac users: *Alt* will display as *Option*.)

d. With the insertion point in the blank paragraph at the top of the document, type the following text, pressing Enter after the first two lines.

Magical Park Corporation
314 North Street
Baltimore, MD 21203

e. Select the first two lines of the heading you just typed, and then on the **Layout tab**, set **Spacing After** to **0 pt**.

f. Click to position the insertion point to the right of the postal code, press and hold Ctrl + Shift and then press ↑ three times to select all three lines. Click the **Home tab**, change the **Font Size** to **18**, and then apply **Bold** and **Center**. Click the **Developer tab**, and then in the **Code group**, click **Stop Recording**. **Save** your document.

3 Click anywhere in the first cell of the table. On the **Developer tab**, in the **Code group**, click **Record Macro**. In the **Record Macro** dialog box, in the **Macro name** box, type **Table_Style** Be sure the **Store macro in** box displays *All Documents (Normal.dotm)*.

a. Under **Assign macro to**, click the **Button** icon. In the **Word Options** dialog box, in the left pane with **Quick Access Toolbar** selected, under **Choose commands from**, click **Normal.NewMacros.Table_Style**. Click **Add**. (Mac users: Use the technique you practiced in Activity 7.04 to assign this as a keyboard shortcut using the letter T.)

b. On the right side of the **Word Options** dialog box, click to select **Normal.NewMacros.Table_Style**. Below the list of commands, click **Modify**.

c. In the **Modify Button** dialog box, under **Symbol**, in the first row, click the round gray bullseye symbol. Click **OK** two times.

d. With the insertion point in the table, click the **Table Tools Design tab**, and then in the **Table Styles group**, click **More**. In the **Table Styles** gallery, under **Grid Tables**, in the fourth row, click the last style.

e. Click the **Table Tools Layout tab**, in the **Cell Size group**, click **AutoFit**, and then click **AutoFit Contents**. In the **Table group**, click **Properties**. In the **Table Properties** dialog box, under **Alignment**, click **Center**, and then click **OK**. Click the **Developer tab**, and then in the **Code group**, click **Stop Recording**. **Save** your document.

4 From the files you downloaded for this project, open the file **w07C_Press_Release**. Display the **Save As** dialog box, navigate to your **Word Chapter 7** folder. In the lower portion of the dialog box, click the **Save as type arrow**, and then from the list, click **Word Macro-Enabled Document**. In the **File name** box, using your own name, type **Lastname_Firstname_7C_Press_Release** and then click **Save**.

(continues on next page)

Chapter Review

a. Insert the file name in the footer, and then close the footer. Click the **Developer tab**, and then in the **Code group**, click **Record Macro**. In the **Macro name** box, type **AutoClose** Click the **Store macro in arrow**, and then click your **Lastname_ Firstname_7C_Press_Release (document)**. Click **OK**. (Mac users: AutoClose may not be available. Insert the current date in your header, select the last format, move to Step 5.)

b. Click the **Insert tab**, in the **Header & Footer group**, click **Header**, and then from the displayed list, click **Edit Header**.

c. Press Ctrl + A, and then press Delete. On the **Header & Footer Tools Design tab**, in the **Insert group**, click **Date & Time**. In the **Date and Time** dialog box, click the last format to display the time, and then click **OK**.

d. On the **Header & Footer Tools Design tab**, in the **Close group**, click **Close Header and Footer**. Click the **Developer tab**, and then in the **Code group**, click **Stop Recording**.

5 Click anywhere in the first cell of the table. On the **Quick Access Toolbar**, click the black bullseye button to run the *Table_Style* macro and format the table. (Mac users: On the Developer tab, in the Code group, click Macros; click Table_Style, click Run.)

a. On the **Developer tab**, in the **Code group**, click **Macros**. In the **Macros** dialog box, select the **Heading** macro, and then click **Edit**.

b. In the code for the **Heading** macro, locate the postal code **21203**. Position the insertion point to the right of *3*, press Backspace, and then type **1**

c. Near the top of the **Visual Basic Editor** window, click **File**, and then click **Close and Return to Microsoft Word**. (Mac users: Display the menu bar, click Word, click Close and Return to Microsoft Word.)

d. Press Ctrl + Home, and then press Alt + Ctrl + G to run the *Heading* macro. Click anywhere in the document to deselect the text.

6 Display **Backstage** view, click the **Info tab**, and then **Show All Properties**.

a. In the **Tags** box, type **schedule, press release** In the **Subject** box, type your course name and section number. If necessary, edit the author name to display your name. On the left click **Save**.

b. Click the **Developer tab**, and then in the **Code group**, click **Macros**. In the **Macros** dialog box, delete the **Heading** macro and then delete the **Table_Style** macro. **Close** the **Macros** dialog box.

c. Display **Backstage** view. On the left, click **Home**, and then click **Options**. In the **Word Options** dialog box, click **Quick Access Toolbar**. On the right side of the window, click **Normal. NewMacros.Table_Style**, click **Remove**. In the **Word Options** dialog box, on the left, click **Customize Ribbon**, and then on the right, deselect the **Developer tab**. Click **OK**. (Mac users: You do not need to remove anything from the Quick Access Toolbar. To deselect the Developer tab, display the menu bar, click Word, Preferences, Ribbon & Toolbar.)

d. **Close** Word, and then click **Save** to save your documents.

7 Submit your two Word files as directed by your instructor.

End You have completed Project 7C | END

Chapter Review

Apply 7B skills from these Objectives:

5. Modify the Layout of a Document
6. Format Graphic and Text Elements in a Word Document

Skills Review | **Project 7D Resort Facilities**

In the following Skills Review, you will format a document, insert graphics, and link text boxes to create a brochure containing information about Magical Park Corporation's resorts. Your completed document will look similar to Figure 7.46.

Project Files

For Project 7D, you will need the following files:

w07D_Resort_Facilities
w07D_Resort_Reviews
w07D_Pools
w07D_Room
w07D_Resort_Bullet
You will save your file as:
Lastname_Firstname_7D_Resort_Facilities

Project Results

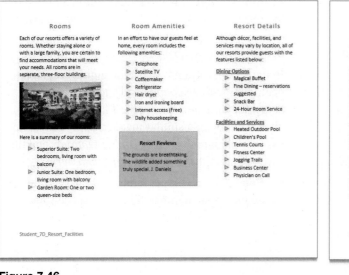

Figure 7.46

(continues on next page)

Chapter Review

1 From the files you downloaded with this project, open the file **w07D_Resort_Facilities**. Using your own name, save the document in your **Word Chapter 7** folder as **Lastname_Firstname_7D_Resort_Facilities**

a. Insert the file name in the footer. On the **Layout tab**, in the **Page Setup group**, click **Orientation**, and then click **Landscape**. In the **Page Setup group**, click **Margins**, and then click **Narrow**. In the **Page Setup group**, click **Columns**, and then click **Three**.

b. On **Page 1**, in the first column, click to position the insertion point to the left of the paragraph *Room Amenities*. In the **Page Setup group**, click **Breaks**, and then under **Page Breaks**, click **Column**. In the second column, position the insertion point to the left of the paragraph *Resort Details*. Using the technique you just practiced, insert a **Column** break.

c. On **Page 2**, position the insertion point to the left of the paragraph *Resorts Division*, and then using the technique you practiced, insert a **Column** break. Press Ctrl + End, and then insert a **Column** break. (Mac users: Press command ⌘ + fn + → to move to the end.)

d. In the **Page Setup group**, click **Size**, and then at the bottom of the list, click **More Paper Sizes**. In the **Page Setup** dialog box, under **Paper Size**, click the **Paper size arrow**, scroll down, and then click **Custom size**. Set the **Width** to 9". Set the **Height** to 7". Click **OK**, and then **Save** your document. (Mac users: Display the menu bar. Click File, Page Setup, Paper Size arrow, Manage Custom Sizes. Enter the Width and Height; click OK two times. Change the orientation back to Landscape if necessary.)

2 On **Page 1**, in the first column, select the paragraph *Rooms*. Change the **Font Size** to **14**, click the **Font Color button arrow**, and then in the fifth column, click the last color. **Center** the paragraph.

a. With the paragraph still selected, on the **Home tab**, in the **Font group**, click the **Dialog Box Launcher**. In the **Font** dialog box, click the **Advanced tab**. Under **Character Spacing**, click the **Spacing arrow**, and then click **Expanded**. Click the **By spin box up arrow** to **1.2 pt**. Click **OK**. (Mac users: Display the menu bar. Click Format, Font.)

b. In the **Clipboard group**, double-click **Format Painter**. Select each of the following paragraphs to apply the format: *Room Amenities*, *Resort Details*, and *About Our Resorts*. Click **Format Painter** one time to turn it off.

c. On **Page 1**, in the first column, select the last three paragraphs beginning with *Superior Suite*. In the **Paragraph group**, click **Bullets**.

d. On **Page 1**, in the third column, select the paragraph *Dining Options*. Apply **Bold** and **Underline**. Click the **Font Color button arrow**, and then in the fifth column, the fifth color.

e. In the **Paragraph group**, click **Line and Paragraph Spacing**, and then click **Remove Space After Paragraph**. In the **Clipboard group**, click **Format Painter**, and then in the third column, apply the format to the paragraph *Facilities and Services*. (Mac users: Click Line and Paragraph Spacing, Line Spacing Options, change Spacing After to 0 pt.)

f. In the second column, select the eight paragraphs beginning with *Telephone* and ending with *Daily Housekeeping*, and then in the **Paragraph group**, click **Bullets**. In a similar manner, apply bullets to the four paragraphs below *Dining Options*, and the seven paragraphs below *Facilities and Services*.

g. On **Page 2**, in the first column, in the last paragraph, locate the phone number. Select the space following *(702)*. From the **Insert tab**, display the **Symbol** dialog box, and then from the **Special Characters tab**, insert a **Nonbreaking Space**. Select the hyphen following *555*. From the **Insert tab**, display the **Symbol** dialog box, and then from the **Special Characters tab**, insert a **Nonbreaking Hyphen**. **Save** your document.

3 Press Ctrl + Home. On the **View tab**, in the **Show group**, select the **Gridlines** check box.

a. On the **Insert tab**, in the **Text group**, click **Text Box**, and then click **Draw Text Box**. On **Page 1**, in the second column, position the ✛ pointer at the beginning of the column break formatting mark. Drag to the right until you are one gridline past the column break formatting mark, drag down **12** squares, and then release the mouse button. On the **Format tab**, in the **Size group**, click in the **Height** box, type **1.5** and then click in the **Width** box. Type **2.25** and then press Enter.

(continues on next page)

Chapter Review

b. On **Page 2**, in the second column, click to position the insertion point to the left of *Resorts Division*. On the **Insert tab**, in the **Text group**, click **Text Box**, and then click **Draw Text Box**. In the second column, position the ⊞ pointer at the top margin one gridline to the left of the beginning of the paragraph *Resorts*. Drag to the right **18** squares until the border is three squares to the right of *Corporation*, and then drag down until the bottom of the text box is aligned with the line below the text *Lodging Program for* (in the first column). Release the mouse button. On the **Format tab**, in the **Size group**, click in the **Height** box. Type **3** and then click in the **Width** box. Type **2.4** and then press Enter.

c. On the **Format tab**, in the **Arrange group**, click **Wrap Text**, and then click **Top and Bottom**. Scroll, if necessary, to display a portion of both text boxes simultaneously. On **Page 1**, in the second column, click the text box to select it. On the **Format tab**, in the **Text group**, click **Create Link**. On **Page 2**, point to the text box, and then click to create a link.

d. If necessary, on Page 1, click to position the insertion point in the text box. On the **Insert tab**, in the **Text group**, click the **Object button arrow**, and then click **Text from File**. From the files you downloaded with this project, select the file **w07D_Resort_Reviews**, and then click **Insert**.

e. In the second text box, click to the left of the text *I am*, type **More Reviews** and then press Enter. Select the text you just typed. Apply **Bold** and **Center**.

f. With the second text box selected, on the **Drawing Tools Format tab**, in the **Shape Styles group**, click **More**. In the **Shape Styles** gallery, in the fourth row, click the second shape style. In a similar manner, apply the shape style to the first text box.

g. On the **View tab**, in the **Show group**, clear the **Gridlines** check box to hide the gridlines. **Save** your document.

4 On **Page 2**, in the second column, select the five paragraphs below the text box. Apply **Bold** and **Center**. On the **Home tab**, in the **Font group**, click **Text Effects and Typography**, and then in the second row, click the second text effect.

a. On **Page 2**, in the third column, position the insertion point in the blank paragraph. Type **OUR RESORTS** Press Enter two times, and then type **Your home away from home!**

b. Select the paragraph you just typed, change the **Font Size** to **14**, apply **Italic**, and **Center**. On the **Home tab**, in the **Font group**, click **Text Effects and Typography**. In the **Text Effects** gallery, in the first row, click the second effect.

c. Select the first paragraph—*OUR RESORTS*. Change the **Font Size** to **20**, and then apply **Bold** and **Center**. On the **Home tab**, in the **Font group**, click **Text Effects and Typography**, and then in the first row, click the second effect. **Save** your document.

5 On **Page 1**, in the first column, position the insertion point in the blank paragraph. On the **Insert tab**, in the **Illustrations group**, click **Pictures**. In the **Insert Picture** dialog box, navigate to the files you downloaded with this project, select the file **w07_Room**, and then click **Insert**.

a. On the **Picture Tools Format tab**, in the **Adjust group**, click **Artistic Effects**. In the **Artistic Effects** gallery, in the fourth row, click the second effect.

b. On **Page 2**, in the third column, click in the blank paragraph. On the **Insert tab**, in the **Illustrations group**, click **Pictures**. In the **Insert Picture** dialog box, navigate to the files you downloaded with this project, select the file **w07D_Pools**, and then click **Insert**.

c. On the **Format tab**, in the **Adjust group**, click **Artistic Effects**. In the **Artistic Effects** gallery, in the third row, click the second effect.

d. Position the insertion point to the left of the paragraph *OUR RESORTS*, and then press Enter three times. **Save** your document.

6 On **Page 1**, in the first column, select the three bulleted paragraphs. On the **Home tab**, in the **Paragraph group**, click the **Bullets button arrow**, and then click **Define New Bullet**.

a. In the **Define New Bullet** dialog box, under **Bullet character**, click **Picture**. In the **Insert Pictures** dialog box, to the right of **From a file**, click **Browse**. (Mac users: Use Finder to navigate to your files for this project.)

(continues on next page)

Chapter Review

b. In the **Insert Picture** dialog box, navigate to the files you downloaded with this project, select **w07D_ Resort_Bullet**, and then click **Insert**. Click **OK**.

c. In the second column, select the bulleted list. In the **Paragraph group**, click the **Bullets button arrow**. Under **Recently Used Bullets**, click the **Resort Bullet**. In the same manner, apply the **Resort Bullet** to the two bulleted lists in the third column. **Remove** the picture bullet from the Bullet Library.

d. Press Ctrl + Home. Display Backstage view, click the **Info tab**, and click **Show All Properties**. In the **Tags** box, type **facilities, graphics, reviews** In the **Subject** box, type your course name and section number. If necessary, edit the author name to display your name.

e. On the left, click **Save**. In the upper right corner of the Word window, click **Close**. As directed by your instructor submit your Word file.

You have completed Project 7D   **END**

Content-Based Assessments (Mastery and Transfer of Learning)

| MyLab IT Grader | Mastering Word | Project 7E Collegiate Expo |

Apply 7A skills from these Objectives:

1. Create Macros
2. Run Macros
3. Edit a Macro in the Visual Basic Editor
4. Use a Built-in Word Macro

In the following Mastering Word project, you will create macros to assist with editing a document that will be sent to college students who are registered for the Collegiate Expo conducted by Magical Park Corporation. Your completed document will look similar to Figure 7.47.

Project Files for MyLab IT Grader

1. In your **MyLab IT** course, locate and click **Word 7E Collegiate Expo**, Download Materials, and then Download All Files.
2. Extract the zipped folder to your Word Chapter 7 folder. Close the Grader download screens.
3. Take a moment to open the downloaded **Word_7E_Collegiate_Expo_Instructions**; note any recent updates to the book.

Project Results

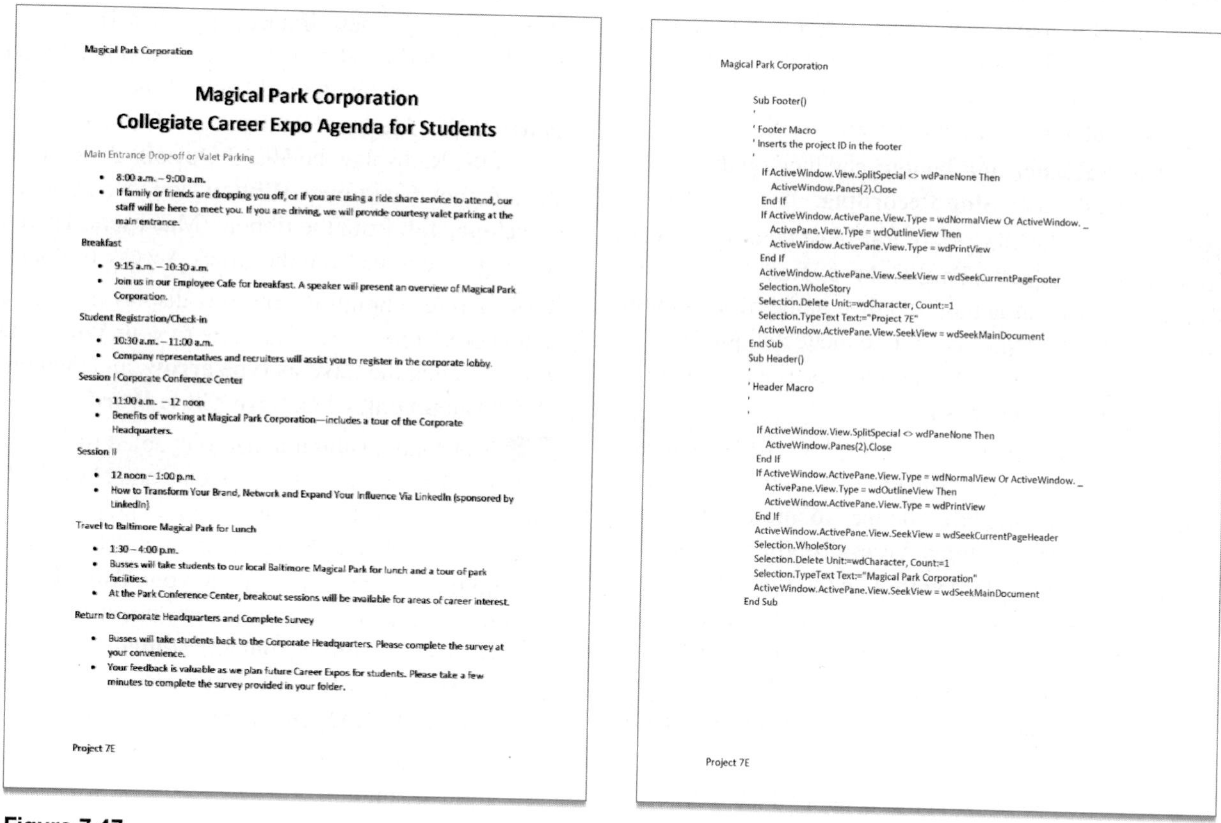

Figure 7.47

For Non-MyLab Submissions

For Project 7E, you will need:
w07E_Collegiate_Expo

In your Word Chapter 7 folder, save the file as a Word Macro-Enabled Document as:
Lastname_Firstname_7E_Collegiate_Expo

After you have named and saved your document as a Word Macro-Enabled Document, on the next page, begin with Step 2. After Step 8, save and submit your Word document and/or your Macro-enabled Word document as directed by your instructor.

(continues on next page)

Mastering Word: Project 7E Collegiate Expo (continued)

1 Navigate to your **Word Chapter 7 folder**, and then double-click the Word file you downloaded from **MyLab IT** that displays your name—**Student_Word_7E_Collegiate_ Expo**. If necessary, at the top, click **Enable Editing**. Display the **Save As** dialog box, and then save the file in your **Word Chapter 7** folder as a **Word Macro-Enabled Document**.

2 Display the **Developer tab**, and then if necessary, change your Macro Security setting to **Disable all macros with notification**. Select the first two lines that form the title and change the **Font Size** to **22**. Display the **Record Macro** dialog box, and then in the **Macro name** box, type **Footer**

Be sure the **Store macro in** box displays *All Documents (Normal.dotm)*. In the **Description** box, type **Inserts the project ID in the footer**

Assign the **Keyboard** shortcut key [Alt] + [Ctrl] + [J]. Click the **Insert tab**. In the **Header & Footer** group, click **Footer**, and then click **Edit Footer**. Press [Ctrl] + [A], press [Delete], and then type **Project 7E**

Click **Close Header and Footer**, and then on the **Developer tab**, click **Stop Recording**.

3 Select the heading *Main Entrance Drop-off or Valet Parking* and change the **Font Color** to **Red**. Display the **Record Macro** dialog box, and then in the **Macro name** box, type **Header** (Mac users: Use the technique you practiced in Activity 7.04 to assign this as a keyboard shortcut using the letter H.)

Be sure the **Store macro in** box displays *All Documents (Normal.dotm)*. Click the **Button** icon, and then in the **Word Options** dialog box, add the **Normal.NewMacros. Header** macro to the **Quick Access Toolbar**. Click **Modify**, and then under **Symbol**, in the first row, click the third button—a blue circle containing a blue i. Click the **Insert tab**, click **Header**, and then click **Edit Header**. Press [Ctrl] + [A], press [Delete], and then type **Magical Park** Click **Close Header and Footer**. On the **Developer tab**, click **Stop Recording**.

4 In the fourth bullet point, in the first sentence, change *Cafeteria* to **Cafe**

Display the **Macros** dialog box, select the **Header** macro, and then click **Edit**. Near the bottom of the **Header** macro code, position the insertion point to the right of *Park*, press [Spacebar], and then type **Corporation** Press [Ctrl] + [A] to select all of the text in the Visual Basic window, right-click over the selected text, and then click **Copy**. Click **File**, and then click **Close and Return to Microsoft Word**. Press [Ctrl] + [Home]. On the Quick Access Toolbar, click the **Header** macro button. (Mac users: Use the keyboard shortcut you created for the Header macro.)

5 Press [Ctrl] + [End] and then press [Ctrl] + [Enter] to insert a new page. Press [Backspace] one time to turn off the bullets, and then press [Ctrl] + [V] to paste the text from the Visual Basic window.

6 Display Backstage view, if necessary, click the **Info tab**, and then at the bottom, click **Show All Properties**. In the **Tags** box, type **expo agenda, macros** In the **Subject** box, type your course name and section number. If necessary, edit the author name to display your name. On the left click **Save**.

7 From the **Developer tab**, display the **Macros** dialog box, click the **Macros in arrow**, and then click **All active templates and documents**. Delete the **Header** and **Footer** macros.

From Backstage view, if necessary, click **Home**, display the **Word Options** dialog box, and then click **Quick Access Toolbar**. On the right side of the window, click **Normal.NewMacros.Header**, click **Remove**, and then click **OK**. Redisplay the **Word Options** dialog box, on the left click **Customize Ribbon**, and then remove the **Developer tab** from the ribbon. (Mac users: There is nothing to remove from the Quick Access Toolbar.)

8 Before submitting your file, display the **Save As** dialog box, if necessary, navigate to your **Word Chapter 7** folder, click the **Save as type arrow**, and then click **Word Document**. Click **Save**. Close **Word**.

9 You cannot submit a macro-enabled file for grading in **MyLab IT**. In **MyLab IT**, locate and click the Grader Project **Word 7E Collegiate Expo**. In **step 3**, under **Upload Completed Assignment**, click **Choose File**. In the **Open** dialog box, navigate to your **Word Chapter 7 folder**, and then click your *Word document* (not your Macro-enabled Word document) **Student_Word_7E_ Collegiate_Expo** file one time to select it. In the lower right corner of the **Open** dialog box, click **Open**.

The name of your selected file displays above the Upload button.

10 To submit your file to **MyLab IT** for grading, click **Upload**, wait a moment for a green **Success!** message, and then in **step 4**, click the blue **Submit for Grading** button. Click **Close Assignment** to return to your list of **Course Materials**.

You have completed Project 7E **END**

Content-Based Assessments (Mastery and Transfer of Learning)

In the following Mastering Word project, you will format a document, insert graphics, and link text boxes to create a leaflet containing information for Magical Park Corporation's employees. Your completed document will look similar to Figure 7.48.

Apply 7B skills from these Objectives:

5. Modify the Layout of a Document
6. Format Graphic and Text Elements in a Word Document

Project Files for MyLab IT Grader

1. In your **MyLab IT** course, locate and click **Word 7F First Aid**, Download Materials, and then Download All Files.
2. Extract the zipped folder to your Word Chapter 7 folder. Close the Grader download screens.
3. Take a moment to open the downloaded **Word_7F_First_Aid_Instructions**; note any recent updates to the book.

Project Results

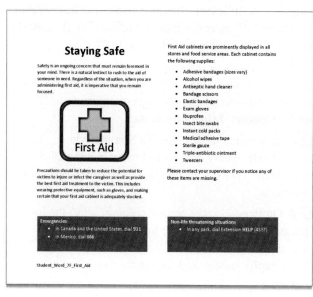 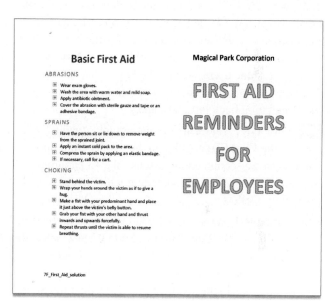

Figure 7.48

For Non-MyLab Submissions

For Project 7F, you will need:
w07F_First_Aid
w07F_Contact_Information
w07F_Medical
w07F_Medical_Bullet

In your Word Chapter 7 folder, save your document as:
Lastname_Firstname_7F_First_Aid

After you have named and saved your document, on the next page, begin with Step 2.
After Step 17, save and submit your file as directed by your instructor.

(continues on next page)

1 Navigate to your **Word Chapter 7 folder**, and then double-click the Word file you downloaded from **MyLab IT** that displays your name—**Student_Word_7F_First_Aid**. If necessary, at the top, click **Enable Editing**.

2 Insert the file name in the footer. On the **Layout tab**, in the **Page Setup group**, change the **Orientation** to **Landscape**, and then change the **Columns** to **Two**. On **Page 1**, in the first column, position the insertion point to the left of the fourth paragraph that begins *First Aid cabinets*, and then insert a **Column** break. In the second column, position the insertion point to the left of the paragraph *Basic First Aid*, and then press Ctrl + Enter to create a new page.

3 On **Page 2**, position the insertion point to the left of *Magical Park Corporation*, and then insert a **Column** break. Display the **Page Setup** dialog box, change the **Paper Size** to **Custom size**, and then change the **Width** to **10"** (make sure your page Height is 8.5"). **Save** your document. (Mac users: Access the Page Setup dialog box from the File tab on the menu bar; if necessary, change the Orientation back to Landscape.)

4 On **Page 1**, select the first paragraph *Staying Safe*. Change the **Font Size** to **28**, and then apply **Bold** and **Center**. In the second column, select the 13 paragraphs beginning with *Adhesive* and ending with *Tweezers*, and then apply **Bullets**.

5 On **Page 1**, in the second column, select all the text, and then change the **Font Size** to **12**. On **Page 2**, select the first paragraph—*Basic First Aid*. Change the **Font Size** to **26**, apply **Bold** and **Center**. Display the **Font Color** gallery, and then in the sixth column, click the fifth color.

6 Select the paragraph *ABRASIONS*. Change the **Font Size** to **14**. Display the **Font Color** gallery, and then in the sixth column, click the first color. From the **Font** dialog box, set the **Spacing** to **Expanded** by **1.4 pt**. Activate **Format Painter** for multiple use, and then apply the format to the paragraphs *SPRAINS* and *CHOKING*. Turn off the Format Painter.

7 Select the four paragraphs below *ABRASIONS*, and apply **Bullets**. In a similar manner, apply **Bullets** to the paragraphs below *SPRAINS* and *CHOKING*.

8 On **Page 2**, in the second column, select the first paragraph—*Magical Park Corporation*. Change the **Font Size** to **18**, and then apply **Bold** and **Center**.

9 On **Page 1**, in the second paragraph, in the fourth line, select the space to the right of *first*, and then insert a nonbreaking space. In a similar manner, in the third paragraph, in the third line, select the space to the right of *first*, and then insert a nonbreaking space. **Save** your document.

10 Display the document **Gridlines**. On **Page 1**, at the bottom of the first column, draw a **Text Box** that begins at the left margin, 4 gridlines below the last paragraph. Drag down 9 squares (1.12 inches), and then drag to the right until the border of the text box aligns with the end of the third paragraph mark (3.63 inches).

11 At the bottom of the second column, locate the **Page Break indicator**. In the second column, draw a **Text Box**, beginning 6 gridlines below the left side of the **Page Break indicator**, the same size as the first text box (height of 1.12 inches; width of 3.63 inches). Be sure the **Shape Width** of both text boxes is **3.63"**.

12 Position the insertion point in the first text box, and then create a link to the second text box. From the files downloaded with this project, insert text from the file **w07F_Contact_Information.docx**.

13 To both text boxes, apply a **Shape Style**; in the **Shape Style** gallery, in the third row, click the third shape style. Turn off the display of Gridlines. **Save** your document.

14 On **Page 2**, in the second column, select the last four paragraphs. Change the **Font Size** to **48**, and then apply **Center**. Display the **Text Effects and Typography** gallery, and then in the first row, click the third effect.

15 On **Page 1**, position the insertion point at the end of the second paragraph that begins *Safety is*, and then press Enter one time. With your insertion point positioned in the blank paragraph, from the files you downloaded with this project, insert the picture file **w07F_Medical.jpg**. Change the **Shape Height** to **2"**. Display the **Artistic Effects** gallery, and then apply the **Photocopy** effect. **Center** the picture. If necessary, drag the text boxes up or down so that their top edges align.

16 On **Page 2**, select the first list. Define a new bullet using the file **w07F_Medical_Bullet.jpg**, and then apply it to the bulleted list. Apply the medical bullet to the remaining lists in the column.

(continues on next page)

17 Display the document properties. In the **Tags** box, type **first aid, leaflet** and in the **Subject** box, type your course name and section number. If necessary, edit the author name to display your name. On the left, click **Save**. Remove the medical bullet from the Bullet Library. **Close** Word.

18 In **MyLab IT**, locate and click the Grader Project **Word 7F First Aid**. In **step 3**, under **Upload Completed Assignment**, click **Choose File**. In the **Open** dialog box, navigate to your **Word Chapter 7 folder**, and then click your **Student_Word_7F_First_Aid** file one time to select it. In the lower right corner of the **Open** dialog box, click **Open**.

The name of your selected file displays above the Upload button.

19 To submit your file to **MyLab IT** for grading, click **Upload**, wait a moment for a green **Success!** message, and then in **step 4**, click the blue **Submit for Grading** button. Click **Close Assignment** to return to your list of **Course Materials**.

You have completed Project 7F | END

MyLab IT Grader

Mastering Word   Project 7G Park Letter

Apply 7A and 7B skills from these Objectives:

1. Create Macros
2. Run Macros
3. Edit a Macro in the Visual Basic Editor
4. Use a Built-in Word Macro
5. Modify the Layout of a Document
6. Format Graphic and Text Elements in a Word Document

In the following Mastering Word Project, you will edit a letter by inserting graphics and modifying text. You will also create and record a macro. Your completed document will look similar to Figure 7.49.

Project Files for MyLab IT Grader

1. In your Course Materials, locate and click **Word 7G Park Letter**, Download Materials, and then Download All Files.
2. Extract the zipped folder to your Word Chapter 7 folder. Close the Grader download screens.
3. Take a moment to open the downloaded **Word_7G_Park_Letter_Instructions**; note any recent updates to the book.

Project Results

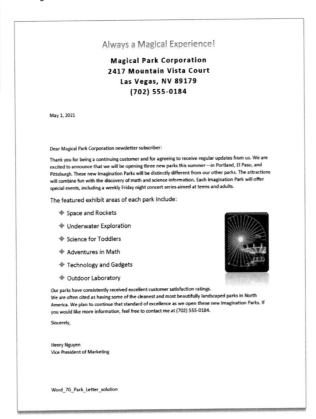

Figure 7.49

For Non-MyLab Submissions

For Project 7G, you will need:

w07G_Park_Letter
w07G_Ride
w07G_Imagination_Bullet

In your Word Chapter 7 folder, save your document as:

Lastname_Firstname_7G_Park_Letter

After you have named and saved your document, on the next page, begin with Step 2.
After step 10, save and submit your file as directed by your instructor.

(continues on next page)

Mastering Word: Project 7G Park Letter (continued)

1 Navigate to your **Word Chapter 7 folder**, and then double-click the Word file you downloaded from **MyLab IT** that displays your name—**Student_Word_7G_Park_Letter**. If necessary, at the top, click **Enable Editing**.

2 Save your file in your **Word Chapter 7** folder as a Word Macro-Enabled Document. Display the **Developer tab**, and then if necessary, change your Macro Security setting to **Disable all macros with notification**.

Insert the file name in the footer. Select the first four paragraphs. Change the **Font Size** to **16**, and then apply **Bold** and **Center**. Click anywhere to deselect the text.

Display the **Record Macro** dialog box, and then in the **Macro name** box, type **Header** Be sure the **Store macro in** box displays *All Documents (Normal.dotm)*. In the **Description** box, type **Inserts the corporate slogan in the header**

Assign the Keyboard shortcut key [Alt] + [Ctrl] + [J]. Click the **Insert tab**. In the **Header & Footer group**, click **Header**, and then click **Edit Header**. Type **Always a Magical Experience!** Select the text you just typed. From the **Home tab**, display the **Text Effects and Typography** gallery, and then in the second row, click the second effect. Change the **Font Size** to **20** and then **Center** the text. On the **Header & Footer Tools Design tab**, click **Close Header and Footer**, and then on the **Developer tab**, click **Stop Recording**.

3 Select the first four paragraphs, and then from the **Font** dialog box, change the **Spacing** to **Expanded** by **1.5 pt**.

4 Select the seven paragraphs that begin with *The featured exhibit* and end with *Outdoor Laboratory* and then change the **Font Size** to **14**. Select the six paragraphs below the paragraph that begins *The featured exhibit*, and then apply **Bullets**.

5 In the paragraph that begins *Our parks*, locate the phone number, change the space to a nonbreaking space, and then change the hyphen to a nonbreaking hyphen. **Save** your document.

6 Position the insertion point to the right of the paragraph that begins *The featured exhibit*—following the colon. From the files you downloaded with this project, insert the picture **w07G_Ride.jpg**. Display the **Artistic Effects** gallery, and then apply the **Glow Diffused** effect. Display the **Picture Styles** gallery, and apply the **Reflected Bevel, Black** picture style.

7 Change **Wrap Text** to **Square**, and then change the **Shape Height** to **1.6"** With the picture selected, display the **Layout** dialog box and click the **Position tab**. Change the **Horizontal Alignment** to **Right** relative to **Margin** and the **Vertical Absolute** position to **4.5"** below the **Margin**.

8 Select the bulleted list. By using the image **w07G_Imagination_Bullet.jpg** file you downloaded with this project, define a new bullet, and then apply it to the bulleted list. Press [Ctrl] + [Home]. Remove the picture bullet from the **Bullet Library**.

9 From the **Developer tab**, display the **Macros** dialog box, click the **Macros in arrow**, and then click **All active templates and documents**. **Delete** the **Header** macro.

Display the **Word Options** dialog box, on the left click **Customize Ribbon**, and then remove the **Developer** tab from the ribbon.

Display the document properties. In the **Tags** box, type **letter, graphics** and in the **Subject** box, type your course name and section number. If necessary, edit the author name to display your name. On the left, click **Save**.

10 In the upper right corner of the Word window, click **Close** [×].

(continues on next page)

Mastering Word: Project 7G Park Letter (continued)

11 In **MyLab IT**, locate and click the Grader Project **Word 7G Park Letter**. In **step 3**, under **Upload Completed Assignment**, click **Choose File**. In the **Open** dialog box, navigate to your **Word Chapter 7 folder**, and then click your **Student_Word_7G_Park_Letter** file one time to select it. In the lower right corner of the **Open** dialog box, click **Open**.

The name of your selected file displays above the Upload button.

12 To submit your file to **MyLab IT** for grading, click **Upload**, wait a moment for a green **Success!** message, and then in **step 4**, click the blue **Submit for Grading** button. Click **Close Assignment** to return to your list of **Course Materials**.

You have completed Project 7G | **END**

Content-Based Assessments (Critical Thinking)

Apply a combination of the 7A and 7B skills.	**GO! Fix It** **Project 7H Employer Letter**	IRC
	GO! Make It **Project 7I Engineering Fair**	IRC
	GO! Solve It **Project 7J Job Support**	IRC
	GO! Solve It **Project 7K Attendance Memo**	

Project Files

For Project 7K, you will need the following files:

w07K_Attendance_Memo

w07K_Coaster

You will save your files as:

Lastname_Firstname_7K_Attendance_Memo

Open the file **w07K_Attendance_Memo** and save it to your **Word Chapter 7** folder as a macro-enabled document with the file name **Lastname_Firstname_7K_Attendance_Memo** Insert the file name in the footer. Create a macro that inserts the text **Magical Park Recruitment** center-aligned in the header. Assign the macro to the Quick Access Toolbar as a button. In the lower portion of the memo, insert the picture **w07K_Coaster**. Position it attractively, resize as necessary, and add an artistic effect. Paste images of the Quick Access Toolbar and macro code as the second page in the document. Add appropriate document properties. Delete the macro you created, and then submit your file as directed by your instructor.

Mastering Word: Project 7K Attendance Memo (continued)

Performance Element		Performance Level		
		Exemplary: You consistently applied the relevant skills	**Proficient: You sometimes, but not always, applied the relevant skills**	**Developing: You rarely or never applied the relevant skills**
	Create a macro	The macro is created and displays as a button on the Quick Access Toolbar.	The macro is created but does not display as a button on the Quick Access Toolbar.	A macro is not created.
	Format document and picture	Formatting is attractive and appropriate.	Adequate formatting but difficult to read or unattractive.	Either there is no formatting or it is inadequate.
	Paste image	Image is pasted correctly.	Image pasted incorrectly.	No images are pasted in the document.

You have completed Project 7K | END

Outcomes-Based Assessments (Critical Thinking)

Rubric

The following outcomes-based assessments are *open-ended assessments*. That is, there is no specific correct result; your result will depend on your approach to the information provided. Make *Professional Quality* your goal. Use the following scoring rubric to guide you in *how* to approach the problem and then to evaluate *how well* your approach solves the problem.

The *criteria*—Software Mastery, Content, Format and Layout, and Process—represent the knowledge and skills you have gained that you can apply to solving the problem. The *levels of performance*—Professional Quality, Approaching Professional Quality, or Needs Quality Improvements—help you and your instructor evaluate your result.

	Your completed project is of Professional Quality if you:	Your completed project is Approaching Professional Quality if you:	Your completed project Needs Quality Improvements if you:
1-Software Mastery	Choose and apply the most appropriate skills, tools, and features and identify efficient methods to solve the problem.	Choose and apply some appropriate skills, tools, and features, but not in the most efficient manner.	Choose inappropriate skills, tools, or features, or are inefficient in solving the problem.
2-Content	Construct a solution that is clear and well organized, contains content that is accurate, appropriate to the audience and purpose, and is complete. Provide a solution that contains no errors of spelling, grammar, or style.	Construct a solution in which some components are unclear, poorly organized, inconsistent, or incomplete. Misjudge the needs of the audience. Have some errors in spelling, grammar, or style, but the errors do not detract from comprehension.	Construct a solution that is unclear, incomplete, or poorly organized, contains some inaccurate or inappropriate content, and contains many errors of spelling, grammar, or style. Do not solve the problem.
3-Format and Layout	Format and arrange all elements to communicate information and ideas, clarify function, illustrate relationships, and indicate relative importance.	Apply appropriate format and layout features to some elements, but not others. Overuse features, causing minor distraction.	Apply format and layout that does not communicate information or ideas clearly. Do not use format and layout features to clarify function, illustrate relationships, or indicate relative importance. Use available features excessively, causing distraction.
4-Process	Use an organized approach that integrates planning, development, self-assessment, revision, and reflection.	Demonstrate an organized approach in some areas, but not others; or, use an insufficient process of organization throughout.	Do not use an organized approach to solve the problem.

Apply a combination of the 7A and 7B skills.

GO! Think   **Project 7L College Flyer**

Project Files

For Project 7L, you will need the following file:

New blank Word document

You will save your files as:

Lastname_Firstname_7L_College_Flyer

Magical Park conducts a college recruitment job fair every year. Magical Park's corporate office is located at 314 North Street, Baltimore, MD 21201. Search the Internet for the types of job opportunities that are available for college graduates at a theme park. Save a new macro-enabled document as **Lastname_Firstname_7L_College_Flyer** and in the new document, create a flyer indicating the types of jobs available at Magical Park. Use fictitious information for the date, time, and location. Create a macro for recruitment fair contact information that will run somewhere in the flyer; the name of a person to contact and his or her contact information. Create an AutoClose macro that will automatically insert the date and time in the header—only in this document. Format the document to create a professional appearance. Use the Online Pictures command to find and insert a picture of a roller coaster somewhere in the flyer. Insert a text box in the flyer that contains fictitious comments from current employees who were recruited at a previous recruitment fair. Insert images of the contact information and AutoClose macro codes, insert the file name in the footer, and add appropriate document properties. Delete the macros you created. Submit your Word document as directed by your instructor.

You have completed Project 7L   **END**

GO! Think   **Project 7M Jobseeker Tips**   **IRC**

You and GO!   **Project 7N Personal Letterhead**   **IRC**

Creating Merged Documents

8
WORD 2019

Martin Valigursky/Shutterstock

In This Chapter

GO! to Work with Word

In this chapter, you will use data sources with mail merge to create letters, envelopes, postcards, and a directory. Mail merge provides a time-saving and convenient way to produce personalized mass mailings, such as customized letters and envelopes. You can construct your own table of data or use an existing file. You can also sort and filter the data to specify what information will be used. For example, you might want to send individual letters to customers who purchased a specific cruise. You can also use a data source with mail merge to generate a directory— for example, a list of company employees and their phone extensions.

The projects in this chapter relate to **Caribbean Customized**, which specializes in exciting cruises in the Caribbean, including excursions to islands and the mainland in North and Central America. With its tropical beauty and cultural diversity, the Caribbean region offers lush jungles, freshwater caves, miles of white sand beaches, ancient ruins, and charming cities. Ships are innovative and include rock-climbing walls and extensive spa facilities. A variety of accommodations are available on each ship to meet the needs and budgets of a wide array of travelers. The food and entertainment are rated as exceptional by all.

PROJECT 8A Customer Letters

Project Activities

Caribbean Customized is launching a new rewards program for its valued customers. Lucinda Parsons, the president of the company, has asked you to create a document describing the Emerald Program that can be sent to all customers who previously booked multiple cruises. In Activities 8.01 through 8.07, you will create a customized form letter and envelope. This will enable the company to send a personalized letter to the targeted group of customers. Your completed documents will look similar to Figure 8.1.

Project Files for **MyLab IT** Grader

1. In your storage location, create a folder named **Word Chapter 8**.
2. In your **MyLab IT** course, locate and click **Word 8A Customer Letters**, Download Materials, and then Download All Files.
3. Extract the zipped folder to your Word Chapter 8 folder. Close the Grader download screens.
4. Take a moment to open the downloaded **Word_8A_Customer_Letters_Instructions**; note any recent updates to the book.

Project Results

GO Project 8A
Where We're Going

Figure 8.1 Project 8A Customer Letters

For Non-MyLab Submissions
For Project 8A, you will need:
w08A_Customers
w08A_Letters_Main

In your storage location, create a folder named **Word Chapter 8**.
In your Word Chapter 8 folder, save your documents as:
Lastname_Firstname_8A_Letters_Main
Lastname_Firstname_8A_Letters_Merged
Lastname_Firstname_8A_Envelopes_Main
Lastname_Firstname_8A_Envelopes_Merged

Open w08A_Letters_Main, and then Save it as Lastname_Firstname_8A_Letters_Main. After you have named and saved your document, on the next page, begin with step 2.

Objective 1 Merge a Data Source and a Main Document

GO! Learn How
Video W8-1

Mail merge is a Word feature that joins a *data source* with a *main document* to create a customized document, such as mailing labels. The data source, containing categories of information such as names and addresses, can be stored in a variety of formats—a Word table, an Excel worksheet, an Access table or query, or an Outlook contact list. Placeholders for the customized information from the data source are inserted in the main document, which contains the text or formatting that remains constant. You can use the Mail Merge Wizard or the commands on the Mailings tab to create personalized letters, envelopes, labels, or directories.

Activity 8.01 | Creating and Applying a Character Style

A *character style* contains formatting characteristics that you apply to text—for example, font name, font size, font color, and bold emphasis. You can create a style to apply consistent formatting throughout a document.

1 Navigate to your **Word Chapter 8 folder**, and then double-click the Word file you downloaded from **MyLab IT** that displays your name—**Student_Word_8A_Letters_Main**.

This letter contains information regarding the Emerald Program developed by Caribbean Customized.

MAC TIP   To display group names on the ribbon, display the menu, click Word, click Preferences, click View, select the Show group titles check box.

2 Select the second and third paragraphs of the document containing the company address. On the **Home tab**, in the **Styles group**, click the **Dialog Box Launcher** to display the Styles pane.

MAC TIP   On the Home tab, in the Styles group, click Styles Pane.

3 In the **Styles** pane, click **New Style**. In the **Create New Style from Formatting** dialog box, under **Properties**, in the **Name** box, type **Letter Emphasis** and then click the **Style type arrow**. Click **Character**.

4 Under **Formatting**, change the **Font Size** to **12**, and then apply **Bold** B and **Italic** _I_. Click the **Font Color arrow**, and then under **Theme Colors**, in the fifth column, click the last color. Compare your screen with Figure 8.2.

A preview of the style formatting applied to the first line of the selected text displays.

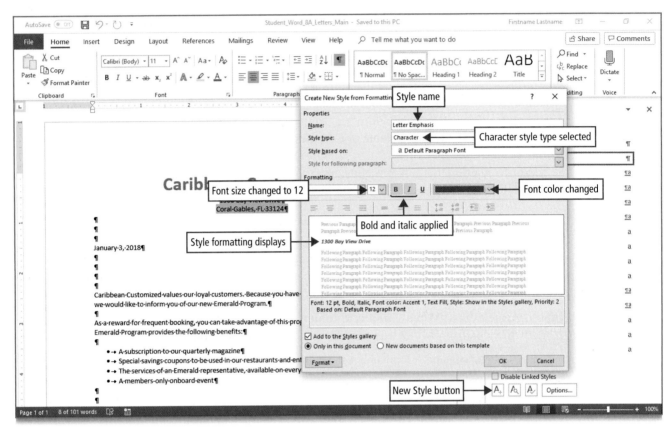

Figure 8.2

5 Click **OK** to create the style, and then **Close** ☒ the **Styles** pane.

🖥 **MAC TIP**   Select the two lines of the company address. On the Home tab, in the Styles group, click Letter Emphasis.

---

6 Press Ctrl + End to move to the end of the document, and then select the text **Lucinda Parsons, President**. On the **Home tab**, in the **Styles group**, point to **Letter Emphasis**. Compare your screen with Figure 8.3.

The style that you created displays in the Styles gallery and can be applied to text in this document.

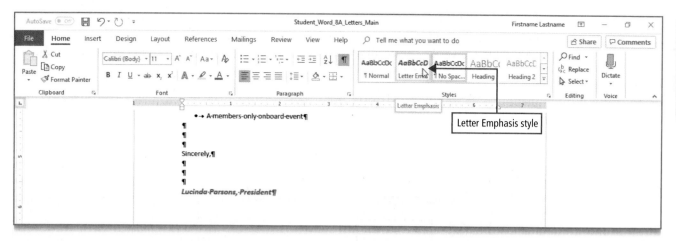

Figure 8.3

7 Click **Letter Emphasis** to apply the style to the selection.

8 Save your changes.

Activity 8.02 | Selecting a Mail Merge Data Source and Defining the Main Document

A data source is comprised of *fields*, categories—or columns—of data, and *records*. A record is a row of information that contains the data for one entity—for example, information about one customer. In this Activity, you will select an Excel file as a data source and you will use the commands on the Mailings tab to define the main document.

1 Click the **Mailings tab**. In the **Start Mail Merge group**, click **Start Mail Merge**, and then click **Letters**.

2 On the **Mailings tab**, in the **Start Mail Merge group**, click **Select Recipients**, and then click **Use an Existing List**.

3 In the **Select Data Source** dialog box, navigate to the files you downloaded with this project, locate and select **w08A_Customers**, and then click **Open**.

The w08A_Customers file is an Excel workbook that includes names and addresses for current and potential customers.

🖥️ **MAC TIP**   If a message displays indicating that the file must be opened using the Excel Workbook text converter, click Yes. If a password dialog box displays, enter your Mac password and then click Always Allow. In the Open Workbook dialog box, type A1:I16 and then click OK. Close any message bars that display. Skip step 4.

---

4 In the **Select Table** dialog box, if necessary, select **'Customer Information'**, which is the name of the worksheet in the w08A_Customers file that contains the customer mailing data. At the lower left of the dialog box, verify that the **First row of data contains column headers** check box is selected and select it if it is not. Compare your screen with Figure 8.4.

The worksheet contains column headers in row 1. The column headers will comprise the field names used in the mail merge.

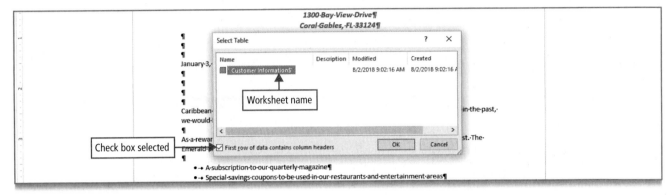

Figure 8.4

5 Click **OK**, and then **Save** 🖫 your document.

Although visually nothing appears to happen, when you designate a data source, the file—in this case, the Excel file—is linked to the main document based on the current locations of both files.

MORE KNOWLEDGE | **Using Outlook as a Data Source**

You can use an Outlook Contacts list as a data source. To use the Contacts list, on the Mailings tab, in the Start Mail Merge group, click Select Recipients. Then, from the list, click Choose from Outlook Contacts. In the Choose Profile dialog box, select the folder where your Outlook Contacts list is stored, and then click OK.

Activity 8.03 | **Filtering Records**

Expert 4.3.1

You can *filter* a data source to apply a set of criteria to display specific records—for example, information only for customers that live in a particular state. Because the Emerald Program is available only to individuals who have previously toured with Caribbean Customized, you will filter the data source to display only existing customers.

1 On the **Mailings tab**, in the **Start Mail Merge group**, click **Edit Recipient List**. In the **Mail Merge Recipients** dialog box, under **Refine recipient list**, click **Filter**.

🖥 **MAC TIP** In the Start Mail Merge group, click Filter Recipients.

2 In the **Filter and Sort** dialog box, on the **Filter Records tab**, click the **Field arrow**, scroll as necessary, and then click **Booked Cruise**. Click the **Comparison arrow**, and then if necessary, click **Equal to**. In the **Compare to** box, type **Yes** and then compare your screen with Figure 8.5.

> The data source will be filtered to display only those records where the Booked Cruise field is equal to Yes.

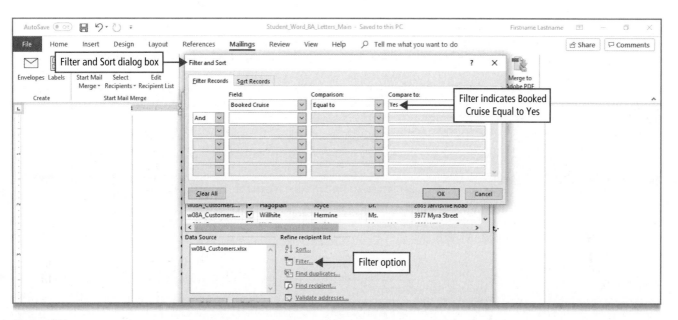

Figure 8.5

3 Click **OK**. In the **Mail Merge Recipients** dialog box, scroll horizontally and vertically as necessary, and notice that in the Booked Cruise field only three records with *Yes* display.

> Three customers have previously booked a cruise and qualify for the Emerald Program.

4 Click **OK** to close the **Mail Merge Recipients** dialog box, and then **Save** the document.

Activity 8.04 | Inserting Merge Fields

MOS
Expert 4.3.2

You are creating a *form letter*—a letter with standardized wording that can be sent to many different people. Each letter can be customized by inserting *merge fields*—placeholders that represent specific information in the data source. In this Activity, you will insert appropriate merge fields.

1 Click in the blank paragraph above the paragraph that begins *Caribbean Customized values*. On the **Mailings tab**, in the **Write & Insert Fields group**, click **Address Block**. In the **Insert Address Block** dialog box, take a moment to examine the various settings associated with this dialog box, and then click **OK**. In the document, notice that the **Address Block merge field** is inserted. Compare your screen with Figure 8.6.

A standard feature of a business letter is the *inside address*—the name and address of the recipient of the letter. The *Address Block* is a predefined merge field that includes the recipient's name, street address, city, state, and postal code. The Insert Address Block dialog box provides options for changing the way the inside address displays. You are inserting the Address Block merge field as a placeholder for the inside address. Each merge field in a main document is surrounded by double angle brackets—characters used to distinguish where data will be populated.

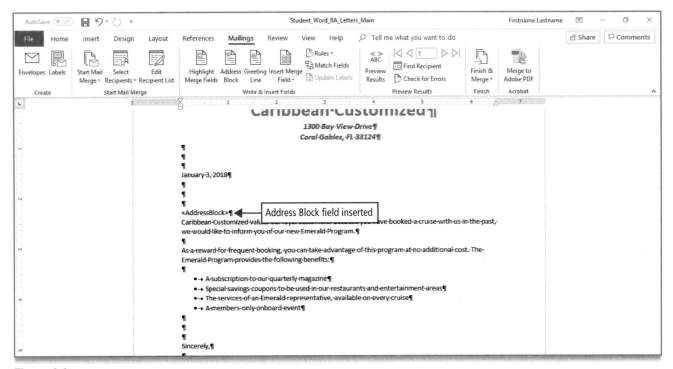

Figure 8.6

⌨ **MAC TIP** In the Write & Insert Fields group, click Insert Merge Field. Click Title, press ⎵spacebar, and then use the same process to insert the First_Name and Last_Name fields, being sure to press ⎵spacebar between the two field names. Press ⏎enter and then insert the Street_Address field. Press ⏎enter and insert the City field. Type a comma (,) and press ⎵spacebar. Insert the State field, press ⎵spacebar, and then insert the Postal_Code field.

---

2 Press ⏎Enter two times, and then in the **Write & Insert Fields group**, click **Greeting Line**. In the **Insert Greeting Line** dialog box, under **Greeting line format**, in the box on the right— the **Punctuation** box, click the **Punctuation arrow**, and then click **:** (the colon). Compare your screen with Figure 8.7.

Another standard feature of a business letter is the *salutation*—or greeting line. The *Greeting Line* is a predefined merge field that includes an introductory word, such as *Dear*, and the recipient's name. When using a business letter format, a colon usually follows the salutation. The Insert Greeting Line dialog box allows you to choose the introductory word and punctuation that displays in the salutation.

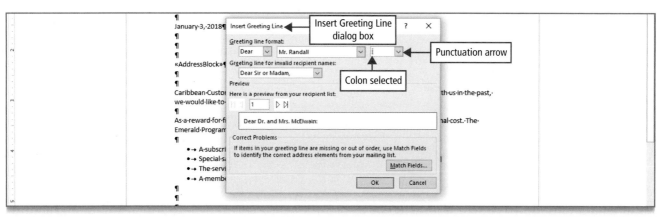

Figure 8.7

3 Click **OK**, and then press [Enter] to insert a blank line.

The Greeting Line merge field is inserted in the document and is used as a placeholder for the salutation.

4 Scroll down, and then position the insertion point in the *second* blank line below the bulleted text. On the **Mailings tab**, in the **Write & Insert Fields group**, click the **Insert Merge Field** arrow. Be careful to click the arrow, not the button.

5 In the list of merge fields, click **Title**, and then press [Spacebar]. Click the **Insert Merge Field** arrow again, and then click **Last_Name**. To the right of the **Last_Name** field, type , (a comma). Compare your screen with Figure 8.8.

The Title and Last_Name merge fields are inserted within the paragraph. Merge fields can be inserted at any location, so it is important to add spaces or punctuation as required.

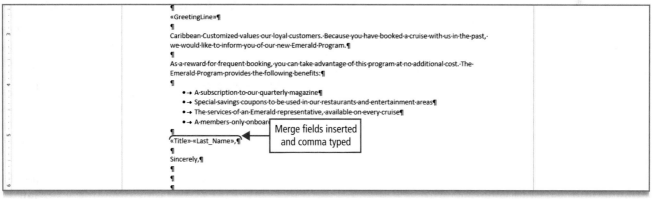

Figure 8.8

6 Press [Spacebar], and then type **please contact us at (305) 555-0768 if you are interested in enrolling in our Emerald Program.** Compare your screen with Figure 8.9.

Formatting and editing of your main document is complete.

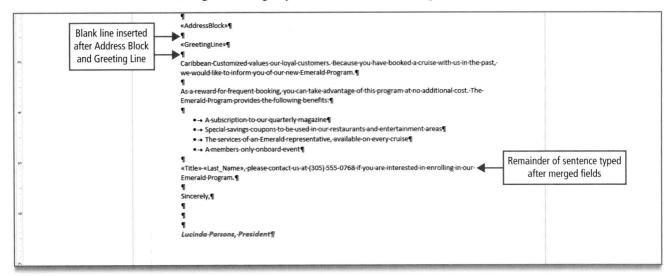

Blank line inserted after Address Block and Greeting Line

Remainder of sentence typed after merged fields

Figure 8.9

7 **Save** your document.

Activity 8.05 | Previewing Results and Validating Merged Data

Expert 4.3.3

After the merge fields are added to the form letter, you can preview the letters one at a time. Before you complete the merge process, it is a good idea to scan the letters to check for spelling, punctuation, and spacing errors. If you find an error, correct it in the main document before completing the merge. You can use the Check for Errors feature to specify how to handle errors that may occur during the merge process.

1 Press [Ctrl] + [Home]. On the **Mailings tab**, in the **Preview Results group**, click **Preview Results**. Notice that the merge fields are replaced with specific information from the data source. Compare your screen with Figure 8.10.

Previewing the merged results allows you to see how each record will display in the letter. By default, the displayed information—in this case, the customer information—is from record 1, as indicated in the Go to Record box.

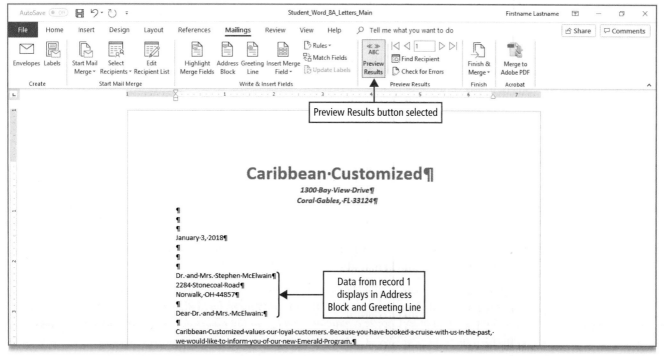

Figure 8.10

> **2** On the **Mailings tab**, in the **Preview Results group**, click **Next Record** ▷, and then scroll your document so that the date displays at the top of the document and the signature line is visible at the bottom. Compare your screen with Figure 8.11.
>
> In the Go to Record box, record 2 displays. You can use the navigation buttons to preview how other letters will display after the merge. In the paragraph following the bulleted list, the *Title* and *Last_Name* merge fields are replaced with data from record 2.

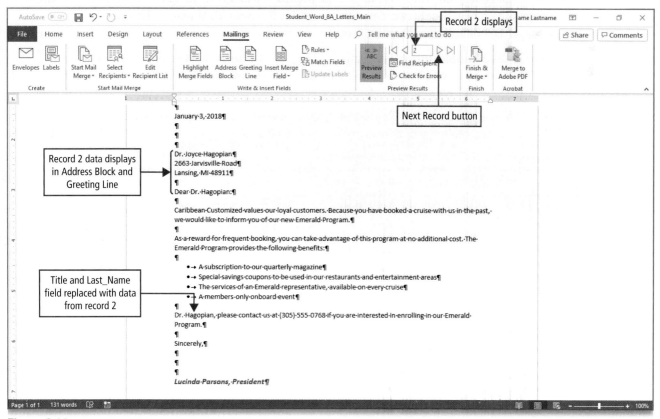

Figure 8.11

3 On the **Mailings tab**, in the **Preview Results group**, click **Last Record** ▷. In the **Go to Record** box, notice that record **3** displays and the record's information from the data source displays in the inside address, salutation, and last paragraph of the letter.

4 On the **Mailings tab**, in the **Preview Results group**, click **First Record** ◁. In the **Go to Record** box, notice that record **1** displays.

5 On the **Mailings tab**, in the **Preview Results group**, click **Preview Results** to turn off the preview and display the merge fields in the letter.

6 On the **Mailings tab**, in the **Preview Results group**, click **Check for Errors**.

 MAC TIP   Skip steps 6–8.

---

7 In the **Checking and Reporting Errors** dialog box, click to select the first option that begins **Simulate the merge**, and then click **OK**.

> By simulating the merge, you can designate how to handle errors that might occur during the final merge process. If there are any errors, the *Invalid Merge Field* dialog box displays with the options to *Remove Field* or to *Choose a matching field from the Fields in Data Source list*. In this case, there are no errors reported.

8 Click **OK** to close the Microsoft Word message box.

Activity 8.06 | Merging to a New Document

MOS

Expert 4.3.4

Recall that your form letter is the main document containing the merge fields. You can print the letters directly from the main document or merge all of the letters into one Word document that you can edit. You will finish the merge process by merging the data source and the main document to a new, single document that contains the individual letters. This new document will no longer be connected to the data source.

1 On the **Mailings tab**, in the **Finish group**, click **Finish & Merge**, and then click **Edit Individual Documents** to display the **Merge to New Document** dialog box. Compare your screen with Figure 8.12.

> Although *All* is selected by default, you can use the Merge to New Document dialog box to specify which records you want to merge to a new document.

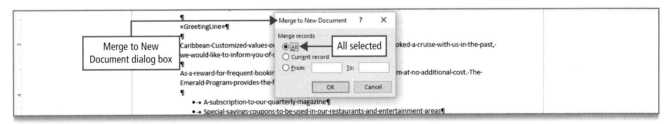

Figure 8.12

2 In the **Merge to New Document** dialog box, click **OK** and then scroll the document to view the results of the merge.

> A new merged document displays with *Letters1 – Word* in the title bar. Based on the filtered recipient list, three letters display.

3 ▸ Press Ctrl + Home, and then scroll to view the bottom of **Page 1**. Compare your screen with Figure 8.13.

The status bar indicates that there are three pages—the individual letters. Each page, or letter, is separated by a Next Page section break.

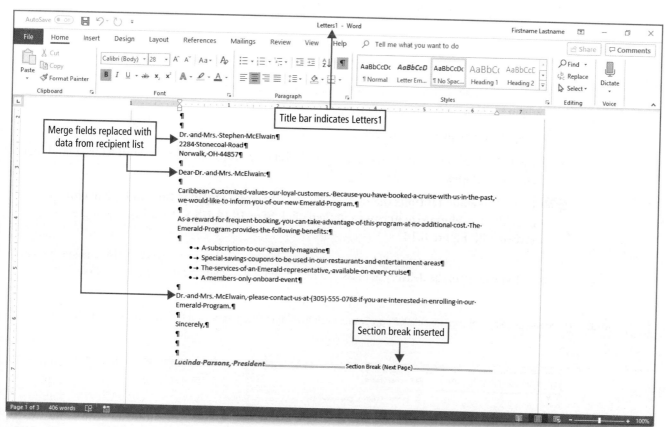

Figure 8.13

4 ▸ Display the **Save As** dialog box. Navigate to your **Word Chapter 8** folder, and then using your name, **Save** the document as **Lastname_Firstname_8A_Letters_Merged**

5 ▸ Insert a footer with the file name, and then **Close** the footer area.

6 ▸ Display the document **Properties**. In the **Tags** box, type **customer letters, merged** and then in the **Subject** box, type your course name and section number. If necessary, edit the author name to display your name.

7 ▸ **Save** your changes, and then close the document.

8 ▸ In the displayed document—the main document—scroll to the bottom of the page, and then insert the file name in the footer. **Close** the footer area.

9 ▸ Click the **File tab**, and then click **Show All Properties**. In the **Tags** box, type **customer letters, main** and then in the **Subject** box, type your course name and section number. If necessary, edit the author name to display your name.

10 ▸ **Save** 🖫 and **Close** your main document but leave Word open.

GO! Learn How
Video W8-2

You can use mail merge to create envelopes from a data source, and you can specify the envelope size and text formatting. Additionally you can include electronic postage, if the appropriate software is installed on your computer.

Activity 8.07 | Using Mail Merge to Create Envelopes

Expert 4.3.4

The same data source can be used with any number of main documents of different types. In this Activity, you will use mail merge to create envelopes for the form letters using the same filtered data source.

1 Display a new blank document.

2 Click the **Mailings tab**. In the **Start Mail Merge group**, click **Start Mail Merge**, and then click **Envelopes**.

3 In the **Envelope Options** dialog box, on the **Envelope Options tab**, under **Envelope size**, click the **Envelope size arrow**, and then click **Size 10 (4 1/8 × 9 1/2 in)**. Compare your screen with Figure 8.14.

> In the Envelope Options dialog box you can select an envelope size. You can also change the font formatting for the delivery address and return address by clicking the appropriate Font button.

MAC TIP In the Envelope dialog box, click Page Setup, click the Paper Size arrow, and then click Envelope #10. Click OK.

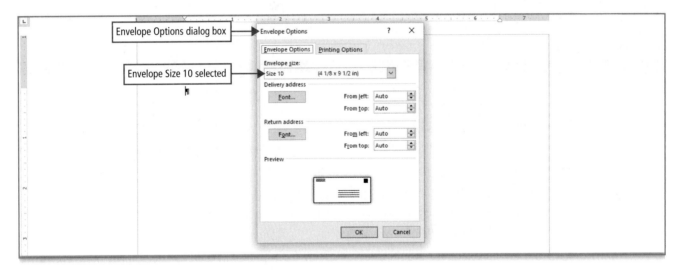

Figure 8.14

4 Click **OK** to display your Word document with the Envelope Size 10 margins and paper size applied. Display the **Save As** dialog box, and then navigate to your **Word Chapter 8** folder. Save the document as **Lastname_Firstname_8A_Envelopes_Main** and **Zoom** your document so that it displays at **100%**.

MAC TIP If the envelope displays in Portrait orientation, on the Layout tab, click Orientation, and then click Landscape.

5 On the **Mailings tab**, in the **Start Mail Merge group**, click **Select Recipients**, and then click **Use an Existing List**. In the **Select Data Source** dialog box, navigate to the files you downloaded with this project, select the file **w08A_Customers**, and then click **Open**.

MAC TIP If a message displays indicating that the file must be opened using the Excel Workbook text converter, click Yes. If a password dialog box displays, enter your Mac password and then click Always Allow. In the Open Workbook dialog box, type A1:I16 and then click OK. Close any message bars that display. Skip step 6.

6 In the **Select Table** dialog box, with **'Customer Information'** and the **First row of data contains column headers** check box selected, click **OK**.

7 On the **Mailings tab**, in the **Start Mail Merge group**, click **Edit Recipient List**. In the **Mail Merge Recipients** dialog box, under **Refine recipient list**, click **Filter**.

MAC TIP In the Start Mail Merge group, click Filter Recipients.

8 In the **Filter and Sort** dialog box, on the **Filter Records tab**, click the **Field arrow**, scroll as necessary, and then click **Booked Cruise**. Click the **Comparison arrow**, and then click **Equal to**. In the **Compare to** box, type **Yes** Compare your screen with Figure 8.15.

The data source will be filtered to display only those records where the Booked Cruise field is equal to Yes.

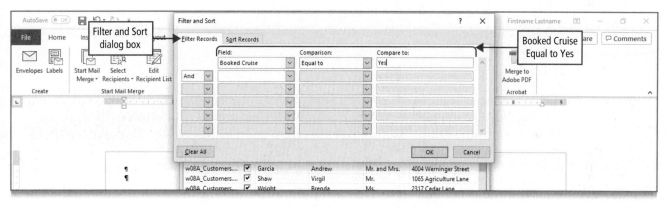

Figure 8.15

9 Click **OK** two times to close the dialog boxes.

10 In the upper left corner of the envelope, if a return address displays, delete the existing text. Type the following return address, pressing Enter after the first and second lines. Compare your screen with Figure 8.16.

Caribbean Customized

1300 Bay View Drive

Coral Gables, FL 33124

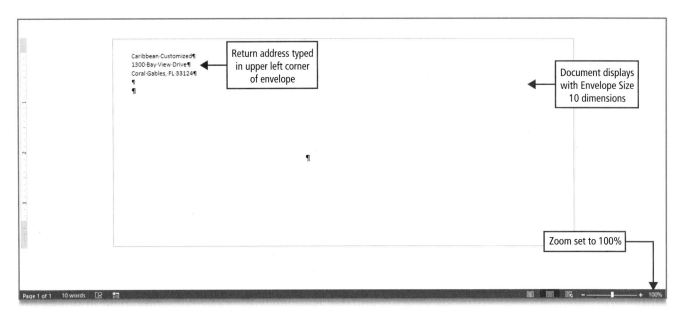

Figure 8.16

11 In the center of the document, position the insertion point to the left of the paragraph mark. On the **Mailings tab**, in the **Write & Insert Fields group**, click **Address Block**. In the **Insert Address Block** dialog box, click **OK** to insert the Address Block merge field in the document.

> A text box displays to indicate the position of the delivery address.

MAC TIP In the center of the envelope, select and delete the text Drag fields into this box or type text. In the Write & Insert Fields group, click Insert Merge Field. Click Title, press spacebar, and then use the same process to insert the First_Name and Last_Name fields, being sure to press spacebar between the two field names. Press enter and then insert the Street_Address field. Press enter and insert the City field. Type a comma (,) and press spacebar. Insert the State field, press spacebar, and then insert the Postal_Code field. Click Finish & Merge, and then click Edit Individual Documents. Skip step 12.

12 On the **Mailings tab**, in the **Preview Results group**, click **Check for Errors**. In the **Checking and Reporting Errors** dialog box, click to select the third option that begins **Complete the merge without pausing**, and then click **OK**. Compare your screen with Figure 8.17.

> By selecting this option, the merge is completed and any errors are reported in a new document. In this case, there are no errors. Notice that the document contains three pages—consisting of individual envelopes—separated by Next Page section breaks. Because the delivery address is in a text box, Word positions the section breaks below the return address.

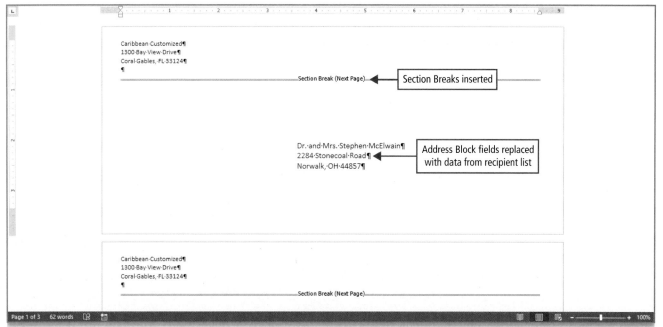

Figure 8.17

13 Display the **Save As** dialog box, navigate to your **Word Chapter 8** folder, and then save the document as **Lastname_Firstname_8A_Envelopes_Merged** Display the document properties. In the **Tags** box, type **customer envelopes, merged** and then in the **Subject** box, type your course name and section number. If necessary, edit the author name to display your name. **Save** your document.

14 To submit your merged letters and envelopes in **MyLab IT**, you will combine your merged letters and merged envelopes into one file. Press Ctrl + A to select all of the merged envelopes. On the **Home tab**, in the **Clipboard group**, click **Copy**.

15 Click the **File tab**, and then **Open** your **Lastname_Firstname_8A_Letters_Merged** file. Press Ctrl + End to move to the end of the last merged letter. On the **Home tab**, in the **Clipboard group**, click **Paste** to paste the three merged envelopes at the end of the document.

16 Save 🖫 and Close ✕ all open documents.

For Non-MyLab Submissions Determine What Your Instructor Requires
As directed by your instructor, submit your completed Word file.

---

17 In **MyLab IT**, locate and click the Grader Project **Word 8A Customer Letters**. In **step 3**, under **Upload Completed Assignment**, click **Choose File**. In the **Open** dialog box, navigate to your **Word Chapter 8 folder**, and then click your **Lastname_Firstname_8A_Letters_Merged** file one time to select it. In the lower right corner of the **Open** dialog box, click **Open**.

The name of your selected file displays above the Upload button.

18 To submit your file to **MyLab IT** for grading, click **Upload**, wait a moment for a green **Success!** message, and then in **step 4**, click the blue **Submit for Grading** button. Click **Close Assignment** to return to your list of **Course Materials**.

MORE KNOWLEDGE **Printing an Envelope or Label from Selected Data**

To print a single envelope or label from selected data, in any document, select the name and address you want to use. On the Mailings tab, in the Create group, click Envelopes for an envelope or Labels for a label. In the Envelopes and Labels dialog box, you can edit the delivery address and make other changes, and then click Print.

You have completed Project 8A   **END**

PROJECT 8B

Cruise Postcards

Project Activities

Caribbean Customized is offering a special cruise to loyal customers. Maria Ramirez, Cruise Consultant, has asked you to create postcards to advertise the cruise. In Activities 8.08 through 8.17, you will use mail merge to create the postcards. You will also create a contact list for customers who are going on the cruise. Your completed files will look similar to Figure 8.18.

Project Files for MyLab IT Grader

1. In your **MyLab IT** course, locate and click **Word 8B Cruise Postcards**, Download Materials, and then Download All Files.
2. Extract the zipped folder to your Word Chapter 8 folder. Close the Grader download screens.
3. Take a moment to open the downloaded **Word_8B_Cruise_Postcards_Instructions**; note any recent updates to the book.

Project Results

GO! Project 8B

Where We're Going

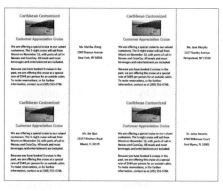
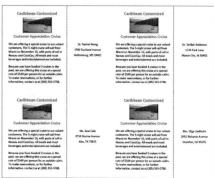

Figure 8.18 Project 8B Cruise Postcards

For Non-MyLab Submissions

For Project 8B, you will need:

Two new blank Word documents
w08B_Cruise_Clients
w08B_Cruise
w08B_Appreciation_Cruise
w08B_Directory_Data

In your Word Chapter 8 folder, save your documents as:

Lastname_Firstname_8B_Postcards_Main
Lastname_Firstname_8B_Postcards_Merged
Lastname_Firstname_8B_Directory_Main
Lastname_Firstname_8B_Directory_Merged

Start with a new blank Word document and save the file as Lastname_Firstname_8B_Postcards_Main. After you have named and saved your document, on the next page, begin with step 2.

GO! Learn How
Video W8-3

During the merge process you can modify information in the data source and arrange the records in a particular order. For example, you may want to add new records or display the records in alphabetical or numerical order based on a specific field.

Activity 8.08 | Using an Access Database as a Mail Merge Data Source

Devon Marshall, Database Coordinator for Caribbean Customized, has asked you to create a postcard mail merge using a table in an Access *database*. A database is an organized collection of facts about people, events, things, or ideas related to a particular topic or purpose.

1 Navigate to your **Word Chapter 8 folder**, and then double-click the Word file you downloaded from **MyLab IT** that displays your name—**Student_Word_8B_Postcards_Main**.

2 On the **Mailings tab**, in the **Start Mail Merge group**, click **Start Mail Merge**, and then click **Labels**. In the **Label Options** dialog box, under **Label information**, click the **Label vendors arrow**, and then click **Avery US Letter**. Under **Product number**, scroll as necessary, and then click **3263 Postcards**. Compare your screen with Figure 8.19.

A description of the selected label displays under Label information on the right side of the Label Options dialog box. In addition to labels, some product numbers are designated as business cards, name tags, or—in this case—postcards.

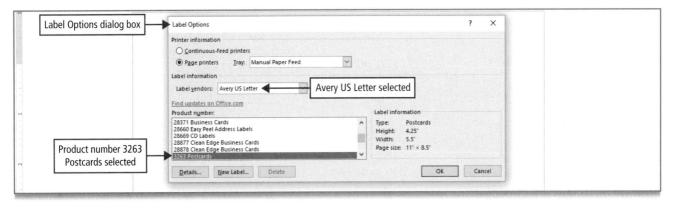

Figure 8.19

3 In the **Label Options** dialog box, click **OK**. Verify that the gridlines—dashed lines—display in the document. If necessary, click the Layout tab, and then in the Table group, click View Gridlines to display the gridlines.

The postcard template is a table consisting of four cells.

4 On the **Mailings tab**, in the **Start Mail Merge group**, click **Select Recipients**, and then click **Use an Existing List**. In the **Select Data Source** dialog box, navigate to your student data files for this chapter, select **w08B_Cruise_Clients**, and then click **Open**.

In the second, third, and fourth cells, notice that the <<Next Record>> field displays. When you are using a label template, the <<Next Record>> field indicates that the contents of the first label will be propagated to the remaining cells of the table during the mail merge process.

MAC TIP The records from the Access database have been copied into a Word file. In the Select Data Source dialog box, use the file Mac_8B_Cruise_Clients.

Activity 8.09 | Managing a Recipient List by Editing a Data Source

MOS
Expert 4.3.1

In this Activity, you will you will edit the data source.

1 On the **Mailings tab**, in the **Start Mail Merge group**, click **Edit Recipient List**. In the **Mail Merge Recipients** dialog box, under **Data Source**, click **w08B_Cruise_Clients. accdb**, and then click **Edit**.

You can edit a data source during the merge process by changing existing data or by adding or deleting records.

MAC TIP Click Edit Recipient List. In the Edit List Entries dialog box, click the Next Record arrow several times until ID 7 displays. Click the Minus (-) button to delete the ID 7 record. Click the Add (+) button to create a new record. In the ID field, type 9. Skip steps 2–5 and continue with step 6.

2 In the **ID** field, scroll as necessary, and locate the cell containing 7. To the left of the cell in the ID field, click the row selector box—the small square to the left of the row. Compare your screen with Figure 8.20.

Clicking the row selector box selects an entire record. This is useful if you want to delete a record.

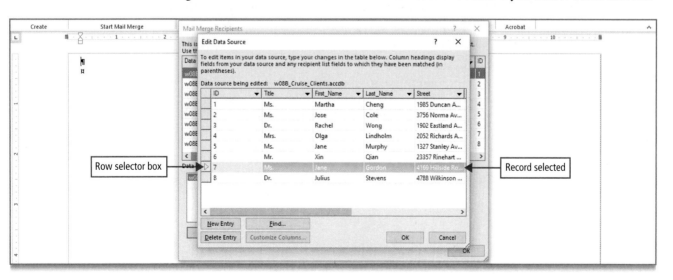

Figure 8.20

3 In the **Edit Data Source** dialog box, click **Delete Entry**. In the **Microsoft Word** message box, click **Yes** to confirm the deletion of the record.

4 In the **Edit Data Source** dialog box, click **New Entry**. Notice that a new record line displays below the last current record with ID *0*. Compare your screen with Figure 8.21.

In the new record line, you can add new client information to the data source.

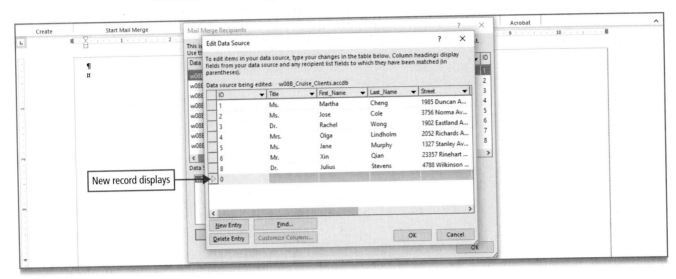

Figure 8.21

5 In the new record line, in the **ID** field, position the insertion point to the right of **0**. Type **9** and then press `Tab`. In the **ID** field, notice that *9* displays, without the default *0*.

It is not necessary to delete the default 0 when entering data in cells containing numbers.

6 In the cell in the **Title** field, type **Dr.** and then press `Tab`. Type the following text in the remaining cells of the row, pressing `Tab` after each entry *except* the last entry.

First_Name	Last_Name	Street	City	State	Postal_Code	Cruises_Booked
Delilah	Robinson	1234 Park Lane	Mason City	IA	50401	3

7 Click **OK**. In the **Microsoft Word** message box, click **Yes** to update your recipient list and save the changes to w08B_Cruise_Clients. Compare your screen with Figure 8.22 and leave the **Mail Merge Recipients** dialog box open for the next activity.

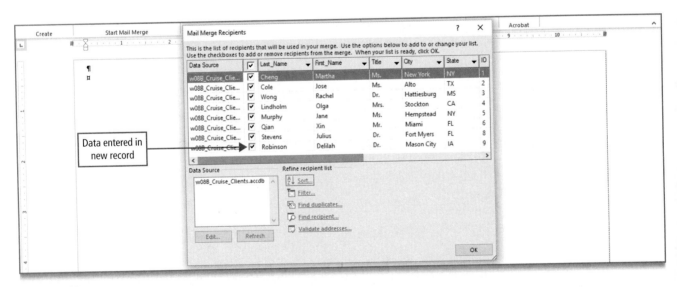

Figure 8.22

Activity 8.10 | Sorting a Recipient List

Sorting a data source by postal code can be useful if you want a mailing to qualify as *bulk mail*. Bulk mail is a large mailing, sorted by postal code, which is eligible for reduced postage rates, available from the United States Postal Service.

1 In the **Mail Merge Recipients** dialog box, scroll to display the **Postal_Code** field. To the right of **Postal_Code** click the **arrow**, and then click **Sort Ascending**. Compare your screen with Figure 8.23.

By sorting the records, when the merge process is complete, the individual postcards will display in order by postal code.

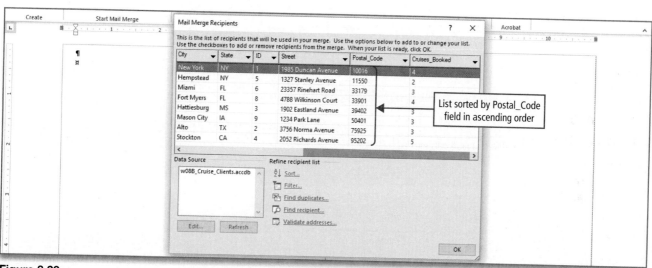

Figure 8.23

MAC TIP In the Start Mail Merge group, click Filter Recipients. In the Query Options dialog box, click Sort Records. Click the Sort By arrow, and then click Postal_Code.

---

2 Click **OK**, and then **Save** 🖫 your changes.

Activity 8.11 | Creating a Nested Table in the Main Document

In Word documents, you can create a *nested table*—a table inserted in a cell of an existing table. In this Activity, you will create a nested table to simplify formatting the postcard, and then add text and merge fields.

1 Press `Ctrl` + `Home` to position the insertion point at the top of the first label. Click the **Insert tab**, and then in the **Tables group**, click **Table**. Under **Insert Table**, click the cell in the first row and second column to create a 2 x 1 table. Compare your screen with Figure 8.24.

A table containing one row and two columns displays within the first cell of the original table. You create a nested table whenever you insert a table within an existing cell.

Figure 8.24

2 With the insertion point in the first cell of the nested table, drag to the right to select both cells in the new nested table. Under **Table Tools**, on the **Design tab**, in the **Borders group**, click the **Borders button arrow**, and then click **No Border**.

3 With the cells still selected, click the **Table Tools Layout tab**, and then in the **Cell Size group**, click in the **Table Row Height** box, type **4.25** and then press Enter. Compare your screen with Figure 8.25.

The row height of the nested table matches the height of the label.

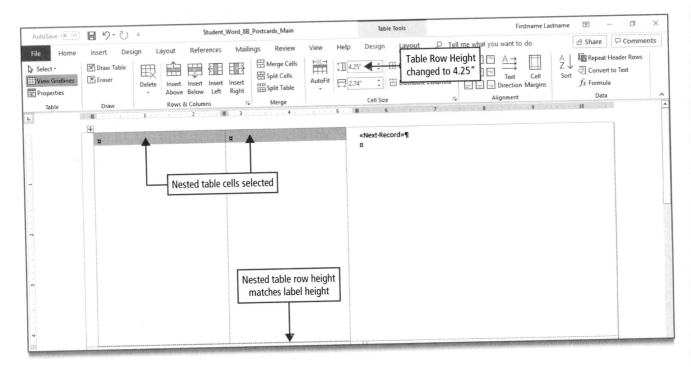

Figure 8.25

4 Position the insertion point in the second cell of the nested table. Under **Table Tools**, click the **Design tab**. In the **Borders group**, click the **Line Style arrow**, and then click the third line style—the dashed border. Click the **Line Weight arrow**, and then click **1 1/2 pt**. Click the **Pen Color button arrow**, and then under **Theme Colors**, in the last column, click the last color. In the **Borders group**, click the **Borders button arrow**, and then click **Left Border**. Compare your screen with Figure 8.26.

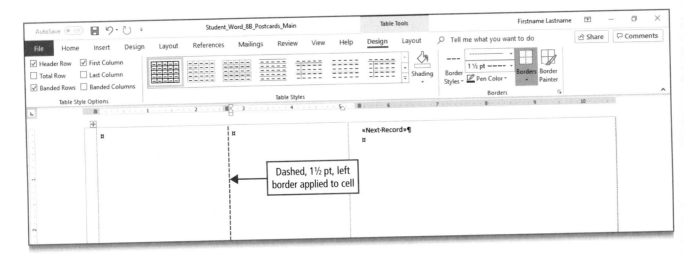

Figure 8.26

5 If necessary, display the rulers. Point to the dashed green border in the nested table to display the resize pointer ⟨⫶⟩, and then drag to the right until the border aligns at approximately **3 inches on the horizontal ruler**. Compare your screen with Figure 8.27, and then **Save** ⟨⊞⟩ your document.

> This border will visually separate the message from the delivery address in the completed postcards.

Figure 8.27

Activity 8.12 | Adding Text and Merge Fields to the Main Document

MOS

Expert 4.3.2

In this Activity, you will insert and format text from a file, insert a picture, and then add merge fields to the postcard main document.

1 Click in the first cell of the nested table, and then click the **Insert tab**. In the **Text group**, click the **Object button arrow**, and then click **Text from File**. Navigate to the files you downloaded with this project, select the file **w08B_Appreciation_Cruise**, and then click **Insert**.

2 At the top of the postcard, select the postcard title—*Caribbean Customized*. Change the **Font Size** to **16**, apply **Bold** ⟨B⟩, **Center** ⟨≡⟩ the text, and then change the **Font Color**—in the last column, the fifth color. Click the **Layout tab**, and then in the **Paragraph group**, change the **Spacing Before** to **18 pt**.

3 Click in the blank paragraph below the postcard title. Click the **Insert tab**, and then in the **Illustrations group**, click **Pictures**. From the files you downloaded with this project, insert **w08B_Cruise**, and then on the **Picture Tools Format tab**, in the **Picture Styles group**, click **Picture Effects**. Point to **Bevel**, and then under **Bevel**, in the first row, click the first style. With the picture selected, on the **Home tab**, click **Center** ⟨≡⟩. Compare your screen with Figure 8.28.

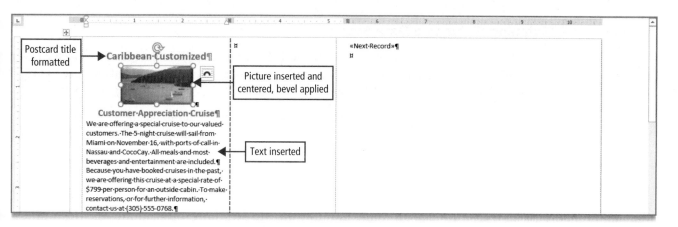

Figure 8.28

4 Position the insertion point anywhere in the paragraph that begins *We are offering*. Click the **Layout tab**. In the **Paragraph group**, click the **Spacing Before spin box up arrow** to **12 pt**, and then click the **Spacing After spin box up arrow** to **12 pt**.

5 In the paragraph that begins *Because you have booked*, position the insertion point to the right of *booked*, and then press ⌨Spacebar. Click the **Mailings tab**. In the **Write & Insert Fields group**, click the **Insert Merge Field button arrow**, and then click **Cruises_Booked**. Compare your screen with Figure 8.29.

The Cruises_Booked field contains the number of cruises previously booked by each customer. By inserting this merge field, you can personalize the postcards.

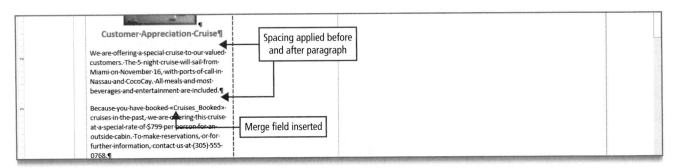

Figure 8.29

6 **Save** 🖫 your changes.

Objective 4 Match Fields and Apply Rules

GO! Learn How
Video W8-4

The data source that you use in a mail merge may not include the same field names that are used in the Address Block or Greeting Line merge fields. The **Match Fields** feature maps the predefined field names to the field names in your data source. You can apply **rules**—conditional Word fields—that allow you to determine how the merge process is completed. This allows you to personalize the final document in additional ways—for example, inserting a specific date in a letter based on the department field in a data source with employee information.

Activity 8.13 | Matching Fields to a Data Source

The Address Block and Greeting Line merge fields include specific field names—such as Last Name, Address 1, and Postal Code. In this Activity, you will use the Match Fields feature to map the Address Block fields to your data source fields to display the delivery address correctly.

1 In the nested table, click to the right of the green dashed border to position the insertion point in the second cell of the nested table. On the **Mailings tab**, in the **Write & Insert Fields group**, click **Address Block**. Compare your screen with Figure 8.30.

In the Preview box only the name, city, and state of the customer display.

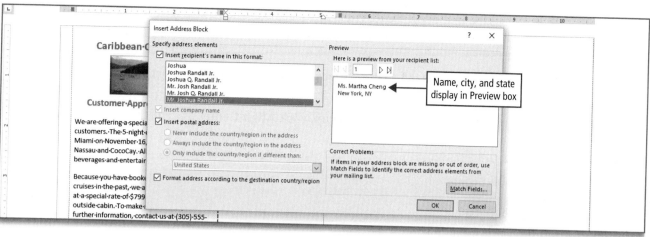

Figure 8.30

💻 **MAC TIP** In the Write & Insert Fields group, click Insert Merge Field. Click Title, press spacebar, and then use the same process to insert the First_Name and Last_Name fields, being sure to press spacebar between the two field names. Press enter and then insert the Street field. Press enter and insert the City field. Type a comma (,) and press spacebar. Insert the State field, press spacebar, and then insert the Postal_Code field. Select all of the field names, and then change the Font Size to 11. Skip steps 2–5 and continue with step 6.

2 In the **Insert Address Block** dialog box, under **Correct Problems**, click **Match Fields**. In the **Match Fields** dialog box, click the **Address 1 arrow**, and then from the displayed list, click **Street**.

3 Click the **Postal Code arrow**, and then click **Postal_Code**. Compare your screen with Figure 8.31.

Word did not recognize the Street and Postal_Code fields in the data source, so it was necessary to associate them with the predefined Address 1 and Postal Code fields, respectively. When you are working with a data source, it is important to remember that *every* character is interpreted by Word. For example, the underscore in Postal_Code caused the field not to be recognized as the predefined Postal Code field.

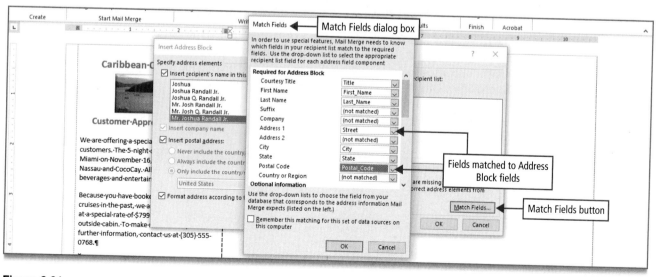

Figure 8.31

4 Click **OK**. In the **Microsoft Word** message box, when asked if you want to match this field to a Unique Identifier, click **Yes**. Notice that the Preview box displays the complete mailing address.

5 Click **OK** to insert the Address Block merge field in the document.

6 With the insertion point in the second cell of the nested table, under **Table Tools**, click the **Layout tab**. In the **Alignment group**, click **Align Center** ⊟, and then compare your screen with Figure 8.32.

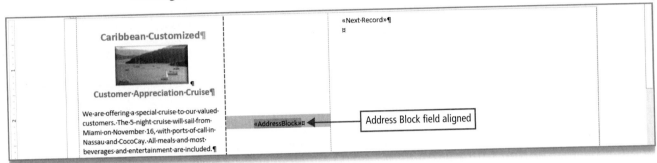

Figure 8.32

7 Save 🖫 your changes.

Activity 8.14 | Applying Rules to a Merge

You can apply rules to add a decision-making element to the mail merge process. In this Activity, you will add a rule that will place different cruise prices in the individual postcards, based on the number of cruises the customer has booked.

1 In the first cell of the nested table, in the last paragraph, delete the text *$799*. Do *not* delete the surrounding space formatting marks.

2 With the insertion point positioned between the two space formatting marks, on the **Mailings tab**, in the **Write & Insert Fields group**, click **Rules**, and then click **If . . . Then . . . Else**.

3 In the **Insert Word Field: IF** dialog box, under **IF**, click the **Field name arrow**, scroll as necessary, and then click **Cruises_Booked**. Click the **Comparison arrow**, and then click **Greater than or equal**. In the **Compare to** box, type **3** In the **Insert this text** box, type **$549** In the **Otherwise insert this text** box, type **$699** Compare your screen with Figure 8.33.

The If . . . Then . . . Else rule allows you to set a condition so that specific text is inserted if the condition is met, and different text is inserted if the condition is not satisfied. In this case, if the number of cruises booked is greater than or equal to 3, during the merge process, Word will insert the text $549. Otherwise, Word will insert the text $699.

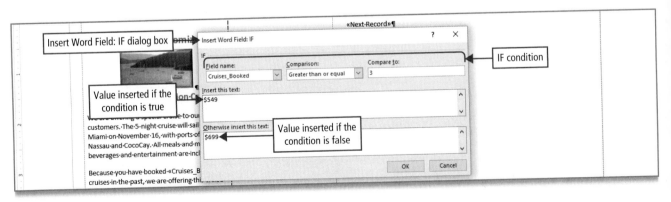

Figure 8.33

4 Click **OK**. Notice that $549 is inserted as the default value for the rule.

5 On the **Mailings tab**, in the **Write & Insert Fields group**, click **Update Labels**. In the **Preview Results group**, click **Preview Results**. Compare your screen with Figure 8.34.

The number of cruises booked, the text for the rule, and the mailing addresses display for each record.

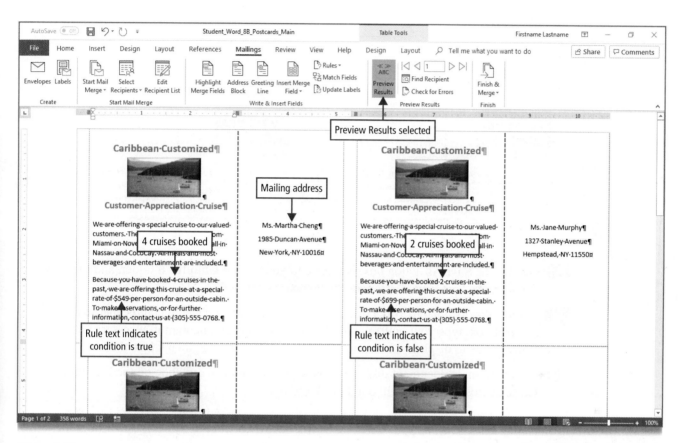

Figure 8.34

6 On the **Mailings tab**, in the **Preview Results group**, click **Preview Results** to turn off the preview.

7 In the **Finish group**, click **Finish & Merge**, and then click **Edit Individual Documents**. In the **Merge to New Document** dialog box, click **OK**. If any words are flagged as spelling errors, right-click and Ignore All. Compare your screen with Figure 8.35.

The new document, *Labels1*, contains the postcards with the merged data. Notice that the rule text—cruise price—agrees with the number of cruises booked. By default, a blank page is included at the end of the document.

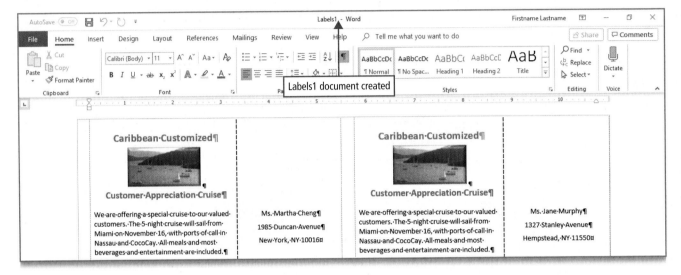

Figure 8.35

8 Display the **Save As** dialog box. Navigate to your **Word Chapter 8** folder, and then save the document as **Lastname_Firstname_8B_Postcards_Merged**

9 Display the document **Properties**. In the **Tags** box, type **cruise postcards, merged** In the **Subject** box, type your course name and section number, and then if necessary, edit the author name to display your name. **Save** your document, and then **Close** the file.

10 With your main document displayed, **Save** your document, and then on the **File tab**, click **Close** to close the document but leave Word open.

Objective 5 | Create a Data Source and a Directory

GO! Learn How
Video W8-5

Previously in this chapter, you used mail merge to create documents that contain individual components—such as letters, envelopes, and postcards. You can also use mail merge to create a *directory*—a single list of selected data records using specified fields from a data source. For example, a directory might contain the names, departments, and phone numbers for company employees.

Activity 8.15 | Formatting a Directory Main Document

Maria Ramirez, Cruise Consultant, has asked you to create a directory that lists emergency contact information, which is recorded on paper forms, for customers booked on the Customer Appreciation Cruise.

1 From the files you downloaded with this project, open **Student_Word_8B_Directory Main**.

NOTE If you are *not* submitting your project in **MyLab IT** for grading, begin a new blank document and save the file as Lastname_Firstname_8B_Directory_Main.

2 On the **Layout tab**, in the **Page Setup group**, click **Margins**, and then click **Narrow**.

The Narrow margin setting adjusts all margins to 0.5".

3 Click the **Mailings tab**. In the **Start Mail Merge group**, click **Start Mail Merge**, and then click **Directory**. Click **Select Recipients**, and then click **Use an Existing List**. Navigate to the files you downloaded with this project, select **w08B_Directory_Data**, and then click **Open**. In the **Select Table** dialog box, click **OK**.

> **MAC TIP** If a message displays indicating that the file must be opened using the Excel Workbook text converter, click Yes. If a password dialog box displays, enter your Mac password and then click Always Allow. In the Open Workbook dialog box, in the Cell Range box, type a1:f6 and then click OK. Close any message bars that display.

4 To set a left tab stop, at the left end of the horizontal ruler, verify that the **Left Tab** button ⌊L⌋ displays. On the ruler, click at **2.5 inches on the horizontal ruler**. To set two additional left tab stops, click at **4.5 inches** and then at **5.5 inches on the horizontal ruler**. Compare your screen with Figure 8.36.

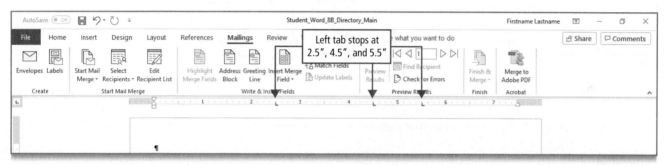

Figure 8.36

5 On the **Mailings tab**, in the **Write & Insert Fields group**, click the **Insert Merge Field** arrow. In the list, click **Title**, and then press Spacebar. Click the **Insert Merge Field arrow** again, click **First_Name**, and then press Spacebar. Click the **Insert Merge Field arrow** again, click **Last_Name**, and then press Tab.

6 Click the **Insert Merge Field** arrow, click **Contact_Name**, and then press Tab. Use the same technique to insert the **Relationship** field, being sure to press Tab after you insert the field. Then, insert the **Home_Phone** field and press Enter. Compare your screen with Figure 8.37.

All of the merge fields from the data source are inserted on the first line of the document. When the directory is created, all the information for one record—a customer—will display on a single line. The tab between the fields will display the data in columns, creating a professional appearance. Pressing Enter after the last field adds a new paragraph so that when the data is merged, each record will display on a separate line.

Figure 8.37

> **MAC TIP** Select the entire line of field names, and then if necessary, change the Font Size to 11.

7 **Save** 🖫 your changes.

Activity 8.16 | Merging Files to Create a Directory

Expert 4.3.4

When completing the merge process for a directory, all of the data represented by the merge fields is displayed in a single document.

1 On the **Mailings tab**, in the **Preview Results group**, click **Preview Results**.

Because you are creating a directory, only one record—the first record—displays.

2 On the **Mailings tab**, in the **Finish group**, click **Finish & Merge**, and then click **Edit Individual Documents**. In the **Merge to New Document** dialog box, click **OK**. Compare your screen with Figure 8.38.

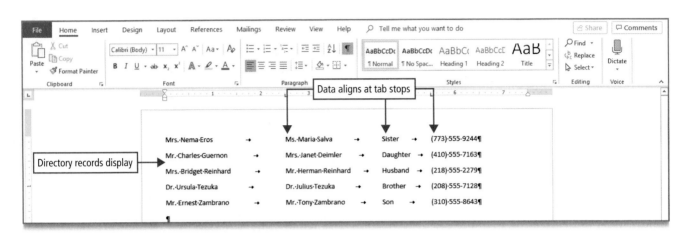

Figure 8.38

Activity 8.17 | Editing a Directory

In the final merged directory, you can add additional elements, such as a title and headings, to improve the appearance of the final document.

1 With the insertion point at the beginning of the document, press Enter, and then press ↑.

2 Type the following text, pressing Enter after each line including the last line.

Caribbean Customized
Customer Appreciation Cruise
Emergency Contact List

3 Select the first paragraph, and then change the **Font Size** to **28**. On the **Layout tab**, in the **Paragraph group**, change the **Spacing Before** to **24 pt**. Select the second and third paragraphs, and then change the **Font Size** to **16**.

4 Position the insertion point in the blank paragraph immediately above the first customer record. Type **Customer** press Tab, and then type **Contact** Press Tab, type **Relationship** press Tab, and then type **Phone Number**

5 Select the column heading text that you just typed, and then apply **Bold** B and **Underline** U. Deselect the text, and then compare your screen with Figure 8.39.

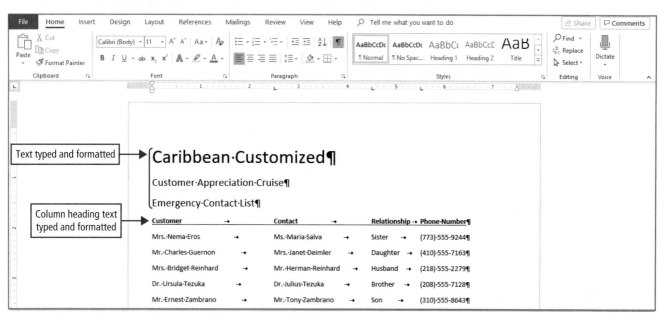

Figure 8.39

6 **Save** the document in your **Word Chapter 8** folder as **Lastname_Firstname_8B_Directory_Merged**

7 Display the document **Properties**. In the **Tags** box, type **directory, merged** and then in the **Subject** box, type your course name and section number. If necessary, edit the author name to display your name. **Save** your document.

8 To submit your merged postcards and directory in **MyLab IT**, you will combine your merged postcards and merged directory into one file. **Open** your **Lastname_Firstname_8B_Postcards_Merged** file. Press Ctrl + A to select all of the merged postcards. On the **Home tab**, in the **Clipboard group**, click **Copy** and then **Close** ✕ the file.

9 With your **Lastname_Firstname_8B_Directory_Merged** file open, press Ctrl + End to move to the end of the document. On the **Layout tab**, in the **Page Setup group**, click **Breaks**, and then under **Section Breaks**, click **Next Page** to insert a new section in the document.

10 On the **Home tab**, in the **Clipboard group**, click **Paste** to paste the merged postcards at the end of the document.

11 **Save** 🖫 and **Close** ✕ all open documents.

For Non-MyLab Submissions Determine What Your Instructor Requires

As directed by your instructor, submit your completed Word file.

12 In **MyLab IT**, locate and click the Grader Project **Word 8B Cruise Postcards**. In **step 3**, under **Upload Completed Assignment**, click **Choose File**. In the **Open** dialog box, navigate to your **Word Chapter 8 folder**, and then click your **Lastname_Firstname_8B_ Directory_Merged** file one time to select it. In the lower right corner of the **Open** dialog box, click **Open**.

The name of your selected file displays above the Upload button.

13 To submit your file to **MyLab IT** for grading, click **Upload**, wait a moment for a green **Success!** message, and then in **step 4**, click the blue **Submit for Grading** button. Click **Close Assignment** to return to your list of **Course Materials**.

You have completed Project 8B **END**

Microsoft Office Specialist (MOS) Skills in This Chapter	
Project 8A	**Project 8B**
Expert 2.3.1 Create paragraph and character styles	**Expert 4.3.1** Manage recipient lists
Expert 4.3.4 Create merged documents, labels, and envelopes	**Expert 4.3.2** Insert merged fields
Expert 4.3.1 Manage recipient lists	**Expert 4.3.4** Create merged documents, labels, and envelopes
Expert 4.3.2 Insert merged fields	
Expert 4.3.3 Preview merge results	

Build Your E-Portfolio

An E-Portfolio is a collection of evidence, stored electronically, that showcases what you have accomplished while completing your education. Collecting and then sharing your work products with potential employers reflects your academic and career goals. Your completed documents from the following projects are good examples to show what you have learned: 8G, 8K, and 8L.

GO! For Job Success

Project Management

Your instructor may assign these questions to your class, and then ask you to think about them or discuss them with your classmates:

Project management is a discipline that identifies and plans for the resources required to complete a defined set of tasks to achieve a stated goal. Project managers develop timelines, coordinate resources, organize and motivate cross-functional groups working on the project, and forecast and monitor costs. Size and complexity of projects vary: Construction and architecture projects might entail building a new highway or skyscraper; software projects develop new software products or upgrades of existing products. Administrative projects might include meeting and event planning.

Project managers must have skills in a variety of areas including accounting, management, forecasting, and writing. What are some other skills that would be valuable in project management?

What "soft" skills do you think are required to be a successful project manager?

To assure that the corporate strategy translates into projects actually being implemented, many organizations have implemented a Project Management Office, which assures alignment between strategy and projects so that the right projects move forward at the right time and right budget. What do you think are some other benefits to both executives and project managers of using a Project Management Office?

g-stockstudio/ Shutterstock

End of Chapter

Summary

The mail merge feature joins a main document with a data source—for example, an Excel spreadsheet or an Access table—to create personalized documents such as letters, envelopes, mailing labels, and directories.

Filter the data source to display specific records or sort the data source to display records in a specific order. Predefined merge fields or individual merge fields determine the placement of data in the document.

Match Fields maps predefined field names to the field names in the data source. Apply a rule to check criteria—for example, to insert a specific date based on a particular field—when completing the merge process.

When performing a mail merge, you can edit a data source to add new records, delete records, and customize the field names. A directory is a single list of records using specified fields from a data source.

GO! Learn It Online

Review the concepts and key terms in this chapter by completing these online challenges, which you can find at **MyLab IT**.

Chapter Quiz: Answer matching and multiple choice questions to test what you learned in this chapter.

Lessons on the GO!: Learn how to use all the new apps and features as they are introduced by Microsoft.

MOS Prep Quiz: Answer questions to review the MOS skills that you practiced in this chapter.

Your instructor may assign one or more of these projects to help you review the chapter and assess your mastery and understanding of the chapter.

Project	Apply Skills from These Chapter Objectives	Project Type	Project Location
8A MyLab IT	Objectives 1–2 from Project 8A	**8A Instructional Project (Grader Project)** Instruction Guided instruction to learn the skills in Project 8A.	In **MyLab IT** and in text
8B MyLab IT	Objectives 3–5 from Project 8B	**8B Instructional Project (Grader Project)** Instruction Guided instruction to learn the skills in Project 8B.	In **MyLab IT** and in text
8C	Objectives 1–2 from Project 8A	**8C Skills Review (Scorecard Grading)** Review A guided review of the skills from Project 8A.	In text
8D	Objectives 3–5 from Project 8B	**8D Skills Review (Scorecard Grading)** Review A guided review of the skills from Project 8B.	In text
8E MyLab IT	Objectives 1–2 from Project 8A	**8E Mastery (Grader Project)** Mastery and Transfer of Learning A demonstration of your mastery of the skills in Project 8A with extensive decision making.	In **MyLab IT** and in text
8F MyLab IT	Objectives 3–5 from Project 8B	**8F Mastery (Grader Project)** Mastery and Transfer of Learning A demonstration of your mastery of the skills in Project 8B with extensive decision making.	In **MyLab IT** and in text
8G MyLab IT	Objectives 1–5 from Projects 8A and 8B	**8G Mastery (Grader Project)** Mastery and Transfer of Learning A demonstration of your mastery of the skills in Projects 8A and 8B with extensive decision making.	In **MyLab IT** and in text
8H	Combination of Objectives from Projects 8A and 8B	**8H GO! Fix It (Scorecard Grading)** Critical Thinking A demonstration of your mastery of the skills in Projects 8A and 8B by creating a correct result from a document that contains errors you must find.	IRC
8I	Combination of Objectives from Projects 8A and 8B	**8I GO! Make It (Scorecard Grading)** Critical Thinking A demonstration of your mastery of the skills in Projects 8A and 8B by creating a result from a supplied picture.	IRC
8J	Combination of Objectives from Projects 8A and 8B	**8J GO! Solve It (Rubric Grading)** Critical Thinking A demonstration of your mastery of the skills in Projects 8A and 8B, your decision-making skills, and your critical thinking skills. A task-specific rubric helps you self-assess your result.	IRC
8K	Combination of Objectives from Projects 8A and 8B	**8K GO! Solve It (Rubric Grading)** Critical Thinking A demonstration of your mastery of the skills in Projects 8A and 8B, your decision-making skills, and your critical thinking skills. A task-specific rubric helps you self-assess your result.	In text
8L	Combination of Objectives from Projects 8A and 8B	**8L GO! Think (Rubric Grading)** Critical Thinking A demonstration of your understanding of the chapter concepts applied in a manner that you would outside of college. An analytic rubric helps you and your instructor grade the quality of your work by comparing it to the work an expert in the discipline would create.	In text
8M	Combination of Objectives from Projects 8A and 8B	**8M GO! Think (Rubric Grading)** Critical Thinking A demonstration of your understanding of the chapter concepts applied in a manner that you would outside of college. An analytic rubric helps you and your instructor grade the quality of your work by comparing it to the work an expert in the discipline would create.	IRC
8N	Combination of Objectives from Projects 8A and 8B	**8N You and GO! (Rubric Grading)** Critical Thinking A demonstration of your understanding of the chapter concepts applied in a manner that you would in a personal situation. An analytic rubric helps you and your instructor grade the quality of your work.	IRC

Glossary

Glossary of Chapter Key Terms

Address Block A predefined merge field that includes the recipient's name and address.

Bulk mail A large mailing, sorted by postal code, that is eligible for reduced postage rates, available from the United States Postal Service.

Character style A type of style that contains formatting that can be applied to selected text and does not include formatting that affects paragraphs.

Data source A list of variable information, such as names and addresses, that is merged with a main document to create customized form letters or labels.

Database An organized collection of facts about people, events, things, or ideas related to a particular topic or purpose.

Directory A single list of records using specified fields from a data source.

Fields In a mail merge, a category—or column—of data.

Filter A set of criteria applied to fields in a data source to display specific records.

Form letter A letter with standardized wording that can be sent to many different people.

Greeting Line A predefined merge field that includes an introductory word, such as *Dear*, and the recipient's name.

Inside address The name and address of the person receiving the letter; positioned below the date line.

Mail merge A Word feature that joins a main document and a data source to create customized letters or labels.

Main document In a mail merge, the document that contains the text or formatting that remains constant.

Match Fields A Word feature that maps predefined field names to the field names in a data source.

Merge field In a mail merge, a placeholder that represents specific information in the data source.

Nested table A table inserted in a cell of an existing table.

Record All of the categories of data pertaining to one person, place, thing, event, or idea, and which is formatted as a row in a database table.

Rules Conditional Word fields that allow you to determine how the merge process is completed.

Salutation The greeting line of a letter, such as *Dear Sir*.

Chapter Review

Skills Review	Project 8C Eastern Cruise

Apply 8A skills from these Objectives:

1. Merge a Data Source and a Main Document
2. Use Mail Merge to Create Envelopes

In the following Skills Review, you will create a form letter, customized for current customers, that announces a new cruise offered by Caribbean Customized. You will also create envelopes to accompany the merged letters. Your completed documents will look similar to Figure 8.40.

Project Files

For Project 8C, you will need the following files:

New blank Word document

w08C_Eastern_Main

w08C_Eastern_Customers

You will save your files as:

Lastname_Firstname_8C_Eastern_Main—not shown in figure

Lastname_Firstname_8C_Eastern_Merged

Lastname_Firstname_8C_EasternEnv_Main—not shown in figure

Lastname_Firstname_8C_EasternEnv_Merged

Project Results

Figure 8.40

(continues on next page)

Chapter Review

1 Start Word. Navigate to your student files, open the file **w08C_Eastern_Main**, and then **Save** the document in your **Word Chapter 8** folder as **Lastname_Firstname_8C_Eastern_Main** If necessary display the rulers and formatting marks. For any words flagged as a spelling error, click Ignore All.

a. Click the **Mailings tab**. In the **Start Mail Merge group**, click **Start Mail Merge**, and then click **Letters**. In the **Start Mail Merge group**, click **Select Recipients**, and then click **Use an Existing List**. In the **Select Data Source** dialog box, navigate to your student data files, select the file **w08C_Eastern_Customers**, and then click **Open**. (Mac users, in the Excel Workbook text converter message box, click Yes. In the Open Workbook dialog box, type A1:H15 and then click OK. Close any message bars that display. In the Start Mail Merge group, click Filter Recipients. Skip steps b and c.)

b. In the **Select Table** dialog box, verify that **'Cruise Customers'** and the **First row of data contains column headers** check box are selected. Click **OK**.

c. On the **Mailings tab**, in the **Start Mail Merge group**, click **Edit Recipient List**. In the **Mail Merge Recipients** dialog box, under **Refine recipient list**, click **Filter**.

d. In the **Filter and Sort** dialog box, on the **Filter Records tab**, click the **Field arrow**, scroll as necessary, and then click **Repeat Customer**. Click the **Comparison arrow**, and then if necessary, click **Equal to**. In the **Compare to** box, type **Yes** Click **OK** two times to close the dialog boxes.

e. Select and **Center** the first paragraph, and then change the **Font Size** to **28**. Select the second and third paragraphs containing the company address. Change the **Font Size** to **16**, and then **Center** the paragraphs.

f. In the blank paragraph following the date, click to position the insertion point, and then press Enter three times. Click the **Mailings tab**, and then in the **Write & Insert Fields group**, click **Address Block**. In the **Insert Address Block** dialog box, click **OK**. (Mac users, in the Write & Insert Fields group, click Insert Merge Field. Click Title, press Spacebar, and then use the same process to insert the First_Name and Last_Name fields, being sure to press Spacebar between the two field names. Press Enter and then insert the Street_Address field. Press Enter and insert the City field. Type a comma (,) and press Spacebar. Insert the State field, press Spacebar, and then insert the Postal_Code field.)

g. Press Enter two times, and then in the **Write & Insert Fields group**, click **Greeting Line**. In the **Insert Greeting Line** dialog box, under **Greeting line format**, in the box on the right—the **Punctuation** box, click the **Punctuation arrow**, and then click **:** (the colon). Click **OK**, and then press Enter. (Mac users, type Dear and then press Spacebar. Insert the Title field. Press Spacebar, insert the Last_Name field, and then type : (a colon). Press Enter.)

2 In the paragraph that begins *Because*, select the word *Because*, and then press Delete. On the **Mailings tab**, in the **Write & Insert Fields group**, click the **Insert Merge Field** arrow, and then click **Title**. Press Spacebar, and then click the **Insert Merge Field arrow** again. Click **Last_Name** and then type **, because** Press Spacebar and then **Save** your changes.

a. On the **Mailings tab**, in the **Preview Results group**, click **Check for Errors**. In the **Checking and Reporting Errors** dialog box, select the option that begins **Simulate the merge**, and then click **OK**. In the **Microsoft Word** message box, click **OK**. (Mac users, skip this step.)

b. On the **Mailings tab**, in the **Finish group**, click **Finish & Merge**, and then click **Edit Individual Documents**. In the **Merge to New Document** dialog box, click **OK**.

c. Display the **Save As** dialog box, and then navigate to your **Word Chapter 8** folder. Save the document as **Lastname_Firstname_8C_Eastern_Merged** and then insert the file name in the footer.

d. Display the document **Properties**. In the **Tags** box, type **eastern cruise letters, merged** In the **Subject** box, type your course name and section number. If necessary, edit the author name to display your name. **Save** your changes, and then **Close** the document to display your main document.

e. In the main document, insert the file name in the footer, and then display the document **Properties**. In the **Tags** box, type **eastern cruise letters, main** In the **Subject** box, type your course name and section number. If necessary, edit the author name to display your name. **Save** your document, and then **Close** the document but leave Word open.

(continues on next page)

Chapter Review

3 Start a new document. Click the **Mailings tab**. In the **Start Mail Merge group**, click **Start Mail Merge**, and then click **Envelopes**. In the **Envelope Options** dialog box, on the **Envelope Options tab**, under **Envelope size**, click **Size 10 (4 1/8 × 9 1/2 in)**. Click **OK** and then **Save** the document in your **Word Chapter 8** folder, with the file name **Lastname_Firstname_8C_EasternEnv_Main** (Mac users, in the Envelope dialog box, click Page Setup, click the Paper Size arrow, and then click Envelope #10. Click OK. If the envelope displays in Portrait orientation, on the Layout tab, click Orientation, and then click Landscape.)

a. On the **Mailings tab**, in the **Start Mail Merge group**, click **Select Recipients**, and then click **Use an Existing List**. In the **Select Data Source** dialog box, navigate to your student data files, select **w08C_Eastern_Customers**, and then click **Open**. In the **Select Table** dialog box, verify that **'Cruise Customers'** and the **First row of data contains column headers** check box are selected, and then Click **OK**. (Mac users, in the Excel Workbook text converter message box, click Yes. In the Open Workbook dialog box, type A1:H15 and then click OK. Close any message bars that display.)

b. On the **Mailings tab**, in the **Start Mail Merge group**, click **Edit Recipient List**. In the **Mail Merge Recipients** dialog box, click **Filter**. In the **Filter and Sort** dialog box, on the **Filter Records tab**, click the **Field arrow**, scroll as necessary, and then click **Repeat Customer**. Click the **Comparison arrow**, and then if necessary, click **Equal to**. In the **Compare to** box, type **Yes** Click **OK** two times to close the dialog boxes. (Mac users, in the Start Mail Merge group, click Filter Recipients.)

c. Type the following return address, pressing Enter after the first and second lines.

Caribbean Customized
1300 Bay View Drive
Coral Gables, FL 33124

d. In the center of the document, position the insertion point to the left of the paragraph mark. On the **Mailings tab**, in the **Write & Insert Fields group**, click **Address Block**. In the **Insert Address Block** dialog box, click **OK**. (Mac users, in the Write & Insert Fields group, click Insert Merge Field. Click Title, press Spacebar, and then use the same process to insert the First_Name and Last_Name fields, being sure to press Spacebar between the two field names. Press Enter and then insert the Street_Address field. Press Enter and insert the City field. Type a comma (,) and press Spacebar. Insert the State field, press Spacebar, and then insert the Postal_Code field.)

e. On the **Mailings tab**, in the **Preview Results group**, click **Check for Errors**. In the **Checking and Reporting Errors** dialog box, select the third option that begins **Complete the merge without pausing**, and then click **OK**. (Mac users, on the Mailings tab, in the Finish group, click Finish & Merge, and then click Edit Individual Documents to display the Merge to New Document dialog box. Click OK.)

4 **Save** the document in your **Word Chapter 8** folder, with the file name **Lastname_Firstname_8C_EasternEnv_Merged** Insert the file name in the footer. Display the document **Properties**. In the **Tags** box, type **customer envelopes, merged** In the **Subject** box, type your course name and section number. If necessary, edit the author name to display your name. **Save** your document, and then **Close** the file and display the main document.

5 In the main document, insert the file name in the footer. Display the document **Properties**. In the **Tags** box, type **customer envelopes, main** In the **Subject** box, type your course name and section number. If necessary, edit the author name to display your name. **Save** and submit as directed, and then **Close** Word.

You have completed Project 8C | **END**

Chapter Review

Apply 8B skills from these Objectives:

3. Edit and Sort a Data Source
4. Match Fields and Apply Rules
5. Create a Data Source and a Directory

In the following Skills Review, you will use mail merge to create name tags for customers taking the Caribbean cruise by selecting a label option, editing records, and sorting the data source. You will create a new data source and match fields to create a list of Southern Caribbean cruise employees and their addresses. Your completed documents will look similar to the ones shown in Figure 8.41.

Project Files

For Project 8D, you will need the following files:

Two new blank Word documents

w08D_Cruise_Customers

w08D_List

You will save your files as:

Lastname_Firstname_8D_NameTags_Main—not shown in figure

Lastname_Firstname_8D_NameTags_Merged

Lastname_Firstname_8D_Employee_List

Project Results

Figure 8.41

(continues on next page)

Chapter Review

1 Start Word and display a new blank document. If necessary, display the rulers and formatting marks.

a. Click the **Mailings tab**. In the **Start Mail Merge group**, click **Start Mail Merge**, and then click **Labels**. In the **Label Options** dialog box, under **Label information**, click the **Label vendors arrow** and select **Avery US Letter**, and then in the **Product number** box, scroll as necessary and click **5392 Name Badges Insert Refills**. Click **OK**. Click the **Table Tools Layout tab**, and then in the **Table group**, if necessary, click View Gridlines to display gridlines. Navigate to your **Word Chapter 8** folder, and then **Save** the document as **Lastname_Firstname_8D_NameTags_Main**

b. On the **Mailings tab**, in the **Start Mail Merge group**, click **Select Recipients**, and then click **Use an Existing List**. In the **Select Data Source** dialog box, navigate to your student data files for this chapter, select **w08D_Cruise_Customers**, and then click **Open**. (Mac users, use the file Mac_8D_Cruise_Customers.)

c. On the **Mailings tab**, in the **Start Mail Merge group**, click **Edit Recipient List**. In the **Mail Merge Recipients** dialog box, at the lower left, under **Data Source**, click **w08D_Cruise_Customers**, and then click **Edit**. (Mac users, Click Edit Recipient List. Click the Add (+) button to create a new record.)

d. In the **Edit Data Source** dialog box, click **New Entry** to add a new record. In the new record line, in the **First_Name** field, type **Lawrence** and then press ⎇ Tab. In the **Last_Name** field, type **Forbus** and then press ⎇ Tab. In the **Country** field, type **USA** and then click **OK**. In the **Microsoft Word** message box, click **Yes** to update your recipient list.

e. In the **Mail Merge Recipients** dialog box, immediately to the right of **Last_Name**, click the **arrow**, and then click **Sort Ascending**. Click **OK**. (Mac users, in the Start Mail Merge group, click Filter Recipients. In the Query Options dialog box, click Sort Records.)

2 Select the entire table, click the **Table Tools Layout tab**, and then in the **Alignment group**, click **Align Center**.

a. Click in the first cell of the table. Type **Caribbean Customized** and then press ⏎ Enter two times. Select the text you just typed, change the **Font Size** to **16**, apply **Bold**, and then change the **Font Color**—in the last column, click the fifth color.

b. Click to position the insertion point in the last blank paragraph. Click the **Mailings tab**. In the **Write & Insert Fields group**, click the **Insert Merge Field button arrow**, and then click **First_Name**. Press Spacebar, click the **Insert Merge Field button arrow**, and then click **Last_Name**. Press Enter two times. Select the merge fields you just inserted, change the **Font Size** to **20**, and then change the **Font Color**— under **Theme Colors,** in the last column, click the last color.

c. In the last blank paragraph, click to position the insertion point. Type **Southern Caribbean Cruise** select the text, change the **Font Size** to **16**, and then apply **Italic**.

d. On the **Mailings tab**, in the **Write & Insert Fields group**, click **Update Labels**. In the **Finish group**, click **Finish & Merge**, and then click **Edit Individual Documents**. In the **Merge to New Document** dialog box, click **OK**.

e. **Save** the document in your **Word Chapter 8** folder, as **Lastname_Firstname_8D_NameTags_Merged**

f. Display the document **Properties**. In the **Tags** box, type **name tags, merged** In the **Subject** box, type your course name and section number. If necessary, edit the author name to display your name. **Save** your document, and then **Close** the file.

g. With the main document displayed, display the document **Properties**. In the **Tags** box, type **name tags, main** and then in the **Subject** box, type your course name and section number. If necessary, edit the author name to display your name. **Save** your document. **Close** the document but leave Word open.

3 Display a **New** blank document. On the **Home tab**, in the **Styles group**, change the style to **No Spacing**.

a. Click the **Mailings tab**, in the **Start Mail Merge group**, click **Start Mail Merge**, and then click **Directory**. On the **Mailings tab**, in the **Start Mail Merge group**, click **Select Recipients**, and then click **Use an Existing List**. Navigate to your student data files, select **w08D_List**, and then click **Open**. In the **Select Table** dialog box, click **OK**.

b. On the **Mailings tab**, in the **Write & Insert Fields group**, click **Address Block**. In the **Insert Address Block** dialog box, under **Correct Problems**, click **Match Fields**. In the **Match Fields** dialog box, click the **State arrow**, and then from the displayed list, click **State/Province**. Click **OK** two times to close the dialog boxes.

(continues on next page)

Chapter Review

c. Position the insertion point to the right of the *Address Block* merge field, if necessary, and then press Enter two times. On the **Mailings tab**, in the **Finish group**, click **Finish & Merge**, and then click **Edit Individual Documents**. In the **Merge to New Document** dialog box, click **OK**.

4 With the insertion point at the beginning of the document, press Enter two times and then press Ctrl + Home. Type **Southern Caribbean Employees** and then select the text that you typed. Change the **Font Size** to **16**, and then change the **Font Color**—in the last column, click the fifth color.

a. Display the **Save As** dialog box. Navigate to your **Word Chapter 8** folder, and save the document as **Lastname_Firstname_8D_Employee_List** Insert the file name in the footer.

b. Display the document **Properties**. In the **Tags** box, type **employee list** and then in the **Subject** box, type your course name and section number. If necessary, edit the author name to display your name. **Save** your document, and then **Close** the document. **Close** Word without saving the main document. Submit as directed.

You have completed Project 8D | **END**

8
WORD

MyLab IT Grader **Mastering Word** **Project 8E Hospitality**

Apply 8A skills from these Objectives:

1. Merge a Data Source and a Main Document
2. Use Mail Merge to Create Envelopes

In the following Mastering Word project, you will use mail merge to filter a data source and customize a form letter to employees who have been selected for the hospitality team for the Ultimate Southern cruise. Your completed documents will look similar to the ones shown in Figure 8.42.

Project Files for MyLab IT Grader

1. In your **MyLab IT** course, locate and click **Word 8E Hospitality**, Download Materials, and then Download All Files.
2. Extract the zipped folder to your Word Chapter 8 folder. Close the Grader download screens.
3. Take a moment to open the downloaded **Word_8E_Hospitality_Instructions**; note any recent updates to the book.

Project Results

Figure 8.42

For Non-MyLab Submissions

For Project 8E, you will need:

New blank Word document
w08E_Hospitality_Team
w08E_Hospitality_Main

In your Word Chapter 8 folder, save your documents as:

Lastname_Firstname_8E_Hospitality_Main
Lastname_Firstname_8E_Hospitality_Merged
Lastname_Firstname_8E_HospitalityEnv_Main
Lastname_Firstname_8E_HospitalityEnv_Merged

Open w08E_Hospitality_Main and Save it as Lastname_Firstname_8E_Hospitality_Main.
After you have named and saved your document on the next page, begin with step 2.
After step 9, save and submit your file as directed by your instructor.

(continues on next page)

1 ▶ Navigate to your **Word Chapter 8 folder**, and then double-click the Word file you downloaded from **MyLab IT** that displays your name—**Student_Word_8E_Hospitality**.

2 ▶ Select the two lines of the company address, apply **Bold**, and then change the **Font Color**—in the fifth column, click the last color. Create a **Character Style** named **Letter Emphasis** and then apply the **Letter Emphasis** style to the last line in the letter—**James Vaughn, Human Resources Manager**. (Mac users, if necessary, apply the Letter Emphasis style to the two lines of the company address.)

3 ▶ Create a **Letters** mail merge document. As the data source, from the files you downloaded with this project, select the file **w08E_Hospitality_Team**. (Mac users, use the range A1:H10.) **Filter** the data source so that the **Job Title** field is **Not equal to Fitness instructor**

4 ▶ Position the insertion point in the blank paragraph following the date, press [Enter] three times, and then insert the **Address Block** merge field. Press [Enter] two times, insert the **Greeting Line** merge field. Press [Enter]. (Mac users, insert the Title field, press [Spacebar], and then use the same process to insert the First_Name and Last_Name fields. Press [Enter] and then insert the Street_Address field. Press [Enter] and insert the City field. Type a comma (,) and press [Spacebar]. Insert the State field, press [Spacebar], and then insert the Postal_Code field. Press [Enter] two times. Type Dear and then press [Spacebar]. Insert the Title field. Press [Spacebar], insert the Last_Name field, and then type a comma. Press [Enter].)

5 ▶ Locate the paragraph that begins *Please report*, and then in the *second* sentence, position the insertion point to the left of *on*. Type **work as** and then press [Spacebar]. Insert the **Job_Title** merge field, and then press [Spacebar]. Finish the merge to **Edit Individual Documents**.

6 ▶ **Save** the document in your **Word Chapter 8** folder as **Lastname_Firstname_8E_Hospitality_Merged** and then insert the file name in the footer. Display the document **Properties**. As the **Tags** type **hospitality, letters** and as the **Subject** include your course name and section number. Display your name as the author. **Save** your changes, and then **Close** the document.

7 ▶ **Save** and **Close** the main document but leave Word open. In a **New** document, start an **Envelopes** mail merge using **Size 10 (4 1/8 × 9 1/2 in)**. **Save** the document to your **Word Chapter 8** folder as **Lastname_Firstname_8E_HospitalityEnv_Main** (Mac users, change the Orientation to Landscape.) As the data source, from the files you downloaded with this project, select the file **w08E_Hospitality_Team**. (Mac users, use the range A1:H10.) **Filter** the data source so that the **Job Title** field is **Not equal to Fitness instructor**

8 ▶ Type the following return address on three lines. (Mac users, select and delete the text box that contains the return address. Position the insertion point in the blank paragraph in the upper left corner of the envelope, and then type the return address.)

Caribbean Customized
1300 Bay View Drive
Coral Gables, FL 33124

9 ▶ In the center of the document, insert the **Address Block** merge field. (Mac users, delete the text in the middle of the envelope, and then insert the same address fields that you used in step 4.) **Save** the document and then **Finish & Merge** to **Edit Individual Documents**. **Save** the merged envelopes to your **Word Chapter 8** folder as **Lastname_Firstname_8E_HospitalityEnv_ Merged** and then select and **Copy** the entire document. **Open** your **Lastname_Firstname_8E_Hospitality_ Merged** document, and then press [Ctrl] + [End]. **Paste** the three merged envelopes to the end of the document. **Save** and **Close** all open files.

10 ▶ In **MyLab IT**, locate and click the Grader Project **Word 8E Hospitality**. In **step 3**, under **Upload Completed Assignment**, click **Choose File**. In the **Open** dialog box, navigate to your **Word Chapter 8 folder**, and then click your **Lastname_Firstname_8E_Hospitality_ Merged** file one time to select it. In the lower right corner of the **Open** dialog box, click **Open**.

The name of your selected file displays above the Upload button.

11 ▶ To submit your file to **MyLab IT** for grading, click **Upload**, wait a moment for a green **Success!** message, and then in **step 4**, click the blue **Submit for Grading** button. Click **Close Assignment** to return to your list of **Course Materials**.

You have completed Project 8E END

Content-Based Assessments (Mastery and Transfer of Learning)

Mastering Word   Project 8F Cruise Ships

In the following Mastering Word project, you will use mail merge and sort a data source to create jewel case labels for DVDs containing information about Caribbean Customized cruises and ships. Additionally, you will create a directory listing customer information. Your completed files will look similar to the ones shown in Figure 8.43.

Project Files for MyLab IT Grader

1. In your **MyLab IT** course, locate and click **Word 8F Cruise Ships**, Download Materials, and then Download All Files.
2. Extract the zipped folder to your Word Chapter 8 folder. Close the Grader download screens.
3. Take a moment to open the downloaded **Word_8F_Cruise_Ships_Instructions**; note any recent updates to the book.

Project Results

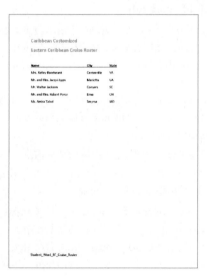

Figure 8.43

For Non-MyLab Submissions

For Project 8F, you will need:
Two new blank Word documents
w08F_Ships_Data
w08F_Eastern_Data

In your Word Chapter 8 folder, save your documents as:
Lastname_Firstname_8F_Ships_Main
Lastname_Firstname_8F_Ships_Merged
Lastname_Firstname_8F_Cruise_Roster

Begin with a new blank document. After you have named and saved your document as Lastname_Firstname_8F_Ships_Main, on the next page, begin with step 2. After step 15, save and submit your file as directed by your instructor.

(continues on next page)

Mastering Word: Project 8F Cruise Ships (continued)

1 Navigate to your **Word Chapter 8 folder**, and then double-click the Word file you downloaded from **MyLab IT** that displays your name—**Student_Word_8F_Ships_Main**.

2 Start a **Labels** mail merge using **Avery US Letter**, and change the **Product Number** to **8962 DVD Labels**. From the files you downloaded with this project, select **w08F_Ships_Data** as the data source. (Mac users, use the Mac_8F_Ships_Data file.)

3 On the **Table Tools Layout tab**, change the **Alignment** for the entire table to **Align Center**. In the first cell, type **Caribbean Customized** and then press Enter two times. Insert the **Cruise_Name** merge field, and then press Enter three times. Insert the **Ship** merge field and press Enter. Type **Captain** and then press Spacebar. Insert the **Captain** merge field.

4 Select the first paragraph, change the **Font Size** to **22**, and change the **Font Color**—in the last column, click the fifth color.

5 Select the third paragraph, which contains the *Cruise_Name* field. Be sure to include the paragraph mark following the field name. Change the **Font Size** to **24**, and change the **Font Color**—in the last column, click the last color. Select the sixth and seventh paragraphs, change the **Font Size** to **20**, and change the **Font Color**—in the last column, click the fifth color.

6 Position the insertion point in the blank paragraph below the *Cruise_Name* merge field. Create an **If . . . Then . . . Else** rule so that if the **Days** field is **Greater than or equal** to **7** then the text **Extended Tour** is inserted. Leave the **Otherwise insert this text** box blank.

7 Select the **Extended Tour** text, change the **Font Size** to **14**, and then apply **Bold**.

8 Update the labels, and then **Finish & Merge** to **Edit Individual Documents**. **Save** the document to your **Word Chapter 8** folder as **Lastname_Firstname_8F_Ships_Merged** and then **Close** the document. **Save** and **Close** the main document but leave Word open.

9 Start a **New** blank document and start a **Directory** mail merge. From the files you downloaded with this project, use **w08F_Eastern_Data** as the data source. (Mac users, use the range A1:E6.) **Sort** the data source to display the **Last** field in ascending order.

10 On the horizontal ruler, set left tabs at the **2.5-inch mark** and **3.5-inch mark**. Insert the **Title** merge field, press

Spacebar, insert the **First** merge field, press Spacebar, and then insert the **Last** merge field. Press Tab, insert the **City** merge field, press Tab, insert the **State** merge field, and then press Enter. Finish the merge to **Edit Individual Documents**.

11 With the insertion point at the beginning of the document, press Enter. In the blank paragraph, type **Caribbean Customized** and then press Enter. Type **Eastern Caribbean Cruise Roster** and then press Enter two times. Select the first two paragraphs, change the **Font Size** to **16**, apply **Bold**, and then change the **Font Color**—in the last column, click the first color.

12 In the blank line above the list, type **Name** press Tab, type **City** press Tab, type **State** and then select the text you typed and apply **Bold** and **Underline**.

13 **Save** the document to your **Word Chapter 8** folder as **Lastname_Firstname_8F_Cruise_Roster** and then insert the file name in the footer. Display the document properties. In the **Tags** type **customers, roster** and in the **Subject** type your course and section number. Under **Related People**, be sure that your name displays as **Author**. **Save** your document.

14 Open your **Lastname_Firstname_8F_Ships_Merged** document, select the entire document, and then **Copy** the selection. **Close** the document.

15 Display your **Lastname_Firstname_8F_Cruise_Roster** document, and then press Ctrl + End. On the **Layout tab**, in the **Page Setup group**, click **Breaks**, and then under **Section Breaks**, click **Next Page**. **Paste** the merged labels to the end of the document. **Save** your document, and then **Close** all open documents. Do not save the directory main document.

16 In **MyLab IT**, locate and click the Grader Project **Word 8F Cruise Ships**. In **step 3**, under **Upload Completed Assignment**, click **Choose File**. In the **Open** dialog box, navigate to your **Word Chapter 8 folder**, and then click your **Lastname_Firstname_8F_Cruise_Roster** file one time to select it. In the lower right corner of the **Open** dialog box, click **Open**.

The name of your selected file displays above the Upload button.

17 To submit your file to **MyLab IT** for grading, click **Upload**, wait a moment for a green **Success!** message, and then in **step 4**, click the blue **Submit for Grading** button. Click **Close Assignment** to return to your list of **Course Materials**.

You have completed Project 8F | **END**

MyLab IT Grader

Mastering Word | **Project 8G Entertainers**

In the following Mastering Word project, you will create a letter to recruit entertainers for next year's Caribbean Customized cruises. You will filter the data source, match fields, and insert merge fields to modify the form letter. Your completed documents will look similar to the ones shown in Figure 8.44.

Project Files for MyLab IT Grader

1. In your **MyLab IT** course, locate and click **Word 8G Entertainers**, Download Materials, and then Download All Files.
2. Extract the zipped folder to your Word Chapter 8 folder. Close the Grader download screens.
3. Take a moment to open the downloaded **Word_8G_Entertainers_Instructions**; note any recent updates to the book.

Project Results

Figure 8.44

For Non-MyLab Submissions

For Project 8G, you will need:

New blank Word document
w08G_Entertainers
w08G_Entertainers_Letter

In your Word Chapter 8 folder, save your documents as:

Lastname_Firstname_8G_Entertainers_Letter
Lastname_Firstname_8G_Entertainers_Merged
Lastname_Firstname_8G_Entertainers_Directory

Open w08G_Entertainers_Letter and Save it as Lastname_Firstname_8G_Entertainers_Letter.
After you have named and saved your document, on the next page, begin with step 2.
After step 14, save and submit your file as directed by your instructor.

(continues on next page)

Mastering Word: Project 8G Entertainers (continued)

1 Navigate to your **Word Chapter 8 folder**, and then double-click the Word file you downloaded from **MyLab IT** that displays your name—**Student_Word_8G_Entertainers_Letter**.

2 Select the two-line company address. Apply **Bold**, change the **Font Size** to **12**, and change the **Font Color**—in the second to last column, click the fifth color. Create a **Character** style named **Address** and then apply the style to the last line of the document—*Mark Graber, Entertainment Director*.

3 Start a **Letters** mail merge using the file you downloaded with this project—**w08G_Entertainers** as the data source. (Mac users, use the range A1:I16.) Sort the data source to display the **Postal Code** field in ascending order, and then filter the list to create letters for entertainers whose **Role** is **Singer**

4 Position the insertion point in the blank paragraph following the date, and then press Enter three times. Insert the **Address Block** merge field, matching the field **Street** with the **Address 1** field. (Mac users, insert the Title field, press Spacebar, and then use the same process to insert the First_Name and Last_Name fields. Press Enter and then insert the Street field. Press Enter and insert the City field. Type a comma (,) and press Spacebar. Insert the State field, press Spacebar, and then insert the Postal_Code field.)

5 Press Enter two times, insert the **Greeting Line** merge field, and then press Enter. (Mac users, type Dear and then press Spacebar. Insert the Title field. Press Spacebar, insert the Last_Name field, and then type a comma. Be sure to press Enter after the comma.)

6 Locate the paragraph that begins *Because you have*, and then position the insertion point to the right of *past*, before the comma. Press Spacebar, type **as a** and then press Spacebar. Insert the **Role** merge field.

7 Finish the merge to **Edit Individual Documents**. **Save** the document in your **Word Chapter 8** folder as **Lastname_Firstname_8G_Entertainers_Merged** and then **Close** the document. **Save** and **Close** the main document but leave Word open.

8 In a **New** document, create a **Directory** mail merge using the **w08G_Entertainers** file as the data source. (Mac users, use the range A1:I16.) Sort the data source to display the **Role** field in ascending order.

9 On the horizontal ruler, set left tabs at the **3-inch mark** and the **5-inch mark**. Insert the **First_Name** merge field, press Spacebar, and then insert the **Last_Name** merge field. Press Tab, insert the **Home_Phone** merge field, press Tab, and then insert the **Role** merge field. Press Enter. Finish the merge to **Edit Individual Documents**.

10 At the top of the document, insert a blank line. In the blank line, type **Caribbean Customized** and then press Enter. Type **Available Entertainers** and then press Enter. Type **Name** press Tab, type **Home Phone** press Tab, and then type **Talent**

11 Select the first two paragraphs, change the **Font Size** to **16**, and apply **Bold**. Select the third paragraph, and apply **Bold** and **Underline**.

12 **Save** the document in your **Word Chapter 8** folder as **Lastname_Firstname_8G_Entertainers_Directory** and then insert the file name in the footer. Add document properties that include the **Tags directory, merged** and as the **Subject** your course name and section number. Display your name as the author. **Save** the document.

13 **Open** your **Lastname_Firstname_8G_Entertainers_Merged** document, select the entire document, and then **Copy** the selection. **Close** the document. Display your **Lastname_Firstname_8G_Entertainers_Directory** document. Move to the end of the document, insert a **Next Page** section break, and **Paste** the selection to the end of the document.

14 **Save** your document, and then **Close** all open documents. Do not save the directory main document.

15 In **MyLab IT**, locate and click the Grader Project **Word 8G Entertainers**. In **step 3**, under **Upload Completed Assignment**, click **Choose File**. In the **Open** dialog box, navigate to your **Word Chapter 8 folder**, and then click your **Lastname_Firstname_8G_Entertainers_Directory** file one time to select it. In the lower right corner of the **Open** dialog box, click **Open**.

The name of your selected file displays above the Upload button.

16 To submit your file to **MyLab IT** for grading, click **Upload**, wait a moment for a green **Success!** message, and then in **step 4**, click the blue **Submit for Grading** button. Click **Close Assignment** to return to your list of **Course Materials**.

You have completed Project 8G | END

Content-Based Assessments (Critical Thinking)

Apply a combination of the 8A and 8B skills.			
	GO! Fix It	**Project 8H Marketing Plan**	**IRC**
	GO! Make It	**Project 8I Business Cards**	**IRC**
	GO! Solve It	**Project 8J Planning Session**	**IRC**
	GO! Solve It	**Project 8K Shipping Information**	

Project Files

For Project 8K, you will need the following files:

New blank Word document

w08K_Shipping_Information

You will save your file as:

Lastname_Firstname_8K_Shipping_Merged

Using mail merge, create labels using Avery US Letter 5352 Mailing Labels. Use **w08K_Shipping_Information** as the data source, sort the data in ascending order by Zip_Code, and apply a filter to display only individuals on the Southern cruise. Include the Address Block merge field and match fields as necessary. Format the document so that the labels display attractively and then merge the labels. Save the merged document to your **Word Chapter 8** folder as **Lastname_Firstname_8K_Shipping_Merged** and then submit your file as directed by your instructor. Do not save the main document.

		Performance Level		
		Exemplary	**Proficient**	**Developing**
Performance Criteria	**Select a mailing label**	The correct mailing label is selected.	A mailing label template is used, but an incorrect label is selected.	No label template is used.
	Sort and filter the data source	The data source is sorted and filtered.	The data source is not sorted or it is not filtered.	The data source is neither sorted nor filtered.
	Match fields in the Address Block	All fields are matched and display correctly in the Address Block.	The Address Block is inserted but the fields are not matched.	No fields are matched or the Address Block is not inserted.
	Insert text and merge fields in labels	The labels are merged and formatted appropriately.	The labels are merged but are not formatted appropriately.	The labels are not merged.

You have completed Project 8K **END**

Rubric

The following outcomes-based assessments are *open-ended assessments*. That is, there is no specific correct result; your result will depend on your approach to the information provided. Make *Professional Quality* your goal. Use the following scoring rubric to guide you in *how* to approach the problem and then to evaluate *how well* your approach solves the problem.

The *criteria*—Software Mastery, Content, Format and Layout, and Process—represent the knowledge and skills you have gained that you can apply to solving the problem. The *levels of performance*—Professional Quality, Approaching Professional Quality, or Needs Quality Improvements—help you and your instructor evaluate your result.

	Your completed project is of Professional Quality if you:	Your completed project is Approaching Professional Quality if you:	Your completed project Needs Quality Improvements if you:
1-Software Mastery	Choose and apply the most appropriate skills, tools, and features and identify efficient methods to solve the problem.	Choose and apply some appropriate skills, tools, and features, but not in the most efficient manner.	Choose inappropriate skills, tools, or features, or are inefficient in solving the problem.
2-Content	Construct a solution that is clear and well organized, contains content that is accurate, appropriate to the audience and purpose, and is complete. Provide a solution that contains no errors of spelling, grammar, or style.	Construct a solution in which some components are unclear, poorly organized, inconsistent, or incomplete. Misjudge the needs of the audience. Have some errors in spelling, grammar, or style, but the errors do not detract from comprehension.	Construct a solution that is unclear, incomplete, or poorly organized, contains some inaccurate or inappropriate content, and contains many errors of spelling, grammar, or style. Do not solve the problem.
3-Format and Layout	Format and arrange all elements to communicate information and ideas, clarify function, illustrate relationships, and indicate relative importance.	Apply appropriate format and layout features to some elements, but not others. Overuse features, causing minor distraction.	Apply format and layout that does not communicate information or ideas clearly. Do not use format and layout features to clarify function, illustrate relationships, or indicate relative importance. Use available features excessively, causing distraction.
4-Process	Use an organized approach that integrates planning, development, self-assessment, revision, and reflection.	Demonstrate an organized approach in some areas, but not others; or, use an insufficient process of organization throughout.	Do not use an organized approach to solve the problem.

Outcomes-Based Assessments (Critical Thinking)

Apply a combination of the 8A and 8B skills.

GO! Think	Project 8L Health Insurance

Project Files

For Project 8L, you will need the following files:

New blank Word document

w08L_Insurance_Data

You will save your files as:

Lastname_Firstname_8L_Insurance_Main

Lastname_Firstname_8L_Insurance_Merged

Caribbean Customized is changing to a new health insurance provider—MediCertain—at the beginning of the year. MediCertain offers a variety of plans for employees. James Vaughn, Human Resources Manager, is conducting information sessions for employees during November in Conference Room D at 9:30 a.m. The Administrative department will meet on November 1; all other departments will meet on November 3. The enrollment period begins November 10 and ends November 30.

Create a memo to department managers from Mr. Vaughn, informing them of the new provider and the scheduled time for the department's information session. Save the document as **Lastname_Firstname_8L_Insurance_Main**

Start a Letters mail merge using the memo that you created and use the data source w08L_Insurance_Data. Insert appropriate merge fields in the memo, and create a rule to display the date of the session based on the department. Format the memo in a professional manner. Save the merged document as **Lastname_Firstname_8L_Insurance_Merged** and then add appropriate properties to the merged and main documents. Submit your files as directed by your instructor.

You have completed Project 8L	END

GO! Think	Project 8M Training	IRC

You and GO!	Project 8N Invitation	IRC

Creating Forms, Customizing Word, and Preparing Documents for Review and Distribution

9

WORD 2019

PROJECT 9A

Outcomes
Create and protect a customized form with content controls.

Objectives
1. Create a Customized Form
2. Convert Text to a Table and Insert Content Controls in a Table
3. Modify and Protect a Form
4. Complete a Form

PROJECT 9B

Outcomes
Customize Word and prepare documents for review and distribution.

Objectives
5. Create a Custom Ribbon Tab
6. Create Style, Color, and Font Sets
7. Convert a Table to Text
8. Prepare a Document for Review and Distribution

In This Chapter

 GO! To Work with Word

In this chapter, you will create a form, which is a structured document that includes fields—such as check boxes—that assist the person entering information into the form. You can save a form as a template, protect a form from unauthorized changes, and then make the form available to others for completion in Word. In this chapter, you will also create a custom ribbon tab to improve your productivity when using Word. You will also prepare a document for distribution. For example, when a document that requires a signature is sent electronically, the recipient can digitally sign the file. Removing document properties and personal information is another way to prepare a document for distribution.

The projects in this chapter relate to **Laurales Herbs and Spices**. After ten years as an Executive Chef, Laura Morales started her own business, which offers quality products for cooking, eating, and entertaining available for purchase in retail stores and online. In addition to herbs and spices, there is a wide variety of condiments, confections, jams, sauces, oils, and vinegars. Later this year, Laura will add a line of tools, cookbooks, and gift baskets. The company name is a combination of Laura's first and last names, and also the name of an order of plants related to cinnamon.

Project Activities

In Activities 9.01 through 9.14, you will create a form to measure customer satisfaction. Chelsea Warren, Marketing Vice President, wants to get feedback from customers regarding the quality of products and services offered by Laurales Herbs and Spices. You will customize the form and save it as a template so that it can be completed by individual users. To test the form prior to distribution, you will enter customer information in the survey form. Your completed document will look similar to Figure 9.1.

 ## Project Files for **MyLab IT Grader**

1. In your storage location, create a folder named **Word Chapter 9**.
2. In your **MyLab IT** course, locate and click **Word 9A Customer Survey**, Download Materials, and then Download All Files.
3. Extract the zipped folder to your Word Chapter 9 folder. Close the Grader download screens.
4. Take a moment to open the downloaded **Word_9A_Customer_Survey_Instructions**; note any recent updates to the book.

Project Results

GO! Project 9A
Where We're Going

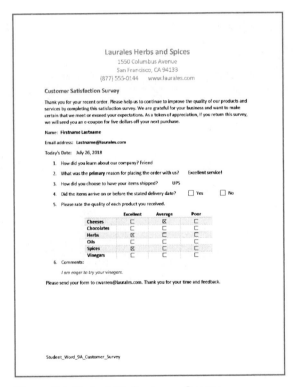

Figure 9.1 Project 9A Customer Survey

For Non-MyLab Submissions

For Project 9A, you will need:
w09A_Customer_Survey

In your storage location, create a folder named **Word Chapter 9**
In your Word Chapter 9 folder, save your document as:
Lastname_Firstname_9A_Customer_Survey

After you have named and saved your document, on the next page, begin with Step 2.

Objective 1 Create a Customized Form

ALERT Because Office 365 is a cloud-based subscription service that receives continuous updates, you may encounter some variations in what appears on your screen and what is shown in this instruction. Microsoft Office 365 is fully installed on your PC or Mac; no internet access is necessary to create or edit documents. When you *are* connected to the internet, you will receive monthly upgrades and new features, so you always have the latest versions of Office apps as soon as they are available. Your subscription gives you continuous free access to the latest innovations and refinements.

A *form* is a structured document that has *static text*—descriptive text such as headings and labels—and reserved spaces, or *content controls*, for information to be entered by the person filling in the form. A content control is a data entry field in a form in which a particular type of information, such as a name or date, is supplied by the person entering information into the form. For example, you can create a survey form that provides a place to enter text or choose a specific entry from a list. You can also protect the form to restrict changes made by the person completing the form.

Activity 9.01 | Displaying the Developer Tab

MAC TIP Although MAC TIPS are included where possible, this project is best suited for a Windows-based PC. Some commands in this project are not available on a Mac.

MOS
Expert 1.1.7

Insert content controls into forms that will be filled in electronically. You access content controls from the Developer tab; by default, the Developer tab does not display on the ribbon.

GO! Learn How
Video W9-1

1 Navigate to your **Word Chapter 9** folder, and then double-click the Word file you downloaded from **MyLab IT** that displays your name—**Student_Word_9A_Customer_Survey**. If necessary, at the top click **Enable Editing**.

2 Click the **File tab**, and then click **Options**. Compare your screen with Figure 9.2.

Use the Word Options dialog box to add and update settings for Word, for your documents, for your personal information, and for your preferences. Categories of options display on the left.

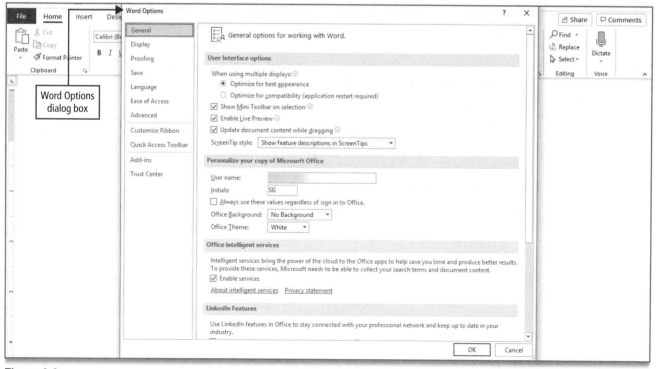

Figure 9.2

3 In the **Word Options** dialog box, on the left, click **Customize Ribbon**.

MAC TIP Display the menu bar, click Word, click Preferences, click Ribbon & Toolbar, click the + button, click New Tab, and then click the Developer check box.

4 On the right, in the **Main Tabs** list, locate and then click to select the **Developer** check box. Compare your screen with Figure 9.3.

Main tabs that display on the ribbon are indicated with a checkmark.

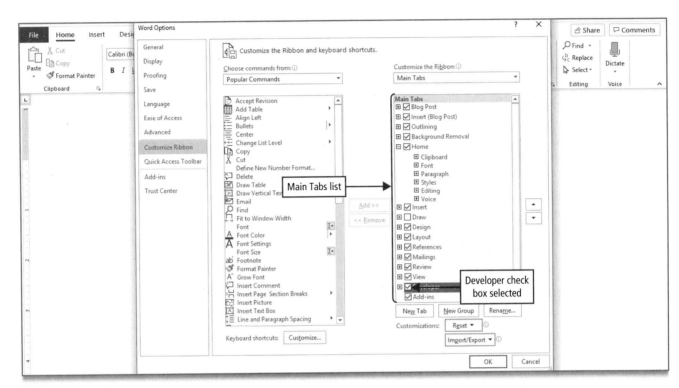

Figure 9.3

5 Click **OK** to close the **Word Options** dialog box. On the ribbon, locate and then click the **Developer tab**. Compare your screen with Figure 9.4.

On the Developer tab, you can extend the capabilities of Word. For example, you can create a form and then distribute the form for people to complete. You can integrate content controls with other applications to store the information that people have entered into the completed form. Content control commands are located in the Controls group.

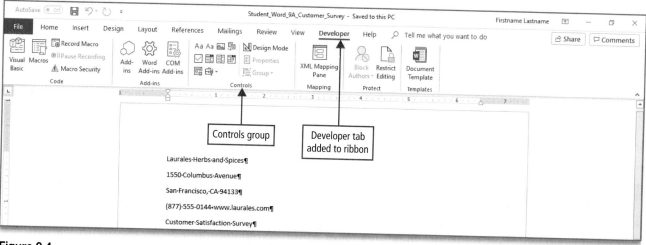

Figure 9.4

> **6** Select the first three paragraphs of the document. From the **Layout tab**, set **Spacing After** to **0 pt**.

> **7** Select the first paragraph of the document—*Laurales Herbs and Spices*. Change the **Font Size** ⌈11 ▾⌉ to **18**, apply **Bold** ⌈B⌉, click the **Font Color button arrow** ⌈A ▾⌉, and then in the eighth column (gold colors), click the fifth color. Center the paragraph.

> **8** Select the next three paragraphs—the address, phone, and website information. Change the **Font Size** ⌈11 ▾⌉ to **14**, and then click **Font Color** ⌈A ▾⌉. Center the paragraphs.

>> Recall that the Font Color button will retain its most recently used color.

> **9** Select the fifth paragraph—*Customer Satisfaction Survey*. Change the **Font Size** ⌈11 ▾⌉ to **14**, apply **Bold** ⌈B⌉, click the **Font Color button arrow** ⌈A ▾⌉, and then in the eighth column (gold colors), click the last color. **Save** ⌈🖫⌉ your document.

Activity 9.02 | Inserting a Plain Text Content Control

Expert 4.1.3

The ***Plain Text content control*** inserts a field in the form that enables the person completing the form to insert ***unformatted text***—plain text—in the document. You will add several plain text content controls to this form so that the customer filling out the form can provide personal information and comments.

> **1** Locate the paragraph *Name*, and then scroll as necessary so that the paragraph displays near the top of your screen. Click to position the insertion point to the right of *Name*—after the colon, and then press ⌈Tab⌉.

> **2** On the ribbon, click the **Developer tab**, and then in the **Controls group**, click **Design Mode**.

>> Turning on ***Design Mode*** enables you to edit content controls in a document.

💻 **MAC TIP**   In the Legacy Controls group, click Text Box. Design Mode may not be available.

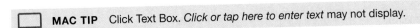

3 In the **Controls group**, click **Plain Text Content Control** [Aa]. At the insertion point, notice that a field with the default text *Click or tap here to enter text.* displays. Compare your screen with Figure 9.5.

The default text serves as a placeholder and also assists the person filling in the form to know what to do.

🖥 **MAC TIP** Click Text Box. *Click or tap here to enter text* may not display.

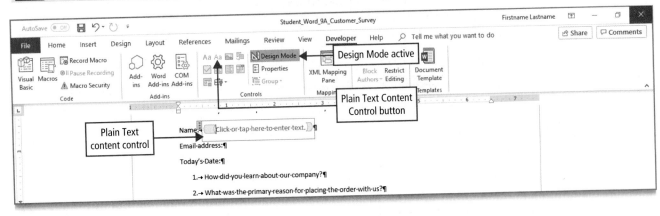

Figure 9.5

4 Locate the paragraph *Email address*. Click to position the insertion point to the right of the colon, press [Tab], and then in the **Controls group**, click **Plain Text Content Control** [Aa].

🖥 **MAC TIP** Click Text Box.

5 Scroll to view the bottom of the page. Above the last paragraph that begins *Please send*, click to position the insertion point in the blank paragraph.

6 Press [Tab] two times, and then in the **Controls group**, click **Plain Text Content Control** [Aa].

🖥 **MAC TIP** Click Text Box.

7 Click in a blank area of the document to deselect the content control, and then compare your screen with Figure 9.6.

Figure 9.6

8 **Save** 🖫 your document.

| MORE KNOWLEDGE | Inserting a Rich Text Content Control |

The Controls group includes a *Rich Text content control* that enables the person filling in the form to add text with most types of formatting, such as formats available on the mini toolbar. The Rich Text content control also allows for the insertion of tables and graphics.

Activity 9.03 | Inserting a Date Picker Content Control and Modifying Field Properties

MOS
Expert 4.1.4

The *Date Picker content control* enables the person filling out the form to select a date from a calendar. In this Activity, you will insert the Date Picker content control and then specify the format for displaying the date.

1 Locate the paragraph *Today's Date*. Click to position the insertion point to the right of the colon, and then press Tab one time.

2 On the **Developer tab**, in the **Controls group**, click the **Date Picker Content Control** button. Notice that the default text *Click or tap to enter a date.* displays in the content control.

🖥 **MAC TIP** The Date Picker control may not be available. Click to add Text Box and move to Activity 9.04.

---

3 With the **Date Picker content control** selected, in the **Controls group**, click **Properties**. In the **Content Control Properties** dialog box, under **Date Picker Properties**, in the **Display the date like this** box, click the third style—your date will differ. Compare your screen with Figure 9.7.

In the Content Control Properties dialog box, you can modify settings for a content control—in this instance, the date format MMMM d, yyyy. The date selected by the customer filling in the form will display in the format you specify.

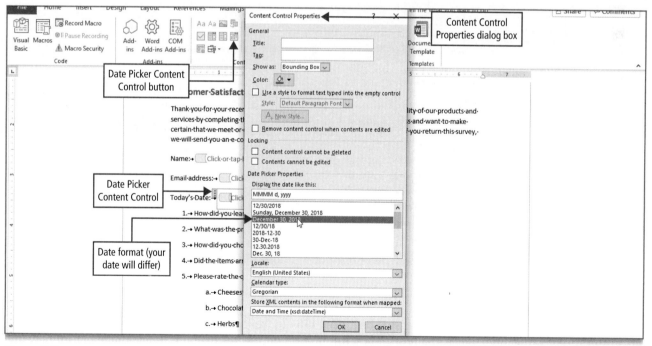

Figure 9.7

4 Click **OK** to close the **Content Control Properties** dialog box, and then **Save** your document.

Activity 9.04 | Inserting a Drop-Down List Content Control

MOS
Expert 4.1.2,
Expert 4.1.3

The ***Drop-Down List content control*** enables the person filling in the form to select a specific item from a list, which is created by the designer of the form. By providing a list, you limit the available choices and ensure acceptable responses. You will use the Drop-Down List content control to solicit information regarding company awareness and shipping options.

1 ▶ Locate the paragraph that begins *1. How did you learn about*. Click to position the insertion point to the right of the question mark, and then press Tab one time.

2 ▶ In the **Controls group**, click **Drop-Down List Content Control** 🔲. With the **Drop-Down List content control** selected, in the **Controls group**, click **Properties**.

💻 **MAC TIP** In the Legacy Controls group, click Combo Box, click Options, click in the Drop-down item box and type *Internet*, click the + button, and then move Step 4 to add additional items to the list.

---

3 ▶ In the lower portion of the **Content Control Properties** dialog box, under **Drop-Down List Properties**, click **Add**. In the **Add Choice** dialog box, click in the **Display Name** box, type **Internet** and notice that as you type, the text in the **Value** box changes to match what you type in the **Display Name** box. Compare your screen with Figure 9.8.

The Add button enables you to specify the items that will be included in the Drop-Down List content control. Each item in the list is identified by a name and a value. The display name is the text that will display to customers filling out the form when they view the list.

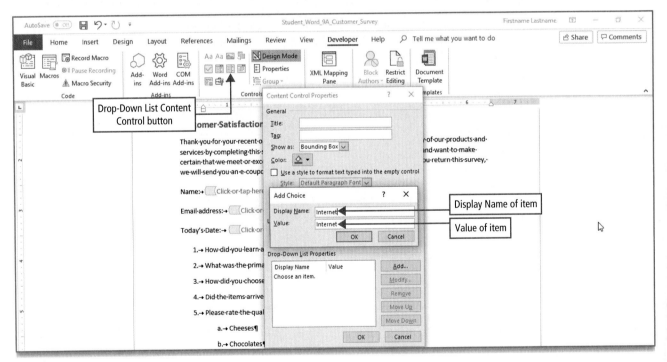

Figure 9.8

4 ▶ In the **Add Choice** dialog box, click **OK**. In the lower portion of the **Content Control Properties** dialog box, click **Add**. In the **Add Choice** dialog box, click in the **Display Name** box, type **Magazine** and then click **OK**.

5 ▶ Using the technique you just practiced, **Add** the choices **Television** and **Friend**

6 In the **Content Control Properties** dialog box, under **Drop-Down List Properties**, click **Friend**, and then click **Move Up** three times. Compare your screen with Figure 9.9.

It is helpful for the person filling out the form if the items in the list are in alphabetical order. You can use the Move Up and Move Down buttons to modify the order of the items.

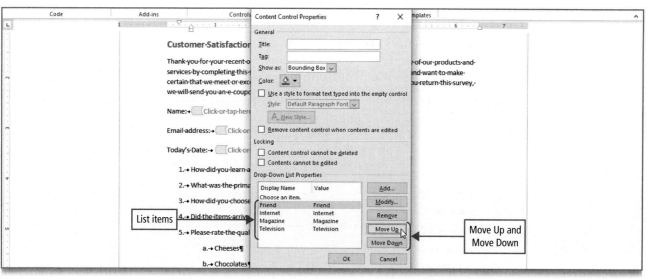

Figure 9.9

7 Click **OK**, and then on the **Developer tab**, in the **Controls group**, click **Design Mode** to turn off Design Mode. In the inserted **Drop-Down List content control**, click the **Drop-Down List arrow**, and then compare your screen with Figure 9.10.

The listed items are the various ways that a customer might have learned about the company. When Design Mode is turned off, you can view the document as it will be seen by the person filling in the form. The term *Choose an item.* displays by default.

MAC TIP *Choose an item* may not display. The first item displays.

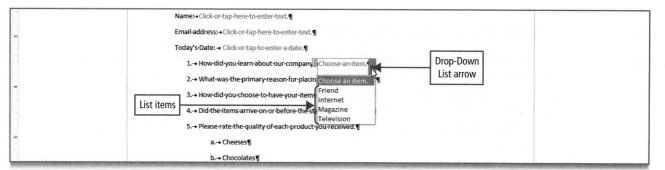

Figure 9.10

Activity 9.05 | Inserting an Additional Drop-Down List Content Control

Expert 4.1.3

1 Click anywhere in the black text to deselect the Drop-Down List content control. On the **Developer tab**, in the **Controls group**, click **Design Mode** to turn on Design Mode.

2 Locate the paragraph that begins *3. How did you choose*. Click to position the insertion point to the right of the question mark, and then press Tab one time.

3 In the **Controls group**, click **Drop-Down List Content Control** ⊞, and then in the **Controls group**, click **Properties**.

MAC TIP In the Legacy Controls group, click Combo Box, click Options, click in the Drop-down item box, and then add items as instructed below.

4 In the **Content Control Properties** dialog box, click **Add**. By using the techniques you have practiced, add three choices for this control—one each for **FedEx** and **UPS** and **USPS** and then compare your **Content Control Properties** dialog box with Figure 9.11.

The three items in the list represent the shipping providers used by Laurales Herbs and Spices.

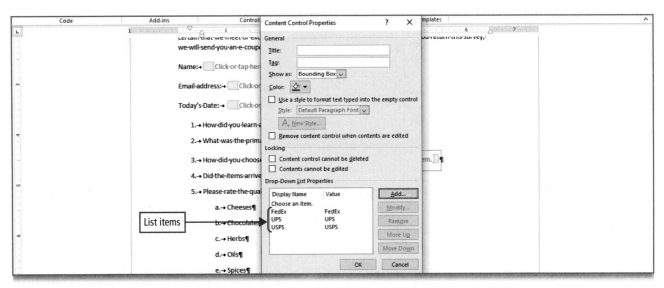

Figure 9.11

5 In the **Content Control Properties** dialog box, click **OK**, and then **Save** 🖫 your document.

Activity 9.06 | Inserting a Combo Box Content Control

A *Combo Box content control*, which is similar to a Drop-Down List content control, enables the customer filling out the form to select from an existing list and also to enter in new text. In this Activity, you will add a Combo Box content control that asks customers to indicate why they place orders with Laurales Herbs and Spices. The Combo Box will allow the customer to enter a reason that is different from the listed items. (On a Mac, the combo box only works as a way to add drop-down items.)

MOS
Expert 4.1.3

1 Locate the paragraph that begins *2. What was the primary*. Select the word **primary**, and then apply **Bold** B. On the same line, click to position the insertion point after the question mark, and then press Tab one time.

2 On the **Developer tab**, in the **Controls group**, click **Combo Box Content Control** ⊞, and then in the **Controls group**, click **Properties**.

MAC TIP In the Legacy Controls group, click Combo Box, then click Options. In the Drop-Down Form Field Options, click in the Drop-down item box, and add items as instructed.

3 In the **Content Control Properties** dialog box, under **Drop-Down List Properties**, click **Add**. In the **Add Choice** dialog box, in the **Display Name** box, type **Price** and then click **OK**.

4 In a similar manner, **Add** the choices **Quality** and **Selection**

5 In the **Content Control Properties** dialog box, under **Drop-Down List Properties**, click the default text *Choose an item.* and then click **Modify**.

6 In the **Modify Choice** dialog box, in the **Display Name** box, click to position the insertion point to the left of the period, and then press Spacebar one time. Type **or type another reason** and then click **OK**. Compare your screen with Figure 9.12.

> Recall that a Combo Box content control allows the person filling out the form to insert new text. In this instance, you want to provide the customer with the option to enter a reason that is not already listed for choosing Laurales Herbs and Spices.

MAC TIP This command may not be available.

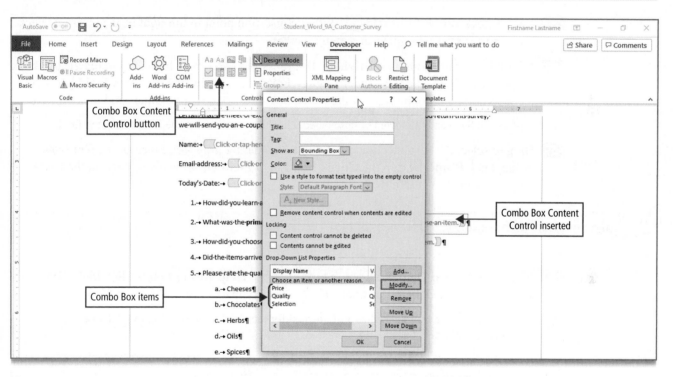

Figure 9.12

7 In the **Content Control Properties** dialog box, click **OK**, and then **Save** 🖫 your changes.

Activity 9.07 │ Inserting and Modifying a Check Box Form Field

Legacy controls are fields you use in designing a form for persons who possess older versions of Word. A *Check Box form field* is a legacy control that enables the customer to select, or not select, a specific option. For purposes of this instruction, you are adding content controls and legacy controls in the same form. In this Activity, you will add two check box form fields and then modify their properties.

1 Locate the paragraph that begins *4. Did the items arrive.* Click to position the insertion point to the right of the question mark, and then press Tab one time.

2 On the **Developer tab**, in the **Controls group**, click **Legacy Tools** 🖳▾, and then under **Legacy Forms**, point to **Check Box Form Field** ☑. Compare your screen with Figure 9.13.

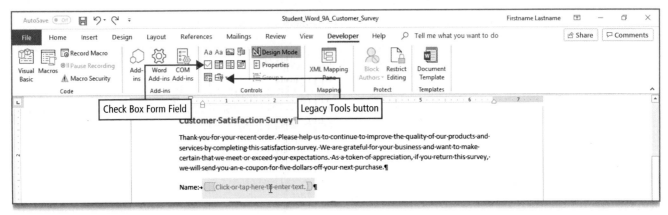

Figure 9.13

3 Click **Check Box Form Field** ☑. With the insertion point to the right of the inserted check box, press Spacebar two times, and then type **Yes**

4 With the insertion point to the right of *Yes*, press Tab two times. In the **Controls group**, click **Legacy Tools** 🖳▾, and then under **Legacy Forms**, click **Check Box Form Field** ☑. With the insertion point to the right of the check box, press Spacebar two times, and then type **No**

A check box can be selected or deselected when the person using the form clicks the field.

5 Drag to select the first check box—it will turn a darker gray—and then in the **Controls** group, click **Properties**. In the **Check Box Form Field Options** dialog box, in the lower left corner, click **Add Help Text**.

🖥 **MAC TIP** Add Help Text may not be available.

6 In the **Form Field Help Text** dialog box, click the **Help Key (F1) tab**, click in the **Type your own** box, and then type **Click here for Yes** Compare your screen with Figure 9.14.

As the customer completes the form, the text for the check box form field will display in a Help message box when the F1 key is pressed.

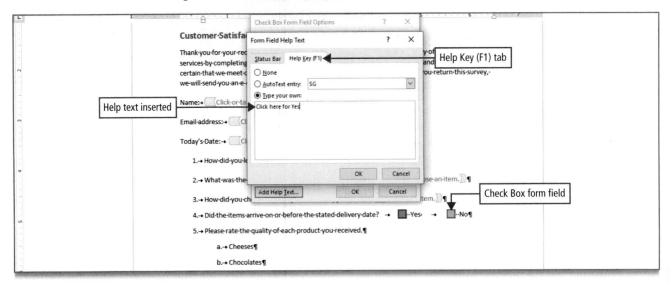

Figure 9.14

7 Click **OK** two times to close the dialog boxes. By using the technique you just practiced, select the second check box, display the **Form Field Help Text** dialog box, click the **Help Key (F1) tab**, and then type Click here for No Click **OK** two times to close the dialog boxes. **Save** 🖫 your document.

MORE KNOWLEDGE | **Deleting Form Fields and Content Controls**

To delete a form field or content control, select the field you want to remove, and then press Del.

Objective 2 | **Convert Text to a Table and Insert Content Controls in a Table**

You can select any text and convert it to a table. Typically, you will need to make some decisions about how many columns you will want in the table. If you convert paragraphs of text, your table will result in a single column, but Word offers easy-to-use options to format the text into a useful table. You can also insert content controls into a table so that your form can have multi-column choices for customers filling out your form.

Activity 9.08 | Converting Text to a Table

3.1.1

1 Select the six paragraphs formatted with lowercase letters—beginning with *a. Cheeses* and ending with *f. Vinegars*. On the **Home tab**, in the **Paragraph group**, click **Numbering** 🔢▾ to turn off the numbered format. Click the **Insert tab**, in the **Tables group**, click **Table**, and then click **Convert Text to Table**.

2 In the **Convert Text to Table** dialog box, under **Separate text at**, be sure the **Paragraphs** option button is selected. Click **OK**, and then compare your screen with Figure 9.15.

Recall that a table is a useful tool to display information in an organized format.

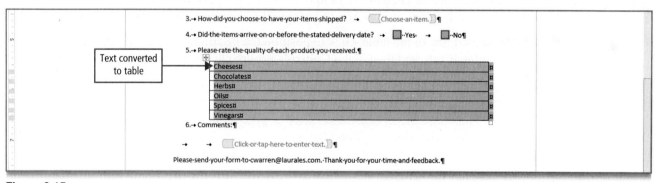

Figure 9.15

3 In the first cell of the table, click to position the insertion point to the right of *Cheeses*. Point slightly above the top right corner of the cell, and then click the **One-Click Row/Column Insertion** button ⊕ three times to insert three additional table columns.

4 Click in the first cell of the table, and then under **Table Tools**, click the **Layout tab**. In the **Rows & Columns group**, click **Insert Above** to insert a new row at the top of the table.

5 In the first row of the table, click to position the insertion point in the second cell. Type **Excellent** press Tab, type **Average** press Tab, and then type **Poor**

6 ▶ Under **Table Tools**, click the **Design tab**, in the **Table Styles group**, click **More** ⊟. In the **Table Styles** gallery, under **Grid Tables**, in the second row, click the fifth (gold) style. Click the **Table Tools Layout tab**, in the **Table group**, if necessary click **View Gridlines** to display dotted gridlines around the table.

7 ▶ On the **Table Tools Layout tab**, in the **Table group**, click **Select**, and then click **Select Table** to select the entire table. In the **Cell Size group**, in the **Height** box, type **0.2** In the **Cell Size group**, in the **Width** box, type **1** and then press ⏎.

8 ▶ In the **Table group**, click **Properties**. In the **Table Properties** dialog box, on the **Table tab**, under **Alignment**, click **Center**. Click **OK**, click outside of the table to deselect the table, and then compare your screen with Figure 9.16.

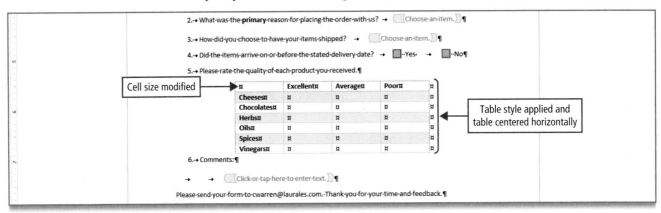

Figure 9.16

9 ▶ **Save** 🖫 your document.

Activity 9.09 | Inserting a Check Box Content Control

MOS
Expert 4.1.3

A **Check Box content control** is a field that enables the person filling in the form to select, or not select, a specific option. In this Activity, you will add several check boxes to the form.

1 ▶ In the second row of the table, click to position the insertion point in the second cell. Click the **Developer tab**, and then in the **Controls group**, click **Check Box Content Control** ☑. Compare your screen with Figure 9.17.

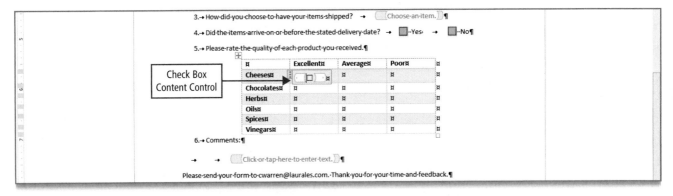

Figure 9.17

2 ▶ In the current cell, with the insertion point blinking to the left of the check box, on the content control, click **Select Field** ⦂ to select the **Check Box content control**. On the **Home tab**, in the **Clipboard group**, click **Copy**.

🖳 **MAC TIP** Drag to select.

---

3 ▶ In the second row, click in the third cell, and then press Ctrl+V to paste the Check Box content control in the cell. Press Tab, and then press Ctrl+V to paste the Check Box content control.

> You can copy and paste content controls in the same manner as text and graphics.

4 ▶ In a similar manner, paste the **Check Box Content Control** in the remaining empty cells of the table.

5 ▶ Point slightly above the second column of the table to display the ↓ pointer, and then drag to the right to select the second, third, and fourth columns of the table. On the **Table Tools Layout tab**, in the **Alignment group**, click **Align Center** 📄. Click outside of the table to deselect it, and then compare your screen with Figure 9.18. **Save** 🖫 your document.

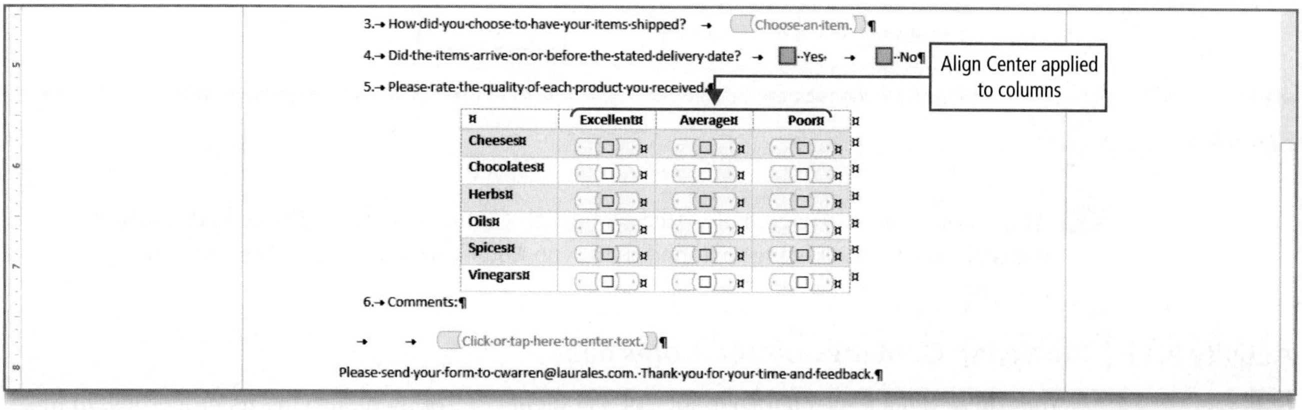

Figure 9.18

MORE KNOWLEDGE | **Inserting Other Controls**

The Picture content control enables you to insert an image—for example, a photo for identification. Use the Building Block Gallery content control to insert a building block in a content control—which enables you to add specific text. The Repeat Section content control contains other controls and repeats the contents as needed.

Objective 3 | **Modify and Protect a Form**

You can manage the information provided by the person filling in the form by modifying the properties of content controls. In addition, when a form is distributed, you can protect it so that the static text and content controls cannot be edited or removed by the person filling out the form.

Activity 9.10 | **Editing Text in a Content Control**

You can customize the placeholder text that displays in content controls.

1 ▶ Locate the paragraph that begins *Name*, and then in the same paragraph, click anywhere in the text *Click or tap here to enter text* to select the **Plain Text content control** that you inserted earlier.

2 In the **Plain Text content control**, select the existing text *Click or tap here to enter text.* and then type **Enter your first and last name.**

3 To the right of the text *Email address*, in the **Plain Text content control**, select the existing text, and then type **Enter your email address.** Click in a blank area of the document to deselect the content control, and then compare your screen with Figure 9.19.

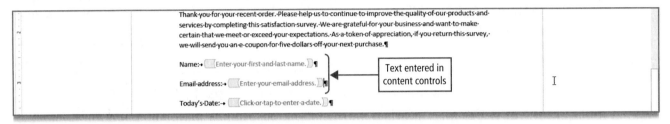

Figure 9.19

4 At the bottom of the page, below the paragraph *Comments*, in the **Plain Text content control**, select the existing text, and then type **Enter your comments. Save** 🖫 your document.

Activity 9.11 | Modifying Content Control Properties

You can designate the characteristics of a content control by modifying its properties. In this Activity, you will assign a title and style to plain text content controls.

1 In the paragraph that begins *Name*, click anywhere inside the **Plain Text content control** to select it.

2 Click the **Developer tab**, and then in the **Controls group**, click **Properties**.

3 In the **Content Control Properties** dialog box, in the **Title** box, type **Name**

Assigning a title that displays on the content control makes it easier to identify it.

4 In the **Content Control Properties** dialog box, under **General**, select the **Use a style to format text typed into the empty control** check box. Click the **Style arrow**, and then click **Strong**. Compare your screen with Figure 9.20.

Styles for a content control work in the same manner as other text in a document. In addition to the displayed styles, you can create a new style. In this instance, when the customer types his or her name, the text will be formatted with the Strong style.

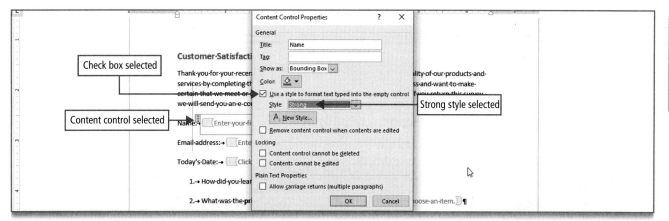

Figure 9.20

5 Click **OK**. Notice that the title *Name* displays on the Plain Text content control.

6 Click anywhere inside the **Plain Text content control** for *Email* to select it.

7 In the **Controls group**, click **Properties**. In the **Content Control Properties** dialog box, in the **Title** box, type **Email Address** and then under **General**, click to select the **Use a style to format text typed into the empty control** check box. Click the **Style arrow**, click **Strong**, and then click **OK**.

8 At the bottom of the page, above the last paragraph of the document, click inside the **Plain Text content control** for *Comments* to select it.

9 In the **Controls group**, click **Properties**. In the **Content Control Properties** dialog box, in the **Title** box, type **Comments** and then under **General**, click to select the **Use a style to format text typed into the empty control** check box. Click the **Style arrow**, click **Quote**, and then click **OK**.

The customer's comments will be formatted with the Quote style.

10 **Save** 🖫 your document.

Activity 9.12 | Restricting Editing and Using a Password to Protect a Form

Expert 1.2.1,
Expert 1.2.2

The purpose of providing a form is to have individuals enter data only in the content controls you have created without editing other text or modifying any formats in the form document. To do so, Word enables you to protect the form to restrict the entry of data only into the control fields you have created. In this Activity, you will apply restrictions and add a password to safeguard the form.

1 Press Ctrl + Home to move to the top of your form. On the **Developer tab**, in the **Controls group**, click **Design Mode** to turn off Design Mode.

When you finish designing a form, you must turn off Design Mode before you can restrict the form and distribute the form for use.

2 On the **Developer tab**, in the **Protect group**, click **Restrict Editing** to display the **Restrict Editing** pane.

By restricting the formatting and editing, you can control the changes the person filling out the form can make in the form. Item 1, if selected, restricts formatting changes. Item 2 defines how the document can be edited.

MAC TIP Click Protect Form; no pane displays.

3 In the **Restrict Editing** pane, under **2. Editing restrictions**, click to select the **Allow only this type of editing in the document** check box.

4 Click the **Allow only this type of editing in the document arrow**, and then click **Filling in forms**. Compare your screen with Figure 9.21.

This option restricts the use of the document so that the person filling in the form can only fill in the content controls in the document.

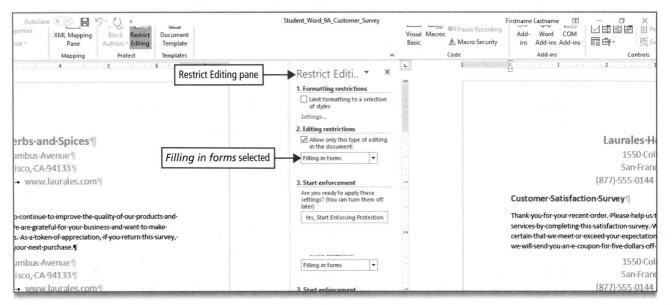

Figure 9.21

5 In the **Restrict Editing** pane, under **3. Start enforcement**, click **Yes, Start Enforcing Protection**.

Before you begin enforcing protection, you should always confirm that all elements of the document display correctly.

6 In the **Start Enforcing Protection** dialog box, in the **Enter new password (optional)** box, type **survey15** Notice that as you type, the characters are replaced with bullets.

A *password* is a code to gain access to a file—in this instance, the customer survey document.

7 In the **Reenter password to confirm** box, type **survey15** and then compare your screen with Figure 9.22.

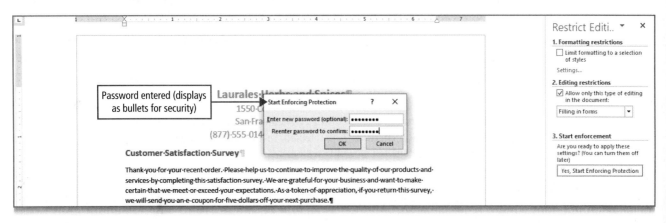

Figure 9.22

8 Click **OK** and notice that the first content control is selected.

> By restricting the editing to filling in forms, only the content controls are accessible in the document.

9 In the **Restrict Editing** pane, at the bottom, click **Stop Protection**. Click in the **Password** box, and type the password **survey15** and click **OK**.

> For this instruction, you will not use a password on the form.

10 **Close** ⊠ the **Restrict Editing** pane, which still has editing restrictions set to *Filling in forms*. Click at the top of the document title to deselect the *Name* control, and then **Save** 🖫 your document.

MORE KNOWLEDGE | **Adding a Password to Any Document**

You can add a password to any document to prevent unauthorized persons from making changes. At the bottom of the Save As dialog box, click Tools, and then click General Options. In the General Options dialog box, in the Password to open or Password to modify box, type a password. Click OK to close the General Options dialog box. In the Confirm Password dialog box, type the password again, and then click OK. Save the document.

Objective 4 | **Complete a Form**

After the form is protected, it can be distributed to others by sending it as an email attachment, and then the recipient can complete the form in Word. Typically, you create a form and then save it as a ***template*** so that it can be used repeatedly without changing the original document. A template is a predefined structure that contains basic document settings, such as fonts, margins, and available styles, and can also store elements such as building blocks and content controls.

Activity 9.13 | **Completing a Form**

In this Activity, you will complete the customer satisfaction survey. In actual use, be sure to save your form as a template so that it can reused.

1 In the paragraph that begins *Name*, click in the **Plain Text content control**, and then using your own name, type **Firstname Lastname** and then compare your screen with Figure 9.23.

> Your name is formatted with the Strong style—the style you selected in the Content Control Properties dialog box.

Figure 9.23

2 ▶ Press [Tab], and then in the paragraph that begins *Email address*, in the **Plain Text content control**, using your own last name, type **Lastname@laurales.com**

> Because the form is protected—only filling in information is allowed—you can move from one content control to the next by pressing [Tab].

3 ▶ Press [Tab], click the **Date Picker content control arrow** to display the calendar, and then at the bottom of the calendar, click **Today**.

> The date displays with the format you selected in the Content Control Properties dialog box. In the Date Picker content control, you can navigate in the calendar to select any date.

MAC TIP   Enter today's date.

---

4 ▶ Press [Tab]. To the right of the paragraph that begins with *1*, click the **Drop-Down List content control arrow**, and then click **Friend**.

5 ▶ Press [Tab]. To the right of the paragraph that begins *2*, click the **Combo Box content control arrow**, click **Choose an item or type another reason.** and then type **Excellent service!**

> Recall that you modified the default text in the list to read *Choose an item or type another reason.* The user of the form can type a response that differs from the listed items.

6 ▶ Press [Tab]. To the right of the paragraph that begins *3*, click the **Drop-Down List content control arrow**, and then click **UPS**.

7 ▶ In the table, in the **Cheeses** row, in the **Average** column, click the check box. In the **Herbs** row, in the **Excellent** column, click the check box. In the **Spices** row, in the **Excellent** column, click the check box.

8 ▶ Below the paragraph that begins *6. Comments*, click the **Plain Text content control** that indicates *Enter your comments* and then type **I am eager to try your vinegars.** Click in a blank area of the document to deselect the content control, and then compare your screen with Figure 9.24.

> The text is formatted with the Quote style—the style you selected in the Content Control Properties dialog box.

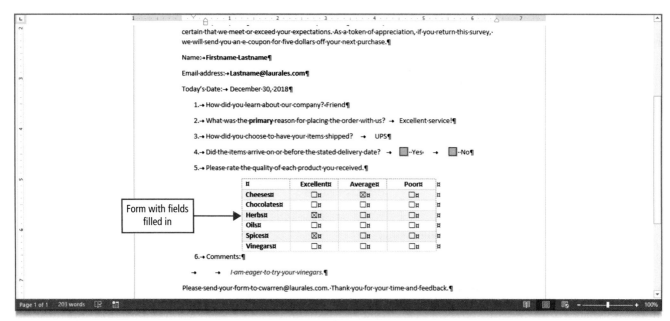

Figure 9.24

Activity 9.14 | Removing the Developer Tab from the Ribbon

1 Press Ctrl + Home, and then insert the **File Name** in the footer.

2 Click the **File tab**, and then click **Show All Properties**. In the **Tags** box, type **customer survey, tested** In the **Subject** box, type your course name and section number. If necessary, edit the author name to display your name. On the left, click **Save** to save your document and return to the Word window.

3 Click the **File tab**, on the left click **Options**. In the **Word Options** dialog box, on the left click **Customize Ribbon**. In the **Main Tabs** list, locate and then click to clear the **Developer** check box. Click **OK** and notice that the Developer tab no longer displays on the ribbon.

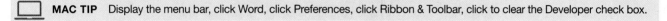 **MAC TIP**   Display the menu bar, click Word, click Preferences, click Ribbon & Toolbar, click to clear the Developer check box.

4 In the upper right corner of the Word window, click **Close** ✕.

For Non-MyLab Submissions Determine What Your Instructor Requires for Submission
As directed by your instructor, submit your completed Word document.

5 In **MyLab IT**, locate and click the Grader Project **Word 9A Customer Survey**. In **step 3**, under **Upload Completed Assignment**, click **Choose File**. In the **Open** dialog box, navigate to your **Word Chapter 9 folder**, and then click your **Student_Word_9A_ Customer_Survey** file one time to select it. In the lower right corner of the **Open** dialog box, click **Open**.

The name of your selected file displays above the Upload button.

6 To submit your file to **MyLab IT** for grading, click **Upload**, wait a moment for a green **Success!** message, and then in **step 4**, click the blue **Submit for Grading** button. Click **Close Assignment** to return to your list of **Course Materials**.

You have completed Project 9A   END

Moving Agreement

Project Activities

In Activities 9.15 through 9.22, you will create a document pertaining to an upcoming office move. Laurales Herbs and Spices is relocating its administrative offices. To help ensure that no items are lost or damaged, Rachel Enders, who is in charge of the move, has asked each employee to sign an agreement indicating that everything has been properly packed, labeled, and is ready to be moved. You will customize the ribbon to increase your efficiency in creating the agreement and insert a signature line. Your completed document will look similar to Figure 9.25.

Project Files for MyLab IT Grader

1. In your **MyLab IT** course, locate and click **Word 9B Moving Agreement**, Download Materials, and then Download All Files.
2. Extract the zipped folder to your Word Chapter 9 folder. Close the Grader download screens.
3. Take a moment to open the downloaded **Word_9B_Moving_Agreement_Instructions**; note any recent updates to the book.

Project Results

GO! Project 9B
Where We're Going

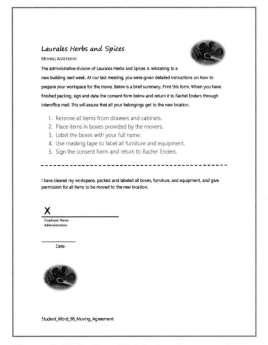

Figure 9.25 Project 9B Moving Agreement

For Non-MyLab Submissions

For Project 9B, you will need:
w09B_Moving_Agreement
w09B_Logo_Photo

In your Word Chapter 9 folder, save your document as:
Lastname_Firstname_9B_Moving_Agreement

After you have named and saved your document on the next page, begin with Step 2.
There are two Optional Activities at the end of this Project. If assigned to you, you will need two additional files:
w09B_Paid_Time_Off_optional
w09B_Language_optional

Objective 5 Create a Custom Ribbon Tab

ALERT   Because Office 365 is a cloud-based subscription service that receives continuous updates, you may encounter some variations in what appears on your screen and what is shown in this instruction. Microsoft Office 365 is fully installed on your PC or Mac; no internet access is necessary to create or edit documents. When you *are* connected to the Internet, you will receive monthly upgrades and new features, so you always have the latest versions of Office apps as soon as they are available. Your subscription gives you continuous free access to the latest innovations and refinements.

The ribbon consists of tabs, and each tab contains groups of related commands. You can personalize Word and improve your efficiency by adding commands that you use frequently to an existing tab or by creating a new custom tab.

Activity 9.15 | Creating a Custom Ribbon Tab

MAC TIP   Although MAC TIPS are included where possible, this project is best suited for a Windows-based PC. Some commands in this project are not available on a Mac.

1 Navigate to your **Word Chapter 9 folder**, and then double-click the Word file you downloaded from **MyLab IT** that displays your name—**Student_Word_9B_Moving_Agreement**. If necessary, at the top click **Enable Editing**.

2 Select the paragraph *Moving Agreement*, and then on the **Home tab**, in the **Font group**, click the **Dialog Box Launcher** ⌐ to display the **Font** dialog box.

MAC TIP   Right-click the selected paragraph, click Font to open Dialog Box Launcher.

3 On the **Font tab**, under **Font style**, click **Bold**. Under **Effects**, select the **Small caps** check box. Click **OK**.

4 ▶ Click the **File tab**, and then click **Options**. In the **Word Options** dialog box, on the left click **Customize Ribbon**, and then compare your screen with Figure 9.26.

The Customize Ribbon tab of the Word Options dialog box displays a list of Popular Commands on the left and a list of Main Tabs on the right. Under Main Tabs, recall that the check marks to the left of tab names indicate tabs that are currently available on the ribbon. You can expand or collapse the view of tabs and groups by clicking ⊞ or ⊟ respectively. By default, Home is selected and expanded to display the groups on the Home tab.

🖥 **MAC TIP**   Display the Word menu, click Word, click Preferences, click Ribbon & Toolbar, click the + button, click New Tab.

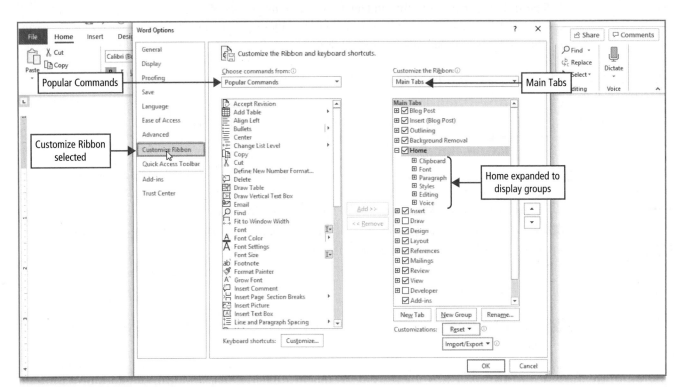

Figure 9.26

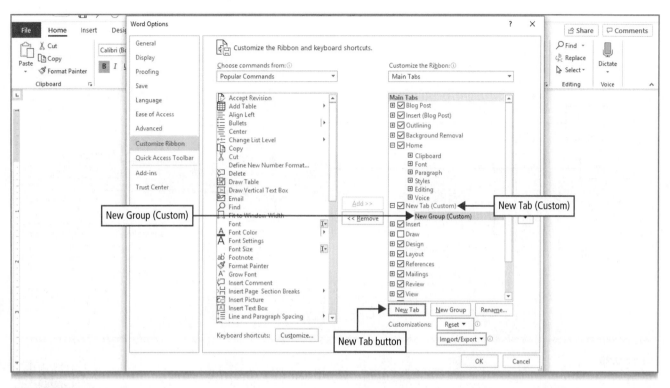

5 In the **Word Options** dialog box, on the right below the **Main Tabs** list, with **Home** selected, in the lower right corner, click **New Tab**, and then compare your screen with Figure 9.27.

In the Main Tabs list, *New Tab (Custom)* displays in expanded view with *New Group (Custom)* indented and selected.

Figure 9.27

6 Click **New Tab (Custom)** to select it, and then in the lower right corner of the **Word Options** dialog box, click **Rename**. In the **Rename** dialog box, in the **Display name** box, type **My Commands** and then click **OK**.

☐ **MAC TIP** Click the Settings symbol, then click Rename.

7 Click **New Group (Custom)** to select it, and then at the bottom right of the **Word Options** dialog box, click **Rename**. In the **Rename** dialog box, in the **Display name** box, type **Common Tasks** and then click **OK**. Leave the **Word Options** dialog box open for the next Activity.

☐ **MAC TIP** Click the Settings symbol, then click Rename.

Activity 9.16 │ Adding Commands to a Ribbon Tab

Commands are arranged within groups on a tab. You can add any command directly to a tab, but it is good practice to add related commands to a group.

1 In the **Word Options** dialog box, near the top on the left, locate the **Choose commands from** box, and notice that *Popular Commands* displays.

2 In the list under **Popular Commands**, scroll as necessary, click **Print Preview and Print**, and then to the right of the list, click **Add**. In the **Main Tabs** list, notice that **Print Preview and Print** displays below the **Common Tasks (Custom)** group you created. Compare your screen with Figure 9.28.

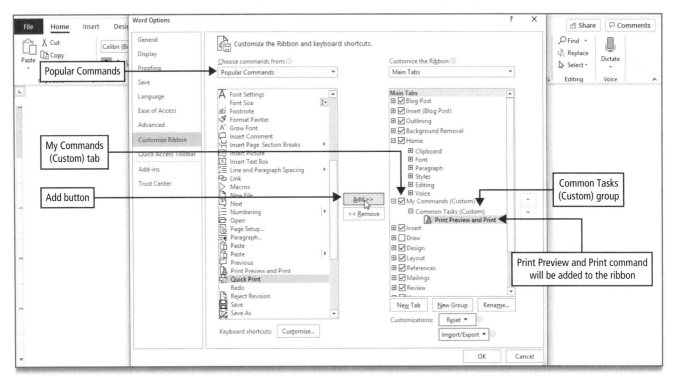

Figure 9.28

3 In the **Word Options** dialog box, click the **Choose commands from arrow**, and then click **All Commands**.

In the *Choose commands from* box, you can select a different group of available commands.

4 Under **All Commands**, scroll as necessary, click **Edit Footer**, and then click **Add**. In the **Main Tabs** list, notice that in the **Common Tasks (Custom)** group, **Edit Footer** displays below **Print Preview and Print**.

5 Click the **Choose commands from arrow**, and then click **File tab**.

6 In the **File tab** list, click **Close File**, and then click **Add**.

The Close command closes a document and keeps Word open.

7 In the **Main Tabs** list, with **Close File** selected, to the right of the **Main Tabs** list, click **Move Up** ▲ two times. Click **Edit Footer**, click **Move Up** ▲ one time, and then compare your screen with Figure 9.29.

The commands are displayed in alphabetical order. You can use the Move Up and Move Down buttons to arrange tabs, groups, and commands in any order.

MAC TIP Add Quick Print instead of Print Preview & Print. Add the Close button from All commands, then click and drag to reposition the buttons.

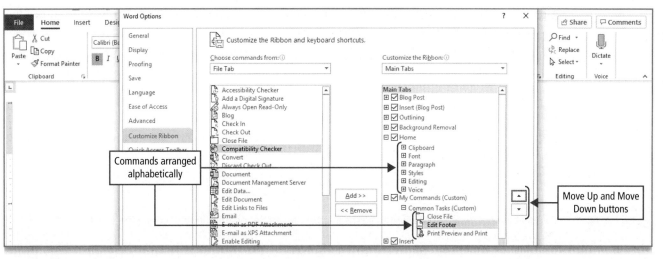

Figure 9.29

8 ▶ In the lower right corner, click **OK** to close the **Word Options** dialog box, and notice that your custom tab *My Commands* displays to the right of the **Home tab** on the ribbon.

9 ▶ Click the **My Commands tab**, and then notice that the **Common Tasks group** displays on the left and includes the three commands you added.

10 ▶ On the **My Commands tab**, in the **Common Tasks group**, click **Edit Footer**. In the **Insert group**, click **Document Info**, and then click **File Name** to insert the file name in the footer. **Close** the footer area.

11 ▶ If necessary, select the paragraph *Moving Agreement*, and then change the **Font Color** ▣ ▾—in the last column (green colors), click the last color.

12 ▶ **Save** ▣ your document.

Objective 6   Create Style, Color, and Font Sets

You can create custom elements for your documents, and this is commonly done in large organizations where every document must have the same look and feel. For example, if you visit the website for Microsoft or for Apple or for Google, you will notice that every page presents a similar style of fonts, colors, and layouts. This visual consistency demonstrates how a company wants to present itself to the public.

Think about the various publications at your college—the college catalog, the course schedule, the website pages, news releases. You will probably notice that your college attempts to use similar fonts, colors—for example the school colors—and layouts for its publications.

Activity 9.17 | Creating a Custom Font Set

Expert 3.2.2

1 ▶ Click anywhere to deselect the subtitle. On the **Design tab**, in the **Document Formatting group**, click **Fonts**, and then at the bottom, click **Customize Fonts**.

2 In the **Create New Theme Fonts** dialog box, click the **Heading font arrow**, scroll down the alphabetic list, and then click **Segoe Print**.

Segoe, typically pronounced SEE-goh, is a family of fonts that Microsoft uses for its online and printed materials. In August of 2012, Microsoft updated its corporate logo for the first time in 25 years with a new logo using one of the Segoe fonts.

3 Click the **Body font arrow**, scroll down as necessary, and then click **Segoe UI Semilight**.

4 In the **Name** box, select the existing text, type **Laurales 9B** and then compare your screen with Figure 9.30.

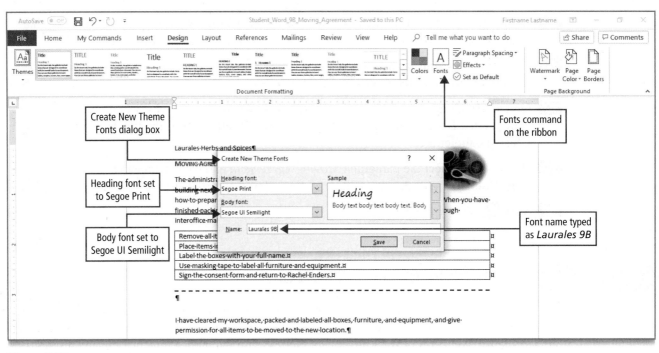

Figure 9.30

5 At the bottom of the **Create New Theme Fonts** dialog box, click **Save**, and notice that the Body font—Segoe UI Semilight—is applied to the body text.

6 Select the paragraph *Laurales Herbs and Spices*, and then on the **Home tab**, in the **Font group**, click the **Font Color arrow**. Under **Theme Colors** in the fifth column, click the first color (blue color).

7 With the paragraph still selected, in the **Styles group**, click the **More** button ⏷, and then click **Heading 1**. Click anywhere in the document to deselect the title, and then compare your screen with Figure 9.31.

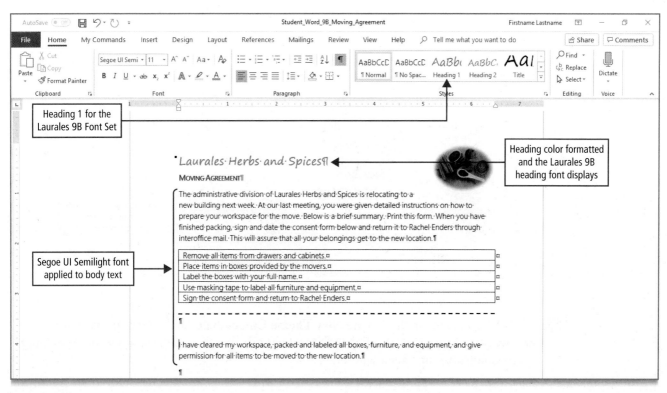

Heading 1 for the Laurales 9B Font Set

Heading color formatted and the Laurales 9B heading font displays

Segoe UI Semilight font applied to body text

Figure 9.31

MORE KNOWLEDGE **Deleting a Custom Font Set**

To delete a custom font set, on the Design tab, in the Document Formatting group, click Fonts, point to the font set name, right-click, click Delete, and then click Yes.

Activity 9.18 | Creating a Custom Color Set

MOS
Expert 3.2.1

1 On the **Design tab**, in the **Document Formatting group**, click **Colors**, and then at the bottom, click **Customize Colors**.

MAC TIP Select the text *Laurales Herbs and Spices*. Display the Font color gallery, click More Colors, click Color Palettes. By using the arrow, find and click Web Safe Colors. In the Search box type *003300* and select the color, click OK. Select *MOVING AGREEMENT* and apply Web Safe Color 660000. Move to Activity 9.19.

2 In the **Create New Theme Colors** dialog box, click the **Accent 1 arrow**. Below the color palette, click **More Colors**, in the **Colors** dialog box, click the **Standard tab**, and then in the seventh (widest) row, click the first color. Compare your screen with Figure 9.32.

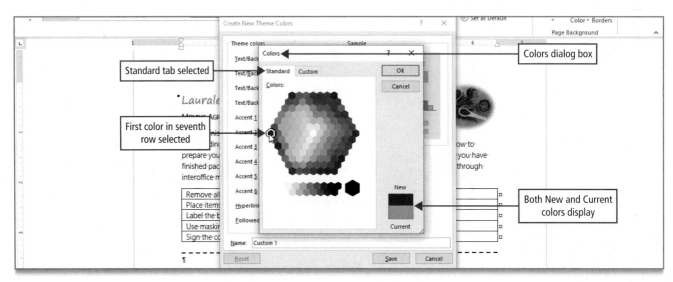

Figure 9.32

3 Click **OK**, and then in the **Create New Theme Colors** dialog box, click the **Accent 6 arrow**. Click **More Colors**, click the **Standard tab**, and then in the last row, click the third color. Compare your screen with Figure 9.33.

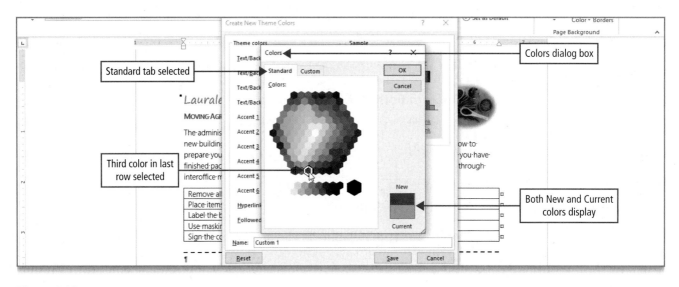

Figure 9.33

4 Click **OK**, and then at the bottom of the dialog box, in the **Name** box, type **Laurales 9B** Click **Save**. Notice the change in color for the title *Laurales Herbs and Spices* and the heading *Moving Agreement*. Compare your screen with Figure 9.34.

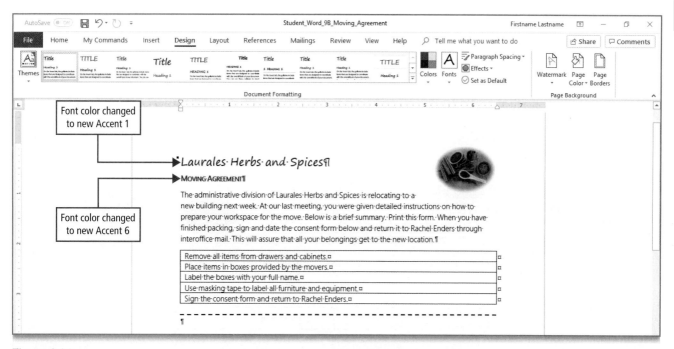

Figure 9.34

MORE KNOWLEDGE | **Deleting a Custom Color Set**

To delete a custom color set, on the Design tab, in the Document Formatting group, click Colors, point to the color set name, right-click, click Delete, and then click Yes.

Activity 9.19 | Creating a Custom Style Set

MOS

1.2.2,
Expert 3.2.4

A *style set* is a group of settings for the Font and Paragraph properties of your document. In this Activity, you will create a style set that uses line spacing of 1.5 lines.

1 On the **Home tab**, in the **Paragraph group**, click **Line and Paragraph Spacing** ⌄, and then click **1.5**.

The line spacing for the paragraphs changes to 1.5. By default, the line spacing within a table is single spacing.

2 On the **Design tab**, in the **Document Formatting group**, click the **More** button ⊡, and then compare your screen with Figure 9.35.

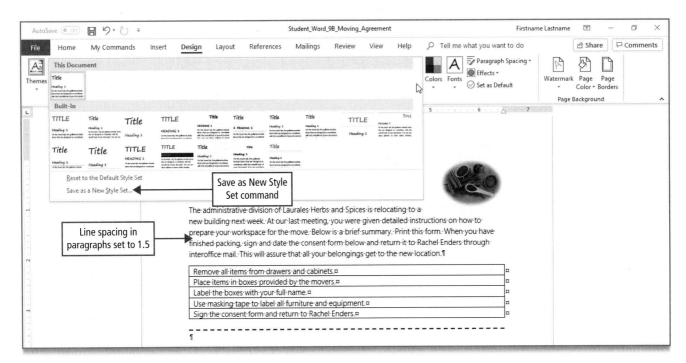

Figure 9.35

3 At the bottom of the gallery, click **Save as a New Style Set**, and then in the **File name** box, type **Laurales 9B**

For each user, style sets are stored in the username area of the C drive on the computer.

4 Click **Save** to save the style and close the dialog box. On the **Design tab**, in the **Document Formatting group**, click the **More** button, and then under **Custom**, point to the first style. Compare your screen with Figure 9.36.

> So long as you are using this computer with the same signed-on user, this Style Set will be available to you.

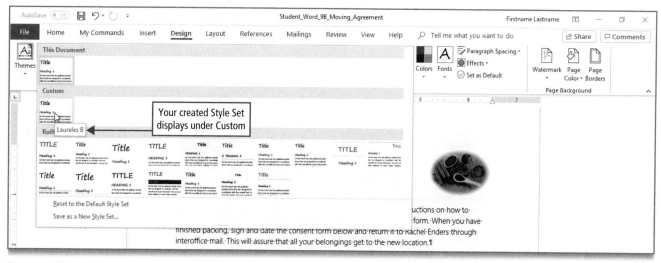

Figure 9.36

5 Click in a blank area of the document to close the gallery without making any selections, and then **Save** your document.

> **MORE KNOWLEDGE** | **Deleting a Custom Style Set**
>
> To delete a custom style set, on the Design tab, in the Document Formatting group, click the More button. Under Custom, point to the custom style, right-click, click Delete, and then click Yes.

Objective 7 | Convert a Table to Text

You can convert a Word table to text if you decide a table is not an appropriate format for the information. For example, a table with only one column might be easier to read if formatted as text.

Activity 9.20 | Converting a Table to Text

3.1.2

1 Click anywhere in the table. On the **Table Tools Layout tab**, in the **Data group**, click **Convert to Text**.

2 In the **Convert Table to Text** dialog box, under **Separate text with**, if necessary, click the **Paragraph marks** option button, and then compare your screen with Figure 9.37.

You can choose how the content of the table cells will be separated—by paragraph marks, tabs, commas, or any other single character.

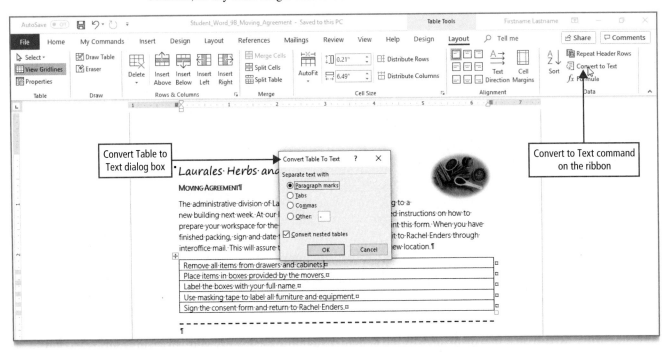

Figure 9.37

3 In the **Convert Table to Text** dialog box, click **OK**. Notice that the table is replaced with five paragraphs.

4 With all five paragraphs selected, on the **Home tab**, in the **Font group**, change the **Font Size** 11 to 14, apply **Bold** B, and then change the **Font Color** A —in the eighth column (gold colors) click the last color.

5 On the **Home tab**, in the **Paragraph group**, click **Numbering**. Press Ctrl + Home, and then compare your screen with Figure 9.38.

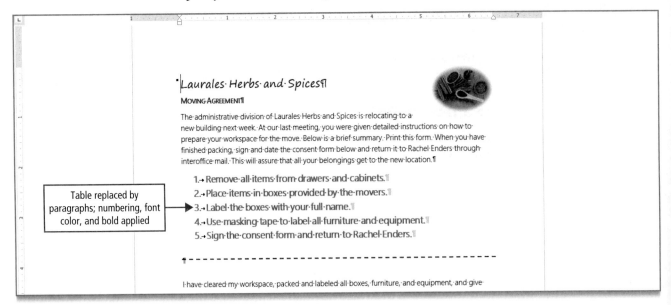

Figure 9.38

6 **Save** your document.

Objective 8 Prepare a Document for Review and Distribution

Activity 9.21 | Managing Document Versions and Inserting a Signature Line

MOS
Expert 1.1.2

AutoRecover, if turned on, automatically saves versions of your file while you are working on it, and also helps to recover unsaved documents. The AutoRecover option in Word helps you protect your files in case your computer hardware fails or if you accidentally close a file without saving.

A *signature line* is an element you can add to a document that specifies who should sign the document. In this Activity, you will add a signature line indicating that an employee signature is required to confirm that items are ready to be moved.

1 Click the **File tab**, on the left click **Options**, and then in the **Word Options** dialog box, on the left, click **Save**.

⌨ **MAC TIP** To set the AutoRecover option, on the menu bar, click Word, click Preferences, under Output and Sharing click Save.

2 Be sure the **Save AutoRecover information every** box is selected—the default is 10 minutes. Also, be sure the **Keep the last AutoRecovered version if I close without saving** box is selected.

With these two check boxes selected, you will never lose more than 10 minutes of work, and if you accidently close a file without saving your latest changes, you can recover the last autosaved version.

3 By clicking the down spin box arrow, change the number of minutes to **1**, and then compare your screen with Figure 9.39.

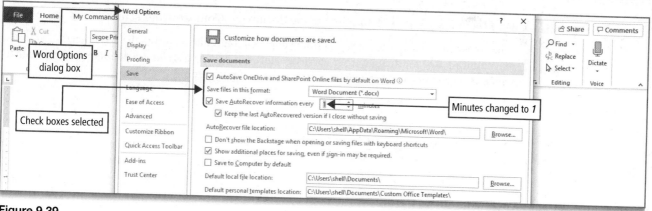

Figure 9.39

4 In the lower right corner, click **OK** to close the **Word Options** dialog box.

5 In your document, below the paragraph that begins *I have cleared*, click to position the insertion point in the empty paragraph.

⌨ **MAC TIP** In the empty paragraph, type *Employee Name* and press ENTER and then type *Administration* and then move to Step 9.

6 ▶ Click the **Insert tab**. In the **Text group**, click the **Signature Line button arrow**, and then click **Microsoft Office Signature Line**.

7 ▶ In the **Signature Setup** dialog box, in the **Suggested signer** box, type **Employee Name** In the **Suggested signer's title** box, type **Administration** and then compare your screen with Figure 9.40.

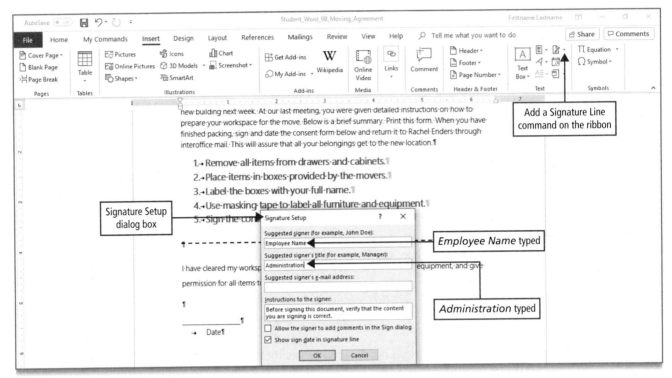

Figure 9.40

8 ▶ Click **OK** to insert the signature line in the document. Compare your screen with Figure 9.41.

The signer can sign a hard copy—a printed copy. Or, the signer can sign the document electronically by inserting an image of a signature or by using a *stylus*—a pen-like device—with a *tablet PC*—a computer that enables you to write on the screen.

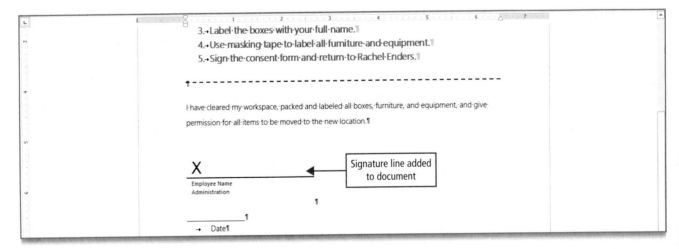

Figure 9.41

9 Click the **File tab**, on the left be sure that **Info** is selected, and then to the right, under **Info**, click **Manage Document**. Compare your screen with Figure 9.42.

Here you can recover unsaved documents, or open a version of the document that has been saved in the last minute. In the Figure, several minutes have elapsed so there are several versions—yours may differ.

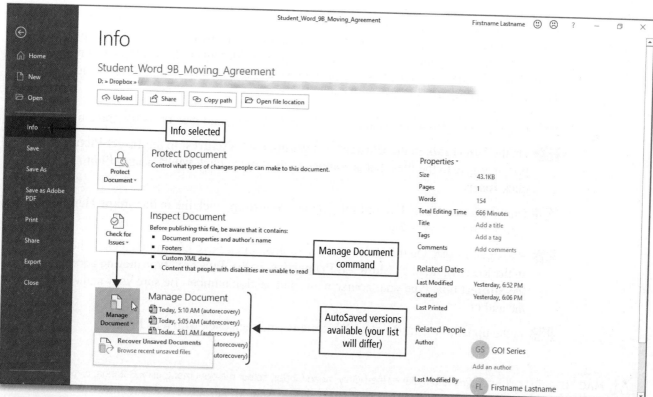

Figure 9.42

10 In the upper left, click **Back** ⬅, and then click **Save** 💾.

11 Click the **File tab**, on the left click **Options**, and then in the **Word Options** dialog box, on the left, click **Save**.

12 In the Save AutoRecover information every box, set the minutes back to the default of **10** minutes. Also, be sure the **Keep the last autosaved version if I close without saving** box is selected.

13 In the lower right corner, click **OK**.

ALERT   **Do you see a banner below the ribbon?**

If you open a file that contains a signature line, but the document has not been digitally signed, you may see a banner below the ribbon stating that the document needs to be signed. For purposes of this instruction, you can ignore such a banner.

Activity 9.22 | Marking a Document as Final

Expert 1.2.2

After all changes have been made, a document can be identified as a final version—making it a *read-only file*. A read-only file can be viewed but not changed.

The Mark as Final command is not a security feature; anyone can remove the Mark as Final status from the document and edit it. However, marking a document as final lets people with whom you are sharing the document know that you consider this to be a complete version of the document. Marking a document as final also prevents others from making inadvertent changes if they are just reading the document on their screen.

1 Press Ctrl + End to move to the end of your document, and then press Enter three times.

2 On the **Insert tab**, in the **Illustrations group**, click **Pictures**. In the **Insert Picture** dialog box, navigate to the files that accompany this Project, click **w09B_Logo_Photo**, and then click **Insert**.

3 On the **Picture Tools Format tab**, in the **Size group**, click the in the **Shape Height** box, type **1** and then press Enter.

4 Press Ctrl + Home. On the Quick Access Toolbar, click **Save** 🖫, and then click the **File tab**. In the lower right, click **Show All Properties**. In the **Tags** box, type **moving agreement** In the **Subject** box, type your course name and section number. Be sure your name displays as the author.

5 In the upper left, click **Protect Document**, and then click **Mark as Final**.

MAC TIP To Lock a document to make it Read-Only, open Finder, select the document, click Settings, click Get Info, under General, select the Locked check box.

6 In the **Microsoft Word** dialog box, click **OK** to confirm that the document will be marked as final.

7 In the **Microsoft Word** message box indicating that the document has been marked as final, click **OK**. Compare your screen with Figure 9.43.

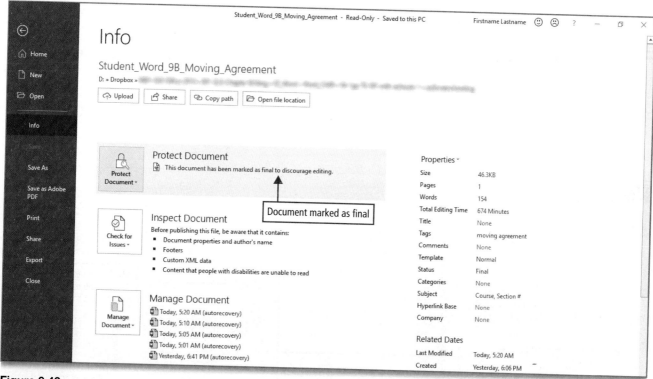

Figure 9.43

8 In the upper left corner, click **Back** ⊖, and then compare your screen with Figure 9.44.

The title bar indicates that this is a read-only file. A MARKED AS FINAL banner displays above the document, the commands on the ribbon are hidden, and a Marked as Final icon displays on the status bar. The viewer will be able to read the document but not make any changes.

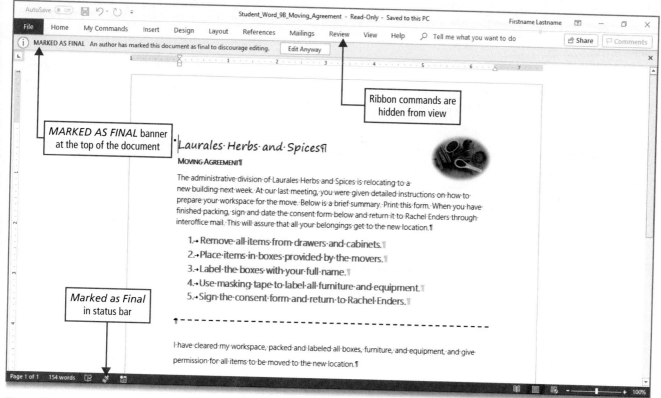

Figure 9.44

9 Click the **Home tab** to display the commands. Notice that most of the buttons on the ribbon are unavailable—dimmed.

10 Click the **My Commands tab**, and then in the **Common Tasks group**, click **Close** to close your document.

11 Point to the **My Commands tab**, right-click, and then click **Customize the Ribbon**. In the **Word Options** dialog box, in the **Main Tabs** list, right-click **My Commands (Custom)** as shown in Figure 9.45.

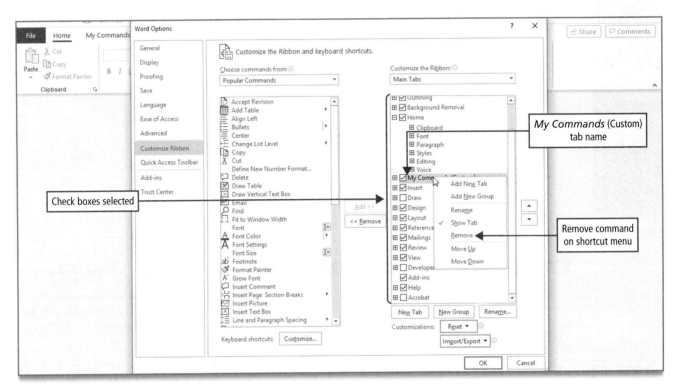

Figure 9.45

12 On the shortcut menu, click **Remove**. Click **OK** to close the dialog box, and notice that your custom tab no longer displays on the ribbon.

MAC TIP Display the menu bar, click Word, click Preferences, click Ribbon & Toolbar to access the dialog box. Your document must be open to complete this action.

---

13 In the upper right corner of the Word window, click **Close** ✕

For Non-MyLab Submissions   Determine What Your Instructor Requires for Submission
As directed by your instructor, submit your completed Word document.

---

14 In **MyLab IT**, locate and click the Grader Project **Word 9B Moving Agreement**. In **step 3**, under **Upload Completed Assignment**, click **Choose File**. In the **Open** dialog box, navigate to your **Word Chapter 9 folder**, and then click your **Student_Word_9B_Moving_Agreement** file one time to select it. In the lower right corner of the **Open** dialog box, click **Open**.

> The name of your selected file displays above the Upload button.

15 To submit your file to **MyLab IT** for grading, click **Upload**, wait a moment for a green **Success!** message, and then in **step 4**, click the blue **Submit for Grading** button. Click **Close Assignment** to return to your list of **Course Materials**.

ALERT **Optional Activities**

The following two Activities are optional; they are not included in the 9B **MyLab IT** Grader project. Complete these Activities if they are assigned by your instructor.

Activity 9.23 | Maintaining Backward Compatibility

There may be times when you want a document to be available to persons using versions of Word older than Word 2007. In order to make a document backward compatible, you must save it as a Word 97–2003 document with the file extension .doc.

Some of the features that behave differently and document elements that are not available when editing .doc files—among others—include: text effects are removed, content controls are converted to static content, SmartArt graphics are converted to a single image, building blocks and AutoText entries might lose some information, bibliography and citations are converted to static text.

1 From the files that accompany this Project, open the file **w09B_Paid_Time_Off_optional**. Click the **File tab**, click **Save As**, click **Browse**, and then navigate to your **Word Chapter 9** folder.

2 At the bottom of the **Save As** dialog box, click the **Save as type arrow**, and then compare your screen with Figure 9.46.

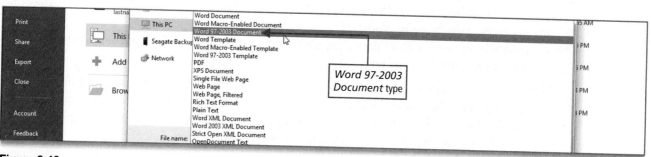

Figure 9.46

3 On the list, click **Word 97–2003 Document**. Using your own name, in the **File name** box, type **Lastname_Firstname_9B_Paid_Time_Off_optional** and then click **Save**. Compare your screen with Figure 9.47. Note: If the dialog box does not display, study the figure, and then proceed to the next step.

The Microsoft Word Compatibility Checker dialog box indicates that some features in the current document are not supported in an older version of Word. The Summary box indicates the elements of the document that may be modified.

 MAC TIP   *Word 97-2004 displays.*

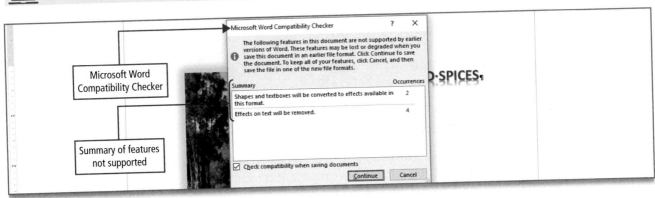

Figure 9.47

4 In the **Microsoft Word Compatibility Checker** dialog box, click **Continue**. Notice the Word Art mirroring effect applied to *Laurales Herbs and Spices* no longer displays and that *[Compatibility Mode]* displays in the title bar.

5 In the upper right corner of the Word window, click **Close** ✕. If directed by your instructor to do so, submit your original Word file.

Activity 9.24 | Configure Language Options in Documents

MOS
Expert 1.3.1

By default, your installation of Office uses a single language, and the Proofing tools on the Review tab use the default language when you use commands such as Spelling & Grammar.

If your document contains text in multiple languages, you can add other editing languages for use when checking spelling. From the Word Options dialog box, you can change these settings for any document you create in Word.

Additionally, with a Word document displayed, you can display the Language dialog box and specify language for selected text.

1 From the files that accompany this Project, open the file **w09B_Language_optional**. Click the **File tab**, click **Save As**, click **Browse**, and then navigate to your **Word Chapter 9** folder. In the **Save as type** box, if necessary, change to **Word Document**. Using your own name, save the file as **Lastname_Firstname_9B_Language_optional**

2 To install another editing language, click the **File tab**, on the left, click **Options**, and then in the **Word Options** dialog box, on the left, click **Language**.

 MAC TIP   On the menu bar, click Word, click Preferences, click Spelling & Grammar, click Dictionaries.

3 Under **Choose Editing Languages**, click the **Add additional editing languages arrow**, scroll down, and then click **Spanish (Latin America)**. Compare your screen with Figure 9.48.

🖥️ **MAC TIP**   Click Spanish.

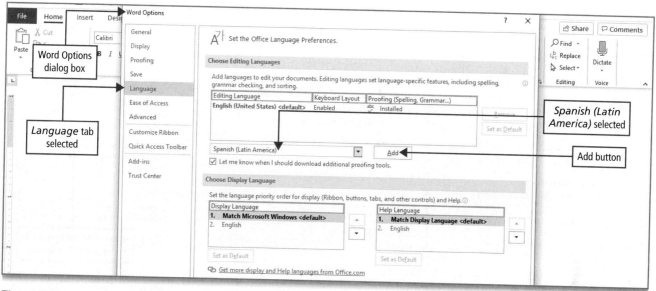

Figure 9.48

4 Click **Add**; the language you select may not be installed on your system, in which case you can download it by following the screen prompts.

5 In the lower right corner of the dialog box, click **Cancel**.

6 To check spelling in a document in a different language, select the last paragraph of the document, which is a translation of the paragraph above in Spanish.

7 With the paragraph selected, click the **Review tab**, in the **Language group**, click **Language**, and then click **Set Proofing Language**. Scroll down as necessary, and then click **Spanish (Latin America)**. Click **OK**.

8 On the **Review tab**, in the **Proofing group**, click **Check Document**, if necessary, click **Result** and then compare your screen with Figure 9.49.

The word *progroma* should be spelled *programa*.

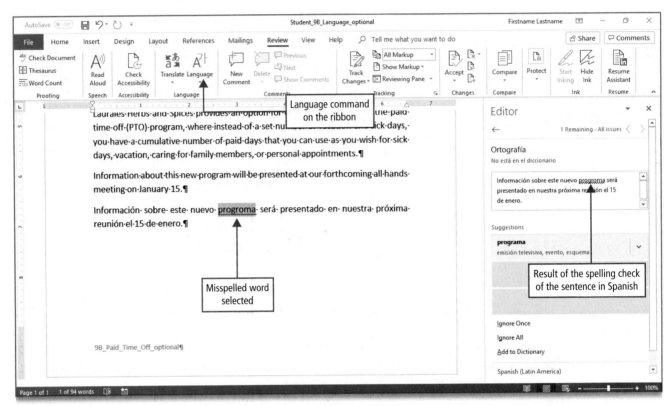

Figure 9.49

9 Under **Suggestions**, click **programa**. If necessary, in the message box, click **OK**.

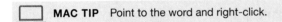
MAC TIP   Point to the word and right-click.

10 **Save** 🖫 your document. In the upper right corner of the Word window, click **Close** ⊠. If directed by your instructor to do so, submit your Word file.

You have completed the Optional Activities for Project 9B   **END**

wavebreakmedia/Shutterstock, Monkey Business Images/Fotolia, Ivanko80/Shutterstock, Monkey Business Images/Shutterstock

Microsoft Office Specialist (MOS) Skills in This Chapter

Project 9A	Project 9B
3.1.1 Convert text to tables	**1.2.2** Apply style sets
1.1.7 Expert: Display hidden ribbon tabs	**3.1.2** Convert tables to text
4.1.2 Expert: Modify field properties	**1.1.2 Expert:** Manage document versions
4.1.3 Expert: Insert standard content controls	**1.2.1 Expert:** Restrict editing
4.1.4 Expert: Configure standard content controls	**1.2.1 Expert:** Protect documents by using passwords
	1.3.1 Expert: Configure editing and display languages
	3.2.1 Expert: Create custom color sets
	3.2.2 Expert: Create custom font sets
	3.2.4 Expert: Create custom style sets

Build Your E-Portfolio

An E-Portfolio is a collection of evidence, stored electronically, that showcases what you have accomplished while completing your education. Collecting and then sharing your work products with potential employers reflects your academic and career goals. Your completed documents from the following projects are good examples to show what you have learned: 9G, 9K, and 9L.

GO! For Job Success

Discussion: Personal Technology

Your instructor may assign this discussion to your class and then ask you to think about, or discuss with your classmates, these questions.

Personal technology has evolved beyond smartphones and now includes wearable devices like watches and fitness bands that enable you check emails and calendars on your wrist and to track health data such as heart rate. Wearables also provide opportunities for businesses to provide better service and safer workplaces. In a manufacturing environment, smart goggles, badges, and sensors in clothing can detect unsafe conditions or provide real-time information to improve productivity. At a retail store, associates with wearables can access up-to-date inventory data and customer information to provide better service and streamline operations.

Wearable technology also gives employers greater ability to track and monitor employees. In an open office environment, requiring employees to scan a badge every time they enter a cube or conference room is efficient if employees need to be contacted or there is an emergency. Movement and location information of field employees like sales staff or delivery drivers is vital business data. On the other hand, wearables allow employers to also monitor personal data like heart rate, physical activity, and sleep patterns.

g-stockstudio/ Shutterstock

How could employees with hands-free, wearable devices improve efficiency in a restaurant or enhance care in a hospital?

What are some disadvantages for employees of wearable tracking technology?

Could there be advantages to employees if their stress and fatigue levels were monitored?

End of Chapter

Summary

Adding content controls and protecting the document makes it easy for the user to complete a form. By saving the document as a template, the form can be used repeatedly without changing the original file.

Add titles in content controls to clarify the purpose for the user. Add items to Drop-Down Lists and Combo Boxes to provide choices for the user to select. Format static text to improve the form's appearance.

Personalize the ribbon to improve efficiency. In the Word Options dialog box, display the Developer tab, add frequently used commands to existing tabs and groups, or create your own custom tabs and groups.

Add consistency to your documents by creating custom font, color, and style sets. Convert a table to text if it makes the information more readable. Word helps you to recover previous versions of your documents.

GO! Learn It Online

Review the concepts, key terms, and MOS skills in this chapter by completing these online challenges, which you can find at **MyLab IT**.

Chapter Quiz: Answer matching and multiple choice questions to test what you learned in this chapter.

Lessons on the GO!: Learn how to use all the new apps and features as they are introduced by Microsoft.

MOS Prep Quiz: Answer questions to review the MOS skills that you practiced in this chapter.

Project Guide for Word Chapter 9

Your instructor will assign Projects from this list to ensure your learning and assess your knowledge.

Project	Apply Skills from These Chapter Objectives	Project Type	Project Location
9A MyLab IT	Objectives 1–4 from Project 9A	**9A Instructional Project (Grader Project)** **Instruction** Guided instruction to learn the skills in Project 9A.	In **MyLab IT** and in text
9B MyLab IT	Objectives 5–8 from Project 9B	**9B Instructional Project (Grader Project)** **Instruction** Guided instruction to learn the skills in Project 9B.	In **MyLab IT** and in text
9C	Objectives 1–4 from Project 9A	**9C Skills Review (Scorecard Grading)** **Review** A guided review of the skills from Project 9A.	In text
9D	Objectives 5–8 from Project 9B	**9D Skills Review (Scorecard Grading)** **Review** A guided review of the skills from Project 9B.	In text
9E MyLab IT	Objectives 1–4 from Project 9A	**9E Mastery (Grader Project)** **Mastery and Transfer of Learning** A demonstration of your mastery of the skills in Project 9A with extensive decision making.	In **MyLab IT** and in text
9F MyLab IT	Objectives 5–8 from Project 9B	**9F Mastery (Grader Project)** **Mastery and Transfer of Learning** A demonstration of your mastery of the skills in Project 9B with extensive decision making.	In **MyLab IT** and in text
9G MyLab IT	Objectives 1–8 from Projects 9A and 9B	**9G Mastery (Grader Project)** **Mastery and Transfer of Learning** A demonstration of your mastery of the skills in Projects 9A and 9B with extensive decision making.	In **MyLab IT** and in text
9H	Combination of Objectives from Projects 9A and 9B	**9H GO! Fix It (Scorecard Grading)** **Critical Thinking** A demonstration of your mastery of the skills in Projects 9A and 9B by creating a correct result from a document that contains errors you must find.	IRC
9I	Combination of Objectives from Projects 9A and 9B	**9I GO! Make It (Scorecard Grading)** **Critical Thinking** A demonstration of your mastery of the skills in Projects 9A and 9B by creating a result from a supplied picture.	IRC
9J	Combination of Objectives from Projects 9A and 9B	**9J GO! Solve It (Rubric Grading)** **Critical Thinking** A demonstration of your mastery of the skills in Projects 9A and 9B, your decision making skills, and your critical thinking skills. A task-specific rubric helps you self-assess your result.	IRC
9K	Combination of Objectives from Projects 9A and 9B	**9K GO! Solve It (Rubric Grading)** **Critical Thinking** A demonstration of your mastery of the skills in Projects 9A and 9B, your decision making skills, and your critical thinking skills. A task-specific rubric helps you self-assess your result.	In text
9L	Combination of Objectives from Projects 9A and 9B	**9L GO! Think (Rubric Grading)** **Critical Thinking** A demonstration of your understanding of the Chapter concepts applied in a manner that you would outside of college. An analytic rubric helps you and your instructor grade the quality of your work by comparing it to the work an expert in the discipline would create.	In text
9M	Combination of Objectives from Projects 9A and 9B	**9M GO! Think (Rubric Grading)** **Critical Thinking** A demonstration of your understanding of the Chapter concepts applied in a manner that you would outside of college. An analytic rubric helps you and your instructor grade the quality of your work by comparing it to the work an expert in the discipline would create.	IRC
9N	Combination of Objectives from Projects 9A and 9B	**9N You and GO! (Rubric Grading)** **Critical Thinking** A demonstration of your understanding of the Chapter concepts applied in a manner that you would in a personal situation. An analytic rubric helps you and your instructor grade the quality of your work.	IRC

Glossary

Glossary of Chapter Key Terms

AutoRecover option A Word option that automatically saves versions of your file while you are working on it, and also helps to recover unsaved documents.

Check Box content control A content control that allows the user to select, or not select, a specific option.

Check Box form field A legacy control that allows the user to select, or not select, a specific option.

Combo Box content control A content control that allows the user to select an item from a list or enter new text.

Content control A data entry field where the particular type of information is supplied by the user.

Date Picker content control A content control that allows the user to select a date from a calendar.

Design Mode A command that enables the user to edit content controls that are inserted in a document.

Digital certificate (Digital ID) A file that contains information about a person and is used to electronically sign a document.

Drop-Down List content control A content control that allows the user to select a specific item from a list.

Form A structured document that has static text and reserved spaced for information to be entered by the user.

Legacy control A field used in designing a form for persons who possess older versions of Word.

Password A code that is used to gain access to a file.

Plain Text content control A content control that enables the user to enter unformatted text.

Read-only file A file that can be viewed but not changed.

Rich Text content control A content control that enables the user to enter text and apply formatting.

Signature line An element added to a document that specifies who should sign the document.

Static text Descriptive text such as labels or headings.

Style set A group of settings for the Font and Paragraph properties of your document.

Stylus A pen-like device used for writing on an electronic document.

Tablet PC A computer with a monitor that allows you to write on the screen.

Template A predefined structure that contains basic document settings, such as fonts, margins, and available style, and can also store elements such as building blocks and content controls.

Unformatted text Plain text without any special formatting applied.

Chapter Review

Apply 9A skills from these Objectives:

1. Create a Customized Form
2. Convert Text to a Table and Insert Content Controls in a Table
3. Modify and Protect a Form
4. Complete a Form

Skills Review	Project 9C Meeting Reservation Form

In the following Skills Review, you will add content controls to create a form for reserving space for meetings at Laurales Herbs and Spices headquarters office, and then fill in the form. Your completed document will look similar to Figure 9.50.

Project Files

For Project 9C, you will need the following file:

w09C_Reservation_Form

You will save your files as:

Lastname_Firstname_9C_Reservation_Form_Completed

Lastname_Firstname_9C_Reservation_Form (you will not submit this file)

Project Results

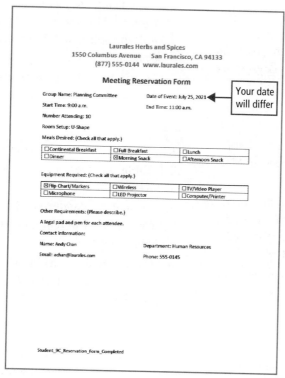

Figure 9.50

(continues on next page)

Chapter Review

1 From the files that accompany this Project, open the file **w09C_Reservation_Form**. Click the **File tab**, on the left click **Save As**, click **Browse**, and then in the **Save As** dialog box, navigate to your **Word Chapter 9** folder. Using your own name, save the file as **Lastname_Firstname_9C_Reservation_Form** and if necessary, display the rulers and formatting marks.

a. Click the **File tab**, and then click **Options**. On the left side of the **Word Options** dialog box, click **Customize Ribbon**. (Mac Users: Click Word on the menu bar, click Preferences, then click Ribbon & Toolbar.)

b. In the **Main Tabs** list, locate and then if necessary click to select the **Developer** check box. Click **OK** to close the **Word Options** dialog box.

2 Locate the text *Group Name*. Position the insertion point to the right of the colon, and then press Spacebar one time.

a. Click the **Developer tab**, and then in the **Controls group**, click **Design Mode** to turn on Design Mode.

b. In the **Controls group**, click **Plain Text Content Control**. (Mac Users: Click Text box. Design Mode may not be available.)

c. In a similar manner, click to the right of the colon for each of the following terms—*Start Time*, *End Time*, and *Number Attending*—press Spacebar, and then insert a **Plain Text Content Control**.

d. Locate the text *Date of Event*. Position the insertion point to the right of the colon, press Spacebar, and then in the **Controls group**, click **Date Picker Content Control**. (Mac Users: Date Picker may not be available. Insert Text Box. Move to Step 3.)

e. With the **Date Picker content control** selected, in the **Controls group**, click **Properties**. In the **Content Control Properties** dialog box, under **Date Picker Properties**, in the **Display the date like this** box, click the third style. Click **OK**.

3 Locate the text *Room Setup*. Position the insertion point to the right of the colon, press Spacebar, and then in the **Controls group**, click **Drop-Down List Content Control**. (Mac Users: Click Combo Box, then click Options to open the Drop-Down Form Field Options.)

a. With the **Drop-Down List content control** selected, in the **Controls group**, click **Properties**. In the **Content Control Properties** dialog box, under **Drop-Down List Properties**, click **Add**. In the **Add Choice** dialog box, in the **Display Name** box, type **Banquet** Click **OK**. (Mac Users: Type *Banquet* and then click the + button to add.)

b. Using the same technique, add the following choices to the **Drop-Down List content control**:
Classroom
Hollow Square
U-Shape

c. Click **OK** to close the dialog box. Select the two paragraphs that begin *Continental* and *Dinner*. Click the **Insert tab**. In the **Tables group**, click **Table**, and then click **Convert Text to Table**. In the **Convert Text to Table** dialog box, click **OK**.

d. In the table, click to position the insertion point to the left of *Continental*. On the **Developer tab**, in the **Controls group** click **Check Box Content Control**. Position the insertion point to the left of *Full Breakfast*, and then insert another Check Box Content Control.

e. In a similar manner, insert a **Check Box Content Control** to the left of each of the remaining items in the table.

4 Select the two paragraphs that begin *Flip Chart* and *Microphone*. Click the **Insert tab**. In the **Tables group**, click **Table**, and then click **Convert Text to Table**. Click **OK**.

a. Using the technique you just practiced, insert a **Check Box Content Control** to the left of all the items in the table.

b. Click to position the insertion point in the blank paragraph above *Contact Information*. Click the **Developer tab**, and then in the **Controls group**, click **Plain Text Content Control**. (Mac Users: Click Text Box.)

c. Below *Contact Information*, locate the text *Name*. Click to position the insertion point to the right of the colon, and then press Spacebar.

d. In the **Controls group**, click **Plain Text Content Control**. (Mac Users: Click Text Box.)

e. In a similar manner, to the right of the colon for each of the following items—*Department*, *Email*, and *Phone*—press Spacebar, and then insert a **Plain Text Content Control**. (Mac Users: Click Text Box.)

5 To the right of the paragraph that begins *Name*, click in the **Plain Text content control**, and then type **Enter your first and last name.** (Mac Users: After selecting the text, click Options. In the Default text box type *Enter your first name and last name.*)

a. To the right of the paragraph that begins *Email*, click in the **Plain Text content control**, and then type **Enter your work email address.**

Chapter Review

b. To the right of *Name*, click in the **Plain Text content control** to select it. On the **Developer tab**, in the **Controls group**, click **Properties**. In the **Content Control Properties** dialog box, in the **Title** box, type **Name** Select the **Use a style to format text typed into the empty control** check box. Click the **Style arrow**, click **Strong**, and then click **OK**.

c. To the right of *Email*, click in the **Plain Text content control** to select it. On the **Developer tab**, in the **Controls group**, click **Properties**. In the **Content Control Properties** dialog box, in the **Title** box, type **Email Address** Select the **Use a style to format text typed into the empty control** check box. Click the **Style arrow**, click **Strong**, and then click **OK**. (Mac Users: Commands in Steps b. and c. above may not be available.)

6 ▶ Press Ctrl + Home. On the **Developer tab**, in the **Controls group**, click **Design Mode** to turn off Design Mode.

a. On the **Developer tab**, in the **Protect group**, click **Restrict Editing**. (Mac Users: Click Protect Form. Save your document and move to Step 7.)

b. In the **Restrict Editing** pane, under **2. Editing restrictions**, select the **Allow only this type of editing in the document** check box. Click the **Allow only this type of editing in the document arrow**, and then click **Filling in forms**.

c. In the **Restrict Editing** pane, under **3. Start enforcement**, click **Yes, Start Enforcing Protection**.

d. In the **Start Enforcing Protection** dialog box, click **OK** without entering a password. **Close** the **Restrict Editing** pane, and then **Save** your document.

7 ▶ Click the **File tab**, click **Save As**, click **Browse**, and then in the **Save As** dialog box, navigate to your **Word Chapter 9** folder. In the File name box, using your own name, type **Lastname_Firstname_9C_Reservation_Form_Completed** and then click **Save**.

a. In the content control following *Group Name*, type **Planning Committee** Press Tab, click the **Date Picker content control arrow**, and then click **Today**. Continue filling in the form using the information shown below.

Start Time	9:00 a.m.
End Time	11:00 a.m.
Number Attending	10
Room Setup	U-Shape
Meals Desired	Morning Snack
Equipment Required	Flip Chart/Markers
Other Requirements	**A legal pad and pen for each attendee.**
Name	**Andy Chan**
Department	**Human Resources**
Email	**achan@laurales.com**
Phone	**555-0145**

b. Click the **Developer tab**, and then in the **Protect group**, click **Restrict Editing**. At the bottom of the **Restrict Editing** pane, click **Stop Protection**. **Close** the **Restrict Editing** pane. Press Ctrl + Home, and then insert the file name in the footer. (Mac Users: Click Protect Form.)

c. Click the **File tab**, and then click **Show All Properties**. In the **Tags** box, type **meeting reservation, completed** In the **Subject** box, type your course name and section number. If necessary, edit the author name to display your name. On the left, click **Save**.

d. Click the **File tab**, on the left click **Options**. In the **Word Options** dialog box, on the left click **Customize Ribbon**. In the **Main Tabs** list, locate and then click to clear the **Developer** check box. Click **OK**, and notice that the Developer tab no longer displays on the ribbon. (Mac Users: Click Word on the toolbar and click Preferences. Click Ribbon & Toolbar.)

e. **Save** 🖫 your document. In the upper right corner of the Word window, click **Close** ⊠. Submit your document as directed by your instructor.

You have completed Project 9C | END

Chapter Review

Apply 9B skills from these Objectives:

5. Create a Custom Ribbon Tab
6. Create Style, Color, and Font Sets
7. Convert a Table to Text
8. Prepare a Document for Review and Distribution

Skills Review   Project 9D Privacy Policy

In the following Skills Review, you will finalize a document that explains the privacy policy of Laurales Herbs and Spices. Your completed document will look similar to Figure 9.51.

Project Files

For Project 9D, you will need the following files:

w09D_Privacy_Policy

w09D_Logo_Photo

You will save your file as:

Lastname_Firstname_9D_Privacy_Policy

Project Results

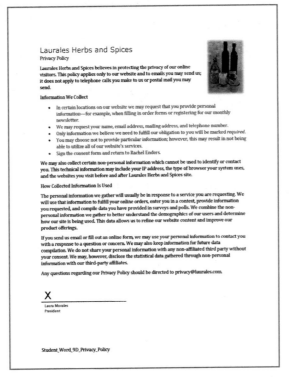

Figure 9.51

(continues on next page)

Chapter Review

1 From the files that accompany this Project, open the file **w09D_Privacy_Policy**.

a. Click the **File tab**, on the left click **Save As**, click **Browse**, and then in the **Save As** dialog box, navigate to your **Word Chapter 9** folder. Using your own name, save the file as **Lastname_Firstname_9D_Privacy_Policy**

2 Click the **File tab**, and then on the left click **Options**. In the **Word Options** dialog box, on the left, click **Customize Ribbon**.

a. Below the **Main Tabs** list, with **Home** selected, click **New Tab**. In the list, click **New Tab (Custom)**, and then at the bottom of the list, click **Rename**. In the **Rename** dialog box, in the **Display name** box, type **9D Commands** and then click **OK**.

b. In the list, click **New Group (Custom)**, and then click **Rename**. In the **Rename** dialog box, in the **Display name** box, type **Frequent Tasks** and then click **OK**.

c. With **Frequent Tasks (Custom)** selected, in the upper left portion of the dialog box, click the **Choose commands from arrow**, and then click **All Commands**. Under **All Commands**, scroll as necessary, click **Edit Footer**, and then between the two lists, click **Add**. From the list of **All Commands**, locate and click **Insert Picture**, and then click **Add**. Click **OK** to close the **Word Options** dialog box. (Mac Users: To create a custom ribbon tab, click the Word menu, and then click Preferences. In the dialog box, click Ribbon & Toolbar. Click the + button, and then click New Tab.)

3 On the ribbon, click the **9D Commands tab** that you just created. In the **Frequent Tasks group**, click **Edit Footer**, and then insert the file name in the footer. **Close** the footer area.

a. Select the paragraph *Laurales Herbs and Spices*. Change the **Font Color**—in the fifth column, click the first color.

b. Select the paragraph *Privacy Policy*, and then change the **Font Color**—in the last column, click the last color.

c. Press [Ctrl] + [Home]. Click the **9D Commands tab**, and then in the **Frequent Tasks group**, click **Pictures**. In the **Insert Picture** dialog box, navigate to the files that accompany this Project, select the picture **w09D_Logo_Photo**, and then click **Insert**.

d. With the picture selected, on the **Picture Tools Format tab**, in the **Size group**, click in the **Shape Height** box, type **1.75** and press [Enter].

e. In the **Arrange group**, click **Position**, and then under **Text Wrapping**, in the first row, click the third wrapping style—**Position in Top Right with Square Text Wrapping**. Click anywhere to deselect the picture.

4 On the **Design tab**, in the **Document Formatting group**, click **Fonts**, and then at the bottom, click **Customize Fonts**. (Mac Users: Create a New Theme may not be available on a Mac.)

a. In the **Create New Theme Fonts** dialog box, click the **Heading font arrow**, scroll down the list, and then click **Verdana**.

b. Click the **Body font arrow**, scroll down, and then click **Cambria**. In the **Name** box, name the Font set **Laurales 9D** and click **Save**.

c. Select the paragraph *Laurales Herbs and Spices*, and then on the **Home tab**, in the **Styles group**, click the **Heading 1** style.

5 On the **Design tab**, in the **Document Formatting group**, click **Colors**, and then at the bottom, click **Customize Colors**. (Mac Users: Create New Theme Colors may not be available on a Mac.)

a. In the **Create New Theme Colors** dialog box, click the **Accent 1 arrow**. Click **More Colors**, click the **Standard tab**, and then in the seventh (widest) row, click the next to last color.

b. Click **OK**, and then click the **Accent 6 arrow**. Click **More Colors**, click the **Standard tab**, and then in the first row, click the next to last color.

c. Click **OK**, in the **Name** box type **Laurales 9D** and then click **Save**.

6 Click anywhere in the table. On the **Table Tools Layout tab**, in the **Data group**, click **Convert to Text**.

a. In the **Convert to Table to Text** dialog box, click **OK**.

b. With the five paragraphs selected, on the **Home tab**, in the **Font group**, change the **Font Color**—in the fifth column (purple colors), click the last color. (Mac Users: Display the Font Color gallery, click More Colors, click Color Wheel. With the crosshair cursor, select a dark purple color. Apply the color to the Heading and the five paragraphs just selected.)

c. In the **Paragraph group**, click **Bullets**.

(continues on next page)

Chapter Review

7 Press Ctrl + End. On the **Insert tab**, in the **Text group**, click the **Signature Line button arrow**, and then click **Microsoft Office Signature Line**.

a. In the **Signature Setup** dialog box, in the **Suggested signer** box, type **Laura Morales** In the **Suggested signer's title** box, type **President** and then click **OK**.

b. **Save** your document. (Mac Users: Signature box may not be available. Insert a 1x1 table. Remove all borders except the bottom. Type *X* apply Bold and increase the Font Size to 16. Click in the paragraph below the table. Type *Laura Morales* and Press ENTER one time. Type *President* then select Laura Morales and change Spacing After to 0 pt.)

8 From **Backstage** view, click **Show All Properties**. In the **Tags** box, type **privacy policy** In the **Subject** box, type your course name and section number. Be sure your name displays as the author.

a. On the left, click **Protect Document**, and then click **Mark as Final**.

b. In the **Microsoft Word** message box, click **OK**. In the second **Microsoft Word** message box, click **OK**.

c. On the left, click **Options**, and then in the **Word Options** dialog box, click **Customize Ribbon**. In the **Main Tabs** list, right-click **9D Commands (Custom)**, and then on the shortcut menu, click **Remove**. Click **OK**, and then **Close** Word. (Mac Users: On the menu bar, click Word, click Preferences, click Ribbon & Toolbar to access the dialog box.)

9 Submit your Word document as directed by your instructor.

You have completed Project 9D | **END**

MyLab IT Grader	Mastering Word	Project 9E Ergonomic Study

In the following Mastering Word project, you will create a form for the IT Department at Laurales Herbs and Spices. The department plans to survey employees regarding health issues related to their workstations. Your completed document will look similar to Figure 9.52.

Apply 9A skills from these Objectives:

1. Create a Customized Form
2. Convert Text to a Table and Insert Content Controls in a Table
3. Modify and Protect a Form
4. Complete a Form

Project Files for MyLab IT Grader

1. In your **MyLab IT** course, locate and click **Word 9E Ergonomic Study**, Download Materials, and then Download All Files.
2. Extract the zipped folder to your Word Chapter 9 folder. Close the Grader download screens.
3. Take a moment to open the downloaded **Word_9E_Ergonomic_Study_Instructions**; note any recent updates to the book.

Project Results

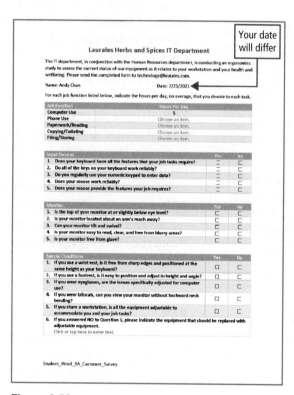

Figure 9.52

For Non-MyLab Submissions

For Project 9E, you will need:
w09E_Ergonomic_Study

In your Word Chapter 9 folder, save your document as:
Lastname_Firstname_9E_Ergonomic_Study

After you have named and saved your document, on the next page, begin with Step 2.
After Step 14, save and submit your file as directed by your instructor.

(continues on next page)

1 Navigate to your **Word Chapter 9 folder**, and then double-click the Word file you downloaded from **MyLab IT** that displays your name—**Student_Word_9E_ Ergonomic_Study**. If necessary, at the top, click **Enable Editing**. If necessary, add the **Developer tab** to the ribbon.

2 Select the first paragraph, change the **Font Size** to **16**, apply **Bold**, and then change the **Font Color**—in the last column, click the last color. Center the paragraph.

3 Including the tab marks and the paragraph marks, select the six paragraphs that begin with *Job Function* and end with *Filing/Storing*. Display the **Convert Text to Table** dialog box, be sure the number of columns is **2** and the text is separated at **Tabs**, and then convert the text to a table.

4 To all four tables in the document, apply the same table style—in the **Grid Tables** gallery, in the fourth row, click the last table style.

5 On the **Developer tab**, turn on **Design Mode**. Locate the text *Name*, position the insertion point to the right of the colon, press [Spacebar] one time, and then insert a **Plain Text Content Control**. (Mac Users: Insert a Text Form Field using the Text Box tool.)

6 Locate the text *Date*, position the insertion point to the right of the colon, press [Spacebar] one time, and then insert a **Date Picker Content Control**. (Mac Users: Insert a Text Form Field using the Text Box tool. Date Picker Content Control may not be available.)

7 In the first table, in the second row, click in the second cell, and then insert a **Drop-Down List Content Control**. Display the **Content Control Properties** dialog box, and then display the **Add Choice** dialog box. In the **Display Name** box, type **1** and click **OK** to add the **Value**. In a similar manner, add the numbers **2** through **8** (in numerical order) to the list. Click the **Select Field** button to select the entire control, copy the content control, and then paste it into the remaining empty cells in the first table. Select the second column, and then **Align Center**. (Mac Users: Click Combo Box, then click Options to add the values.)

8 In the second table, below **Yes**, position the insertion point in the first empty cell, and then insert a **Check Box Content Control**. Copy the content control, and then paste it into the remaining empty cells in all three tables. For the second, third, and fourth tables, select the second and third columns, and then **Align Center**.

9 In the fourth table, in the last row, click to position the insertion point in the first cell. On the **Table Tools Layout tab**, in the **Rows & Columns group**, click **Insert Below**. With all three cells selected, in the **Merge group** click **Merge Cells**, and then in the **Alignment group**, click **Align Center Left**.

10 On the **Home tab**, in the **Paragraph group**, click **Numbering** to continue numbering with 6. Click in the cell, and then type **If you answered NO to Question 5, please indicate the equipment that should be replaced with adjustable equipment.** Press [Enter], press [Backspace] one time to remove the auto number, and then insert a **Plain Text Content Control**. Turn off **Design Mode**—your document reverts to one page. **Restrict Editing** to only **Filling in forms**. Do not use a password. **Close** the **Restrict Editing** pane. (Mac Users: Click Text Box. Click Protect Form.)

11 In the content control following **Name**, type **Andy Chan**

12 To the right of **Date**, click the **Date Picker content control arrow**, and then click **Today**. To the right of *Computer Use*, click the **Drop–Down List content control arrow**, and then click **5**. (Mac Users: Type today's date. Deselect Protect Form.)

13 Press [Ctrl] + [Home], and then insert the file name in the footer. Click the **File tab**, and then click **Show All Properties**. In the **Tags** box, type **ergonomic study** In the **Subject** box, type your course name and section number. If necessary, edit the author name to display your name. Remove the **Developer tab** from the ribbon.

14 On the left, click **Save**. In the upper right corner of the Word window, click **Close** [X].

15 In **MyLab IT**, locate and click the Grader Project **Word 9E Ergonomic Study**. In **step 3**, under **Upload Completed Assignment**, click **Choose File**. In the **Open** dialog box, navigate to your **Word Chapter 9 folder**, and then click your **Student_Word_9E_Ergonomic_Study** file one time to select it. In the lower right corner of the **Open** dialog box, click **Open**.

The name of your selected file displays above the Upload button.

16 To submit your file to **MyLab IT** for grading, click **Upload**, wait a moment for a green **Success!** message, and then in **step 4**, click the blue **Submit for Grading** button. Click **Close Assignment** to return to your list of **Course Materials**.

You have completed Project 9E **END**

Mastering Word | **Project 9F Staffing Needs**

Apply 9B skills from these Objectives:

5. Create a Custom Ribbon Tab
6. Create Style, Color, and Font Sets
7. Convert a Table to Text
8. Prepare a Document for Review and Distribution

In the following Mastering Word project, you will create a memo from George Tillman, Director of Human Resources, explaining staffing needs for next year at Laurales Herbs and Spices. Your completed document will look similar to Figure 9.53.

Project Files for MyLab IT Grader

1. In your **MyLab IT** course, locate and click **Word 9F Staffing Needs**, Download Materials, and then Download All Files.
2. Extract the zipped folder to your Word Chapter 9 folder. Close the Grader download screens.
3. Take a moment to open the downloaded **Word_9F_Staffing_Needs_Instructions**; note any recent updates to the book.

Project Results

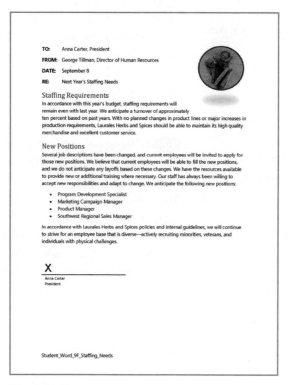

Figure 9.53

For Non-MyLab Submissions

For Project 9F, you will need:
w09F_Staffing_Needs
w09F_Logo_Photo

In your Word Chapter 9 folder, save your document as:
Lastname_Firstname_9F_Staffing_Needs

After you have named and saved your document, on the next page, begin with Step 2.
After Step 12, save and submit your file as directed by your instructor.

(continues on next page)

1 Navigate to your **Word Chapter 9 folder**, and then double-click the Word file you downloaded from **MyLab IT** that displays your name—**Student_Word_9F_Staffing_Needs**. If necessary, at the top, click **Enable Editing**.

2 Display the **Word Options** dialog box, and then on the left click **Customize Ribbon**. On the right, be sure **Main Tabs** are displayed and that **Home** is selected. Create a **New Tab**, in the **Main Tabs** list select **New Tab (Custom)**, and then **Rename** the tab as **9F Commands** In the list click **New Group (Custom)**, and then **Rename** the group as **Frequent Tasks** (Mac Users: To create a custom ribbon tab, click the Word menu, and then click Preferences. In the Word Preferences dialog box, click Ribbon & Toolbar. Click the + button, and then click New Tab.)

3 On the left, display **All Commands**, and then **Add** the following commands to the **Frequent Tasks group**: **Edit Footer** and **Insert Picture**. Click **OK** to close the **Word Options** dialog box. From the new **9F Commands tab**, add the **File Name** to the footer.

4 Select the paragraphs *Staffing Requirements* and *New Positions*, and then change the **Font Color**—in the fifth column, click the last color.

5 Press Ctrl + Home to move to the top of the document, and then from the **9F Commands tab**, insert the picture **w09F_Logo_Photo** from the files that accompany this Project. Set the height of the picture to **2"** and then from the **Picture Tools Format tab**, in the **Arrange group**, set the **Position** to **Position in Top Right with Square Text Wrapping**— the third option under **With Text Wrapping**.

6 Create a new font set using **Cambria** as the **Heading font** and **Segoe UI** as the **Body font**. Name the font set **Laurales 9F** Select *Staffing Requirements* and *New Positions*, and then apply the **Heading 1** style. (Mac Users: Creating a new font set may not be available.)

7 Create a new color set. Change **Accent 1** to the first color in the last row of the **Standard** colors. Change **Accent 4** to the first color in the seventh (widest) row of the **Standard** colors. Name the color set **Laurales 9F** (Mac Users: Creating a new color set may not be available.)

8 Convert the table to text by separating the text with paragraph marks. Apply **Bullets** to the four new paragraphs.

9 In the blank paragraph at the end of the document, insert a **Microsoft Office Signature Line** with **Anna Carter** as the Suggested signer and her title **President** (Mac Users: Signature Line may not be available on a Mac.)

10 Display the document properties. As the **Tags** type **staffing needs** In the **Subject** box, type your course name and section number. Be sure your name displays as the author.

11 Mark the document as final, and then in the Word Options dialog box, remove the custom ribbon tab **9F Commands**. (Mac Users: To lock a document and then make it Read-Only, open Finder, select the document you want to protect, click Settings, and then click Get Info. Under General, select the Locked check box. Click Word on the menu bar and click Preferences. Click Ribbon & Toolbar to access the dialog box.)

12 In the upper right corner of the Word window, click **Close** ✕.

13 In **MyLab IT**, locate and click the Grader Project **Word 9F Staffing Needs**. In **step 3**, under **Upload Completed Assignment**, click **Choose File**. In the **Open** dialog box, navigate to your **Word Chapter 9 folder**, and then click your **Student_Word_9F_Staffing_Needs** file one time to select it. In the lower right corner of the **Open** dialog box, click **Open**.

The name of your selected file displays above the Upload button.

14 To submit your file to **MyLab IT** for grading, click **Upload**, wait a moment for a green **Success!** message, and then in **step 4**, click the blue **Submit for Grading** button. Click **Close Assignment** to return to your list of **Course Materials**.

You have completed Project 9F | END

Apply 9A and 9B skills from these Objectives:

1. Create a Customized Form
2. Convert Text to a Table and Insert Content Controls in a Table
3. Modify and Protect a Form
4. Complete a Form
5. Create a Custom Ribbon Tab
6. Create Style, Color, and Font Sets
7. Convert a Table to Text
8. Prepare a Document for Review and Distribution

In the following Mastering Word Project, you will create a custom form that will be used by employees to evaluate training seminars at Laurales Herbs and Spices. Your completed document will look similar to Figure 9.54.

Project Files for MyLab IT Grader

1. In your Course Materials, locate and click **Word 9G Seminar Evaluation**, Download Materials, and then Download All Files.
2. Extract the zipped folder to your Word Chapter 9 folder. Close the Grader download screens.
3. Take a moment to open the downloaded **Word_9G_Seminar_Evaluation_Instructions**; note any recent updates to the book.

Project Results

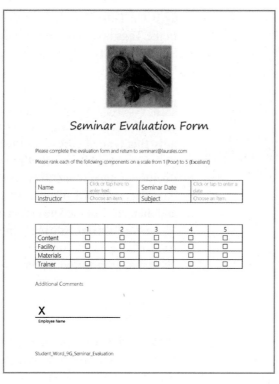

Figure 9.54

For Non-MyLab Submissions
For Project 9G, you will need:
w09G_Seminar_Evaluation
w09G_Logo_Photo

In your Word Chapter 9 folder, save your document as:
Lastname_Firstname_9G_Seminar_Evaluation

After you have named and saved your document, on the next page, begin with Step 2.
After step 15, save and submit your file as directed by your instructor.

(continues on next page)

Mastering Word: Project 9G Seminar Evaluation (continued)

1 Navigate to your **Word Chapter 9 folder**, and then double-click the Word file you downloaded from **MyLab IT** that displays your name—**Student_Word_9G_Seminar_Evaluation**. If necessary, at the top, click **Enable Editing**.

2 Insert the file name in the footer of the document. Press Ctrl + Home. From your project files, **Insert** the picture **w09G_Logo_Photo**. Change the **Height** to **2"** and then press Ctrl + E to center the picture

3 Position the insertion point in the empty paragraph immediately below the picture. Type **Seminar Evaluation Form** and then press Enter. Select the paragraph you just typed, and then change the **Font Color**—in the last column (green colors), click the last color. (Mac Users: Skip to Step 6.)

4 Create a new color set. Change **Accent 1** to the first color in the last row of the **Standard** colors. Change **Accent 6** to the third color in the last row of the **Standard** colors. Name the color set **Laurales 9G**

5 Create a new font set using **Segoe Print** for the **Heading font** and **Segoe UI Light** for the **Body font**. Name the font set **Laurales 9G** Apply the **Heading 1** style to the title *Seminar Evaluation Form*, center the heading, and then change the **Font Size** to **24**.

6 Convert the first table to text separated with paragraph marks.

7 If necessary, display the Developer tab on the ribbon. On the **Developer tab**, turn on **Design Mode**. In the first table, in the cell to the right of *Name*, insert a **Plain Text Content Control**. (Mac Users: Insert Text Box.)

8 In the cell to the right of *Seminar Date*, insert a **Date Picker Content Control**, and then change the format to **M/d/yy**—the fourth display choice. (Mac Users: Date Picker Content Control may not be available; insert Text Box.)

9 In the cell following *Instructor*, insert a **Drop-Down List Content Control**, and then add the following names: (Mac Users: Insert Combo Box, click Options to add names.)

> **Alvin Barnes**
> **Charles Corbin**
> **Susan Parrish**

10 In the first table, in the last cell, insert a **Drop-Down List Content Control**, and then add the following topics:

> **Customer Service**
> **Employee Benefits**
> **Microsoft Office**
> **Safety Issues**

11 In the second table, insert a **Check Box Content Control** in each of the empty cells. Turn off **Design Mode**.

12 In the blank paragraph at the end of the document, insert a **Microsoft Office Signature Line**. As the **Suggested signer** type **Employee Name** (Mac Users: Signature Line may not be available.)

13 Click the **File tab**, and then **Show All Properties**. In the **Tags** box, type **seminar evaluation form** In the **Subject** box, type your course name and section number. Be sure your name displays as the author. On the left, click **Save** to return to your document.

14 Press Ctrl + Home. Display the **Restrict Editing** pane. Under **2. Editing restrictions**, select the **Allow only this type of editing in the document** check box. Click the **Allow only this type of editing in the document arrow**, and then click **Filling in forms**. **Save** your document. Display the **Word Options** dialog box, and then remove the **Developer tab** from the ribbon. Close the **Restrict Editing pane**. (Mac Users: In the pane, click Protect Form. Under 3 Start Enforcement click Yes, Start Enforcing Protection. Do not add a password.)

15 In the upper right corner of the Word window, click **Close** ☒.

16 In **MyLab IT**, locate and click the Grader Project **Word 9G Seminar Evaluation**. In **step 3**, under **Upload Completed Assignment**, click **Choose File**. In the **Open** dialog box, navigate to your **Word Chapter 9 folder**, and then click your **Student_Word_9G_Seminar_Evaluation** file one time to select it. In the lower right corner of the **Open** dialog box, click **Open**.

> The name of your selected file displays above the Upload button.

17 To submit your file to **MyLab IT** for grading, click **Upload**, wait a moment for a green **Success!** message, and then in **step 4**, click the blue **Submit for Grading** button. Click **Close Assignment** to return to your list of **Course Materials**.

You have completed Project 9G | END

Outcomes-Based Assessments (Critical Thinking)

Apply a combination of the 9A and 9B skills.			
GO! Fix It	**Project 9H Complaint Form**		**IRC**
GO! Make It	**Project 9I Phone Request**		**IRC**
GO! Solve It	**Project 9J Accident Report**		**IRC**
GO! Solve It	**Project 9K Staff Promotion**		

Project Files

For Project 9K, you will need the following files:

New blank Word document

w09K_Promotion_Data

You will save your file as:

Lastname_Firstname_9K_Staff_Promotion

Anna Carter, President of Laurales Herbs and Spices, needs to fill the position of Executive Assistant. She would like to promote an individual from within the company. She has identified ten candidates; however, she wants the department managers to identify the strengths and weaknesses of the individuals. Create a memorandum from Ms. Carter to department managers, including the current date and an appropriate subject line. In the body of the memo, design a form that includes appropriate content controls to select the name of the individual being evaluated and rate the candidate on a variety of skills using a five-point scale ranging from Poor to Excellent. Information regarding candidates' names and required skills can be found in the student file **w09K_Promotion_Data**. Save the document as a Word template with the file name **Lastname_Firstname_9K_Staff_Promotion** Insert the file name in the footer and add appropriate document properties. Restrict editing to filling in the form. Print your document or submit electronically as directed by your instructor.

<table>
<thead>
<tr><th rowspan="2">Performance Element</th><th></th><th colspan="3">Performance Level</th></tr>
<tr><th></th><th>Exemplary: You consistently applied the relevant skills</th><th>Proficient: You sometimes, but not always, applied the relevant skills</th><th>Developing: You rarely or never applied the relevant skills</th></tr>
</thead>
<tbody>
<tr><td></td><td>Insert and format text</td><td>All required information is included and the document is formatted as a memo.</td><td>Some information is missing or the document is not formatted as a memo.</td><td>No specific information is included and the document is not formatted as a memo.</td></tr>
<tr><td></td><td>Insert content controls</td><td>Appropriate content controls are used and required items are added.</td><td>Some content controls are inappropriate or some required items are missing.</td><td>No content controls are inserted.</td></tr>
<tr><td></td><td>Insert 5-point rating scale</td><td>The scale allows for 5 ratings and displays appropriately with skills and content controls.</td><td>The scale does not contain 5 ratings or does not display appropriately with skills and content controls.</td><td>There is no scale.</td></tr>
<tr><td></td><td>Save as template and restrict editing</td><td>The document is saved as a template and is restricted to filling in forms.</td><td>The document is not saved as a template or is not restricted to filling in forms.</td><td>The document is not saved as a template and the form is not restricted.</td></tr>
</tbody>
</table>

You have completed Project 9K **END**

Rubric

The following outcomes-based assessments are *open-ended assessments*. That is, there is no specific correct result; your result will depend on your approach to the information provided. Make *Professional Quality* your goal. Use the following scoring rubric to guide you in *how* to approach the problem and then to evaluate *how well* your approach solves the problem.

The *criteria*—Software Mastery, Content, Format and Layout, and Process—represent the knowledge and skills you have gained that you can apply to solving the problem. The *levels of performance*—Professional Quality, Approaching Professional Quality, or Needs Quality Improvements—help you and your instructor evaluate your result.

	Your completed project is of Professional Quality if you:	**Your completed project is Approaching Professional Quality if you:**	**Your completed project Needs Quality Improvements if you:**
1-Software Mastery	Choose and apply the most appropriate skills, tools, and features and identify efficient methods to solve the problem.	Choose and apply some appropriate skills, tools, and features, but not in the most efficient manner.	Choose inappropriate skills, tools, or features, or are inefficient in solving the problem.
2-Content	Construct a solution that is clear and well organized, contains content that is accurate, appropriate to the audience and purpose, and is complete. Provide a solution that contains no errors of spelling, grammar, or style.	Construct a solution in which some components are unclear, poorly organized, inconsistent, or incomplete. Misjudge the needs of the audience. Have some errors in spelling, grammar, or style, but the errors do not detract from comprehension.	Construct a solution that is unclear, incomplete, or poorly organized, contains some inaccurate or inappropriate content, and contains many errors of spelling, grammar, or style. Do not solve the problem.
3-Format and Layout	Format and arrange all elements to communicate information and ideas, clarify function, illustrate relationships, and indicate relative importance.	Apply appropriate format and layout features to some elements, but not others. Overuse features, causing minor distraction.	Apply format and layout that does not communicate information or ideas clearly. Do not use format and layout features to clarify function, illustrate relationships, or indicate relative importance. Use available features excessively, causing distraction.
4-Process	Use an organized approach that integrates planning, development, self-assessment, revision, and reflection.	Demonstrate an organized approach in some areas, but not others; or, use an insufficient process of organization throughout.	Do not use an organized approach to solve the problem.

Outcomes-Based Assessments (Critical Thinking)

Apply a combination of the 9A and 9B skills.

| GO! Think | Project 9L Computer Equipment |

Project Files

For Project 9L, you will need the following file:

New blank Word document

You will save your files as:

Lastname_Firstname_9L_Computer_Equipment

Lastname_Firstname_9L_Computer_Request

Every three years, the IT department of Laurales Herbs and Spices updates computer equipment and software for the administrative staff. Employees may choose either a desktop or laptop computer. Other options include, but are not limited to, a choice of printers or a scanner. In conjunction with the new computer rollout, the IT department wants to prioritize training needs by asking employees to select a topic—File Management, Microsoft Office, or Website Development—that would be most helpful to them.

Create a questionnaire that can be sent to the administrative staff. Include appropriate text and content controls for the employee's name, the current date, and types of computer equipment and training. Restrict editing the document to filling in forms. Save the document as a Word template with the file name **Lastname_Firstname_9L_Computer_Equipment** Using the template, create a new document and complete the form, using your name as the employee. Save the document as **Lastname_Firstname_9L_Computer_Request** Add appropriate document properties, and mark the document as final. In your template, stop protection, insert the file name in the footer, and add appropriate document properties. Print both documents or submit electronically as directed by your instructor.

You have completed Project 9L | END

| GO! Think | Project 9M Vacation Compensation | IRC |

| You and GO! | Project 9N Cover Page | IRC |

Working with Long Documents

WORD 2019

PROJECT 10A

Outcomes
Create, navigate, and inspect a master document and subdocuments, and modify footers.

Objectives
1. Create a Master Document and Subdocuments
2. Manage a Master Document and Subdocuments
3. Navigate and Inspect the Master Document
4. Create and Modify Headers and Footers

PROJECT 10B

Outcomes
Work with and format long documents and create an index, table of contents, and table of figures.

Objectives
5. Create an Index
6. Create a Table of Contents
7. Create a Table of Figures
8. Control the Flow and Formatting of Pages and Text

ivanoel/Shutterstock

In This Chapter

GO! To Work with Word

When several people work on a document, keeping track of the different versions can be difficult. In this chapter, you will create a master document and subdocuments from a multipage file to allow parts of the document to be edited while maintaining the integrity of the complete document. The navigation features in Word allow you to view and edit the final master document. Additionally, you will create navigational and reference aids for a long document, including a table of contents, a table of figures, and an index. Defining the flow of text on the pages of the document will improve readability.

The projects in this chapter relate to the **City of Tawny Creek**, a growing community located between Los Angeles and San Diego, about 20 miles from the Pacific shore. Just 10 years ago, the population was under 100,000; today it has grown to almost 300,000. Community leaders have always focused on quality of life and economic development in decisions on housing, open space, education, and infrastructure, making the city a model for other communities its size around the United States. The city provides many recreational and cultural opportunities with a large park system and thriving arts community.

PROJECT 10A Autumn Schedule

Project Activities

In Activities 10.01 through 10.12, you will create a master document with several subdocuments. The finished document will be a description of the autumn activities offered by the City of Tawny Creek. Your completed documents will look similar to Figure 10.1.

Project Files for **MyLab IT Grader**

1. In your storage location, create a folder named **Word Chapter 10**.
2. In your **MyLab IT** course, locate and click **Word 10A Autumn Schedule**, Download Materials, and then Download All Files.
3. Extract the zipped folder to your Word Chapter 10 folder. Close the Grader download screens.
4. Take a moment to open the downloaded **Word_10A_Autumn_Schedule_Instructions**; note any recent updates to the book.

Project Results

GO! Project 10A
Where We're Going

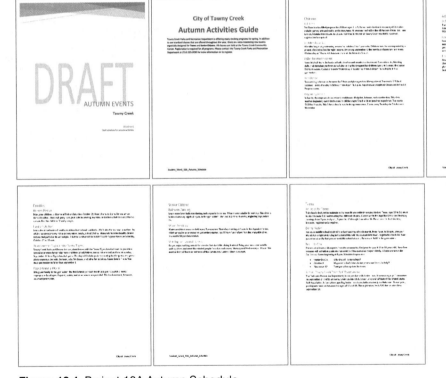

Figure 10.1 Project 10A Autumn Schedule

For Non-MyLab Submissions
For Project 10A, you will need:
w10A_Autumn_Schedule
w10A_Teens

In your storage location, create a folder named **Word Chapter 10**.
In your Word Chapter 10 folder, save your documents as:
Lastname_Firstname_10A_Autumn_Schedule
Lastname_Firstname_10A_Teens

In your Word Chapter 10 folder, create a folder named Project 10A. Save the w10A_Autumn_Schedule file in the Project 10A folder. After you have named and saved your document, on the next page, begin with Step 3.

| Objective 1 | **Create a Master Document and Subdocuments** |

GO! Learn How
Video W10-1

You can organize a long document into sections—a ***master document*** and ***subdocuments***—to make it easier to work with different parts of the document. A master document is a Word document that serves as a container for the different parts of a document. A subdocument is a section of the document that is linked to the master document. Changes made in the subdocument are reflected in the master document. Using subdocuments enables the individuals collaborating on a project to edit the various sections of the document without altering the entire long document. Each individual can work on a specific section, and then the sections can be integrated into the final document.

Activity 10.01 | Using the Outlining Feature and Creating a Master Document

Using a master document allows you to maintain consistent formatting and styles across all of the subdocuments even though different people are working on the sections. ***Outline view*** displays the overall organization, or hierarchy, of parts of a document, including headings, subheadings, and subordinate text.

1 Navigate to your **Word Chapter 10 folder**, and then double-click the Word file you downloaded from **MyLab IT** that displays your name—**Student_Word_10A_Autumn_Schedule**.

2 Open the **Word Chapter 10** folder. Create a folder named **Project 10A** and then **Save** the document to your **Project 10A** folder. If necessary, display the rulers and formatting marks.

3 On the **View tab**, in the **Views group**, click **Outline**. If necessary, change the Zoom level to 100%. Compare your screen with Figure 10.2.

Outline view makes it easy to view the different levels in a document. The paragraphs formatted with the Heading 1 or Heading 2 style are designated as Level 1 or Level 2 headings and display with a gray plus sign bullet—indicating that subordinate levels display below those paragraphs. Level 2 paragraphs are indented. All other paragraphs are indented and display with a smaller gray bullet to indicate ***body text***. Outline view does not display paragraph alignments—in this case, the first two paragraphs do not display as centered.

MAC TIP   To display group names on the ribbon, display the menu, click Word, click Preferences, click View, select the Show group titles check box.

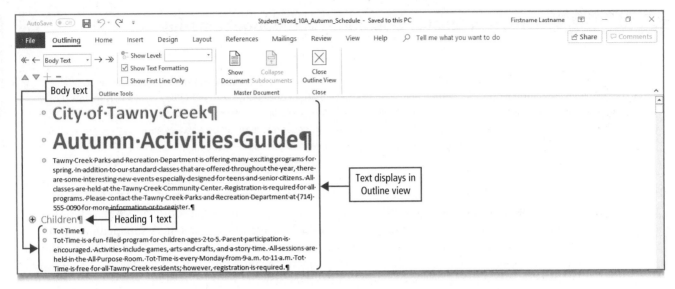

Figure 10.2

> **4** Click to position the insertion point to the left of the paragraph *Children*. Compare your screen with Figure 10.3.
>
>> On the Outlining tab, in the Outline Tools group, the Outline Level box displays Level 1. Paragraphs formatted with Heading 1 are the top-level paragraphs in the document.

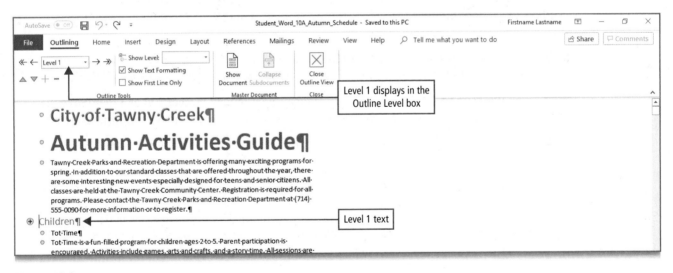

Figure 10.3

> **5** Immediately below the paragraph *Children*, click to position the insertion point to the left of the paragraph *Tot Time*. On the **Outlining tab**, in the **Outline Tools group**, click the **Outline Level arrow** Body Text ▾, and then compare your screen with Figure 10.4.
>
>> You can set up to 9 levels for specific paragraphs and you can change a paragraph to Body Text by using Outline view.

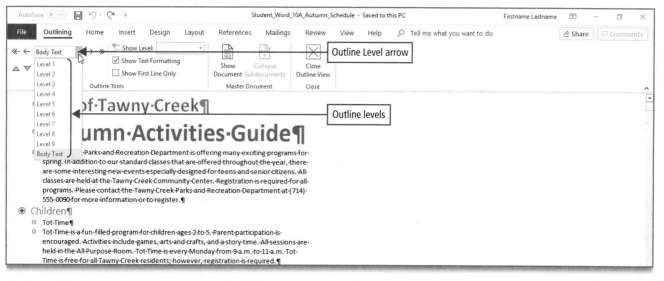

Figure 10.4

6 ▶ Click **Level 2**, and then notice that a gray bullet containing a plus sign displays to the left of *Tot Time* and the text formatting is changed.

> The *Tot Time* paragraph is assigned a Level 2 heading and the Heading 2 style is applied.

7 ▶ Click to position the insertion point in the paragraph *Ballet for Preschoolers*. On the **Outlining tab**, in the **Outline Tools group**, click **Demote** →.

> The Demote button moves a selected paragraph to a lower level. In this case, the paragraph is changed from a Level 1 to a Level 2 and the Heading 2 style is applied.

8 ▶ If necessary, scroll down to the view the *Tap Dance* paragraph, and then click to position the insertion point in the paragraph *Tap Dance*. On the **Outlining tab**, in the **Outline Tools group**, click **Promote** ←. Compare your screen with Figure 10.5.

> The Promote button moves a selected paragraph to a higher level. In this case, the paragraph is changed from a Level 3 to a Level 2 and the Heading 2 style is applied. The *Tot Time*, *Toddler Aquatics*, *Ballet for Preschoolers*, *Tap Dance*, and *Beginning Karate* paragraphs all display as Level 2 under the Level 1 *Children* paragraph.

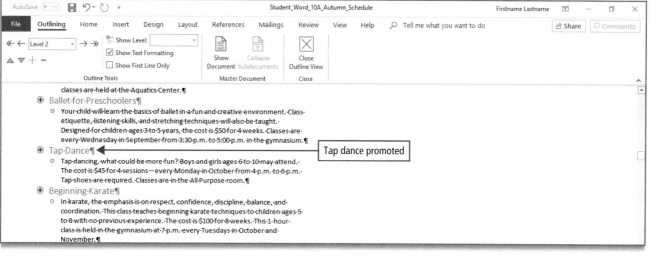

Figure 10.5

9 ▶ Press `Ctrl` + `Home`, and then click to the left of *Children*. Drag down to select all remaining paragraphs in the document. On the **Outlining tab**, in the **Master Document group**, click **Show Document** to toggle it on, and then click **Create**. Press `Ctrl` + `Home`, and then scroll down slightly so that the Children paragraph is at the top of the Word window. Compare your screen with Figure 10.6.

The first heading level in the selection determines where each subdocument is created. In this instance, the Level 1 headings of the document are used to create subdocuments. A light gray border displays around each subdocument, and a subdocument icon displays to the left of the first line of each new subdocument.

Continuous section breaks define the beginning and end of each subdocument. Recall that a ***section break*** is a mark that stores the section formatting information, such as the margins, page orientation, headers and footers, and sequence of page numbers. A continuous section break indicates that the section will begin on the same page of the document.

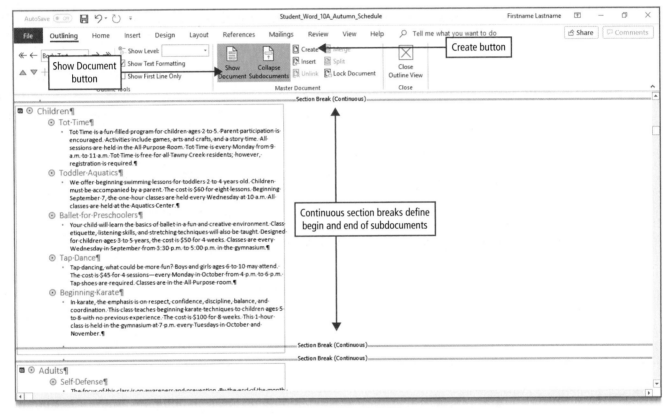

Figure 10.6

10 ▶ **Save** 🖫 your changes.

Activity 10.02 | Collapsing and Displaying Subdocuments

When a master document is created, the subdocuments display in expanded form—all text in the document is visible. You can collapse one or more subdocuments to hide a portion of the text.

1 On the **Outlining tab**, in the **Master Document group**, click **Collapse Subdocuments**. Compare your screen with Figure 10.7.

The subdocuments are collapsed and display as hyperlinks. Each subdocument is saved as a separate document in the same location as the master document—in this case, your Project 10A folder. The file name of the subdocument is created from the heading text of the subdocument. In this case, the subdocuments are named *Children*, *Adults*, *Families*, and *Senior Citizens*. The files for a master document and its subdocuments are usually stored in the same folder.
When the master document is collapsed, the Lock icon displays next to the links for all subdocuments. When a subdocument is locked, no one else can make changes to it.

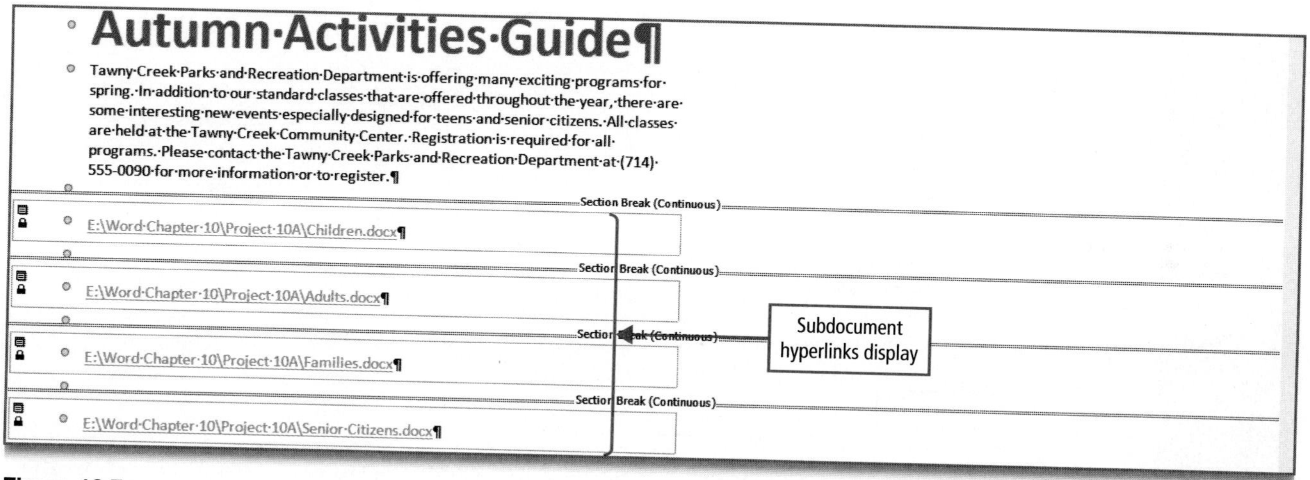

Autumn·Activities·Guide¶
Tawny·Creek·Parks·and·Recreation·Department·is·offering·many·exciting·programs·for·spring.·In·addition·to·our·standard·classes·that·are·offered·throughout·the·year,·there·are·some·interesting·new·events·especially·designed·for·teens·and·senior·citizens.·All·classes·are·held·at·the·Tawny·Creek·Community·Center.·Registration·is·required·for·all·programs.·Please·contact·the·Tawny·Creek·Parks·and·Recreation·Department·at·(714)·555-0090·for·more·information·or·to·register.¶
Section Break (Continuous)
E:\Word·Chapter·10\Project·10A\Children.docx¶
Section Break (Continuous)
E:\Word·Chapter·10\Project·10A\Adults.docx¶
E:\Word·Chapter·10\Project·10A\Families.docx¶
Section Break (Continuous)
E:\Word·Chapter·10\Project·10A\Senior·Citizens.docx¶
Subdocument hyperlinks display

Figure 10.7

MORE KNOWLEDGE **Locking a Subdocument**

If you want to lock a specific subdocument, position the insertion point in the subdocument, and then on the Outlining tab, in the Master Document group, click the Lock Document button.

2 Point to the **Word Chapter 10\Project 10A\Children.docx** hyperlink, press and hold down Ctrl, and then click the link to open the *Children* subdocument. Notice that the subdocument displays in a new window with the default Office theme applied.

MAC TIP Point to the hyperlink and click. If a message box displays, click OK.

3 **Close** ✕ the **Children** document.

Because you opened the *Children* subdocument by clicking the hyperlink, the color of the hyperlink changes in the master document.

4 **Save** your changes.

Activity 10.03 | Inserting an Existing File as a Subdocument

Any existing document can be inserted as a subdocument in a master document. The subdocuments must be expanded when inserting a new document.

1 On the **Outlining tab**, in the **Master Document group**, click **Expand Subdocuments**. From the files you downloaded with this project, **Open** the file **w10A_Teens**.

The first paragraph is formatted with the Heading 1 style, and the four paragraph headings are formatted with the Heading 2 style.

2 Display the **Save As** dialog box, navigate to your **Project 10A** folder, and then compare your screen with Figure 10.8.

The four subdocuments that were saved when you created the master document display in your Project 10A folder along with your master document.

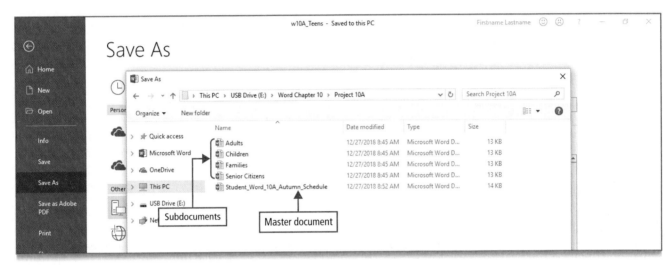

Figure 10.8

3 **Save** the file in your **Project 10A** folder as **Lastname_Firstname_10A_Teens** and then **Close** ✕ the *Teens* document.

4 In the **Student_Word_10A_Autumn_Schedule** document, press Ctrl + End. On the **Outlining tab**, in the **Master Document group**, if necessary, click Show Document to toggle it on, and then click **Insert**. In the **Insert Subdocument** dialog box, navigate to your **Project 10A** folder, select **Lastname_Firstname_10A_Teens**, and then click **Open**.

The existing document is inserted as a subdocument. Because Heading 1 and Heading 2 styles were applied in the *Teens* document, the respective levels are maintained in the subdocument.

5 **Save** 🖫 your changes, and then compare your screen with Figure 10.9.

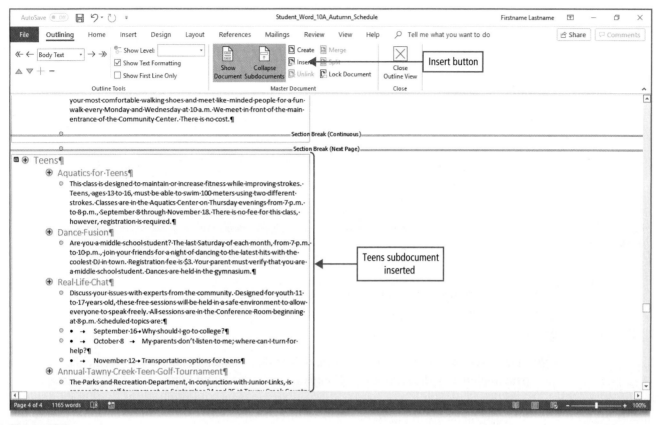

Figure 10.9

| Objective 2 | **Manage a Master Document and Subdocuments** |

GO! Learn How
Video W10-2

There are two ways to edit a subdocument—by editing the master document or by editing the subdocument.

Activity 10.04 | **Editing a Master Document and Subdocuments**

1 In the master document, under *Teens*, locate the paragraph under *Dance Fusion*. Change the registration fee from *$3* to **$4** and then **Save** the document.

The changes to a subdocument can be made in the master document.

2 **Open** your **Lastname_Firstname_10A_Teens** file. Compare your screen with Figure 10.10.

The change that you made to the cost for Dance Fusion displays as $4 in this subdocument. When changes are made to the master document, they are also reflected in the subdocument.

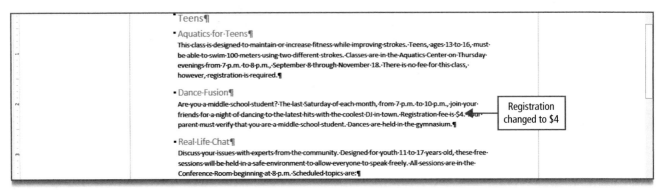

Figure 10.10

3 In the **Lastname_Firstname_10A_Teens** document, locate the paragraph below *Real Life Chat*. In the second sentence, change the ages from *11 to 17* to **13 to 16**

4 **Save** 🖫 your changes, and then **Close** ⊠ the **Lastname_Firstname_10A_Teens** document.

5 In the **Student_Word_10A_Autumn_Schedule** document, under *Teens*, locate the paragraph below *Real Life Chat*. Compare your screen with Figure 10.11.

Your 10A_Autumn_Schedule document reflects the change you made in your 10A_Teens document for ages 13 to 16.

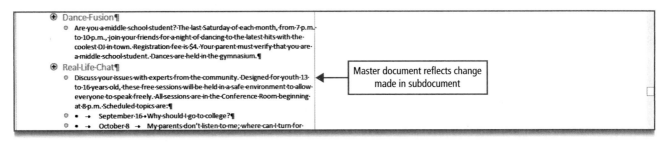

Figure 10.11

6 On the **Outlining tab**, in the **Close group**, click **Close Outline View**. **Save** 🖫 your changes.

Objective 3 Navigate and Inspect the Master Document

GO! Learn How
Video W10-3

After all subdocuments have been edited, it is important to view the master document and, if necessary, make any final revisions. Word provides several features for examining a document—such as browsing the document by pages or locating a specific item. In a long document, these features enable you to navigate quickly to the sections you want to review.

Activity 10.05 | Using the Navigation Pane to View a Document

1 Press **Ctrl** + **Home**. Click the **View tab**, and then in the **Show group**, select the **Navigation Pane** check box. Notice that the **Navigation** pane displays to the left of your document. Near the top of the **Navigation** pane, click **Pages**. Compare your screen with Figure 10.12.

The Navigation pane contains three ways to browse your document—by headings, by pages, or by using the results of a search. The Navigation pane displays *thumbnails*—graphical representations of pages—for all the pages in your document. In this case, the current page—where the insertion point is located—displays and is selected in the Navigation pane.

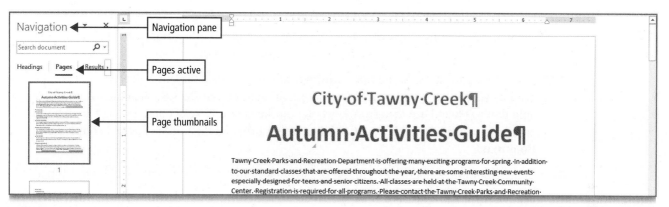

Figure 10.12

🖥 **MAC TIP**   In the Navigation Pane, if necessary, click Thumbnails Pane.

2 In the **Navigation** pane, click the thumbnail for page **3**. Notice that the top of **Page 3** displays.

3 Near the top of the **Navigation** pane, click **Headings**. Compare your screen with Figure 10.13.

In the Navigation pane, the individual headings in your document display.

🖥 **MAC TIP**   In the Navigation Pane, click Document Map.

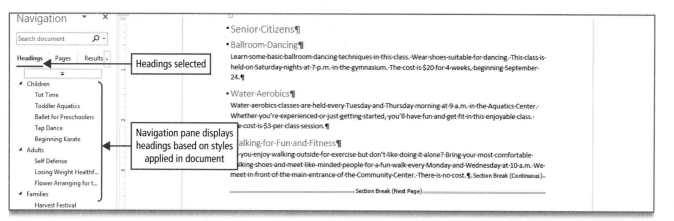

Figure 10.13

4 In the **Navigation** pane, under **Children**, click the heading **Beginning Karate**. Notice the *Beginning Karate* heading displays at the top of your screen. Leave the Navigation pane open for the next activity.

MORE KNOWLEDGE **Rearranging the Content in a Document**

You can drag and drop a tab in the Browse Headings list to move a heading or subheading and all related paragraphs to a new location in the document.

Activity 10.06 | Creating Bookmarks

MOS
1.1.2

A ***bookmark*** identifies the exact location of text, a table, or other object that you name for future reference. You can use bookmarks to locate specific parts of a document quickly.

1 In the **Navigation** pane, click the **Adults** heading. In the document, select the text for the heading *Adults* but do *not* select the paragraph mark that follows the heading. If necessary, hold down Shift and use the arrow keys on your keyboard to select and deselect so that the paragraph mark is *not* selected. Click the **Insert tab**, and then in the **Links group**, click **Bookmark**.

2 In the **Bookmark** dialog box, in the **Bookmark name** box, type **Adults** and then compare your screen with Figure 10.14.

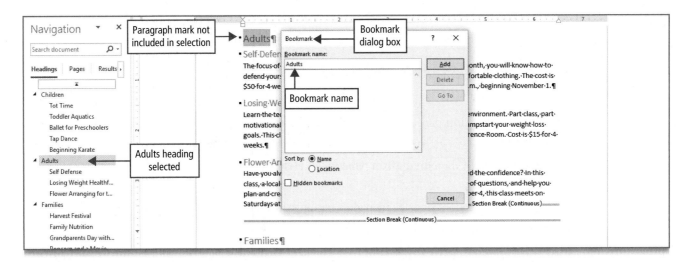

Figure 10.14

3 Click **Add**.

4 In the **Navigation** pane, click the heading **Children**. In the document, select the text for the heading *Children* but do *not* select the following paragraph mark. In the **Links group**, click **Bookmark**. In the **Bookmark** dialog box, in the **Bookmark name** box, type **Children** and then click **Add**.

5 Use the same selection technique and then insert bookmarks for the *Families* heading and the *Teens* heading, using the **Bookmark name Families** and **Teens** respectively.

When bookmarks are added to a document, by default they are listed in alphabetical order by name.

6 In the document, select the heading text *Senior Citizens*. In the **Links group**, click **Bookmark**. In the **Bookmark** dialog box, in the **Bookmark name** box, type **Senior_Citizens** and then click **Add**.

> Bookmark names cannot include spaces; however, you can insert an underscore between the two words in a bookmark name.

7 Press Ctrl + Home. In the **Navigation** pane, click the **Search document arrow**, and then click **Go To**.

🖥 **MAC TIP**   On the menu, click Edit, point to Find, and then click Go To.

---

8 In the **Find and Replace** dialog box, with the **Go To tab** selected, in the **Go to what** box, scroll as necessary and then click **Bookmark**. Click the **Enter bookmark name arrow**, and then compare your screen with Figure 10.15.

> All five bookmarks display in alphabetical order.

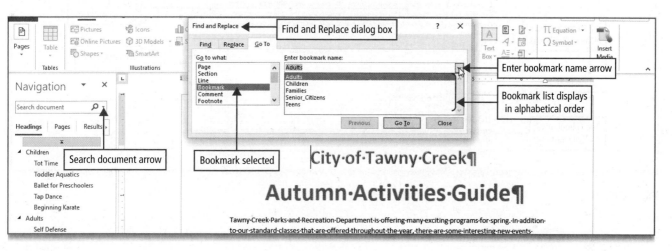

Figure 10.15

9 From the list, click **Teens**, and then click **Go To**. **Close** ☒ the **Find and Replace** dialog box, and then **Close** ☒ the **Navigation** pane.

> The section of the document that begins with the bookmark *Teens* displays and the *Teens* heading is selected.

10 **Save** 🖫 your changes.

MORE KNOWLEDGE   **Defining a Bookmark for a Range of Pages**

To define a bookmark for a range of pages—or paragraphs—select the paragraphs you want to include, and then on the Insert tab, in the Links group, click Bookmark. In the Bookmark dialog box, type a name for the bookmark, and then click Add.

Activity 10.07 | Creating Cross-References

> A *cross-reference* is a text link to an item that displays in another location in the document, such as a heading, a caption of a figure, or a footnote. Cross-references function as internal hyperlinks that enable you to move quickly to specific locations in a document.

1 Press `Ctrl` + `Home`. In the paragraph that begins *Tawny Creek Parks and Recreation*, in the second sentence, select the text *teens*, being careful not to select any spaces.

> When creating a cross-reference, either select text or place the insertion point where you want the cross-reference to display in your document. In this case, you want the cross-reference to display instead of the word *teens*.

2 On the **Insert tab**, in the **Links group**, click **Cross-reference**. In the **Cross-reference** dialog box, click the **Reference type arrow**, and then click **Bookmark**. If necessary, click the Insert reference to arrow to display Bookmark text, and select the Insert as hyperlink check box.

ANOTHER WAY   On the References tab, in the Captions group, click Cross-reference.

3 Under **For which bookmark**, click **Teens**, and then compare your screen with Figure 10.16.

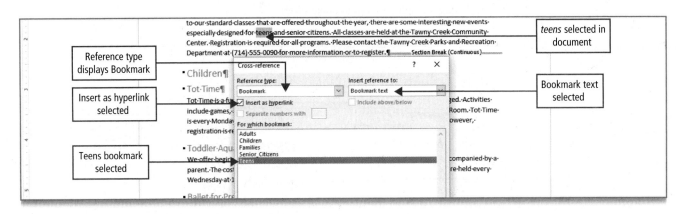

Figure 10.16

4 In the **Cross-reference** dialog box, click **Insert**, and then click **Close**.

> The text you selected when you created the bookmark replaces the existing text in the paragraph. In this case, *Teens* is capitalized.

5 Click anywhere in the text *Teens*. Notice that it displays as a gray box representing a field—a cross-reference. Double-click to select the entire field *Teens*, and then apply **Bold** `B`.

MAC TIP   Do *not* click the Teens cross-reference. Click before the T in Teens, drag to select Teens, and then apply Bold.

6 In the same sentence, select the text *senior citizens*. On the **Insert tab**, in the **Links group**, click **Cross-reference**.

7 In the **Cross-reference** dialog box, if necessary, click the **Reference type arrow**, and then click **Bookmark**. Be sure the **Insert reference to** box displays **Bookmark text**, and the **Insert as hyperlink** check box is selected. Under **For which bookmark**, click **Senior_Citizens**. Click **Insert**, and then click **Close**.

> The formatting of the inserted bookmark text matches the rest of the paragraph, except the underscore is replaced with a space.

8 Select the *Senior Citizens* cross-reference text, and then apply **Bold** `B`. Deselect the text.

> **9** Point to the **Teens** cross-reference. Compare your screen with Figure 10.17.

A ScreenTip displays, indicating how to activate the hyperlink.

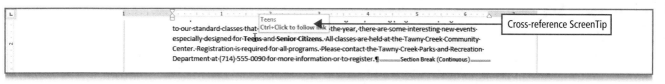

Cross-reference ScreenTip

Figure 10.17

> **10** Hold down Ctrl, and when the 🖱 pointer displays, click **Teens**.

The Teens section of the document displays at the bookmark location.

🖥 **MAC TIP** Point to the Teens cross-reference and click.

> **11** Press Ctrl + Home. **Save** 💾 your changes.

Activity 10.08 | Reviewing Word Count and Readability Statistics

The *word count* of a document indicates the number of words, paragraphs, pages, and characters in a document. If the document will be distributed to a group of people, you may want to determine the ease of readability based on the average number of syllables per word and words per sentence by viewing the *readability statistics*. Readability Statistics is a Spelling and Grammar tool that analyzes a document and determines the reading level of the text.

> **1** On the **Review tab**, in the **Proofing group**, click **Word Count**. Compare your screen with Figure 10.18.

The Word Count dialog box indicates how many words, paragraphs, pages, and characters are contained in the document. In addition, the word count displays on the status bar in Word.

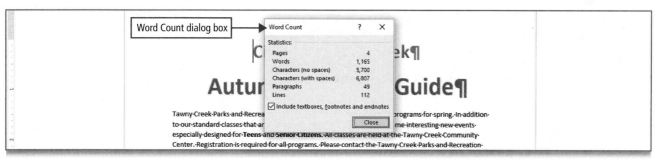

Word Count dialog box

Figure 10.18

> **2** Click **Close** to close the **Word Count** dialog box.

> **3** Click the **File tab**, and then click **Options**. In the **Word Options** dialog box, click **Proofing**. Under **When correcting spelling and grammar in Word**, select the **Show readability statistics** check box to turn on the display of readability statistics. Click **OK**.

🖥 **MAC TIP** On the menu, click Word, and then click Preferences. Click Spelling & Grammar, and then click Show readability statistics. Close the dialog box.

4 On the **Review tab**, in the **Proofing group**, click **Check Document**.

You must complete a spelling and grammar check to review the readability statistics.

5 If the Editor pane displays, click the Results button, and then ignore each error that displays. Compare your screen with Figure 10.19.

In the Readability Statistics dialog box, under Readability, two readability ratings display. The Flesch Reading Ease score is based on a 100-point scale—the higher the score, the easier it is for the reader to understand the document. The Flesch-Kincaid Grade Level score displays the reading level based on U.S. grade levels. For example, 8.0 indicates that the document can be comprehended by a student reading at an eighth grade level.

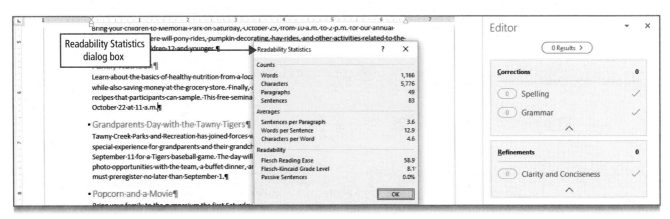

Figure 10.19

6 Click **OK** to close the **Readability Statistics** dialog box, and then close any other message boxes and panes that display, Click the **File tab**, and then click **Options**. In the **Word Options** dialog box, click **Proofing**. Under **When correcting spelling and grammar in Word**, clear the **Show readability statistics** check box. Click **OK**.

> **MAC TIP** On the menu, click Word, and then click Preferences. Click Spelling & Grammar, and then clear the Show readability statistics check box. Close the dialog box.

Activity 10.09 | Finalizing a Master Document

To prepare a master document for distribution, you should remove the links to the subdocuments.

1 If necessary, press Ctrl + Home. On the **View tab**, in the **Views group**, click **Outline**. On the **Outlining tab**, in the **Master Document group**, click **Show Document** to toggle it on. If necessary, in the Master Document group, click Expand Subdocuments. If a Microsoft Word message box displays, click OK to save changes to the master document.

2 To the left of the paragraph *Children*, click the **Subdocument** icon 🔳 to select the entire *Children* subdocument. Compare your screen with Figure 10.20.

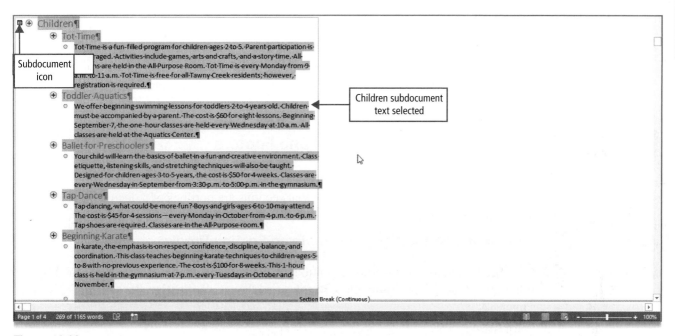

Figure 10.20

3 With the *Children* subdocument selected, in the **Master Document group**, click **Unlink**.

The Children paragraph and all subordinate paragraphs are no longer linked to a subdocument. The Subdocument icon and gray border surrounding the text no longer display.

4 Scroll to display the **Adults** heading, and then click the **Subdocument** icon 🔳 to select the entire *Adults* subdocument. In the **Master Document group**, click **Unlink**.

5 In a similar manner, **Unlink** the subdocuments **Families**, **Senior Citizens**, and **Teens**.

6 Above the paragraph *Children*, click to position the insertion point to the right of the first bullet for *Section Break (Continuous)*. Compare your screen with Figure 10.21.

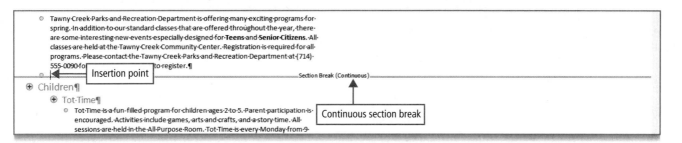

Figure 10.21

7 Press Delete to remove the **Section Break (Continuous)**. In a similar manner, delete all instances of **Section Break (Continuous)** and **Section Break (Next Page)**.

The section breaks are no longer needed because the subdocuments are no longer defined.

🖥 **MAC TIP** Position the insertion point to the left of each heading that follows each section break. For example, click to the left of the Children heading. Hold down command ⌘ and press delete. Some headings are preceded by two section breaks. Be sure to delete all breaks, including the one at the end of the document.

> **8** On the **Outlining tab**, in the **Close group**, click **Close Outline View**.

> **9** Press Ctrl + Home, and then **Save** 🖫 your changes.

MORE KNOWLEDGE | **Opening a Master Document**

If you open a master document, the subdocuments are collapsed and display as hyperlinks. To view the entire document, on the View tab, in the Views group, click Outline. On the Outlining tab, click the Expand Subdocuments button.

Objective 4 | **Create and Modify Headers and Footers**

You can display different headers and footers on the first page, odd pages, and even pages in a document by inserting section breaks. Recall that sections are portions of a document that can be formatted differently.

GO! Learn How
Video W10-4

Activity 10.10 | Inserting and Formatting Odd and Even Section Breaks

2.3.3

> **1** On **Page 1**, position the insertion point to the left of the paragraph *Children*. On the **Layout tab**, in the **Page Setup group**, click **Breaks**, and then under **Section Breaks**, click **Even Page**.

The paragraph *Children* displays at the top of Page 2.

> **2** Press Ctrl + Home, and then compare your screen with Figure 10.22.

An ***Even Page section break*** is inserted at the end of Page 1. An Even Page section break is a formatting mark that indicates the beginning of a new section on the next even-numbered page.

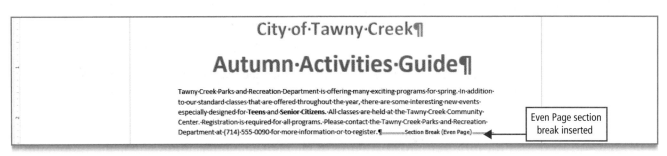

Figure 10.22

> **3** On **Page 2**, under the *Beginning Karate* paragraph, click to position the insertion point at the end of the paragraph that begins with *In karate*. On the **Layout tab**, in the **Page Setup group**, click **Breaks**, and then under **Section Breaks**, click **Odd Page**. If a blank paragraph displays at the top of page 3, delete it.

The paragraph *Adults* displays at the top of Page 3. An ***Odd Page section break*** is inserted on Page 2. An Odd Page section break is a formatting mark that indicates the beginning of a new section on the next odd-numbered page.

> **4** Using the same technique, insert an **Even Page** section break at the end of the paragraph below *Flower Arranging for the Novice* and *Walking for Fun and Fitness*. Insert an **Odd Page** section break at the end of the paragraph below *Popcorn and a Movie*. Scroll through your document and delete any blank paragraphs that display at the top of each page.

5 On **Page 2**, double-click in the footer area. On the **Header & Footer Tools Design tab**, in the **Options group**, select the **Different Odd & Even Pages** check box. Scroll to display the bottom of **Page 2** and the top of **Page 3**. Compare your screen with Figure 10.23.

At the bottom of Page 2, the text *Even Page Footer – Section 2* displays on the footer tab. At the top of Page 3, the text *Odd Page Header – Section 3* displays on the header tab. By inserting section breaks and selecting different formatting options, you can insert different text or objects in the various sections of the document.

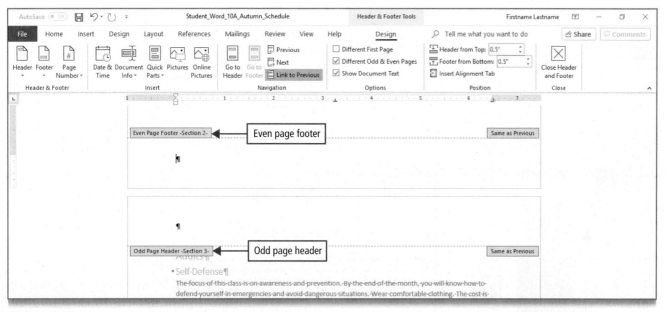

Figure 10.23

6 With the insertion point in the footer **Even Page Footer – Section 2**, press Tab two times, and then type **City of Tawny Creek**

7 On the **Header & Footer Tools Design tab**, in the **Navigation group**, click **Next**. Notice that the insertion point displays in the footer *Odd Page Footer – Section 3*.

8 With the insertion point in the *Odd Page Footer – Section* 3 footer, insert the **File Name**. In the **Navigation group**, click **Next**. Compare your screen with Figure 10.24.

The right-aligned text *City of Tawny Creek* displays. Because this is an even page footer, the file name does not display.

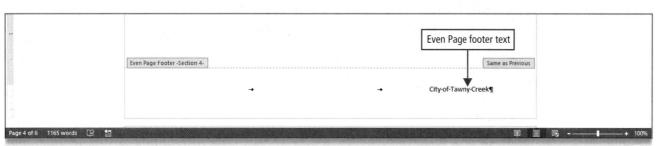

Figure 10.24

9 In the **Navigation group**, click **Previous** three times to display the footer **Odd Page Footer – Section 1**. In the **Close group**, click **Close Header and Footer**. **Save** your changes.

Activity 10.11 | Inserting a Cover Page

A ***cover page*** is the first page of a document that provides introductory information—for example, the title, the author, a brief description, or a date.

1 Press Ctrl + Home. Click the **Insert tab**, and then in the **Pages group**, click **Cover Page** to display the **Cover Page** gallery. Compare your screen with Figure 10.25.

The Cover Page gallery contains predesigned cover page styles.

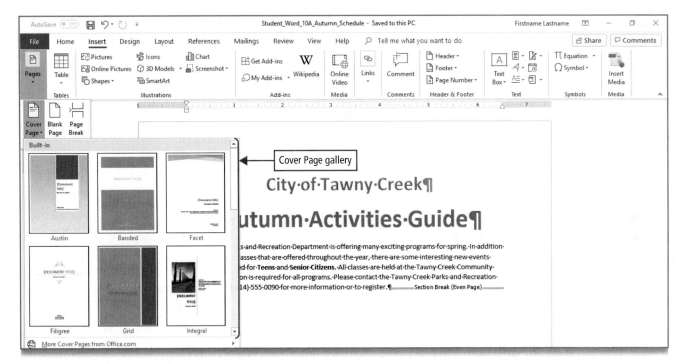

Figure 10.25

2 In the **Cover Page** gallery, locate and click **Facet**.

The cover page, which contains text placeholders, is inserted on a new first page of the document.

3 If necessary, scroll down and then click in the **Document title** placeholder. Type **autumn events** and notice that although the text is typed in lowercase, the placeholder is formatted to display text in All caps. Below the title, click in the **Document subtitle** placeholder. Type **Tawny Creek** and then click in the **Abstract** placeholder. Be sure that the Abstract field is active, and then type **Draft schedule for autumn activities**

4 Scroll to view the bottom of the page, and then click in the **Email address placeholder** to display the text box enclosing the Author and Email placeholders. Click the text box dashed border, and then press Delete to delete the text box. Compare your screen with Figure 10.26.

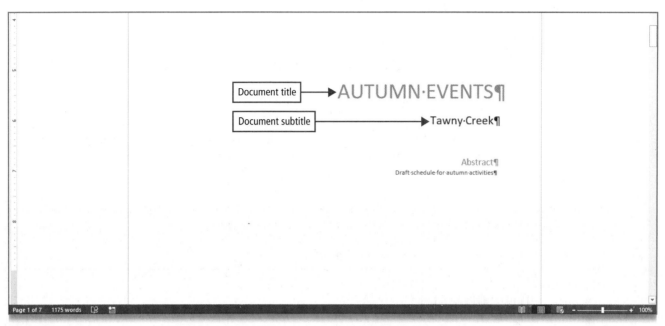

Figure 10.26

5 Press Ctrl + Home, and then **Save** 🖫 your document.

Activity 10.12 | Inserting a Watermark

1.2.4

A ***watermark*** is a text or graphic element that displays behind document text. You add a watermark to identify the status of a document or to create a visual impact. In this Activity, you will add a watermark to indicate that the Autumn Events schedule is a draft document.

1 With the insertion point at the top of **Page 1**, click the **Design tab**, and then in the **Page Background group**, click **Watermark**. Scroll down, and then under **Disclaimers**, click the second watermark style—**Draft 2**. Scroll down to view the cover page title, subtitle, and abstract, and then compare your screen with Figure 10.27.

The word DRAFT displays on the background of the page in a light gray. The watermark only displays on page 1 because the document is divided into sections. A watermark displays on the pages within the section in which the watermark is inserted.

> **MAC TIP** In the Insert Watermark dialog box, click the Text option button. Click the Text arrow, and then click DRAFT. Click OK. In your Mac document, the watermark displays on all pages.

Figure 10.27

MORE KNOWLEDGE | **Inserting a Picture as a Watermark**

To insert a picture as a watermark, on the Design tab, in the Page Background group, click Watermark. In the Watermark gallery, click Custom Watermark. In the Printed Watermark dialog box, select Picture watermark, and then click Select Picture. In the Insert Pictures dialog box, navigate to the location of the image, and then click Insert. Change the Scale and Washout options as desired, and then click OK.

2 Display the document **Properties**.

The Title and Subtitle placeholders in the cover page are linked to the Title and Subject document properties respectively. The text *autumn events* may display in the Title box and the text *Tawny Creek* may display in the Subject box. For this project, you will not enter a Subject in the document properties.

3 In the **Tags** box, type **autumn schedule** and then **Save** and **Close** ✕ your document.

For Non-MyLab Submissions Determine What Your Instructor Requires
As directed by your instructor, submit your completed Word file.

4 In **MyLab IT**, locate and click the Grader Project **Word 10A Autumn Schedule**. In **step 3**, under **Upload Completed Assignment**, click **Choose File**. In the **Open** dialog box, navigate to your **Word Chapter 10 folder**, open your **Project 10A** folder, and then click your **Student_Word_10A_Autumn_Schedule** file one time to select it. In the lower right corner of the **Open** dialog box, click **Open**.

The name of your selected file displays above the Upload button.

5 To submit your file to **MyLab IT** for grading, click **Upload**, wait a moment for a green **Success!** message, and then in **step 4**, click the blue **Submit for Grading** button. Click **Close Assignment** to return to your list of **Course Materials**.

You have completed Project 10A **END**

PROJECT

10B Reference Guide

Project Activities

In Activities 10.13 through 10.25, you will add an index, a table of contents, and a table of figures to a document that describes the City of Tawny Creek. Your completed document will look similar to Figure 10.28.

Project Files for MyLab IT Grader

1. In your **MyLab IT** course, locate and click **Word 10B Reference Guide**, Download Materials, and then Download All Files.
2. Extract the zipped folder to your Word Chapter 10 folder. Close the Grader download screens.
3. Take a moment to open the downloaded **Word_10B_Reference_Guide_Instructions**; note any recent updates to the book.

Project Results

GO! Project 10B

Where We're Going

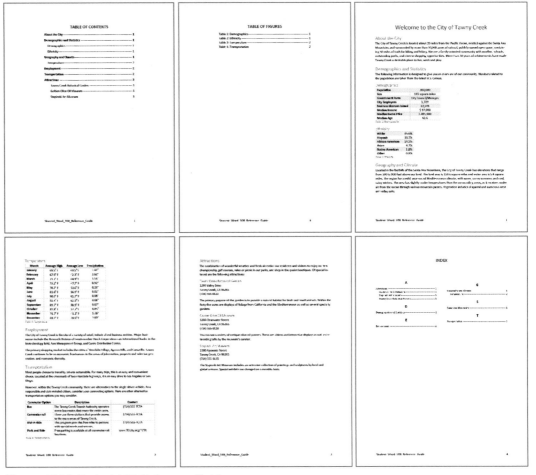

Figure 10.28 Project 10B Reference Guide

For Non-MyLab Submissions

For Project 10B, you will need:

w10B_Reference Guide

In your Word Chapter 10 folder, save your document as:

Lastname_Firstname_10B_Reference_Guide

After you have named and saved your document, on the next page, begin with Step 2.

Objective 5 | Create an Index

GO! Learn How
Video W10-5

An *index* is a compilation of topics, names, and terms accompanied by page numbers that displays at the end of a document. Each entry indicates where the *index entry* can be found. An index entry is a word or phrase that is listed in the index. To create an entry, you mark the words you want to include in the index as an index entry.

Activity 10.13 | Inserting Page Numbers

1 Navigate to your **Word Chapter 10 folder**, and then double-click the Word file you downloaded from **MyLab IT** that displays your name—**Student_Word_10B_Reference_Guide**.

2 If necessary, display the rulers and formatting marks. **Ignore All** spelling errors.

MAC TIP To display group names on the ribbon, display the menu, click Word, click Preferences, click View, select the Show group titles check box.

3 Insert the file name in the footer. With the insertion point to the right of the file name, press Tab two times. On the **Header & Footer Tools Design tab**, in the **Header & Footer group**, click **Page Number**, and then click **Current Position** to display the **Page Number** gallery. Compare your screen with Figure 10.29.

The page numbers in the document are used as a reference in the index. The Page Number gallery provides built-in formats for inserting the page number.

MAC TIP Click Page Number, and then click Page Number again. Click OK, close the footer, and then skip Step 4.

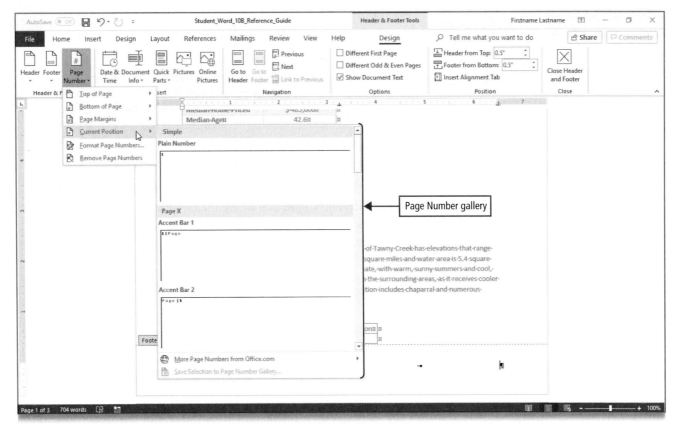

Figure 10.29

4 In the **Page Number** gallery, under **Simple**, click the first style—**Plain Number**. Notice that the page number *1* is inserted in the footer at the right margin. In the **Close group**, click **Close Header and Footer**.

5 On **Page 1**, below *Temperature*, click in the first cell of the table. On the **Table Tools Design tab**, in the **Table Styles group**, click **More**. Under **Grid Tables**, in the first row, click the second style. Compare your screen with Figure 10.30.

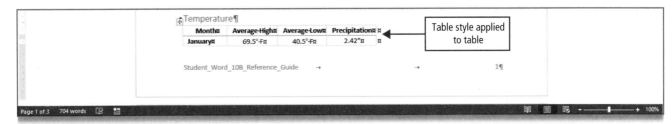

Figure 10.30

6 Scroll to the bottom of **Page 2**, and then apply the same formatting to the table in the *Transportation* section.

7 Save your changes.

Activity 10.14 | Marking Index Main Entries

Expert 3.3.1

An index *main entry* is a word, phrase, or selected text used to identify the index entry.

1 ▶ Press [Ctrl] + [Home]. In the paragraph below the heading *About the City*, select the text **Santa Ana Mountains**.

When creating an index, you must first identify which terms will be used for index entries—in this case, the selected text *Santa Ana Mountains* will be used as an index entry.

2 ▶ Click the **References tab**, and then in the **Index group**, click **Mark Entry** to display the **Mark Index Entry** dialog box. Compare your screen with Figure 10.31, and then take a moment to read the description of the dialog box features in the table shown in Figure 10.32.

Santa Ana Mountains displays in the Main entry box. When text is selected, by default it displays in the Main entry box.

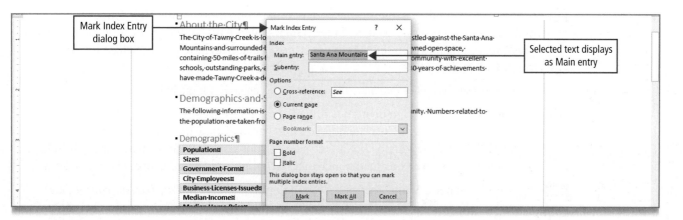

Figure 10.31

Mark Index Entry Dialog Box Features	
Feature	**Description**
Main entry	The word, phrases, or selected text that will be used to identify the index entry.
Subentry	A more specific term that refers to the main entry. For example, the index entry *Transportation* could have subentries for *Automobiles*, *Buses*, and *Trains*.
Cross-reference	An entry that refers the reader to another topic that provides more information. For example, the main entry *England* might be listed in the index as *See United Kingdom*.
Current page	The index entry is marked with the current page number.
Page range	The index entry is marked with a range of page numbers.
Page number format	These options control how the page number will display in the index.
Mark	Marks only the selected text.
Mark All	Marks all occurrences of the selected text in the document.

Figure 10.32

> **3** In the **Mark Index Entry** dialog box, click **Mark All**, and then **Close** the **Mark Index Entry** dialog box. Notice that the index entry displays to the right of the selected text. Compare your screen with Figure 10.33.

> After you mark text as an index entry, Word inserts an *index entry field*, to the right of the selected text. An index entry field is code containing the identifier *XE* and the term to be used in the index. The code is formatted as *hidden text*—nonprinting text. Because you clicked the Mark All button, the occurrence of *Santa Ana Mountains* at the bottom of Page 1 is also marked.

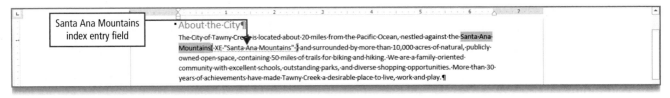

Figure 10.33

> **4** On **Page 1**, select the heading *Demographics and Statistics*. On the **References tab**, in the **Index group**, click **Mark Entry**. In the **Mark Index Entry** dialog box, with *Demographics and Statistics* displayed in the **Main entry** box, click **Mark**, but do not close the **Mark Index Entry** dialog box.

> The text *Demographics and Statistics* is marked as an entry for the index.

> **5** Click in the document, and then select the paragraph *Geography and Climate*. If necessary, point to the **Mark Index Entry** dialog box title bar to display the pointer, and then drag the **Mark Index Entry** dialog box to the side of your screen. With the paragraph still selected, click in the **Main entry** box, and notice that *Geography and Climate* displays. Click **Mark**.

> **6** In a similar manner, **Mark** entries for the paragraphs *Employment*, *Transportation*, and *Attractions*. **Save** your document and leave the **Mark Index Entry** dialog box open for the next Activity.

Activity 10.15 | Marking Index Subentries and Using an AutoMark File

> An index *subentry* is a more specific term that refers to the main entry. In this Activity, you will mark subentries for the Attractions main entry.

> **1** Below *Attractions*, locate the text *Tawny Creek Botanical Garden*, and then position the insertion point to the right of *Garden*. In the **Mark Index Entry** dialog box, click in the **Main entry** box. Type **Attractions** and then click in the **Subentry** box. Type **Tawny Creek Botanical Garden** and then click **Mark**. Compare your screen with Figure 10.34.

> The text *Tawny Creek Botanical Garden* is added as an index subentry under *Attractions*. The index entry field displays the main entry text, a colon, and the subentry text.

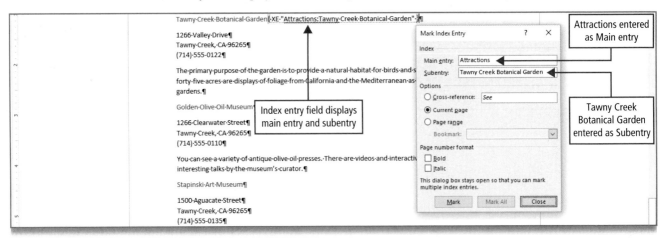

Figure 10.34

2 Position the insertion point to the right of the text *Golden Olive Oil Museum*. In the **Main entry** box, type **Attractions** and in the **Subentry** box, type **Golden Olive Oil Museum** Click **Mark**.

3 Use the same technique to mark the **Stapinski Art Museum** as a **Subentry** under the **Attractions Main entry**, and then **Close** the **Mark Index Entry** dialog box.

4 Save 🖫 your changes.

5 In the **Index group**, click **Insert Index**. In the **Index** dialog box, click **AutoMark** to display the **Open Index AutoMark File** dialog box.

> If a document contains words that are frequently used as index entries, the words can be saved as an *AutoMark file*. An AutoMark file contains a two-column table that is used to mark words that will be used as index entries. The first column lists the terms to be searched for in the document. The second column lists the corresponding entries. In the Open Index AutoMark File dialog box, you can select an AutoMark file to automatically insert index entries in a document.

6 In the **Open Index AutoMark File** dialog box, click **Cancel**.

Activity 10.16 | Inserting an Index

MOS
Expert 3.3.2

After text or phrases have been marked as index entries, the next step is to insert the index. Generally, an index is inserted on a separate page at the end of a document.

1 Press Ctrl + End, and then press Ctrl + Enter to insert a manual page break.

MAC TIP To insert a page break, press command ⌘ + Enter.

2 With the insertion point at the top of the new page, type **INDEX** and then press Enter two times.

3 Select the *INDEX* paragraph you just typed. Change the **Font Size** to **16**, apply **Bold** B, and then change the **Font Color** A ·—in the fifth column, click the last color. **Center** ☰ the text.

4 Position the insertion point in the last blank paragraph at the end of the document. On the **References tab**, in the **Index group**, click **Insert Index** to display the **Index** dialog box.

5 In the **Index** dialog box, on the **Index tab**, click the **Formats arrow**, and then click **Classic**. Click the **Right align page numbers** check box. Compare your screen with Figure 10.35.

> The Index dialog box allows you to select your own options, including predefined index formats, and then preview the selection. You can also create your own index format using a template.

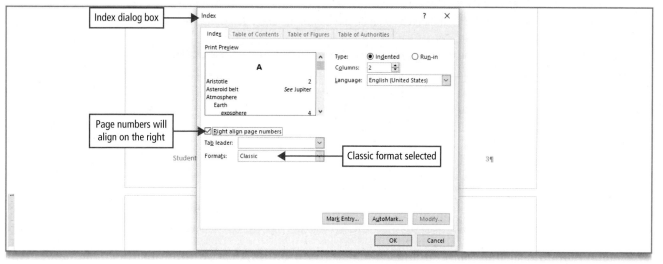

Figure 10.35

> **6** Click **OK**, and then compare your screen with Figure 10.36.

> The index is inserted in a two-column format. Word distributes the text evenly between the two columns. The main entries display alphabetically and the marked subentries display under the *Attractions* main entry.

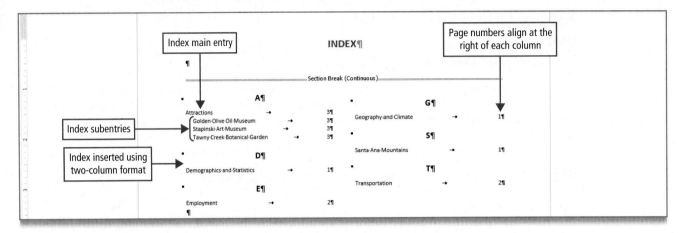

Figure 10.36

> **7** Save 🖫 your changes.

Activity 10.17 | Updating an Index

Expert 3.3.3

After an index has been inserted into a document, the index can be updated if you want to include additional words in the index or if the page numbers in the document change.

> **1** Scroll to the bottom of **Page 1**, and position the insertion point to the right of *Temperature*.

> **2** On the **References tab**, in the **Index group**, click **Mark Entry**. In the **Mark Index Entry** dialog box, in the **Main entry** box, type **Geography and Climate** and then click in the **Subentry** box. Type **Temperature** and then click **Mark**. **Close** the **Mark Index Entry** dialog box.

> **3** Press Ctrl + End. Click anywhere in the index entries, and notice that under the *Geography and Climate* main entry, the newly marked subentry—*Temperature*—does not display in the existing index.

> Because the index is a field, it displays as shaded text.

> **4** On the **References tab**, in the **Index group**, click **Update Index**. Compare your screen with Figure 10.37.

> The index is updated to include the additional entry *Temperature*.

🔄 **ANOTHER WAY** Right-click the Index field, and then from the shortcut menu, click Update Field.

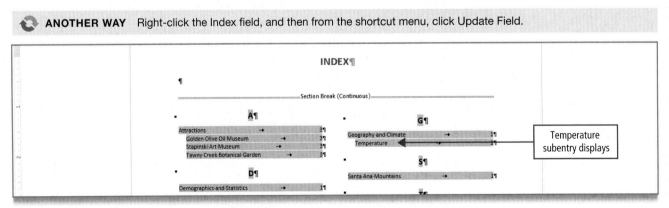

Figure 10.37

> **5** Save 🖫 your changes.

A **table of contents** is a list of a document's headings and subheadings, marked with the page numbers on which those headings and subheadings occur. Many times a table of contents will be abbreviated and referred to as a **TOC**. The TOC is a useful way to navigate a long document because clicking the heading or subheading in the TOC moves you to the page of the heading or subheading you clicked. In most instances, a table of contents displays at the beginning of a document.

GO! Learn How
Video W10-6

Activity 10.18 | Assigning Heading Levels

1 Press Ctrl + Home. At the beginning of **Page 1**, select the second paragraph—*About the City*.

2 On the **References tab**, in the **Table of Contents group**, click **Add Text**. Notice *Level 1* is selected.

> The Add Text button is used to identify the entries that will be included in the table of contents. Each entry in the TOC is identified by a heading level—Level 1 being the highest. When text is formatted with a heading style, Word matches the heading style number with the corresponding level number and automatically adds it to the TOC. In this case, Level 1 is selected because the text is formatted with the Heading 1 style. You can change the level for selected text or add unformatted text to the TOC by assigning the appropriate level.

3 On **Page 3**, select the paragraph *Tawny Creek Botanical Garden*. In the **Table of Contents group**, click **Add Text**, and then click **Level 3**. In a similar manner, assign **Level 3** to the paragraphs *Golden Olive Oil Museum* and *Stapinski Art Museum*. Compare your screen with Figure 10.38.

> Because these paragraphs were not formatted with a Heading style, you must assign a level for the terms to display in the TOC. By selecting *Level 3*, the paragraphs are formatted with the *Heading 3* style.

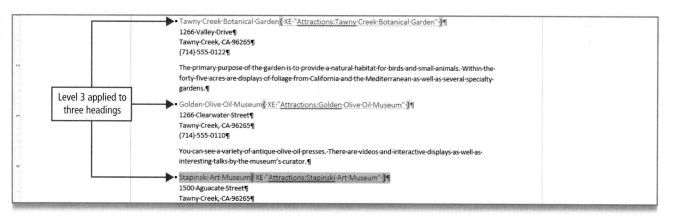

Level 3 applied to three headings

Figure 10.38

4 Press Ctrl + Home, and then **Save** your changes.

Activity 10.19 | Creating and Formatting a Table of Contents

4.2.1, 4.2.2

A table of contents can be customized to include formatting. Any formatting added to the TOC will not affect the rest of the document. It is a good idea to format the TOC to make it stand out from the rest of the document.

1 With the insertion point at the beginning of the document, click the **Layout tab**. In the **Page Setup group**, click **Breaks**, and then under **Section Breaks**, click **Next Page**.

A table of contents is typically displayed as a separate, first page of a document.

2 Press Ctrl + Home to move to the beginning of the document. Click the **Home tab**, and then in the **Styles group**, click **Normal**.

3 Type **TABLE OF CONTENTS** and then press Enter two times.

4 Select the paragraph you just typed. Change the **Font Size** to **16**, apply **Bold** B, and then click **Font Color** A ⋅ to apply the most recently used font color. **Center** the text.

5 On **Page 1**, position the insertion point in the blank paragraph to the left of the section break. Click the **References tab**, and then in the **Table of Contents group**, click **Table of Contents**. Compare your screen with Figure 10.39.

You can insert a built-in table of contents by clicking the style you want, or you can click Custom Table of Contents to create your own TOC style.

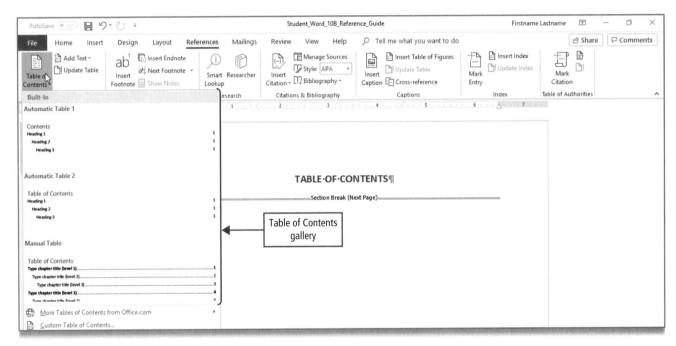

Figure 10.39

6 Below the **Table of Contents** gallery, click **Custom Table of Contents**.

7 In the **Table of Contents** dialog box, under **Web Preview**, if necessary, select the Use hyperlinks instead of page numbers check box. Notice that the **Print Preview** box displays the table of contents format with Heading 2 and Heading 3 indented. Compare your screen with Figure 10.40.

A hyperlink will enable a reader of a document to click a page number in the TOC and move to that part of the document. The Show levels box displays *3*—representing the three heading levels assigned to specific text in the document. By using the Formats arrows, you can select a formatting style for the TOC. The Options button allows you to indicate the headings levels that will be used in the TOC. The Modify button allows you to change the formatting of the TOC—for example, fonts, paragraphs, and tabs.

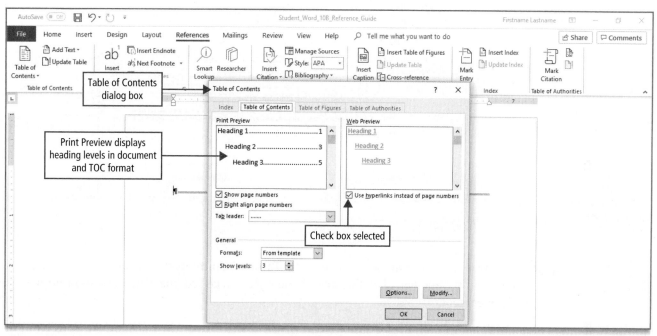

Figure 10.40

8 In the **Table of Contents** dialog box, click **Modify**. In the displayed **Style** dialog box, under **Styles**, if necessary, click to select TOC 1.

Under Preview, the current format for Heading Level 1 displays along with a description of the specific format elements.

9 In the **Style** dialog box, click **Modify**. In the **Modify Style** dialog box, under **Formatting**, click **Bold** [B]. Compare your screen with Figure 10.41.

In the TOC all text assigned Heading Level 1 will display in bold.

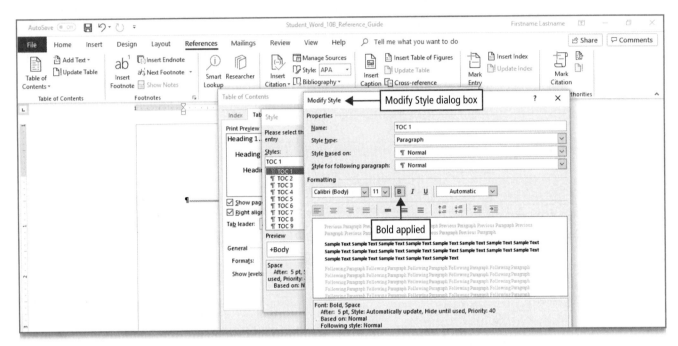

Figure 10.41

10 Click **OK** two times. On the left side of the **Table of Contents** dialog box, click the **Tab leader arrow**, and then click the second line style—a dashed line. Click **OK** to insert the table of contents.

A **tab leader** is a dotted, dashed, or solid line used to connect related information and improve the readability of a line.

11 Drag to select the entire table of contents, do not include the TABLE OF CONTENTS title. Click the **Home tab**, and then in the **Font group**, click the **Font Color arrow** [A▾]. Under **Theme Colors**, in the second column, click the first color—**Black, Text 1**. Click in a blank area of the page, and then compare your screen with Figure 10.42.

All document headings display with the related page number. If a document is edited and page numbers change, you can update the TOC to reflect the changes.

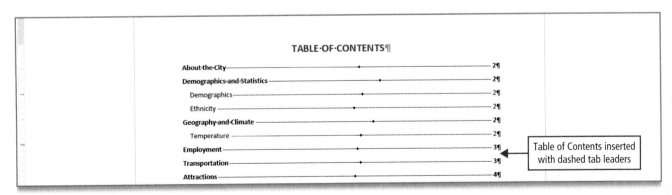

Figure 10.42

12 Point to the *Attractions* entry in the table of contents to display the ScreenTip, which indicates the entry is a hyperlink. Press and hold Ctrl and click **Attractions**.

> The insertion point moves to Page 4 where the related text begins and is positioned to the left of the *Attractions* heading.

MAC TIP Click Attractions to move to the Attractions heading in the document.

13 **Save** 🖫 your changes.

Objective 7 | Create a Table of Figures

GO! Learn How
Video W10-7

A *table of figures* is a list of the figure captions in a document. In most instances, a table of figures displays at the beginning of a document, on a separate page following the table of contents.

Activity 10.20 | Inserting and Modifying Captions and Creating a Table of Figures

MOS

Expert 3.4.1, 3.4.2, 3.4.3

In this Activity, you will add captions to the four tables in the document, and then create the table of figures.

1 On **Page 2**, in the first table—below the heading *Demographics*, click in the first table cell. Click the **References tab**, and then in the **Captions group**, click **Insert Caption**.

2 In the **Caption** dialog box, in the **Caption** box, with the insertion point to the right of *Table 1*, type a colon, and then press Spacebar. Type **Demographics** and then click the **Position arrow**. Click **Below selected item** and then compare your screen with Figure 10.43.

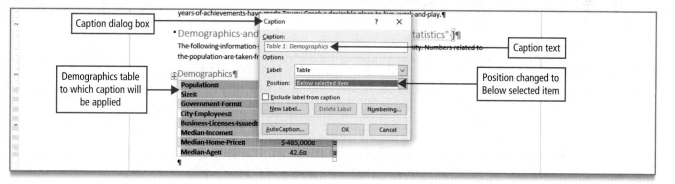

Figure 10.43

3 Click **OK** to display the caption below the table.

Recall that a caption is a title that is added to a Word object and is numbered sequentially.

4 Under **Ethnicity**, click in the first table cell and then insert a caption. In the **Caption** dialog box, under **Caption**, with the insertion point to the right of *Table 2*, type a colon, and then press Spacebar. Type **Ethnicity** and notice that the **Position** box displays *Below selected item.* Click **OK**.

5 In a similar manner, below the third table in the document, insert the caption **Table 3: Temperature** and then, below the fourth table, insert the caption **Table 4: Transportation**

Because the Temperature table is split across two pages, the caption displays at the bottom of the table—on Page 3.

6 Press Ctrl + Home. Click to position the insertion point in the last paragraph of **Page 1**—to the left of the section break. Press Ctrl + Enter to insert a manual page break. Notice that the insertion point moves to the first paragraph on the new, second page.

7 Type **TABLE OF FIGURES** and then press Enter. Press Ctrl + Home and then use **Format Painter** to copy the formatting from the **Table of Contents** text to the **Table of Figures** text.

8 Click to position the insertion point in the blank paragraph to the left of the section break. On the **References tab**, in the **Captions group**, click **Insert Table of Figures**. In the **Table of Figures** dialog box, click the **Tab leader arrow**, and then click the second line style—the dashed line.

The Table of Figures dialog box is similar to the Table of Contents dialog box and provides many of the same options.

9 Click **OK** to insert the table of figures. Compare your screen with Figure 10.44.

The captions and their respective page numbers display, separated by the dashed line tab leader.

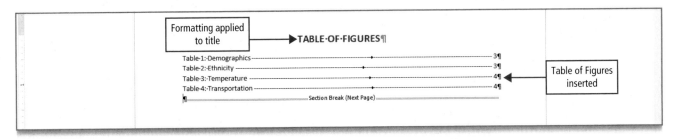

Figure 10.44

10 Point to the *Temperature* entry in the table of figures to display a ScreenTip, which indicates the entry is a hyperlink. Press and hold Ctrl, and then click the **Temperature** entry.

The insertion point moves to Page 4 and is positioned to the left of the *Table 3: Temperature* caption.

11 Save your changes.

Objective 8 | Control the Flow and Formatting of Pages and Text

GO! Learn How
Video W10-8

Recall that page breaks and section breaks allow you to control how text, tables, page numbers, and other objects display in your document. It is important that text flows smoothly and page numbers display properly. The process of arranging and numbering the pages in a document is called *pagination*.

Activity 10.21 | Hiding White Space and Applying Hyphenation

In Print Layout view, to maximize your view of the document, you can hide the white spaces at the top and bottom of each page as well as the gray space between the pages. *Hyphenation* is a feature that enables control of how words are split between two lines, resulting in a less ragged edge at the right margin.

1 Scroll up to display the bottom of **Page 3** and the top of **Page 4**. Position the mouse pointer between the pages until it changes to the **Double-click to hide white space** pointer ⊞, and then double-click. Compare your screen with Figure 10.45.

The white space, including the footer, at the top and bottom of the pages and the gray space between the pages no longer displays. You must be in Print Layout view to use the Hide White Space feature.

Month¤	Average·High¤	Average·Low¤	Precipitation¤	¤
January¤	69.5°·F¤	40.5°·F¤	2.42"¤	¤
February¤	67.9°·F¤	42.3°·F¤	3.62"¤	¤
March¤	71.7°·F¤	44.9°·F¤	1.14"¤	¤
April¤	73.1°·F¤	47.7°·F¤	0.92"¤	¤

Temperature{XE·"Geography·and·Climate:Temperature"·}¶

White space hidden

Figure 10.45

2 Click the **Layout tab**, and then in the **Page Setup group**, click **Hyphenation**. Compare your screen with Figure 10.46.

None is selected because the hyphenation feature is turned off by default. Selecting *Automatic* will cause Word to automatically hyphenate the entire document. If you modify the document, as you work Word will change the hyphenation as necessary. Selecting *Manual* allows you to decide how specific words should be hyphenated. You can select *Hyphenation Options* to modify hyphenation settings for either automatic or manual hyphenation.

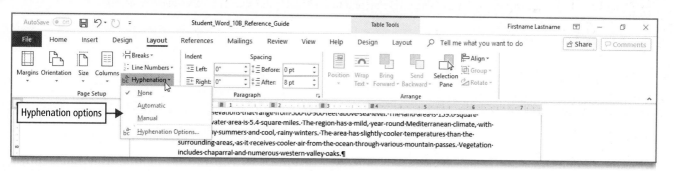

Hyphenation options

Figure 10.46

3 Click **Hyphenation Options**. In the **Hyphenation** dialog box, select the **Automatically hyphenate document** check box, and then in the **Limit consecutive hyphens to** box, type **2**

If several consecutive lines of text contain words that could be hyphenated, Word applies hyphens on only two consecutive lines.

4 Click **OK** to close the **Hyphenation** dialog box. Click the **Home tab**, and then hide the formatting marks.

To view how hyphenation will be applied in the final document, it is useful to hide the formatting marks for the Mark Entry references.

5 ▶ Scroll through the document and notice that on **Page 3**, in the paragraph below the *About the City* heading, in the second line, notice that the word *containing* is hyphenated and in the last paragraph on Page 3, the word *western* is hyphenated.

ALERT   **Different Words Are Hyphenated**

Depending on the width of your screen, word wrapping may cause your text to display differently. The hyphenated word may display on a different line, or the word may display without any hyphenation.

---

6 ▶ Scroll to display the bottom of **Page 3** and the top of **Page 4**. Point to the gray border separating the two pages, and then when the **Double-click to show white space** pointer ⊞ displays, double-click. Notice the white space at the top and bottom of the page and the gray space between the pages display.

7 ▶ Save 🖫 your changes.

Activity 10.22 | Setting Paragraph Pagination Options by Keeping Paragraphs Together on a Page

Expert 2.2.2

There are times when it may enhance the readability and appeal of text to keep paragraphs together on the same page. For example, a bulleted list may be separated and displayed on two pages, but you may want to keep the entire list together on a single page.

1 ▶ If necessary, scroll the document so that the Temperature table, which is split across Pages 3 and 4, displays.

2 ▶ At the bottom of **Page 3**, above the table, drag to select the paragraph *Temperature,* the table, and the *Temperature* caption.

3 ▶ On the **Home tab**, in the **Paragraph group**, click the **Dialog Box Launcher** ⌐ to display the **Paragraph** dialog box.

🖵   **MAC TIP**   Point to the selection, hold down ⌊control⌋ and then click. On the shortcut menu, click Paragraph.

---

4 In the **Paragraph** dialog box, click the **Line and Page Breaks tab**, and then under **Pagination**, select the **Keep with next** check box. Compare your screen with Figure 10.47, and then take a moment to study the table in Figure 10.48.

The *Keep with next* command causes two elements, such as paragraphs, to display together on the same page. For example, it is good practice to keep a heading together with the paragraph of text that follows it. In this case, Word will keep the entire selection—the paragraph and the table—together on the same page.

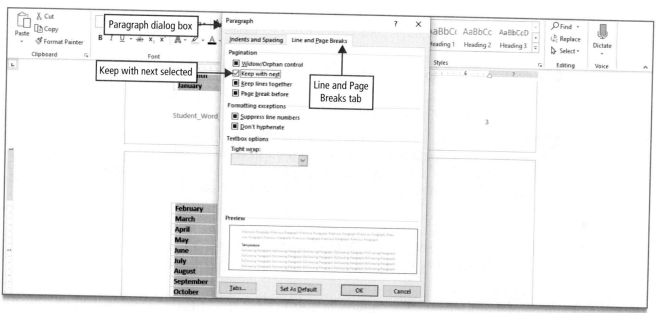

Figure 10.47

Pagination Commands	
Command	**Description**
Widow/Orphan control	Prevents a paragraph from splitting to display a single line at the top—widow—or bottom—orphan—of a page.
Keep with next	Causes two elements, such as paragraphs, to display together on the same page. For example, a heading will display on the same page as the paragraph of text that follows it.
Keep lines together	Prevents a page break from occurring within a paragraph.
Page break before	Forces a page break to occur before a paragraph.

Figure 10.48

5 Click **OK**. Deselect the text, and notice that the paragraph *Temperature* is at the top of the page, above the table.

The heading paragraph *Temperature* refers to the information in the table. Keeping the paragraph and table together on the same page improves readability.

6 Display formatting marks, and then **Save** 🖫 your changes.

Because Mark Entry formatting marks are displayed in some paragraphs, the hyphenation of the document changes when formatting marks are displayed.

Activity 10.23 | Changing Page Settings and Splitting the Window, and Formatting Page Numbers

When a document contains section breaks, you can change the page settings—such as orientation or margins—and page numbering formats for different sections. In this Activity, you will change the page margins for the TOC and table of figures, modify the page numbering for the document, and then update the TOC, table of figures, and index to reflect the changes you made.

1 Press Ctrl + Home. Click the **Layout tab**. In the **Page Setup group**, click **Margins**, and then click **Wide**.

The left and right margins in Section 1 of the document—Page 1 and Page 2—are changed to 2 inches.

2 Click the **View tab**, and then in the **Window group**, click **Split**.

The *Split Window* feature displays a document in two panes so that you can view or work on different parts of the document at the same time.

3 In the top pane, scroll as necessary to display the top of **Page 2**—the paragraph *Table of Figures*—and then click to the left of the word *Table*. In the bottom pane, scroll as necessary to display the top of **Page 3**—the paragraph that begins *Welcome to*—and then click to the left of the word *Welcome*. Compare your screen with Figure 10.49.

Recall that you changed the margins for *Section 1*, which includes the *Table of Figures* page. In the top pane, the horizontal ruler displays left and right margins set to 2 inches. In the bottom pane that displays the beginning of *Section 2*, the horizontal ruler displays the default left and right margin set to 1 inch.

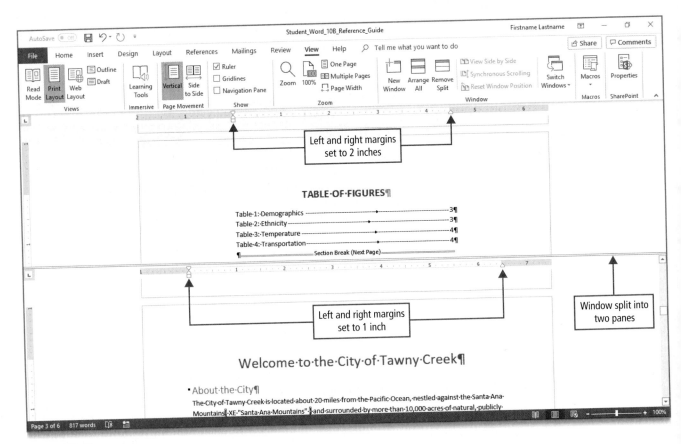

Figure 10.49

4 In the **Window group**, click **Remove Split** to return the document to a single full screen. **Save** your document.

Activity 10.24 | Formatting Page Numbers and Updating the Table of Contents, Table of Figures, and Index

MOS
Expert 3.3.3

Page numbers on the Table of Contents and Table of Figures pages are commonly formatted as roman numerals. In this activity, you will modify the page numbering for the document, and then update the TOC, table of figures, and index to reflect the changes you made.

1 Press [Ctrl] + [Home], and then scroll to the bottom of **Page 1**. Right-click in the footer area, and then click **Edit Footer**.

🖥️ **MAC TIP** Double-click in the footer area.

---

2 In the footer, select the page number **1**. On the **Header & Footer Tools Design tab**, in the **Header & Footer group**, click **Page Number**, and then click **Format Page Numbers**.

In the Page Number Format dialog box, you can modify page number styles.

3 In the **Page Number Format** dialog box, click the **Number format arrow**, and then click the fifth numbering style—**i, ii, iii**. Compare your screen with Figure 10.50.

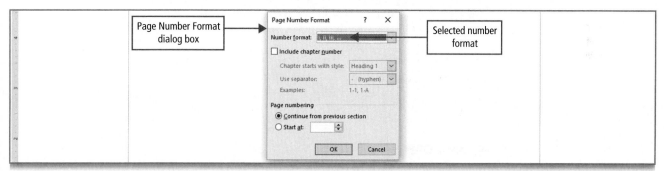

Figure 10.50

4 Click **OK**, and notice that the page number changes to *i*.

5 Scroll to the bottom of **Page 3**. Notice that the page number retains the original numbering style—*3*. Click to position the insertion point anywhere in the footer area on **Page 3**.

At the top left of the footer area, the *Footer - Section 2* tab displays. Page 3 begins Section 2. When you created the TOC page, you inserted a Next Page section break. The TOC and table of figures are in Section 1 of the document. At the top right of the footer area, the *Same as Previous* tab displays.

6 In the **Navigation group**, click **Link to Previous** to toggle it off. Notice that the *Same as Previous* tab no longer displays at the top right of the footer area on **Page 3**. Compare your screen with Figure 10.51.

By clicking the Link to Previous button, the footer for Section 2—the rest of the document—is no longer linked to the footer for Section 1—the first two pages. The Section 2 footer can be modified without affecting the Section 1 footer.

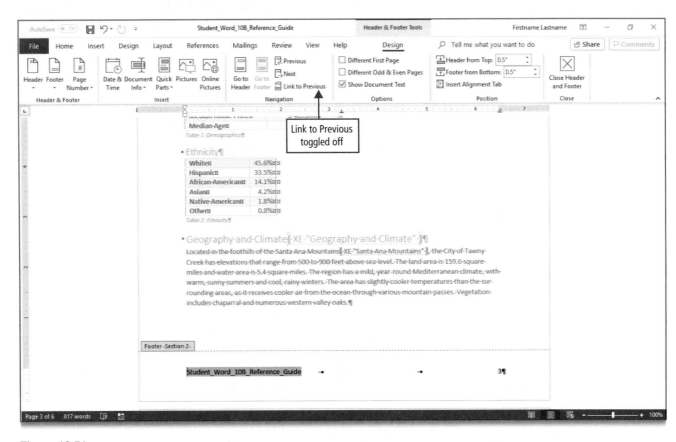

Figure 10.51

7 In the footer, select the page number **3**. In the **Header & Footer group**, click **Page Number**, and then click **Format Page Numbers**. In the **Page Number Format** dialog box, under **Page numbering**, click the **Start at** option button, and then compare your screen with Figure 10.52.

You can use the Start at option to select the first page number that should display in a new section of a document. By default, the number *1* displays in the Start at box.

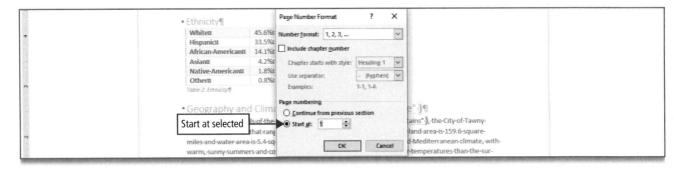

Figure 10.52

8 Click **OK**. Notice that the page number *1* displays in the footer on the third page of the document. In the **Close group**, click **Close Header and Footer**.

9 Press Ctrl + Home. On the **References tab**, in the **Tables of Contents** group, click **Update Table**. In the **Update Table of Contents** dialog box, with the **Update page numbers only** option button selected, click **OK** to update the page numbers in the TOC. Click in the blank paragraph below the TOC, and then compare your screen with Figure 10.53.

> Because you inserted breaks and changed page numbering styles, it is necessary to update the page numbers for the TOC, table of figures, and the index.

ANOTHER WAY Right-click anywhere in the Table of Contents, and then click Update Field.

TABLE·OF·CONTENTS¶

About·the·City ———— 1¶
Demographics·and·Statistics——— 1¶
   Demographics ——— 1¶
   Ethnicity ——— 1¶
Geography·and·Climate——— 1¶
   Temperature ——— 2¶ ◄——— Page numbers updated
Employment ——— 2¶
Transportation ——— 2¶
Attractions——— 3¶

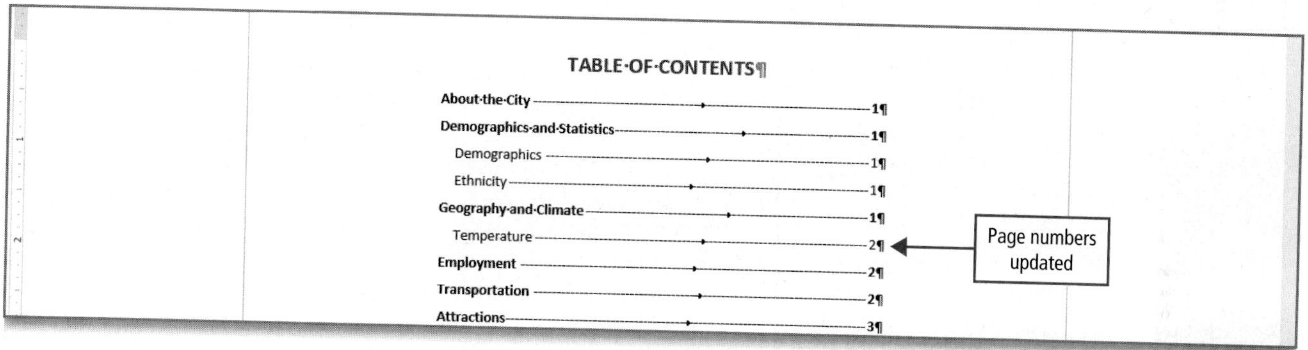

Figure 10.53

10 On the second page of the document, right-click in the **Table of Figures**, and then click **Update Field**. In the **Update Table of Figures** dialog box, with the **Update page numbers only** option button selected, click **OK**.

MAC TIP Select the Table of Figures. On the References tab, in the Captions group, click the Update Table button. Click OK.

11 Press Ctrl + End. Right-click in the **index**, and then click **Update Field**.

> When updating an index, changes are made automatically.

MAC TIP Point to the index, hold down control, and then click to display the shortcut menu. Click Update Field.

12 Save 🖫 your changes.

Activity 10.25 | Configuring Documents to Print, Printing Sections, and Setting Print Scaling

You can modify print settings to suit your needs. For example, you may want to print a range of pages or scale the printout for a specific paper size.

1 Press Ctrl + Home. Click the **File tab**, and then click **Print**.

2 Under **Settings**, click **Print All Pages**. Compare your screen with Figure 10.54.

A list of *Document* and *Document Info* settings displays. You can print specific pages, selected portions of a document, or information related to the document.

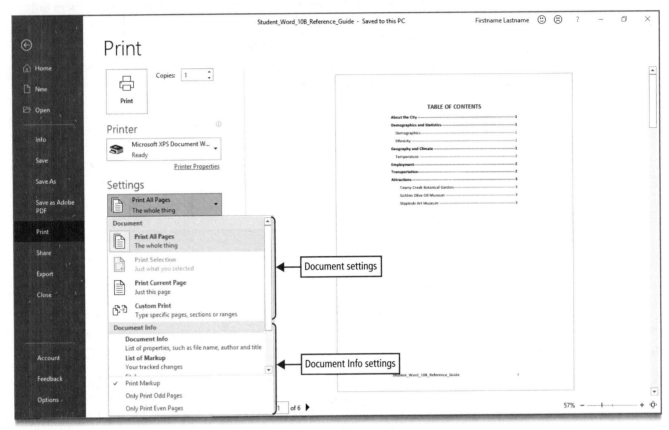

Figure 10.54

3 In the list, scroll as necessary, and then click **Custom Print**. Notice the button immediately below Settings displays *Custom Print* and the insertion point is in the *Pages* box.

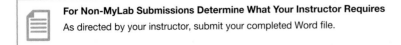
MAC TIP   View the options in the Print dialog box, click Cancel, and then skip to Step 6.

4 Immediately below **Custom Print**, point to **Pages**, and take a moment to read the ScreenTip.

The ScreenTip contains information for printing specific pages, a range of pages, or specific sections of a document. For example type *p1s1* to print the first page in section 1.

5 Under **Settings**, click **1 Page Per Sheet**, and then point to **Scale to Paper Size**.

In the main list, you can select the number of pages on which you want to print your document. In the secondary list, you can select the paper size for the printed document.

6 Display the document **Properties**. In the **Tags** box, type **reference guide** and in the **Subject** box, type your course name and section number. If necessary, edit the author name to display your name.

7 Save 🖫 your changes and **Close** Word.

📄 **For Non-MyLab Submissions Determine What Your Instructor Requires**
As directed by your instructor, submit your completed Word file.

---

8 In **MyLab IT**, locate and click the Grader Project **Word 10B Reference Guide**. In **step 3**, under **Upload Completed Assignment**, click **Choose File**. In the **Open** dialog box, navigate to your **Word Chapter 10 folder**, and then click your **Student_Word_10B_Reference_Guide** file one time to select it. In the lower right corner of the **Open** dialog box, click **Open**.

The name of your selected file displays above the Upload button.

9 To submit your file to **MyLab IT** for grading, click **Upload**, wait a moment for a green **Success!** message, and then in **step 4**, click the blue **Submit for Grading** button. Click **Close Assignment** to return to your list of **Course Materials**.

You have completed Project 10B | **END**

wavebreakmedia/Shutterstock, Monkey Business Images/Fotolia, Ivanko80/Shutterstock, Monkey Business Images/Shutterstock

Microsoft Office Specialist (MOS) Skills in This Chapter	
Project 10A	**Project 10B**
1.1.2 Link to locations within documents	**1.3.3** Modify print settings
1.2.4 Configure page background elements	**4.2.1** Insert tables of contents
2.3.3 Change page setup options for a section	**4.2.2** Customize tables of contents
	Expert 2.2.2 Set paragraph pagination options
	Expert 3.3.1 Mark index entries
	Expert 3.3.2 Create indexes
	Expert 3.3.3 Update indexes
	Expert 3.4.1 Insert figure and table captions
	Expert 3.4.2 Configure caption properties
	Expert 3.4.3 Insert and modify a table of figures

Build Your E-Portfolio

An E-Portfolio is a collection of evidence, stored electronically, that showcases what you have accomplished while completing your education. Collecting and then sharing your work products with potential employers reflects your academic and career goals. Your completed documents from the following projects are good examples to show what you have learned: 10G, 10K, and 10L.

GO! For Job Success

Social Media

Your instructor may assign these questions to your class, and then ask you to think about them or discuss them with your classmates:

You know that you should avoid making social media posts about your employer and never post anything negative about your boss or coworkers. There have been incidents, however, when people lost their jobs over social media posts made on their personal accounts during non-work hours that had nothing to do with their employers. Employers who take this action usually do so in response to an employee post that degrades others or involves illegal activity.

g-stockstudio/Shutterstock

> Do you think an employer should have the right to fire an employee for making a personal social media post that makes negative comments about coworkers or about the company?

> What would you do if you saw a coworker's post that included negative comments about the company?

> What is your employer's or school's policy on social media?

End of Chapter

Summary

When a document is created or edited by several people, one efficient way of assembling or editing the document is to create a master document and subdocuments. Unlink the subdocuments to create a final document.

To navigate to specific locations in a document, use bookmarks, cross-references, and the Navigation pane. Insert section breaks to create different footers on odd and even pages. Include a cover page for interest.

An index indicates where specific text is located in the document. A table of contents helps the reader go directly to specific topics. The reader can use a table of figures to navigate to graphic elements.

Apply hyphenation and pagination options to improve readability. Modify page numbers to differentiate introductory pages—for example, a table of contents—from the main pages of the document.

GO! Learn It Online

Review the concepts and key terms in this chapter by completing these online challenges, which you can find at **MyLab IT**.

Chapter Quiz: Answer matching and multiple choice questions to test what you learned in this chapter.

Lessons on the GO!: Learn how to use all the new apps and features as they are introduced by Microsoft.

MOS Prep Quiz: Answer questions to review the MOS skills that you practiced in this chapter.

Project Guide for Word Chapter 10

Your instructor will assign Projects from this list to ensure your learning and assess your knowledge.

		Project Guide for Word Chapter 10		
Project	**Apply Skills from These Chapter Objectives**	**Project Type**		**Project Location**
10A MyLab IT	Objectives 1–4 from Project 10A	**10A Instructional Project (Grader Project)** Guided instruction to learn the skills in Project 10A.	Instruction	In **MyLab IT** and in text
10B MyLab IT	Objectives 5–8 from Project 10B	**10B Instructional Project (Grader Project)** Guided instruction to learn the skills in Project 10B.	Instruction	In **MyLab IT** and in text
10C	Objectives 1–4 from Project 10A	**10C Skills Review (Scorecard Grading)** A guided review of the skills from Project 10A.	Review	In text
10D	Objectives 5–8 from Project 10B	**10D Skills Review (Scorecard Grading)** A guided review of the skills from Project 10B.	Review	In text
10E MyLab IT	Objectives 1–4 from Project 10A	**10E Mastery (Grader Project)** A demonstration of your mastery of the skills in Project 10A with extensive decision making.	Mastery and Transfer of Learning	In **MyLab IT** and in text
10F MyLab IT	Objectives 5-8 from Project 10B	**10F Mastery (Grader Project)** A demonstration of your mastery of the skills in Project 10B with extensive decision making.	Mastery and Transfer of Learning	In **MyLab IT** and in text
10G MyLab IT	Objectives 1-8 from Projects 10A and 10B	**10G Mastery (Grader Project)** A demonstration of your mastery of the skills in Projects 10A and 10B with extensive decision making.	Mastery and Transfer of Learning	In **MyLab IT** and in text
10H	Combination of Objectives from Projects 10A and 10B	**10H GO! Fix It (Scorecard Grading)** A demonstration of your mastery of the skills in Projects 10A and 10B by creating a correct result from a document that contains errors you must find.	Critical Thinking	IRC
10I	Combination of Objectives from Projects 10A and 10B	**10I GO! Make It (Scorecard Grading)** A demonstration of your mastery of the skills in Projects 10A and 10B by creating a result from a supplied picture.	Critical Thinking	IRC
10J	Combination of Objectives from Projects 10A and 10B	**10J GO! Solve It (Rubric Grading)** A demonstration of your mastery of the skills in Projects 10A and 10B, your decision-making skills, and your critical thinking skills. A task-specific rubric helps you self-assess your result.	Critical Thinking	IRC
10K	Combination of Objectives from Projects 10A and 10B	**10K GO! Solve It (Rubric Grading)** A demonstration of your mastery of the skills in Projects 10A and 10B, your decision-making skills, and your critical thinking skills. A task-specific rubric helps you self-assess your result.	Critical Thinking	In text
10L	Combination of Objectives from Projects 10A and 10B	**10L GO! Think (Rubric Grading)** A demonstration of your understanding of the chapter concepts applied in a manner that you would outside of college. An analytic rubric helps you and your instructor grade the quality of your work by comparing it to the work an expert in the discipline would create.	Critical Thinking	In text
10M	Combination of Objectives from Projects 10A and 10B	**10M GO! Think (Rubric Grading)** A demonstration of your understanding of the chapter concepts applied in a manner that you would outside of college. An analytic rubric helps you and your instructor grade the quality of your work by comparing it to the work an expert in the discipline would create.	Critical Thinking	IRC
10N	Combination of Objectives from Projects 10A and 10B	**10N You and GO! (Rubric Grading)** A demonstration of your understanding of the chapter concepts applied in a manner that you would in a personal situation. An analytic rubric helps you and your instructor grade the quality of your work.	Critical Thinking	IRC

Glossary

Glossary of Chapter Key Terms

AutoMark file A Word document that contains a two-column table used to mark words as index entries.

Body text Text that does not have a heading style applied.

Bookmark A link that identifies the exact location of text, a table, or other object.

Continuous section break A mark that defines the beginning and end of each subdocument.

Cover page The first page of a document that provides introductory information.

Cross-reference A text link to an item that appears in another location in the document, such as a heading, a caption, or a footnote.

Even Page section break A formatting mark that indicates the beginning of a new section on the next even-numbered page.

Hidden text Nonprinting text—for example, an index entry field.

Hyphenation A feature that enables control of how words are split between two lines, resulting in a less ragged edge at the right margin.

Index A compilation of topics, names, and terms accompanied by page numbers that displays at the end of a document.

Index entry A word or phrase that is listed in the index.

Index entry field Code, formatted as hidden text and displaying to the right of an index entry, containing the identifier XE and the term to be included in the index.

Keep with next A formatting feature that causes two elements, such as paragraphs, to display together on the same page.

Master document A Word document that serves as a container for the different parts of a document.

Main entry A word, phrase, or selected text used to identify the index entry.

Odd Page section break A formatting mark that indicates the beginning of a new section on the next odd-numbered page.

Outline view A document view that displays the overall organization, or hierarchy, of the document's parts, including headings, subheadings, and subordinate text.

Pagination The process of arranging and numbering the pages in a document.

Readability statistics A Spelling and Grammar tool that analyzes a document and determines the reading level of the text.

Section break A mark that stores the formatting information for a section of a document.

Split Window A Word feature that displays a document in two panes so that you can view or work on different parts of the document at the same time.

Subdocument A section of a document that is linked to the master document.

Subentry A more specific term that refers to the main entry.

Table of contents (TOC) A list of a document's headings and subheadings, marked with the page numbers where those headings and subheadings occur.

Table of figures A list of the figure captions in a document.

Thumbnail A graphical representation of a page.

Watermark A text or graphic element that displays behind document text.

Word count A Word feature that indicates the number of words, paragraphs, pages, and characters in a document.

XE Code identifying an index entry.

Chapter Review

Apply 10A skills from these Objectives:

1. Create a Master Document and Subdocuments
2. Manage a Master Document and Subdocuments
3. Navigate and Inspect the Master Document
4. Create and Modify Headers and Footers

In the following Skills Review, you will create a master document and subdocuments for events happening during the summer in the City of Tawny Creek. Your completed document will look similar to Figure 10.55.

Project Files

For Project 10C, you will need the following files:

w10C_Summer_Calendar

w10C_Shakespeare_Festival

You will save your files as:

Lastname_Firstname_10C_Summer_Calendar

Lastname_Firstname_10C_Shakespeare_Festival (not shown in figure)

Project Results

Figure 10.55

(continues on next page)

Chapter Review

Skills Review: Project 10C Summer Calendar (continued)

1 Start Word. From your student files, locate and open the file **w10C_Summer_Calendar**. If necessary, display the rulers and formatting marks. Display the **Save As** dialog box, and then open your **Word Chapter 10** folder. Create a folder named **Project 10C** and then save the document in your **Project 10C** folder as **Lastname_Firstname_10C_Summer_Calendar**

a. Click the **View tab**. In the **Views group**, click **Outline** to change to Outline view. Click to position the insertion point to the left of *Tawny Creek Half-Marathon and Marathon*. Drag down to select all remaining paragraphs in the document.

b. On the **Outlining tab**, in the **Master Document group**, click **Show Document** to turn it on, and then click **Create**. Press Ctrl + Home.

c. On the **Outlining tab**, in the **Master Document group**, click **Collapse Subdocuments**. In the **Microsoft Word** message box, click **OK**. On the **Outlining tab**, in the **Master Document group**, click **Expand Subdocuments**, and then **Save**.

2 From your student files, locate and open the file **w10C_Shakespeare_Festival**.

a. Display the **Save As** dialog box, and then navigate to your **Project 10C** folder. Save the file as **Lastname_Firstname_10C_Shakespeare_Festival** and then **Close** the *Shakespeare Festival* document.

b. In the master document, press Ctrl + End to move to the end of the document. In the **Master Document group**, click **Insert**. Navigate to your **Project 10C** folder, select **Lastname_Firstname_10C_Shakespeare_Festival**, and then click **Open** to insert the subdocument.

c. In the master document, under *Summer Shakespeare Festival*, in the second bulleted item, change the month from *July* to **August**

d. On the **Outlining tab**, in the **Close group**, click **Close Outline View**. **Save** your changes.

3 Press Ctrl + Home. Click the **View tab**, and then in the **Show group**, select the **Navigation Pane** check box.

a. In the **Navigation** pane, with the **Headings** tab displayed, click the **Tawny Creek Music Festival** heading. Select the heading *Tawny Creek Music Festival*, using the Shift and arrow keys as necessary so that the paragraph mark is not selected. (Mac users, if necessary, in the Navigation pane, display the document map.)

b. Click the **Insert tab**, and then in the **Links group**, click **Bookmark**. In the **Bookmark** dialog box, in the **Bookmark name** box, type **Tawny_Creek_Music_Festival** and then click **Add**. Press Ctrl + Home.

4 In the **Navigation** pane, click the **Search document arrow**, and then click **Go To**. (Mac users, on the menu, click Edit, point to Find, and then click Go To.) In the **Find and Replace** dialog box, in the **Go to what** box, click **Bookmark**.

a. Below the **Enter bookmark name** box, which displays *Tawny_Creek_Music_Festival*, click **Go To**. **Close** the **Find and Replace** dialog box, and then **Close** the **Navigation** pane.

b. Press Ctrl + Home. In the paragraph that begins *Whether you're a resident*, in the second sentence, select the text **Music Festival**, being careful not to select the space to the left or the period on the right.

c. On the **Insert tab**, in the **Links group**, click **Cross-reference**.

d. In the **Cross-reference** dialog box, click the **Reference type arrow**, and then click **Bookmark**. If necessary, click the **Insert reference to arrow** to display **Bookmark text**, and select the **Insert as hyperlink** check box.

e. Under **For which bookmark**, with *Tawny_Creek_Music_Festival* selected, in the **Cross-reference** dialog box, click **Insert**, and then click **Close**.

5 Move your mouse pointer over the **Tawny Creek Music Festival** cross-reference. Press and hold Ctrl, and when the 🖑 pointer displays, click **Tawny Creek Music Festival**. (Mac users, click the cross-reference, do not press Ctrl.)

a. Press Ctrl + Home. Click the **File tab**, and then click **Options**. In the **Word Options** dialog box, click **Proofing**. Under **When correcting spelling and grammar in Word**, select the **Show readability statistics** check box to turn on the display of readability statistics. Click **OK**. (Mac users, on the menu, click Word, and then click Preferences. Click Spelling & Grammar, and then click Show readability statistics. Close the dialog box.)

b. On the **Review tab**, in the **Proofing group**, click **Check Document** and ignore any grammar corrections.

(continues on next page)

Chapter Review

c. Click **OK** to close the **Readability Statistics** dialog box. Click the **File tab**, and then click **Options**. In the **Word Options** dialog box, click **Proofing**. Under **When correcting spelling and grammar in Word**, clear the **Show readability statistics** check box. Click **OK**. (Mac users, on the menu, click Word, and then click Preferences. Click Spelling & Grammar, and then clear the Show readability statistics check box. Close the dialog box.)

6 Press Ctrl + Home. On the **View tab**, in the **Views group**, click **Outline**. If the subdocument icons do not display, on the Outlining tab, in the Master Document group, click Show Document.

a. To the left of the paragraph *Tawny Creek Half-Marathon and Marathon*, click the **Subdocument** icon to select the entire subdocument. In the **Master Document group**, click **Unlink**.

b. In a similar manner, **Unlink** the subdocuments *Farmer's Market, Tawny Creek Music Festival*, and *Summer Shakespeare Festival*.

c. Above the paragraph *Tawny Creek Half-Marathon and Marathon*, click to position the insertion point to the right of the first bullet for **Section Break (Continuous)**, and then press Delete. In a similar manner, delete all instances of **Section Break (Continuous)** and **Section Break (Next Page)** that display. (Mac users, position the insertion point to the left of each heading that follows each section break. Hold down command ⌘ and press Delete. Some headings are preceded by two section breaks. Be sure to delete all breaks, including the one at the end of the document.)

d. On the **Outlining tab**, in the **Close group**, click **Close Outline View**.

7 Position the insertion point at the end of the paragraph under *Summer Calendar Highlights*. Click the **Layout tab**. In the **Page Setup group**, click **Breaks**, and then under **Section Breaks**, click **Even Page**. Under *Farmer's Market*, position the insertion point at the end of the paragraph that begins *What will you find*, and then insert an **Even Page** section break.

a. Insert **Odd Page** section breaks at the end of the paragraphs that begin *The mission of this event* and *This year marks*.

b. Scroll through the document and delete any blank paragraph marks that display at the top of each page.

c. At the bottom of **Page 2**, double-click in the footer area. On the **Header & Footer Tools Design tab**, in the **Options group**, select the **Different Odd & Even Pages** check box.

d. On **Page 2**, click in the **Even Page** footer, press Tab two times, and then type **Tawny Creek Events**

e. On **Page 3**, in the **Odd Page** footer, insert the file name.

f. In the **Close group**, click the **Close Header and Footer** button. **Save** your changes.

8 Press Ctrl + Home. Click the **Insert tab**. In the **Pages group**, click **Cover Page**, and then click the **Ion (Light)** style.

a. Click in the **Document title** placeholder, and then type **Summer Calendar**

b. Click in the **Document Subtitle** placeholder, and then type **Event Highlights**

c. In the upper right corner of the page, Click in the **Year** placeholder, and then type **2020**

d. In the **Author** placeholder, below the subtitle, if necessary, delete the existing text, and then type your first and last names.

e. On the **Design tab**, in the **Page Background group**, click **Watermark**, and then under **Disclaimers**, click **Draft 2**. (Mac users, in the Insert Watermark dialog box, click the Text option button. Click the Text arrow, and then click DRAFT. Click OK.)

f. Display the document **Properties**. In the **Author** box, verify that your first and last names display. In the **Tags** box, type **summer calendar** and then in the **Subject** box, type your course name and section number.

g. **Save** and **Close** your document and submit as directed.

You have completed Project 10C | **END**

Chapter Review

Skills Review | Project 10D Job Descriptions

Apply 10B skills from these Objectives:

5. Create an Index
6. Create a Table of Contents
7. Create a Table of Figures
8. Control the Flow and Formatting of Pages and Text

In the following Skills Review, you will add an index, a table of contents, and a table of figures to the listing of job descriptions for the City of Tawny Creek. Your completed document will look similar to Figure 10.56.

Project Files

For Project 10D, you will need the following file:

w10D_Job_Descriptions

You will save your file as:

Lastname_Firstname_10D_Job_Descriptions

Project Results

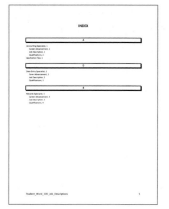

Figure 10.56

(continues on next page)

Chapter Review

1 Start Word. From your student files, open the file **w10D_Job_Descriptions**. Save the file in your **Word Chapter 10** folder as **Lastname_Firstname_10D_Job_Descriptions** and if necessary, display the rulers and formatting marks. If any words are flagged as spelling errors, right-click the first occurrence of each, and then click **Ignore All**.

a. Insert the file name in the footer. With the insertion point to the right of the file name, press [Tab] two times. On the **Header & Footer Tools Design tab**, in the **Header & Footer group**, click **Page Number**, and then click **Current Position**. (Mac users, click Page Number, and then click Page Number again. Click OK, close the footer, and then skip to Step c.)

b. In the **Page Number** gallery, under **Simple**, click **Plain Number**. In the **Close group**, click **Close Header and Footer**.

c. Under *Accounting Specialist*, click in the first cell of the table. Click the **Table Tools Design tab**, and then in the **Table Style Options group**, clear the **Header Row** check box. In the **Table Styles group**, click **More**, and then under **Grid Tables**, in the first row, click the fourth style.

d. Press [Ctrl] + [Home], and then **Save** your changes.

2 Under *Administrative Support Positions*, select the text *Application Tips*. Click the **References tab**, and then in the **Index group**, click **Mark Entry**. In the **Mark Index Entry** dialog box, click **Mark**.

a. Click in the document, and then select the paragraph *Accounting Specialist*. If necessary, point to the **Mark Index Entry** dialog box title bar, and then drag the **Mark Index Entry** dialog box to the side of your screen. With the paragraph selected, click in the **Mark Index Entry** dialog box, click **Mark**.

b. Without closing the **Mark Index Entry** dialog box, in a similar manner, **Mark** entries for *Data Entry Specialist* and *Records Specialist*.

3 On **Page 1**, position the insertion point to the right of *Job Description*. In the **Mark Index Entry** dialog box, click in the **Main entry** box. Type **Accounting Specialist** and then in the **Subentry** box, type **Job Description** and click **Mark**.

a. On **Page 2**, position the insertion point to the right of *Qualifications*. In the **Main entry** box, type **Accounting Specialist** and in the **Subentry** box, type **Qualifications** and then click **Mark**.

b. Still on **Page 2**, position the insertion point to the right of *Career Advancement*. Create the **Main entry** box **Accounting Specialist** and the **Subentry Career Advancement**

c. Using the technique you just practiced, under the paragraph heading *Data Entry Specialist*, mark *Job Description*, *Qualifications*, and *Career Advancement* as subentries for the main entry **Data Entry Specialist**

d. In a similar manner, under the paragraph heading *Records Specialist*, mark subentries for *Job Description*, *Qualifications*, and *Career Advancement* as subentries for the main entry **Records Specialist**

e. **Close** the **Mark Index Entry** dialog box and then **Save** your changes.

4 Press [Ctrl] + [End], and then press [Ctrl] + [Enter] to insert a manual page break. (Mac users, press [command ⌘] + [Enter].) With the insertion point at the top of the new page, type **INDEX** and then press [Enter]. Select the text *INDEX*, including the paragraph mark, change the **Font Size** to **16**, apply **Bold**, and **Center** the text.

a. Click in the blank paragraph below the INDEX title. On the **References tab**, in the **Index group**, click **Insert Index** to display the **Index** dialog box.

b. In the **Index** dialog box, on the **Index tab**, click the **Formats arrow**, and then click **Fancy**. On the right side of the **Index** dialog box, click the **Columns spin box down arrow** to **1**. Click **OK**.

c. On **Page 1**, select the first paragraph with italic formatting—*Application Tips*. In the **Table of Contents group**, click **Add Text**, and then click **Level 3**. In a similar manner, assign **Level 3** to the remaining nine italicized paragraph headings. Press [Ctrl] + [Home], and then **Save** your changes.

5 With the insertion point at the beginning of the document, click the **Layout tab**. In the **Page Setup group**, click **Breaks**, and then under **Section Breaks**, click **Next Page**. Press [Ctrl] + [Home] to move to the beginning of the document. Click the **Home tab**, and then in the **Styles group**, click **Normal**.

a. Type **TABLE OF CONTENTS** and then press [Enter] two times. Select the text you just typed, including the paragraph mark, change the **Font Size** to **16**, and then apply **Bold** and **Center**.

(continues on next page)

Chapter Review

b. Click to position the insertion point to the left of the section break. Click the **References tab**, and then in the **Table of Contents group**, click **Table of Contents**. In the **Table of Contents** gallery, click **Custom Table of Contents**. In the **Table of Contents** dialog box, if necessary, select the Use hyperlinks instead of page numbers check box.

c. Under **General**, click the **Formats arrow**, and then click **Fancy**. Click **OK**, and then **Save** your changes.

6 On **Page 2**, below the heading *Accounting Specialist*, in the first table, click in the first cell. On the **References tab**, in the **Captions group**, click **Insert Caption**.

a. In the **Caption** dialog box, in the **Caption** box, with the insertion point to the right of *Table 1*, type a colon, press Spacebar, and then type **Accounting Specialist** Click the **Position arrow**, and then click **Below selected item**. Click **OK**.

b. On **Page 3**, click in the first cell of the table. In the **Captions group**, click **Insert Caption**. In the **Caption** dialog box, in the **Caption** box, with the insertion point to the right of *Table 2*, type a colon, press Spacebar, and then type **Data Entry Specialist** Click **OK**.

c. In a similar manner, insert the caption **Table 3: Records Specialist** below the third table in the document. Click **OK**.

7 Press Ctrl + Home. Click to position the insertion point in the last paragraph of the page—to the left of the section break. Press Ctrl + Enter to insert a manual page break.

a. Type **TABLE OF FIGURES** and then press Enter. Select the text you just typed, change the **Font Size** to **16**, apply **Bold**, and **Center**.

b. Click to position the insertion point in the last paragraph on **Page 2**—to the left of the section break. On the **References tab**, in the **Captions group**, click **Insert Table of Figures**.

c. In the **Table of Figures** dialog box, under **General**, click the **Formats arrow**, and then click **Distinctive**. Click **OK**, and then **Save** your changes.

d. Click the **Layout tab**. In the **Page Setup group**, click **Hyphenation**, and then click **Automatic**.

8 Press Ctrl + Home, and then scroll to the bottom of **Page 1**. Double-click in the footer area, and then in the footer, select the page number.

a. On the **Header & Footer Tools Design tab**, in the **Header & Footer group**, click **Page Number**, and then click **Format Page Numbers**.

b. In the **Page Number Format** dialog box, click the **Number format arrow**, and then click the fifth numbering style—**i, ii, iii**. Click **OK**.

c. On **Page 3**, in the footer, select the page number 3. In the **Header & Footer group**, click **Page Number**, and then click **Format Page Numbers**. In the **Page Number Format** dialog box, under **Page numbering**, click the **Start at** option button. With *1* displayed in the **Start at** box, click **OK**. In the **Close group**, click **Close Header and Footer**.

9 On the **References tab**, in the **Tables of Contents group**, click **Update Table**. In the **Update Table of Contents** dialog box, with the **Update page numbers only** option button selected, click **OK**.

a. On **Page 2**, click to position the insertion point in the table of figures. Right-click, and then click **Update Field**. In the **Update Table of Figures** dialog box, with the **Update page numbers only** option button selected, click **OK**. (Mac users, select the Table of Figures. On the References tab, in the Captions group, click the Update Table button. Click OK.)

b. Press Ctrl + End. Click to position the insertion point in the index, right-click, and then click **Update Field**. (Mac users, point to the index, hold down Ctrl, and then click to display the shortcut menu. Click Update Field.)

c. Display the document **Properties**. In the **Tags** box, type **job list** and in the **Subject** box, type your course name and section number. If necessary, edit the author name to display your name.

d. **Save** and **Close** your document, and then submit as directed.

You have completed Project 10D | **END**

Mastering Word	Project 10E Council Topics

Apply 10A skills from these Objectives:

1. Create a Master Document and Subdocuments
2. Manage a Master Document and Subdocuments
3. Navigate and Inspect the Master Document
4. Create and Modify Headers and Footers

In the following Mastering Word project, you will create a master document and subdocuments for a document that summarizes topics to be discussed at the February meeting of the Tawny Creek City Council. Your completed documents will look similar to Figure 10.57.

Project Files for MyLab IT Grader

1. In your **MyLab IT** course, locate and click **Word 10E Council Topics**, Download Materials, and then Download All Files.
2. Extract the zipped folder to your Word Chapter 10 folder. Close the Grader download screens.
3. Take a moment to open the downloaded **Word_10E_Council_Topics_Instructions**; note any recent updates to the book.

Project Results

Figure 10.57

For Non-MyLab Submissions

For Project 10E, you will need:
w10E_Council_Topics
w10E_Agenda_Item

In your Word Chapter 10 folder, save your documents as:
Lastname_Firstname_10E_Council_Topics
Lastname_Firstname_10E_Agenda_Item

Create a folder named Project 10E and save your w10E_Council_Topics file in the Project 10E folder. After you have named and saved your document, on the next page, begin with Step 2.

After Step 12, save and submit your file as directed by your instructor.

(continues on next page)

Content-Based Assessments (Mastery and Transfer of Learning)

1 Navigate to your **Word Chapter 10 folder**, and then double-click the Word file you downloaded from **MyLab IT** that displays your name—**Student_Word_10E_Council_Topics**. Display the **Save As** dialog box, navigate to your **Word Chapter 10** folder, and create a folder named **Project 10E** Save the file in your **Project 10E** folder.

2 If necessary, display the rulers and formatting marks. Select the first paragraph of the document, change the **Font Size** to **28**, apply **Center**, and then change the **Text Effects and Typography**—in the first row, click the third effect. Select the second paragraph, change the **Font Size** to **28**, apply **Bold**, and then apply **Center**.

3 Apply the **Heading 1** style to the paragraphs that begin *Repurpose, Comments,* and *Green* and then display the document in **Outline** view. Beginning with the paragraph that begins *Repurpose,* select all the remaining paragraphs in the document. Create a master document and then **Save** your changes.

4 From your student files, open the file **w10E_Agenda_Item**. Save the file in your **Project 10E** folder as **Lastname_Firstname_10E_Agenda_Item** and then **Close** the document.

5 At the end of your *Council Topics* document, insert your file **Lastname_Firstname_10E_Agenda_Item** document as a subdocument. In the master document, under *Madison Street Widening Project,* in the last sentence, change the cost from *$1.6* to **$1.8** and then **Close Outline View** and **Save** your changes.

6 Select the entire heading that begins *Green Tawny Creek Program* being careful not to select the paragraph mark. Add a **Bookmark** with the **Bookmark name Agreement_Amendment**

7 In the paragraph below the document subtitle, at the end of the second sentence, select the text **Green Tawny Creek Program**. **Insert** a cross-reference that is linked to the *Agreement_Amendment* bookmark.

8 In **Outline** view, be sure that **Show Document** is active. **Unlink** all of the subdocuments and then delete all of the section breaks in the document. **Close** Outline view. Insert **Even Page** section breaks at the end of the paragraphs that begin *The following topics* and *Note that all.* Insert **Odd Page** section breaks at the end of the paragraphs that begin *During the past* and *City Renew, Inc.* Delete any blank paragraphs at the top of each page.

9 On **Page 2**, display the footer and select the **Different Odd & Even Pages** check box. On **Page 2**, in the footer, press `Tab` two times. Type **Tawny Creek** and then on **Page 3**, in the footer, insert the file name. Close the footer.

10 Press `Ctrl` + `Home`, and then insert the **Retrospect** cover page. In the **Document title** placeholder, type **Agenda Topics** and in the **Document Subtitle** placeholder, type **City Council**

11 Select and delete the shape that contains the *Author, Company Name,* and *Company Address* placeholders so that the entire filled shape is deleted. On the cover page, insert the **Draft 2** watermark. (Mac users, in the Insert Watermark dialog box, click the Text option button. Click the Text arrow, and then click DRAFT. Click OK.)

12 Display the document properties. In the **Tags** box, type **council topics** and then **Save** and **Close** your document. Do *not* change the Author or Subject properties.

13 In **MyLab IT**, locate and click the Grader Project **Word 10E Council Topics**. In step 3, under **Upload Completed Assignment**, click **Choose File**. In the **Open** dialog box, navigate to your **Word Chapter 10** folder, open your **Project 10E folder**, and then click your **Student_Word_10E_Council_Topics** file one time to select it. In the lower right corner of the **Open** dialog box, click **Open**.

The name of your selected file displays above the Upload button.

14 To submit your file to **MyLab IT** for grading, click **Upload**, wait a moment for a green **Success!** message, and then in step 4, click the blue **Submit for Grading** button. Click **Close Assignment** to return to your list of **Course Materials**.

You have completed Project 10E | **END**

Apply 10B skills from these Objectives:

5. Create an Index
6. Create a Table of Contents
7. Create a Table of Figures
8. Control the Flow and Formatting of Pages and Text

In the following Mastering Word project, you will add an index, a table of contents, and a table of figures to a document containing frequently asked questions and answers related to doing business with the City of Tawny Creek. Your completed document will look similar to Figure 10.58.

Project Files for MyLab IT Grader

1. In your **MyLab IT** course, locate and click **Word 10F Business FAQ**, Download Materials, and then Download All Files.
2. Extract the zipped folder to your Word Chapter 10 folder. Close the Grader download screens.
3. Take a moment to open the downloaded **Word_10F_Business_FAQ**; note any recent updates to the book.

Project Results

Figure 10.58

For Non-MyLab Submissions

For Project 10F, you will need:
w10F_Business_FAQ

In your Word Chapter 10 folder, save your document as:
Lastname_Firstname_10F_Business_FAQ

After you have named and saved your document, on the next page, begin with Step 2.
After Step 15, save and submit your file as directed by your instructor.

(continues on next page)

Content-Based Assessments (Mastery and Transfer of Learning)

Mastering Word: Project 10F Business FAQ (continued)

1 Navigate to your **Word Chapter 10 folder**, and then double-click the Word file you downloaded from **MyLab IT** that displays your name—**Student_Word_10F_Business_FAQ**.

2 If necessary, ignore any spelling errors that display. Insert the file name in the footer, and then press Tab two times. Insert a **Plain Number** page number and then close the footer.

3 Select the first paragraph, change the **Font Size** to **22**, apply **Bold**, and then apply **Center**.

4 Apply the **Heading 1** style to the paragraph headings that begin *Construction*, *Small Business*, *General Instructions*, *Zoning*, and *Special Events*. For each *Heading 1* paragraph, mark the heading text as a **Main entry** for the index.

5 Apply the **Heading 2** style to the paragraphs *Concessions*, *Signs*, and *Town Services*. For each *Heading 2* paragraph, type the paragraph text as a **Subentry** for the **Main entry Special Events Ordinances**

6 For each table, deselect the **Header Row** and **First Column** check boxes, and then in the **Table Styles gallery**, under **Grid Tables**, in the first row, click the second style. Apply the following captions to the three tables positioned below the selected item: Table 1: **Concessions** and Table 2: **Signs** and Table 3: **Town Services**

7 At the end of the document, press Enter. Type **INDEX** and then press Enter two times. Select the *INDEX* paragraph you just typed, change the **Font Size** to **16**, apply **Bold**, and then apply **Center**. In the last paragraph of the document, insert an index with the **Classic** format. Change the **Columns** to **1** and select the **Right align page numbers** check box.

8 Press Ctrl + Home, and then insert a **Next Page** section break. Press Ctrl + Home, and then apply the **Normal** style. Type **TABLE OF CONTENTS** and then press Enter two times. Select the text you typed, change the **Font Size** to **16**, apply **Bold**, and then apply **Center**.

9 Click to the left of the paragraph mark at the beginning of the section break line, and then insert a table of contents with the **Classic** format. **Save** your changes.

10 If necessary, click to position the insertion point to the left of the section break. Press Ctrl + Enter. (Mac users, press command ⌘ + Enter.) Type **TABLE OF FIGURES** and then press Enter. Select the text you typed, change the **Font Size** to **16**, apply **Bold**, and then apply **Center**.

11 To the left of the section break, insert a table of figures with the **Classic** format. **Save** your changes.

12 Press Ctrl + Home. Change the **Hyphenation** to **Automatic**.

13 On **Page 1**, in the footer, change the **Number format** to **i, ii, iii**. On the third page of the document, change the **Page numbering** to **Start at** the number **1**.

14 Update the **Table of Contents** and **Table of Figures** with the **Update page numbers only** option button selected, and then update the **Index**.

15 Display the document **Properties**. In the **Tags** box, type **business FAQ** and in the **Subject** box, type your course name and section number. If necessary, edit the author name to display your name. **Save** and **Close** your document.

16 In **MyLab IT**, locate and click the Grader Project **Word 10F Business FAQ**. In step 3, under **Upload Completed Assignment**, click **Choose File**. In the **Open** dialog box, navigate to your **Word Chapter 10** folder, and then click your **Student_Word_10F_Business_FAQ** file one time to select it. In the lower right corner of the **Open** dialog box, click **Open**.

The name of your selected file displays above the Upload button.

17 To submit your file to **MyLab IT** for grading, click **Upload**, wait a moment for a green **Success!** message, and then in step 4, click the blue **Submit for Grading** button. Click **Close Assignment** to return to your list of **Course Materials**.

You have completed Project 10F **END**

Content-Based Assessments (Mastery and Transfer of Learning)

Mastering Word Project 10G Chamber Programs

Apply 10A and 10B skills from these Objectives:

1. Create a Master Document and Subdocuments
2. Manage a Master Document and Subdocuments
3. Navigate and Inspect the Master Document
4. Create and Modify Headers and Footers
5. Create an Index
6. Create a Table of Contents
7. Create a Table of Figures
8. Control the Flow and Formatting of Pages and Text

In the following Mastering Word project, you will create a master document and subdocuments related to the programs offered by Tawny Creek's Chamber of Commerce. The final document will include an index, a table of contents, and a table of figures. Your completed documents will look similar to Figure 10.59.

Project Files for MyLab IT Grader

1. In your **MyLab IT** course, locate and click **Word 10G Chamber Programs**, Download Materials, and then Download All Files.
2. Extract the zipped folder to your Word Chapter 10 folder. Close the Grader download screens.
3. Take a moment to open the downloaded **Word_10G_Chamber_Programs_Instructions**; note any recent updates to the book.

Project Results

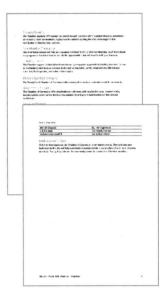

Figure 10.59

For Non-MyLab Submissions

For Project 10G, you will need:

w10G_Chamber_Programs
w10G_Ambassadors_Club

In your Word Chapter 10 folder, save your document as:

Lastname_Firstname_10G_Chamber_Programs
Lastname_Firstname_10G_Ambassadors_Club

Create a folder named Project 10G and save your w10G_Chamber_Programs file in the Project 10G folder. After you have named and saved your document, on the next page, begin with Step 2.

After Step 17, save and submit your file as directed by your instructor.

(continues on next page)

1 Navigate to your **Word Chapter 10 folder**, and then double-click the Word file you downloaded from **MyLab IT** that displays your name—**Student_ Word_10G_Chamber_Programs**. Navigate to your **Word Chapter 10** folder, and then create a folder named **Project 10G Save** the document in your **Project 10G** folder.

2 Apply the **Heading 1** style to the paragraphs *Networking*, *Special Events*, *Workshops and Seminars*, and *Other Chamber Services*.

3 Apply the **Heading 2** style to the paragraphs that begin *Morning*, *Lunches*, *Ribbon*, *Business Training*, *New Member*, *Industrial*, *Government*, and *Recycling*.

4 Beginning with the paragraph *Networking*, select all remaining text in the document and then create a master document.

5 From the files you downloaded with this project, open the file **w10G_Ambassadors_Club**. Save the file in your **Project 10G** folder as **Lastname_ Firstname_10G_Ambassasors_Club** and then **Close** the document. At the end of the master document, **Insert** the **Lastname_Firstname_10G_Ambassadors_Club** file as a subdocument.

6 In the *Ambassadors Club* subdocument, change the word *various* to **numerous** and then **Save** your changes. **Unlink** all subdocuments, remove all section breaks, and then **Close Outline View**. On **Page 1**, in the footer, insert the file name on the left and a **Plain Number** page number on the right.

7 Apply the following captions to the four tables, positioned **Above selected item**.

    Table 1: Appliances

    Table 2: Glass and Aluminum

    Table 3: Old Tires

    Table 4: Scrap Metal

8 If a blank paragraph displays below the *Scrap Metal* table, delete it. Beginning on **Page 1**, for each *Heading 1* paragraph—*Networking*, *Special Events*, *Workshops and Seminars*, *Other Chamber Services*, and *Ambassador's Club*, use the **Mark Entry** dialog box to **Mark** the text as a **Main entry**.

9 Below each *Heading 1* paragraph, mark each *Heading 2* paragraph as a **Subentry** using the appropriate *Heading 1* text for the **Main entry**.

10 At the end of the document, insert a manual page break, type **INDEX** and then press Enter two times. Select the text you typed, change the **Font Size** to **16**, apply **Bold**, and then apply **Center**. In the last paragraph, insert an index with the **Formal** format and the page numbers right aligned.

11 Press Ctrl + Home, and then insert a **Next Page** section break. Press Ctrl + Home, and then apply the **Normal** style. Type **TABLE OF CONTENTS** and then press Enter two times. Select the text you typed, change the **Font Size** to **16**, apply **Bold**, and then apply **Center**. Click to the left of the paragraph mark in the Section Break line, and then insert a table of contents with the **Formal** format. **Save** your changes.

12 On **Page 1**, position the insertion point in the last paragraph of the page—to the left of the section break, and then insert a manual page break. Type **TABLE OF FIGURES** and then press Enter. Select the text you typed, change the **Font Size** to **16**, apply **Bold**, and then apply **Center**. Click to the left of the paragraph mark in the Section Break line, and then insert a table of figures with the **Formal** format. **Save** your changes.

13 On **Page 1**, in the footer, change the page number format to **i, ii, iii**. On **Page 3**, change the **Page numbering** to **Start at** the number **1**.

14 Update the **Table of Contents** and **Table of Figures** with the **Update page numbers only** option button selected, and then update the **Index**.

15 Press Ctrl + Home. Display the **Cover Page** gallery, and then insert the **Retrospect** cover page. In the **Document Title** placeholder, type **Chamber of Commerce** and in the **Document Subtitle** placeholder, type **Program Descriptions**

16 Select and delete the shape that contains the *Author*, *Company Name*, and *Company Address* placeholders so that the entire filled shape is deleted. On the cover page, insert a **Draft 2** watermark. (Mac users, in the Insert Watermark dialog box, click the Text option button. Click the Text arrow, and then click DRAFT. Click OK.)

(continues on next page)

Mastering Word: Project 10G Chamber Programs (continued)

17 Display the document properties. In the **Tags** box, type **chamber programs** and then if necessary, edit the author name to display your name. **Save** and **Close** your document.

18 In **MyLab IT**, locate and click the Grader Project **Word 10G Chamber Programs**. In step 3, under **Upload Completed Assignment**, click **Choose File**. In the **Open** dialog box, navigate to your **Word Chapter 10** folder, open your **Project 10G folder**, and then click your **Student_Word_10G_Chamber_Programs** file one time to select it. In the lower right corner of the **Open** dialog box, click **Open**.

The name of your selected file displays above the Upload button.

19 To submit your file to **MyLab IT** for grading, click **Upload**, wait a moment for a green **Success!** message, and then in step 4, click the blue **Submit for Grading** button. Click **Close Assignment** to return to your list of **Course Materials**.

You have completed Project 10G **END**

Apply a combination of the 10A and 10B skills.

GO! Fix It	Project 10H Boards Summary	IRC
GO! Make It	Project 10I Internship Program	IRC
GO! Solve It	Project 10J Health Department	IRC
GO! Solve It	Project 10K Volunteer Program	

Project Files

For Project 10K, you will need the following file:

w10K_Volunteer_Program

You will save your file as:

Lastname_Firstname_10K_Volunteer_Program

Open the file **w10K_Volunteer_Program** and save it to your **Word Chapter 10** folder as **Lastname_Firstname_10K_Volunteer_Program** Insert the file name and page number in the footer. Format the title paragraphs and apply Heading 1 styles to paragraph headings. Format the tables attractively and insert captions. Create a table of contents and table of figures on separate pages. Create an index that displays main headings as well as specific names for departments and organizations. Hyphenate and paginate the document. Modify the page number format for the first two pages. Add appropriate document properties. Print your document or submit electronically as directed by your instructor.

		Performance Level	
	Exemplary:	**Proficient:**	**Developing:**
Format tables and insert captions	All tables are formatted attractively and appropriate captions are inserted.	At least one table is not formatted or an appropriate caption is not inserted.	No tables are formatted and no captions are inserted.
Create table of contents and table of figures	The table of contents and table of figures are created correctly.	The table of contents or table of figures is not created correctly.	The table of contents and table of figures are not created.
Create index	The index is created and includes appropriate entries.	The index is created but some entries are missing.	The index is not created.
Hyphenate and paginate	The document is hyphenated and paginated appropriately.	The document is not hyphenated or is not paginated appropriately.	The document is not hyphenated and is not paginated appropriately.
Insert and format page numbers	Page numbers are inserted in the footer and formatted correctly.	Page numbers are inserted in the footer but not formatted correctly.	Page numbers are not inserted in the footer.

Performance Element (row label, left side)

You have completed Project 10K | END

Rubric

The following outcomes-based assessments are *open-ended assessments*. That is, there is no specific correct result; your result will depend on your approach to the information provided. Make *Professional Quality* your goal. Use the following scoring rubric to guide you in *how* to approach the problem and then to evaluate *how well* your approach solves the problem.

The *criteria*—Software Mastery, Content, Format and Layout, and Process—represent the knowledge and skills you have gained that you can apply to solving the problem. The *levels of performance*—Professional Quality, Approaching Professional Quality, or Needs Quality Improvements—help you and your instructor evaluate your result.

	Your completed project is of Professional Quality if you:	Your completed project is Approaching Professional Quality if you:	Your completed project Needs Quality Improvements if you:
1-Software Mastery	Choose and apply the most appropriate skills, tools, and features and identify efficient methods to solve the problem.	Choose and apply some appropriate skills, tools, and features, but not in the most efficient manner.	Choose inappropriate skills, tools, or features, or are inefficient in solving the problem.
2-Content	Construct a solution that is clear and well organized, contains content that is accurate, appropriate to the audience and purpose, and is complete. Provide a solution that contains no errors of spelling, grammar, or style.	Construct a solution in which some components are unclear, poorly organized, inconsistent, or incomplete. Misjudge the needs of the audience. Have some errors in spelling, grammar, or style, but the errors do not detract from comprehension.	Construct a solution that is unclear, incomplete, or poorly organized, contains some inaccurate or inappropriate content, and contains many errors of spelling, grammar, or style. Do not solve the problem.
3-Format and Layout	Format and arrange all elements to communicate information and ideas, clarify function, illustrate relationships, and indicate relative importance.	Apply appropriate format and layout features to some elements, but not others. Overuse features, causing minor distraction.	Apply format and layout that does not communicate information or ideas clearly. Do not use format and layout features to clarify function, illustrate relationships, or indicate relative importance. Use available features excessively, causing distraction.
4-Process	Use an organized approach that integrates planning, development, self-assessment, revision, and reflection.	Demonstrate an organized approach in some areas, but not others; or, use an insufficient process of organization throughout.	Do not use an organized approach to solve the problem.

Outcomes-Based Assessments (Critical Thinking)

Apply a combination of the 10A and 10B skills.

GO! Think	Project 10L Technology Plan

Project Files

For Project 10L, you will need the following files:
Two new blank Word documents
You will save your files as:
Lastname_Firstname_10L_Technology_Plan
Lastname_Firstname_10L_Maintenance

The City of Tawny Creek is developing a new technology plan. Search online for information related to city or state technology plans. Using the data you find, in your own words, create a report—including headings and subheadings—that explains the steps required to develop a plan. These steps should include the following topics: a vision statement, the goals, a needs assessment, design and purchase, and implementation. Define what each step means; do not enter specific data. Save your file as **Lastname_Firstname_10L_Technology_Plan**

Create a master document with subdocuments for each step. Save a second, new document as **Lastname_Firstname_10L_Maintenance** and then create information defining maintenance. Insert this file as a subdocument in the master document. Unlink the subdocuments. Insert at least one bookmark and related cross-reference. For each document, insert the file name in the footer and add appropriate document properties. Print both documents or submit electronically as directed by your instructor.

	You have completed Project 10L	END

GO! Think	Project 10M City Parks	IRC

You and GO!	Project 10N Personal Journal	IRC

Appendix

MICROSOFT OFFICE SPECIALIST WORD 2019			
Obj Number	**Objective text**	**Activity**	**Page Number**
1.0 Manage Documents			
1.1	**Navigate within documents**		
1.1.1	Search for text	2.16, 3.11	197, 250
1.1.2	Link to locations within documents	1.17, 10.06	127, 670
1.1.3	Move to specific locations and objects in documents	3.11	250
1.1.4	Show and hide formatting symbols and hidden text	1.01, 2.01	105, 171
1.2	**Format documents**		
1.2.1	Set up document pages	Office Features 1.10, 1.17, 7.10	115, 127, 503
1.2.2	Apply style sets	2.22, 4.13, 9.19	207, 336, 625
1.2.3	Insert and modify headers and footers	1.15, 2.01	120, 171
1.2.4	Configure page background elements	1.05, 6.08, 10.12	110, 439, 680
1.3	**Save and share documents**		
1.3.1	Save documents in alternative file formats	3.14	256
1.3.2	Modify basic document properties	1.16, 2.10, 2.20, 3.12	122, 183, 205, 251
1.3.3	Modify print settings	Online Supplemental	
1.3.4	Share documents electronically	Online Supplemental	
1.4	**Inspect documents for issues**		
1.4.1	Locate and remove hidden properties and personal information	1.16	122
1.4.2	Locate and correct accessibility issues	1.1.6	
1.4.3	Locate and correct compatibility issues	1.1.6	
2.0 Insert and Format Text, Paragraphs, and Sections			
2.1	**Insert text and paragraphs**		
2.1.1	Find and replace text	2.16	197
2.1.2	Insert symbols and special characters	3.25, 7.12	276, 507
2.2	**Format text and paragraphs**		
2.2.1	Apply text effects	3.24, 7.15	275, 512
2.2.2	Apply formatting by using Format Painter	2.04, 7.11	176, 504
2.2.3	Set line and paragraph spacing and indentation	1.19, 1.20, 1.21, 3.01, 3.02, 4.14	130, 131, 133, 237, 238, 337
2.2.4	Apply built-in styles to text	2.22, 4.01	207, 315
2.2.5	Clear formatting	1.11	116
2.3	**Create and configure document settings**		
2.3.1	Format text in multiple columns	3.15, 3.16, 7.10	262, 264, 503

MICROSOFT OFFICE SPECIALIST WORD 2019			
Obj Number	**Objective text**	**Activity**	**Page Number**
2.3.2	Insert page, section, and column breaks	3.08, 3.15, 3.17, 7.10	248, 262, 265, 503
2.3.3	Change page setup options for a section	10.10	676
3.0 Manage Tables and Lists			
3.1	**Create tables**		
3.1.1	Convert text to tables	9.08	607
3.1.2	Convert tables to text	9.19	625
3.1.3	Create tables by specifying rows and columns	2.01	171
3.2	**Modify tables**		
3.2.1	Sort table data	Online Supplemental	
3.2.2	Configure cell margins and spacing	2.07	179
3.2.3	Merge and split cells	2.07	179
3.2.4	Resize tables, rows, and columns	2.05	177
3.2.5	Split tables	Online Supplemental	
3.2.6	Configure a repeating row header	Online Supplemental	
3.3	**Create and modify lists**		
3.3.1	Format paragraphs as numbered and bulleted lists	1.22, 1.23, 2.04, 7.11	134, 135, 176, 504
3.3.2	Change bullet characters and number formats	1.24, 4.10, 7.17	137, 329, 515
3.3.3	Define custom bullet characters and number formats	4.10, 7.17	329, 515
3.3.4	Increase and decrease list levels	2.04, 4.09	176, 327
3.3.5	Restart and continue list numbering	Online Supplemental	
3.3.6	Set starting number values	Online Supplemental	
4.0 Create and Manage References			
4.1	**Create and manage reference elements**		
4.1.1	Insert footnotes and endnotes	3.03	240
4.1.2	Modify footnote and endnote properties	3.04	241
4.1.3	Create and modify bibliography citation sources	3.05, 3.06	244, 245
4.1.4	Insert citations for bibliographies	3.05, 3.07, 3.09	244, 247, 249
4.2	**Create and manage reference tabs**		
4.2.1	Insert tables of contents	10.19	690
4.2.2	Customize tables of contents	10.19	690
4.2.3	Insert bibliographies	3.09	249
5.0 Insert and Format Graphic Elements			
5.1	**Insert illustrations and text boxes**		
5.1.1	Insert shapes	1.11	116
5.1.2	Insert pictures	1.04, 3.19, 7.16	109, 268, 513
5.1.3	Insert 3D models	1.17	127
5.1.4	Insert SmartArt graphics	1.27	143

\multicolumn{4}{c	}{**MICROSOFT OFFICE SPECIALIST WORD 2019**}
Obj Number	**Objective text**	**Activity**	**Page Number**
5.1.5	Insert screenshots and screen clippings	3.23	274
5.1.6	Insert text boxes	1.13, 7.14	118, 509
5.2	**Format illustrations and text boxes**		
5.2.1	Apply artistic effects	1.09, 7.16	114, 513
5.2.2	Apply picture effects and picture styles	1.08, 7.16	114, 513
5.2.3	Remove picture backgrounds	3.20	271
5.2.4	Format graphic elements	1.12, 1.14, 3.21, 3.22, 7.16	117, 119, 272, 273, 513
5.2.5	Format SmartArt graphics	1.28	144
5.2.6	Format 3D models	1.17	127
5.3	**Add text to graphic elements**		
5.3.1	Add and modify text in text boxes	7.14	509
5.3.2	Add and modify text in shapes	1.12	117
5.3.3	Add and modify SmartArt graphic content	1.27	143
5.4	**Modify graphic elements**		
5.4.1	Position objects	1.07, 3.18, 3.19	112, 266, 268
5.4.2	Wrap text around objects	1.05, 3.18	110, 266
5.4.3	Add alternative text to objects for accessibility	Office Features 1.14	119
6.0 Manage Document Collaboration			
6.1	**Add and manage comments**		
6.1.1	Add comments	6.13	447
6.1.2	Review and reply to comments	6.13	447
6.1.3	Resolve comments	6.14	450
6.1.4	Delete comments	6.14	450
6.2	**Manage change tracking**		
6.2.1	Track changes	6.17	456
6.2.2	Review tracked changes	6.18	457
6.2.3	Accept and reject tracked changes	6.18	457
6.2.4	Lock and unlock change tracking	6.17	456

\multicolumn{4}{c	}{**MICROSOFT OFFICE EXPERT WORD 2019**}
Obj Number	**Objective text**	**GO! Activity**	**Page Number**
1.0 Manage Document Options and Settings			
1.1	**Manage documents and templates**		
1.1.1	Modify existing document templates	Online Supplemental	
1.1.2	Manage document versions	5.16, 9.21	395, 629
1.1.3	Compare and combine multiple documents	6.2	432
1.1.4	Link to external document content	Online Supplemental	

MICROSOFT OFFICE EXPERT WORD 2019			
Obj Number	**Objective text**	**GO! Activity**	**Page Number**
1.1.5	Enable macros in a document	7.01, 7.02, 7.04, 7.05, 7.06	487, 488, 492, 494, 496
1.1.6	Customize the Quick Access toolbar	1.07, 7.04	19, 492
1.1.7	Display hidden ribbon tabs	7.02, 9.01	488, 597
1.1.8	Change the Normal template default font	Online Supplemental	
1.2	**Prepare documents for collaboration**		
1.2.1	Restrict editing	9.12, 9.22	611, 632
1.2.2	Protect documents by using passwords	9.12	611
1.3	**Use and configure language options**		
1.3.1	Configure editing and display languages	9.24	636
1.3.2	Use language-specific features	Online Supplemental	
2.0 Use Advanced Editing and Formatting Features			
2.1	**Find, replace, and paste document content**		
2.1.1	Find and replace text by using wildcards and special characters	5.23	404
2.1.2	Find and replace formatting and styles	5.22	403
2.1.3	Apply Paste Options	Online Supplemental	
2.2	**Configure paragraph layout options**		
2.2.1	Configure hyphenation and line numbers	6.11	443
2.2.2	Set paragraph pagination options	10.22	696
2.3	**Create and manage styles**		
2.3.1	Create paragraph and character styles	8.01	543
2.3.2	Modify existing styles	3.04	241
2.3.3	Copy styles to other documents or templates	5.01	371
3.0 Create Custom Document Elements			
3.1	**Create and modify building blocks**		
3.1.1	Create QuickParts	6.05	435
3.1.2	Manage building blocks	6.03, 6.12	433, 443
3.2	**Create custom design elements**		
3.2.1	Create custom color sets	6.06, 9.18	437, 623
3.2.2	Create custom font sets	6.06, 9.17	437, 621
3.2.3	Create custom themes	6.07	438
3.2.4	Create custom style sets	9.19	625
3.3	**Create and manage indexes**		
3.3.1	Mark index entries	10.14	685
3.3.2	Create indexes	10.16	687
3.3.3	Update indexes	10.24	699
3.4	**Create and manage tables of figures**		
3.4.1	Insert figure and table captions	5.11, 10.20	388, 693

\multicolumn{4}{c}{**MICROSOFT OFFICE EXPERT WORD 2019**}
Obj Number	**Objective text**	**GO! Activity**	**Page Number**
3.4.2	Configure caption properties	5.11, 10.20	388, 693
3.4.3	Insert and modify a table of figures	10.2	665
4.0 Use Advanced Word Features			
4.1	**Manage forms, fields, and controls**		
4.1.1	Add custom fields	5.09	383
4.1.2	Modify field properties	9.04, 9.11	602, 610
4.1.3	Insert standard content controls	9.02, 9.05, 9.06, 9.09	599, 603, 604, 608
4.1.4	Configure standard content controls	9.03	601
4.2	**Create and modify macros**		
4.2.1	Record simple macros	7.03, 7.04	490, 492
4.2.2	Name simple macros	7.03, 7.04	490, 492
4.2.3	Edit simple macros	7.07	498
4.2.4	Copy macros to other documents or templates	Online Supplemental	
4.3	**Perform mail merges**		
4.3.1	Manage recipient lists	3.27, 8.03, 8.09	280, 546, 561
4.3.2	Insert merged fields	3.28, 8.04, 8.12	282, 547, 565
4.3.3	Preview merge results	3.29, 8.05	283, 550
4.3.4	Create merged documents, labels, and envelopes	3.28, 8.06, 8.07, 8.16	282, 552, 554, 572

Glossary

Address Block A predefined merge field that includes the recipient's name and address.

AdjustListIndents A built-in macro used to modify the indenting of a bulleted or numbered list.

Alignment The placement of paragraph text relative to the left and right margins.

Alignment guide A green vertical or horizontal line that displays when you are moving or sizing an object to assist you with object placement.

All Markup A Track Changes view that displays the document with all revisions and comments visible.

American Psychological Association (APA) One of two commonly used style guides for formatting research papers.

Area chart A chart type that shows trends over time.

Artistic effects Formats applied to images that make pictures resemble sketches or paintings.

Ascending The order of text sorted alphabetically from A to Z or numbers sorted from the smallest to the largest.

Author The owner, or creator, of the original document.

AutoClose A macro that will automatically run when closing a document.

AutoCorrect A feature that corrects common typing and spelling errors as you type, for example changing *teh* to *the*.

AutoFit A table feature that automatically adjusts column widths or the width of the entire table.

AutoFit Contents A table feature that resizes the column widths to accommodate the maximum field size.

AutoMark file A Word document that contains a two-column table that is used to mark words as index entries.

AutoRecover A feature that helps prevent losing unsaved changes by automatically creating a backup version of the current document.

AutoRecover option A Word option that automatically saves versions of your file while you are working on it, and helps to recover unsaved documents.

Balloon The outline shape in which a comment or formatting change displays.

Bar chart A chart type that shows a comparison among related data.

Bibliography A list of cited works in a report or research paper; also referred to as Works Cited, Sources, or References, depending upon the report style.

Body The text of a letter.

Body text Text that does not have a heading style applied.

Bookmark A link that identifies the exact location of text, a table, or other object.

Brightness The relative lightness of a picture.

Building blocks Reusable pieces of content or other document parts—for example, headers, footers, and page number formats—that are stored in galleries.

Building Blocks Organizer A feature that enables you to view—in a single location—all of the available building blocks from all the different galleries.

Bulk mail A large mailing, sorted by postal code, which is eligible for reduced postage rates, available from the United States Postal Service.

Bulleted list A list of items with each item introduced by a symbol such as a small circle or check mark, and which is useful when the items in the list can be displayed in any order.

Bullets Text symbols such as small circles or check marks that precede each item in a bulleted list.

Caption A label that is added to a Word object and numbered sequentially.

Category axis The area of the chart that identifies the categories of data.

Cell The box at the intersection of a row and column in a Word table.

Cell margins The space inside a table cell between the text and the cell borders—top, bottom, left, and right.

Center alignment The alignment of text or objects that is centered horizontally between the left and right margin.

Change Case A formatting command that allows you to quickly change the capitalization of selected text.

Character spacing A Word feature that enables you to change the default spacing constraints between characters.

Character style A style, indicated by the symbol a, that contains formatting characteristics that you apply to text, such as font name, font size, font color, bold emphasis, and so on.

Chart A visual representation of numerical data.

Chart area The entire chart and all its elements.

Chart data range The group of cells with red, purple, and blue shading that is used to create a chart.

Chart Elements A Word feature that displays commands to add, remove, or change chart elements, such as the title, legend, gridlines, and data labels.

Chart Filters A Word feature that displays commands to define what data points and names display on a chart.

Chart style The overall visual look of a chart in terms of its graphic effects, colors, and backgrounds.

Check Box content control A content control that enables the user to select, or not select, a specific option.

Check Box form field A legacy control that enables the user to select, or not select, a specific option.

Citation A note inserted into the text of a research paper that refers the reader to a source in the bibliography.

Collaboration The action of working together with others as a team in an intellectual endeavor to complete a shared task or achieve a shared goal.

Column break indicator A dotted line containing the words *Column Break* that displays at the bottom of the column.

Column chart A chart type that shows a comparison among related data.

Column Width A Learning Tools command that changes the width of the line length to fit more or less text on each line; options include Very Narrow, Narrow, Moderate, or Wide.

Combine A Track Changes feature that allows you to review two different documents containing revisions, both based on an original document.

Combo Box content control A content control that enables the user to select an item from a list or enter new text.

Comment A note that an author or reviewer adds to a document. ; or, in a macro procedure, a line of text that is used solely for documentation.

Compare A Track Changes feature that enables you to review differences between an original document and the latest version of the document.

Complimentary closing A parting farewell in a business letter.

Content control A data entry field where the particular type of information is supplied by the user.

Contiguous Items that are adjacent to one another.

Continuous section break A mark that defines the beginning and end of each subdocument.

Contrast The difference between the darkest and lightest area of a picture.

Cover letter A document that you send with your resume to provide additional information about your skills and experience.

Cover page The first page of a document that provides introductory information.

Crop A command that removes unwanted or unnecessary areas of a picture.

Crop handles Handles used to define unwanted areas of a picture.

Crop pointer The pointer used to crop areas of a picture.

Cross-reference A text link to an item that appears in another location in the document, such as a heading, a caption, or a footnote.

Data labels The part of a chart that displays the value represented by each data marker.

Data markers The shapes in a chart representing each of the cells that contain data.

Data points The cells that contain numerical data used in a chart.

Data range border The blue line that surrounds the cells containing numerical data that display in the chart.

Data series In a chart, related data points represented by a unique color.

Data source A document that contains a list of variable information, such as names and addresses, that is merged with a main document to create customized form letters or labels.

Database An organized collection of facts about people, events, things, or ideas related to a particular topic or purpose.

Date & Time A command with which you can automatically insert the current date and time into a document in variety of formats.

Date Picker content control A content control that enables the user to select a date from a calendar.

Dateline The first line in a business letter that contains the current date and which is positioned just below the letterhead if a letterhead is used.

Descending The order of text sorted alphabetically from Z to A or numbers sorted from the largest to the smallest.

Design Mode A command that enables the user to edit content controls that are inserted in a document.

Direct formatting The process of applying each format separately, for example bold, then font size, then font color, and so on.

Directory A single list of records using specified fields from a data source.

Document gridlines Nonprinting horizontal and vertical lines used to assist in aligning graphics and other elements in a document.

Dot leader A series of dots preceding a tab that guides the eye across the line.

Drag-and-drop A technique by which you can move, by dragging, selected text from one location in a document to another.

Drawing objects Graphic objects, such as shapes, diagrams, lines, or circles.

Drop-Down List content control A content control that enables the user to select a specific item from a list.

Editor A digital writing assistant in Word that flags misspellings, grammatical errors, and writing style issues.

Em dash A punctuation symbol used to indicate an explanation or emphasis.

Embedding The process of inserting an object, such as a chart, into a Word document so that it becomes part of the document.

Enclosures Additional documents included with a business letter.

Endnote In a research paper, a note placed at the end of a document or chapter.

Even Page section break A formatting mark that indicates the beginning of a new section on the next even-numbered page.

Federal registration symbol The symbol ® that indicates that a patent or trademark is registered with the United States Patent and Trademark Office.

Field A placeholder for data.

Fields In a mail merge, categories—or columns—of data.

Filter A set of criteria applied to fields in a data source to display specific records.

Flip A command that creates a reverse image of a picture or object.

Floating object A graphic that can be moved independently of the surrounding text characters.

Footnote In a research paper, a note placed at the bottom of the page.

Form A structured document that has static text and reserved spaced for information to be entered by the user.

Form letter A letter with standardized wording that can be sent to many different people.

Formatting marks Characters that display on the screen, but do not print, indicating where the Enter key, the Spacebar, and the Tab key were pressed; also called nonprinting characters.

Formula A mathematical expression that contains functions, operators, constants, and properties, and returns a value to a cell.

Function A predefined formula that performs calculations by using specific values in a particular order.

Graphics Pictures, charts, or drawing objects.

Greeting Line A predefined merge field that includes an introductory word, such as *Dear*, and the recipient's name.

Hanging indent An indent style in which the first line of a paragraph extends to the left of the remaining lines and that is commonly used for bibliographic entries.

Header row The first row of a table containing column titles.

Hidden text Nonprinting text—for example, an index entry field.

Hyphenation A feature that enables control of how words are split between two lines, resulting in a less ragged edge at the right margin.

Icon Picture composed of straight and curved lines.

Indenting Moving the beginning of the first line of a paragraph to the right or left of the rest of the paragraph to provide visual cues to the reader to help divide the document text and make it easier to read.

Index A compilation of topics, names, and terms accompanied by page numbers that displays at the end of a document.

Index entry A word or phrase that is listed in the index.

Index entry field Code, formatted as hidden text and displaying to the right of an index entry, containing the identifier XE and the term to be included in the index.

Ink Revision marks made directly on a document by using a stylus on a Tablet PC.

Inline object An object or graphic inserted in a document that acts like a character in a sentence.

Inside address The name and address of the person receiving the letter; positioned below the date line.

Justified alignment An arrangement of text in which the text aligns evenly on both the left and right margins.

Keep lines together A formatting feature that prevents a single line from displaying by itself at the bottom of a page or at the top of a page.

Keep with next A formatting feature that causes two elements, such as paragraphs, to display together on the same page.

Kerning A character spacing option that automatically adjusts the spacing between pairs of characters, with a specified minimum point size, so that words and letters appear equally spaced.

Layout The placement and arrangement of the text and graphic elements on a slide.

Layout Options A Word feature that displays commands to control the manner in which text wraps around a chart or other object.

Leader character Characters that form a solid, dotted, or dashed line that fills the space preceding a tab stop.

Learning Tools Features in Word that add visual changes to assist with reading fluency and comprehension.

Left alignment An arrangement of text in which the text aligns at the left margin, leaving the right margin uneven.

Legacy control A field used in designing a form for persons who possess older versions of Word.

Legend The part of a chart that identifies the colors assigned to each data series or category.

Letterhead The personal or company information that displays at the top of a letter and that commonly includes a name, address, and contact information.

Line break indicator A non-printing character in the shape of a bent arrow that indicates a manual line break.

Line chart A chart type that shows trends over time.

Line spacing The distance between lines of text in a paragraph.

LinkedIn A professional networking website that focuses on business and employment-oriented services and on which you can build and share your professional identify and connect with others in your field of interest.

Linked style A style, indicated by the symbol a, that behaves as either a character style or a paragraph style, depending on what you select.

List style A style that applies a format to a list.

Live Layout A feature that reflows text as you move or size an object so that you can view the placement of surrounding text.

Lock Tracking A feature that prevents reviewers from turning off Track Changes and making changes that are not visible in markup.

Macro A set of commands and instructions that can be grouped as a single command to accomplish a task automatically.

Macro virus A macro that causes files to be erased or damaged by inserting unauthorized code.

Mail merge A Word feature that joins a main document and a data source to create customized letters or labels.

Main document In a mail merge, the document that contains the text or formatting that remains constant.

Main entry A word, phrase, or selected text used to identify the index entry.

Main Tabs An area in the Customize Ribbon portion of the Word Options dialog box.

Manual column break An artificial end to a column to balance columns or to provide space for the insertion of other objects.

Manual line break A break that moves text to the right of the insertion point to a new line while keeping the text in the same paragraph.

Manual page break The action of forcing a page to end and placing subsequent text at the top of the next page.

Margins The space between the text and the top, bottom, left, and right edges of the paper.

Markup The formatting Word uses to denote a document's revisions visually.

Markup area The space to the right or left of a document where comments and formatting changes display in balloons.

Master document A Word document that serves as a container for the different parts of a document.

Match Fields A Word feature that maps predefined field names to the field names in a data source.

Memorandum (Memo) A written message sent to someone working in the same organization.

Merge A table feature that combines two or more adjacent cells into one cell so that the text spans across multiple columns or rows.

Merge field In a mail merge, a placeholder that represents specific information in the data source.

Modern Language Association (MLA) One of two commonly used style guides for formatting research papers.

Multilevel list A list in which the items display in a visual hierarchical structure.

Multiple Pages A zoom setting that decreases the magnification to display several pages of a document.

Nameplate The banner on the front page of a newsletter that identifies the publication.

Nested table A table inserted in a cell of an existing table.

Newsletter A periodical that communicates news and information to a specific group.

No Markup A Track Changes view that displays the document in its final form—with all proposed changes included and comments hidden.

No Paragraph Space The built-in paragraph style—available from the Paragraph Spacing command—that inserts *no* extra space before or after a paragraph and uses line spacing of 1.

Nonbreaking hyphen A formatting mark that prevents a hyphenated word or phrase from being displayed on two lines.

Nonbreaking space A formatting mark that keeps two words together so that both words will wrap even if only the second word would normally wrap to the next line.

Noncontiguous Items that are not adjacent to one another.

Nonprinting characters Characters that display on the screen, but do not print; also called formatting marks.

Normal The default style in Word for new documents and which includes default styles and customizations that determine the basic look of a document; for example, it includes the Calibri font, 11 pt font size, line spacing at 1.08, and 8 pt spacing after a paragraph.

Normal template The template that serves as a basis for all Word documents.

Note In a research paper, information that expands on the topic, but that does not fit well in the document text.

Numbered list A list that uses consecutive numbers or letters to introduce each item in a list.

Numerical data Numbers that represent facts.

Object anchor The symbol that indicates to which paragraph an object is attached.

Odd Page section break A formatting mark that indicates the beginning of a new section on the next odd-numbered page.

Office Presentation Service A Word feature to present your Word document to others who can watch in a web browser.

One-click Row/Column Insertion A Word table feature with which you can insert a new row or column by pointing to the desired location and then clicking.

Organizer A dialog box where you can modify a document by using styles stored in another document or template.

Original A Track Changes view that displays the original, unchanged document with all revisions and comments hidden.

Outline view A document view that displays the overall organization, or hierarchy, of the document's parts including headings, subheadings, and subordinate text.

Page break indicator A dotted line with the text *Page Break* that indicates where a manual page break was inserted.

Page Color A Learning Tools command that changes the color of the page to make the text easy to scan and consume.

Pagination The process of arranging and numbering the pages in a document.

Paragraph style A style, indicated by, that includes everything that a character style contains, plus all aspects of a paragraph's appearance; for example text alignment, tab stops, line spacing, and borders.

Parenthetical references References that include the last name of the author or authors and the page number in the referenced source.

Password A code that is used to gain access to a file.

PDF Reflow The ability to import PDF files into Word so that you can transform a PDF back into a fully editable Word document.

Picture effects Effects that enhance a picture, such as a shadow, glow, reflection, or 3-D rotation.

Picture styles Frames, shapes, shadows, borders, and other special effects that can be added to an image to create an overall visual style for the image.

Pie chart A chart type that shows the proportion of parts to a whole.

Placeholder text Non-printing text that holds a place in a document where you can type.

Plain Text content control A content control that enables the user to enter unformatted text.

Procedure A block of programming code that performs one or more tasks.

Quick Parts All of the reusable pieces of content that are available to insert into a document, including building blocks, document properties, and fields.

Quick Tables Tables that are stored as building blocks.

Read Aloud A Learning Tools command that reads text out loud and highlights each word as it is read; this command is available in both Word and Outlook.

Read Mode A view in Word that optimizes the Word screen for the times when you are reading Word documents on the screen and not creating or editing them.

Read-only file A file that can be viewed but not changed.

Readability statistics A Spelling and Grammar tool that analyzes a document and determines the reading level of the text.

Recolor A feature that enables you to change all colors in the picture to shades of a single color.

Record All of the categories of data pertaining to one person, place, thing, event, or idea, and which is formatted as a row in a database table.

Recording The process of creating a macro while performing specific actions in a document.

Researcher A Word feature that helps you find topics and reliable sources for a research paper; for sources that you select, citation information is available.

Resume Assistant A feature in Word with which you can see suggestions from LinkedIn to help you update your resume.

Reveal Formatting A pane that displays the formatted selection and includes a complete description of formats applied.

Reviewer An individual who reviews and marks changes on a document.

Reviewing Pane A separate scrollable window that shows all of the changes and comments that currently display in a document.

Revisions Changes made to a document.

Rich Text content control A content control that enables the user to enter text and apply formatting.

Right alignment An arrangement of text in which the text aligns at the right margin, leaving the left margin uneven.

Rotation handle A symbol with which you can rotate a graphic to any angle; displays above the top center sizing handle.

Rules Conditional Word fields that allow you to determine how the merge process is completed.

Salutation The greeting line of a letter, such as *Dear Sir.*

Scale A command that resizes a picture to a percentage of its size.

Screen Clipping A tool with which you can take a quick snapshot of part of a screen, and then add it to your document.

Screenshot An image of an active window on your computer that you can paste into a document.

Section A portion of a document that can be formatted differently from the rest of the document.

Section break A double dotted line that indicates the end of one section and the beginning of another section; the section break mark stores the formatting information for a section of a document..

Shapes Lines, arrows, stars, banners, ovals, rectangles, and other basic shapes with which you can illustrate an idea, a process, or a workflow.

Show Preview A formatting feature that displays a visual representation of each style in the Styles pane.

Signature line An element added to a document that specifies who should sign the document.

Simple Markup The Track Changes view that indicates revisions by vertical red lines in the left margin and indicates comments by icons in the right margin.

Single spacing The common name for line spacing in which there is *no* extra space before or after a paragraph; uses line spacing of 1.

Skype A Microsoft product with which you can make voice calls, make video calls, transfer files, or send messages—including instant messages and text messages—over the Internet.

Small caps A font effect that changes lowercase letters to uppercase letters, but with the height of lowercase letters.

Smart Lookup A Word feature with which you can get more information about text you select; shows definitions, images, and results from various online sources.

SmartArt A designer-quality visual representation of your information that you can create by choosing from among many different layouts to effectively communicate your message or ideas.

Sorting The action of ordering data, usually in alphabetical or numeric order.

Spin box A small box with an upward- and downward-pointing arrow that lets you move rapidly through a set of values by clicking.

Split A table feature that divides selected cells into multiple cells with a specified number of rows and columns.

Split Table A table feature that divides an existing table into two tables in which the selected row—where the insertion point is located—becomes the first row of the second table.

Split Window A Word feature that displays a document in two panes so that you can view or work on different parts of the document at the same time.

Static text Descriptive text such as labels or headings.

Style guide A manual that contains standards for the design and writing of documents.

Style Inspector A pane that displays the name of the selected style with formats applied and contains paragraph- and text-level formatting options.

Style A group of formatting commands, such as font, font size, font color, paragraph alignment, and line spacing, that can be applied to a paragraph with one command.

Style set A collection of character and paragraph formatting that is stored and named.

Styles pane A pane that displays a list of styles and contains tools to manage styles.

Stylus A pen-like device used for writing on an electronic document.

Subdocument A section of a document that is linked to the master document.

Subentry A more specific term that refers to the main entry.

Subject line The optional line following the inside address in a business letter that states the purpose of the letter.

Suppress A Word feature that hides header and footer information, including the page number, on the first page of a document.

Syllables A Learning Tools command that shows breaks between syllables of words.

Synchronous scrolling The setting that causes two documents to scroll simultaneously.

Synonyms Words with the same or similar meaning.

Tab stop A specific location on a line of text, marked on the Word ruler, to which you can move the insertion point by pressing the Tab key, and which is used to align and indent text.

Table An arrangement of information organized into rows and columns.

Table of contents (TOC) A list of a document's headings and subheadings, marked with the page numbers where those headings and subheadings occur.

Table of figures A list of the figure captions in a document.

Table style A style that includes formatting for the entire table and specific table elements, such as rows and columns.

Tablet PC A computer with a monitor that e you to write on the screen.

Team A group of workers tasked with working together to solve a problem, make a decision, or create a work product.

Template An existing document that you use as a starting point for a new document; it opens a copy of itself, unnamed, and then you use the structure—and possibly some content, such as headings—as the starting point for a new document.

Text box A movable, resizable container for text or graphics.

Text effects Decorative formats, such as shadowed or mirrored text, text glow, 3-D effects, and colors that make text stand out.

Text from File A command to insert text from another file into your document.

Text Highlight Color A Word command with which you can apply a highlight color to selected text.

Text pane A pane that displays to the left of a SmartArt graphic and is used to type text and edit text in a SmartArt graphic.

Text wrapping The manner in which text displays around an object.

Theme A predefined set of colors, fonts, and line and fill effects that look good together and is applied to an entire document by a single selection.

Theme template A stored, user-defined set of colors, fonts, and effects that can be shared with other Office programs.

Thesaurus A research tool that provides a list of synonyms.

Thumbnail A graphical representation of a page.

Toggle button A button that can be turned on by clicking it once, and then turned off by clicking it again.

Track Changes A feature that makes a record of the changes made to a document.

Value axis The area of a chart that displays a numerical scale based on the numerical data in a chart.

Variable In an equation, a letter that represents a value.

VBA The abbreviation for Visual Basic for Applications—a programming language used to create macros.

Vertical change bar A line that displays in the left margin next to each line of text that contains a revision.

View Side by Side A view that displays two open documents in separate windows, next to each other on the screen.

Visual Basic Editor An editor that enables you to view and edit existing macro code or create a new macro.

Visual Basic for Applications (VBA) A programming language used to create macros.

Watermark A text or graphic element that displays behind document text.

Wildcard A special character such as * or ? that is used to search for an unknown term.

Word count A Word feature that indicates the number of words, paragraphs, pages, and characters in a document.

Word Options A collection of settings that you can change to customize Word.

Word wrap The feature that moves text from the right edge of a paragraph to the beginning of the next line as necessary to fit within the margins.

Works Cited In the MLA style, a list of cited works placed at the end of a research paper or report.

Writer's identification The name and title of the author of a letter placed near the bottom of the letter under the complimentary closing—also referred to as the *writer's signature block*.

Writer's signature block The name and title of the author of a letter placed near the bottom of the letter, under the complimentary closing—also referred to as the *writer's identification*.

XE Code identifying an index entry.

Index

Ignore All, 407
Illustrations group, 39
images
    building blocks and, 435–437
    collecting images from multiple
        documents, 396–397
Importing/Exporting, 371
Increase Indent command,
    328–329
indenting
    AdjustListIndents, 500
    defining, 239
    hanging indents, 249
    of lists, 327–329
    paragraphs, 131–133, 238–240
    in research paper formatting, 238–240
    text, 131–133
index entry field, 686
indexing
    AutoMark files in, 686–687
    creating, 683–688
    defining, 683
    hidden text in, 686
    index entry field, 686
    inserting into document, 687–688
    inserting page numbers in, 683–685
    main entries in, 685–686
        alphabetical display of, 688
    margins for, 698
    subentries in, 686–687
    updating, 688
    XE identifier in, 686
Info tab, 8, 38
information handouts
    aligning paragraphs in, 128–130
    creating with Google Docs,
        147–148
    indenting text in, 131–133
    inserting icons in, 145–146
    line spacing of, 130–131
    lists in
        bulleted lists, 134–135
        customizing bullets, 137–139
        numbered lists, 135–137
    paragraphs, space before and after,
        133–134
    setting margins in, 127–128
    SmartArt
        inserting, 143–144
        sizing and formatting, 144–145
    tab stops
        modifying, 141–142
        setting, 139–141
Ink, 453
inline objects, 109
input devices, 47
Insert Caption, 388
Insert Chart dialog box, 341
Insert Hyperlink dialog box, 273
Insert tab, 399
    Illustrations group, 39
        Insert Chart dialog box in, 341

inserting. *See also* adding; Word
    documents
    AutoText, 442–443
    bookmarks, 39
    charts, 341–344
        Insert Chart dialog box, 341
    columns in tables, 386
    comments, 447–450
    content controls, 488
    cover pages, 678–679
    current date, 195–197
    dates, 195–197
    document information, 37–38
    existing files as subdocuments, 666–667
    fields in footers, 120–121
    footers, 37–38
        fields in, 120–121
    footnotes, 240–241
    footnotes in research papers, 240–241
    graphics, 508
    icons, 145–146
    index into documents, 687–688
    Insert Caption, 388
    Insert Chart dialog box, 341
    Insert Hyperlink dialog box, 273
    Insert tab, 399
        Illustrations group, 39, 341
    links in documents, 274
    manual line breaks, 191–193
    merge fields, 547–550, 571
    nonbreaking hyphens, 507–508
    nonbreaking spaces, 507–508
    One-Click Row/Column Insertion, 178–
        179, 383–385
    pictures, 565
        in newsletters, 266–268
        in Word documents, 109
    pictures in newsletters, 266–268
    Quick Parts, 442–443
    Quick Tables, 442–443
    rows in tables, 386
    saved files into PowerPoint, 66
    saved files into presentations, 66
    shapes, 116–117
    signature lines, 628–630
    SmartArt graphics in Word documents,
        143–144
    special characters, 399–400
    symbols, 275–276, 330
    text
        from another document, 107
        from file, 173–176
    text boxes, 118–119
    text from files, 173–176
    3D models, 39
    watermarks, 680–681
insertion points, 11, 375
    defining, 47
inside addresses, 552
    defining, 194, 548
Inspect Document, 38
Intelligent Services, 400

Intense Reference, 335–336
Internet of Things, 465
Inverse page color, 210
italics, 29–30, 399

J

JPEG files, 64
Jump List, 54
justified alignment, 129
    in column text, 265
    defining, 128

K

keep lines together formatting, 317
keep source formatting check box, 36
Keep with next command, 697
keep with next formatting, 317
kerning, 504–506
keyboard shortcuts
    defining, 13, 66
    for movement, 33–34
    using, 32–36
keyboards, 50
KeyTips, 25
keywords, 38

L

labels
    excluding captions from, 388
    personalized, 543
    printing, 558
landscape orientation, 25
language options, 635–636
layout, 331–332
    Column Layout, 255
    of documents, 127–134
    Live Layout, 111–112
    modifying, 503–508
    of paragraphs, 127–134
    Print Layout view, 106, 393, 695
Layout Options, 22, 349
    text wrap settings in, 109
    wrapping text around picture using,
        110–111
leader characters, 142
Learning Tools, 210–211
left alignment, 128–129
legacy controls, 605–607
legends, 344, 346
letterheads, 191
letters
    form letters, 547
    personalized, 543
    printing, 552
line break indicators, 192, 279
line spacing, 624
    default, 106
    options for, 130
    setting, 130–131

inserting icons, 145–146

inserting pictures, 109

inserting SmartArt graphics in, 143–144

inserting tables into, 200–201

inserting text from another, 107

line spacing, 130–131

lists, 134–139

managing and modifying sources for, 249–250

page borders, 115–116

paragraph spacing, 133–134

presenting online, 186–187

printing, 122–123

setting margins, 127–128

Word documents (.docx), 487

Word Editor, 201–206

Word files, 80–83

Word Macro-Enabled Documents (.docm), 487

Word Macro-Enabled Templates (.dotm), 487

Word objects, 388–389

Word Options, 395

Customize Ribbon, 338–339

defining, 338

saving and, 393

Word Templates (.dotx), 487

creating, 208–210

Word templates, creating, 208–210

word wrap, 106

WordPad Desktop app, 78

Works Cited, 244–245

wrapping text, 22

around pictures, 110–111

settings for, 109

writer's identifications, 194

writer's signature blocks, 194

X

XE identifier, 686

XML Paper Specification, 41

XPS files, 41

Z

zip, 10

zipped files

downloading and extracting, 11–14, 65–66

extracting with File Explorer, 73–74

zipped folders, 65

Zoom group, 376–377, 394

zoom levels

changing, 25–26

Object, 255

Page Width, 25–26

Zoom slider, 25–26

zooming

defining, 40

Multiple Pages zoom setting, 376

Page Width zoom, 25–26

from View tab, 394